7

3/04
2

LOUIS XIV

LOUIS XIV

IAN DUNLOP

ST. MARTIN'S PRESS ⚜ NEW YORK

www.stmartins.com

ISBN 0-312-26196-9

First published in Great Britain by Chatto & Windus

First U.S. Edition: August 2000

10 9 8 7 6 5 4 3 2 1

To
DEIRDRE
With all my Love

Contents

List of Illustrations

The Collège des Quatre Nations. I. Silvestre. Louvre. Cabinet des Dessins. © R.M.N. 95CN19609.

The Colannade du Louvre. S. Leclerc. Cabinet des Estampes. C51875.

Colbert. C. Le Febvre. Versailles. © R.M.N. 96DN1862.

Père de La Chaise. P. Simon. Versailles. © R.M.N. 95DN24882.

Saint-Germain, baptism of Grand Dauphin. P. Brissart. Cabinet des Estampes. C97474.

The Tuileries. J. Rigaud. Cabinet des Estampes. C32135.

Meudon in the days of Louvois. I. Silvestre. Cabinet des Dessins. 3036.

Louvois. By courtesy of the Duke of Buccleuch. Photo Antonia Reeve.

Michel Le Tellier. R. Nanteuil. Trustees of the British Museum.

Vauban's fortifications of Lille. Photo Maison Vauban.

Vauban. Artist unknown. The Louvre. Photo Bulloz.

Turenne. C. Le Brun. Versailles. © R.M.N. 74DN620.

Bosseut. P. Drevet after Rigaud. Trustees of the British Museum.

The Dragonnades. G. Engelmann. Cabinet des Estampes. B55445.

Versailles, the 'Enveloppe', garden side. Ian Dunlop.

Versailles, the 'Enveloppe', entrance side. I. Silvestre. Cabinet des Estampes. 74C60788.

Versailles, the 'Enveloppe', north side. I. Silvestre. Cabinet des Estampes. 74C63879.

Marly. A. Guillaumot. Cabinet des Esampes. 74C68782.

The Machine de Marly. P.-D. Martin. Versailles. © R.M.N. 73DN4356.

Versailles, north gardens. J.-B. Martin. Versailles. © R.M.N. 89EE964.

The Grand Canal at Versailles. A. Perelle. Cabinet des Estampes. 56B6114.

The Poop of *Le Soleil Royal*. J. Bérain. Louvre. © R.M.N. MV23718.

The duchesse de Bourgogne. F. Gobert. Versailles. © R.M.N. 84EN1763.

The duchesse d'Orléans. H. Rigaud. Versailles. MV2084.

Fénelon. Vivien. Versailles. MV3658.

Mme de Maintenon. Artist unknown. By permission of the Duke of Buccleuch.

J.-B. Van Loo. In a private collection.

Creation of the Order of Saint-Louis. J. Marot. Versailles. © R.M.N. 71DN6321.

Louis with his son, grandson, great-grandson and the duchesse de Ventadour. Attributed to J. De Troy or N. Largillière. Wallace Collection.

Les Invalides from the south. Artist unknown. Cabinet des Estampes. C168461.

Les Invalides from the north. P.-D. Martin. Musée Carnavalet. Photothèque des Musées de la Ville de Paris. 87CAR1824A.

Versailles, the Grande Chapelle. Artist unknown. Archives Nationales. 01/1782 no 7.

Versailles, the Grande Chapelle. C. Cochin. Cabinet des Estampes. 73DN4341.

Preface

'Perhaps', wrote Voltaire of the memoirs of Mme de Caylus, 'the spirit of Philosophy, which reigns in our day, will not be too impressed by the little affairs of the Court which are the subject of these memoirs: we want to know what were the reasons for these wars; what the financial resources; why the navy declined after having been brought to the highest perfection . . . But all these themes having been more or less exhausted in the histories of the century of Louis XIV, we can look with pleasure on these little details which enable us to understand many individuals who are still remembered: these details are even useful, on more than one occasion, to throw light on the important events.'

Voltaire is pleading the cause of what the French call *la petite histoire*. But if the study of the weightier matters of the reign could have been regarded as exhausted even in Voltaire's day, how much more so must that be true today.

This book is an attempt to portray one of the greatest characters who have played an important role on the stage of French history: Louis XIV. He was also perhaps one of the most elusive. 'It must be acknowledged', wrote the Duke of Berwick – an illegitimate son of James II of England – 'that no prince has ever been so little known as this one.' If that could be said by someone who had open access to Louis and who was closely associated with some of his most important ventures, what hope has the historian with only documents as a guide? I would myself claim to know quite a lot *about* Louis: I would not claim to *know* him. I am not trying to reassess his reign. There are plenty of recent works in English, American and French which supply this need. This book is in many ways complementary to these studies.

'Tout écrivain est peintre', wrote La Bruyère, 'et tout excellent écrivain, excellent peintre.' I have tried to paint Louis, and to help my readers to see him, as his contemporaries saw him. It is no use trying to fit their accounts into a sort of 'identikit'. They each saw him through a slightly different lens and in a slightly different light.

I have tried to avoid passing judgements. But in order to write a book of this length, the author must be highly selective. I may be influenced in my selection by what is in fact a judgement or even a prejudice. But I hope that in choosing to quote *this* piece of material rather than *that* one I have been more influenced by the image which has been slowly emerging in my mind than by some preconceived idea. Those who know a lot more about Louis than I do may be disappointed at some of my omissions, but I leave the general readers, to whom this book is chiefly addressed, to form their own judgements on Louis.

I have tried to paint Louis against his proper background, so much of which was his own creation, and to set him in the context of the many brilliant personalities who adorned his reign. As Voltaire himself wrote: 'It is not only the life of Louis XIV that I claim to write. I want to try and paint for posterity not the actions of a single man, but the spirit of the men in the most enlightened age that there has ever been.' Later in the eighteenth century Cardinal Maury made the same point. 'It is with this august cortège of immortal genius', he declared, 'that Louis XIV faces the judgement of posterity, backed by all the great men who had reached and retained their positions through his discretion.' To Louis this was an important aspect of the art of administration. 'In a great state', he said in the memoirs which he wrote for his son, 'there are always men suited to any sort of activity. The only thing is to know them and put them in place.' This was the real greatness of Louis: his ability to encourage and to make use of the talents of others. As Chateaubriand wrote: 'It is the voice of genius of all kinds which sounds from the tomb of Louis: from the tomb of Napoleon only the voice of Napoleon is heard.'

If we are to picture the members of this 'august cortège' we need to be able to put them in their proper setting. Horace Walpole understood this when he sent an 'enchanting little landscape' of his creation at Strawberry Hill to his friend Sir Horace Mann with the words: 'I could rest no longer with the thought of your having no idea of the place of which you hear so much, for it is uncomfortable in so intimate an acquaintance as ours not to be exactly master of every spot where one another is writing or reading or sauntering.'

But if a reconstruction in the imagination of the vanished glories of the architectural background may help us to see these men and women of genius more vividly, they will in turn bring a new life and a new interest to Saint-Germain and Versailles, to Fontainebleau and Chambord, filling their rooms with memories and decking the gardens with all the colourful paraphernalia of the Court of France.

It was a very different world from that in which we live today and many of the quotations which I record here are inserted chiefly to emphasise this difference. The need to make a deliberate effort to appreciate the *Grand Siècle* is underlined by Lytton Strachey: 'Their small, bright world is apt to seem uninteresting and out of date unless we spend some patient sympathy in the discovery of the real charm and real beauty that it contains.'

How do we discover what that 'small, bright world' was like? The visible memorials of Louis' reign are among the most precious documents: Versailles – in spite of the alterations of his successors – has much to tell us about the way he saw his role as King. His passion for building, second only to his enthusiasm for warfare, was a dominant force in his life. It is not possible to understand Louis without appreciating this. The Trianon de Marbre is more evocative of his private life, if such a term may be used of him. The Hôtel des Invalides, the aqueduct at Maintenon, the remains of Vauban's fortifications, and even the grounds that are all that survive of Marly, add to our perception of the gargantuan scale of the architectural undertakings of the reign. Further afield, Fontainebleau and Chambord still have the strange power of an ancient building to throw back across the centuries the fading echoes of a bygone age. To restore these monuments in the imagination to their pristine condition is the business of the topographer: the resurrection of the past within the framework of the present.

The great monuments of literature, drama and music of which the *Grand Siècle* provided the climate for so many, are, of course intact. We are probably nearest to the atmosphere of Louis' reign as we turn the pages of La Fontaine, Boileau or La Bruyère, or give ourselves up to the enchantment of Mme de Sévigné's letters, to the clear logic and exquisite irony of Pascal, to the high-pitched hyperbole of Bossuet's *Oraisons Funèbres* or the simple clarity of Bourdaloue's sermons.

Less easy to approach are those more ephemeral manifestations of the spirit of the age – the *Ballets de Cour* in which the young Louis frequently danced, and danced extremely well. In recent years there has been an increase of interest in these, and the important part which they played in preparing Louis for his role as *le Roi Soleil*, and in the propaganda for the new regime, is now widely recognised.

I am not aware that any have been revived upon the stage. Our knowledge of the exact choreography may not be sufficient. But two occasions stand out in my own experience. One was a production of Molière's masterpiece *Le Bourgeois Gentilhomme* accompanied by the *entrées de ballet* to the music of Lully; the other was a concert in the Chapel at

Versailles of Lully's motet *Plaude, Laetare Gallia*, written for the baptism of the Dauphin. They were experiences never to be forgotten.

In other forms of literature, particularly in their letters and memoirs, the men and women of the age provide copious material. But they also confront the historian with a problem. Some of the memoirs are regarded, and rightly, as 'subject to caution'. This has led certain historians, faced with a number of undoubted inaccuracies, to treat them as untrustworthy. And yet it is barely credible that anyone should have written memoirs which contained no truth at all. A picture can be true in its overall impression even if it is inaccurate in certain details.

Two of the greatest writers – one of memoirs and the other of letters – on the life of the Court are the two most obviously guilty of prejudice, exaggeration and even downright error: the duc de Saint-Simon and Lise-lotte von der Pfalz, who succeeded Princess Henrietta-Anne of England as the wife of Louis' brother, the duc d'Orléans. With both one is obliged, in the language of the rifle range, to 'aim off for wind'. But I would rather risk a shot than leave them unquoted. I return to Lytton Strachey on the subject of Saint-Simon. 'Throughout the endless succession of his pages the enormous panorama unrolls itself, magnificent, palpitating, alive.' That is the impression I would like to give of the *Siècle de Louis XIV*.

Louis emerges to my mind as a man whose foremost concern in life was what it meant to be a King – 'de faire son métier de Roi'. Within that overarching concern he appears to have two dominant passions – the art of war and the arts of peace, and, within the arts of peace, the expression of what it meant to him to be a King in the building and decorating of his palaces. I merely observe that his love of war brought France into humiliation and earned her the hatred of Europe, whereas his love of architecture and the related arts gave France its position as the cultural centre to which all Europe looked. 'Who could have told', asked Montesquieu, 'that the King established the greatness of France by building Versailles and Marly?'

Ian Dunlop
Selkirk, 1999

Introduction

Voltaire begins his *Siècle de Louis XIV* with a quick sketch of the history of France in which he seeks to account for his country's repeated failure to achieve the greatness of which it was capable. He turns a typically blind eye to the twelfth-century 'Renaissance', when France became, in the words of Odo de Châteauroux, 'the oven in which the intellectual bread of humanity was cooked', and to the awe-inspiring achievement of the builders of the Ile de France, christened by Jean Gimpel 'La Croisade des Cathédrales'. To Voltaire, as to nearly all of his contemporaries, the term 'gothic' was an expression of contempt, but not always the sort of contempt which is bred of familiarity.

For Voltaire was a child of the sixteenth-century Renaissance. For nine hundred years, he claims, 'the genius of the French had nearly always been stultified beneath a gothic government, amid divisions and civil wars, having no fixed laws or customs, changing every two centuries a language which always remained uncouth; the nobles, subject to no discipline, knowing only warfare and idleness, the churchmen living in ignorance and disorder, and the people, with no industry, sunk in their misery'. Now, at the end of the sixteenth century, hope was renewed, but it was not to last. 'Henri le Grand was in process of delivering France from the calamities and barbarities into which thirty years of religious wars had plunged her when he was murdered in his own capital in the middle of his people whose welfare he was just beginning to restore.' The Time of Troubles – those thirty years, which had not been without heroes – culminated in the murder of Henri III on 2 August 1589, which left his successor 'not so much a throne to ascend as a crown to be conquered'. But France needed more than conquering: she needed rebuilding.

For the last of the Valois had left respect for the monarchy at a low ebb. Charles de Cossé, comte de Brissac, had been blatantly outspoken: the people, he said, had grown strangely colder – 'merveilleusement refroidi' – in the love which the French had always felt for their sovereign.

The sixteenth century had ended in disaster. 'It was not France', wrote Etienne Pasquier, 'that emerged from the forty years of conflict, but the carcass of France.' To the proud monarchy of the first Valois succeeded in 1589 a King 'with his shirt in tatters and doublet out at the elbows'. But Henri de Navarre, the legitimate successor to Henri III, was endowed with those qualities which the French most admire. According to Francesco Vendramini, the Venetian ambassador at the turn of the century, 'the Spaniards say that His Majesty fights like a devil and forgives like a god'. When he made his manifesto – 'We are all Frenchmen and fellow citizens of the same fatherland' – men listened. When he added: 'We must be brought to agreement by reason and kindness, not by severity and cruelty, which serve only to arouse men' – they responded. But not Paris. Henri de Navarre, although the legitimate heir to the throne, was a Protestant, a Huguenot. The Catholic League, under the duc de Mayenne, was still in control of the capital. The Cardinal de Bourbon was proclaimed King. Henri saw that to be the master of France but not the master of Paris was to be unable to rule. He had on several occasions refused to renounce his religion in order to gain the throne. But now that he had won his throne he was prepared to reconsider the matter. Having refused to accept the first draft for his recantation, he agreed to a revision of it. On 25 July 1593, he was received into the Roman Catholic Church at Saint-Denis.

On 27 February 1594 he was crowned at Chartres Cathedral, Reims being in the hands of the League, and, as Henri IV, was to become the most popular King in the history of France. The power of the League had been broken. Mayenne fled, leaving Paris in the able hands of its Governor, the comte de Brissac. Brissac, although a devout Catholic, was statesman enough to realise that further resistance would be not only useless but counter-productive. In the early hours of 22 March 1594, he opened the gates of the capital to the royalist troops. Popular relief expressed itself in the ditty:

> Tu est sauvé, Paris; et ton gouverneur Brissac
> A gardé ton navire et du *bris* et du *sac.*

Henri IV and his minister Maximilien de Béthune, baron de Rosny, whom he later created duc de Sully, had the gigantic task of rebuilding a France that was in ruins. They were men of a stature equal to the task of restoring prosperity to a desolate land. Of the state of desolation, the Venetian ambassador Vendramini reported to the Senate that he saw 'destruction everywhere . . . a great part of the cattle had disappeared, so that ploughing is no longer possible'. For lack of beasts of burden, peasants themselves drew the plough 'and served as animals, with ropes over their shoulders'. Not unnaturally their sufferings tended to dehumanise them. 'The people are not what they used to be – courteous and honest; war and the sight of blood has made them sly, coarse and barbarous.' The first need was to restore prosperity and self-esteem to the labourer. 'I want there to be no peasant in my kingdom', said Henri, 'so poor that he is unable to have a chicken in his pot every Sunday.'

The King and his minister had also to find some means of pacifying the bitter hatred between the Catholics and the Huguenots. Sully, himself a staunch Protestant, was particularly well suited to the task of establishing religious peace. He was a man in advance of his times – one of the few who were already ecumenical. As his biographer Marie-Madeleine Martin puts it: 'Sully was the best example of that attitude, which was most unusual in his day, of a man of unswerving loyalty to his religion and yet very open to the reasonings of his adversaries.'

Naturally the defection of the King to 'the beast of Rome' placed him in a difficult relationship with his former Huguenot supporters. The best which he could do was to offer them the compromise of the Edict of Nantes in 1598. Some of the provisions were useful, and, indeed, the least that he could offer – the right to worship in certain places according to their beliefs; the right to make wills; the right of their clergy to hold both regional and national synods; the eligibility of Huguenots for any State employment. But there were other provisions which were to prove counter-productive. The Huguenots were accorded about 150 strongholds and castles, including such places as La Rochelle, Saumur and Montpellier, which made them appear as a state within the State. But the Edict worked for a time and enabled the peace which was so necessary for the huge task of rebuilding France which confronted Henri IV and Sully.

But they were great builders also in the literal sense of the word. 'If you do not come to Paris in the next two years', wrote Malherbe to a friend, 'you will no longer recognise it.'

Henri also set about continuing the work on the Château Neuf at Saint-Germain and invited the Italian Thomas Francini to adorn and embellish its gardens with the grottoes and waterworks for which they were so justly famous.

Set in a noble forest, placed on the high ground of the Hauts de Seine and overlooking the wide meanders of the river, the Château de Saint-Germain reaped the advantages of a free air and a fine prospect. Louis le Gros had built a castle here in about 1120. A century later Saint Louis had enriched it with the beautiful Sainte-Chapelle which still exists. But

François I had regarded Saint-Germain as ripe for reconstruction. 'He had the old buildings pulled down', writes Du Cerceau, 'without, however, altering the foundations ... which form a rectangle gone mad.' The ground plan is, in fact, a five-sided figure, devoid of right angles, of which the shortest side is that occupied by the Sainte-Chapelle. François put the architect Pierre Chambiges, the builder also of Chantilly, in charge of the reconstruction, but Du Cerceau claims that 'the King took such an interest in the building that one might almost say that he was the architect'.

It is an amazing structure, dignified in the grandeur of its conception, crude in the pettiness of its ornament; a palace of the Renaissance in the size and regularity of its windows; a château of the late Middle Ages in the vaulting of its ceilings and its many corkscrew staircases. It is both – and yet it is neither. It lacks the Italian refinement of Lescot's work at the Louvre without retaining the flamboyant magnificence of Chantilly.

In only one respect was the new Saint-Germain well in advance of its time. It was provided with a flat roof which offered the most delightful walk to the inmates of the palace. 'This terrace', claims Du Cerceau, 'is, I think, the first of its sort in Europe and a thing worthy to be seen and considered.'

The view from this rooftop walk was magnificent, but one had to climb up to the roof to enjoy it, for the château was set well back on its site. Henri II, who succeeded François I in 1547, commissioned Philibert de l'Orme to design the 'Château Neuf', a sort of annexe to the castle on the very edge of the high ground which would command the view directly from its windows and the terraces of its gardens. Seen from the river it dominated the colline du Pecq and clothed its slopes with masonry. Beneath the actual château the ground was cut back into two perpendicular faces, adorned with arcades and pilasters. Each of these two faces was traversed by an enormous ramp.

It was along the terraces thus formed that Henri IV created his grottoes. They give an insight into the mind of the seventeenth century, with their moving figures and changing scenery. One was particularly remarkable – the Grotte de la Demoiselle qui joue des Orgues. The lady's fingers were activated by water so that she played her organ producing a music (so claims a document of 1644) 'hardly inferior to the best of concerts'.

The Château Neuf served as a sort of 'royal lodge' where the King and Queen could be housed in greater comfort and in greater privacy than in what was now called the 'Vieux Château'. Considerable work was also carried out at Fontainebleau and the Louvre, but the latter remained unfinished.

It was from the Louvre, on Friday 14 May 1610, that Henri set out to visit Sully, who was ill at the time. He went informally, without guards, accompanied only by a few friends At the corner of the rue de la Ferronerie there was a blockage caused by a pig, and the coach had to stop. It happened that François Ravaillac, a Catholic fanatic who had vowed to kill the King, was standing at the corner. He seized his opportunity, thrust himself into the coach and stabbed the King twice in the heart. By the time the coach had regained the Louvre, Henri IV was dead.

Ravaillac died a hideous death, but he had himself to thank: he had killed the only man in France who was likely to have had mercy upon him. When the surgeons performed the post-mortem on the King, they found 'all his members healthy and in good state' and said that in the course of nature he could have lived another twenty years. It is a matter of wistful speculation as to what might have been the future of France if Henri IV had been spared those twenty years.

Louis XIII was nine at the time of his father's death. His mother, Marie de Medici, with the approval of the Parlement de Paris, became Regent, but she soon came under the influence of an Italian named Concini and his wife Eleanore. Concini was given the title of maréchal d'Ancre. Favourites are seldom viewed with favour by the Court and Concini was widely detested. The young Louis, however, was also falling under the sway of a favourite – Charles d'Albert, seigneur de Luynes, at first his page and then his closest companion; from companion he progressed to confidant and from confidant to confederate; together they planned the assassination of Concini. On Monday 14 April 1617, the main entrance to the Louvre, between the two surviving towers of the château of Philippe-Auguste, was closed on the pretext that the King was to go hunting. Concini had to use the narrow passage called *la planchette*. As he entered it he was shot in the face at point-blank range by Vitry, Louis' captain of the guard. When Louis was informed he said to Vitry: 'Merci, grand merci à vous; à cette heure je suis Roi.'

The murder of her favourite brought the King and his mother into open hostility. Marie was exiled to Blois, but she managed to escape and to rally supporters. Finally, on Friday 7 August 1620 Louis attacked her army at Ponts-de-Cé, near Angers, and routed them. A reconciliation was negotiated and took place in the Chambre de Judith – so named after its tapestry – in the magnificently restored Château de Brissac. One of the architects of this reconciliation was Armand du Plessis, Bishop of Luçon, soon to be Cardinal de Richelieu.

The Venetian ambassador Angelo Carrario (usually called 'Correr' in French) has left one of the most succinct appraisals of Richelieu. Louis was so much subjugated by him that the Cardinal appeared 'rather to command as king than to operate as minister; he was only minister in name and it was precisely only in name that he was not king; he had been made the sole director of war and of peace, the distributor of finances, the dispenser of Crown appointments and ecclesiastical dignities; in fact it was he alone who had the disposition of everything, as a sovereign and a despot. His Majesty, very often, was not even informed as to what he was deliberating on or doing even in matters of the greatest importance.'

'The Cardinal therefore had to maintain at all costs his standing with the King,' continues Carrario; 'I am going to say something very different from the general belief and which is perhaps not even evident to Your Serenity – that he does not entirely possess the sincere and cordial affection of His Majesty . . . that he is more esteemed than loved. It was due to circumstances and not to the goodwill of the King that he came into favour, and it is necessity that maintains him in it . . . and, if I may go so far as to say so, it is fear rather than the King's goodwill towards him.'

The abbé de Choisy completes the portrait. 'Richelieu, born to command other men, a generous friend and a cruel enemy, kept on the same table his Machiavelli and his Breviary . . . He brought the House of Austria low and put paid to its aspirations to universal monarchy.'

Richelieu had less to fear from enemies abroad than from enemies at home. Louis was susceptible to favourites of either sex and a favourite could endanger the Cardinal's position. 'The *petit coucher du Roi*', he used to say, 'causes me more anxiety than the whole of Europe.' He humiliated the *grands seigneurs*, enforced the obedience of the Parlement, imprisoned princes, had the King's brother, Gaston d'Orléans, the heir presumptive to the throne, exiled; he saw the Queen Mother, his enemy, die in a foreign land, he treated the reigning Queen, Louis' wife Anne of Austria, with harshness and almost as a criminal. Above all he dominated the spirit of his master who esteemed him, 'who feared him, but who did not love him, for the terror with which he inspired him'. This fear, or terror, was compared by Loménie de Brienne with the feelings of a schoolboy for an over-severe headmaster.

It seems that Louis did not have much taste for kingship. His character was marked by a love of sobriety both in the adornment of his person and in the satisfaction of his appetites; he ate little and drank less; he was deeply devout and gave most of the money reserved for his personal expenditure to the poor. But he compensated for his lack of outward show by a majesty that was natural to him, for he was a man of magnificent physique and robust constitution and a horseman without equal. 'The King on foot is King of his subjects,' wrote Antoine de Pluvinel: 'the King mounted is King of Kings.'

Like most of the Bourbon family, Louis XIII was a mighty hunter and on a number of occasions he rode so far from Saint-Germain that he did not return that night, but slept, often only on straw, at a little hamlet in the Val de Galie called Versailles. In due course he decided to build here a little hunting lodge.

One of the earliest public references to Versailles was made by the maréchal de Bassompierre while addressing the Notables who met in 1627. He drew attention to the unfinished condition of most of the royal palaces, claiming that the King 'was not inclined to building and that the finances of France will not be exhausted by the erection of sumptuous edifices, unless one were to reproach him with the wretched little château at Versailles, the construction of which would not furnish matter for pride to a simple gentleman'. Saint-Simon, whose father often accompanied Louis on his hunting expeditions, called the original house a 'petit château de cartes'. It was 24 metres in length, 6 in breadth, and had two short wings.

Mme de Motteville states that this smallness was deliberate – 'in order to admit only a few people and not to be disturbed in the peace and quiet which he sought here from the importunities of the Court'.

Perhaps Louis' feelings for his little place on the edge of the forest can best be appreciated from his words to the Père Dinet, his confessor, shortly before he died. 'If God gives me back my health,' he said, 'as soon as I see my Dauphin attain his majority, I will set him in my place and retire to Versailles with four of your fathers, to converse with them of things divine, and to have no thoughts but of the concerns of my soul and my salvation.' Versailles, however, was not destined to become the monastic retreat of royalty.

The reference to a Dauphin brings the future Louis XIV onto the stage. In February 1638, Louis XIII had solemnly placed France, 'our Person, our State, our Crown and all our subjects', under the direct protection of the Virgin Mary. The announcement of the King's Vow coincided with the announcement that the Queen, after twenty-two years of marriage, was at last pregnant. 'The two events', writes François Bluche, 'were seen as cause and effect and there was great public rejoicing.'

The circumstances attending the conception may have owed as much to chance as to prayer. Louis XIII had favourites – for 'mistresses' would be the wrong word – among the fairer sex. In 1637 the King's chaste affections were attracted by Mlle de La Fayette. The affair was complicated but not concluded by her taking the veil and one of the strange turning points of history is connected with this. The story is told by Mme de Motteville, whose closeness to Louis' Queen, Anne of Austria, gives a particular interest to her memoirs. She recounts the story, but she begins with the words: 'It is believed . . .' One day in December, when the King was visiting Mlle de La Fayette at the convent of Les Filles Sainte-Marie, 'the weather was so bad that he could not return to sleep at Saint-Germain as he had planned, and was obliged to go to the Louvre and avail himself of half the Queen's bed'. A child was conceived and to many it seemed to be literally the answer to their prayers – *l'enfant du miracle*.

To one man, however, there was an even deeper cause for thanksgiving. Pierre de La Porte, who had the position of Porte-manteau Ordinaire in the household of the Queen, was also the agent through whom she passed her secret correspondence to her brother, the King of Spain – even when France and Spain were at war. In August 1637, Richelieu had La Porte arrested and sent to the Bastille, where he was alternately bribed with promises and threatened with torture. With great courage and presence of mind he managed not to say anything incriminating and a scandal, which could have resulted in the Queen's being sent back to Spain, was avoided. Had this occurred the conception of Louis XIV could never have taken place. To La Porte, therefore, *l'enfant du miracle* was 'l'enfant de mon silence'.

I

The Birth of Louis XIV

In early September 1638, the Court of Saint-Germain was in a state of excited, if anxious, expectancy. The Queen was approaching childbirth. The dangers to the life of both the mother and the child were enough cause for anxiety in any family, but with a royal childbirth everything depended upon the sex of the child. Gaston d'Orléans was Louis XIII's only brother. His persistent intriguing and treachery against his brother and the Queen Regent rendered him an undesirable successor to the throne.

It had been the same with the birth of Louis XIII, which is recorded in some detail. Henri IV had been so confident that Marie de Medici would provide him with an heir that he had even appointed Jean Héroard, a week before the child was born, 'to serve as Physician to my son, the Dauphin'. The Court was at Fontainebleau and outside the royal apartments, in the Cour de l'Ovale, the couriers, ready booted for their journeys, were awaiting the signal to gallop off with their despatches.

The poor Queen was therefore tormented by the fear, not uncommon in the circumstances, that the child would be a girl. The King had made a private arrangement with the midwife that if it was a boy her first words would be: 'Warm me a cloth', but when the moment came there was something about her expression which caused him to doubt the message. The Queen cried out in Italian. 'Is it a male?' At this moment the midwife, who had given the baby the kiss of life, uncovered the appropriate portion of his anatomy. The King rushed to the Queen's side: 'Rejoice, my love,' he cried, 'God has given us our heart's desire: we have a fine son!'

There are no similar details available for the birth of Louis XIV. Perhaps the most interesting account of the event came from the pen of the Venetian ambassador Angelo Carrario. On Sunday 5 September he wrote to the Doge: 'This morning, a little before twelve o'clock, the Queen, by an auspicious delivery, has enriched France with a Dauphin. The King, together with his brother, the Princesses of the Blood and some of the great officers of the Crown . . . chose to assist her throughout, supporting her for a long time in his own arms. On perceiving the infant to be as fine a one and as healthy and well formed as could be desired, he immediately proceeded to the Church . . . and after a Te Deum had been chanted . . . he returned to the Queen's apartments.

'Happening to be at Saint-Germain at that moment for the purpose of speaking with the Secretary Savigny, I was so fortunate as to kiss His Majesty's hands and to be the first of foreign ministers to offer him such congratulations as became so great an occasion . . . taking me by the hand and leading me to the cradle in which the Dauphin lay, having had all the curtains raised that I might the better see him, he said: "Here is a miraculous effect of the Almighty's grace, for well may I give this title to so fine an infant: twenty-two years have I been married, and four luckless miscarriages has my wife had." '

The messengers who brought the news to Paris would normally have crossed the Seine by the Pont de Neuilly, but the bridge was down and the news had to be communicated to those on the other side by means of pre-arranged gesticulations. The birth of a daughter was to be signalled by arms crossed on the chest; that of a son by the throwing of hats into the air. The news that it was a boy was transmitted with an appropriately impressive salvo of headgear.

'The joy of the people is boundless,' continues Carrario; 'throughout the city one walks through fire, and in many places, principally in the houses of the aristocracy, fountains of wine are seen to flow, thus increasing the gladness of men's hearts; nothing is heard but shouts of joy and congratulations.' Richelieu himself recorded that 'such great rejoicings as these, for this new favour shown by Heaven to the Kingdom of France, were never seen before'.

It was an age still deeply concerned with horoscopes. Racine records that 'the constellation of the Dauphin was composed of nine stars . . . and he was born on a Sunday, the day of the Sun. Like the rays and light of the sun he will bring radiance to France and her allies.' Louis seems to have been predestined to the title of 'the Sun King' – le Roi Soleil. Racine continues, somewhat inconsequentially, 'Already, in January 1639, he was at the breast of his ninth wet-nurse; they all left him in haste because he maltreated their breasts.'

This was because he was born with two teeth. 'He bit the nipples of those who had not enough milk to satisfy him', wrote the surgeon Dionis, 'until they bled.' The Dutch jurist Grotius saw a special significance in this: 'the Dauphin is not content with sucking his nurses dry, he tears them with his teeth. Let France's neighbours be on their guard against such precocious voracity.'

As was usual, Louis XIV had been provisionally baptised – *ondoyé* – at the time of his birth. This ceremony was performed in the little oratory of the King's apartment at the Château Neuf at Saint-Germain. The real ceremony of baptism was deferred until the boy was four and a half, by which time he had a brother, Philippe, born in 1640. This took place in the Sainte-Chapelle in the Vieux Château. Cardinal Mazarin was god-father and the princesse de Condé was godmother. The Bishop of Meaux, Dominique Séguier, as Grand Aumônier, administered the sacrament.

The ceremony was of course recorded in the *Gazette* and of course described with a maximum of adulation. Robed in a mantle of silver taffeta Louis was 'beautiful as an angel, displaying in all his actions a modesty and a decorum extraordinary in one of his age'. After the baptism he was taken to see his dying father, who asked him his name. 'Louis XIV,' came the reply. 'Not yet, my son,' said the King, 'but you will be soon.'

On Wednesday 14 May 1643, Louis XIII died in the Château Neuf at Saint-Germain. It was Ascension Day. Séguin, the Queen's Premier Médecin, told Mme de Motteville that the King had asked him how long he had to live. Séguin felt his pulse and answered: 'Sire, Your Majesty might have two or three hours at the most.' The King joined his hands and raised his eyes to heaven. 'Eh bien, mon Dieu,' he said; 'j'y consens, et de bon coeur.' Giustinian recounts how Louis had ordered that the curtains of his bed be drawn aside. From his window he could see the single spire of Saint-Denis – 'ce doigt silencieux levé vers le ciel' – the last resting place of the Kings of France. 'Voici ma chambre,' he said; 'je m'en vais.'

The accession of Louis XIV was immediately followed by one of the most brilliant victories in the history of France, the battle of Rocroi. It formed a fitting preface to the reign. Henri d'Orléans, duc d'Aumâle, born in 1822, fourth son of King Louis-Philippe, gives a vivid account of the whole campaign. Described by the brothers Goncourt as 'the typical cavalry officer of the old school', he had inherited from his godfather, the last of the Condé dynasty, not only the vast estates of Chantilly but also the important archives. He had all the taste for precision of the scholar and all the understanding of the art of war of the professional soldier. He was well qualified to write of the battles and the generals of the Condé family.

In 1643, towards the end of Louis XIII's reign, the armies of France were fighting the House of Habsburg on all her frontiers. In the north, at the army in Picardy, 'the most threatened, the least lucky and the most essential of our armies', wrote the duc d'Aumâle, there was no general.

One of the most difficult and delicate tasks confronting a ruler is the choice of military leaders in time of war. Richelieu was no bad judge. In Picardy his choice seemed to be between Henri de la Tour d'Auvergne, later to be vicomte de Turenne, and Louis de Bourbon, duc d'Enghien, later to be prince de Condé. The first was thirty-one years old, the second ten years younger. It was finally decided that the duc d'Enghien should have the army in Picardy.

'Most great commanders', wrote Voltaire, 'have reached that position by degrees. This prince was born a general; the art of war seemed in him to be a natural instinct; the Swedish Torstenson was the only one in Europe other than him to have, at the age of twenty, this genius which can dispense with experience.'

Arriving at Amiens on 17 April, the duc d'Enghien found himself in the most discouraging situation. The death of Richelieu a few months previously had brought about a sudden relaxation of discipline and many officers went absent without leave. 'All the captains of the Gardes Ecossaises', wrote Enghien to his father, 'have gone to Paris without my permission; the Swiss officers have all gone too. The troops have no officers and will not march without them.' Money was short, horses were scarce and fodder was scarcer still; the artillery was unable to move. The imminent prospect of the death of the King, by releasing foreign soldiers from their oaths of allegiance, made desertions more and more to be expected. Morale was low; the soldiers, writes the duc d'Aumâle, had 'that air of depression and resignation which comes from habitual defeat'.

Enghien's opposite number, commanding the Spanish troops in Flanders, was Don Francisco Melo, a most experienced officer. Under him the Spanish infantry, the *tercios viejos*, had the reputation of being invincible. Their discipline was magnificent and their firepower devastating. Melo's plan was to cross the Meuse and attack Rocroi. He would then advance towards Reims, ravaging Champagne on his way, and enter the valley of the Marne, which was the high road to the capital. 'The Spaniards', wrote the contemporary historian Le Laboureur, 'boasted that they were going to have their winter quarters in Paris.' On 15 May Melo arrived with his army before Rocroi. The manoeuvre had been accomplished with perfect precision and amazing speed.

Rocroi, once an isolated village in a marshy plain, had been identified by François I as a site of potential military importance. By 1643 it had been encircled by a wall with five bastions and a deep moat. At the moment when Melo encamped before it, there were but 400 men in the garrison.

On 14 May the French arrived at Saint-Quentin. Although Enghien would not learn it until two days later, the King died at two forty-five that afternoon. Four days later Enghien reached Rocroi. He had some 23,000 troops, about two thirds infantry and one third cavalry – in other words eighteen battalions and thirty-two squadrons. Melo had between 26,000 and 28,000. His artillery, eighteen pieces, was superior to that of the French.

The night of the 18th was spent in battle order. Enghien had put a new spirit into the troops and morale was high. Most importantly his orders were clear: 'Everyone was told exactly what he had to do.' Bossuet, preaching his *oraison funèbre*, tells how, on the night of the battle, 'which he had to pass in the presence of the enemy, like a vigilant captain, he was the last to retire to rest – but never did he rest more peacefully. On the evening of so great a day . . . he is untroubled, so completely is he in his natural element; it is well known that the next day, at the hour agreed, this second Alexander had to be awakened from a profound sleep.'

At three o'clock on Tuesday 19 May the battle began. By between five and six a.m. Enghien's left flank had been routed and the centre was in retreat. Enghien himself had been more successful on the right wing, but he returned to face a desperate situation. 'A few minutes' respite for the horses to regain their breath', wrote Aumâle, 'were sufficient to enable him to decide on a new plan of action, an original conception of which no other battle offers an example.'

Turning his troops 'avec un élan incomparable' he attacked the enemy in the rear and threw them into irretrievable disorder. Only the *tercios viejos*, the cream of the Spanish infantry, remained intact. Enghien now turned upon these; a first, a second and a third time he was repulsed, but on his fourth charge the phalanx, at the end of their strength and at the end of their ammunition, yielded. All who were not killed were taken prisoner.

The Spanish lost 7,000 or 8,000 killed, 6,000 or 7,000 captured, all their artillery was taken and with it enough money to pay the French army for a month. The French lost about 2,000 killed and as many wounded.

Begun at three in the morning, the battle of Rocroi was over by ten-thirty. It was, wrote Aumâle, 'the most complete and resounding victory won by our troops for over a century . . . Enghien had assumed all the responsibility; the honour for the victory belongs to him and to no one else.'

The news of the victory took only one day to reach Paris; in due course it was followed by the trophies of the battle. It required fifty cavalry officers and a hundred picked soldiers to parade them through the streets from the Louvre to Notre-Dame. 'Your standards', wrote the duc de Longueville to Enghien, his brother-in-law, 'have filled all Paris with rejoicing.'

As for Enghien himself, his main concern was to follow up his victory. He saw at once that the capture of Thionville, opening up control of the valley of the Moselle, would, at a single stroke, protect the French army in Alsace from attack in the rear, open the way to the conquest of Flanders and drive a wedge between the Spanish Netherlands and Germany.

Enghien did not ask for anything for himself as a reward for his victory, but he did press urgently for the Court's recognition of the contribution made by the comte de Gassion, his second-in-command. But Gassion was a Huguenot. Already the Court had made promises to Turenne, who was at that time still a Huguenot, and the Queen Regent could not bring herself to offer the marshal's baton to Gassion. Two other names were put forward by Enghien, Sirot and Quincé. Both were met with silence. More importantly a new Lieutenant-General had to be appointed as second-in-command. The prince de Condé advised the appointment of Turenne, or, failing that, Châtillon or La Meilleraie. Any of these would have been acceptable to Enghien. Instead, the Queen Regent gave the post to the duc d'Angoulême, an illegitimate son of Charles IX and Marie Touchet. He was just over seventy, with a far from respectable record and an unfortunate susceptibility to gout. 'I very much fear', wrote the duc de Longueville to Enghien, 'that on account of his age and his infirmities he cannot be of much use to you; you will find him complaisant and always in agreement with the last speaker.'

The disappointment and frustration of the duc d'Enghien stand out clearly in his letters. On 7 June, he wrote to his father from Maubeuge: 'The question of M. de Gassion is of so great importance that I am obliged to press it, and the greatest pleasure that you can give me would be to settle the matter promptly . . . Everyone in the army, who wants this thing, is waiting in expectation to see whether I have enough credit to bring this off. Judge if that is not of great importance to me . . . it is vital to me that the soldiers can see that I am able to acknowledge the services which they have rendered.' Then, turning to his plan to attack Thionville, he adds: 'I beg you to assist me in my original plan in which I am proceeding with diligence.'

On 8 June Michel Le Tellier, Secretary of State for War, wrote: 'At last the Queen has acceded to your advice regarding the siege of Le Chenet' (code for Thionville) . . . 'I assure you that from this quarter you will lack for nothing at all. I will take every care to obtain for you all that you may desire.'

On the same day the duc d'Enghien wrote to the Queen Regent. His tone is peremptory. He demands the full co-operation of the marquis de Gesvres and his troops, but he adds: 'Even if he does not do so I will not give up the pursuit of my first project, hoping that Your Majesty will assist me with all things necessary to the success of a project that is so advantageous to the well-being of your State.' He goes on to remind her that he has asked for a marshal's baton for Gassion and that nothing has been done about it: 'now, I am obliged to say to Your Majesty that I find the minds of the chief commanders so strongly embittered and alienated that if Your Majesty does not give them this satisfaction I will hardly dare to answer for them.'

The prince de Condé found means of suppressing his son's letter before it reached the Queen.

Rocroi was the turn of the tide – a booster for French morale and a blow to Spanish complacency. The capture of Thionville was strategically more important and it was accomplished with the same disregard for his personal safety that Enghien had exhibited at Rocroi.

Another triumph for France, the capture was also another jewel in the crown of the House of Condé, which aroused Cardinal Mazarin's fears. To Enghien it was intolerable that he should have to keep on begging for money with which to pay his troops and for rewards with which to recompense his officers. But his constant demands were an embarrassment to the Government. 'I can see that your cause will fare badly,' his father wrote to him on 25 August; 'your services will not be recognised, your friends and allies will be badly treated and your enemies promoted.' Soldiers and politicians are not always playing the same game. Mazarin was ungenerous, to say the least, and Enghien was not unnaturally affronted. A rift began at this time which was later to assume disastrous proportions.

During all this military and political activity one little side-light is shed on the character of the new King. Soon after the capture of Thionville the Queen Regent wrote to the duc d'Enghien: 'My son the King takes such a pleasure in consulting the plan [of the defences and siege operations] that he will not part with it and took it off to his room where he keeps it.' At a very early age Louis began to be attracted by the paraphernalia of military exercises. This comes out clearly in the picture painted of Louis during his infancy in the memoirs of Louis-Henri Loménie de Brienne, second son of Henri-Auguste, comte de Brienne, Secretary of State for Foreign Affairs.

At the age of about seven, Louis-Henri was placed in the Household of the King, who was two and a half years his junior. 'All I can remember', he writes, 'is that Mme de Lasalle, *femme de chambre* to the Queen Regent, and placed by Her Majesty with the King her son, received us pike in hand and drums beating at the head of the company of Children of Honour, which was already numerous and was under her command . . . She had on a hat covered with black plumes and wore a sword at her side.' She gave them each a musket and kissed them on the forehead; she was not lacking in intelligence, but she adapted herself to the age of the King and she acted like a child with the children.

She made them do drill and the King, 'though still an infant, took an extreme pleasure in this. His amusements all had something to do with war; his fingers were always tapping on the drum and as soon as his little hands could hold the sticks he had hung round his neck a large drum just like those of the Cent-Suisses, which he was continually beating. It was his greatest pleasure.'

The young Louis' military tastes soon extended to a love of weapons. When Brienne first used a small gun, 'which made quite a lot of noise . . . the King clapped his hands and wanted to shoot too, but he was not allowed to handle firearms until after he was seven. The first shot he fired scored a bull's eye.'

Other sources complete the picture of Louis as a small child. Angelo Contarini, Envoy Extraordinary from the Republic of Venice, gives, in a despatch written on Louis' fifth birthday, a charming little portrait. 'His Majesty has an alert mind, and the beauty of his disposition is an indication of high qualities as yet undeveloped. He is of sturdy build and has an animated if rather serious expression, but it is a seriousness full of charm. He rarely laughs, even at play. He insists that his three-year-old brother, the duc d'Anjou, shall show him respect and obedience. He knows and understands that he is King and intends to be treated as such. And when, occasionally, the Queen his mother reproves him, he replies that the time is coming when he will be master. When the Ambassadors talk to the Regent he does not listen, but when they address him he is very attentive . . . In short, unless his life and education play him false, he promises to be a great King.'   .

In the meantime he was subject to the authority of his mother and his tutors. Although his valet La Porte suggests that he was rather spoilt, the rod was not spared.

Marie du Bois, seigneur de Lestoumière, also a valet, recorded an occasion when a slight difference of opinion between Louis and his mother developed into a crisis of authority. 'I will make you understand', she said, 'that it is I who have authority and not you. It is too long since you have had a beating. I will show you that you can be spanked at Amiens as well as in Paris.' It was only to be expected in those days. When the future Louis XIII was about six his father wrote to his governess, the marquise de Montglat, 'I desire and order you to whip him every time he shows stubbornness or does anything wrong, knowing as I do that nothing in the world can be of greater profit to him than that; I know this from experience having profited by it myself, for at his age I was frequently whipped.'

It is possible that Henri IV's grandson was whipped frequently also, but on this occasion the threat was enough. Louis wept with rage and resentment. 'I was deeply moved', comments Du Bois, 'to see my master crying so bitterly. That went on for some time. Then, suddenly, he went of his own accord and threw himself on his knees beside the Queen ... "Maman," he said, "please forgive me. I promise never to do anything but what you want." The Queen kissed her son tenderly and they became good friends again.'

Of his relations with his younger brother, a typical letter would state that 'Mama and I are in good health' and would end 'believe me always to be your affectionate and kind *petit papa*, LOUIS. Given at Amiens this first day of July, 1647.' The term *petit papa* was often used by elder brothers.

In October 1650, when Louis was nine. Abraham de Wicquefort, a Dutchman who was the representative in Paris of the Duke Augustus of Wolfenbuttel, noted that Mazarin had a model fortification constructed in the gardens of the Palais-Royal. There is an engraving of it by Israel Silvestre in the Cabinet des Estampes, which gives the date 1650, showing a very considerable structure. It included all the paraphernalia of defence. Louis, says Wicquefort, 'was preparing to take it by assault with a company of seventy or eighty young noblemen ... all dressed in the same way, that is in grey cloth with black shoulder sashes and collars of gold lace'. The inscription on the engraving states that it was made 'for the diversion of the King'. No doubt it was also intended for his instruction. Louis' playtime, in fact, was constantly cultivating his taste for military exercises.

His lessons, however, were constantly extolling the virtues of peace. Louis' tutor, who assumed his responsibilities once the King was seven and had been transferred from female to male tutelage, was Hardouin de Péréfixe, later to be Bishop of Rodez and ultimately Archbishop of Paris. Péréfixe wrote most of the textbooks which he used, among which his *Institutio Principis* was direct instruction in the art of ruling. 'Do not desire war. Remain at peace until a just cause or some great necessity such as the safety of the State or the need to defend your allies compels you, almost in spite of yourself, to have recourse to arms. And do this in such a way that all can see that you only desire the peace of the realm.'

In one respect Péréfixe already saw the young Louis as superior to his grandfather, Henri IV: 'God has given you an advantage that King Henri did not possess: a majestic presence, an almost divine appearance and carriage, a figure and a beauty worthy of the ruler of world empire, which charm the eye and compel the respect of all.' That looks more like flattery than praise, but the Venetian ambassador Nani, who was under no necessity to flatter, reported much the same thing: 'If fortune had not made him a great king, it is certain that nature gave him the appearance thereof.'

Louis' religious education had its beginnings, of course, at a very early age. He was devoted to his mother Anne of Austria and his mother was devoted to the rituals of the Catholic Church. When not occupied with affairs of state she seems to have spent most of her time in one church or another.

On 28 October 1649, in the month after Louis' eleventh birthday, Anne of Austria wrote to the Jesuit father, Florent de Montmorency: 'The King, my son, having, by the grace of God, arrived at an age when it is necessary to begin to give him a Director of Conscience, in order that he may be able as soon as possible to adopt a way of life which conforms with the title, which is his by birth, of His Most Christian Majesty and the Eldest Son of the Church, I remembered having given my word to the fathers of your company that, when the time came, I would make my choice from among them.' Her choice fell upon the Père Paulin, who was at once captivated by the young Louis: 'indeed, no lamb could be more meek and tractable than our King'. La Porte, at about the same time, asserted that Louis was 'very ready to learn and yields always to reason'. On Christmas Day, 1649, Louis and his brother, now known as *le petit Monsieur*, received their first Communion at the Midnight Mass in the Church of Saint-Eustache. The two boys had been confirmed earlier in the month in the private chapel of the Palais-Royal. The young King, wrote the reporter to the *Gazette*, 'showed many signs of a great inclination to piety'.

In these first eleven years of Louis' life one can see foreshadowed some of the tendencies which were to mark his character and influence his attitude to his role as King. But already his country had entered into the disastrous period of political dissension and civil war which is known as the Fronde.

Louis was at a most impressionable age. During the Fronde he was to suffer deep humiliation at the hands of the Parlement de Paris and of some of the upper aristocracy and Princes of the Blood. But at the same time he became increasingly aware of the natural love of the French for their legitimate King. The cry which came from the hearts of his suffering people was 'Vive le Roi tout seul!'

2

The Fronde

Louis XIII had provided in his will for a Regency Council which would have limited the powers of his widow as Regent. She immediately persuaded the Parlement de Paris to set aside the will and thus became the sole ruler of France. Marie de Medici, the widow of Henri IV, had received the same position. 'The custom', noted Voltaire with a touch of sarcasm, 'which gave the regency to mothers of Kings, seemed then to Frenchmen a law almost as fundamental as that which deprives females of the crown. The Parlement de Paris, having decided this matter on two occasions, that is to say having declared by its own decrees the right of mothers, thus appeared to have conferred the regency' (and therefore to have the right to appoint the ruler); 'it regarded itself as the King's tutor and each councillor believed himself to have some share in the sovereignty'.

But to have the authority of a regent conferred upon one was no guarantee of possessing the qualities requisite for its exercise. To have married a King and to have given birth to a Dauphin were the only qualifications. Anne of Austria was a woman incapable of holding in her hands the reins of government; 'au commencement', it was said, 'la Reine ne savait rien de rien'. She therefore had to rely on someone else to govern for her. Her choice, perhaps pre-conditioned by Richelieu, fell upon Cardinal Mazarin. Voltaire has assessed the situation admirably: 'the Cardinal had over her the influence which a clever man must have over a woman born with enough weakness to be dominated but with enough strength to persist in her choice'.

As early as May 1631 the Venetian ambassador Sagredo wrote in a despatch: 'Mazarin, my most Serene Highness, is agreeable and personable; he is civil, shrewd, dissembling, eloquent, persuasive and impassive, indefatigable at work, circumspect, far-seeing, secretive, full of resources; in a word he possesses all those qualities which go to make up a skilful negotiator. His first attempt was a masterly stroke. Anyone who appears with such brilliance on the world's stage must cut there a great and fine figure.'

For eighteen years – with two short intervals of prudent self-exile – Mazarin was to be the ruler of France. He attracted the hatred of the people, the Parlement and the Princes of the Blood to a degree that has seldom been surpassed in French history. So far as the people of Paris were concerned, they often had no other means of expressing their hatred than by being rude about him. No insult was too gross, no term of abuse too outrageous 'against this wretched tyrant, cheat, impostor, clown, buffoon, Italian thief, held here in common odium by everybody'. Licentious lampoons poured from the gutter press and became known as 'mazarinades'. In due course one appeared with the title 'The custodian of the Queen's bed'.

The combination, however, at a more serious level, of a weak Regent and an unpopular, foreign First Minister, offered to the Parlement an opportunity to try to increase its own power at the expense of that of the monarchy. As so often, it was the need of the Crown to raise money, especially in time of war, which opened the doors to the opposition. A tax had to be 'registered' by the members of the Parlement, but, if they refused, the King could impose a *lit de justice* at which he overrode their refusal and compelled the registration of the tax.

The Parlement, however, could not invoke, as the Parliament did in England, the principle 'No taxation without representation', for the Parlement was not elected by, and its members did not, except in their own imagination, represent the people. But in their own different ways – for their functions had little in common – the Parlement de Paris and the Houses of Parliament in London were both determined, during the same decade, to modify the royal power in their respective countries. In England they were successful – but England recognised no *lit de justice*; in France the monarchy emerged more absolute than before – but France had no Cromwell. Nevertheless there was a serious clash in France between the Crown and the Parlement: it was called the 'Fronde'. The word meant a sling, a weapon which can be lethal but which was not, in the seventeenth century, used in serious warfare.

The Fronde was one of the most complex and confusing episodes in the history of France. It seems that every possible permutation of alliance between the Parlement, the people of Paris and the Princes of the Blood make it difficult – and sometimes unnecessary – to follow. But certain scenes stand out by virtue of their intrinsic interest or the light which they shed on the character of the times or the developing outlook of the young Louis.

Richelieu had established not so much the absolute supremacy of the

Crown as that of its First Minister. After his death the duc de La Rochefoucauld was astonished and dismayed to find that Richelieu still reigned. 'I
arrived at the Court, which I found as much in subjection to his will as
it had been during his life.' He had chosen Mazarin to succeed him, 'and
thus was assured of reigning more absolutely after his death than the
King his Master had been able to do during the thirty-three years of his
reign'.

The Italian Mazarin had been naturalised in April 1639, but he was
regarded as a foreigner – an impression which was somewhat enhanced
by his imperfect command of French pronunciation. He appointed another
Italian, Particelli d'Emery, to the lucrative and all-important post of Contrôleur des Finances. D'Emery was a disaster and this left the flank of the
Crown open to attack. The marquis de Montglat saw in him one of
the causes of all the trouble. 'He sought every possible means of finding
money to be able to continue the war and to satisfy the Cardinal's cupidity,
which was insatiable. Since he [Emery] was a hard and pitiless person he
could not have cared less if he had ruined everybody in order to gratify
his benefactor.' The partisans – a polite but sarcastic word for the extor-
tioners – enforced their exactions with such rigour that 'they took the
very furniture and livestock from the labourers, who were obliged to
abandon everything and leave their land uncultivated. The misery of the
peasants, contrasted with the opulence of the businessmen who were given
such high interest on the money which they advanced that they became
rich in less than no time, caused everyone to murmur.' This gave the
complexion of social morality to an opposition which, originating in
the Parlement, 'seemed', says Alphonse Feillet, 'to give the character of
legality to resistance'.

In January 1648, the Avocat Général, Omer Talon, addressed a remonstrance to the Regent. 'For the last ten years the country has been in
ruins; the peasants are reduced to sleeping on straw, their furniture having
been sold for the payment of taxes which they are not able to meet ...
These unfortunates have no possessions of their own except for their
souls, which cannot be sold at auctions ... Reflect, Madame, on this
public misery. This evening, in the quiet of your Oratory, consider the
calamity facing the provinces, where the hopes of peace, the honours of
victory, the glory of countries conquered can none of them feed those
who have no bread.'

Anne of Austria, whose one ambition was to pass on the royal
supremacy intact to her son, merely met the remonstrances of the Parlement with dictatorial anger: 'Taisez-vous! Je ne veux pas vous entendre.'

The active opposition of the Parlement dates from 13 May 1648, when
a meeting was held in the Chambre Saint-Louis in the former Palais de la

Cité, where some of the independent bodies such as the Cours des Comptes, Cours des Aides and Conseil de l'Hôtel de Ville made common cause. Mazarin had lost the Parlement, the bourgeois of Paris and the people. The aristocracy could be won only by constant bribery, mostly in the form of lucrative posts, but the Regent's early and senseless extravagance in this respect had made her more enemies than friends. Her main support came from the duc d'Orléans and the prince de Condé (the duc d'Enghien, victor of Rocroi, had succeeded his father as prince de Condé in December 1646), but as ever it was at a price. Mazarin handled Gaston d'Orléans by making him governor of Languedoc and by encouraging him to believe that his current favourite, the abbé de La Rivière, could be given a cardinal's hat. Condé was given the governorship of Champagne.

One of the more impartial recorders of the Fronde was Abraham de Wicquefort, who was the representative of the Duke August of Wolfenbuttel, a relative of the Duke of Brunswick. He is clearly well informed as well as being an eye-witness of some of the dramas. On 19 June 1648 he described a new and dangerous alliance. It was no longer just the Parlement and the Court who were involved in the dispute: 'the people are beginning to take an interest in this affair'. On 11 August 1648, the Chambre Saint-Louis produced a sort of charter – 'la réforme de l'état'. It contained twenty-seven articles of which the most interesting resembled the English Habeas Corpus: 'that no subject of the King could be detained for more than twenty-four hours without being interrogated and referred to his normal judge'.

On 28 August Wicquefort reported the victory on the 20th by Condé's troops at Lens – news which 'has so filled the Court with joy as to stifle all the rest'. The duc de La Rochefoucauld goes even further: 'Le Conseil du Roi regarda ce grand succès comme un coup du Ciel.' The young Louis, not yet ten years old, exclaimed: 'The Parlement will be annoyed by this!'

It was the sorry truth. It seemed to the marquis de Montglat that the moment of triumph was snatched from France by the selfishness of the members of the Parlement. 'The French, invincible in the face of their enemies, could only be conquered by themselves.' Had the money needed by Condé to follow up the victory of Lens been forthcoming, the submission of the Low Countries would have been virtually certain – 'but this great good fortune was brought to a sudden stop by the internal troubles which befell the kingdom and by the spirit of faction of those who put their private interest before the good and the greatness of the State'.

On Wednesday 26 August, a solemn Te Deum was sung in Notre-Dame in thanksgiving for the victory. Confident in the strength which this gave to her position and blind to the reality of the situation, the Queen Mother ordered the arrest of three prominent members of the Parlement – Broussel, du Blanc Mesnil (both known as *pères du peuple*) and Charton – as they were returning from the Cathedral. Broussel was the most important of the three because of his widespread popularity. He is described by La Rochefoucauld as 'a person of an old-fashioned probity ... and all the more accredited because his age and his lack of wealth put him beyond the reach of envy'.

The arrest was handled with incompetence and provoked an uprising. The coach in which Broussel was being taken into custody broke down and while he was being transferred to another he was recognised by the crowd. 'This', writes Wicquefort, 'caused such a change in the temper of the people that in less than half an hour one saw almost the whole city rise up in revolt and chains across the roads everywhere.'

Wicquefort confirms, in this instance, the memoirs of one of the more colourful figures of the Fronde, Jean-François de Gondi, coadjutor, or Assistant Bishop, to his uncle, the Archbishop of Paris, and later to be Cardinal de Retz. His egocentricity was such that his memoirs need to be treated with caution, but his powers of describing an episode or of capturing an atmosphere are considerable.

'I cannot express to you', wrote Retz, 'the consternation which arose in Paris in the first quarter of an hour after the abduction of Broussel and the commotion in the second. Sadness, or rather dejection, took hold of even the children; people looked at one another but said nothing. Suddenly they broke out; they became excited, they started running and yelling, they shut up the shops.'

The royal family, meanwhile, had regained the Palais-Royal and had dined quietly. The valet Du Bois had left his horse at the entrance in readiness for a visit and when he went to mount it he found the square in front of the palace filled with troops and the guards doubled. He returned to the Queen's apartment. 'I had not been there long before I realised that it was a situation of red-hot alarm.' He was soon armed with pistols and out in the streets. 'Stones were flying about everywhere, hurled from the windows: chains were being drawn across the roads; the barricades were up: the chaos was so great that no one was safe. By the end of the day Paris was in an extraordinary uproar which announced some great disorder.'

The next day, Thursday 27 August, the situation was if anything worse. The Parlement decided to go in a body to the Palais-Royal and demand the release of Broussel. The président de Mesmes, writes La Rochefoucauld, 'told the Regent that it was no longer a case for deliberation and that it was an absolute necessity to yield to the will of the people who refused to listen to the voice of the Magistrate and who had lost all sense of respect and obedience, in short, that they were the masters. The Queen said that she would not give way at all and that, holding in her hand as she did, the sacred trust of the authority of the King her son, she would never consent to its violation by giving in to the passions of the multitude.' It was not for nothing that La Rochefoucauld had observed that the Queen Regent was 'by nature incapable of fear'.

In the end the Queen had to agree to the release of Broussel, but on condition that the Parlement confined its attention to matters of law. After the return of Broussel, writes de Retz, 'the barricades were destroyed, the shops were opened and in less than two hours Paris seemed quieter than I had ever seen it on Good Friday'. The peace, however, was not to last for long. The agitators were still unsatisfied and violence continued.

In all these scenes of danger the young King – he was now just ten – showed a courage and a concern for others which did him great credit. Du Bois records how Louis' brother, the young duc d'Anjou, was overcome with fear. 'The King did his best to reassure him, going so far as to draw his little sword, which he did with an admirable grace, caressing his trembling young brother, keeping close to him and saying the most charming things in the world, but remaining calm, with the air of some great general who, in the face of some sudden alarm can find the words to put a new heart into all who hear him. Finally he had the kindness to take Monsieur back to his own room and put him to bed.'

The last months of the year 1648 were for the Cardinal and the Regent 'the winter of their discontent'. Condé wanted a cardinal's hat for his brother the prince de Conti; Gaston d'Orléans had been encouraged to expect one for his favourite the abbé de La Rivière. The Pope refused to grant more than one. The Parlement continued to press for its right to have its say in the affairs of State. The coadjutor de Retz preached against the money-borrowing of the Crown – 'this public consecration of usury' (a practice forbidden in the Bible) – and rated Mazarin 'the most convinced Jew that there was in Europe'. He succeeded in mobilising the clergy of Paris into solid opposition. A few days after Christmas the hostility of the people of Paris became once more apparent.

'Thus ended the year 1648,' writes Mme de Motteville; 'it had not been a happy one . . . France was in such a position that it could not continue thus for long. Either the King must recover his power, or his subjects would deprive him of what was left of it. Everything had passed beyond the normal boundaries; order was overturned and the French, from having too many masters, no longer recognised any.'

Secure in what she believed to be the support of Condé, Anne felt ready for strong action. Together with Condé, Gaston d'Orléans and Mazarin she decided, says Mme de Motteville, 'to punish [Paris] by the strongest measures, and she was resolved henceforth to speak to her subjects through the mouths of her cannons'. First, however, it was imperative to get the King and the Court out of Paris.

The secret was well guarded. The duc d'Orléans told neither his wife nor his daughter; the prince de Condé said nothing to his mother or to his sister, the duchesse de Longueville; Mme de Motteville had not the slightest inkling that such a flight was planned. 'On 5 January,' she writes, 'the Eve of Epiphany ... I went to the Queen's rooms where I was accustomed to pass the greater part of the day. I found her in her petit cabinet, calmly watching the King as he played and leaning nonchalantly on the corner of the table; she seemed to think only of what she was seeing ... Presently Mme de la Trémouille caught my eye; I leant over towards her and she said in a very low voice: "It is noised abroad in Paris that the Queen leaves tonight." ' Mme de Motteville refused to believe it.

At last the ladies retired to bed. 'As soon as we had left, the doors of the Palais-Royal were closed with orders that they should not be reopened ... The maréchal de Villeroy allowed the King to sleep until three in the morning, then he woke him up, together with Monsieur, to get them into the carriage which was waiting at the garden gate of the Palais-Royal.' The royal party assembled without any difficulty at the rendezvous in the Cours la Reine. Only the duchesse de Longueville refused to accompany them, claiming her pregnancy as her excuse. But it was a nerve-racking experience for all. 'Never has a night been so filled with horror and agitation.'

The departure from Paris was well organised and successful: the arrival at Saint-Germain was not. No thought at all had been given to the problems of taking up residence here during the small hours. The palace was entirely unfurnished and in no condition to receive anyone, let alone a King and his suite. 'The King, the Queen and all the Court', complains Mme de Motteville, 'found themselves in this place with no beds, no officers, no furniture, no linen and without anything at all that might be necessary for the service of the royal family and all those who had come with them. Madame la duchesse d'Orléans slept the first night on straw, and Mademoiselle also. All those who followed the Court shared the same lot, and, in a few hours, straw at Saint-Germain became so dear that money could not buy it.' Orléans' daughter, Mademoiselle de Montpensier, records the experience herself. 'I lay in a very beautiful room in the attics, with beautiful painting and beautiful gilding, large but with very little fire and no glass in the windows, which is not agreeable in January.'

On 2 January 1649 the Parlement had issued a remonstrance in which can be seen one of the main themes of the Fronde. 'The elevation of a particular person', it ran, 'to too high a position of authority is contrary to the policy of maintaining public order in any sort of government, but especially of monarchies, of which the fundamental law is that there is only one master, both in title and in practice.' Concini and Richelieu are cited as examples of this too great favour and power. The early hopes of the Parlement in the regency of Anne of Austria had been disappointed. Mazarin, 'a pupil of Richelieu nourished with his ambitious maxims and fashioned by his artifices, in succeeding to his ministry, had succeeded also to his designs'.

It was just at this time of deep humiliation that the royal family received the news from England of the execution of Charles I. Jean Vallier was a Maître d'Hôtel du Roi whose journal covers the period of the Fronde; he was firmly on the side of the King and felt the frondeurs publicised Mazarin's errors to win power for themselves. He described the impact of the event in England: 'The news arrived in the city of the most horrible and detestable act of parricide that has ever been committed by Christians.' He accused the English Parliament of 'satiating their implacable hatred of his sacred person'; of having forced him 'to answer for his actions, like some criminal of no importance, before a little underling of a judge'; he castigates 'those two pests of the human race', Cromwell and Fairfax, and glorifies Charles for meeting his death 'with all the piety and courage worthy of a great King'.

On 23 March 1649, Condé made an inflammatory speech in the Parlement. It was reported by the Venetian ambassador, Michiel Morosini. 'With this statement the Princes aimed at winning over all the people, and the Parlement itself, to regard as satisfactory only an agreement which would lead to the Cardinal's exit from the Kingdom, and in fact it was so effective that the people desire nothing but war and the great men desire no concession other than the Minister's departure. The Court, when it heard of such an extravagant demand, was for a long time agitated and confused, but finally resolved to consider whether, in fact, it should agree to Mazarin's departure, and after many hours it was decreed, as on other occasions, that he should remain, since the King could never agree to such a weak action as to obey his subjects, the Cardinal's supporters having quoted the example of England, in which the disturbances began as a result of the King submitting to the demands of his subjects, who demanded a favourite minister of his, after which their extravagant pretensions grew to such an extent that they ended by bringing their King to the block and the axe.'

Louis commented on the English in his memoirs: 'This subjugation, which forces the sovereign to take the law from his people, is the last calamity that can fall upon a man of our rank ... It is not merely power that a people assembled attributes to itself; the more you give it, the more it pretends to; the more you favour it, the more it despises you; and when this power is once in its possession, it is held so strongly that one cannot take it away without extreme violence.'

By mid-January 1650 Wicquefort was feeling short of information, 'because of the sterility of the news at this season of the year', when suddenly, on Tuesday 19 January, 'the whole city was filled with the astounding report of the biggest thing that has happened during the regency – the arrest of M. le Prince [Condé], the prince de Conti [his brother] and the duc de Longueville [their brother-in-law]'. All three had been specially required to attend the Council at the Louvre. On entering the Galerie Dorée, where the Council usually met, they were entertained in conversation by the Chancellor Séguier until Guitault, Capitaine des gardes du corps de la Reine, entered with half a dozen of the guard and arrested them. Dumbfounded but helpless, they were taken, not without mishaps, to Vincennes. The firing of a cannon informed the occupants of the Palais-Royal that the mission had been accomplished.

The manner in which the arrest had been contrived gave rise to much hostile criticism, but Mazarin said 'in a loud voice ... that Her Majesty had only taken this momentous resolution because she believed there to be no other remedy against the great evil which threatened the whole kingdom with inevitable ruin'.

The Princes were, of course, allowed their own servants and were lodged in what had served Charles V as a royal palace, but they were in strict custody. As a precaution against Condé's escape, the Mass was always said in French, lest, in the course of the liturgy, some communication might be made to him in Latin which the guards would not understand.

Having seen the three Princes safely incarcerated in the donjon of Vincennes, the Regent decided, in spite of the harsh weather, to take the King, not yet twelve and a half years old, into Normandy.

Normandy was one of the chief areas that supplied food to Paris and the duc de Longueville was its governor. Its loyalty to the Crown had to be won. 'That is why our young Monarch and his august mother', stated the *Gazette*, 'are proceeding to this province, for it has always been observed in France that the presence of the King is worth an army and that it is a safeguard against rebellions.' The people of Rouen forced the duchesse de Longueville to leave the town and gave a hearty welcome to the young King.

The King and his mother left Paris on 1 February 1650 and arrived at Rouen two days later. It was hardly a royal progress. The comte d'Harcourt, who commanded the royalist troops, could provide only a scant escort. 'He had little money and few troops; but the authority of the legitimate power has often as much strength as the largest battalions. The King and Queen were received at Rouen with great manifestations of joy, such as were deserved by a young King whose beauty and whose innocence could not fail to please these people.'

At the beginning of April the King and his mother went on a similar mission to Burgundy, of which Condé was governor. Here it was necessary to capture Bellegarde before they could enter Dijon. Once again the presence of the King was decisive. Mme de Motteville writes: 'The King, in spite of his youth, went to the camp and showed himself to his army. The soldiers were absolutely delighted to see him and accepted without complaining that this was the only payment they would receive. The presence of this young Monarch, putting new spirit into those who fought for him, gave them a new strength.'

Early in 1651, a year after the imprisonment of the Princes, things still looked as bad as ever. Gaston d'Orléans was determined to obtain the release of the Princes and the dismissal of Mazarin. The marquise de Montglat (who wrote memoirs as well as her husband) tells how supporters of the Cardinal were urging the Regent to take the King out of Paris and place herself at the head of the army, refusing to liberate the Princes, maintaining Mazarin in power and forcing Gaston d'Orléans and the Parlement into submission. When Gaston heard of this he was determined to frustrate it no matter what the cost was. On 6 February, Mazarin went into prudent self-exile at Schloss Brühl near Cologne.

On the night of 9 February, the Palais-Royal was virtually in a state of siege. The Queen feared that Gaston's real design was to force her into a convent, seize the King's person, get rid of Mazarin and become Regent himself. Gaston sent M. des Ouches, captain of the Swiss Guards, to discover if the King had already left. The Queen assured him that she had no intention of taking the King out of the capital. Des Ouches said that he had orders to see the King with his own eyes. After a moment's hesitation Anne commanded the maréchal de Villeroy to conduct des Ouches to the King's bedroom: 'Having opened the curtains of his bed, he held a candle close to his face so that he could be recognised.'

Mme de Motteville again takes up the tale. Des Ouches did all that he could to convince the people of Paris that 'he had just seen the King, who was asleep, and advising them to follow the example of their Master. They replied that they wanted to see him themselves.' They went straight to the Palais-Royal and demanded to do so. His mother, continues Mme de Motteville, 'immediately ordered all the doors to be opened and that they should be conducted to Louis' room. The rioters were delighted by this openness; they came to the bedside of the King, where the curtains had been drawn back.' It worked. Their old love for their King returned and they gave him a thousand benedictions. 'For a long time they watched him sleeping and were lost in admiration ... They had come as people filled with anger; they left as subjects filled with tenderness.' The next day, at his mother's direction, Louis signed the order for the release of the Princes.

On 5 September 1651, Louis reached his thirteenth birthday, the date fixed for his coming of age. Two days later he held a solemn *lit de justice* in the Parlement. The account of it, copied into Mme de Motteville's memoirs from the reports printed at the time, makes an astonishing contrast with the chronicles of discord and devastation which typify the Fronde. It is like the interruption of one serene and lovely day in a month of stormclouds.

There were many English refugees in Paris at the time and John Evelyn went to visit his friend Thomas Hobbes. 'From his window we saw the whole equipage and glorious cavalcade of the young French Monarch, Louis XIV, passing to Parliament when first he took the kingly government upon him.'

All the dramatic heraldry of kingship, all the gilded paraphernalia of the Court, all the pomp of civic pride and ecclesiastical grandeur were paraded before the eyes of the delighted people of Paris. 'Then came abundance of footmen and pages of the King,' continues Evelyn, 'new-liveried with white and red feathers; next, the garde du corps and other officers; and lastly appeared the King himself ... like a young Apollo, in a suit so covered with rich embroidery that one could perceive nothing of the stuff under it; he went almost the whole way with his hat in his hand, saluting the ladies and acclamators, who had filled the windows with their beauty and the air with "Vive le Roi!" He seemed a prince of a grave yet sweet countenance.' The official record completes the account: 'His Majesty ... appeared to be of so tall a stature that it was difficult to believe that he had not left fourteen behind him.' He was mounted on a light bay charger whose high spirits frequently caused it to rear in a majestic caracole which revealed Louis as 'already one of the finest horsemen of the realm'. The seemingly endless cavalcade jingled along the rue Saint-Honoré from the Palais-Royal to the Châtelet, and across the Pont au Change, and drew up at the entrance to the Palais de Justice.

Every street and every window along the route was filled with spectators; 'the cries of "Vive le Roi!" only interrupted by tears of joy, rising to the very heavens, opened the hearts of all and followed His Majesty right to the steps up to the Sainte-Chapelle'. In this beautiful Gothic shrine, illuminated by some of France's finest stained glass, a low Mass was celebrated by the Bishop of Bayeux, after which the King was conducted to the Grande Chambre where he took his seat upon the *lit de justice*. In a reverent silence he addressed the body which had so recently sought to restrict his royal power. 'Messieurs – I have come to my Parlement to tell you that, following the law of my State it is my wish to take the government upon myself; and I hope with God's grace that it will be with piety and justice. My Chancellor will make my intentions known to you in greater detail.'

It was the moment for the Queen Mother to step down. Mme de Motteville assures us that 'she saw the ending of her regency with real joy; if this were mixed with a little sadness it was that she had not handed over to the King her son a sovereign authority as absolute as she would have wished'. She did not cling to power but was often heard to say: 'Qu'il soit le Maître et que je ne sois plus rien.' Inclining slightly in her seat, she addressed her son: 'Monsieur – this is the ninth year since, in accordance with the last wish of the late King, my most honoured Lord, I have taken charge of your education and of the government of your State . . . Now that the law of the realm calls you to the government of this monarchy, I hand over to you, with great satisfaction, the authority which was conferred upon me to rule it.' Louis answered: 'Madame – I thank you for the care which you were pleased to take of my education and of the administration of my Kingdom. I beg that you will continue to give me your good advice, and I desire that, next to myself, you will be the chief of my council.' The Queen now rose to her feet and went to salute her son, 'but His Majesty, coming down from the *lit de justice*, went to her and embraced and kissed her. The Chancellor then caused the doors to be opened and the public to be admitted, and the Sieur Guiet, Clerk of the Court, read aloud the edicts brought by the King against blasphemy and duelling and the declaration of the innocence of the prince de Condé.'

Condé, however, was not present at Louis' side as second Prince of the Blood. He had left Paris to take up arms against his King and was negotiating an alliance with France's enemy, the King of Spain. The second Fronde – the Fronde des Princes – had started. It was an expression both of Condé's insatiable lust for power and of the bitter hostility of the Princes of the Blood to the rule of Mazarin. Condé, by his lineage, was the last of the great feudal magnates. The blood of the connétable de Bourbon and of the duc de Montmorency, sometimes as ready to bear arms against their sovereign as for him, flowed in his veins. The duchesse de Nemours relates that Condé used to say that the whole of the war was only worth describing in burlesque verse and himself called it 'la guerre des pots de chambre'.

Condé's first move was to Bourges, the capital of Le Berry, of which he was Governor. Leaving his brother Conti to ferment sedition in Bourges, he moved on to Bordeaux. Louis and his council agreed to act swiftly. At the end of September, Louis wrote to the Mayor of Bourges announcing his intention to visit 'sa bonne ville' immediately. The Mayor assured him that 'as soon as His Majesty should approach, his loyal subjects would take arms to receive him and to drive out M. le prince de Condé'.

On 2 October the royal cortège, with its little army, left Fontainebleau for Bourges. 'The joy and excitement of the King', wrote Mazarin to his nephew the duc de Mercoeur, 'exceeded all bounds. The prince grows bigger every day, both in body and in spirit.'

On 8 October Louis was received with acclamations by the people of Bourges. In return for their loyalty he ordered the destruction of the Grosse Tour which had long been a symbol of subjection. On the same day he issued a declaration against Condé and Conti and their sister the duchesse de Longueville, together with the duc de Nemours and the duc de La Rochefoucauld.

It seems that Louis was beginning to feel his royal authority. The Parlement, though not in open rebellion, was still a danger to his position in Paris. In January 1652, a deputation from the Parlement came to present a remonstrance to Louis while he was at Poitiers. Louis took the document from the Premier Président, Pomponne de Bellièvre, and said that he would bring the matter before his Council. Bellièvre was beginning to explain that it was the right of the Magistrates to present their own petitions when Louis cut him short. 'You may go, sir. I have spoken.'

In the meantime Mazarin, summoned by Louis from his exile at Schloss Brühl and supported by a considerable army, had entered France. By 16 January he was in the Loire valley and was soon able to join Louis at Poitiers. He had been branded by the Parlement as 'traitor, thief and enemy of the peace of Christendom' and some had presumed to put a price upon his head. 'This head,' wrote Mme de Motteville, 'attacked on all sides and with a price upon it, was the only one strong enough to re-establish order.'

Meanwhile Gaston d'Orléans, after much dithering, had gone over to the side of the rebels. With him came his daughter, Mademoiselle de Montpensier.

The Grande Mademoiselle played, in the words of her biographer Victoria Sackville-West, 'a pseudo-heroic part in the whole absurd, abortive affair ... The Fronde and Mademoiselle were, in a way, made for each other.' During the Fronde des Princes she actually entered Orléans – the capital of her father's apanage – by escalade, climbing up a ladder and being pushed through a hole in a door. She was greeted with shouts of joy of 'Vive le Roi! Vive les Princes! et point de Mazarin!' She was then carried shoulder-high through the streets. 'My joy made me quite beside myself,' she admitted; 'everyone was kissing my hands and I was in fits of laughter at seeing myself in so entrancing a situation.'

While the Grande Mademoiselle was being transported with delight, the peasants and the paupers of France were being reduced to the last stages of misery and famine. La Porte, valet de chambre to the young King, describes a horrific scene: 'When the mothers died, the children died soon afterwards,' he wrote; 'I saw, on the bridge of Melun, by which the Court passed soon afterwards, three children on top of their dead mother. One of them was still trying to suckle.'

In 1651 reports – *les Relations* – were being received from all over the country. From Saint-Quentin, to pick a single example: 'Out of 450 sick, the inhabitants, who were unable to look after them, drove out 200, whom we saw dying one by one on the high road ... Their ordinary diet was of mice, for which they hunted; they devoured roots which animals would not eat, in fact it is impossible to describe what we have seen ... We can assure you that we have seen with our own eyes, between Reims and Rethel, herds – not of cattle but of men and women going out into the fields and grubbing in the earth like pigs in the hope of finding a few roots ... but they become so feeble that they no longer have the strength to seek their livelihood ... the curé of Boult, whose letter we enclose, assured us that he had buried three parishioners who died of hunger; the rest have lived on chopped straw mixed with earth, from which they make a food which cannot be called bread.' At Port-Royal Mère Angélique Arnauld wrote to Mère Agnès: 'I enclose a sample of the bread which the poor eat; you may judge to what extremity they are reduced.'

Their suffering was of no consequence to the prince de Condé and his peers. Personal pride and personal ambition were his only motives. The motives of the Grande Mademoiselle are less obvious. 'I have some knowledge of the sentiments of this princess,' claimed Mme de Motteville; 'everything that Mademoiselle ever did was always ruined by her temperament, which made her go too far and too fast.'

The portraits of her all agree in showing a large, heavy-featured face which is at best dull and at worst inane. The large canvas painted by Pierre Bourgignon, which used to hang in the Salle des Gardes at her Château de Saint-Fargeau, is an example of the latter. She is posing as an Amazon in a plumed helmet, which looks invincibly ridiculous; with her left hand she exhibits an oval portrait of her father. One can understand how she thoroughly enjoyed the opportunities offered to her by the Fronde for playing at soldiers.

What the soldiers were playing at is another story. The letters of Mère

Angélique Arnauld in the year 1652 paint an appalling picture. 'France is utterly desolate,' she wrote on 28 June, 'there is no province which is not at the extremity of suffering. Paris and its surrounding country are the most ill-treated. All the villages round here are total deserts, and those few inhabitants who remain have taken to the woods, the others having died of hunger or having been slaughtered by the soldiers . . . The same has happened in one of our villages – Mondeville – and, it has to be said, on all sides . . . There is no obedience or discipline in any of the armies, and it seems that the soldiers are possessed by the devil.'

The letters of the Mère Angélique read like the texts to the engravings of Jacques Callot – *Les Grandes Misères de la Guerre* (the word 'Grande' refers not to the magnitude of the misery but to the size of the copper plate and distinguishes these from *Les Petites Misères*), though these were in fact engraved during the Thirty Years War (1618–48). In one scene a large tree has already twenty-one men hanging from its branches, their feet still reaching down for the ground that is no longer there. Another man is about to be turned off the ladder; a second kneels at its foot to receive a final absolution; two more are engaged in a last-minute game of dice; others look up at the dangling figures as they await their turn to join the number. The scene affords a chilling sense of the cheapness of human life. In another engraving the scene is of soldiers turned brigands raiding a farmhouse. Over a large fire the wretched master of the house is hanging head downwards from a meat-hook, while an older man, perhaps some faithful steward, is held with his feet in the fire until he reveals some hoard of treasure which may not even exist. In the next room a soldier prepares to rape a woman without so much as troubling to remove his hat.

No deterrent might seem too spectacular in the face of these diabolical crimes, and Callot offers the grim reality of such punishment. On a high scaffold a man is spread-eagled upon a cartwheel. The executioner has raised his flail to smash the bones of his arms and legs and leave him on the wheel to die of pain. In another plate – *Les Châtiments* – he invites our judgement on the meeting of inhumanity with equal inhumanity. But in the darkness of this Valley of the Shadow of Death the bright light of Christian charity was not completely extinguished. The age of the Fronde produced at least one priest who earned, if anyone ever did, the title of Saint – Vincent de Paul, known commonly as Monsieur Vincent.

Son of a peasant farmer from the district of Les Landes, he received ordination in the year 1600. He soon attracted the attention of Emmanuel de Gondi, brother of the Archbishop of Paris, and joined his household. Emmanuel was the Général des Galères and it was through him that Vincent had one of his first experiences of human degradation and suffering at its worst. The living death of the convicts condemned to man the galleys was described by Henri Martin as 'l'enfer anticipé' – a foretaste of Hell.

Monsieur Vincent soon established a deep but chaste relationship with Louise de Marillac, the veuve Legras: he was *le Père des Pauvres*, she *la Mère*. The offspring of their partnership was the association of Christian ladies – les Filles de la Charité. But it is one thing to have a heart breaking with compassion for suffering humanity and another to have the mind of an administrator capable of keeping a vast number of projects moving steadily forward. The rare combination of those two gifts was the key to the success of Monsieur Vincent. The Filles de la Charité, l'Oeuvre des Enfants Trouvés, the Hospice du Nom de Jésus for geriatric patients, and the army of Missionnaires were organised on a nationwide scale.

In 1648, with the outbreak of the Fronde, Monsieur Vincent was sixty-eight years old, but he at once accepted the new demands with which the near-anarchy of the provinces confronted him. On 22 May 1651, the Mayor of Rethel wrote to him: 'No one so far, with the exception of Your Reverence and your followers, has had compassion on our sufferings. For the last two years Champagne as a whole and this town in particular are only kept going by the charities which you have dispensed.' Those words could have been written from almost anywhere in France.

If Monsieur Vincent was the hero of those dark days, the prince de Condé was the villain of the piece. An anonymous sonnet of the period begins:

> Condé, l'unique auteur de nos plus grands malheurs,
> Par qui toute la France, aujourd'hui désolée,
> Ne parait plus qu'un grand et triste mausolée,
> Et l'on confond partout et le sang et les pleurs.

> [Condé, the sole author of our greatest misfortunes,
> Through whom all France, today laid waste,
> Seems no more than one vast, miserable mausoleum
> And on all sides the blood is mingled with tears.]

The portraits of Condé at Chantilly do not do him justice. Both David Teniers le Jeune and Juste Egmont show a face upon which one would not trouble to bestow a second glance. He has rather a long nose and that is about all. But Coysevox gives us a very different picture, both in his bronze bust and in the medallion struck to mark his funeral. The face is unforgettable; here we can see, in Bossuet's words, 'un Prince du sang qui portait la victoire dans ses yeux' – a face that could have put a new spirit into the troops before Rocroi. There is something farouche about his blazing eyes and wild, unkempt appearance. He had, as Primi Visconti observed, 'l'air d'un brigand'.

Madame de Motteville gives a thumbnail sketch in which she does not descend to flattery: 'He was not handsome; his face was of an ugly shape. His eyes were a vivid blue and in his expression was a look of pride. His nose was aquiline, his mouth most displeasing because it was too large and the teeth too prominent, but in his whole countenance there was something great and proud, something of the eagle.'

Mademoiselle was chiefly of interest to the prince de Condé because she was immensely rich. With a little encouragement from him she raised and paid a regiment of her own. 'I must confess', she wrote, 'that I went a bit childish and rejoiced at the sound of the trumpets.'

From Orléans, where Mademoiselle reigned supreme, the Prince's party was able to enter Paris while the King's army was waiting and watching on the north-east of the city. The encounter took place on 2 July 1652. It was one of the hottest days of the year – 'il faisait un chaud horrible ce jour-là', wrote Mademoiselle, who describes her own share in the battle. 'The enemy' (and that term included the King) 'numbered more than 12,000 men; Monsieur le Prince only had 5,000 and he held out against them for the space of seven or eight hours . . . He was everywhere. The enemies have said that he must be a demon, for it was not humanly possible to do all that he did. He took part in all the attacks.'

During this whole day the Queen Mother was at the Couvent des Carmes at Saint-Denis, kneeling in prayer before the exposed Sacrament, except for those moments, adds Mme de Motteville, 'when she went to the grille to learn of the death of some member of the King's party'. But she suffered also from the deaths on the other side. 'The crime of her enemies did not efface the regret which she felt at their loss.' A civil war is often the saddest of all wars.

Towards the end of the day Condé came to see Mademoiselle at a house near the Porte Saint-Antoine. 'He was in a pitiful condition,' she wrote; 'the dust was inches deep upon his face, his hair was all in tangles; his shirt and collar were covered with blood, although he had not himself been wounded; his cuirass had been battered all over and he held his sword in his hand, having lost its scabbard. He said to me: "You are looking at a man in utter despair; I have lost all my friends." '

It was then that Mademoiselle performed the one action for which she is remembered in popular history – she ordered the cannons of the Bastille to fire on the King's troops. It was probably the stupidest thing that this stupid woman ever did. She was hoping to marry Louis. La Porte related that Mademoiselle took two hours telling him why she had shut the gates of Orléans against the King, 'charging me to tell the Queen Mother, and she gave me to understand that giving her the King in marriage would be the best way to bring about a good peace'. Her action, however, was counter-productive.

'I went to the Bastille,' she wrote, 'which I had never seen before, and walked for some time on top of the towers and I had the cannons changed; they were all aimed towards the town; I had them turned towards the river and the faubourg to defend the bastion. I looked through a telescope and saw, on the heights of the Charonne, a large crowd and even some coaches, from which I rightly judged that the King was there.' Further east, towards Bagnolet, the royal army was manoeuvring into position. She could see the generals deploying their cavalry. Turenne and La Ferté began to advance towards Paris. It was then that it happened – 'two or three volleys were fired from the cannons of the Bastille, as I ordered when I left it'.

Mazarin, observing her action from a safe distance, remarked: 'Elle a tué son mari!'

3
Ballet, the Coronation and Illness at Mardyck

On 24 December 1652, when Louis was just over fourteen, the Venetian ambassador, Giovanni Sagredo, noted that 'a very rich and costly ballet is being laid on; for more than four months Torelli has been busy making the machines for it. The King applies himself all day long exclusively to learning this ballet . . . Gambling, dancing and the comedy are his only concerns, and this in order to divert his attention away from matters of greater weight and importance.' Sagredo was perhaps a little puritanical in implying that ballet was something lightweight and that Louis would have been better employed on Latin grammar and syntax. The Ballet de Cour was much more than a costly and frivolous entertainment.

The word 'ballet' can be misleading. The modern mind must dispel any image of *Les Sylphides* or *Petrouchka*. The abbé de Pure, writing in 1667, described it as 'a dumb show in which the gestures and movements convey the meaning which could have been expressed in words'. It was divided into a number of entries, much as a comedy was divided into scenes, but with no sequential connection. Ballets were performed from within the most elaborate scenery, much of which could be moved by the most elaborate mechanism. Monsters could arise from the deep; the chariot of Apollo could cross the sky; some deity from ancient Rome – the *deus ex machina* – could descend and put the earth to rights; the divinities of the infernal regions could rise from their underworld and palaces collapse upon themselves. Some of the most ambitious of these sets were designed by Giacomo Torelli. In the Ballet de Cour most of the leading roles were taken by members of the Court and particularly by members of the royal family, who had received instruction in the art of Terpsichore just as they had been trained in fencing and shooting and horsemanship. Exactly what they had been trained to do remains obscure. There is something ephemeral about a dance. We often know the scenery; we often know the music;

we know most of the verses which accompanied the entries; but we do not know the precise choreography.

The recital of verses or of songs often accompanied the dance. It was the writer of these verses who was the true author of the ballet. He set the theme. By far the most important of these authors was Benserade. He had been baptised Isaac, which may have been appropriate, for Isaac means 'laughter'. He was a great success at Court. In 1697 Louis himself paid tribute to Benserade in granting the *privilège du Roi* to the first edition of his Works: 'In his verses which he wrote for the ballets at the beginning of our reign, the manner in which he combined together the character of the persons dancing with that of the personalities whom they represented was a sort of personal secret which he copied from no one and which, perhaps, no one will ever copy from him.'

But if Benserade knew how to mix the character of the actor with that of his role, he knew also how to mix entertainment with propaganda. On 23 February 1653, during the week before Shrove Tuesday, Benserade produced the *Ballet de la Nuit* – the one complained of by Sagredo. The Jesuit priest Ménestrier, a contemporary authority on 'les ballets anciens et modernes', was full of enthusiasm for this particular one. It opened with the setting of the sun and the figure of Night, in a chariot drawn by owls, moved across the sky. Shepherds returned from their folds, the moon and the stars appeared and were observed by Ptolemy and Zoroastra. There followed an alternation of dreams and nightmares, in some of which Louis played an ordinary part. Ballets which are true to their art, wrote Ménestrier, 'have an admirable variety of all sorts of actions and all sorts of passions. It is in this that the *Ballet de la Nuit* seems to me inimitable; one sees the characters of all sorts of people.' As entertainment it was clearly first class. It was this that made it the perfect introduction to the moral which came at the end. The climax was reached with the appearance of the Morning Star, the 'Dayspring from on high', which banished all the dreams. It was danced by Louis' brother. His verses proclaimed his role.

> Le Soleil qui me suit, c'est le jeune LOUIS.
> La troupe des astres s'enfuit
> Dès que ce grand Roi s'avance;
> Les nobles clartés de la Nuit,
> Qui triomphaient en son absence,
> N'osent soutenir sa présence:
> Tous ces volages feux s'en vont évanouis.
> Le Soleil qui me suit, c'est le jeune LOUIS.

[The sun which follows me is the young LOUIS.
The company of the stars are put to flight
Once this great King advances;
The noble luminaries of the night,
Which triumphed in his absence,
Dare not endure his presence:
All these inconstant lights depart extinguished.
The Sun which follows me is the young LOUIS.]

This paved the way for the entrance of Louis himself in a costume scintillating with gold which repeated again and again the radiating shafts of sunlight and with an explosion of ostrich plumes to crown the whole. In his horoscope, described by Racine, it had been predicted that 'like the rays and light of the sun he will bring radiance to France and her allies'. Now that destiny was about to be fulfilled. *Le Roi Soleil* had appeared upon the stage.

Most of the ballets took place in the Grande Salle of the former Hôtel de Bourbon, just outside the Louvre. It was known as the Petit Bourbon and was used as the Court theatre until the opening, in 1662, of Vigarani's magnificent new opera house at the Tuileries. The Petit Bourbon was accessible to all. 'Everyone comes', complained Mlle de Montpensier, 'without invitation. There are all sorts and conditions of men. The places at the back are occupied by the canaille.' Performed before such an audience the ballet offered a real opportunity for propaganda. 'It has not been underlined sufficiently', writes Jean-Christian Petitfils, 'the extent to which Mazarin's fêtes announced the personal reign of the King.'

This exaltation of monarchy found its echo in the hearts of a people, who, after years of near-anarchy, could now identify their patriotic fervour with the cause of the King. The cry of 'Vive le Roi tout seul!' was to be answered.

But the expectation of a strong lead from the top created also a sense of the greatness of the people thus led. Two years after the *Ballet de la Nuit* came the *Ballet du Temps*, in which the minutes, the hours, the days, the weeks, the months and the years reached their climax in the *Siècle d'Or*, represented by Louis. The *Gazette* for 3 December 1654 saw in it 'a good omen that we should enjoy, during the years of his reign, the delights which go with a happy age'. Mazarin and Benserade were using the ballet astutely as a means of indoctrinating the public; they must also have considered the effect which this was to have on Louis himself.

In the *Ballet des Plaisirs de la Ville et de la Campagne* Louis, referred to as a demi-god, took the part of *le Génie de la Danse*. According to the strict choreography all had to take their time from him:

31

Et malheur à qui ne danse
De cadence avec lui.

Sometimes the other dancers added a note of interest, at least to the historian. In 1654, the year of the Coronation, the cast of *Les Noces de Thétis et de Pelée* included two of the children of Charles I: the Duke of York, later to be James II, and the Princess Henriette-Anne, later to marry Louis' brother. Mlle Mancini, soon to be Louis' first love, and Mlle de Mortemart, later to be Mme de Montespan, also danced.

The marriage of Peleus and Thetis was not an obvious choice of theme. It is difficult to see any connection between the title roles and anyone in the Court of France. In ancient mythology, however, it had always been represented as a particularly sumptuous affair and was attended by all the Gods with the exception of Eris, the Goddess of Discord. Louis appeared in various roles, some of which he danced with the musician Lully: he appeared as Apollo, as a Fury and, in the last *entrée*, as La Guerre.

Cent oracles fameux ont prédit à la Terre;
Pour avoir une bonne paix
Qu'il fallait une bonne guerre.

Brandishing a sword in one hand and a lighted flambeau in the other, his swirling kilt or tunic and the enormous mane built up by the feathers on his helmet, create the impression of something farouche and savage. It is more like the war dance of some Zulu warrior or Red Indian chief. Only the legs and shoes are those of the *honnête homme*.

The confusions of the Fronde and the continued presence of Spanish troops in northern France had caused the Coronation of Louis XIV to be postponed. It finally took place on 7 June 1654. He was still three months short of his sixteenth birthday.

La Grande Mademoiselle was not invited. She was in exile at Saint-Fargeau in Burgundy. In view of her recent behaviour that was hardly surprising. She records in her memoirs that she would have regarded it as beneath her dignity to go incognito, and then, with a touch of 'sour grapes', claimed that she did not really want to see it anyway. 'When one knows the Court and all the people in it, and when one has read the book of the words, it is as if one had seen it.' She was clearly well informed. 'What is remarkable about this coronation is that nobody there was what they should have been.'

She was referring chiefly to a group known as the Twelve Peers of France, whose presence was necessary. Six of them were lay and six

ecclesiastical. They were the Dukes of Burgundy, Normandy and Aqui-
taine; the Counts of Flanders, Champagne and Toulouse; the Archbishop
of Reims and the Bishops of Laon and Langres – all of whom were also
dukes – and the Bishops of Beauvais, Noyon and Chalons – all of whom
were also counts.

Their proper function had been to act as a high court to arbitrate in
disputes between the King and his tenants-in-chief. At the Coronation
they had a ceremonial function, which was to 'uphold' the crown when
it was placed on the King's head. They had long since lost any political or
juridical importance. The bishops, of course, performed their ecclesiastical
functions, but the titles of the lay peers were either obsolete or held as
courtesy titles by the King's brothers or sons. For the Coronation the
King nominated whom he chose to act as Duke of Normandy, Duke of
Burgundy, Count of Flanders and so on. It was naturally to the members
of the royal family and the Princes of the Blood that these roles were
normally given, but in 1654, owing to their behaviour during the Fronde,
most of these were in disgrace.

Of the royal family, apart from Anne of Austria only Louis' brother,
Philippe d'Anjou, a boy of thirteen, and the duc de Vendôme – a natural
son of Henri IV and Gabrielle d'Estrées – were present. The ceremony
should have been performed by the Archbishop of Reims, but the titular
archbishop at the time was a duke of the house of Savoy who was not
even in priest's orders. His senior suffragan, Simon Legras, Bishop of
Soissons, had to assume the functions of his office. The bishops elect
of Laon and Langres had not yet been consecrated. This meant that the
ecclesiastical peers all moved up two places and the Archbishops of
Bourges and Rouen were brought in to fill the gaps at the bottom. Thus
it was that the Bishop of Beauvais, representing the Bishop of Laon,
was accompanied by the Bishop of Chalons, representing the Bishop of
Beauvais. As for the six lay peers, the four vacancies were filled by the
Dukes of Elbeuf, Candale, Roannez and Bournonville who were, wrote
la Grande Mademoiselle, 'so little suited to be in the places usually
occupied by the Princes of the Blood'. She appears to have forgotten the
reason for the absence of the latter.

The Cathedral of Reims – later than Chartres, earlier than Amiens –
marks the point of emergence of the fully developed Gothic style. The
French Gothic could truly be described as royal. All the great cathedrals
built on Capetian territory symbolise the marriage between the royal and
the ecclesiastical authority, but Reims more than any, for it was here, at the
beginning of every reign, that the solemnisation of that marriage was re-
enacted. The requirements of a coronation dictated a layout which Reims
shares with Westminster Abbey. The canons' stalls were situated in the

two eastern bays of the nave and enclosed to the west by a pulpitum or choir screen. This left the entire area of the crossing available for the considerable personnel and the complex ritual of the anointing and crowning. The High Altar stood between the two easternmost piers of the crossing.

The Coronation rite, with its biblical precedent in the idea of 'the Lord's anointed', made the King of France God's lieutenant in the land. Voltaire, in his *Siècle de Louis XIV*, claimed that the French regarded their King 'as a sort of Divinity'. The rite also symbolised the marriage between the Crown and the Church – the coalition which had resulted in the centralisation and unification of France at the expense of feudalism. 'The unit of the Crown and the Church,' wrote Viollet-le-Duc, 'the alliance of these two powers to form a nationality, gave rise to the cathedrals of Northern France.'

The architectural decorations of Reims Cathedral make many allusions to this royal role. Kings line the gallery over the west front; kings, and the Archbishops who crowned them, look down from the stained glass windows of the clerestory; the statues round the west rose window are also concerned with kingship – Saul anointed by Samuel, Solomon crowned by Nathan. They also illustrate the virtues expected of a king: Courage, by David killing Goliath; Justice, by Solomon giving the baby back to its true mother. At the summit God is seen blessing kings.

Above the rose window the statues depict the baptism of Clovis. All good Frenchmen believed that the oil used for this sacrament had been brought by a dove from Heaven. It was preserved in an ampulla – *la Sainte Ampoule* – and used for the anointing of all subsequent kings. This anointing was held to be even more significant than the crowning and the proper term in French for the whole ceremony is *le Sacre*. *La Sainte Ampoule* was kept at the Abbey of Saint-Rémi, not far from the Cathedral.

The whole Cathedral, up to the level of the triforium, had been hung with 'the richest and most beautiful of the tapestries of the Crown'. A baldachino of four Corinthian columns provided a sumptuous setting for the altar. On the south side of the crossing a 'tribune' – something between a small grandstand and a large box at the opera – had been built to house the Queen Mother and some of her ladies; this was answered on the north side by a sort of tent, of blue velvet covered with fleurs de lys, which served as a confessional, for the King was required to be *réconcilié* before receiving the sacrament.

Some of the regalia, including the crown, sword and spurs of Charlemagne, were kept in the royal Abbey of Saint-Denis. Four members of the community were appointed to transport these to the Abbey of Saint-

Rémi de Reims. One of them, Père Tixier, has left his account of the occasion. The great day started for them with a Mass at two-thirty in the morning, after which they were each allowed 'a finger of wine'. At four o'clock they were taken in a coach to the Cathedral.

There was already a huge crowd, some 3,000 or 4,000, outside the west front. 'It is unbelievable', insists Tixier, 'the difficulty we had in elbowing our way through the crowd and making them give way.' They found the great doors shut. Someone, however, told them of a little side door, to which they now made their way. There was a large crowd here as well, including a number of bishops who had also been shut out. Once within the nave, having feared again and again for the safety of their precious regalia, they felt that their troubles were over. They were not. The Grand Master of the Ceremonies, seeing that they were wearing albs, refused to let them into the choir. It is not very clear why. They had no choice but to disrobe. Then, and only then, were they able to place the sacred objects, which were indispensable to the rite of coronation, upon the altar.

In the French ceremony only twelve peers wore the ermine-lined mantles and coronets of their assumed rank. They were the six lay peers, three Marshals of France, the Grand Maître, the Grand Chambellan and the Premier Gentilhomme de la Chambre du Roi. The coronets were not put on, as in England, at the moment of the King's crowning, but were worn throughout the service.

At half past six in the morning the six lay peers made their ceremonial entrance into the Cathedral, where they were joined by the six ecclesiastical peers, and together they processed to the Archbishop's palace to summon the King. The Bishops of Beauvais and Chalons came first to the King's bedroom. Twice they knocked and twice the Grand Chambellan replied: 'Le Roi dort.' The third time they were admitted.

Louis, far from being asleep, was already dressed in a tunic of white satin. The other robed and coroneted personnel now joined them and they led the King in great ceremony to his place in the crossing of the cathedral.

The clergy of the Cathedral now went down to the west end to receive the Grand Prieur of Saint-Rémi and his precious burden of the *Sainte Ampoule*. He was mounted on a white horse and rode beneath a canopy upheld by four more horsemen. At the choir screen the cavalcade drew rein and the ampulla was carried reverently to the altar. Horses could not be admitted to the choir.

The Bishop of Soissons now mixed a drop of the sacred chrism with some more oil and proceeded to anoint the King seven times – on his forehead, his stomach, between the shoulders and upon each shoulder and in the crook of each arm. The tunic was made so as to open at these places. With each application of the oil the Bishop proclaimed in Latin: 'I anoint you King.' This conferred upon the King the minor orders of the Church but not, of course, priesthood, which would have involved celibacy. There was thus an ecclesiastical significance in the royal robes with which the King was now vested by the Grand Chambellan – a blue dalmatic, such as a deacon wore, and over that the blue coronation robe, covered with fleurs de lys and lined with ermine. It was draped over his left arm 'like a priest's chasuble' and made to hang so that the King's right hand was free.

The ring was now placed upon the third finger of Louis' right hand in token of the Holy Faith by means of which he was to 'drive out the enemy . . . to extirpate heresy, to reunite your subjects and to attach them to steadfastness in the Catholic faith'. The formula provided most of the religious agenda for Louis' reign.

When it came to the crowning, the Chancellor mounted the altar steps and summoned the Twelve Peers: 'Monsieur le duc d'Anjou, qui représentez le duc de Bourgogne, présentez vous à cet acte.' One by one the lay peers took up their positions on the north side of the altar and the ecclesiastical peers on the south side. Taking the crown of Charlemagne from the altar the Bishop held it for a moment over the King's head. The duc d'Anjou and the Bishop of Beauvais reached out and held it also, while the other peers extended their right hands towards it. The gesture resembled that of priests concelebrating.

In 1665 the newly founded manufactory of the Gobelins began a series of sixteen tapestries entitled the *Histoire du Roy*. One of the first to come off the looms represented the actual moment of the crowning. But Le Brun, who provided the cartoon, instead of showing the peers making their gesture towards the crown, has grouped them informally so that none seems to be taking the slightest interest in the ritual and they are apparently more intent on catching the artist's eye.

Once crowned, Louis was conducted to his throne on the top of the choir screen, with the Twelve Peers to either side of him, who now paid their homage, kissing the King on the cheek and saying: 'Vivat Rex in aeternum.' With them came the Aide, the Maître and the Grand Maître des Cérémonies. The first of these, Nicolas Sainctot, was Introducteur des Ambassadeurs – a post which always called for a thorough knowledge of protocol. It was largely through his efforts that everyone knew what to do in all this elaborate ritual and it is in his memoirs that the most authentic account of the Coronation of Louis XIV is to be found.

While the Twelve Peers were offering their homage, the great west doors were opened and the public flooded in, drowning the efforts of the musicians with their shouts of 'Vive le Roi!' The heralds showered them with specially minted gold and silver coins with, on one side, the profile of Louis wearing his crown and on the reverse the dove descending with the ampulla. Salvos of artillery were fired in the square in front of the cathedral and thousands of terrified doves were released. The medieval rite had included the element of popular acclaim – 'Laudamus, volumus, fiat!' (We praise him! We approve him! Let him be King!) It is perhaps significant of the times that the people were now invited only to admire, not to approve. In the eyes of his subjects Louis was now not just their legitimate ruler: he was the Lord's Anointed. In his own eyes, as he stated in his memoirs, the *Sacre* made the Monarch 'plus auguste, plus inviolable et plus saint'.

'We have great and high hopes that something good will come from the *sacre*,' wrote Guy Patin, Dean of the Faculty of Medicine at the Sorbonne; 'they say that the spirit of the King has been awakened.'

It seems that the Coronation gave Louis a new sense of security and almost of divinity in his kingship. One of the most important areas in which he needed to express his royal authority was in his relations with the Parlement de Paris. On 20 March 1665, he confronted this august assembly. According to ancient custom the Chancellor spoke in his name. Séguier laid much stress on the need for a satisfactory peace with Spain, but he insisted on the necessity for new financial resources with which to make an honourable end to the war. He concluded by expressing his deep desire that the Parlement 'would give once more the proof of its attachment to the service of the King and of the State, and would set the example to his subjects of perfect fidelity and obedience'. The measures put forward were duly registered by the Parlement.

Next day, however, some of the younger members of the Chambre des Enquêtes claimed that they had been inhibited from debating by the presence of the King and called for a fresh look at the issues. On 13 April the entire Parlement reassembled without any authority and without having even informed Mazarin. The news of this act of insubordination reached Louis while he was hunting at Vincennes. He left the hunt, rode straight to the Palais de Justice and burst into the Grande Chambre in his hunting coat and riding boots with his whip still in his hand – 'an outfit', comments the marquis de Montglat, 'not in common use before that day'. The scene is described in the chronicle known as the *Journal d'un Bourgeois de Paris pendant la Fronde*.

'The King sat down and surveyed the assembly. Then he spoke. "Everyone knows how much trouble your assemblies have stirred up in my state and how many dangerous results they have produced. I have been informed that you still claim the right to continue them, under the pretext of deliberating on those edicts which have just recently been published and read in my presence. I have come here on purpose in order to forbid you [pointing at Messieurs des Enquêtes] to continue, which I do absolutely, and to you, Monsieur le Premier Président [pointing at him] to allow or permit them, whatever earnest representations Messieurs des Enquêtes might make." '

This was certainly a high-handed act of authority, but there is a difference between the exercise of authority and absolutism. Louis' biographer John Wolf sums it up thus: 'In reading Louis' memoirs it becomes clear that the expression of absolutism is tempered by the fact that Louis also understood that he ruled a kingdom in which history and tradition created an infrastructure of rights, customs and privileges, limiting the action of power; royal absolutism did not imply the right to arbitrary political action even in the mind of so absolute a King as Louis.'

Needless to say, Louis was not only conscious of his kingly power; he was conscious also of his young virility. It was widely believed that he owed his sexual initiation to Mme de Beauvais, one of his mother's ladies; if so, it did not lead to any continuing relationship. The girls with whom Louis most naturally consorted were Mazarin's nieces. The one to whom he was to become most strongly attached was the least attractive physically – Marie Mancini.

One important person to note the passage of Louis from childhood to adolescence was his valet de chambre, Marie Du Bois. In early April 1655, he began his 'quarter' as valet de chambre. It was nearly two years since they had seen each other. 'The King was in Paris, and, for someone who was only seventeen years and a few months old [Du Bois should have said "sixteen"], I found him so accomplished that my joy knew no bounds. I observed the whole change that had come over him from the first day that I was on duty and I want to set down here how he passed his day.

'As soon as he awoke, he recited the Office of the Holy Spirit and said his rosary. That done, his Preceptor, Hardouin de Péréfixe, entered and supervised his studies, that is to say either in the Holy Scriptures or the history of France. That done, he got out of bed. At that point we entered, the two valets only, who were on duty for the day and the ordinary usher. On getting out of bed he seated himself on the *chaise percée* in the same room with the alcove in which he slept; he remained on it for more or less half an hour. He then passed into his Grande Chambre, where there were ordinarily the princes and *grands seigneurs* who were waiting to assist at his *lever*. He was in his dressing gown and went up to them and spoke to them, one after the other, in so informal a manner that they were enchanted. Then he sat in his chair and washed his hands, face and mouth. After he had wiped himself dry he took off his night-cap, which was tied round his head because there was so much hair underneath it.

'He said his prayers beside his bed with his chaplains in attendance and with everyone on their knees, no one daring to stand up or speak or make any sound – the usher would have sent them out of the room. After the King had prayed he sat in his chair. He had his hair combed and was brought his light clothes, breeches of sergette and a vest of Holland cambric. He then passed into the large cabinet which is behind the ante-room where he did his exercises.' This room seems to have been equipped as a gymnasium. 'He vaulted with an admirable lightness, having his horse set at its highest, and alighted on it like a bird and made no more sound when landing in the saddle than if a pillow had been placed on it. Next he did some fencing and exercises with the pike. He went back to the alcove room where he practised dancing and, returning to his Grande Chambre, changed his clothes and had breakfast.

'He went up to the apartment of Cardinal Mazarin . . . he saw him in private and each day summoned one of the Secretaries of State who made his reports, from which – and from other more secret sources – the King learned about matters of state for an hour or an hour and a half.'

It was often said that Mazarin deliberately denied Louis a good education and excluded him from the affairs of the State in order to keep the control in his own hands. The abbé de Choisy, for instance, suggested that Mazarin 'did not intend so much to make of him a great prince as a man who was soft, tender and complaisant, who, satisfied with his *maisons de plaisance* and with his command of the Musketeers, would leave him master of the State'. Perhaps the most extreme statement of the case, and the best known, is that of Saint-Simon: 'Le Cardinal avait tenu le roi dans la plus entière ignorance et la plus honteuse dépendance.' But Saint-Simon had his own particular prejudice. It must be remembered also that he was born only in 1675, a quarter of a century after the period under consideration.

The Venetian ambassador, Giovanni-Baptisto Nani, writing in 1648 when Louis was ten years old, had referred to the Cardinal's control of the young King's education, but suggests a somewhat different motive. 'He has taken upon himself the position of Governor to the King and his brother in order to be able to command his affection in due course.' In this he succeeded. The affection between the Cardinal and the King was almost like that of father and son.

In April 1654, just two months before the Coronation, Sagredo had repeated the accusation against Mazarin, 'who deliberately keeps the King diligent in the exercise of his amusements in order to turn him away from more solidly important matters; while His Majesty is occupied with the running of a wooden machine on the stage, the Cardinal, on the theatre of France, is motivating and running all the machines of state "à son bon plaisir" '.

The dates of such comments are important. The turning point seems to have been the Coronation. Shortly after it the maréchal du Plessis, who was Governor to Louis' brother Philippe, notes that there were, 'apart from certain sessions of the Council, ordinary days set aside for the Councils which were held in the presence of the King'. He goes on to state that the business dealt with on these occasions was seldom of any consequence. The motive behind this could well have been a sound one. It could have been Mazarin's intention to initiate his pupil's political education by easy stages; to accustom him first to the procedure and personnel of the Council and then, as he gained confidence, to let him in on the more complex and serious issues. It makes sense as an educational method.

In 1660 Nani, on a second embassy to France, describes Louis' daily visits to Mazarin's apartment. 'There the Cardinal informs him of everything, instructs him and shapes him in such a way that, if His Majesty observes his clear advice and strong principle . . . there can be no doubt that, unless he falls into the power of some other minister, he will become a very great prince.'

The apparent ease with which Louis took over the running of the State machine the day after Mazarin's death is the strongest evidence that he had already learnt a lot about it. In July 1661 Louis gave audience to the abbé Fantoni, emissary of Marie de Gonzague, Queen of Poland, and talked with him for two hours on the affairs of his country. Fantoni, wrote Colbert, 'could not believe that a prince who had only been talking of affairs for four months could know so much without some sort of a miracle'. He did not know, adds Colbert, 'that during the life of the Cardinal no affair of any consequence arose on which he was not fully informed'.

Loménie de Brienne, writing a few years later, says the same. He affirms that 'this Prince never failed to attend the Council in His Eminence's room; he never failed to receive a long lesson in politics after the Council. The Cardinal, they say, hid nothing from him.' Even Choisy comes round to the admission that Mazarin 'held council with Fouquet, Lionne and the Secretaries of State and did not want anyone to speak of affairs if the King were not present'.

Choisy, in fact, says much which reverses his original accusation. 'One day, when the maréchal de Gramont flattered him (Mazarin) on his ever-lasting power based on the feebleness of the King, he replied: "You don't know him. There is enough there to make four kings and one *honnête homme.*" ' That was Anne's expressed intention. Mazarin wrote: 'she is more interested than anyone to see you become not only the greatest King in the world but also the most *honnête homme*'.

There remains the question of the academic side of Louis' education, the effectiveness of which was also widely doubted. Here the most important witness is Louis himself. In 1694, when he was visiting Mme de Maintenon's Academy for Young Ladies at Saint-Cyr and was congratulating the directress, the Mère Priolo, on her father's work of history, which was written in Latin, he admitted that he could not understand it – 'For I am an ignoramus; I did not receive so good an education as that which I offer at Saint-Cyr.'

In the portion of his memoirs written in 1666, Louis stated for the benefit of the Grand Dauphin: 'when one is a child, one regards study as mere vexation; when one first enters into public affairs one regards it as a bagatelle of no use; but when one's faculty for reasoning begins to become serious, one recognises, at last but too late, how important it is to apply oneself to it when one still has time'. There could be something autobiographical about that statement. Choisy tells us that 'study was tedious to him, as it is to all children'. It seems also that the education of royal princes was badly handled in most European countries. Lord Bolingbroke asserted that the education of Louis XIV had been 'as bad as that of other princes from all points of view'.

Mme de Maintenon observed of the Grand Dauphin that 'at the age of five or six he knew a thousand words in Latin, but not a single one when he became his own master'. There is nothing strange about this. One has only to consider how many Englishmen, after eight or nine years of private education, are still incapable of speaking French, let alone of answering a despatch in Latin. For Latin was not at that time a dead language. It was still the official language in all correspondence with the Imperial and Papal Courts. In 1664 the Venetian ambassador, Alvise Grimani, records how Louis, determined to deal with affairs of state at first hand, asked his former tutor Péréfixe to renew his lessons in Latin.

Twenty years previously, in 1644, just at the time when Péréfixe was starting the education of his royal pupil, a new textbook had appeared – *La Nouvelle Méthode pour apprendre, facilement et en peu de temps, la langue latine*. Louis, in according his *privilège du Roi* to the fourth edition, makes it clear that 'we ourselves used it to learn the rudiments of the Latin tongue'.

Some of Louis' exercise books have survived and are today in the Bibliothèque Nationale. As so often in the education of princes, the subject-matter consisted mostly of pious precepts and edifying exhortations, but the exhortations were in Latin and this at least provided

Louis with an introduction to the language. To take a single example –
one of them reads: 'I know that the first duty of a Christian Prince is to
serve God, and that piety is the foundation of all the royal virtues.' There
follows its translation into Latin, written in the same unformed, childish
hand, and signed Ludovicus.

Mazarin was more of a father than a godfather to Louis. Towards the
end of 1654 he wrote: 'it depends on yourself to become the most glorious
King that has ever been, God having given you all the necessary qualities,
all that is now needed is for you to put them to good effect, which you
will do with ease, acquiring by the application which you accord to public
affairs the knowledge and experience which are required; and, all the
same, that need not prevent you from taking your recreation'. 'I will die
happy', he wrote on another occasion, 'when I see you prepared to govern
by yourself.'

If we make due allowance for the real hatred which many Frenchmen
felt for Mazarin, it is possible to discount nearly all the hostile criticism
of Louis' education. If we look at the real mutual esteem and affection
which existed between the King and the Cardinal, the idea that Mazarin
tried deliberately to stunt his godson's growth loses credibility. The depth
of this affection became particularly apparent when Louis nearly died
during the campaign of 1658 before Dunkirk.

In August 1657 Louis was reconciled with the Grande Mademoiselle.
Looking for an opportunity to make her peace with him after her hostile
behaviour during the Fronde, she got him talking about his campaigns –
it was just after the capture of Montmédy. It was a subject which he liked
to talk about. He was very proud of his Musketeers and his Gardes du
Corps and he asked her what she thought of their greatcoats. 'I said that
they were very fine.' He continued: 'There is nothing so beautiful as the
two Blue Squadrons; you shall see, for they will provide your escort.'
Their trumpeters were regarded as the best in the world and they were
very smartly dressed. Louis asked if Mademoiselle had ever heard their
timbals. 'Yes, Sire,' she answered, 'I have heard them.' 'And where was
that?' This was the moment for which she was waiting. 'I smiled and said
to him, in the most respectful manner: "In the foreign troops who were
with us during the war. The memory of it is not very agreeable to me,
because it was at that time that I caused Your Majesty much displeasure.
I ask your pardon; I ought to do so on my knees . . . I beg you to believe
that there is nothing which I hope for more passionately than to find
opportunities to do as much for you as I once did against you." ' Louis
was nothing if not magnanimous and his response was worthy of his
grandfather. 'I am very ready to believe what you say,' he replied; 'let us

talk no more about the past.' Louis continued to talk about military matters.

In May 1658 Louis was with his army making a concerted attack on Dunkirk with the aid of English troops sent by Cromwell. In his element when on campaign, he liked to live at close quarters with his troops. On 27 May Mazarin told Colbert that he was trying to persuade Louis not to stay at Mardyck, just west of Dunkirk, not only because it was insalubrious but because the courtiers were eating all the food which was wanted for the soldiers. 'You will easily believe', he concluded, 'that my words did not please him and produced no effect. He is the master, but nothing will prevent me from telling him always what I believe would be in his interest.'

On 14 June the spectacular victory won by Turenne at the battle of the Dunes led to a successful attack on Dunkirk. Mardyck was a very unhealthy place and the weather was extremely hot. 'The air', wrote Mme de Motteville, 'was infected by the dead bodies which had lain there, half buried in the sand, from previous years, without having rotted away, for the dryness of the land prevented it. There were no facilities at Mardyck: there was a shortage of water and of everything else.' On Sunday 30 June, Louis was obliged to admit to Mazarin that he needed rest. The Cardinal persuaded him to agree to move to Calais. 'You cannot imagine the difficulty which I had in disposing him to leave,' he wrote to the Queen. By now the physicians were beginning to take alarm. Vallot noted in his journal: 'His Majesty did not spare himself by day or by night from hardship or fatigue and took no rest in a place where the air was infected and the water putrid.' The result was almost inevitable: Louis became seriously ill.

'The King came back from the army', wrote la Grande Mademoiselle, 'sick of a very dangerous and unremitting fever. During the next five or six days all the news was very bad.' Guy Patin, writing from Paris, could take a professional interest in the King's disease, but he was also concerned for the religious and political aspects of the case. 'The Blessed Sacrament', he wrote to his friend Spon, 'is exposed on every altar and the Prayers of the Forty Hours are being said in the churches. I pray God that he may be cured, for I would dread grave disorders at Court and throughout the country if he were to die . . . It is being said in public that he is in danger from his disease and from his doctors – Vallot, Guénot and Daquin.'

It is interesting to note the different attitudes of those who described the event – some alarmist, some concealing the real danger. While Mlle de Montpensier and Mme de Motteville feared the worst, the *Gazette* treads lightly over Louis' illness, not referring to it until the worst was over. The first mention comes on 9 July: 'There is every reason to hope that, with the help of Heaven, our fears will be seen to have turned into transports of joy.'

Mazarin seems to have revealed less than the full truth. Either the doctors withheld their information from him, or he withheld it from Turenne and the English ambassador, Sir William Lockhart. He wrote to both on Wednesday 3 July. To Turenne he says that if anyone else had the same malady 'it would be counted as nothing; the physicians assure me that there is not the least shadow of a danger'. To Lockhart he writes: 'I do not think there is anything to fear . . . it is true that in a case where health is so precious, Your Excellency will understand that I have great anxieties.'

Vallot's entry, however, for the same day records 'an increase in the fever accompanied by a disturbing redoubling of all the symptoms'. Louis' condition was becoming steadily worse. On Thursday 4 July, Vallot described the symptoms: 'Having taken note of his convulsive movements and of the swelling, or rather puffiness of his whole body, which is an unmistakable sign of something seriously malignant, I resolved, on account of this puffiness (which resembled that which comes after a snake bite) and of the delirium in his mind, which spelt ruin if we did not apply immediately the necessary remedies, I resolved in my anxiety to propose two remedies.' They were entirely predictable. One was a thorough purging and the other the letting of blood.

On 5 July Vallot prescribed an emetic wine or antimony. It did not have the desired effect. The next day a special courier, despatched to the duc d'Orléans, brought la Grande Mademoiselle a letter stating that the antimony had not worked and that the doctors had given up hope. 'I was deeply afflicted, as may easily be imagined: the King is my first cousin; he treats me well; but above all it is a fearful thing to see a young King die.'

The prospect of Louis' death meant that all eyes were turned towards his brother Philippe d'Anjou. 'While the King was with the army', continues Mademoiselle, 'Monsieur, instead of being with him, remained with the Queen like a child – yet he is already seventeen. The Queen led her usual life of praying and gambling.' The prospect of Philippe succeeding to the throne alarmed his aunt. 'I was very fond of Monsieur, but I did not see that it would be to his advantage, in his present state, being too much of a child, to take the government upon himself . . . it is not that he is devoid of wit, but as yet he lacks solidity, having neither knowledge nor experience.'

Mme de Motteville was not present at Calais, but she had the story from the lips of the Queen herself. The King's illness did not respond to the treatment which he was given. 'He was fifteen days in extreme danger and the Queen felt all the pain that her love for him must have caused her.' The one thing that sustained her was the behaviour of Philippe d'Anjou. 'She admitted to me that on this occasion she was infinitely satisfied by the good disposition of Monsieur. He showed her all the tenderness possible and obviously appeared to dread losing the King. When the Queen told him he must no longer go near him for fear of catching his disease he burst into tears and was for some time incapable of pronouncing a single word. The Queen, from whom I had these particular details, was very grateful to him for this.'

At midnight on Saturday 6 July Louis received Holy Communion. 'Everyone was edified by the devotion with which His Majesty did this,' wrote Mazarin to Colbert on the Sunday; 'yesterday his mind was wandering and he was asking me a thousand irrelevant questions; His Majesty then summoned me to come closer. I thought he was still delirious, but he said to me in a low voice these very words: "You are a man of a strong sense of will and you are the best friend that I have. I therefore beg you to let me know when I am in extremis, because the Queen would never dare to do so for fear of aggravating my condition." His Majesty desired that I should give him my promise that I would do so. I can tell you that those words pierced my heart.'

Meanwhile all France was waiting with bated breath for what seemed to be the inevitable news. 'Everyone in Paris', claimed Mademoiselle, 'was in an agony of suspense. The news came that the King had received the Viaticum and that the Queen and the Cardinal had left his room in a state of despair.' Mademoiselle was misinformed. The King had received Communion, not the Viaticum; that is only administered when a person is held to be in extremis.

The night between Sunday and Monday, 7–8 July, appears to have been critical. On the Monday Louis was bled once again. 'This remedy', wrote Vallot, 'did not greatly reduce either the fever or the symptoms.' The other physicians were summoned to a consultation and Mazarin invited to join them. Vallot admitted to him that 'some master stroke was needed to save the King'.

It was at this point, on Monday 8 July, that Mazarin wrote one of his most revealing letters. It was to the Duke of Modena. 'I find it difficult to begin this letter,' he wrote, 'because I have to say to Your Highness that the King has been ill for the last eight days . . . His Majesty concealed for two days the fact that he was ill because his desire was to be with his army. I did all that I could to make him decide at least to come for one or two days to see the Queen, after which he could return to the army; but all my remonstrances were in vain.'

He then outlines the course of the illness up to date. Louis seemed to be beginning to respond to treatment, 'but with all that and with the assurance which the physicians give that they will deliver the King from this malady . . . I admit to Your Highness that I am a prey to the strangest anxieties and that nothing will deliver me from them until I see the King cured. It is some consolation to me to share my pain with you in relating in detail all that has passed in this unhappy event; and I can swear to you, as a man of honour, that, although the King is my master and benefactor, I give no consideration to that in this experience and even less to the great personal interest that I have in his preservation, but simply that he is the most lovable of princes that I have ever seen and that, if I may be permitted to speak in such a way, he is the best friend that I have and that he has been so kind as to say to me on many occasions that it is as my friend and not as my master that he relates to me.'

Louis, in fact, made a miraculous recovery. To some this was attributed to the medicaments administered; to others it was the direct operation of God.

Guy Patin, perhaps wise after the event, wrote to his friend Falconet: 'I have always believed that he would recover and I wanted to lay a wager with certain persons. The King is a well-built young prince, large and strong, who is still under twenty; who hardly drinks any wine, who is in no way debauched and no part of his body is damaged or in any way affected . . . They are continuing here the prayers and processions for his health, and I am delighted to see the devotion of the people for his convalescence. He is a prince worthy of their love.' He concludes: 'I myself feel for him the strongest possible affection, beyond that which the French naturally have for their Prince.'

4
Louis' Marriage

On 7 October 1658, when Louis had just turned twenty, la Grande Mademoiselle wrote a pen portrait of him: 'He has a lofty air, dignified, proud, courageous and pleasing, something very majestic and moderate in his expression and the most beautiful hair imaginable, both in its colour and in its curls. He has shapely legs and a good deportment... His manner is reserved and he speaks little, but to people with whom he feels at ease he is a good conversationalist, never saying anything that is not absolutely to the point. He has good taste and discernment and a naturally good temper. He is charitable and generous and plays the part of a King without demeaning himself.'

Louis had by this time a mistress, a Mlle de La Motte d'Argencourt, one of his mother's ladies-in-waiting. 'Among other attractive qualities,' wrote Bussy-Rabutin, 'for she was very beautiful, she danced to perfection and it was this which caused the King to fall in love with her.' She became the first of a long line to exchange Louis' bed for a cell in a nunnery. She was succeeded in Louis' bed by one of Mazarin's nieces, Marie Mancini. This was to become a more serious affair, but, as Mme de Motteville observed, 'while the King was becoming involved, almost imperceptibly, in a passionate love affair, all Europe was watching to see in which direction he would turn for his choice of a wife; and all those princesses who could reasonably aspire to this honour were eagerly awaiting the outcome of his choice'.

Only two candidates were seriously considered: both were cousins of Louis. One was the Princess Marguerite de Savoie. She was first cousin by marriage to the comtesse de Soissons, a niece of Mazarin, who thereby had reasons for privately preferring this match. The other was the Infanta of Spain, Marie-Thérèse. She was a niece of the Queen Mother, a person who longed for peace between France and Spain, a peace which could be sealed with this marriage. For a long time this had seemed out of the question, for Philip IV of Spain had no son and his daughter was heir-presumptive to the throne. But now a son had been born and the position was altered.

Bussy-Rabutin described the first move. 'The Cardinal had invited the duchesse de Savoie to meet Louis and his Court at Lyon and to bring the princesses her daughters with her ostensibly for the purpose of marrying her eldest to the King.' Marguerite, apart from being obviously eligible, combined somewhat Latin good looks with a lively spirit. In all probability she would have made him a good wife. Louis' affections, however, were still deeply engaged with Marie Mancini. Bussy described her as 'ugly, fat, short and with the look of an inn-keeper's wench, but with the wit of an angel, so that when listening to her one forgot that she was ugly. The King would have married her had not the Cardinal opposed it.'

It is clear from his letters that Mazarin was seriously worried. On 16 July 1659, he wrote to his godson warning him of the dangers of such a liaison. 'I beseech you', he concluded, 'to think of your glory, your honour, the service of God and the good of your realm.' It was the right note to sound. Louis put his duty to France before the dictates of his heart. Marie's parting words were: 'Ah! Sire; vous êtes Roi, vous m'aimez, et je pars.' She was married off to the constable Lorenzo de Colonna.

Mazarin was probably by this time in favour of a match between the King and the Infanta of Spain. The Queen Mother was already determined. In 1658 the Venetian ambassador Nani had written: 'It is certain that by reminding Cardinal Mazarin how, at the time of the barricades and the civil war, she had risked herself and the monarchy at personal cost in order to defend him, so she demanded in return that he should do all in his power to make her niece her daughter-in-law with peace as her dowry, promising to maintain him in overall charge of affairs in such a way that he would have no less authority in the State in peace than he had had in times of war.'

The real purpose of the meeting at Lyon may have been to push Philip IV into agreeing with the Franco-Spanish marriage. The ruse, if it was a ruse, was successful. The moment Philip heard of the Savoy affair he exclaimed: 'It cannot and shall not take place', and he despatched a special envoy, the marquis de Pimentel, to offer Louis his daughter's hand in marriage. In late January 1659, the King and his mother were back in Paris and during the spring Pimentel and Mazarin were busy preparing a draft treaty.

The events leading up to the marriage were long drawn out and there were times when it looked as if the whole negotiation would collapse.

One of those to record how the news was received in Paris was Guy

Patin. Without being really rich or noble, he was both well off and well connected, a man widely held in high esteem. He was also a great letter writer. His regular correspondents were men of his own profession who lived remote from Paris. Patin himself admits that what he says may not always reflect the truth – which is at least honest of him. 'I write to you the news that I hear; among it there is some that is false.' But his letters make it clear that dependable news was not always easy to come by.

On 1 January 1659, he wrote to his friend Falconet: 'It is thought likely here that the King will marry the Infanta of Spain, and everyone who is a good Frenchman wants this very much. That will put an end to the war and she will be the Queen of Peace.'

On 13 May he stated: 'The peace has not yet been made – but it is being negotiated.' But progress was slow and nothing certain. On 6 August he was becoming impatient: 'There is no doubt about the peace and the marriage, but no one knows upon what conditions.' On the 15th he learnt that the First Ministers of France and Spain were to meet, though neither could make any move which could be construed as admitting the superiority of the other's King. Mazarin and Don Luis de Haro had both reached the banks of the Bidassoa, frontier river between France and Spain – but in which country were they to meet? Should there be any sort of meeting before negotiations began and if so in accordance with what etiquette? Did Mazarin's position as a Prince of the Church outweigh Don Luis' status as a Grand d'Espagne?

Mazarin removed the possibility of his crossing into Spain by taking to his bed with a severe attack of gout. It may well have been genuine, for he was crying out in pain, but this was a well-known trick – *l'expédient du lit* – and could only be used with caution. It was, after all, a game which two could play.

There was, however, an island on the Bidassoa called the Ile des Faisans, the ownership of which had been disputed between France and Spain for centuries. It looked as if this might provide neutral ground for a meeting. Footbridges had to be built out from either bank and a building constructed with a French apartment at one end, a Spanish apartment at the other and a room that was common to both in the middle.

On 10 August Mazarin wrote to Le Tellier that the marquis de Pimentel had come to see him 'and I agreed with him down to the smallest detail as to what should be done on one side and on the other when we meet, that is to say the number of guards which we shall bring, the personnel which is to accompany us to the island, and remain there for the duration of the conference, and even the quality of the tapestries which we will hang in the room which is common to both countries. I had no difficulty in agreeing to these bagatelles and informed him that neither Don Luis' reputation nor my own would be in any way affected if the tapestries of one were not so rich as those of the other . . .' That is what Mazarin said to Pimentel. To Le Tellier he added in confidence that the tapestries which he had himself brought were far superior to those of Don Luis.

It was not until 13 August that the first meeting actually took place. The articles of the peace treaty signed in June in Paris and ratified by the Spanish King, were not, however, regarded as final. Spain still hoped to obtain certain marginal improvements. Each side knew that the other could not afford to renew so costly a war, but Don Luis knew that Mazarin's personal reputation was at stake; he could not afford a breakdown of the negotiations; even a serious delay could have been dangerous.

They were a well-matched pair, for Don Luis de Haro concealed behind his exquisite courtesy a tenacity which equalled that of Mazarin. He brought up the whole issue of the reinstatement of the prince de Condé. To the Spanish Condé was an honoured ally who had saved them from defeat: to the French he was a traitor who had offered his services to the enemy of France in time of war, an incarnation of fronde and feudalism.

In most of the passages of arms it seems that Mazarin had the edge over his adversary. 'Understand', said the hidalgo, 'that my master, the King of Spain, would never find another ally if he fails to keep his word with an ally so distinguished as Condé.' 'An ally?' answered Mazarin; 'subjects who revolt against their king . . . can in no case be qualified as allies; the only "allies" are sovereign princes who alone have the freedom to contract an alliance.' To Le Tellier, Mazarin complained that the Spanish appeared to accept the maxim that 'rebellion is not in France a crime, but a means of improving one's condition'. On 6 September they were still arguing about Condé but three days later a special courier arrived in Paris with the news that the peace treaty had been agreed and that the royal marriage would take place on 24 October. Guy Patin notes, however, that since Louis and Marie-Thérèse were cousins, a dispensation of the Pope was required before they could marry.

On 19 September it was reported that the Spanish were still standing firm on the full reinstatement of the prince de Condé, but a compromise was finally reached: he would be reinstated as Governor of Burgundy and his son, the duc d'Enghien, was to receive the important charge of Grand Maître de la Maison du Roi. A court official told Patin that the wedding would not now take place until May in the following year.

While these tedious negotiations were dragging on, a special ambassador was sent to Madrid to seek the hand of the Infanta, Marie-Thérèse, in marriage. Louis chose for this important task the maréchal duc de Gramont. Gramont was Governor of Béarn and lived close to the frontier. He knew Spain and the Spanish well and he spoke their language fluently. He was well suited to the part he was to play.

On 28 September he set out for the Alcasar, the royal palace, of Madrid. He was received by Philip IV in the Salon. It was an occasion which emphasised the difference between the two countries. The Spanish hidalgos, forbidden to appear before the King in anything but the most sober attire, formed an impressive contrast with the multicoloured and gilded finery of the French. Gramont himself admitted that the Spanish courtiers had 'an air of grandeur and of majesty which I have seen nowhere else'.

However, when Gramont tried to talk about the project of the royal marriage he found the stiff Spanish etiquette fairly inhibiting. At his first interview with the Infanta he was not allowed to mention the subject of the wedding. All that he could do was to present her with a letter from her aunt, Anne of Austria, together with the words: 'My respect and my silence may indicate to Your Royal Highness that which I have not the temerity to mention.' Marie-Thérèse confined herself to the question: 'How is the Queen my aunt?'

A second interview was hardly more encouraging. Gramont wrote to Mazarin: 'I thought that the Catholic King having declared to me that he gave his daughter, the Infanta, to the King in marriage, I was free to expand a little more than I had done at my first audience . . . and I imagined that on this second occasion I might have a response less dry than on the first.' All that the Infanta could say was: 'Tell my aunt that I will always be obedient to her will.' Gramont recognised, however, that the Infanta had never yet spoken so many words to any man except her father. 'Your Eminence will understand that without some special gift of the Holy Spirit to penetrate the depths of her heart, it is somewhat difficult for me to speak thereof with any certainty.'

When Gramont returned to Saint-Jean-de-Luz on 10 November, he found that the prince de Condé was to be forgiven. The reconciliation took place on 27 January 1660, at Aix en Provence, when Louis was travelling south to collect his bride from the Spanish frontier. Condé began to make his humble apologies but Louis interrupted him. 'My cousin,' he said, 'after the great services which you have rendered to the Crown, I am far from having any remembrance of a behaviour which harmed no one but yourself.' Condé's reaction to this reception was to remark, a little later: 'A pardon so proudly conceded made it clear to me that I had a master.' Mme de Motteville observed that Condé had become a different person, 'equally great in humility and gentleness as he had been in his victories'.

Condé, for his part, made atonement for the years of the Fronde by commissioning a large painting by Lecomte for the Galerie des Batailles at Chantilly. It was entitled *Le Repentir*. Condé is seen declining the fanfares of Fame, while at his feet Clio, the Muse of History, tears out the offending pages from her register.

On 23 March 1660, Patin wrote: 'It is said that the King's marriage is put off for another month. I pray God that the Spaniards are not deceiving us.' He did not appreciate the capacity of the Spanish for procrastination. There was an old saying in the Spanish colonies: 'If death came from Spain, we should be immortal.'

When the Pope's dispensation had been received, Louis wrote to ask Philip for permission to enter into correspondence with his future bride. He ended his letter: 'Je suis, Monsieur mon frère et oncle, bon frère et nepheu de Votre Majesté.' It was usual for kings to address one another as 'brother', whatever other relationship they might have had. Philip sent word to Anne of Austria that Louis had his permission to write to Marie-Thérèse who would reply 'even if it might cause her to blush'.

Louis' first letter was dated 24 March from Avignon. It was addressed a little prematurely 'à la Reine'. 'Now that circumstances are such as will enable me to live with Her as with another self, I am delighted to begin by assuring Her by these lines that this happiness could never have come to anyone who desired it more passionately or who felt himself more lucky to possess it than I.'

The letter never reached the Infanta. Philip changed his mind and stated that the time had not yet come. The Bishop of Fréjus, who had been sent to Spain to represent Louis at the marriage by proxy, tried to persuade Marie-Thérèse to accept the letter, but she refused to do anything without her father's permission. All that she managed to say about her future bridegroom was 'that which I say for the Queen my aunt may be understood also for the King'. It is unlikely that those words brought a blush to her cheeks.

It was only later, when she was free from Spanish protocol, that she would admit to having fallen in love with Louis from the portraits of him sent by his mother. She used to find pretexts to pass through the room where they hung and make her curtsy to them. In one he was wearing a hat with a blue ostrich feather *panache*: she called him 'my cousin with the blue plume'. This romantic side to her nature probably came from her mother, Elizabeth de France, a daughter of Henri IV.

On 8 May the French Court arrived at Saint-Jean-de-Luz – in those days a large and prosperous town on account of the whale fishery. Householders were turned out of their homes in order to give room to the King and his followers.

The negotiations between Mazarin and Don Luis, however, were still dragging on. 'There were considerable delays on the part of the Spanish

Court', noted Mme de Motteville, 'about certain villages which they demanded from France. This quibbling disgusted both the Kings and both the Courts were distressed by it; there was murmuring on both sides and in Saint-Jean-de-Luz it was whispered that the marriage might still be called off.'

On 19 May the welcome news arrived that England had offered the crown to Charles II. 'For a long time', wrote Mme de Motteville, 'this people, detesting tyranny, sighed for the legitimate rule of their King.'

On 1 June the French at Saint-Sebastien had their first sight of the Infanta. She stood, reported the *Gazette*, for more than an hour on a balcony over the street along which the procession of the Blessed Sacrament was passing, and was seen 'with an extraordinary satisfaction by a large number of French who are here, and who acknowledge that they could not have a Queen more worthy of their respect and admiration'.

The abbé Matthieu de Montreuil, a canon of Le Mans Cathedral, wrote a long letter to an unnamed lady in which he states that his eye-witness touches were intended to supplement the accounts in the *Gazette*. In the Church at Saint-Sebastien he describes, behind the tabernacle, 'a hundred little steps which rise right up to the vault, on which stood a million candles which, like so many stars, formed the most dazzling and magnificent ornament that the eye could see'.

On 2 June, in the episcopal palace of Saint-Sebastien, the Infanta had to renounce her claim to the Spanish throne. The reading of the deed of renunciation took one and a half hours. 'All the courtiers,' writes Mademoiselle, 'as they returned from Saint-Sebastien, brought the most detailed accounts to the Queen of the looks and appearance of the Infanta. This gave her the greatest possible pleasure and caused her the greatest possible impatience to see her.'

'She is far more beautiful', wrote Mme de Motteville, 'than any of the portraits which have been seen in France; she has blue eyes, not too large but very bright and pleasing – they seem to be full of joy. Her forehead is high and since the way in which she does her hair leaves it completely uncovered, that makes her face look longer than it would if some of her hair were dressed a little lower. Her nose is beautiful enough and not too large; she has a lovely mouth and very rosy; her complexion is perfect and very white; her cheeks are heavy. She puts on rouge, but not as much as the other ladies do. Her hair is blonde and wonderfully beautiful. She is not very large but seems to have a passably good figure.'

The reason for Mme de Motteville's uncertainty about the girl's figure was that it was obscured by her clothes. 'I found the costumes and hair-styles of Spanish women painful to behold. Their bodies were not clothed in anything stiff enough to make use of their figures ... Their short sleeves were slashed and looked all wrong. They wore little linen and their lace seemed to us to be ugly.' But it was the skirts, enormous farthingales known as *garde-Infantes*, which really spoilt the effect. Mme de Motteville described one as a 'monstrous machine, nearly round; it looked as if there were several hoops of a barrel sewn onto the inside of their skirts . . . When they walked the machine rose and fell and looked most inelegant.'

After renouncing her claim to the Spanish throne, Marie-Thérèse accompanied her father to Fuentarabia. It was on 3 June, *la petite Fête-Dieu*, that Le Tellier was able to announce that the treaty had been fully and finally agreed. It was regarded by the French in Saint-Jean-de-Luz as 'honourable to the King' and received with great jubilation by the courtiers whose only desire was to get back to Paris as soon as possible.

As the result of the endless wrangling between the two plenipotentiaries the terms of the treaty were, for the most part, a complex balance of minor details. But as François Bluche puts it: 'they extended the realm of France and increased its strategic opportunities'. By far the most important issue in the whole treaty was that of the Spanish succession.

Perhaps as the result of too much in-breeding, the Spanish Habsburgs were a sickly line. Marie-Thérèse might yet prove the only legitimate inheritor to their throne. In the clauses of the treaty she specifically renounced her claim, but Mazarin had made a difference between the throne of Spain and the sovereignty of the Low Countries. Thanks to Lionne's subtle wording, he also made the renunciation of her rights conditional on the payment of her dowry – a total of 500,000 écus d'or, to be paid in three instalments, the first on the consummation of the marriage: 'that on condition that the sums are made over to His Most Christian Majesty . . . the said most serene Infanta will rest content with the said dowry and not thereafter sue for any other of her rights'. Bluche sums up: 'If the dowry was unpaid, the renunciation clause would be rendered void.' While establishing peace in Europe, Mazarin had left the door ajar for future hostilities.

In the meantime, however, all was joy as the preparations went forward for the royal wedding.

First the marriage by proxy was to take place on Spanish ground with Don Luis de Haro taking the role of the bridegroom. The decoration of the humble little church at Fuentarabia was entrusted to Velázquez, who hung the walls with tapestries and paintings suited to the occasion. A large contingent of the French Court, including la Grande Mademoiselle and Mme de Motteville, attended this ceremony. 'I was astonished', wrote the latter, 'to see in this place, on such a momentous occasion, so few people present.' The French ladies had a long wait during which Mme de

Motteville conversed in Spanish with some of the clergy. 'They replied to me, and I have to say that they spoke in terms somewhat too gallant to befit a priest.'

At last the King of Spain arrived. According to the abbé Matthieu de Montreuil, 'he walked with a grave and majestic bearing never moving his eyes. He has, to tell the truth, a very fine figure, but his face is lean and his hair scant.' He was dressed soberly in grey embroidered with silver but with two very special jewels – a diamond and a pearl – taken from the royal crown. 'He reverenced the altar,' wrote Mademoiselle; 'he is the most solemn man in all the world. The Infanta followed him, dressed in white satin embroidered with little silver bows and adorned in the Spanish manner with some rather ugly jewellery . . . Her coiffure was contrived with hair that was not her own . . . The King was good-looking rather than handsome, but old and worn out. The Infanta looked to me like a young version of the Queen; I found her extremely pleasing.'

Another witness now appears upon the scene: Mlle de Vandy, a close friend of Mademoiselle's and of the comtesse de Maure. Mlle de Vandy was present at the marriage by proxy and gives a touching little detail. Before the Infanta gave her consent, 'she made her curtsy to the King her father, and he, giving her permission to say "Yes", was so deeply moved that tears came into his eyes'. Beneath all his stiffness and all his gravity he was not incapable of normal human emotions.

The ceremony is described by the abbé Matthieu: 'Don Luis de Haro, who married the Infanta by proxy on behalf of the King of France, held out his hand; she held out her hand towards Don Luis de Haro, but their hands did not touch. When that was done the King took off his hat to the Infanta, no longer as his daughter but as Queen of France.' It used to be the custom for a King's proxy to put one leg, often especially stockinged in white, into the bridal bed, but the abbé hastened to reassure his reader that 'Don Luis de Haro did nothing even approaching such a ceremony'.

After the marriage was over King Philip dined in one room and the new Queen in the next. Mlle de Vandy noted the contrast between the two. 'The King sat at a table with such gravity that he is more like a statue than a human being.' His daughter was very much the opposite. Mademoiselle, who was officially incognito but easily recognisable, attracted her attention. 'Her young Majesty who did not have the deathly gravity of her father, but on the contrary an air of sweetness that was both civil and lively, looked often at the unknown beauty . . . As she left the table she said: "I would very much like to kiss this unknown person", and in fact she did embrace her.' They were not, however, able to converse freely, for the Queen spoke no French and Mademoiselle no Spanish.

On 4 June, the duc de Créqui brought the King's wedding present to Marie-Thérèse, the traditional 'cassette' or coffer. 'It contained all that could be imagined', wrote Mademoiselle, 'in the way of jewellery, gold and diamonds as well as watches, clocks, boxes for beauty spots or sweetmeats, little flasks of all shapes, little cases for scissors, knives or toothpicks . . . You may easily believe that we had never seen a present so magnificent and so elegant.' With it came a letter from Louis. 'To receive at the same time a letter from Your Majesty and the news of the celebration of our marriage and to be on the eve of having the happiness of seeing her, are assuredly subjects of unspeakable joy for me.' Louis, however, did not wait for the next day to catch his first sight of his bride.

On the same day a meeting had been arranged between Philip and his sister Anne of Austria. It is described by the abbé Matthieu. 'The King of Spain bowed his head towards his sister the Queen Mother's hair. It was not an embrace – it was only a half, even only a quarter of one. He did not kiss her at all, nor did anything approaching it. That seemed strange between brother and sister after forty-five years of absence. It was certainly not from coldness, on the contrary, they both had tears in their eyes at the joy of seeing one another again; it is just that the gravity and custom of Spain involve this.' For some time brother and sister talked together. When the painful subject came of the long war between their two countries, Philip made the evasive statement: 'Hélas! Madame, c'est le diable qui l'a faite!'

During all this Marie-Thérèse had sat in silence at her father's side. It had been agreed that Louis could ride past the windows of the Salle des Conférences so that he and Marie-Thérèse could catch a glimpse of each other, but Louis was not satisfied with this. He sent a message to Mazarin to say that 'an unknown man' was asking for the door to be opened. Anne gave her permission. It was a time for Marie-Thérèse to blush. Her father forbade her to show any reaction.

'And when may she?' asked Anne. 'When she has passed through that door,' came the answer. At this moment Philippe d'Anjou had an inspiration. Turning towards her, he said in a low voice: 'What does Your Majesty think of that door?' Marie-Thérèse smiled: 'The door looks to me very beautiful and very good.'

After the meeting Don Luis de Haro entertained a large number of the French to dinner. 'It was a Friday', noted Mademoiselle, 'and they were scandalised to see meat mixed with the fish at the tables of the Spaniards.' The subjects of the Very Christian King were more punctilious in their observance of the fast day than those of his Most Catholic Majesty. But worse was to come. The plays performed by the Spanish comedians, in which religious ceremonies were travestied, were found deeply shocking by most of the French.

On 6 June the two Kings met. They entered the conference room simultaneously and advanced ceremoniously towards the centre line which marked the frontier between their two realms. After an exchange of elaborate compliments, Louis apologised for having caused Philip to undertake so tedious a journey, to which Philip replied that he would have done it on foot if necessary. They then proceeded to business. It lasted at least an hour. Loménie de Brienne, wrote Mlle de Vandy, 'read the text of the treaty in French, naming Cardinal Mazarin first and Don Luis de Haro second; the Spanish Secretary of State then read it again, naming Don Luis before Mazarin'. The two Kings then knelt and swore, each on a separate but identical copy of the Gospels, to maintain the Peace. They then embraced each other, after which, Mlle de Vandy continues, 'the two Kings walked backwards each to his respective door and left the conference room'.

They met again on the following day. This is the moment portrayed in the tapestry of the *Histoire du Roy*. The contrast between the French and Spanish courtiers was only too obvious. The French had spent millions on their lace and their gold braid. The duc de La Rochefoucauld wrote to Mme de Sablé: 'They talk of nothing but of the magnificence of the costumes of the Court; it seems to me hardly a compliment to those who wear them, and that they should wish that these might talk also of themselves.'

The costumes of the Spanish men, including King Philip, revealed a mixture of sensible simplicity and appropriate enrichment, but Marie-Thérèse – the only woman in the picture – exemplified all that Mme de Motteville had criticised in Spanish fashions. Her hair was dressed *en large*, that is to say, it was built out on either side with hair not her own so as to form two great clusters of hair and ribbons, each as large as her face, which seemed to reflect the ugly shape of the farthingale.

On Monday 7 June, Marie-Thérèse said a tearful farewell to her father, and crossed the frontier into France, where she took up residence with her aunt, now officially known as *la Reine Mère*. Louis passed the evening quietly with his family and the new Queen. Mme de Motteville records that 'they had supper together with the same familiarity as if they had been together all their lives'. She was astonished to notice that, although he always pretended that he could not, Louis spoke perfectly good Spanish.

On the following evening, noted the abbé Matthieu, Mazarin received a courier with the news that Charles II had embarked for England to take up his father's throne. His mother, Henrietta-Maria, had already received at Colombes the news of his arrival at Dover.

On Wednesday 9 June, the 'French' wedding took place in the little church of Saint-Jean-de-Luz. The duchesse de Navailles, as Dame d'Honneur, helped Marie-Thérèse to dress. She had great difficulty in fixing the small royal crown, which was worn right on the back of the head. In a very long train lined with ermine and thickly sown with golden fleurs de lys, Marie-Thérèse looked more as if she were going to her coronation than to her wedding. 'The Queen', wrote the abbé Matthieu, 'wore, and kept upon her head during the whole course of the ceremony, a gold crown. Mme de Navailles, her Mistress of the Robes, held it up for her from behind for fear that its weight might be painful to her.' Louis, he noted, was dressed in a suit of cloth of gold covered with black lace. He wore no jewellery but his cloak was heavily embroidered and with the star of the Saint-Esprit on his left shoulder.

Jean Dolce, Bishop of Bayonne, celebrated the nuptial Mass. The great tapestry in the series *Histoire du Roy* shows the moment at which he handed the bridegroom the ring. Standing a little behind Louis is his mother. 'One could easily read,' observed Mme de Motteville, 'in the face of this great Queen, the inner joy in her soul; and this made her look so beautiful that, at the age of fifty-nine, she could almost rival the beauty of the Queen her niece ... but the young Queen had the lovelier complexion ... This happy mother, after the ceremony was over, did us the honour to tell us that, on seeing the Queen going up to the offertory in her royal robes and crown, it seemed to her that there was no other head in the world worthy of this crown.'

That evening, in their modest house at Saint-Jean-de-Luz, the royal family had supper together 'with no more ceremony than usual', writes Mme de Motteville, 'and immediately afterwards the King said that he wanted to go to bed'. 'It is too early,' said the young bride to her aunt, with tears in her eyes. But her desire to please the King overcame her modesty, and as she was being undressed and was told that the King was ready, she said in Spanish to her ladies: 'Hurry, hurry, the King is waiting for me.'

5
Return to Paris and the Death of Mazarin

The day after the wedding, the new Queen went out with her aunt and her husband, 'who was in the greatest joy in the world', writes Mademoiselle; 'they were laughing and jumping for joy ... it was the most beautiful friendship in the world'. Mme de Motteville takes up the same theme: 'It seemed that God had showered his graces on this marriage, for the King showed much tenderness to the Queen, and she to him. He asked her consent to send back to Spain the comtesse de Piego, her cameriere major or dame d'honneur. He pointed out to her that it was not the custom to retain a foreigner in this first position. She replied that she had no other will than his and said that she had left her father, whom she loved tenderly, and her country, in order to give herself entirely to him; that she had done this with all her heart, but that she begged him in return to accord her the favour of always being with him.' Louis responded to this by giving orders to the Grand Maréchal du Logis that the Queen and himself were never to be set apart, no matter how small the house in which they might be lodging. This must have been the happiest day in Marie-Thérèse's life.

The Queen Mother, who recognised in her son a certain tendency to coldness and gravity, was relieved to find that he was responding to the charms of this young wife. She told Mme de Motteville that she had even been thanked by him for having diverted his affections away from Marie Mancini and for giving him the Infanta, who would in all probability 'make him happy as much by her beauty and goodness, as by her desire to please him and by the affection which she felt for him'.

On 15 June the Court set out, with much relief, for Paris. It took them a whole month to reach Fontainebleau. They travelled by way of Bordeaux and Poitiers and from thence to the Château de Richelieu. They stayed here long enough, records the *Gazette*, for Louis to enjoy 'le divertissement de la chasse'. He left on 7 July 'very well pleased with the beauty of this house'. The Château de Richelieu, with its satellite town, was in many ways a precursor of Versailles. It is interesting that Louis should have spent forty-eight hours here at this juncture. La Fontaine found that 'the whole has a beauty, a magnificence and a grandeur worthy of its builder'. In particular he admired a small cabinet 'papered with portraits. Here were Kings, Queens and Richelieus, great lords and greater personalities.' As well as the Kings renowned for their conquests hung portraits of those who had conquered them – in the amorous rather than the military sense – 'enfin, c'est l'histoire de notre nation que ce cabinet'.

Beyond the cabinet was the Grande Galerie. From either end of this imposing apartment Louis XIII and his minister, life-sized and bravely mounted, looked down from their tall gilt frames upon the achievements of their reign. 'The whole length of this room', wrote a German visitor named Brackenhoffer, 'on both sides are large paintings representing the exploits of the King and the Cardinal, and over each a Roman exploit or labour of Hercules by way of comparison.' The whole room, and indeed the whole château, was an apotheosis of Richelieu, in much the same way that Versailles was to become the apotheosis of Louis.

From Richelieu the King and his Court proceeded by way of Amboise and Blois to Chambord, which had been the property of Louis' uncle, Gaston d'Orléans. Chambord was the most important creation of François I – a gargantuan hunting lodge, built remote from anywhere in the middle of an enormous park. Its approach led through a forest stretching for miles on every side and filled with venerable oaks which no man ever planted. The forest opened upon the watery expanses of the park, with its lakes and canals, and then, suddenly, afforded the first glimpse of the buildings – a bewildering medley of white stone and blue slate, of towers upon towers, cupolas upon cupolas, chimneys upon chimneys – creating the impression of an overcrowded chessboard which is the essence of Chambord. 'When one first sees it from afar off', writes Félibien, 'one is astonished at the number of pavilions, towers and turrets which make up the donjon.' As at Richelieu, Louis was here for long enough to be deeply impressed by Chambord and the marvellous facilities which it offered for hunting. Since the death of Gaston, Chambord had become once more the property of the Crown and Louis was to make frequent visits here.

On 13 July, records the *Gazette*, the Court arrived at Fontainebleau, and in the cool of the evening Louis took his young bride out along the canal, 'in a richly decorated *calèche*, the courtiers following in their coaches ... It is impossible to see anything more charming than this promenade around the canal.'

After about a week at Fontainebleau they all moved on – the Queen Mother and Mazarin to Paris, the King and his Queen to Vincennes, where they remained while arrangements were being made for the Queen's state entry into Paris. After this they took up residence in the Louvre.

This was a building which was going to pose one of Louis' more difficult problems. At the beginning of the fifteenth century the duc de Berry, a younger brother of Charles V, had commissioned Pol de Limbourg and his brothers to decorate a book of hours for him. It was to contain miniatures of the royal palaces and châteaux with which he was associated. These are the first really accurate depictions of French medieval architecture and they have a detailed brilliance which brings the whole scene into focus.

For the Louvre, Pol de Limbourg shows the south and east façades, each of which centred on a gatehouse, framed between two towers and surmounted by a tall pavilion roof. The corner towers give birth, above their battlements, to smaller towers capped by *poivrières* with delicately swept profiles. Towers and pavilions are crested with gilded weather-vanes and banners painted with the royal fleurs de lys. Tall white chimney-stacks add an important contribution to the already exciting skyline. The whole complex of pavilions, towers, turrets and chimneys soars to its climax in the great conical roof of the Grosse Tour or Donjon, rising to a height 31 metres above the level of the Court. There is something of the spectacular roofscape of Chambord in the total silhouette thus created.

In 1527 François I decided to replace the old castle with a Renaissance château. He chose a French architect, Pierre Lescot, with whom the sculptor Jean Goujon collaborated closely. Together they produced a façade correctly classical and richly decorated. Their concern seems to have been for ornamental beauty rather than for monumental grandeur. 'In the said year of 1527 in February', wrote the Bourgeois de Paris 'they began to pull down the Grosse Tour du Louvre, by order of the King, in order to convert the Louvre into a "logis de plaisance". It was a great shame to take it down, for it was very beautiful, tall and strong, and was appropriate for keeping prisoners of great distinction.' But François did not want a prison: he wanted a palace. The structure was palatial only in its style and not in its dimensions. François I's Louvre was to have been no larger than that of Charles V. Lescot's wing has a front of only nine windows. By proportioning his façades to so small a building, François created a problem for those who later wanted to enlarge it.

The next difficulty was to arise from the decision of Catherine de Medici to build herself another palace, the Tuileries, outside the line of the fortifications, about a quarter of a mile west of the Louvre. She and her second son Henri III felt it desirable to link the two together. It was Henri IV who made the connection; indeed he seemed to be more interested in joining the Louvre and the Tuileries than in finishing either of them.

The long gallery which he built followed the line of the old city wall and made use of its foundations. The south façade of the Louvre was set back some 60 metres behind the line of this wall. To affect a junction, therefore, a building set at right angles to both was needed. At first-floor level this was entirely occupied by the Petite Galerie or Galerie des Rois.

Beneath this gallery Anne of Austria had created her summer apartment. But on 6 February 1661 fire broke out in the Petite Galerie. The Blessed Sacrament was sent for from the parish church of Saint-Germain l'Auxerrois and was solemnly processed in the direction of the fire. Buckets of water, however, just in case, were being passed by a human chain which was rapidly formed. The gallery was destroyed, but the Queen Mother's rooms were spared. The Blessed Sacrament was processed back to the church, attended by the King and Queen 'and all the Court with the most exemplary devotion'. The gallery was rebuilt and given the new name of Galerie d'Apollon which it retains today.

The connection of the Louvre and the Tuileries was not the least of the problems to confront the successors of Henri IV. These difficulties, however, might have been overcome had there been any persistent determination to do so. But the Kings of France showed a recurrent reluctance to live in Paris. Vincennes and Saint-Germain were in many ways more attractive to them. The many projects for transforming the Louvre into a palace were pursued in a less than whole-hearted fashion. Progress at the Tuileries was steadier and it was often possible for the King to lodge here while the Louvre was under scaffolding. Thus, although the Louvre was for centuries regarded as the seat of the monarchy – rather like Saint James's Palace, in England – it was not often inhabited for any great length of time. Adjoining his wing, Lescot built a corner pavilion to house the King's Apartment. The external architecture was very much plainer than that of the courtyard. This was no doubt deliberate. A palace often reserved its fairest face for its most intimate friends.

But if the outward architecture was austere, the rooms which it contained were of a richness that was something new in France. Walls and ceilings were clothed with wooden panelling of the most ornate workmanship – chiefly by Francisque Scibec. But it was the ceilings which attracted the admiration of most visitors. The seventeenth-century English traveller Thomas Coryat describes what he calls the 'Presence Chamber' – more usually the Grande Antichambre – as 'very fair, being adorned with a wondrous sumptuous roof, which, though it be made but of timber work, yet it is exceedingly richly gilt, and with that exquisite art, that a stranger upon the first view thereof would imagine it were beaten gold'.

The royal apartments, however, suffered from one serious defect: they were badly lit. 'The King's bedroom', wrote Sauval in 1660, 'has not been put right, where at high noon one has to feel one's way about. This darkness is all the more unfortunate in that it obscures the most beautiful room in the world belonging to the greatest King on Earth.'

The palace of the Tuileries presented no particular problems: it was merely far from finished. Philibert de l'Orme's original design is known only from the drawings of Du Cerceau. He shows one of those gigantic buildings which the architects of the Renaissance delighted to imagine. In England, plans for a Whitehall Palace which would have occupied the whole area between St James's Park and the Thames, and which no Stuart King could ever have dreamed of being able to afford, resulted only in the erection of one tiny portion known as the Banqueting House.

The design for the Tuileries shows an architectural extravaganza which would have measured 26 metres by 166 and covered an area ten times that of the Louvre as it then stood. Only some two thirds of the range of buildings on the garden side had been constructed by 1660.

The two most distinctive features of de l'Orme's architecture were the array of dormer windows and a most remarkable oval staircase. The former was to find an admirer in Viollet-le-Duc. 'The decoration of the upper storey, which stood out against the dark tones of the roof, crowned the building in the richest possible manner. It was a truly palatial architecture, both in the strength and nobility of its masses and in the refinement of its detail.'

But the rooms were not only sumptuous – they were comfortable. 'It was the most agreeable habitation in the World', wrote Mlle de Montpensier, 'and one which I greatly loved.'

One of the great attractions was the terrace at first-floor level on either side of the central pavilion. 'There is a most pleasant prospect', wrote Thomas Coryat, 'from that walk into the Tuileries gardens, which is the fairest garden for length of delectable walks that ever I saw.'

On 26 August 1660, the King and Queen made their ceremonial entry into Paris. It was, of course, the occasion for the striking of a commemorative medallion. The catalogue of the medallions gives a concise account of the occasion. 'Everything had been laid out for one of the most superb entries that have ever been seen. The streets were ornamented with foliage, paintings and tapestries, and at various places there had been erected triumphal arches with emblematic figures and inscriptions.'

One of the most interesting of commentators was the abbé Michel de Pure, who wrote in 1668 his *Idée des Spectacles Anciens et Nouveaux*. He saw Paris as the successor to ancient Rome. 'It is much to be desired', he pleaded, 'that the custom in Rome should be observed of erecting triumphal arches, solid and durable, in order to preserve the memory of fine actions and the merits of heroes.' He deplored the construction of merely temporary architecture, but he went on to say that 'if there is anything about us which could be compared with the Roman Triumphs . . . it would doubtless be the Entries which our good cities offer to the sovereigns'.

The good city of Paris had put into the decoration of its triumphal arches all that ingenuity could contrive in the way of symbolic figures and classical allusion. Some of these could never have been made to satisfy the requirement of permanence made by the abbé de Pure. At the Fontaine Saint-Gervais the arch was almost entirely of living vegetation, including a corona of laurel trees which topped the whole structure. Beneath them Apollo was represented attended by Muses and surrounded by musicians. The meaning was reasonably clear – the Arts of Peace had returned and the new Parnassus was in the centre of Paris.

Sometimes, however, the allusions were more cryptic. To decode them one needed a perceptive eye and a thorough knowledge of the ways of ancient Rome. In the Marché Neuf was the figure of Hercules slaying the hydra; beneath him were engraved the letters SPQP – *Senatus populusque Parisinis* – replacing the famous SPQR, *Senatus Populusque Romanus*: Paris was the new Rome.

In order to appreciate such niceties, the spectator needed a long familiarity with the mythology of the Gods and Heroes. It seems odd that the Catholic Church, regenerated by the Council of Trent, should have tolerated paganism in such profusion. But the Jesuits, who managed to gain almost a monopoly in the field of education, made considerable use of Greek and Roman fables. Louis himself had learnt mythology without tears by means of a pack of playing cards designed for the purpose by Desmarets de Saint-Sorlin.

'From eight in the morning until after midday their Majesties, seated on thrones which had been prepared for them at the extremity of the Faubourg Saint-Antoine, received the homages and expressions of allegiance of all the more important corporations and city companies.' The thrones had been placed on a platform, reached by eighteen steps, in front of a large, newly built house, to which it was joined by a gallery of communication. The royal couple, after some four hours of harangues and loyal addresses, were able to retire to this house for a little refreshment.

At two o'clock in the afternoon the procession began. It was so arranged that the uniforms and robes of those partaking formed a steady crescendo of colour and finery. It began with the subfusc of the mendicant friars and clergy, followed by the students and doctors of the University, mostly in black, but with a touch of scarlet. The six Merchant Corporations struck a new note with robes of crimson, violet or blue and trimmed with ermine. The Corporation of Tailors were the first to be on horseback, their mounts adorned with ribbons and their trumpeters clothed in white satin. But the really spectacular array was reserved for the second half of the procession. Mazarin did not take part in the parade, but his retinue led the nobles and princes of the realm. Seventy-two mules, with saddle-cloths of red velvet bordered with gold and muzzles of solid silver, were cheered with an enthusiasm which the Cardinal himself had seldom known. The Chancellor Séguier, enveloped in a long gown of cloth of gold, rode beneath two parasols upheld by pages. He was painted thus by Le Brun and still has a place of honour at the Louvre.

The King himself – preceded by a small army of retainers, the mus-keteers, the pages, the Cent Suisses, the Heralds at Arms and the great officers of the Household – was brilliant in gold and silver embroidery and, wrote Mme de Motteville, 'mounted on a horse well fitted to exhibit him to his subjects'. But he did not outshine the young Queen. Seated like a goddess in a chariot of Roman style that was drawn by six Danish horses, she was covered in diamonds, rubies and pearls 'd'une valeur inestimable'. Her silvery blonde hair, her rosy complexion and white skin, together with the blue of her eyes, set off by the black of her dress, gave the most extraordinary lustre to her beauty. 'The crowds', concludes Mme de Motteville, 'were enraptured at the sight of her, and in their transports of love and joy called down a thousand blessings on her head.'

Among the many thousands of spectators, a certain Françoise d'Au-bigné, wife, and soon to be the widow, of the poet Scarron, recorded her enthusiasm. 'I was all eyes for ten or twelve hours together.' On the following day she sat down to write a long letter to Mme de Villarceaux. She began: 'I will not undertake to give you an account of the entry of the King.' She then proceeded to do so in more than a thousand words. 'I believe that nothing so beautiful could possibly be seen and that the Queen must have gone to bed last night very contented with the husband whom she has chosen.' Every detail of the seemingly endless cavalcade is described in the most superlative language – 'and all with a magnificence which astonished everyone'. Most magnificent of all, of course, was the *Maison du Roi*. 'You could not imagine the beauty of the horses on which the pages of both the Grande and the Petite Ecurie were mounted; they advanced in a series of bounds and they were managed in the most agreeable manner in the world.' The weather was brilliantly fine and the jewels and golden embroidery of the courtiers sparkled in the sun. But Mme Scarron ends on a significant note: 'The King knows perfectly well that he cannot afford expenses of this sort.'

From the windows of the Hôtel de Beauvais the Queen Mother and

Cardinal Mazarin looked down on the processions and listened to the acclamations. Since the death of Louis XIII they had preserved an unbroken partnership. Together they had shared the hardships, the humiliations and the near-disasters of the Fronde. She had seen Mazarin reviled and lampooned in the streets; there had been a price on his head and on more than one occasion he had been forced to quit the country. Together they had watched the young Louis grow in stature and in strength; together they had planned the peace and the marriage which had turned the people of Paris delirious with joy – but the affections of the Parisians are nothing if not fickle.

Mazarin, whose gout had been aggravated by the treatment which he was receiving for the gravel, was by now in decline and he was subject to convulsions which gave rise to fears for his life. 'One day', wrote Mme de Motteville, 'the King asked his advice on some matter; he replied: "Sire, you ask advice from a man who has lost the faculty of reasoning and who talks nonsense." The King, overcome with grief, passed into a little cabinet in the Cardinal's apartment and wept for this man who had served him as godfather, tutor, governor and minister.'

But the end was not yet. Mazarin was spared to witness the beginning of a new age and to see his beloved godson riding into power and popularity on the crest of an enormous wave. Perhaps more than anyone in France at the time he was entitled to say *Nunc dimittis*.

On 3 March 1661 he received Communion and two days later orders were given for the 'prayers of the forty hours' to be said in every church in Paris. This was not normally ordered except for a sovereign.

Daniel Cosnac, Bishop of Valence, happened to arrive at Vincennes just at the moment when Mazarin was about to receive Extreme Unction. 'I found the room completely full of people on their knees. The Cardinal was seated in an armchair beside his bed. He caught sight of me and as soon as the prayers were finished he called out for me to approach. Once I had pushed my way through the crowd, he said to me twice, in the most moving tones and with his eyes fixed on me: "M. de Valence, I ask your forgiveness." ' Cosnac was intrigued to know why, but just at this moment, by the most unfortunate mistiming, Colbert entered, threw himself at Mazarin's feet and asked *his* pardon.

On Wednesday 9 March 1661 Cardinal Mazarin died, as David Ogg puts it, 'in an atmosphere of piety and abundance'. As to his piety, it is not easy for posterity to judge; Mme de Motteville believed that it was genuine. 'The Queen Mother did me the honour of saying, in the presence of the King, that the Cardinal was very small before God; that he had a great sense of humility and hoped that God would have mercy on him.'

But she admitted: 'They are two things which it is difficult to combine: Christian humility and love of the good things of this world.'

That the Cardinal had the latter in abundance was only too evident. The Palais Mazarin, now the Bibliothèque Nationale, and the Château de Vincennes between them certainly housed one of the most remarkable private collections in France. Loménie de Brienne records a scene of the dying Cardinal saying his last farewell to all his treasures. 'I was walking in the new apartments of his palace. I was in the Petite Galerie where there was a tapestry, all of wool, which represented Scipio, done from the designs of Jules Romain; it belonged formerly to the maréchal de Saint-André; the Cardinal possessed nothing more beautiful. I heard him coming by the noise his slippers made, in which he shuffled along like a man languishing after a long illness. I hid behind the tapestry and heard him saying to himself: "I must leave all this!" He stopped at each step, for he was very weak, and went from side to side and, casting his eyes on whatever object attracted his attention, he repeated from the depths of his heart: "I must leave all this!" and then, as he turned: "And that also. How much trouble I took to acquire these things! How can I leave them without regret? I cannot take them with me where I go." I heard these words quite distinctly,' Brienne insists; 'they moved me more deeply, perhaps, than he was moved himself.'

On his death-bed Mazarin urged Louis to take the helm into his own hands and only to have ministers 'in order to listen to their advice'. He also recommended the creation of an inner cabinet – the Conseil Etroit – composed of only the principal ministers of the Crown, all of whom were to be regarded as equal; in other words, there should be no First Minister.

It was the time of Louis' true coming of age. 'Only then', he wrote in his memoirs, 'did it seem to me that I was King: born to be King.' It was perhaps the greatest moment in his life. 'I felt as it were my spirit and my courage rising; I felt myself a different person; I discovered in myself something which I did not know of before, and in my joy I reproached myself for having been so ignorant.'

In April, the month after the death of Mazarin, the Court went to pass the summer at Fontainebleau.

6

The New Reign Begins

Fontainebleau was by far the finest of Louis' palaces. Created by François I around the nucleus of an old castle, it had been greatly enlarged and partly redecorated by Henri IV, but only under Louis XIII had the main forecourt, the Cour du Cheval Blanc, been ennobled with Du Cerceau's magnificent horseshoe staircase. Brantôme, who described the Fontainebleau of François I as 'the most beautiful and pleasant house in all Christendom', went on to claim that Henri IV had left it 'a hundred times better in its decoration and embellishment . . . Briefly, it is a little Paradise in France.'

The word 'Paradise' translates into Tudor English as 'a most parkly ground and romancy pleasant place', and certainly the creation of the gardens at Fontainebleau was one of Henri IV's greatest achievements. 'The walks about the garden are many,' wrote the English traveller Thomas Coryat, 'whereof some are very long and of a convenient breadth.' But the greatest attractions were the little streams which accompanied these sandy paths. 'By most of these walks run very pleasant rivers full of sundry delicate fishes.' Upstream of all of these was 'the principal spring of all, which is called Fountain Beleau, which feedeth all the other springs and rivers, whence the King's palace hath its denomination'.

The spring, released by the excavations of a thirsty hound called Belaud, supplied also one of the principal features of the garden. Sebastien Locatelli, a priest from Bologna who visited Fontainebleau in November 1664, describes a 'marvellous fountain, with four hundred pipes, that throws up as many jets to a height of five or six feet which descend like rain into marble basins; three basins, set one above the other, form a great staircase which seems to be covered with a sheet of silver. The fountain overlooks a canal broad enough to float a large vessel.' It was Henry IV also who had provided Fontainebleau with this Grand Canal. It was 1,100 metres long, took three years to construct and eight days to fill with water. The 'large vessel', in reality a royal barge, was much admired by Italians. Mariani calls it 'a sort of triumphal ship, all gilded and marvellously pompous. While the twelve boatmen, in liveries of red and blue silk, trouble the calm and deep waters with their oars, the King and his brother and the most distinguished ladies of the Court drive along the banks on either side.'

At its farthest extremity, near Avon, the canal was wide enough for the boats to turn. The journey back afforded their occupants 'the vista of the reverse side of the palace, with its great galleries and the four hundred jets supplied by the source which the hound Belaud had discovered'. Henri IV had had 7,000 fruit trees planted in the park on either side of the canal. By 1661 all the plantations had come to their full luxuriance, and in April the tall chimneys and high pavilions of the roof could be seen rising above a cloud of blossom.

It was just at this moment of the year that Louis brought his Court to Fontainebleau. Marie-Thérèse had been pregnant since early February and was to spend the summer here. Louis, says Mme de Motteville, was determined to make their time in this lovely place as enjoyable as possible by the provision of all the *honnêtes plaisirs* that they could have wanted. The abbé de Choisy was in ecstasies: 'all was joy and abundance; the courtiers fared sumptuously and gambled for high stakes. Money flowed freely, every purse was open and the notaries managed to produce as much as the young men wanted. The money-lenders were hard – but who thinks about the terms offered when one needs money? So it was all banquets and ballets and *fêtes galantes*. The comte de Saint-Aignan had all the qualities required of a theatrical producer. He had a theatre put up in one of the alleys of the park at Fontainebleau and the fountains and vistas of the gardens provided the scenery; there was a supper; there was a performance of the latest comedy.'

Ballet, music, comedy: these were the most constant entertainments of the Court. One of Louis' first actions on taking over the government was to establish an Académie Royale de Danse in Paris – 'composed of those most experienced in the said art, to confer among themselves on the subject of the dance, to take such steps as are required and to deliberate on the means of perfecting it'.

The Académie de Danse was followed by the Académie de Musique. The foundation deed contains the interesting clause: 'It is our wish and our pleasure that all gentlemen and ladies may sing there without their being held on that account to do anything derogatory to their titles of nobility.' Louis stated in the preamble to the deed: 'The Sciences and the Arts, being the most considerable ornaments to a State, we have no more agreeable recreation, now that we have given peace to our peoples, than to revive these by summoning to our presence all those who have the reputation of excelling in them, not only within the confines of this Kingdom, but also in other countries.' Among those who came was a young musician from Florence, Jean-Baptiste Lully.

Of the origins and early life of Lully not many facts are available. The lacuna has been filled, for the most part, by fables. Giambattista Lulli (notice the final 'i') was the son of a miller in Florence. He was baptised on 29 November 1632. At the age of fourteen (nearly adult in those days) he was brought to France and placed in the household of la Grande Mademoiselle in the Tuileries. 'He came to France', she records in her memoirs, 'with my late uncle the chevalier de Guise ... I had asked him to bring me an Italian with whom I could converse and learn [the language].'

A tradition has grown up that Giambattista was employed in the kitchens as 'marmiton' or even 'sous-marmiton', and artists have even depicted him as a little ragamuffin playing his violin in the scullery. All that is known for certain is that six years later, in 1652, he is mentioned in Mademoiselle's Household Book with the quality of *valet de chambre*. A *valet de chambre* occupied a position of respect and confidence in a noble or royal household and frequently combined that position with some other distinguished activity.

In the same year, towards the end of October, Mademoiselle was exiled to her Château de Saint-Fargeau in Burgundy. Lulli did not want to share her exile. She gave him leave to go and he made his fortune – 'Car c'est un grand baladin,' she said. The word *baladin* means a buffoon, or someone who plays that part on the stage.

It is possible – even probable – that during his six years at the Tuileries he had come under the influence of Michel Lambert, who was reputed to be the greatest music master in Paris, and whose son-in-law he was to become.

Not long after he left the household of Mademoiselle, on 23 February 1653, Lulli took several parts, mostly of buffoons, in the *Ballet de la Nuit* in which, as we have seen, Louis also danced a number of roles. Loret, in his rhyming chronicle *La Muse Historique*, praises the performance:

> Avec leur appareil grotesque
> Leur bal et musique burlesque
> Causait un divertissement
> Qui faisait rire à tout moment.

A month later, on 16 March, Lulli received official recognition: 'On the assurance that he was given that Baptiste acquitted himself well in the composition of music . . . His Majesty engaged him to serve with the charge of "Compositeur de sa musique instrumentale".'

On 24 July 1662, he married Magdeleine Lambert, whose father was one of the greatest singers of the time and Maître de Musique de la Chambre de sa Majesté. The marriage register was signed by the King, the Queen and the Queen Mother. It was at this point that the name Lulli became 'de Lully'.

'Lully,' writes François Barrière, 'when he appeared, brought about a complete revolution in the art of music.' This revolution is described by Lully's contemporary Charles Perrault. Louis 'ordered him to take charge of the violins, for he played this instrument in a way which no one had ever approached, and His Majesty even created a new group for him which was known as *les petits violons*, who, under instruction, soon equalled and even surpassed the *bande des vingt-quatres*, which was the most renowned in Europe.

'It is true', continues Barrière, 'that they had the advantage of playing pieces composed by M. de Lully – pieces of a sort entirely different from those which had been heard heretofore. Before him, consideration was only given to the top line in music for violins; the bass line, and those in between, were a simple accompaniment and a rough counterpoint, which those who played these parts most often composed as they thought best . . . But M. de Lully gave to all the parts a tune almost as delightful as that of the top line; he introduced the most admirable fugues and above all rhythms that were quite new and unknown to all the masters.

'He introduced into his compositions, in the most agreeable manner, even drums and timbals, instruments which, having only one note, seemed incapable of contributing to the beauty of a harmony; but he managed to give them a rhythm so in keeping with the tunes in which they came, which for the most part were songs of war and triumph, that they touched the heart no less than the more harmonious instruments.

'He had a perfect knowledge of the rules of his art; but whereas those who preceded him had only acquired their reputation by the exact observance of these rules, he distinguished himself particularly by not following them and by putting himself above the rules. A discord or a dissonance was a rock on which even the most able musicians came to grief, but it was precisely on these discords and dissonances that M. de Lully built the most beautiful passages in his compositions by the art which he had of preparing the way for them, of placing them and of resolving them.' The abbé de Choisy joins the chorus in praise of Lully: 'He passed as the greatest man in the world in his art, as original as Corneille and Racine in tragedy, as Molière in comedy.'

Lully was brought into collaboration with Molière in the creation of a new art form, the *comédie-ballet*. It left them both the richer for the experience. Writing for music led Molière to the development of new prose rhythms, while his comedies gradually orientated Lully in the direction of opera, in which he was to achieve his greatest success. Certain of the *comédie-ballets*, notably *La Princesse d'Elides* and *Les Amants Magnifiques*, seemed to point in that direction, while others, such as *Le Bourgeois Gentilhomme*, were the obvious ancestors of the Opéra Comique.

Molière speaks through the mouth of the chevalier Dorante in *La Critique de l'Ecole des Femmes* to reveal his own attitude to his own art – the Comedy, which he contrasts with Tragedy. 'It is much easier to elevate oneself on high-flown sentiments, to defy Fortune in verse, to accuse Destiny and to revile the Gods than to enter properly into the absurdities of Man and to reproduce in an acceptable manner upon the stage the defects of all. When you paint a hero you can do as you like. This is to portray as one pleases, where one is not looking for any resemblance . . . But when your portraits are of real people they must be drawn from nature. It is necessary for them to be true to life and you have done nothing if you have not made them recognisable as the people of your own times . . . In a word, for a serious play it is enough, if one is to avoid disapproval, to talk good sense and to write well. It is a very different matter to win the laughter of the *honnête homme*.'

It seemed that wherever Louis turned he was destined to be served by people of the first quality; it was this that made the century of Louis XIV the *Grand Siècle*. As Voltaire claimed, 'it was a time worthy of the notice of the ages to come, the days when the heroes of Corneille and Racine, the characters of Molière, the symphonies of Lully, quite new to the nation, the voices of Bossuet and Bourdaloue could be heard by Louis Quatorze, by Madame [the duchesse d'Orléans] famous for her good taste, by a Condé, a Turenne, a Colbert, or by this crowd of outstanding men who appeared in all fields. The times will not return when a duc de La Rochefoucauld, author of *Maximes*, at the end of a conversation with a Pascal or an Arnaud, goes to the theatre of Corneille.'

In order that these distinguished authors should be enabled to retain their position Louis was prepared to pay them pensions. A list of those thus honoured survives in the Colbert manuscripts for the year 1663. Of thirty-three beneficiaries, the two who received the highest awards were Mézeray, 'historiographe', 4,000 livres, and Godefroi, 'historiographe du Roi', 3,500. Often the comments are more personal. Molière, 'excellent poète comique', only received 1,000 livres, while Benserade, 'poète français fort agréable', received 1,500. Pierre Corneille, 'premier poète dramatique du monde', was valued at 2,000 whereas Chapelain, 'le plus grand poète français qui ait jamais été', merited 3,000. Since Chapelain presided over this distribution of pensions and praise he may have written his own encomium. In all, these figures add up to nearly 51,000 livres. It was a very practical way in which to encourage the production of great literature.

Charles Perrault, in his collection of *Hommes Illustres*, gives a contemporary view of the emergence of so many men of distinction which gave its greatness to the *Grand Siècle*. 'It seems that Nature takes pleasure, from time to time, in showing her power by the richness of the talents which she distributes among those whom she loves ... Although these times of largess are subject to no rule, it is, all the same, remarkable that this generous mood comes to her most usually when Heaven has decided to give to this earth some great prince who is its ornament; for, as if she felt obliged to prepare the way for this hero in the world, she brings about the birth – either after him or together with him – of a host of men of exceptional merit to receive him and to be either the executors of his great actions or the architects of his magnificence or the heralds of his glory.'

To what extent this is true it is impossible to say. The important fact is that men like Perrault thought it was true; they felt that they were living in one of the great periods of French history, and that feeling must have been a great stimulus to them.

It is certainly true that the advent of Louis XIV coincided with the appearance of three of the most distinguished writers of the age: Molière, La Fontaine and Mme de Sévigné. La Fontaine is the best known. This is probably because he is the most accessible. He is easy to read. The accepted purpose of literature at that time was reduced by La Fontaine to two verbs – to please and to instruct. He realised that if readers are not given pleasure they will not listen to instruction. 'Unadorned moralism produces boredom.' The form of the fable, with its delightful anthropomorphism, was La Fontaine's method of combining pleasure with instruction. The word 'moral' in English has inescapable overtones of rigid ethical principles. It need have no such overtones in French. To say that Molière 'a observé profondément le moral de l'homme' is to say that he takes us deep into human nature. 'We desire novelty and gaiety,' continues La Fontaine. 'I do not call gaiety that which provokes laughter, but a certain charm, an agreeable air which can be given to all sorts of subjects, even the most serious.' It is what T. S. Eliot noted in Andrew Marvell – 'this alliance of levity with seriousness, by which the seriousness is intensified'.

The third name, Mme de Sévigné, brings us into the broad daylight of history. There is a portrait of her by Robert Nanteuil in the Musée Carnavalet. This shows the face of a plump and pleasing person with eyes set widely apart – Bussy described them as 'small and sparkling' – and there is a smile playing about her lips. She was a woman who owed more to her complexion, 'le plus beau teint du monde', than to her features.

But the best portrait of her comes, not from the brush of a painter, but from the pen of a writer – Madame de La Fayette. Her real charm, it seems, existed only in a direct relationship to her powers as a conversationalist. 'Your complexion', writes her friend, 'has a beauty and a flower which insists that you are only twenty' (she was in fact thirty-three at the time). 'Your mouth, your teeth, your hair are incomparable; but I do not need to say such things to you; your mirror will tell you as much, but since it does not amuse you to talk to it, it cannot tell you how attractive you are when you are speaking, and that is what I want to tell you. Know, therefore, Madame, if by chance you do not know already, that your wit adorns and beautifies your person, that there is no one in the world so charming as you are when you are engaged in animated conversation where all constraint is banished. The brilliance of your wit lends such a lustre to your complexion and to your eyes that, although it would seem that wit appeals only to the ear, yet it is certain that yours dazzles the eye and that when one is listening to you, one no longer notices that there is something lacking in the regularity of your features and one assigns to you the most perfect beauty in the world.'

No doubt because of her charm Mme de Sévigné seems to have been adored and adulated wherever she went. One of the earliest glimpses that we have of her comes from the abbé Arnauld of a meeting in 1657. 'It is as if I could see her still now', he writes, 'just as she appeared the first time I had the honour of seeing her, arriving deep in the back of her coach, sitting between her son and her daughter, all three just as the poets represent Latona with the young Apollo and the young Diana on either side, so radiant was the charm both of the mother and of the children.' The daughter, Françoise-Marguerite, later to be comtesse de Grignan, was to become the one consuming passion of her mother's life.

'Love me always, dear daughter,' she wrote on 31 May 1671: 'your friendship is my whole existence; as I said to you the other day, it is all my joy and all my sadness. I admit that the rest of my life is filled with shadows and sorrows when I reflect that so much of it will be passed in separation from you.'

Her friend Simon de Pomponne described their relationship in epigrammatic form. 'It appears that Madame de Sévigné passionately loves Madame de Grignan. Do you want to know the other side of the coin? It is that she loves her passionately!'

It was this, more than anything, which caused her to write the thousands of letters for which she is so justly celebrated. But behind her brilliant skill as a writer there lay this aptitude, it seems no less brilliant, for conversation. Such a gift was all-important in the society in which she lived. 'We need all sorts of people to be able to talk on all sorts of subjects in our conversation,' wrote la Grande Mademoiselle, 'which, to your taste and to mine, is the greatest pleasure in life.'

Today conversation is almost a lost art, although the French are still better at it than the English. It flourishes best in a society in which all the members move at ease and have nothing better to do than to get to know each other; it requires a life of leisure. As long ago as 1829 Sainte-Beuve could write: 'We can only with difficulty today, accustomed as we are to positive occupations, form any true picture of that life of leisure and of talk.'

But conversation requires the presence of the other party. In the event of lengthy separation the art of conversation becomes perforce the art of letter-writing. With Mme de Sévigné three factors combined to make her mistress of the art: her brilliance in conversation, her passionate affection for her daughter and the long periods during which she was separated from her.

Seldom, if ever, can there have been such an outpouring of maternal affection. 'You make me feel all that it is possible to feel of tenderness,' she wrote; 'but if you ever think of me . . . be assured that I continually think of you . . . Nothing can distract me. I am always with you.' This was written in 1670 just after her daughter had left to follow her husband to Provence. 'I see this coach which travels always forward and will never come nearer to me; I am always on the high road; it seems that sometimes I am afraid of its overturning; the rains which fell these last three days threw me into despair; the Rhône [which her daughter had to cross] filled me with the strangest fears. I have the map before my eyes; I know everywhere where you will sleep. Tonight you are at Nevers and on Sunday you will be at Lyon where you will find this letter.'

Mme de Sévigné wrote as she spoke: that is, straight from the heart. 'En vérité,' she admitted, 'il faut bien un peu entre amis laisser trotter les plumes: la mienne a toujours la bride sur le cou.'

The last word may be left to her cousin, Roger de Bussy-Rabutin. 'She is natural, she has a noble facility of expression and sometimes an audacious negligence which is to be preferred to the precision of the academics.' Himself a member of the Académie Française, he was perhaps qualified to judge. But as well as having secured herself a place in Parnassus, Mme de Sévigné is of great value to the historian for the brilliant little portraits of the personalities of the age and the fascinating glimpses which she provides of the life of the Court.

Another chronicler, less gifted but even more informative, was the marquise de Motteville, one of the ladies closest to Anne of Austria and closest, therefore, to events at Court. In April 1661, when the Court arrived at Fontainebleau, there was a new star in its firmament – Henriette-Anne d'Angleterre, the daughter of Charles I and Henrietta-Maria, and the sister of Charles II, his beloved 'Minette'. Since 30 March she had been the wife of Louis' brother Philippe, now duc d'Orléans through the death of his uncle. He was known in the language of the Court as 'Monsieur' and his wife therefore as 'Madame'. Mme de Motteville has left of her one of those portraits in which seventeenth-century France delighted and excelled.

'The princess of England was of more than medium height; she had a very becoming manner and her figure, which was not without defect' (she had one shoulder slightly higher than the other), 'did not appear so marred as in fact it was. Her beauty was not of the most perfect sort, but her whole personal appearance was none the less, on account of her manner and her charm, entirely lovable. Her complexion was very delicate and very pale, but combined with a natural bloom only to be compared with roses and jasmine. Her eyes were small, but sweet and sparkling . . . her lips were vermilion and her teeth as fine and white as one could have wished. She dressed and did her hair in a way which was wholly suited to her person, and there was something about her which made one love her . . . She had not been able to become a Queen, but to remedy this defect it was her wish to reign in the hearts of all honest men and to find her glory in the world by the charm and the beauty of her spirit. One could already see in her [she was only sixteen] the light of reason, and beyond her youth, which had until then concealed her from the public, it was easy to judge that once she found herself on the great stage of the Court of France, she would play one of the leading roles.' Her role, however, was to be greatly complicated and her happiness sadly compromised by the character of her husband.

Philippe d'Orléans was from his earliest childhood fundamentally effeminate. His childhood is described by one of the most extraordinary people to appear upon the crowded stage of seventeenth-century France and to record its eccentricities, François-Timoléon, abbé de Choisy. He was the third son of Gaston d'Orléans' chancellor and of Jeanne-Olympe de Belesbat, a granddaughter of the Chancellor l'Hôpital. It was she who moulded the character of her youngest child. 'She made her son a living doll,' wrote Lescure, who edited Choisy's memoirs, 'dressing him as a woman and giving him the spirit and the nature of a woman.' It was a purely self-regarding plan of action. 'As her whole desire was to remain beautiful,' her son wrote, 'a child of eight or nine years, whom she took with her everywhere, made her appear still young.' His own beauty became 'a living flattery' of hers.

Madame de Choisy was near enough to the Court to be on good terms with the Queen Regent, whose second son, Philippe, was four years older but of the same sexual orientation as François-Timoléon. 'Every time the young Monsieur came to our house, and he came at least two or three times a week, I was dressed as a girl. My ears had been pierced, I had diamonds and beauty spots and other little vanities to which one easily becomes accustomed and from which it is difficult to free oneself. Monsieur, who loved all that sort of thing, was effusively friendly towards me. As soon as he arrived, followed by Cardinal Mazarin's nieces and some of the Queen's young ladies, we began to dress him up and to do his hair. All this was done, it was said, by order of the Cardinal who wanted to make him effeminate for fear that he might vex the King in the way that Gaston d'Orléans had vexed Louis XIII.'

Choisy describes the details of what he wore on each occasion with the precision of an article in a fashion magazine. On one occasion he reaches the climax: 'Je me croirais véritablement femme.'

It was all mixed up with strict religious observance; he was, after all, destined to Holy Orders. He paid the churchwardens of his parish for the right to sit in their only too conspicuous seats. The superior of the Séminaire, however, wrote to Mazarin to complain that François-Timoléon was so beautiful and so attractively dressed that he dared not bring his ordinands, destined to a life of celibacy, to the Mass.

Choisy takes us fairly deep into the psychology of the transvestite. When he was all dressed up and decked out in his diamonds and his beauty spots at a ball or at the comedy, he admitted that 'if I heard someone say in a low voice near me: "What a beautiful person!" I tasted a pleasure within myself to which nothing can be compared, so great it is. Ambition, riches, even love cannot equal it, because we always love ourselves more than we love others.'

It seems that this sort of narcissism was shared by the King's brother. 'I went to the Palais-Royal whenever Monsieur was in Paris. He showed me a thousand kindnesses because our tastes were the same. He would have wished to be able to dress as a woman also, but he dared not because of his high position (princes are prisoners of their grandeur), but in the evening he put on a mob cap, earrings and beauty spots and sat contemplating himself in the mirrors, idolised by his admirers.'

Monsieur is described, of course, by Mme de La Fayette. 'His inclinations were as close to the ways of women as those of his brother were far removed from them. He was beautiful and well built, but of a beauty and a build more befitting a princess than a prince. Also he was more concerned that his beauty should be admired by everyone than to use it to win the hearts of women, although he was continually in their company. His vanity seemed to render him incapable of attachment to anyone but himself.'

These words were written in 1659. Two years later the marriage was arranged between Monsieur and Henriette d'Angleterre. Mme de La Fayette observed that Monsieur went to Le Havre to meet his bride 'with all the eager attentions imaginable and continued until his marriage to pay her his respects in which nothing was lacking but love: to set the heart of this prince on fire was a miracle that was not reserved for any woman in the world'. Monsieur himself claimed, in a tête-à-tête with la Grande Mademoiselle, that he had loved Henriette-Anne for fifteen days.

It was not to her that he lost his heart but to a member of his own sex, the chevalier de Lorraine. This young nobleman, 'fait comme on peint les anges', wrote the abbé de Choisy, ruled Monsieur's heart and household. 'He soon became favourite, master, dispenser of favours and more autocratic with Monsieur than is permissible if one does not wish to be taken for the master, or mistress, of the house.' It did not bode well for the future.

But Philippe d'Orléans was, as Mme de Motteville reminds us, 'a very likeable prince – with plenty of wit, full of kindness, at ease with everyone', and for a short time, in the early summer of 1661, the royal family appeared to be happy and united. The Queen Mother, writes Mme de Motteville, 'by her virtuous conduct had just newly acquired a great reputation; she was loved and revered by all for her gentleness and honest manners, and by her goodness was a source of happiness to high and low'. In particular she was solicitous in her care for the young Queen. 'In fact', resumes Mme de Motteville, 'the whole royal family lived in an atmosphere of peace and concord which was not often to be found . . . I have never seen the Court more beautiful.'

But it was Henriette d'Angleterre who animated the life of the Court. 'It was the middle of the summer,' wrote Jean Loret in *La Muse Historique*; 'Madame went bathing every day. She went in a coach because of the heat, but she returned on horseback, followed by all her ladies, gallantly dressed and with a thousand ostrich feathers on their heads, accompanied by the King and all the younger members of the Court.'

Among the gallantly dressed and magnificently plumed young ladies who attended Madame was a girl of sixteen from the valley of the Loire – Louise de La Vallière. Her first experience of Court life was of this brief period of felicity during that beautiful summer at Fontainebleau.

It was not to last. The Queen, retiring by nature and religious by inclination, was not constituted to be the centre of so brilliant a circle; she was already five months pregnant and, as pleasure succeeded to pleasure in a ceaseless round of balls and ballets, of *fêtes champêtres*, of excursions into the forest and embarkations in gilded gondolas on the Canal, Louis' most natural partner was his sister-in-law. The inevitable happened: 'It began to appear in the eyes of all', observed the marquise de La Fayette, 'that they felt for one another that attraction which is the ordinary precursor of great passions.'

By July it was becoming a serious worry to the Queen Mother. She was supported in this by Monsieur, who was jealous by nature, and by Henrietta-Maria, who arrived at Fontainebleau on 6 July. Faced with their remonstrances, Louis and his sister-in-law began to see the light of reason and the project was approved that he should stage a love affair with one of the ladies-in-waiting – Mlle de Pons or Mlle de Chimerault, both in attendance on the Queen – or with Madame's own *fille d'honneur*, Louise de La Vallière. The first two dropped out and Louise, not yet seventeen, found herself the object of the King's amorous attentions.

But it was the story of the Happy Hypocrite. By wearing the mask of love Louis became the true lover. Louise responded, and as the reality took over from the pretence, Louis, far from making a demonstration of his attachment, became more and more reserved. 'They were very restrained,' wrote Mme de La Fayette; 'he did not see her in Madame's apartments, nor in the excursions by daylight; but on the evening outings he would leave Madame's *calèche* and go to that of La Vallière, who kept her *portière* open, and in the darkness of the night he had many opportunities to speak with her.'

'The King', wrote Choisy, 'was at that time deeply in love with Mlle de La Vallière.' Louise and the abbé had both been attached to the household of the duc d'Orléans. 'I speak of her with pleasure. I spent my childhood with her ... but since she tasted the love of the King she no longer wanted to see her old friends or even to hear mention of them, so exclusively was she occupied with her passion.' Choisy does not appear to have resented this neglect and gives a detailed, but not uncritical, account of her looks and character.

'Mlle de La Vallière was not one of those beauties who are quite perfect and whom one often admires without loving. She was very lovable, and the words of La Fontaine: "Et la grâce, plus belle encore que la beauté" seemed to have been made for her. She had a beautiful complexion, blonde hair, an agreeable smile, blue eyes and a look so tender and at the same time so modest as to win at once both one's esteem and affection. For the rest, she had little enough wit ... but she had no ambition, no designs ...

never forgetting that she was doing something wrong, always hoping to get back onto the paths of righteousness.'

The marquis de Saint-Maurice, who, as ambassador from Savoy, had no need to flatter in his despatches, saw in Louise a 'je ne sais quoi qui sait charmer' – and this was in spite of 'her thinness, her lack of wit, her tantrums and her off-hand manner'. Olivier Lefèvre d'Ormesson, who was not given to flattery either, was more censorious: 'This young lady did not seem to me at all beautiful; her eyes and her complexion were very fine, but she was emaciated, her cheeks were hollow, her mouth and her teeth ugly, the tip of her nose too big and her face too long.'

To these defects Louis was blind. He fell madly in love with Louise and in due course she became his *maîtresse déclarée*. *Le Roi très chrétien, le Fils aîné de l'Eglise*, had broken the seventh Commandment and committed adultery.

On 1 November, All Souls' Day, 1661, Marie-Thérèse fulfilled her primary duty as Queen by providing France with a Dauphin. 'The Queen, in her labour,' writes Mme de Motteville, 'was seriously ill and in peril of her life. When her pains were at their strongest the King seemed so afflicted and so obviously deeply moved by her suffering that he left no room for doubting that the love which he felt for her had a higher place in his heart than all the others. At five in the morning he made his confession and received Communion and, having implored the protection of God, gave himself up wholly to the task of assisting her; she, the meanwhile, in the middle of her suffering was expressing her tenderness for him all the time.' It was touching, but it did not last. Louis was soon back with La Vallière.

It was not without some struggle with his conscience that he had yielded. He was particularly troubled by the effect which his behaviour inevitably had on his relationship with his mother, to whom he was devoted. For some time they were not on speaking terms; the Queen Mother's confessor, however, ordered her to make the first move, but Louis anticipated her. Mme de Motteville describes the scene. 'The King, for his part, by virtue of his good nature and ill-satisfied with himself, came to find her, with the sincere intention of being reconciled with her.' He even went down on his knees and wept bitterly. He said that he had not slept all night at the thought of the pain which he had caused her. But the Queen Mother felt obliged, both by her Christian duty and by her love for her son, to tax him with his shortcomings. 'She told him that he was intoxicated by his own greatness; that he acknowledged no limits to his desires nor to his vengeance. She reminded him of the peril in which he stood regarding his salvation, and in fact said everything which she could to bring him back to his senses and to oblige him at least to desire the power to break those chains which bound him to his sin.'

Louis replied 'with tears of anguish which came from the depths of his heart, where there were still some remains of his former piety, that he knew that he was doing wrong; that he sometimes felt the pangs of shame; that he had done what he could to hold himself back from offending God and to avoid surrendering to his passions, but that he was forced to admit to her that they had become stronger than his reason and that he could no longer resist their violence'. The immediate issue – of whether the ladies of the Court could be obliged to follow in his mistress's suite – had troubled him for a long time but, 'since she wanted it, he had yielded to her'. His mother had to content herself with saying that it was at least something that he could admit that he was doing wrong.

Louis wrote somewhat more dispassionately on the subject in the memoirs which he compiled for his son. 'I will say to you in the first place that, as the prince ought always to be a perfect example of virtue, he would do well to protect himself completely against those weaknesses which are common to the rest of mankind, and all the more so because he can be certain that it is not possible to keep them hidden. And yet, if we should happen in spite of ourselves to fall into one of these deviations, we must at least observe two precautions, which I have always done and felt much the better for. The first – that the time which we devote to our amours should never be to the prejudice of our business, because our first object should always be the maintenance of our glory and our authority, which cannot be achieved without unremitting labour . . . But the second consideration, which is the more difficult and delicate to put into practice, is that, while surrendering our hearts, we remain the masters of our minds; that we keep separate the tenderness of a lover from the decision-making of a sovereign.'

Colbert noted the following words of Louis to his ministers: 'You are all my friends, those who rank first out of all my kingdom in my love and in my confidence. I am young, and women are often a powerful force with those of my age. I order each one of you, if you notice any woman, whosoever she might be, exercising any influence over me or ruling me however slightly, you are to draw my attention to the fact. I will need only twenty-four hours to free myself from it and to give you full satisfaction.'

This says much about Louis' relationships with his ministers and of the primacy which he was to put on attending to the business of ruling France. For Louis expressed his determination to do the job himself – 'de faire son métier de Roi'.

7
Fouquet

In his memoirs Louis dwells on the necessity and on the pleasure of conscientious work. 'There is one thing more, my son, and which I hope you will not learn from your own experience: nothing can be more arduous than complete idleness.' He illustrates his attitude to work from his first taking over of the helm after the death of Mazarin. 'I made it a rule to work regularly twice a day and for two or three hours each time with divers persons, not counting the hours which I would spend on my own account, alone . . . I cannot tell you what fruits I reaped immediately as the result of this decision . . . My early shyness, which a little discernment always brings and which at first afflicted me, especially when I had to speak at any length in public, disappeared completely . . . Finally I experienced an inexpressible pleasure – something which you will not know yourself unless you taste it as I did.'

Louis' decision to 'do his job as King' meant that no minister would succeed to the position of Mazarin. Loménie de Brienne describes the moment at which Louis made known his intentions. It was on 10 March, the day after the death of Mazarin. 'The King asked the princes, dukes and ministers of state . . . to assemble in the Queen Mother's room so that he could explain to them himself that "he had decided to take charge of the State in person and to rely on no one else" [these were his own words] and courteously discharged them from their duties, saying that "when he had need of their good advice, he would call for it" . . . I was ordered to write to all the foreign secretaries to explain the decision that His Majesty had taken to govern his state in person so that they could advise their princes accordingly.'

The people of Paris, meanwhile, had greeted the news of Mazarin's death with joy. 'He had made peace', writes the abbé de Choisy, 'and had promised marvels.' But the marvels did not materialise. There were fireworks, there were ballets, there were carousels: 'we could see the flowers of peace, but we had not yet tasted the fruits. All good men trembled for the State, where they saw no one at the helm: it did not occur to them that the King was capable of governing, even if he were prepared to give himself the trouble. He was handsome, well made and only twenty-two years old. Pleasures assailed him on all sides to anaesthetise his virtue . . . All political thought led to the search for the man who would take over the helm, but no one was obviously in a position to become such a person. There were but three men on the stage – Fouquet, Le Tellier and Lionne . . . We scarcely knew who they were.'

But there was already another name to be reckoned with, that of Jean-Baptiste Colbert. In his last will and testament Mazarin bequeathed 'to Colbert, the house in which he lives . . . and he begs the King to make use of him, for he is faithful'. To begin with the King retained the services of Fouquet, but he was determined to test his honesty. 'In order to secure my guarantees', he wrote in his memoirs, 'I gave him, as contrôleur des finances, Colbert – a man in whom I had every possible confidence.'

Louis asked Fouquet for a complete statement of the financial situation and warned him not to conceal anything, writes the abbé de Choisy, 'saying that he would always make use of him provided that he was satisfied as to his sincerity; that the past was past and forgotten'.

Fouquet consulted his friends Bruant, Delorme and Pellisson, who warned him that it might be dangerous not to paint the picture in its true colours. But Fouquet would not listen. He could not believe that the King, young and pleasure-loving, could continue to bear for long the heavy burden of the State. 'He gave the King, therefore, the State of the expenditure, which he magnified, and of his revenues, which he diminished, making matters seem worse than they were. The King showed these statements every evening to Colbert, who drew his attention to the falsifications. This testing, repeated several times, determined the King to disgrace Fouquet.' 'It is from Pellisson and from Paraire', adds Choisy, 'that I have these particulars.'

No two people could have more aptly personified the change from the old order to the new than Fouquet and Colbert. Even their heraldic achievements seemed to proclaim their opposition. *Fouquet* in old Breton meant a squirrel. With this emblem went the motto 'Quo non ascendam?' (How high shall I not climb?). Colbert's arms were in the form of a rebus – a grass-snake; *couleuvre* in French, *coluberta* in Latin. In early Christian symbolism it stood for prudence. So far as Fouquet was concerned, Colbert was not so much the grass-snake as the snake in the grass. Of the three members of the Conseil Etroit Fouquet was the one who saw himself most clearly as Louis' next First Minister. It was this, insists Choisy, that brought about his fall. 'He allowed himself airs of superiority over the other ministers who were offended and joined together against him.' But it was Colbert who pursued Fouquet with the most relentless tenacity.

The two rivals could hardly have been more different. Fouquet, coming from the highest of parliamentary families but now a *grand seigneur*, rich and extravagant, was an enlightened amateur and a considerable patron of art, drama, literature, learning and science; a lover of luxury, display and magnificent entertainments and ready to spend without counting the cost in order to maintain the lustre of his position. Colbert, who had started as a junior clerk with Le Tellier, and then an intendant under Mazarin, was a serious-minded civil servant, with little fortune of his own, a compulsive worker, an adept of office and ledger and the scrutiny of accounts.

Colbert quickly became Mazarin's *homme de confiance*. Familiar with all the Cardinal's affairs, both public and private, he came to know all about Fouquet's machinations and was offended by his insolent opulence, his excessive expenditure, his scandalous profits. A lover of order, method and economy, Colbert was on a collision course with Fouquet.

It is not possible to understand the drama of the rise and fall of Fouquet without having some knowledge of the financial system which still existed when he came to power. 'The King', writes Colbert's biographer, Inès Murat, 'as a private individual is not rich. His estates hardly yield 80,000 livres a year. The head of the State cannot appeal directly to money-lenders who are suspicious of a king with no credit and in danger of bankruptcy. So the monarch finds himself obliged to proceed by means of the services of the *banquiers*, dealers in ready money. Having become the intermediary between the King or the State on the one hand, and his correspondents or friends on the other, the *banquier* is described as an *homme de finance* or *financier*. Our banquier/financier wants – nothing more natural – to reimburse himself, if possible with interest, for the advances made to the monarch. The King, who is poor, allows him to deduct for his own account one or more financial resources. The financier attains, to a certain degree, the rank of civil servant. But what a strange civil servant who, invested with an authority coming from the State, makes use of this authority for his private affairs and with the blessing of the Prince!'

This had long been the system. Richelieu himself had admitted in his will that the financiers were 'a class apart, injurious to the State, but all the same a necessity'. 'The function of superintendant', continues Inès Murat, 'represents the highest ambition of these financier/civil servants. The superintendant is not accountable. No one can ask to see his accounts, not even the King. He gives an explanation [*il rends raison*] of his administration to the Prince according to his conscience, or his good pleasure. Why, under these circumstances, should he keep a register?'

On 7 February 1653, Abel Servien and Nicolas Fouquet were made joint Surintendants des Finances. The next day Colbert wrote: 'buildings, furniture, silver and other ornaments were for the financiers and tax-farmers who lavished prodigious sums upon them, whereas the buildings of His Majesty were often held up for want of money . . . the royal houses were not kept furnished and there was not so much as a pair of silver andirons for the King's bedroom'.

Three years after the appointment of Servien and Fouquet, Mazarin put about the rumour that he wanted the post for himself. 'The two who occupy that position', wrote Guy Patin, 'are frightened to death; they negotiated for it and bought it in for the sum of three million livres which they gave for the two of them; that is to say that, in order to reimburse themselves, it will be permissible to rob the King and the public of as much as they like and as much as they can in order to build themselves as many fine houses and superb palaces as they shall please.'

The system certainly provided opportunities for great personal enrichment at the top. At the lowest level it created poverty and oppression of the worst sort. Guillaume Lamoignon, the Premier Président of the Parlement de Paris, wrote: 'the people were groaning in all the provinces beneath the hand of the extortioner, and it seems that all their substance and even all their blood would not suffice for the burning greed of the tax collectors. The misery of these poor people has reached the last extremity, partly because of the continuation of the ills which they have endured for so long, partly because of the rise in prices and scarcity of food, almost without precedent, over the last two years.' It was one thing, however, to identify the evils which arose from the system; it was quite another to be able to suggest any more equitable system. The old order continued.

Fouquet's personal wealth and powerful contacts made him the obvious choice for dealing with the tax-farmers and banquiers, and the royal finances had often benefited by his efforts. In July 1656, at the time when the King's troops under Turenne had been forced by Condé and Juan d'Autriche to abandon the siege of Valenciennes, Fouquet managed to produce 900,000 livres at four days' notice. Mazarin wrote to him: 'I know that you have raised this sum on your personal debentures. I owe you a debt of gratitude and I am very deeply touched by the manner in which you dealt with it. I spoke of it at some length to their Majesties; they have charged me to thank you on their behalf for the effort which you have made and to assure you that they will keep it in remembrance.'

The King and his mother even visited Fouquet at his house at Saint-Mandé, adjoining the park at Vincennes.

A year later Mazarin's gratitude seemed to have been forgotten. He claimed the repayment from Fouquet of a personal loan of 300,000 livres in terms which threatened to create a rift between them. Fouquet made an offer which Mazarin rejected, demanding ready money and not promises. Fouquet over-reacted and wrote a somewhat rash letter to the Cardinal, complaining that he listened too readily to scandalous rumours. But Fouquet was a man of a deeply unstable character, vacillating between careless optimism and groundless despondency. Now, afraid that he had offended Mazarin, he became the prey to the deepest anxieties. What if he were to fall from favour and lose his position? During the summer of 1657 he was seriously considering the possibility of his disgrace and drew up a plan of action known as the *projet de Saint-Mandé*. He was unwise enough not only to put his project on paper but to preserve the paper. In his thinking he even foresaw the possibility of his own imprisonment and made provision for a supply of books, the services of a doctor and the need to suborn the prison officers. Madame du Plessis-Bellière, 'to whom I entrust myself completely, and from whom I have never had any secrets or any reservations', was to have charge of his affairs.

On its own, the *projet de Saint-Mandé* hardly looks capable of constituting a threat to the State, but to this precautionary measure was added the purchase and the fortification of Belle-Isle. This island, lying off the entrance to Quiberon Bay, had been granted by Charles IX to the duc de Retz. Among the conditions of this grant was that the defences of the island should be strengthened. It occupied a key position for ships returning to France from America.

In 1658 the duc de Retz, deeply in debt, put Belle-Isle up for sale. Fouquet received from Mazarin the King's mandate to buy it 'in order that this place does not fall into the hands of suspected persons who have not the necessary means to fortify it properly'. The King, recognising that 'there was no one who had given more proofs of his fidelity and zeal than Monsieur Fouquet', invited him to negotiate the purchase 'à l'exclusion de toute autre'. Fouquet thus became the owner of one of the important places in the maritime defences of France. What could be less suspicious than a continuation of the works of fortification neglected by de Retz?

But to this multiplication of walls and bastions must be added the creation of a network of personal allegiances – of men who promised their ultimate loyalty not to the King but to Fouquet. Thus Deslandes, Governor of Concarno, actually signed, on 2 June 1658, a promise 'de n'être jamais à une autre personne que lui', and to serve him 'contre toutes sortes de personnes sans exception'. Did that last clause include the King? Deslandes was one of many. With this strange and strong reaffirmation of the idea of homage Fouquet seems still to belong in outlook to the feudal age. He assured himself of the support of Neuchesne, Commander-in-Chief of the King's Navy, and with his own creature, the marquis de Créqui, put into position as Général des Galères, he could regard himself as invulnerable on Belle-Isle.

Colbert's suspicions were easily aroused. He was looking for evidence enough to bring about his rival's fall. The picture, with all its details, could easily look like a vast conspiracy. But taken as a whole it is difficult to believe. Could Fouquet really have hoped to have lived the rest of his life on an island off Quiberon in open hostility to the King? The whole elaborate structure of the *projet de Saint-Mandé* was not likely to succeed nor did any of these precautions prove necessary, for Mazarin showed no signs of taking offence. In 1658 they faced together one of the most difficult years. On 8 June Mazarin wrote to Fouquet: 'I cannot see any means of subsistence for the coming year.' Fouquet replied: 'I have never yet seen the finances in so bad a way; everyone wanting money and at the same time opposing those who might be able to produce it.' Under such pressure one could not afford to be difficult as to the choice of methods; no expedient could be disregarded. Mazarin's only interest was in ready money, not in properly kept accounts.

It was, however, just at this period that Fouquet felt confident enough to plan one of his most extravagant projects, the creation of the château and gardens on his seigneurial lands of Vaux-le-Vicomte. On 2 August 1656, he signed an agreement with the architect Louis Le Vau.

It was nothing new for a surintendant des finances to provide himself with an impressive mansion. The importance of Vaux-le-Vicomte in architectural history is that it was here that Louis Le Vau, together with the painter Charles Le Brun and the landscape artist André Le Nôtre, learnt to work as a team and to produce that unity of architecture, interior decoration and garden lay-out which distinguishes the *style Louis Quatorze*. They were soon to become the creators of Versailles. Inspired, it seems, by Pietro Cortona's work at the Pitti Palace, the new style at Vaux was described by Anthony Blunt as 'a Baroque tamed by the French classical spirit'. The interior decoration was mostly tapestry. There were originally 143 tapestries, woven from designs by Le Brun. In order to produce them, Fouquet established, at the near-by village of Maincy, a special manufactory which later became the Gobelins in Paris.

Early in 1657 a task force of 18,000 was set to work, levelling the ground for the immense gardens and laying the foundations of the château and its palatial outbuildings. Within a year the shell of masonry was completed.

The size and splendour of Vaux made it an easy target for Fouquet's enemies. 'If I did not speak out', wrote Charles Cotin, 'the very stones themselves would cry aloud; I mean the cut stones, the marble, the porphyry of these sumptuous palaces [the houses of surintendants] where the eyes are dazzled by the gold and blue and fatigued by the façades. I mean these enormous masses of masonry, these mountains made of columns under which the ground groans and gives way; I mean these avenues of transplanted trees which arrived, like their owners, in a single night; avenues to which mighty rivers serve as canals and flow with the tears and the blood of the people; avenues longer and more spacious than the courts of Kings and Queens!' It was the last point which was the most significant. In describing the glories of Vaux as 'sacrileges which rob the legitimate monarchs of the hearts and love of their people', Cotin puts his finger on the vital point: Fouquet was usurping the position which Louis intended for himself alone.

On 10 August the marquise d'Huxelles wrote to Fouquet that the Queen Mother had been criticising him in public. 'The King would like to be rich', she had said, 'and he does not love those who are more so than he, because they undertake things which he cannot do and that he has no doubt that the great wealth of these others has been stolen from him.'

Fouquet, however, took no notice. Wednesday 17 August 1661 was the day chosen for an entertainment at Vaux to which the King and his whole Court were invited and which was designed to be the unveiling of the splendours of the house and gardens and the apotheosis of their owner. The weather was perfect. 'Vaux will never be more beautiful', wrote La Fontaine, 'than it was that evening.'

The King, the Queen Mother, the duc and duchesse d'Orléans, Condé, Longueville and all the Court set out from Fontainebleau at three o'clock and reached Vaux some three hours later.

The arrival at Vaux is still one of the great architectural experiences afforded by France. The whole, vast complex suddenly appears on the right-hand side of the road, a tumultuous compendium of buildings of different heights linked by gargantuan arcades and rows of termes – those great piers of stone crowned each with a double human head facing both ways; but as one moves towards the central axis, offices, outbuildings and forecourts assume progressively their positions in the symmetry to which they were ordained and the château itself appears as the focal point of an artificial setting which extends over hundreds of acres. The whole, huge context of architecture and formal garden serves but to emphasise the importance of the château proper, which is left in splendid isolation.

The royal visit is described in the anonymous *Relation des magnificences faites par M. Fouquet à Vaux-le-Vicomte lorsque le roi y alla.* Louis waited for the cool of the evening before he emerged from the oval Salon and descended the flight of stone steps from the terrace before the château down into the gardens. There were fountains everywhere. 'It is here', continues the *Relation*, 'that Tivoli and Frascati and all that Italy prides itself on possessing . . . must admit that she has nothing to compare with Vaux. To say that a hundred jets of water on either side, each over 10 metres high, formed an alley down which one walked as if between two walls of water, is to say nothing. There were at least a thousand more which made so loud and beautiful a noise that one might have sworn that this was the throne of Neptune.'

Among the many fountains, statues and urns, moved the richly attired members of the Court, their gorgeous costumes 'loaded with plumes and ribbons, forming the most lovely sight that could possibly be imagined'.

As darkness fell, everyone returned to the château where a repast was offered consisting of pheasants, ortolans, quails, partridges, ragouts, bisques and 'toutes sortes de vin en abondance'. Thanks to the provision of the maître d'hôtel, the already famous François Vatel, the tables were re-charged five or six times.

After the supper it was time for the comedy. The stage was set in one of the bosquets of the park, surrounded by fountains and lit with a hundred flambeaux. Here the troop of Molière was to perform *Les Fâcheux*, but Molière himself appeared in his ordinary clothes on the stage claiming to be unprepared with no script and no cast. Then addressing the King in person, he pleaded with him that only by the use of his royal authority could anything happen. Louis gave the sign and immediately a great clam-shell opened and a naiad stepped out. She pronounced the prologue, written by Pellisson, ordering the termes and the trees to speak – which of course they did.

After the performance the King returned to find the château illuminated: 'little lanterns, which had been ranged close to each other along the cornices, made the building stand out as if on fire, and this created a medley of darkness and light which was astonishing to behold'. But even as the courtiers were lost in admiration of the sight, there was a sudden explosion from the direction of the grotto and a tremendous salvo of rockets streaked into the sky – 'as if they wanted to carry their fire to the vaults of heaven' – only to fall again in a thousand different patterns, of fleurs de lys, cyphers and initials, while along the canal a monster whale could be seen moving to the detonation of petards and fireworks within its belly, 'so that fire and water, thus united, became one and the same element'.

As the King left Vaux-le-Vicomte to return to Fontainebleau, he might have seen on the terrace before the château a group of statuary designed by Le Brun. It is described by Mlle de Scudéry (in the tenth volume of *Clélie*). It represents a lion (Louis XIV) protecting a squirrel between its paws from the attacks of a snake.

As the last of the coaches left along the road in the direction of Melun, Fouquet may well have felt that this night had been his high moment of glory. He had given his sovereign and all the Court a never yet surpassed and never to be forgotten experience. All the arts had been pressed into service for the occasion: architecture, painting, sculpture, landscape gardening, hydrodynamics, music, drama, ballet, gastronomy, and pyrotechnics. He must have felt that his position with the King was now secure – that the squirrel, between the paws of the lion, was safe from the snake.

If so, he was never more mistaken in his life. The snake had already triumphed. Three months before the fête de Vaux, on 14 May, Colbert had convinced Louis that the fall of Fouquet was necessary for the attainment of autocracy; that the Surintendant was guilty of *lèse-majesté* and peculation and that he should be put on trial for his life. Louis had even contemplated having him arrested during the fête, but his mother dissuaded him. The arrest was postponed until the following month at Nantes, where Louis was to confront the States of Brittany.

On 24 August Fouquet, accompanied by Hughes de Lionne, Secretary of State for Foreign Affairs, left Fontainebleau, travelling by coach to Orléans where they took 'une fort grande cabane' – a vessel not unlike a royal barge with twelve oarsmen. They were saluted by the young Loménie de Brienne, who noted in his memoirs that 'a moment later another barge went past; in it was M. Le Tellier and M. Colbert. I saluted them also.' His companion, a clerk in the postal service named Ariste, made the comment: 'Those two barges which we can still see are following after each other in such a spirit of rivalry as if the oarsmen were competing for a prize on the Loire. One of the two must come to grief at Nantes.' The abbé de Choisy adds that 'the courtiers were saying openly that this visit would be fatal either to Fouquet or to Colbert'. The general opinion was that it would not be Colbert.

On Thursday 1 September Louis arrived at Nantes, where lodgings had been prepared in the old château. The arrest of Fouquet had been determined for Monday – the King's twenty-third birthday. Earlier on that morning Fouquet, who was just recovering from a bad attack of fever, confided to Brienne: 'Colbert is lost; tomorrow will be the finest day in my life.' When d'Artagnan came to arrest him, Fouquet said that he had believed himself to be 'higher in the opinion of the King than anyone else in the realm'. But Louis was an adept at dissimulation. 'The King is violently against him', wrote La Fontaine to Maucroix, 'and goes so far as to say that he has documents to hand which are enough to hang him.'

The whole arrest was master-minded by Colbert. The draft of his memoir still exists. 'For the execution. The day which will be chosen, on the pretext of a hunt, orders must be given to the musketeers to be mounted and the carriages ready.' He suggests how Louis could best approach d'Artagnan without arousing Fouquet's suspicions; he suggests which valet and which doctor should accompany Fouquet to prison. His recommendations were carried out almost exactly. The document shows how strong was Colbert's position with the King, who evidently agreed with all the provisions.

The trial of Fouquet was a long-drawn-out and confused process. The verdict was reached only at the very end of 1664. Fouquet had to be tricked into selling his post as Procureur-Général so that he could not claim the right to be tried by the Parlement. 'They soon made him walk into a trap', commented Choisy, 'by advising him to sell his charge . . . which he did like an innocent, thus putting the halter round his neck.' In early November 1661, a special judicial tribunal was set up 'to seek out the abuses and malpractices committed in the finances since 1635'. The trial of Fouquet was to be enveloped in a much wider-reaching inquest.

On 15 November the names of the judges were disclosed. The Premier Président Lamoignon, a man thought to be hostile to Fouquet, was to preside. Most of those appointed were either known or believed to be enemies of Fouquet. Lamoignon, however, himself proposed the addition of Olivier Lefèvre d'Ormesson, a man whom Colbert dismissed as 'of limited outlook, ponderous and not really fit for important matters'. He failed to recognise, however, that d'Ormesson was a man of honesty, of integrity and of great courage.

Fouquet was adroit enough to begin his defence by explaining that his methods had been those dictated by Mazarin, who himself had made, without scruple, no distinction between the Treasury of the State and his private fortune – and this was done with the complicity of Colbert. If there was any justification for the financial expedients of Mazarin it was that a long and expensive war did not offer any opportunity for financial reforms.

D'Ormesson, perhaps more than anyone, took note of the skill with which Fouquet defended himself. 'It seemed to me', he wrote, 'that the replies of M. Fouquet were made with much presence of mind and as well expressed as they could have been.' Another of the judges, named Renard, said to Mme de Sévigné: 'One must admit that this man is incomparable; he never spoke so well in the Parlement; he is more in possession of himself than ever.'

Lamoignon had by now been replaced, on Louis' orders, by the Chancellor Séguier, who disliked Fouquet. Mme de Sévigné wrote to Pomponne: '*Puis* [her code name for Séguier] is always afraid of displeasing *Petit* [Colbert]. He apologised to him the other day for M. Fouquet's having spoken at too great length, but that he had been unable to interrupt him.' She had been, in 1654, the object of Fouquet's amorous advances, but if she refused him as a lover, she retained a deep and tender affection for him.

Three years after Fouquet's arrest, in November 1664, the 'instruction' being completed, the trial proper began. It took place in the Arsenal. First, the Chancellor, Séguier, invited the Procureur-Général Chamillart to state his position. 'I require,' he said, 'on behalf of the King, that Nicolas Fouquet should be declared guilty in fact and in law of the crime of peculation, and others mentioned in the process, and, in reparation, condemned to be hanged and strangled until death ensues on a gallows to be erected for that purpose in the courtyard of the Palais.' To the crime of peculation, Chamillart added that of *lèse-majesté* on account of the treasonable notions contained in the *projet de Saint-Mandé*. *Lèse-majesté* carried automatically the sentence of death.

Madame de Sévigné was stunned by the news. 'A judge', she wrote to Pomponne, 'has dared to talk not only of the scaffold but of the cord and the gibbet. I am utterly aghast when I think of such infamy . . . the life that we are living from now until the evening of the verdict is just not life. I am paralysed when I think of that day. If the news is good I will send it to you by a horseman riding hell for leather. If it is not good, I just do not know what I will do, I cannot imagine myself what I would become if my friend, my poor friend . . .' She seems, however, to have been almost more concerned for her own suffering than for Fouquet's. 'If you only knew how unhappy one is if one has a heart made like mine.'

Opinion was divided as to Fouquet's chances. 'People are beginning to think', wrote Condé to the Queen of Poland, 'that the opinion of M. d'Ormesson will be followed; nevertheless the matter is in doubt.' The abbé de Choisy tells how someone was blaming Colbert for his passionate opposition to Fouquet and praising the moderation of Le Tellier. Turenne, who had no love for Le Tellier, replied: 'That is so. I think Colbert is more keen that he should be hanged and that Le Tellier is more afraid that he will not.'

The fatal day, Friday 20 December, came at last. D'Ormesson, as *rapporteur*, was responsible for summing up. It took him eighteen hours to do so. On Friday he gave his conclusions. He rejected the charge of peculation, putting the blame on Mazarin. As to *lèse-majesté*, he described the thought of resistance against the State as 'fort-méchante' but he asserted that the failure to put it into execution 'annihilated the accusation'.

The sentence pronounced by the Court was that of perpetual banishment – a punishment which Fouquet's wife had sought in vain from Louis. It could be said that anyone in possession of so many state secrets as Fouquet would, in exile, be a danger to the State, but from whatever motive Louis altered the sentence to that of perpetual imprisonment. Fouquet was to spend the last twelve years of his life in the castle of Pignerolo, on the borders of Piedmont.

The trial of Fouquet must be seen as an essentially political event. It was also, in a sense that neither the King nor Colbert would have wanted to admit, the trial of Mazarin. Louis XIV, in taking the reins of government into his own hands, wanted to make a clean break with a past that still had its roots in the feudal system. Fouquet, more than anyone, symbolised this past with all its disorder and all its corruption. By condemning Fouquet to an incarceration that was both rigorous and perpetual, Louis proclaimed his rupture with the old system and his determination to replace confusion and anarchy with order and authority. Relentless in pursuit of his prey and inexorable in his refusal to mitigate the sentence, he was not too particular about the methods used to obtain the verdict. It was thanks to the integrity and courage of Olivier Lefèvre d'Ormesson that Louis failed to obtain the sentence of death.

D'Ormesson realised that he could henceforth hope for no preferment or promotion; he sold his charges and retired to the charming little château in Brie Française that bears his name. Built by Androuet du Cerceau and standing off from the shore of a vast *miroir d'eau*, like the house of Narcissus, it became the rendezvous of men and women from the world of art and literature, including some of Fouquet's old friends – Mme de Sévigné, La Fontaine, Le Nôtre, Racine, Boileau and Turenne. Turenne vainly tried to obtain d'Ormesson's return to Court, but when his son André was presented, Louis said to him: 'Try to be as honest as your father.'

8

The Grand Carrousel, Insults to Ambassadors, Jansenism

The birth of the Dauphin, on 1 November 1661, had been greeted with the customary Te Deums and explosions of popular enthusiasm. It was not, however, until June in the following year that Louis laid on one of his great public shows to celebrate the event. It is known today as the 'Carrousel'. At the time it was more often referred to as the 'Courses de Bagues' – tilting at the ring. This immediately links it with the tournaments of the age of chivalry, and it is right that it should. But the word *carrousel* takes us back to the days of classical antiquity. The Père Ménestrier traces its etymology to the Latin *carrus-soli*, in Italian *carozella* – the chariot of the Sun.

In its origins it appears to have been a religious rite, imitating the movement of the stars – an offering to Circe in honour of the God of Light, whose daughter she claimed to be. The God of Light could easily be the ancestor of the Sun King.

Charles Perrault gives us what is almost the official account of the Great Carrousel. In his introduction he suggests that the military exploits of the great and noble may as often be attributed to such unworthy motives as inordinate love of praise, or brutal desire for revenge, as to a genuine love of glory. But this, he argues, is not true of their indulgence in the pleasures of peace. It is in this context that those who seek a true understanding of these men should take note of them: 'It is when they are at their most natural that we ought to paint them if the portrait is to be faithful.'

The great families of the French aristocracy were at their most natural when they were showing off; they were the great masters of the art. The way in which they lived, the way in which they travelled, the way in which they dressed; their architecture, their landscape gardening and their interest in the arts were all conscripted in the interests of display – a display which announced their status and proclaimed their privileges.

Supreme among them was the King himself, whose example they emulated.

It seems also that the people – especially the people of Paris – thoroughly enjoyed the spectacle provided by the major occasions of royal display. The Carrousel was conceived both as a royal tournament and as a public entertainment. The spectacular costumes, the glittering jewel-studded armour; the richly caparisoned chargers and the impressive horsemanship of their riders; the crowds of attendants, which included bears and monkeys; the martial music of trumpets, drums and timbals: all made up a procession which delighted the hearts of the Parisians. The route deliberately chosen made it possible for a very large number to watch it.

'The King,' writes Perrault, 'for whom no pleasure is so sweet as one which he shares with his people, and who knows no greater joy than that which he gives to his subjects, desired that all who were taking part should assemble at the Arsenal, so that, starting from there, they would traverse the whole city from one side to the other.' The arena selected for the tilting, the so-called 'Parterre de Mademoiselle' on the east side of the Tuileries, is still known as the Place du Carrousel.

It was the duc de Gramont, in his capacity of Maréchal de Camp, who master-minded the whole show. 'The job could not have been in better hands', claimed Perrault, 'and it would be difficult to find anyone who combined so much experience of arms with so much of the most delicate gallantry.'

It is possible that Gramont may have been responsible for the conception as well as the choreography. The cast was divided into five groups, each known as a 'quadrille', each representing some particular civilisation and each clothed symbolically and in different colours. Louis, at the head of the first quadrille, was dressed as the Emperor of Rome. Monsieur, the leader of the next one, represented the King of Persia 'who, regarding himself as greater than any King, recognised as his superior only the Sun, whom he worshipped'. His device was the Moon and with it went the motto 'Uno soli minor' – the sun alone is greater than me. Next came the prince de Condé, who was dressed as King of the Turks. This gave him the device of the crescent. Perrault explains: 'like as the crescent becomes larger and brighter according to how much it is exposed to the sun, so the Prince who takes it for his device wishes it to be understood that, since he owes all his greatness and glory to the King, he recognises that his glory will increase in proportion to the favourable regards of His Majesty'. The image, not only of the Sun and the Moon but of the whole solar system, gave a kind of cosmic dimension to the relationship between the King and his subjects.

When it came to the tilting, Perrault continues, 'the King gave further proof of his incredible adroitness, having first carried off the ring after a run in which he won the admiration of all and in which the accuracy, the firmness and the gracefulness were even to be preferred to the address with which he carried off the ring'. The King, however, did not win the first prize. It went to the comte de Saulx who received 'a very rich diamond' from the hands of the Queen Mother. Some competitors had problems caused by the extreme height of their plumed head-dresses and all were incommoded by the brilliance of the sun in their eyes.

'Thus ended this superb fête,' concluded Perrault, 'the magnificence of which surpassed the most famous of tournaments and the memory of which will never die in the minds of those who were fortunate enough to have been witnesses.'

Inès Murat, in her life of Colbert, adds a postscript to the story. It was Louvois who had suggested the idea of the Carrousel to Louis. The marquis de Louvois, Michel Le Tellier's son, had become associated with his father in the office of Secretary of State earlier in the year and was already involved in rivalry with Colbert. It was perhaps with the intention of embarrassing Colbert with the lavish expenditure which the exercise would involve that Louvois favoured the Carrousel. Colbert, however, merely asked the King to keep his intention secret for a week. He then made a temporary transfer to the Royal Treasury of the *octroi* of Paris – that is, the toll levied by the city on all goods consumed within its bounds. The Grand Carrousel was then given full publicity. Inès Murat describes the sequel: 'Hundreds of foreigners pour in from all sides. A few weeks before the date fixed, Colbert explains to the King that the preparations for the celebration are not complete and that it would be advisable to postpone the date by two weeks. This short interval obliges the foreigners to remain in Paris. There is a sudden rise in the expenditure in the city, the *octroi* whereof is temporarily diverted to the profit of the King. The celebration was to yield to the Treasury over a million livres, all expenses paid!'

The Carrousel paraded the King before his people as a person whose position was unique and whose power was shared with nobody. 'There was nothing else in France', wrote Voltaire, 'except a Master and his subjects. He made it clear from the start that he aspired to glory of every sort and that he wished to be as highly esteemed and respected abroad as he was absolute at home.'

The term *céder le pas* – to yield precedence, usually between the rep-resentatives of monarchs – lay at the heart of the matter. The Kings of France had always, if they were strong enough, claimed precedence over all other kings in Europe 'on account of the antiquity of their race and royalty'. Soon after Louis took over the helm in France two incidents occurred in which he demonstrated in no uncertain terms that his precedence was to be acknowledged. They were both recorded in the series of Gobelin tapestries entitled the *Histoire du Roy*. Out of a total of sixteen subjects, which include Louis' coronation, his marriage, two major treaties and seven of his most outstanding military victories, two are devoted to the official reception of apologies for insults to Louis' ambassadors. That these two occasions should have a place in such distinguished company says much about the importance set upon the precedence of the King of France.

The first of these unfortunate incidents took place in London. The ambassador from France, the comte d'Estrades, and the ambassador from Spain, the baron de Watteville, were clearly on course for a collision. In July 1661, when a special embassy arrived from Venice, Charles II suggested that neither ambassador should send his coaches to accompany the procession – a suggestion, records the abbé de Choisy, with which they both complied. But Louis was angry with d'Estrades and on 13 August, he wrote to him from Fontainebleau: 'On the subject of the Ambassadors Extraordinary from Venice in London and on the preparations that you were making to uphold in such an encounter the Prerogatives due to my Crown above all others, it had never crossed my mind that this particular matter should have been concluded as I have heard it was. I cannot conceal from you that I have been deeply wounded by two things; first that my brother King [of England] should have intervened in this matter when there was no need, and rather disobligingly since he seems to have intended to decide upon a complete equality between myself and my brother King of Spain, although he cannot be unaware of how many grounds there are that the pre-eminence belongs to me and that I claim it at all times and in all places; the second is that you should have deferred to the message which he sent to you, which was only a prayer on his part not to send your coaches.' In the following month a new ambassador was to arrive from Sweden. This was a chance for d'Estrades to regain the ground which he had lost.

On 30 September, Samuel Pepys wrote in his diary: 'This morning up by moonshine, at five o'clock to Whitehall to meet Mr Moore at the Privy Seal and there heard of a fray between the two ambassadors of Spain and France; and that this day, being the day of the entrance of an ambassador from Sweden, they intended to fight for the precedence. Our King, I heard, ordered that no Englishman should meddle in the business, but let them do what they would.'

Pepys heard later 'that the Spanish hath got the best of it, and killed three of the French coach horses and several men, and is gone through the City next to our King's coach; at which it was strange to see how all the City did rejoice'. Being 'in all things curious' he 'took oars to Westminster Palace, and run after them through all the dirt and the streets full of people; till at last, at the Mews, I saw the Spanish coach go with fifty drawn swords at least to guard it, and our soldiers shouting for joy. And so I followed the coach, and met it at York House, where the ambassador lies; and there it went in with great state. So then I went to the French house, where I observe still, that there is no men in the world of a more insolent spirit, where they do well, nor before they begin a matter, and more abject if they do miscarry, than these people are; for they all look like dead men, and not a word among them, but shake their heads. The truth is, that the Spaniards were not only observed to fight most desperately, but also they did outwit them; first in lining their own harness with chains so that they could not be cut, then in setting their coach in the most advantageous place, and to appoint men to guard every one of their horses, and others to guard the coach, and others the coachman. And above all in setting upon the French horses and killing them, for by that means the French were not able to stir. There were several men slain of the French' (according to Choisy six killed and twenty-three wounded) 'and one or two of the Spaniards and one Englishman by a bullet. So, having been very much daubed with dirt, I got a coach and home, where I vexed my wife in telling her this story.'

'The news of the affray in London arrived', writes Loménie de Brienne, 'when the Court had just returned to Fontainebleau.' This was after the visit to Nantes during which Fouquet was arrested. Brienne received the despatch at eleven o'clock when the King had just begun his supper. Brienne described to him the events in London. 'The King, without answering me, rose from the table with such a motion of anger that he nearly upset the table, and holding me by the arm led me into the Queen Mother's room to hear the despatch read . . . I have hardly ever seen the King angry apart from this one occasion.' Louis would not finish his supper, in spite of the Queen's entreaties, and made insulting remarks to her about her father which caused that normally meek and subjected woman to rise in anger and openly take her father's side.

Louis vowed that he would oblige all other countries 'to yield to my ambassadors the precedence in all the Courts of Europe'. He immediately withdrew his own ambassador, the Archbishop of Embrun, from Madrid and ordered the Spanish ambassador, Fuensaldagne, to leave France. He broke off negotiations concerning the frontiers between France and the Low Countries and threatened a renewal of the war with Spain. Rather than risk this, Philip IV sent the comte de Fuentes on a special embassy to Paris to apologise to Louis and to assure him that in future the Spanish ambassadors would give precedence to the French.

On 24 March 1662, Fuentes was received in the newly decorated Grand Cabinet du Roi at the Louvre. The scene is depicted in a tapestry which was begun only in 1673. It bears the inscription: 'Audience given by the King Louis XIV to the Spanish Ambassador where he declares in the name of the King his master that in future the Ambassadors of Spain will no longer enter into competition with the Ambassadors of France.'

The other incident took place in Rome about a year after the one in London. Louis was very conscious of the distinction between the Pope as ruler of a secular State and the Pope as the divinely appointed head of the Catholic Church. 'The maxim in France', wrote Voltaire, 'is to regard him as a person who is sacred but involved in affairs, whose feet one should kiss but whose hands one should sometimes tie.' As *Fils aîné de l'Eglise*, Louis was subject to the spiritual authority of the Pope, but diplomatic circumstances which involved Louis' prestige as first King in Europe, could reverse their positions.

Just such a diplomatic circumstance occurred in Rome during the summer of 1662. A new ambassador to Pope Alexander VII, the duc de Créqui, had been appointed. He was a distinguished soldier and held the exalted post of Premier Gentilhomme de la Chambre. His character was noted at Rome as 'lofty, quick-tempered and proud'. Bussy-Rabutin expressed his astonishment that 'one should have been chosen for the embassy to Rome who is the most touchy of all'. D'Artagnan added: 'All that he lacked was the ability to be a little more human.' With a Pope known to be quick to take offence it was not difficult to foresee the dangers that lay ahead. Louis knew Créqui well and his selection of him for this post suggests that he was not too concerned with establishing harmonious relations.

Créqui was given precise instruction by Louis as to the conduct of his embassy. He was to give an 'ostentatious assurance to the Supreme Pontiff of the King's veneration for his person', and he was to adduce as evidence Louis' zeal against the Jansenists and the Huguenots.

But Alexander was a sick man and thought not likely to live long. Much of Créqui's task was preparing the way for the next Conclave to elect a Pope sympathetic to France. What Louis required above all was that the election should be 'free from any consideration other than the service of God . . . that the Pope should have the true sense of being the Father of all . . . who could rule and govern the Holy Church with good result and to the edification of all the faithful'.

The other sensitive area concerned the attitude of France towards the League of Christian Princes against the Turks. Créqui was privately assured that, whatever might be said in public, the King and his Ministers had no intention of joining this league – but required 'that no one should even suspect that this was the true opinion of His Majesty'.

On Friday 2 June the duc de Créqui arrived at the Palazzo Farnese, the French Embassy in Rome. He soon discovered that the French were not popular with the Corsican guards of the Vatican, whose barracks were uncomfortably close neighbours. The situation was potentially explosive. At the end of July, Cardinal Flavio Chigi, nephew of Pope Alexander VII, wrote: 'The frequent acts of insolence committed by the household of the duc de Créqui will in the end bring about some notable inconvenience.'

On 20 August 1662, an incident occurred which was small enough. A cobbler named Marco Vietti, standing in front of the church of Saint Dorothea, observed three Corsican guards proceeding in the direction of the Porte Settiniana and three Frenchmen proceeding in the opposite direction. When they met they started to quarrel. Swords were drawn and what had begun as an argument became a fight. Corsican guards came to the support of their comrades and the fight became a riot which swelled into the proportions of a siege. The Corsicans, armed with arquebuses, were shooting in all directions. Any Frenchman, or suspected Frenchman, was in danger of his life. Cries of 'Kill them! Kill them! They are French!' were heard on all sides.

The duc de Créqui returned in the middle of it all from a visit to the Princess Borghese. He entered the palazzo without difficulty, but shortly after his arrival he went out onto the central balcony. He was greeted by a burst of gunfire. 'I advanced onto the balcony,' he wrote; 'at the same instant, several shots were fired at me.' The duchess also wrote: 'When M. de Créqui was on the terrace, five pistols, loaded with balls, were discharged at him which passed so close to his hair that they grazed it. It is a miracle that he was not killed.'

Louis' demand for an immediate apology from the Pope was not met. The situation was badly handled by both sides. What started as a minor incident ended up as a major diplomatic crisis of which the last scene – the final apology – was represented in a Gobelin tapestry. The detailed study of the evidence made by the comte Charles de Mouy reveals the interplay of exaggerated language and settled prejudice. That a riot had taken place in the course of which several people had been killed or wounded, that the diplomatic immunity of France had been invaded and that shots had been fired at the ambassador, is beyond doubt. That the Vatican was guilty of complicity in the event is highly doubtful, but the Corsican troops were in the Vatican's employ.

In response to Louis' demand for an instant apology, the Cardinal Flavio Chigi offered to call upon the ambassador 'provided that he could be assured that he was in no danger of discourteous proceedings'. That was a gratuitous insult to which Créqui replied that he was a gentleman and, as such, 'incapable of any unworthy action'. Five days after the incident Flavio finally called at the embassy to deliver the Pope's apology. He began by expressing his extreme displeasure at what had occurred and by clearing the Holy See of any responsibility. 'The Corsicans', he admitted, 'were a ferocious people who could not be overmastered.' Créqui pointed out that after five days he was still waiting for assurances that immediate and severe reparation would be made. Chigi replied that a committee had been set up for the purpose. Créqui complained afterwards that he had been 'more scandalised than satisfied by the cardinal's visit'.

Quick action by the Vatican in punishing those guilty might still have saved the situation. Instead, it offered a belated apology, sterile compliments and vague assurances. Two days after the event the gates of the barracks had been thrown open and any who chose were free to depart. Thirty-two Corsicans took the opportunity of leaving Rome. This action on the part of the authorities gave rise to suspicions that they were secretly in sympathy with the rioters. It came out in the evidence that the names of those guilty were perfectly well known in the barracks. Immediate action would have been possible.

On 30 August Louis wrote to Alexander, saying that he was withdrawing his ambassador 'so that no one who concerns my dignity should remain any longer exposed to outrages such as have been unequalled even by the barbarians themselves'. Such intemperate language could only be calculated to increase the tension. Louis acted throughout as one who was convinced of the complicity of the Papal Court. He ended on a note of almost puerile petulance: 'We do not ask anything in this encounter of Your Holiness. You have for so long been in the habit of refusing us everything and have so far shown such aversion for all that concerns our person and our Crown, that we think it best to leave to your own discretion those decisions in accordance with which ours will be guided.'

The situation escalated almost to the point of declaration of war. Not only was the ambassador withdrawn; the papal nuncio was ordered to leave Paris. French troops took possession of the papal state of Avignon. At this Alexander yielded and an agreement was reached on 12 February 1664 by the Treaty of Pisa.

'One can see that in the end', states the *Gazette de France* of 15 March 1664, 'the Supreme Pontiff . . . could not refuse the First Son of the Church a satisfaction which was proportionate to the insult, and that the glory of our Grand Monarque is such that one could not do anything that was wounding to him without being obliged to make him, sooner or later, full atonement.'

Full atonement required, in this case, the erection of a 'pyramid', opposite the Corsican barracks, to commemorate the event. M. de Bourlement, the envoy from Modena who was Louis' agent in the matter, gave his assurance that the pyramid was built 'for all eternity'. It carried the inscription: 'In execration of the odious crime committed on 20 August 1662 by Corsican soldiers, against the duc de Créqui, ambassador of His Most Christian Majesty, the nation of Corsica, in order to perpetuate the memory of this event, has been declared incapable of serving the Apostolic See. By order of our most Serene Lord Alexander, Pope, in accordance with the Peace of Pisa.'

In the meantime the Pope's nephew, Cardinal Flavio Chigi, had been appointed to bring, in a special embassy, the full apology of His Holiness to the King for the insult received. It was conceived as an act of humiliation, but Chigi saw it as an opportunity to reinstate the dignity of the Holy See. He saw himself making a triumphal entry into Paris. His retinue was therefore of the utmost magnificence. On his part, Louis spared no cost in receiving the papal legate with all the pomp and all the consideration for his comfort possible.

Louis was at Fontainebleau. As the Cardinal made his slow but stately progress down the Loire he began to have misgivings. He despatched his *homme de confiance*, Monsignor Ravizza, to Lionne expressing the wish that the King should make a special journey to Paris for the official entry. The duc de Montausier, who had been appointed by Louis to receive the Cardinal, replied that the King had left Paris for the summer and could not, without incommodity, return. Ravizza pleaded that it would be dishonouring to the Legate to receive him 'dans une maison des champs'. Montausier replied that wherever the King was, his honour followed him.

But Louis had to be a little circumspect. There were still certain privileges which he hoped that the Pope might confer, such as the right to nominate to church benefices in the newly acquired Trois-Evêchés – Metz, Toul and Verdun. It was hinted that such a concession might earn Chigi an entry into Paris. Chigi declined to commit himself and Lionne made it clear that the reception would be at Fontainebleau. At Fontainebleau it was. On 19 July 1664, almost two years after the attack on the Palazzo Farnese, Cardinal Chigi was received in Louis' bedroom and read aloud the fulsome papal apology. The apology ended with the words: 'If I and my family had played the slightest part in the outrage of 20 August we would consider ourselves unworthy of the pardon which we would desire and must ask of Your Majesty. Begging him to believe that these words and these sentiments are the expression of a sincere heart which is led, together with all my family, to venerate Your Majesty with the truest devotion.'

The tapestry depicting the incident was not started until 1669 – seven years later. The commemoration was therefore not done in the heat of the moment. But if the insult was not forgotten it was apparently forgiven: in the same year the commemorative pyramid before the Palazzo Farnese was demolished by order of Louis.

Meanwhile Louis was having to be concerned with a purely theological dispute which threatened the peace of the Gallican Church. The rise and fall of Jansenism is not an easy topic for those not trained in theology to understand, nor, since the arguments on both sides are by nature of a hair-splitting nicety and a labyrinthine complexity, does the subject lend itself to simplification. Louis, although well instructed in the Catholic faith, was by no means a theologian. He was, however, obliged to take cognisance of the affair.

The basic question is this: did God create a universe in which there is such a thing as chance and a human race whose members are, at least to a certain extent, free to choose the way in which they act? Or did God create a universe in which, as Calvin claimed, 'no wind ever blows but by the express command of God' and in which human beings are really marionettes whose every movement is controlled by the divine puppet master?

It is more typical of the modern mind – granted that it gives any place at all to a belief in God – to treat as being somewhat uncomplimentary to God the view that the Almighty is responsible for everything which happens, for it makes him solely responsible for every disaster in Nature and every atrocity committed by mankind. It is more acceptable today to attribute a destructive tornado to divinely permitted chance and to attribute non-natural disasters to the selfishness, stupidity or ignorance of the human race. To our forefathers the idea of any limitation, even if self-imposed, on the omnipotence of God seemed derogatory to the divine majesty. But the assertion of any element of free will on the part of his creatures involved just such a limitation and was therefore, to some theologians, anathema.

The problem of the relationship between divine omnipotence and human freedom of choice has attracted the attention of some of the greatest intellects of Christianity. The first and most important exponent of divine omnipotence was Augustine, the fifth-century Bishop of Hippo. His teaching involved a belief in predestination – a belief for which support can be found in the teaching of Saint Paul. The logical conclusion of this train of thought is that God created some people who were irretrievably damned and some who were arbitrarily destined to salvation through the power of divine grace. The fundamental weakness of Augustine's position is in his admission: 'Why he wills to convert some and to punish others, let no one presume to ask.' This is, to many minds, an unacceptable way of dodging the issue.

This argument was revived in 1641 when Cornelius Jansen, Bishop of Ypres, published a book called the *Augustinus*. The Jesuits saw in this an undue emphasis on the efficacy of divine grace and an understatement of the reality of human freedom. The abbé de Saint-Cyran, Jansen's friend and collaborator, was spiritual director of the convent of Port-Royal, where Angélique Arnauld was abbess. In 1643 her brother, Antoine Arnauld, produced a treatise, 'De la Fréquente Communion'. In it he accused the Jesuits of an undue emphasis on free will and an understatement of the reality of grace.

In May 1653, the Pope, Innocent X, issued a bull condemning five propositions allegedly to be found in the *Augustinus*. The Assembly of the French clergy required all clerics to assent to the bull. Arnauld agreed that the five propositions were contrary to Church teaching, but denied that they could be found in the *Augustinus*.

In January 1656, Blaise Pascal published the first of his *Lettres Provinciales* attacking the Jesuits. In October the same year the new Pope, Alexander VII, issued a new bull stating that the five propositions *were* to be found in the *Augustinus*. In 1661 the Assembly of the clergy required all clerics, nuns and schoolmasters to give their assent to the new bull. But the community of Port-Royal, while accepting the ruling of the Pope on doctrine, hesitated to accept his authority on what was, after all, a matter of fact. They agreed to sign a 'Summons' from the archdiocese of Paris which admitted this distinction. They were ordered by the King's Council to retract.

By this time Mazarin was dead and Louis was at the helm. He regarded the behaviour of the nuns of Port-Royal as something in the nature of a revolt. In his memoirs for 1661 he wrote: 'I set myself to destroy Jansenism and to disperse those communities where this spirit of novelty was being fostered, well-intentioned perhaps, but which did not know, or did not wish to know, the dangerous consequences which could have resulted from it.'

Louis had two reasons for disliking Port-Royal and the teachings of the Jansenists. The first was political: a number of important people, such as the duchesse de Chevreuse and the duchesse de Longueville, who had been on the wrong side during the Fronde, were associated with Port-Royal. The second was theological: Louis, whose confessor, the Père Annat, was a Jesuit, naturally inclined to the Jesuit position which regarded Jansenism as next door to Calvinism. The Jesuits seem to have omitted to take the important step of wondering how near Calvinism came to the teaching, accepted as orthodox, of Augustine. Louis had a particular respect for Annat who, he said, 'had a right mind, was disinterested and did not get mixed up in any intrigues'.

Now it was to the Père Annat that Pascal had addressed the seventeenth and eighteenth of his *Lettres Provinciales*. He demolishes one by one the grounds on which Annat had accused him of heresy. 'You suppose in the first place that the author of the Letters belongs to Port-Royal. You then say that Port-Royal had been pronounced heretical; from which you conclude that the author of the Letters is pronounced a heretic.

'So, mon Père, it is not against myself that the main force of the accusation bears, but against Port-Royal, and you only charge me with it because you suppose that I belong to it. I have therefore no great difficulty in defending myself since I have only to tell you that I do not, and to refer you to the letters in which I have said that I stand alone and, in so many words, that I do not belong in any way to Port-Royal.'

Louis may well have been annoyed by this only too successful attack on his esteemed confessor. Pascal is one of the few great names in the *Grand Siècle* who owed nothing to Louis XIV.

For Pascal occupies a high place among the literary giants of the age. According to Voltaire, Pascal had learnt the exactness and precision of the French language from the *Maximes* of the duc de La Rochefoucauld, 'but the first work of genius which appeared in prose was the collection of the *Lettres Provinciales*'.

'Pascal', writes Hugh Fraser Stewart, one of the editors of the *Lettres*, 'is the first to sum up, in his own person and in his writings, the qualities which have given France her pride of place among the civilizing forces of the world.' Above all he stands the test by which Flaubert, that great master of style, judged his own writings: he can be read aloud. To read the *Lettres Provinciales* aloud is to hear the voice of Pascal. It has to be admitted, however, that although he ranks high among the founders of French prose and although he could easily demolish most of the syllogisms of the Jesuits, he did not quite succeed in proving the orthodoxy of Jansenism.

In 1667 Pope Alexander VII died and was succeeded by Clement IX. He was of a more moderate nature than his predecessor, and by the autumn of 1668 Louis had agreed to accept a compromise known as the 'Pax Clementia'.

In the following year a medal was struck by order of Louis bearing the inscription 'Restituta Ecclesiae Gallicanae Concordia' – Concord reestablished in the Gallican Church. The situation is described in the commentary: 'There has arisen among the theologians of France such bitter disputes about the nature of grace that their animosity began to provoke a considerable scandal. The King acted in harmony with the

Pope to eradicate the seeds of division. The Holy Father drew up various letters to the prelates of the realm and His Majesty published edicts which restored the Gallican Church to its former tranquillity.'

Tranquillity, however, was not the most conspicuous feature of the Gallican Church at that time. Daniel Cosnac, Bishop of Valence, has left in his memoirs a picture which illustrates the problems that could and did arise from divided loyalties. The authority structure of the Catholic Church was not as simple as might be supposed. The religious orders had their own hierarchy and often claimed to stand outside the competence of episcopal authority.

Cosnac tells against himself the story of the way in which he obtained preferment. The bishopric of Valence became vacant in June 1654. Then abbé de Cosnac, a member of the household of the prince de Conti, he immediately asked the prince to obtain this appointment for him from Mazarin. Cosnac, however, had not a few enemies in Conti's household and the prince demurred. Cosnac went straight to the princess's bedroom. She was still asleep, but such was Cosnac's insistence that he was not only admitted to her presence, but he managed to persuade her to go straight off, clad only in a dressing gown, to seek the Cardinal.

Mazarin, however, was not a man lightly to give away lucrative appointments. He offered another bishopric which was also vacant but less well endowed. The princess, however, at her chaplain's insistence, renewed her application.

A few days later it happened that Cosnac preached before the Queen and all the Court. As he came down from the pulpit Mazarin approached him and said: 'Monsieur, to nominate you Bishop of Valence at the end of so fine a sermon as you have just preached, that is what is known as receiving the bâton de maréchal de France at the breach; go and thank the King for such an important benefice.'

Cosnac had no sooner fulfilled this demand than he presented himself before the Archbishop of Paris.

'Monseigneur,' he said, 'the King has made me a bishop, and it is now a question of making me a priest.'

'Whenever you like,' answered the Archbishop.

'That is not the only matter,' said Cosnac; 'I must beg you to make me a deacon.'

'Willingly,' said the Archbishop.

'You will not be let off with these two favours,' persisted the abbé; 'for besides the priesthood and the diaconate I must also ask for the sub-diaconate.' 'In God's name,' answered the Archbishop brusquely, 'give me your immediate assurance that you have received the tonsure for fear

Louis at the age of ten, by H. Testelin.
He succeeded to the throne at four and a half and reigned for seventy-two years.

Cardinal Mazarin.
Engraving by
R. Nanteuil.
Mazarin died, writes
David Ogg, 'in an
atmosphere of piety
and abundance.'

The two Queens,
Anne of Austria,
Louis' mother, and
Marie-Thérèse of
Spain, Louis' wife.
They were aunt
and niece.

The Palais Royal. Engraving by La Bessière.
On the left is the theatre which was to become the Comédie Française.

Saint Vincent de Paul, by F. Simon.
'No one,' wrote the Mayor of Rethel,
'with the exception of Your Reverence,
has had compassion on our sufferings.'

The 'Grande Mademoiselle'
with a portrait of her father, by P. de
Bourgignon. She thoroughly enjoyed
the opportunities offered to her by the
Fronde for playing soldiers.

Chantilly in the days of the Grand Condé.
The towers of the medieval fortress rise
behind the Renaissance building of Jean
Bullant. War and Peace were already
juxtaposed in the architecture.
Reconstruction by Ian Dunlop.

André Le Nôtre, by C. Maratti.
The creator of the gardens of
Versailles, Marly, Saint-Cloud
and Chantilly.

The Grande Condé, by A. Coysevox.
He had, as Primi Visconti
observed, 'l'air d'un brigand.'

Cardinal Chigi reads the Pope's apology to Louis in his bedroom at Fontainebleau.
Design for a tapestry by C. Le Brun.

The Queen arriving at Fontainebleau, by I. Silvestre, 1667.
'The cavalcade entered the great forecourt and swung left to draw up before
Du Cerceau's impressive double horseshoe staircase.'

Fontainebleau towards the end of the 17th century.
Attributed to J-B. Martin.

Chambord as Louis first saw it, drawing by I. Silvestre.
Louis often brought his Court here in the autumn for the hunting.

(*Left*) Louise de La Vallière, J. Nocret. Mme de Sévigné compared her with 'a violet which hid in the grass and blushed alike to be a mistress, a mother and a Duchess.' (*Right*) Princess Henrietta Ann, sister of Charles II, sister-in-law of Louis, by P. Lely. Bossuet said of her: 'Madame met her death gently and sweetly as she had ever met all else.'

(*Below*) La Fontaine, *Terre cuite* by Houdon. His aim was to create 'a certain charm, an agreeable air which can be given to all sorts of subjects, even the most serious.' (*Below right*) Mme de Sévigné, by R. Nanteuil. 'There is no one in the world,' wrote Mme de Lafayette, 'so charming as you are when you are engaged in animated conversation.'

Louis in 1664.
Engraving by R. Nanteuil.
After the death of Mazarin, Louis wrote: 'Only then did it seem to me
that I was King – born to be King.'

that this shortage of sacraments will not take you back to the need for baptism.'

In 1687 Cosnac was promoted to be Archbishop of Aix. He ran into trouble immediately. He attempted to remedy alleged abuses among the religious houses of his diocese. He did this in person. In Aix itself there was a convent of the Filles de Saint-Barthélémi. He announced his intention of visiting their church, assuring them in advance that he made no claim against their privileges. The Prioress, the Soeur de Bérulle, immediately opposed the visitation and referred the matter back to the 'general' of her order. The Archbishop arrived and found the church locked and barricaded. 'I honestly thought', he wrote 'that this was by mistake, and I sent one of my ecclesiastics to the parlour, where he found the prioress and begged her, on my behalf, to have the church opened. The prioress replied with a laugh that it was not for me to give orders to her.' She persisted in her disobedience and finally Cosnac decided that he must threaten her with excommunication. 'She made the insolent reply that she would take no more notice of my excommunication than of shaking the dust off her skirt.'

Not content with this, the prioress went and suborned the prior of the monastery of the same order, who had previously agreed to accept an episcopal visitation. 'The prior, with a single monk, was standing at the door of his church and read aloud a paper which he held in his hand in front of some three thousand people, in which he accused me of creating a scandal by entering their church; that this had been done by the use of force, although I had only in my suite three ecclesiastics in their robes and myself in rochet, cape and stole.'

Within a few days the Archbishop found that all the religious orders in Aix closed their doors against him and refused to recognise him as their pastor. They complained to the King that their Archbishop had deprived the people of Aix of the ministrations of his Church. It is interesting that their complaint should have been made to the King. They asked his permission to take the matter to the Pope and to ask him to appoint arbiters to settle the quarrel. 'The King gave permission', continued Cosnac, 'but on the express condition that they asked nothing of the Pope which was not in conformity with the laws and liberties of the Gallican Church or which could be to the prejudice of the rights of His Majesty and of his kingdom.

'At the same time, there being two positions of "Commandeur" in his Order of the Saint-Esprit to be filled by two bishops, His Majesty did me the honour of nominating me for the first of these places.' He had to submit proofs of his *titres de noblesse*, which he was easily able to do, and on 15 May 1701, the Day of Pentecost, Daniel Cosnac had the honour of receiving the Order from the hands of the King. 'The monks', he commented, 'were somewhat mortified by this, seeing that His Majesty honoured me with his affection.'

The mixture of sacred and profane interests is much in evidence in the affairs of Cosnac. His response to being made Archbishop of Aix was to complain in person to Louis that the job, as he had foreseen, was set about with difficulties and that the revenues were lower than those of the Bishoprics of Valence and Die.

Louis was kind but firm. 'Monsieur,' he said, 'I have given you one of the highest positions in my kingdom. I am persuaded that you know how to do it well and that you will do well.' Cosnac's episcopate was to justify Louis' judgement of him. When, in the early years of the eighteenth century, the Huguenots in the Cevennes – known locally as Camisards – rose in rebellion, Cosnac showed himself a vigilant but merciful pastor of his flock.

9
Versailles and La Vallière

Louise de La Vallière was the inspiration responsible for Louis' first taking an interest in the rather uninteresting little house which his father had built at the rather insignificant little hamlet of Versailles. Fouquet's extravagant entertainment at Vaux-le-Vicomte had given Louis the experience of what the team composed of the architect Le Vau, the painter Le Brun and the landscape gardener Le Nôtre was capable of producing – the perfect setting for the music of Lully and the comedies of Molière. Now they were to create a similar setting for Louis' entertainment of his mistress.

The first work of Le Vau was to make the little hunting lodge into a *maison de plaisance* of brick and stone to which Louis could invite a few favoured guests for a few delectable days of brilliant entertainment. This building, the Petit Château, is shown in all its detail by the superb oil painting by Pierre Patel in the Musée de Versailles. Patel has filled his canvas with faultless precision and perfect perspective and, by the skilful use of the shadow cast by a cloud, has brought a vivid sense of reality to the scene. In the centre is the Château, a bright array of brick and stone and slate and gilded lead.

The Château proper is built round three sides of a quadrangle. At each of the four corners, where on an earlier building one would expect a tower, a square pavilion stands almost clear of the main block. Corner touches corner just sufficiently to allow the rooms to connect. The open end of the courtyard is crossed by a double arcade which forms a bridge, a passageway from wing to wing, between two wrought-iron balustrades, all richly gilded. The outer balustrade is continued right round the Château, like a girdle of golden lace, providing an exterior corridor to the rooms of the first floor. For, as was usual in the seventeenth century, the building was one room thick, each room giving access to its neighbour. The whole block stands in a dry moat surrounded by a balustrade.

Mlle de Scudéry, in her 'Promenade de Versailles', gives a vivid idea of the brilliance which this colourful ensemble could produce. 'As the sun, at this moment, was shining in a very clear sky, it seemed ... that it was only to bring out the lustre of all the gold with which the roof of the palace is decorated.' It was, in fact, this external gilding which often impressed visitors most. Sebastien Locatelli, one of the first to leave an account of Versailles under Louis XIV, noted in 1665 that the decorations of the roof 'were covered with gilded copper, which, from a distance, makes a wonderful sight'.

The interior of the Château at this period was described by Sir Christopher Wren, who visited France in 1665. 'Not an inch but is crowded with little Curiosities of Ornaments. The women, as they make here the Language and Fashions, and meddle with politics and philosophy, so they sway also in architecture; Works of Filgrand [filigree] and little Knacks are in great Vogue; but building certainly ought to have the Attribute of the eternal, and therefore the only thing incapable of new Fashions. The masculine furniture of the Palais Mazarine pleas'd me much better.'

In September 1663 Colbert wrote one of his rather rare essays in descriptive writing. It is about Versailles. 'As the King has a particular affection for this house, which it is his pleasure to make the most elegant and the best suited to the reception and entertainment of royal personages at all seasons, it would be difficult to find words to describe the beauty and the appropriateness of the furniture of the apartments, and especially in that of the Queen Mother ... She was surprised to find all these apartments decorated with the two things which are most pleasing to Her Majesty – works of filigree in gold and Chinese silver and jasmins. But China has never seen so many of these works in one place, nor all Italy so many flowers.' It was the perfect setting for the entertainment of the Court. 'Every day there were balls, ballets, comedies, music both vocal and instrumental, violins, promenades and hunting ... and what is very special about this house is that His Majesty has ordained that all those to whom he has accorded an apartment should find it furnished. He provides food for all and even firewood and candles in all the rooms, something which has never been the practice in the royal houses.'

Before the Château proper Patel shows the Cour des Offices. Two symmetrical blocks answer each other across the courtyard, standing back so as to leave clear the vista of the Château itself. Their architecture is dignified but simple, reflecting that of the main building but without its grandeur, as befitted their more humble status. The block to the south of the courtyard contained the stables, capable of housing forty-five horses; that to the north was devoted to the very large kitchens and their staff. To the north of this, Patel shows a square building with a reservoir on its roof. This was the Grotte de Thétis.

Not for long was this colourful jewel allowed to remain in the rough setting of forest and fenland which had contented its founder. To the south Le Vau made use of the falling away of the ground to create an orangery with a great flight of stone steps on either side. After the fall of Fouquet 12,050 seedling orange trees were transferred from Vaux-le-Vicomte to Versailles. On the terrace above the orangery was laid out the Parterre des Fleurs, enclosed by a gilded balustrade and planted with 'a thousand species of flower'. It was particularly dear to Louis, who had a passion for flowers, and its destruction, to make room for Le Vau's enlargements in 1668, led him to the creation of the first Trianon.

To the west of the Château a circular basin, later to take its name from the groups of Latona and her children, with its semi-circular ramps, the Allée Royale or Tapis Vert sloping down to another basin, at first called the Bassin des Cygnes, and the beginnings of the cruciform Canal beyond, already fixed the main lines along which the gardens were to develop. 'Tout y rit, tout y plait, tout y porte à la joie,' exclaimed Mlle de Scudéry, who admired the great diversity of the lay-out. There were wide spaces for carrousels and tournaments, there were retired and intimate walks 'propres à la rêverie d'un amant'. For it was for the pursuit of love, the love of Louis for Louise de La Vallière, that the gardens of Versailles were first created. Here they could be alone in the peace and beauty of Le Nôtre's plantations: here Louis could display before her his brave demeanour and majestic grace in some triumphal pageant.

On 5 May 1664, Louis gave the first and most famous of his entertainments to the Court at Versailles, *Les Plaisirs de l'Ile Enchantée*. Comedies specially written by Molière set to music specially written by Lully and ballets with choreography by the duc de Saint-Aignan ensured a standard of entertainment which can seldom if ever have been surpassed. Although officially the entertainment was offered to the Queen and the Queen Mother, nobody was in any doubt as to its real purpose, for Louise de La Vallière was at that time at the height of her favour. The whole entertainment can be seen as a display of valour and virility by a lover for his mistress.

Everywhere the gardens had been embellished to form the scenery of a pantomime, but a pantomime in which the distinction between the cast and the audience was not always clearly defined. Four thousand candles, besides innumerable flambeaux, lent their lustre to the scene.

The theme of the entertainment was based on a tale by Ariosto. An enchanted island had mysteriously appeared off the coast of France, and from its fairy shores came Roger and his knights to entertain the ladies of the Court. The first evening there was a tournament – a good pretext for the men to show off their masculine physique and comely horsemanship in an impressive costume. The King, as Roger, took care that no one should surpass him, his flame-coloured plumes and silver breastplate, encrusted with precious stones, and the golden fittings of his armour setting off that princely grandeur which was natural to him; 'Jamais un air plus libre, ni plus guerrier, n'a mis un mortel au-dessus des autres hommes.' When Louis had retired from the lists the tournament was won by Louise de La Vallière's brother who received the sword of honour from the hands of the Queen Mother.

It was time now for supper. The service was set to music and almost became a ballet. 'Then, the Knights having retired, came the entrance of the modern Orpheus – you will understand that I mean Lully – at the head of a large troop of musicians who, having advanced towards the Queens with short steps danced to the rhythm of their instruments, divided into two groups one either side of the dais.' The music had been written specially for the occasion – 'Rondeau pour les violons et flûtes allant à la table du Roi'. In the meantime the dishes were carried in procession by gardeners, harvesters, grape-pickers and 'frozen old men carrying ices' who set their pyramids of food upon the tables in time to the music under the watchful eye of Molière as the great god Pan.

The second day, Roger and his knights offered to the Queens the pleasure of a comedy by Molière, *La Princesse d'Elides*, for, as a delicate compliment to the two Queens, he set his scene in Spain. The perspective of the Tapis Vert provided the background for this performance, with the palace of the Enchantress dimly visible across the waters of the Bassin des Cygnes (today the Bassin d'Apollon). The greatest success of the evening was the buffoonery of the valet Lyciscas, played by Molière.

The third day, the setting was the palace of the Enchantress, Alcine, who was borne across the water on a marine monster to address her prologue to the Queen. This was succeeded by a ballet to the music of Lully, leading up to the entrance of Roger who put an end to the spell. With a clap of thunder the whole palace burst into flames and a magnificent display of fireworks ended the three days' entertainment.

But even the disappearance of the enchanted island could not drag Louis away from his charming *maison de plaisance*; further tilting in the dry moat, an al fresco dinner served in the park and the ever famous première of *Tartuffe* filled the following days until 14 July when the Court took once more the road to Fontainebleau.

Tartuffe started a furore which was to last for five years. Its full title is *Tartuffe ou l'Imposteur*, and at face value it was an attack not on true religion but on hypocrisy, which is the greatest enemy of true religion. It was Molière's aim to get people to laugh at themselves and to see their own absurdities. Louis had read the script before its production and found the piece 'fort divertissante'.

But *Tartuffe* could be taken as an attack upon religion itself and it was so taken by both the Parlement and the Church. The President Lamoignon, representing the Parlement, neatly dodged the real issue. 'I am sure it is very good and very informative,' he told Molière, 'but it is not for comedians to instruct men on matters of Christian morals and religion.' Although famous authors wrote famous plays, the theatre was not regarded by the Church as a respectable profession.

Molière had, in fact, provided his own defence in his own script. In Act I, Scene 6, Cléante challenges his brother-in-law Oronte.

> What! Do you make no distinction
> Between hypocrisy and devotion?
> Do you wish to apply to them the same language?

And again later:

> Who are to be more highly valued than the perfectly devout?
> There is nothing in the world more noble or more beautiful
> Than the holy fervour of a genuine zeal.
> Therefore I can see nothing more odious
> Than the made-up outward appearance
> Of an artificial zeal.

Bourdaloue took up the phrase about wearing a mask – which is the literal meaning of hypocrisy – and claimed that Molière 'risked scratching the face while tearing off the mask'. The simile, however, does not apply. The face of the truly devout is not the one behind the mask of the hypocrite.

Hardouin de Péréfixe, Louis' former tutor and now Archbishop of Paris, forbade the performance of the piece in his diocese. But the most extreme attack came from the curé of the Church of Saint Bartholomew, Pierre Roule. He actually claimed that Louis had expressed his anger to Molière, ordered him to make solemn and public penance for the rest of his life for his 'impious and irreligious production and his licentious and libertine poetry, and to do nothing in future so insulting to God, so outrageous to the Church, to religion, to the Sacraments and to those whose office is most necessary for salvation'. Finally he condemned Molière to death by fire, 'a precursor of the fires of Hell'. Roule was guilty of lying: Louis had neither felt nor expressed any such opinion.

The case for the other side was put by the prince de Condé. A play called *Scaramouche Ermite* was performed before the Court. At the end of it the King said to him: 'I would like to know why people who are so scandalised by Molière's comedy do not say a word against *Scaramouche*.' 'The reason for that', replied the prince, 'is that the comedy *Scaramouche* is aimed at God and religion, which are of no concern to these gentry, whereas that of Molière is aimed at themselves, and that is what they cannot endure.'

Louis was not slow to realise that there was more to a fête of this sort than mere entertainment. No one could follow the King to Versailles without his order except those on whom the greatest privilege of all, the *carte blanche*, had been bestowed. The men thus distinguished had the right to wear a blue cloak doubled with silver and gold, similar to that worn by the King himself. 'This sort of distinction', observed la Grande Mademoiselle, 'intrigued the Court.'

The year 1664 was one of heavy expenditure on Versailles – a total of just over 834,000 livres. This included some of the first architectural features of the park.

Twenty minutes' walk in the direction of Saint-Cyr led one to the Ménagerie, a tall, octagonal pavilion surmounted by a rather ecclesiastical-looking dome and cupola, which rose from a wide, octagonal courtyard enclosed by wrought-iron screens. Through each of these screens a gateway gave access to an enclosure which contained birds and animals. An engraving by Perelle shows two elephants and a number of camels, ostriches, flamingos and pelicans. These enclosures could each be overlooked from a balcony in front of one of the windows of the octagonal pavilion. In each of them were certain purely functional buildings, but the Cour de la Volière could boast a bird-cage which was almost a miniature château, with its central corps de logis and dome joined by low wings to end pavilions capped with little pyramidal roofs. It looked more like a small orangery and moved Mlle de Scudéry to exclaim of the birds here 'that those of Venus were not better lodged than those of Mars'.

Every new arrival at the Ménagerie was carefully drawn by the artists of the royal workshops. The Gobelin tapestries of this period are remarkable for the excellence of their animal portraits. Dead bodies were sent to the Académie des Sciences for dissection. In 1681, one of the elephants having died, the Academy was convoked and M. du Verney did the dissecting. It is typical of Louis' wide interests that he was present himself at the autopsy. In this way the arts and the sciences, as well as the guests, profited from the Ménagerie at Versailles.

Louis' privileged companions made frequent visits to the Ménagerie, but if interest in zoology should pall, there was a grotto beneath the central salon equipped with all the concealed jets required for practical joking. Louis was not above entering into the fun. Colbert's agent Petit describes how the King took pleasure in operating the taps 'without being able to avoid being a little bit sprinkled himself'. But the most elaborate system for practical joking of this sort was installed in the Grotte de Thétis. 'L'eau se croise, se joint, s'écarte, se rencontre,' wrote La Fontaine, and woe betide the visitor who sought to escape by taking refuge in the inner sanctuary of the grotto!

The Grotte de Thétis presented towards the Parterre du Nord a simple, single-storeyed façade pierced by three arches and decorated with rustic panels. The arches were closed by wrought-iron gates of a most original design. The head of Apollo was placed in the centre of the middle arch; the gilded bars of all three gates radiated from this centre and became, as it were, the shafts of light from the setting sun.

The gates opened into a vast, vaulted chamber on the opposite wall of which three capacious niches corresponded with the three arches of the façade. These were destined to receive the sculptures from which the grotto took its name. The walls and ceilings were encrusted with shells by Jean de Launay – two years' work. In 1666 a water organ was purchased from the Sieur Denots at Montmorency. It took Denis Joly three years to transport and re-erect this in the grotto.

As at Saint-Germain, the organ was activated by water pressure controlled with the most delicate skill; as at Saint-Germain, the water activated the voices of a whole chorus of songbirds. 'To the sound of the water', wrote Felibien, 'the playing of the organ harmonises with the singing of the little birds . . . and, by an artifice even more surprising, one hears an echo which repeats the gentle music, so that the ears are no less charmed than the eyes.'

It was not until 1666 that the groups of statues by Girardon and Regnaudin were finally positioned in the grotto. Apollo is shown having run his daily course across the sky and descended into the submarine abode of Thétis, where a group of nymphs refresh him after his labours. 'When the sun is tired and has accomplished his task,' wrote La Fontaine, 'he goes down to Thétis and enjoys a little relaxation. In the same way Louis goes off to take his ease.' As the palace of Thétis was to Apollo, so was Versailles to Louis XIV – a place of pleasant recreation and amorous respite. By 1666, however, Mlle de La Vallière was already beginning to yield the first place in the King's affection to Mme de Montespan.

The year began with a serious bereavement, which none the less freed Louis to make public his infidelity. By the beginning of the year it was evident to all that the Queen Mother was terminally ill with cancer of the breast. On Monday 18 January, Mme de Motteville records that the cancer was spreading to her shoulders and that there was no position which she found comfortable. The poor woman said: 'I am suffering a lot. There is no part of my body in which I do not feel very great pain.'

At the customary time, ten in the evening, the Queen Mother said goodnight to the Queen and to Monsieur and Madame. The Archbishop of Auch, her Grand Aumônier, took charge of her spiritual needs, saying the Mass in the little oratory which opened out of the ruelle – the space beside the bed behind the balustrade. It was he who told her what she must have already guessed, that the time had come to prepare herself for death. He advised her to make a confession covering the whole of her life, starting with childhood, through her marriage to the time of her regency. A number of those closest to her were permitted to remain in the room while she made what Mme de Motteville described as 'more like a light-hearted review than a general confession' and added 'certain touches of wit which such an action requires'.

Tuesday 19 January dawned, another day of suffering, and when her ulcers were being dressed it was necessary to provide her with strongly scented sachets. The Archbishop now told her that the time had come to receive the last rites of the Church. 'From this moment', writes Mme de Motteville, 'she showed no signs of fear or of sadness, nor any evidence of weakness either in her words or her actions.' She expressed a desire to speak to the King and asked everyone else to leave the room. It is not known what she said to him. Then she asked to see her younger son.

She was now ready to receive the Viaticum – the anointing with oil which is the last sacrament of the Catholic Church. A procession led by the King and Queen, Monsieur and Madame, followed by Madem-oiselle, the prince de Condé and others, went from the Louvre to the parish church to collect the holy oil. The Archbishop carried the Blessed Sacrament himself. Before he gave the Host to the dying Queen, he reminded her that the position to which her birth and her marriage had raised her was one which she could not take with her into the next world. The supreme importance of the occasion 'brought a light into her eyes and the colour back into her cheeks, and at this moment she appeared so beautiful to all of us – but particularly to the King, who was standing at the foot of the bed, that he turned to Mlle de Beauvais and said in a low voice: "Just look at the Queen my mother; I have never seen her more beautiful." ' This transfiguration reduced everyone in the room to tears – except for Anne herself. 'Presently she looked fixedly at the King and said: "Do what I have told you to do; I tell you again with the Blessed Sacrament upon my lips." The King, with the most profound respect and with his eyes filled with tears and his head bowed, replied that he would not fail to.' No one knew what it was that he promised.

The prince de Condé, who was not a practising Catholic at the time, was leaning against the balustrade. He said to Mme de Motteville: 'I have never seen anything so beautiful. There is a woman worthy of esteem in Eternity.'

Towards midnight on Tuesday only the King and Queen and Mme de Motteville were still in Anne's bedroom. The King, who was leaning against the silver table outside the balustrade, 'regarded in silence the woman who had given him his life and was gently losing hers'. She was sinking fast, but from time to time she recovered moments of lucidity. The Archbishop was reading aloud from the Psalms. When he reached the ninth verse of Psalm 118 – 'It is better to trust in the Lord than to put thy confidence in Princes' – she opened her eyes and said: 'Alas, that is all too true.'

On Wednesday 20 January, between four and five in the morning, Louis' mother breathed her last. Mme de Motteville assures us that she had it from those who slept in his room with him that he spent almost the whole night in tears. The next day he said to the duchesse de Montausier that 'the Queen his mother was not only a great Queen, but deserved to be ranked among the greatest of Kings'.

Somewhat later, Louis described his own feelings in his memoirs. 'This event, although preceded by a long-drawn-out illness, did not fail to affect me so deeply that for several days it made me incapable of giving my mind to any other consideration than the loss which I was sustaining. For, although I have told you continually that a prince must sacrifice all his private emotions for the good of his empire, there are occasions when this principle cannot be put into practice just at first. Nature had formed the bonds which held me to the Queen my mother. But the ties which are formed in the heart by the rapport of spiritual qualities do not break so easily as those which are only the result of blood relationship. The firmness with which this princess upheld my crown, at a time when I could do nothing, was a proof to me of her affection and of her courage. And the respects which I, for my part, paid to her were not just the simple demands of propriety. The habit which I had formed of sleeping under the same roof and eating at the same table with her, the regularity with which I saw her every day in spite of the pressure of work, was not a law to which I subjected myself for reasons of State, but a mark of the pleasure which I took in her company . . . Being unable to endure the sight of the place where this had happened to me, I left Paris within the hour and retreated, in the first instance to Versailles – as a place where it was possible for me to be on my own – and a few days later to Saint-Germain.' It is significant that at such a poignant moment in his life he should have sought the sanctuary of Versailles.

The marquis de La Fare writes of the death of Anne of Austria: 'it did not bring about any change in affairs of state, in which she no longer took a part. But it made a great change in the Court, which began from that day to take on a new complexion. This princess, who had known everybody, knew all about the birth and merits of each; at once proud and polite, she knew, better than anyone else in the world, how to run a Court. Although herself virtuous, she suffered, even with pleasure, that air of gallantry which must exist there in order to make it agreeable and to maintain that standard of politeness which everyone valued in those days but which has since become useless and perhaps even ridiculous.'

With the death of Anne the one restraining influence on Louis' erotic life was removed. The way was open for his long connection with Athenaïs de Montespan. She played her hand carefully and patiently and in the end she triumphed. 'The King's passion for her', writes the marquis de La Fare, 'came into full flower during the voyage that the Queen made in Flanders in the course of the campaign of 1667.'

Athenaïs de Montespan was the second daughter of the duc de Mortemart, prince de Tonnay-Charente. Her mother, Diane, was lady-in-waiting to the Queen. They had two other daughters, the marquise de Thianges and the abbesse de Fontévrault, and a son who took the title of duc de Vivonne. 'These four people', wrote Voltaire, 'went down very well with everyone on account of a special way which they had of mixing conversation with raillery, artlessness and finesse which was known as "l'esprit de Mortemart". They all wrote with a quite particular lightness and grace.'

Athenaïs had married the marquis de Montespan and by the time she appeared at Court was the mother of two children. She is described in some detail by Primi Visconti. 'She had blonde hair, large eyes of an azure blue, the nose aquiline but well shaped, the mouth small and of a bright vermilion and very beautiful teeth – in a word, a perfect face. As for her body, she was of medium height and well proportioned ... Her greatest charm was a grace, a spirit, a certain manner making a witticism which came to please La Vallière to such a point that she could not be without her or speak too well of her to the King. By hearing her so often spoken of, and in such favourable terms, he became curious to know her better and she was soon preferred to her friend.'

Mme de Montespan had played her cards well. Early in 1666 Louis' roving eye, once freed from the thrall of La Vallière, fell first on the princesse de Monaco. The marquis de La Fare wrote: 'While the King was turning his thoughts to the Princess of Monaco, Mme de Montespan began to turn her thoughts to him, and she had the adroitness to do two things at the same time; one was to give the Queen an extraordinarily high opinion of her virtue by receiving Communion in her presence once a week; the other was so to insinuate herself into the good graces of Mlle de La Vallière that she never left her: with the result that she spent most of her time with the King and did all in her power to please him, in which it was not very difficult to succeed, for one with plenty of wit, in the presence of La Vallière who had none.'

Mme de Caylus, in her reminiscences, makes some telling observations on both Louise de La Vallière and Athenaïs de Montespan. 'Mme de La Vallière was born tender-hearted and virtuous: she loved the King but she did not love royalty. The King ceased to love her because of Mme de Montespan. If at the first perception of this, or at least after certain positive proofs of this new passion, Louise had thrown herself into the Carmelites, this action would have been natural and consistent with her character.' She took the other course. She remained on the stage when she no longer had any part to play. She even accepted a place in the suite of her rival. Mme de Montespan had the affectation to make use of her services; 'she gave high praise to her skill and claimed that she could never be content with her attire until she [La Vallière] had put the finishing touches to it'.

'Louise de La Vallière,' continues Mme de Caylus, 'for her part, behaved with all the zeal of a lady's maid whose livelihood depended on the charms which she managed to impart to her mistress.' Louise's nature was more attuned to the convent than to the Court and in 1674 she at last withdrew and became a Carmelite. 'I saw her', continues Mme de Caylus, 'during the last years of her life, and I heard her say, in a tone of voice that went straight to one's heart, the most wonderful things about her condition and of the blessedness which she was already enjoying in spite of the austerity of her penitence.'

The passage from the King's bed to the nun's cell was to become a well-worn path. Louise de La Vallière, Marie-Elizabeth de Ludres, Marie-Angélique de Fontanges and Athenaïs de Montespan all passed that way. 'If this goes on,' wrote Bussy-Rabutin to Mme de Sévigné, 'a sure way for beautiful girls to gain salvation will be lying in the arms of the King. I reckon that, just as he says to those whom he touches for the King's evil: "The King touches you: may God heal you", so he says to the girls whom he loves: "The King embraces you: may God save you." '

A handsome King in the full flowering of his young virility was an object of interest, ambition and concern to most of the members of his Court. 'Let me say once and for all', wrote Primi Visconti in his memoirs, 'that there is no lady of quality who does not have the ambition to become the King's mistress. Numbers of women, both married and single, have declared to me that it would offend neither their husbands nor their fathers nor even God himself if they were to succeed in winning the love of the King. Therefore one must have some indulgence for the King, if he falls into error, with so many devils around him engaged in tempting him. But the worst of it is that the families – the fathers and mothers and even some of the husbands – would make it a subject for vanity.'

It is recorded of the marquis de Montespan's father that he reacted to the news of his daughter-in-law's infidelity to his son by saying: 'God be praised! here at last fortune is beginning to favour our house.' But, as Primi Visconti records, the husband did not take the same view. 'The marquis de Montespan, deeply distressed by the King's passion for his wife, whom he greatly loved, went off to his estates in Gascony, went into mourning and made their children do the same as well as all their domestics. He laid on a funeral just as if the marquise were dead. Later on he was offered 100,000 écus in return for separation from his wife, in payment of the dowry which she owed him; he refused it, saying that he had only a right to 50,000 and that he would take no more at the risk of losing all. In this sort of way', concludes Primi Visconti, 'his behaviour was regarded as extravagant.'

Louis, in his memoirs, reveals a typically androcentric outlook on the female sex. All the blame is put on them. 'They attack the heart of a king like a stronghold. The first concern is to get control of all the positions by which it can be approached. A skilful woman makes it her business first to get rid of all that is not in her interests . . . That feebleness, which is natural to them, often causing them to prefer the pursuit of bagatelles to more important considerations, leads them almost always to make the wrong decision . . . I would willingly concede that a prince whose heart is deeply touched by love, being also always prejudiced by a strong esteem for the one whom he loves, will have difficulty in observing all these precautions – but it is in the difficult situations that we give evidence of our quality.'

It was Mme de Motteville who had the last word: 'The misfortune of our sex is such that men, who made all the rules, have relaxed the strict observance of them for themselves, and it is only in heaven where the commandment that all shall be rewarded according to their works will be applied with equality.'

10

Michel Le Tellier and Colbert

Before the fall of Fouquet Louis had made it clear that he did not intend to have a 'First Minister' of the type of Mazarin or Richelieu. In the Conseil Etroit all were to be equal. It would, however, still have been possible for one of the members of that council to obtain a personal ascendancy over Louis.

Guy Patin, speculating about a possible successor to Mazarin, had put Michel Le Tellier as first choice. 'As for M. Le Tellier, I would prefer him to any other; for he is a good Frenchman and has a good mind. He is not one of those courtiers who are rabid atheists. He believes in God the right way: I know that on good authority. He has a deep understanding of the big issues of the State.' Louis himself said of Le Tellier that 'he was both prudent and wise and of a modesty which I greatly valued'. Mme de Motteville comments favourably on this prudence 'which is natural to him'.

Ezechiel Spanheim, usually a shrewd observer of the Court of France, gives a glowing account of the man and his ministry. 'Finally the position of Chancellor of France having become vacant in 1677, the King, in recognition of his services, honoured him with the highest office of the judiciary, which he held, together with that of Minister of State, until his death in the autumn of 1685. But then he had all the qualities needed to fill the one and the other: a noble presence and an attractive openness; a way that was both honest and winning; a spirit that was gentle and versatile, but also very clear-sighted and very enlightened; the widest experience both in matters of justice and affairs of State and a fine perception together with a deep penetration with which to fathom them.' To this was added one virtue which was personal to him: 'a natural remoteness from anything which resembled pride, so that neither his elevation nor that of his son, the marquis de Louvois, ever led him to leave his established position and to adopt a different way of life'.

His character was reflected in the architecture of Chaville, a dignified but unassuming country house typical of those built in the mid-seventeenth century by men of his class. Chaville lay, as it were, in the shadow of the great Château de Meudon. When Michel Le Tellier's son became marquis de Louvois and minister for war he bought Meudon. His father was content with Chaville.

The abbé de Choisy paints an attractive portrait of the Chancellor which affords an interesting comparison with the line engraving by Nanteuil. 'Michel Le Tellier had been endowed by nature with all the external graces: the face pleasing, the eyes sparkling, the complexion radiant and an understanding smile which predisposes one in his favour. Modest without affectation, careful to make no more parade of his wealth than of his high favour, neither the most brilliant fortune nor the highest position in the State could ever make him forget that his grandfather had been a mere councillor in the Cour des Aides. He never indulged in the vanity of a fine but falsified genealogy.'

In writing those words, Choisy was almost certainly thinking of Colbert, who made a claim, regarded by some historians as difficult to refute and impossible to substantiate, that he could trace his ancestry to a King of Scotland. Seen from the Scottish side the claim has a certain plausibility. On 15 June 1686 the Scottish Parliament registered a 'Bore Brieve' or birth certificate to Charles Colbert, marquis de Seignelay. It contains the words: 'We knowing by clear evidence, ancient writings, friendly letters and other correspondence kept with the ancestors of that old family and by the constant tradition of our forefathers, that that nobleman is descended from Scotland.'

It names an Edward Colbert, baron of Castlehill near Inverness, and his wife Margaret Lindsay. She was the daughter of John Lindsay, baron of Edzall, son of the Earl of Crawford. Crawford had married Lady Mary Gordon, whose mother, the Countess of Huntly, was the fifth daughter of King James I of Scotland. The Colberts of Castlehill used the same heraldic rebus as their French namesakes, 'the serpent azure which they carried in their coat of arms'.

This document, to be found on page 611 of the *Acta Parliamentorum Jacobi VII*, is devoid of dates. But it puts the said Edward Colbert at seven removes from Seignelay. This conflicts with the French genealogy which claims that place for Jehan Colbert, mason, known to be living between 1433 and 1448. Another Scottish document, however, the Public Register of All Genealogies, mentions an Edward Colbert 'who went over to France with Mary [not Margaret] Edzall his spouse about the year 1280, accompanying Christiana de Baliol, niece of King Alexander III, when this princess went there to marry Enguerrand de Guines, Lord of

Coucy'. This register is probably the more trustworthy document. It does not provide undoubted proof of the connection between the two families. It seems odd that the Colberts of Castlehill, who were connected with almost all the great names of Scotland, should reappear after two centuries in Reims as masons, but it is not impossible. The claim may be false, but Colbert could have made it in good faith.

There is a painting of Colbert at Versailles by Claude Lefebvre which can almost be regarded as the official portrait of the minister. It was commissioned by the Académie Royale de Peinture and delivered to them on 30 October 1666. Colbert was by now Surintendant des Bâtiments, Contrôleur Général des Finances and Trésorier des Ordres du Roi. He is represented wearing the imposing black mantle of the Treasurer, with the silver star of the Saint-Esprit sparkling on his left shoulder, and a large lace collar and cuffs. Beside him is a symbolic figure of Atlas upholding the world and on the table at his elbow lies a plan of part of the Tuileries.

'Lefebvre', wrote the critic Dézallier d'Argenville, 'always excelled in portraiture; the truthfulness, the resemblance, the character and the mind of the subject are all combined with the overall colour scheme, the freshness of the tints and an admirable delicacy of touch. The portraits were so true to life that one could almost have spoken to them.'

The portrait fits with the impression which Colbert made on most of his contemporaries. 'His forehead', wrote the abbé de Choisy, 'was habitually furrowed. His deep-set eyes and thick, black eyebrows gave him a look of austerity and at first sight made him look remote and negative.' This was all that some people saw. Choisy, however, knew him better. 'With further acquaintance, when one had become accustomed to him, one found him easy to get on with, prompt and of the most steadfast reliability.'

Although Colbert undoubtedly worked wonders in the world of finance, producing a wealth that no King of France had dreamed of before, his reforms did not bring permanent help to those who needed it most. 'He was solely concerned', continues Choisy, 'to provide the immense sums which were daily demanded of him, but lacked the courage to make representations to his Master, who apparently knew nothing of it, that the people were in a state of misery while there was no talk but of fêtes, of ballets, of illuminations.' Choisy was being unfair. That Louis did know and did care is made clear by his correspondence with his civil servants, which was mostly carried out through Colbert.

Ezechiel Spanheim, who wrote in 1690 a long character sketch and appreciation of Colbert's achievements, sums up thus: 'A great and gifted minister . . . to whom alone the King owes the restoration of his finances, the abolition of the disorder which reigned before him . . . and, as the result, the success of all those great affairs which, thanks to the healthy condition of the said finances, were undertaken and carried out for the benefit of France and for the glory of the King, the upkeep of his army and of his strongholds, the embellishment of his royal houses and the reinstatement of his domains.'

All this was achieved by Colbert's own, almost single-handed effort. 'He was not content, like those who preceded him in office, to concern himself with the broad outlines only and to leave the rest to his clerks, his intendants, *contrôleurs* and other financiers who were customarily employed; he chose to undertake all that himself, to enter into all the details, both of receipts and of expenses ... not wishing to rely on any opinion but his own, so that he brought to the task an application and an unsparing labour which left him no respite.' It is not surprising that Spanheim adds: 'one could have wished him a little more humanity'.

Guy Patin likened him to a block of marble – cold, hard and highly polished. Mme de Cornuel, in the course of an interview, exploded: 'Monseigneur, at least make some sign that you are listening to me!' His first biographer, his contemporary Sandras de Courtilz, wrote: 'He spoke little, never answered straightaway, always wishing to be informed in advance ... He was tireless in his work.'

In November 1676, Mme de Sévigné described an interview with the great minister: 'I went to Saint-Germain, my daughter, to speak about your pension and to whom? To M. Colbert.' Colbert, usually code-named *Petit* in her letters, had deeply upset her by his vicious pursuit of Fouquet. Now he was known as le Nord. 'I was well accompanied,' she continues; 'M. de Saint-Géran, M. d'Aqueville and many others gave me consolation for the ice which I was expecting. It will not cost me much to tell you his answer: "Madame, j'en aurai soin" [Madam, I will see to it].'

Inès Murat sums up: 'The whole figure of the minister evokes the image of saturnine severity, terrifying to those who approached him, but reassuring to the King.' Both were wholly adapted to their respective roles: 'to the one the ostentatious radiance of a monarch who was by nature divine; to the other the rigorous conscientiousness of a minister in the service of the King. Colbert's almost unbelievable capacity for work pleases the King who has, it cannot be denied, a great respect for work. Colbert's methods were in keeping with the character of Louis. Unlike Mazarin they were both lovers of detail – "the detail of everything" was what the King demanded of his minister.'

In many ways Louis and Colbert were complementary to each other and understood each other. Louis was always the master, but he was not a dictator. Colbert was always the servant, but he was not servile. There were times when he could appear very much the opposite. In 1666 Colbert wrote a letter to Louis which was boldly and bravely outspoken. 'I exercise a profession in your service which is without comparison the most difficult of all.' He was referring to his duty to try to restrain the extravagance of the King. This was particularly to be seen in the expenses incurred in war. 'If Your Majesty were aware of all the chaos which is caused in the provinces by the perpetual passage of troops, and how much the people are disgusted by it . . . Your Majesty has made a mixture of your recreation and your warfare that is difficult to disentangle.'

This led to the deplorable contrast between the regular soldiers and the Household Troops, 'heart-breaking for the officers and men and will be their ruin, because the moment a good officer or a good soldier appears in the army he will do all that he can to get into the Household Troops . . . François I and Henri IV never made such distinctions; the latter often made use of all the old army corps for his personal bodyguard.'

Louis did not listen to Colbert in this matter, but he does not seem to have resented the frankness of the criticism. Indeed, he appears to have approved of it. 'What we should be afraid of', he wrote in his memoirs, 'is to be, in case of need, without men who know how and when to contradict us, because our own inclinations are sometimes so clearly evident that the boldest would scruple to oppose them, and yet it is good that there should be some who are capable of taking this liberty. A false complaisance towards us on these occasions could do us more harm than the most dogged contradiction.'

When Colbert began his colossal work of reform, the *Grand Siècle* had not yet entirely freed itself from the toils of the Middle Ages. Much of the *Ancien Régime*, from the pettifoggery of its legal system to the picturesque insalubrity of its great cities, was still a medieval muddle. In spite of the reconstructions of Sully, in spite of the iron rod of Richelieu, the Kingdom which Louis took over in 1661 was a network of interconnecting Augean stables. As he himself wrote: 'le désordre règnait partout'.

The most important centre of unity and uniformity was in the Catholic Church, whose Bishops were appointed by the King. The military Governors, also appointed by the King, were still of considerable importance. The civil power was by now largely exercised by the Intendants – *Intendants de justice, de police et de finance*. Thanks to the Intendants the King was present in his provinces. Colbert believed that an Intendant should not remain for too long in one place and that three years was usually enough.

In order to tackle the problems which faced him, Colbert needed an efficient civil service. Where civil servants were concerned, it was a case of the fewer the better. With regard to the administration of finance he wrote: 'it is certain that the more it can be easily understood and conducted by a smaller number of men, the nearer it will approach perfection'. Apart from being cumbersome, a large civil service would be more likely to elude the control of the central government.

This reduction in quantity, however, needed to be balanced by an improvement in quality. Before appointing men to the post of Intendant, Colbert prepared them for the job by sending them on special missions all over the country, 'in such a way', he wrote, 'that they visit the whole extent of the Kingdom in the course of seven or eight years and become, by this means, capable of the highest offices'.

Colbert's letters to the King left half a page of margin on the left on which he could write his comments. These often reveal an apparently unlimited confidence in his minister – 'It is for you to judge which is better' – 'Whatever you consider appropriate'. On one occasion the King even issued his royal command: 'I order you to do whatever you wish.' But if Colbert's advice was frequently followed it was in every case submitted to Louis' approval. Colbert was authorised to write to such people as Governors or Intendants on behalf of the King.

In November 1662, a year after Louis took over the administration, he sent a circular to all Intendants saying that they were to learn his wishes 'through the letters that Monsieur Colbert would write to them on my behalf'. He reminds them that these letters are to be accepted 'completely and without question . . . I wish you to show the same acceptance towards all that he writes to you.' These letters, which were published by Clément in the late nineteenth century and collated with similar material by Roger Mettam in 1977, show a readiness to give praise when praise was due and to resist firmly the least attempt to neglect or disobey the royal commands, as is shown by a letter in Louis' own hand to the Commandant in Guyenne, written in March 1662. 'I have heard that it has been decided at the Parlement of Bordeaux to send me a remonstrance, suggesting that only 10,000 *setiers* of corn [approximately 45,000 litres] should be allowed to leave my province of Guyenne, instead of the 40,000 *setiers* which I have ordered from there to help the provinces in this region where it has been a bad year; and because I know better than anyone else the needs of my subjects, I add these lines to my earlier letter that I intend, notwithstanding these deliberations or anything else to the contrary, that the amount of corn which I ordered shall be provided and brought here from Guyenne immediately, to be sent to these areas and distributed to these poor people . . . You will therefore inform your Parlement and the consuls of Bordeaux, once and for all, that I expect to be obeyed without any further retort or delay.'

Usually it was Colbert who wrote the royal rebukes. In July 1662 he warned La Barre, the Intendant of Riom, that 'the King has received a number of complaints that, during the weeks of harvest, troops have been used to aid the collection of taxes in your *Généralité* [the area controlled by an Intendant] thus causing widespread disorder and bringing great hardship to the people, who have already suffered a bad year. I have firmly assured His Majesty that you will quickly remedy this situation, and that, in the months of July and August, you will not allow anyone to exert pressure of any kind.' That was a special concession to enable the gathering in of the harvest. In September Colbert was reprimanding the Governor of Upper Poitou for 'refusing to order the troops to go and coerce the parishes which are in arrears with the payments which are due from them ... and that you have even withdrawn from some villages those whom the said Monsieur Pellot [the Intendant] had sent there ... You should issue no instructions about the billeting of troops without his agreement, and you should give all the orders he asks of you when he feels it is appropriate to use the soldiery to compel recalcitrants to pay what they owe; otherwise I shall have no alternative but to inform the King, who, it may be presumed, will not be pleased.'

Louis and Colbert were prepared to hit out in all directions. The nobility were not exempt. They could be subjected to a session of a Court called Les Grands Jours (the Grand Assize). In July 1662, Colbert wrote to the Premier Président du Parlement of Toulouse of an impending visitation. 'I can only say to you that it can produce nothing but a great many benefits, both in re-establishing justice and bringing relief to the people who are oppressed by the violence of the nobility.' Three years later the Grand Assize in Auvergne was described by the Bishop of Nîmes. 'I noticed that throughout the countryside and in Clermont itself there was general terror. All the nobles were taking flight, and there was not a single gentleman who had not examined his conscience, gone over in his mind all the unsavoury aspects of his past life, and tried to make reparation for the wrongs he had committed against his subjects ... Those who had been the tyrants of the poor became their supplicants.' It was noted during these trials that the peasants were very outspoken, 'and that they willingly lodged complaints against the nobles, now that they were not restrained by fear'. The nobility were also attacked on the subject of duelling. To decide a dispute by the sword was to deny the universal nature of royal justice. Voltaire claimed that Louis' firm stance brought about a considerable decrease in duelling – 'une des plus grandes services rendus à la patrie'.

In 1664 Colbert commissioned the Intendants and Maîtres des Requêtes to carry out a general survey of the realm in order to ascertain the state of the Church, of the nobility, of justice and of finances. 'The identification of abuses', writes Inès Murat, 'will be useful for the preparation of a mass of reforms. It is enough to read the results of a survey of Poitou, which Colbert de Croissy sent to his brother, to establish the setting up of a real card index for the police throughout the country.'

Another of Colbert's relatives, his uncle, Henri Pussort, played an important role in these negotiations. He is described by Saint-Simon as 'a great man, but dry, who keeps no company; hard, thorny and difficult to approach, having no amusements and no relaxations. But with all that, a man of great probity, great capacity, great understanding and extremely hard-working.' In April 1667 the *ordonnance civile touchant la reformation de la justice* was registered. It was the first real attempt at the unification and codification of the rules of procedure.

Colbert's reforms were badly received by the provincial parlements, now deprived of the right of remonstrance. In the Instruction of 1663 priority was given to the place of justice. 'As the principal and most important task that His Majesty wants the governors to perform is strongly to uphold justice and to prevent the oppression of the weak by the violence of the powerful.'

The reforms, in fact, were often of a distinctly humanitarian nature. One result of such reforms can be seen in the treatment of trials for sorcery. In July 1670 the Parlement de Rouen condemned a man and two women to be hanged and to have their bodies burnt 'on the simple deposition of a few youths of fourteen or fifteen'. Claude Pellot, the Premier Président (and therefore appointed by the King), wrote to Colbert to say that some thirty more had been arrested in the area between Coutances and Carentan, 'and I am afraid that the more who are condemned, the more will be discovered'. Witch hunts were inclined to be contagious. Colbert's intervention in this case was only just in time. On 19 July Pellot wrote to say that 'we sent a courier to Carentan, where they had been taken for execution and he reached that town on the very day when the sentence was to be carried out. The order also suspended judgement on more than twenty others who were confined in our prisons for the same reason.'

It was the slenderness of the evidence and the severity of the sentencing which concerned Pellot. 'I find it very dangerous, on the evidence of four or five wretches, who often do not know what they are saying, to condemn people to death. It seems to me that the matter is so important that His Majesty should make some ruling about it and then judges should know what proofs are required to condemn such people. For there are some who laugh at it and others who take it seriously and have them burnt and it is a great pity that one should make light in this way of the life of a man.' Colbert and Pellot had only been able to save these particular suspects by obtaining a condemnation by the Great Council of the judgements of the Parlement of Rouen – in spite of the loud protestations of the latter. The councillors were more concerned with their powers and privileges than with any concept of justice.

One can see in all this a real concern for the victims of injustice and oppression. In 1670 Colbert wrote to the Intendant at Tours: 'During your visits make enquiries as to whether the peasants are recovering a little, how they are clothed, how their houses are furnished and whether they make merry on public holidays more than they have of late.' Travellers in France often remarked on the gaiety of the peasants.

Attempts were made to relieve some of the crippling disadvantages under which the peasant laboured. In January 1671, Louis issued a royal proclamation against the seizure of livestock in lieu of taxation. 'As there is nothing more useful in agriculture, nor anything which contributes more to the fertility of the soil than livestock, we have deemed it necessary to deliver them for a time from all forms of seizure and restraint, and in this way to give exhausted lands a period of rest in which to restore themselves, by making the means of increasing fertility more easily available or even to bring new land under cultivation . . . That is why, in our edict of April 1667, we forbade all sergeants-at-arms and other officers of justice to use the methods of seizure.'

A considerable number of these interventions were of a distinctly temporary nature. There is plenty of evidence of a determination on the part of the King and his Minister to discover the facts and of a desire to rectify the wrongs, but it has to be said that they did not succeed. They offered relief rather than remedy. In the case of the seizure of livestock, for instance, an English traveller named Smollett, writing a hundred years later, observed that 'the peasants of France are so wretchedly poor and so much oppressed by their landlords that they cannot afford to enclose their grounds, or give proper respite to their lands by letting them lie fallow or to stock their farms with a sufficient number of black cattle to produce the necessary manure'. But the burden of taxation continued to lie heavily on the shoulders of those who could least afford to pay.

In 1679, with the Peace of Nijmegen just signed, Louis felt that he could be generous, and Colbert saw to it that his generosity did not pass unnoticed. On 17 August he wrote to all Intendants 'announcing a reduction of two million livres in the amount of the *tailles*, and it is important that you should make such generosity widely known so that people may be reminded that although His Majesty asked for considerable help from them to maintain the war effort, he knows equally well how to show them favour and let them taste the fruits of the glorious peace which he has now concluded'.

Colbert's attention to details did not prevent him from having a far wider vision. It was nothing less than to turn France from being a largely agricultural nation into a commercial, mercantile and colonial country somewhat on the lines of England. 'No one before Colbert', wrote Jusserand, 'had so clear an idea of the importance of the navy, commerce, the colonies, of sound finance, of the improvement of communications by roads, rivers and canals.'

Choisy made a brief survey of Colbert's outlook and policies in endeavouring to make France 'sufficient unto itself'. 'Always magnificent in his ideas and nearly always unfortunate in their execution', Colbert 'believed that he could do without the silks of the Levant, the wool of Spain the broadcloth of Holland, the tapestries of Flanders and the horses of England and Barbary. He set up all kinds of industries', continues Choisy, 'which cost more than they were worth. He created an East India Company without possessing the necessary funds and not realising that the French – impatient by nature – would never have the constancy to put money into something for the space of thirty years without gaining any profit from it.' Unlike Choisy, who saw the widespread distribution of raw materials as a divinely ordained opportunity for creating peaceful and friendly co-operation between nations, Colbert believed that the wealth of one country could be obtained only by the impoverishment of another. This was largely because he saw the wealth of a nation almost exclusively in terms of the amount of gold and silver which it possessed. France had no precious metals of its own.

In 1670 Colbert wrote a memorandum to Louis explaining this policy. It was based on the consideration that the total amount of bullion in Europe was limited and that the way to prosperity was 'by increasing the amount of money in public commerce by attracting it from the countries from which it comes; by keeping it within the Kingdom and preventing it from going out again and giving men the means to profit by it'. Such an increase in wealth would enable people to pay more in taxes and the royal revenue would benefit.

One of the exponents of this doctrine, who influenced Colbert, was Jacques Savary who wrote his thesis *Le Parfait Négociant* in 1675. 'Kings', he claimed, 'can also derive great benefits from trade, because, apart from the dues which are paid to them on goods entering or leaving the kingdom, it is indeed true that all the ready money which is in the hands of the merchants and bankers is the source from which the tax-farmers and businessmen draw immense sums of which the King sometimes has need for financing great enterprises.'

Rather than import raw materials, Colbert preferred to import expertise. He invited Dutch, English and Venetian craftsmen to France and subsidised them to improve or initiate industries. They were then forbidden to leave the country. Even when France was at war with Holland it was Dutch workmen who were employed to drain the marshes in the Dauphiné. French engineers were sent to Holland to learn how to improve the navigation rivers and canals.

One of Colbert's most permanent achievements was in the improvement of communications. These were often so slow as to endanger the safe arrival of perishable goods. The journey by road from Paris to Lille took four days, to Lyon eleven. Transport by river or canal was potentially swifter but often made more expensive by landlords exacting tolls to which they were not entitled. To remedy this Colbert set himself with his usual energy.

The rebuilding and re-equipping of the maritime ports – Dunkirk, Le Havre, La Rochelle, Toulon – were among the most lasting results. So was the creation of the Canal des Deux Mers or Canal de Languedoc. This gave direct access from the Atlantic to the Mediterranean by linking the River Garonne to the Golfe du Lion and thus cutting out the 2,000-mile detour round Gibraltar. The canal was 279 kilometres long, 20 metres broad and 2 metres deep. It was the work of Pierre-Paul Riquet and was inaugurated in the presence of Colbert in 1681. Vauban said on this occasion: 'There is one thing lacking to the canal – a statue of Riquet.'

The survival of many of Colbert's constructions was due to his insistence on the best possible materials and the highest possible standards of workmanship. As he wrote to one of his engineers: 'they must be built so solidly that, if it were possible, they would last for ever'.

One of Colbert's aims was to increase the population of France. He attempted to do this by granting a five-year exemption from the *taille* to those who married under the age of twenty. This decree, dated in November 1666, also extended freedom from taxation to 'every father of a family who has ten children living, born in lawful wedlock, who are not Priests or Religious'. Colbert was hostile to monks as being unproductive members of the community and to the clergy who were unreproductive members.

Although Colbert's official allegiance was to the Catholic faith, with certain leanings towards Jansenism, one cannot help suspecting him of a preference for the merit set upon honest, hard work by the 'Protestant ethic' of the Lutheran and the Calvinist. The Church provided for over a hundred *jours fériés* which were days off for workmen. On two occasions Colbert demanded a reduction of these, first by twenty and then by seventeen. His excuse was that 'most of the workers are coarse men who give up to debauchery and disorder these days which were intended for piety and good works'.

Full employment had the additional advantage in Colbert's eyes 'of preserving those employed from such occasions for doing wrong as are inseparable from idleness'. Many of his industries were largely staffed by Huguenots and suffered accordingly when Louis began to persecute them – but that came only after Colbert's death. In 1665 he financed a Dutchman named Van Robais to set up at Abbeville a manufactory of broadcloth. Van Robais gave employment to 1,600 workers and Louis gave them his permission 'to continue to profess the so-called reformed religion'.

Another problem which Colbert tried to overcome was the reluctance of the nobility to have anything to do with trade or commerce. They had in the past even been forbidden to do so on pain of forfeiting their privileges. Their function, after all, was to be men of war. In August 1669 an edict was issued which reversed this. 'Seeing that commerce, and particularly that which goes by sea, is the fertile source from which States draw their wealth, spreading it among their subjects in proportion to their industry and labour, and seeing that there is no more lawful and blameless means of acquiring wealth, and also that it has always been held in high regard by the best ordered nations ... our edicts of May and August 1664, which established the East and West India Companies, state that all persons, no matter what their rank, may join and participate in the companies without loss of nobility or prejudice to their privileges ... it is essential to the welfare of our subjects and to our own satisfaction that we entirely erase the remnants of this universally held belief in the incompatibility of seaborne trade and nobility ... Seaborne commerce shall not cause the loss of noble rank.'

Once again, it is doubtful whether this edict bore much fruit. The French aristocracy would never imitate the English in this respect. A century later the baronne d'Oberkirch could write: 'Anyone who had been *noblesse de robe* could have no place in the high nobility, however ancient his title. Etiquette excluded him from eating with a Prince of the Blood and his wife could never be presented.' This distinction between two levels of nobility was unknown in England. A man might make a fortune in commerce, invest a large sum in the purchase of land and at least be succeeded by a son who obtained a peerage. Such was exactly the story of Josiah Child. He had risen from being a merchant apprentice to the directorship of the East India Company. In 1668 he was made a baronet and was rich enough to buy the house and estate of Wanstead in Essex. In 1715 his son Richard pulled down the old Tudor house and commissioned Colin Campbell to build what was one of the finest palladian palaces in the country. He was first created Viscount Castlemaine and later Earl Tylney. His sister married a son of the Duke of Beaufort. Thus did ancient nobility ally itself with the wealth of new England.

Colbert's design for a maritime France did not really work. 'Because the Frenchman was content with a modest competence at home,' wrote H. A. L. Fisher; 'because he hated and feared the sea, and did not care to risk his fortune on doubtful enterprises at the ends of the earth, Colbert's dream of a great maritime empire and of a world trade promoted by joint stock companies was doomed to disappointment.' If it did fail, it was not for want of trying.

Louis was not slow to express his appreciation of the vigilance of his faithful Minister. 'I have been told that you are not in very good health, and that your keenness to return here will only be harmful to you ... I order you to do nothing that will prevent you from serving me, when you arrive, in all the important tasks which I shall entrust to you. In a word, your health is so vital to me that I wish you to conserve it and to believe that it is my trust in you and my friendship which make me speak in this way.'

Another indication of the nature of Louis' relationship with Colbert is in the part which he played in Louis' family affairs. This, of course, included his mistresses. In 1663 Louise de La Vallière became pregnant. Louis, during the lifetime of his mother, was relatively discreet about his bastards. On this occasion the child was a boy, not destined to live for very long. Colbert was charged with the arrangements for the confinement and for the immediate care of the baby. 'As regards the feeding of the infant', he wrote, 'with the secrecy which the King has required of me, I have enjoined the said Beauchamp and his wife, former domestics of my family ... to whom I have declared, in the interests of secrecy, that one of my brothers, having had a child by a lady of quality, I felt obliged, in order to save his honour, to take care of the child and to entrust to them its nurture – which they have accepted with joy.'

Such stories could easily be multiplied. They reveal Colbert as serving Louis much as he had served Mazarin, as his *homme de confiance*. He possessed what Inès Murat has called 'that agility of mind which enabled him to pass with ease from one area to another and was to play so large a part in creating the impression of being indispensable'. But Colbert was first and foremost a minister – one of the deliberately small Conseil d'en Haut whose members were the men closest to the King.

Louis preferred to pick his highest-ranking ministers from the legal and professional classes rather than from among the higher aristocracy, the *noblesse d'épée*. As he wrote in his memoirs for his son: 'to make clear to you all my thoughts, I felt that it was not in my interest to look for men of higher social standing because, since I needed above all to establish my own reputation, it was important that the public should understand, by the rank of those whom I used, that I had no intention of sharing my authority with them and that they themselves, knowing what they were, should entertain no higher hopes than those which I chose to give them'.

Experience was to confirm that men from the legal and professional classes, such as the Colberts and the Le Telliers, made the best civil servants. Sometimes they acquired titles and were known as *noblesse de robe*. To have been ennobled, however, was to admit that one's ancestors were not noble. These formed, therefore, a kind of 'second-class nobility' not in any way to be confused with the real nobility, the *noblesse d'épée* whose members could trace their ancestry and titles back to before the fourteenth century – 'remonter à la nuit du temps'. These were the military aristocracy whose names had lent their lustre to the battlefields of Europe. Louis referred to these as his 'right arm'. But it was not to these to whom he looked to fill the highest ministerial posts. It was to families such as the Colberts and the Le Telliers that he deliberately turned.

The first Le Tellier of whom a record has survived was a certain Pierre Le Tellier, *marchand bourgeois*, mentioned in 1535. Twenty years later there was a Michel Le Tellier, notary at the Châtelet, and in 1596 Michel Le Tellier the second comes into the light of history with the purchase of the Seigneurie and Château de Chaville, a modest little property near Versailles. It was his grandson, also Michel, born in 1603, who was to become Louis' Chancellor.

It seems also that Louis had a more particular reason for limiting himself, very largely, to two families or 'clans', as they were called. He noted with interest that Charles II was obliged to get rid of his Chancellor, Lord Clarendon. This happened in August 1667. In a letter to Lord Ormonde, Charles admitted: 'the truth is his behaviour and humour was grown so insupportable to myself and to all the world else, that I could no longer endure it, and it was impossible for me to live with it and do those things with the Parliament that must be done or the Government will be lost'.

Louis saw in this a warning to ministers that it was in their own interest to observe a certain modesty in their private fortunes and a lesson to kings to learn 'not to let their creatures grow too great'. He continues, in his memoirs for that year, with advice to the Dauphin on two particular points of importance. The first was the need to 'understand your affairs thoroughly, because a King who does not know them will always be dependent on those who serve him'. The second was the need to share his confidence with several persons, each of whom, 'being by a natural emulation opposed to the advancement of their rivals, the jealousy of the one often serves as a brake on the ambition of the other'.

This was the principle on which Louis acted with the clan Colbert and the clan Le Tellier. The rivalry between them enabled him to resist domination by one party or the other. Not infrequently this rivalry erupted in passionate outbursts, usually by Colbert. In 1666, when Louis was making preparations for his entry into Flanders in the following year, Louvois was put in charge of the War Department. Colbert sent a letter of bitter complaint to Louis which ended on a very personal note. 'Sire; with regard to the assembling of troops and their marching orders, I had not believed that so important a business would be entrusted to a young man of twenty-four with no experience in such matters, a man of very quick temper who imagines that it appertains to the authority of his position to ruin the country and who wants to ruin it because I want to save it!' Colbert was not being honest – or at least not being accurate: Louvois was twenty-seven at the time.

Nevertheless Louis had to keep the peace and he reveals an important side of his character in the way in which he dealt with this situation. Any favour shown by the King to one was likely to be regarded as a direct insult to the other. In 1668 Louvois received the post of Secretary of State for War. Louis had to do something to redress the balance.

In October of that year Colbert was ill. Guy Patin noted: 'Today the King honoured M. Colbert with a visit accompanied by the greatest pomp and ceremony, escorted by the Household Troops with drawn swords. It is said that he has the gout and a touch of dysentery; the fact is that his brain is overworked.' The Venetian ambassador, Giustinian, records that Louis said to Colbert: 'Melancholy begets disease; a little gaiety would bring you healing.' Gaiety is not a word that one would easily associate with Colbert, but his frigid professionalism had at least one endearing feature: he loved dancing. Olivier d'Ormesson records that 'Monsieur Colbert danced extremely well and it was his greatest delight'.

In 1671 the prestigious post of Chancelier des Ordres du Roi became vacant. Colbert's hopes were high, but it was given to Louvois. Saint-Maurice records: 'M. de Louvois received visits, on account of his new dignity, by all the members of the Court except for Colbert. They get on very badly together and it is thought that both father and son have tried to blacken his reputation with the King.'

It was about at this time that Colbert, exasperated by Louvois, flared up in the presence of the King at the council table. It is most instructive to note how Louis dealt with such a situation. First of all he did not act or react in any hurry. On 24 April 1671, two days after the incident, Louis wrote to Colbert: 'I was sufficiently in control of myself, the day before yesterday, to conceal from you the pain that it gave me to hear a man like yourself, whom I have loaded with benefits, speak to me as you did. I have, and still have at this present, a great friendship for you, as is apparent from what I have done, and I think I have given you enough mark of it in telling you that I have kept my feelings in check for a single minute, and that I did not want to say to you in person what I write now in order not to expose you to displeasing me further.

'It is the memory of the services which you have rendered me, as well as my friendship, which give me these sentiments; take advantage of it and do not risk angering me again, for, after having listened to your opinions and to those of your colleagues, and after I have pronounced on all your claims, I do not want to hear anything more said on the matter.'

As a proof of his goodwill Louis proceeded to make a generous offer. 'Consider whether the Ministry of the Marine would not be agreeable to you; if it does not take your fancy and if you would prefer something else – tell me frankly. But after I have made my decision I do not want any answering back. I tell you what my thoughts are so that you may do your work on an assured basis and so that you do not have to make any provisions.' Two days later Louis wrote a second letter, presumably in answer to Colbert's response to the first. 'Do not imagine that my friendship is diminished . . . The marks of preference which you fear that I show to the others ought not to cause you any pain. I want only to avoid injustice and to work for the good of those who serve me.'

The vicissitudes in the Colbert–Le Tellier rivalry were the subject of eager gossip in court and camp. On 2 May 1667, the marquis de Saint-Maurice wrote: 'It is believed that M. de Colbert is not in such high favour; he has powerful enemies and certain people have sent memoranda against him to the King, in which they draw attention to the fact that he takes more than ten million [livres] a year . . . As this minister is not liked it is possible that these impostures against him have been invented.'

Some three weeks later he reported that the ministers had all gone off in the same coach to Colbert's house – 'which caused all Paris to marvel'. Professional rivalry, however, by no means always excludes friendly relationships. A letter from Colbert to Louvois, written just after the capture of Maastricht in June 1673, shows that he could be generous with praise. 'I believe, Monsieur, that you will think it fit that I should rejoice with you over the great and glorious success of the siege of Maastricht.' But the credit for the planning of the operation he gave to the King. 'The credit is yours alone to have executed the orders of the King so well that he lacked nothing for so great an undertaking. It is fitting also that I should thank you for all the civility which you have shown my son. *Je proteste que je suis absolument à vous.*'

By 18 November in the same year the pendulum had swung back. 'M. de Colbert is still in high favour and the King is very satisfied with him on account of the good order into which he has put the direction of finance. His Majesty said the other day at his *coucher* that no kingdom had ever been so well ruled as his; that he had 92 millions in revenue; that with 35 he could pay all expenses so that each year he could save 56 million to spend on the war.'

On 27 September 1671, Saint-Maurice wrote: 'M. Colbert was at Versailles on Tuesday for the first time since his illness. The King treated him extremely well. M. Le Tellier affected to give the highest praise for the good condition into which he had put His Majesty's finances and revenues, assuring me that in the year 1661 he had only had 23 million of revenue in ready money ... He mentions the sum of 1,200,000 livres of revenue from the *services des postes* which would be added to the Trésor Royal in the following year.' This is very nearly the sum quoted by Clément for the year 1680 in his publication of Colbert's letters and papers.

Colbert's family benefited considerably from his rise to power. He had five sisters and three brothers. Four of the sisters were destined to the religious life. This was quite a common family policy as it relieved the father of the necessity of providing them with dowries. It seems improbable that all such young ladies had any real vocation. The eldest of the three brothers, Nicolas, became Bishop, first of Luçon and later of Auxerre. The second, Charles, marquis de Croissy, had a distinguished career as ambassador to England and later as Secretary of State for Foreign Affairs. The youngest, Edouard-François, became Lieutenant-Général des Armées du Roi. Both he and Charles were married to rich heiresses.

In Colbert's own family the daughters fared better. All three became duchesses. Marie-Thérèse married, in 1667, the duc de Chevreuse, son of the duc de Luynes and grandson of the duchesse de Chevreuse who had played an important part in the Fronde. Henriette, the second daughter, married the comte de Saint-Aignan, later to be duc de Beauvilliers. In 1679, Marie-Anne married the duc de Mortemart, nephew of Mme de Montespan. The King contributed 200,000 livres to the dowries of each.

Of Colbert's five sons the most distinguished was Jean-Baptiste, marquis de Seignelay. He succeeded his father as Ministre de la Marine and was considered to be one of the best that France had ever had. Jacques Nicolas, Abbot of Le Bec with an income of 600,000 livres, became at the age of twenty-six coadjutor to the Archbishop of Rouen, whom he succeeded in 1691. According to Saint-Simon he devoted himself to his episcopal duties, but he earned the rebuke of Fénelon for his extravagance in 'improving' the Château de Gaillon: 'Who will correct this mania for building', asked Fénelon, 'if our good bishops themselves authorise this scandal?' It must not be forgotten that the other three sons died on the battlefield.

Colbert lived to see much of his work end in failure. He was even obliged to destroy some of his own reconstructions, going so far as to revert to some of the practices of Fouquet which he had once so sternly condemned. The last few years brought much in the way of disappointment and disillusion which was reflected in his outward bearing. Charles Perrault observed that a great change had come over him. In the early days, when he came into his study, 'we saw him settle down to his work with a look of satisfaction and rubbing his hands together with glee; but now he hardly ever sits down without looking depressed and even sighing. M. Colbert, from being pleasant and easy, has become difficult and difficult to please.' He was beginning to be overwhelmed with a sense of failure.

At some time during the year 1680 – the letter is not dated – he wrote to Louis: 'As regards expenditure, although this is none of my business, I humbly beg Your Majesty to allow me to say to Him that neither in war nor in peace has He ever consulted His financial condition before deciding upon His expenditure, which is so extraordinary as to be without parallel.

'If He would care to look again and compare the present with the past, during the twenty years that I have had the honour to serve you, He will find that, although the receipts have greatly increased, the expenditure has greatly exceeded the receipts and perhaps this will lead Your Majesty to moderate and retrench these excesses and to put a little more proportion in His receipts and expenditure.'

Three years later Colbert was in despair. On 8 June 1683, he wrote again: 'Your Majesty will observe, if it may please Him, that besides the 5,540,887 livres, which is the sum of the expenses that have been paid, there is need, for the expenditure which Your Majesty has, according to the enclosed memorandum, ordered and resolved, of 2,226,500 livres and that these expenses exceed the receipts by 3,600,000.' Louis commented: 'This high expenditure causes me much grief, but some of it was necessary.' Colbert continued: 'All the financial affairs are following their normal course; the Intendants visit their *généralités* and render accounts in all their letters which are full of the misery of the people.' Louis commented: 'Their misery causes me much grief. We will have to do all that we can for the relief of our people.' Two days later he wrote again to Colbert: 'Hasten all the works at Versailles because I might have to shorten this voyage by several days.'

At the end of August Colbert was taken seriously ill. The marquis de Seignelay kept the King informed. In a letter dated 2 September, Paris, at two o'clock in the morning, he stated: 'The illness of my father has become so much worse and his weakness so much greater that the doctors, who understand nothing about this disease . . . have advised him to receive Holy Communion and the Viaticum this night.' Louis replied: 'I am deeply touched by the condition in which your father is. Stay with him as long as is necessary ... I still hope that God will not wish to take him from this world where he is so necessary for the welfare of the State. I wish this with all my heart, with the particular friendship which I have for him and that which I have for you and all your family.'

Colbert died four days later. Louis wrote to his widow a touching letter of condolence. 'If you have lost a husband who was dear to you, I regret the loss of a faithful minister with whom I was fully satisfied.' A tradition grew up that Colbert had died in disgrace. That tradition hardly fits with the correspondence just quoted.

Voltaire was one of the first historians to reinstate Colbert: 'We owe it in all justice to public figures ... to consider the point from which they departed in order the better to judge the changes which they made in their countries. If we compare the administration of Colbert with those which preceded it, posterity would value this man, whose body the mindless populace wanted to tear to pieces after his death, we would have to admit that France had never been so flourishing as in the period between the death of Mazarin and the war of 1689.'

With Colbert dead, Le Tellier and Louvois obtained the appointment of Claude Le Pelletier to replace him. He was both a friend and a relation. The word *pelletier* means a furrier – a dealer in skins. The armorial device of the Le Tellier family was three lizards; that of Colbert a grass-snake. This enabled Choisy to make his *bon mot*: 'The lizard has skinned the grass-snake and sent his skin to Le Pelletier.' The supremacy of Louvois was now assured.

11

Louvois

On the same day on which Colbert died Louvois was appointed to take over his position as Surintendant des Bâtiments. He wrote immediately to the Sieur Lefebvre, Contrôleur des Bâtiments at Versailles: 'The King has done me the honour of making me Surintendant des Bâtiments, I give you notice of this and beg you to use your authority to enforce the continuing without interruption of the work for which you are responsible. I will make a point of being at Versailles early on Wednesday morning and I beg you to let me have a memorandum on all the matters which are in hand, of the number of workmen who are employed at each workshop and the point reached in each project. I beg that I also may find a statement of all that is paid to each workshop which has been under your care during the past weeks and of what you advise they should be paid.'

Simultaneously he wrote to the Contrôleur at Chambord demanding a 'memorandum on the condition and expenditure' by return of post and adding that the work still to be done 'must be of higher quality than in the past'. It was quickly known throughout the workshops that there was now an even firmer hand upon the helm.

A comparison between the average expenditure during the last years of Colbert's administration with that of a similar period under Louvois reveals a rise of about 30 per cent. This rise in the expenditure reflected an increase in the amount of work undertaken rather than any rise in costs. In 1684 Louvois imposed a very detailed tariff – the stonemasons' wages even took into account the hardness of the stone used – but the entrepreneurs were forbidden to pay any extra on the controlled price. The increase in the budget was caused by the multiplication and enlargement of the royal buildings – Versailles, Marly, Trianon, Les Invalides and Saint-Cyr – and by Louis' passion for elaborating his gardens.

Most of Louvois' work as Surintendant des Bâtiments consisted in the maintenance of the system established by Colbert. The Academies were administered with the same attention to detail and discipline. The strictness of this discipline may be judged from the penalties – usually fines – imposed upon faulty or overdue work. The great ebonist Boulle was threatened with imprisonment when two chairs ordered for Meudon failed to arrive on time.

On 31 October 1669, Louvois purchased the Château de Meudon. There could have been no more striking symbol for the rise to power of Louvois, nor could the difference between himself and his father have been more aptly illustrated than by the difference between Meudon and Chaville, the little country house of Pierre Le Tellier which stood, as it were, in its shadow.

Louvois could hardly have seated himself better. Meudon was renowned for its pure air, its beautiful gardens and its incomparable outlook. It was handy for Paris, it was handy for Saint-Germain, but above all it was handy for Versailles, which, it was now becoming clear, Louis was intending to make the definitive seat of the Court and the Government.

Meudon was visited by 'Two Young Dutchmen' in 1657. They admired all that they saw, but particularly they admired the site. 'From this terrace there is a view which is without equal both for its beauty and for its diversity, which is the most happy blend that it would be possible to imagine, for one can see the River Seine meandering across a rich and charming plain, an incredible number of beautiful houses and large villages ... and the whole is so beautifully disposed that one seems to have before one's eyes the picture of an idealised landscape. But what is best about it is that one overlooks in its entirety the biggest, the richest and the most magnificent city in the whole of Christendom.'

The Château was built by Cardinal Sanguin who gave it, in 1527, still unfinished, to his niece the duchesse d'Etampes, a mistress of François I. It was probably completed by 1540. This makes it contemporary with François' buildings at Madrid, Fontainebleau and the later parts of Chambord.

The house stood between four pavilions round three sides of a courtyard. A fifth pavilion marked the centre of the entrance front. These pavilions were elevated above the façades by half a storey and carried their lofty pyramids of roof high above the general silhouette. Together with the tall attendant chimney-shafts they created that deeply indented skyline so dear to the French builder.

It was here, on the garden front of Meudon, that there appeared, for what was probably the first time, what was to become the classical French façade for centuries. Exact in its symmetry, satisfying in its proportions and built throughout with an impressive economy of ornament, the style combined the austerity of an Italian façade with the complexity of a French roofscape. The three pavilions and their two connecting *corps de logis* provided an alignment of five separate roofs of two different heights.

Whether Louvois had any aesthetic interest in architecture is open to doubt. An anecdote by Saint-Simon illustrates the care with which Louis himself superintended the construction of the Trianon de Marbre. He had an eye to detail – 'a pair of compasses in his eye for exactness, proportion and symmetry' – and he noticed a slight irregularity in one of the windows. Louvois was ill-advised enough to argue the point; measurements were taken and the accuracy of the King's observation established. The disconcerted Minister, according to Saint-Simon, retreated, avowing that only another war could save him from disgrace. The war of the League of Augsburg did, in fact, follow soon after this episode, but it can safely be attributed to other causes.

One quality which Louvois shared with his rival Colbert was an astonishing capacity for work. Saint-Maurice describes him as 'indefatigable, bold and prompt and sometimes too much so'. But he added: 'I have never known a man work so hard.'

'M. de Louvois', wrote Dangeau, 'was the greatest man of his kind that has been seen for several centuries. Nothing could be more comprehensive, nothing more fertile, nothing more just than his head for great undertakings. He was indefatigable at his work, and a work which was all day and every day, evaluating, discerning, directing with unimaginable ease all the details of which not even the smallest escaped him. Magnificent in everything, noble in everything, of an open-handed generosity, making to friends and relations presents that were truly princely. The best parent in the world and "Father of the Poor" to whom he never refused anything . . . living at home like a little king and yet with no insolence, talking without embarrassment of his humble origins and of the social difference between himself and his in-laws.' He had married Anne de Souvré, a daughter of one of the most distinguished houses of France.

Louvois' heavy work load made him almost inaccessible. Saint-Maurice tells of constantly attempting to obtain an audience with him and constantly failing – 'In fact no man has ever had so much to do; there are always more coaches and sedan chairs in front of his house than in front of the Tuileries and it is impossible to reach the door of his study.'

Being a hard worker himself, Louvois exacted a similar standard from his clerks. Pierre Clément records that one of these *commis* complained that if he owed it to his goodness that he had a position with a salary of 6,000 livres, he was none the happier for it. 'You require us to be at work from five in the morning until eleven at night, with the result that we could not even spend 200 livres.' Louvois replied with a laugh: 'You will take your ease when you are old.'

The immense scale of Louvois' administration can be appreciated by the fact that his letters, preserved in the Archives de la Guerre, fill 280 fat volumes. According to his biographer André Corvisier his record output for a single day was to have dictated seventy-one letters.

Louvois was the virtual creator of the Archives de la Guerre. Saint-Simon, usually hostile to him, admits that 'he was the first who realised the danger that the despatches and the instructions from the King and his Ministers which were addressed to Generals in the army, to Governors and other war leaders and to the Intendants of the frontiers, would remain in the hands of these individuals, and after them their heirs or even their valets, who could make dangerous use of them'.

In 1688 Louvois gave M. de Bellou, the secretary concerned with secret letters and instructions, the job of collecting the papers concerning the administration of the army. He may have seen no further than the useful-ness which such a collection might be to himself, but no historian of the period can fail to be grateful to him. In 1690 a law was passed requiring those who were inheritors of important military documents to make over to the State such papers as were of administrational or historical importance. The sheer bulk of this collection was impressive. No less than 240 registers, each containing some 100,000 papers, were lodged in the Archives de la Guerre.

Another result of Louvois' zeal for accurate information was in the formation of inventories. In 1683 he commissioned Le Brun, who was, as it were, Keeper of the King's Pictures, to draw up a complete inventory of the royal collections in the Louvre. The list contained 426 items. In the following year he took over all the measured drawings of the Louvre and the Tuileries made by the Sieur Brand and added them to the royal collection. On the death of Le Brun in 1690 he obtained possession of all his drawings. He was always on the lookout for opportunities to purchase the best works of art for the King.

But it was as Secretary of State for War that Louvois was to make his greatest contribution to Louis' reign. He had the best apprenticeship possible – that of working in close collaboration with his father. He was soon master of the smallest details of military administration.

Louvois was well suited to become the right-hand man to the King because he shared Louis' passion for detailed information. To a large extent this was a matter of maintaining a first-rate civil service. So far as the army was concerned it required the right appointments of the Intend-ants d'Armée, the Commissaires as well as the Contrôleurs who were used for special missions. These provided his main source of information.

But Louvois also wanted to see for himself. He undertook a considerable number of tours of inspection. Obviously for one who is to decide the administrative problems of the fortress of Lille, a familiarity with the town, citadel and surroundings of Lille must be a great advantage. Under his father he had been Inspecteur Général of the army and he had learnt the principle that 'when one draws conclusions from a long way off one is liable to make mistakes'.

On his peregrinations he kept up a correspondence with his friend Tilladet which almost constitutes a log-book. He was extremely observant. A small but unimportant entry reveals his prejudice, not untypical of his age, against mountainous scenery. From Barège he wrote: 'If only you could see how frightful this region is and so extraordinary that all the time I have been here I have never seen a single bird of any species. They have too much good sense than to establish themselves here.'

Barège was one of the most therapeutic watering places in France. Louvois immediately saw its possibilities as a recuperation centre for army officers; but it was badly organised. 'The waters here are really marvellous', he wrote, 'and ought to be more highly prized than a gold-mine.' He recommended a modest investment in the place. 'It would not cost 1,000 pistoles to make two beautiful baths in place of the revolting one which is there. Another 1,000 pistoles would create a lodging sufficient for twenty officers in place of the frightful huts which they are obliged to inhabit.'

In May 1668, he spent a week in Flanders. He covered about 200 kilometres, which makes an average of some 30 a day. His journeys were carefully calculated so that he was able to pick up his post-bag at pre-arranged places. A list had been drawn up of the persons whom he was to meet and the subjects to be discussed.

The agenda for another visit to Flanders in December 1676 ranges from such matters of high policy as is implied in his first article – 'talk with M. de La Mothe on what needs to be done against Saint-Omer and Cassel' – to his last conversation, with M. de Souzy, about supplies of fodder, their safe-keeping, and beer – an important item in the life of a soldier.

Louvois' personal appearance and manners did not in any way suggest his undoubted abilities, 'which one would not have expected', wrote Spanheim, 'from a body so heavy and corpulent nor from his appearance which was by nature uncouth . . . nor his haughty manners, both seemingly brusque and hot-headed'. People were also quick to note 'his temperament, spirit and conduct very much the opposite to that of his father'.

Certainly most of the portraits of Louvois show a face that was coarse, not to say boorish, and which seems to corroborate Spanheim's observations. His actions as a minister show him often as ruthless and arrogant and capable of being gratuitously rude to men who deserved his respect.

Spanheim was one of Louvois' fiercest critics. 'I will content myself with mentioning here that which is established and of which no one in the Court of France doubts the truth, and of which I have, besides, incontrovertible proofs. I mean that it is to the counsels of Louvois alone that the public should attribute the undertaking of the present war [the Dutch war] and all the disastrous consequences that it could have had up till now and could have for the future of France itself.'

Spanheim, of course, was a German and he speaks for a Germany outraged by the behaviour of France. He holds Louvois responsible for all the 'sacking, burning, desolation, worse than barbarian treatment and inhumanities without example . . . The terrible effects that the poor Palatinate and its neighbouring towns suffered from the beginning from the violation of treaties and truces, and is still suffering from today [1690] and will be an eternal monument to posterity.'

This, of course, could be taken more as a criticism of Louis than of Louvois. Apologists for Louis have tried to put the blame for the harshness with which the enemies of France were treated on Louvois. Spanheim goes so far as to write of his 'ascendancy over the mind of the King'. But the maxim holds true: 'Le responsable c'est le chef.' Either Louis had the weakness to be dominated and to act against his better judgement or he must be held responsible for at least approving, if not actually instigating, the policies complained of by Spanheim. Louis was not one to be mastered and he must take his own share of responsibility for Louvois' actions, especially in his attitude to the high command of the army.

In the years between 1678 and 1688, a period of relative peace, Louvois set about the perfecting of the military machine which he inherited from his father. It was clear enough that France was going to need it. In 1683 his expenditure required a budget of 54 million livres. That represented nearly 47 per cent of the total expenditure. André Corvisier has worked out that the navy accounted for only 9.5 per cent and the royal buildings 6.27 per cent. By 1690 Louvois could claim a total of 387,000 soldiers.

One of the most important reforms – or attempted reforms – was to the somewhat proprietory attitude of the aristocracy towards their regiments. Nobles were often more concerned with their rights than with their responsibilities. It was an attitude not easily changed. It is illustrated by a short scene described by Mme de Sévigné on 4 February 1689: a confrontation in the gardens of Versailles between Louvois and the young comte de Nogaret. 'The other day M. de Louvois said at the top of his voice: "Monsieur, your company is in a very bad condition." "Monsieur," he answered, "I was not aware of it." "You ought to be aware of it," said

M. de Louvois; "have you seen it?" "No, Monsieur," said M. de Nogaret. "You ought to have seen it." "I will see to it, Monsieur." "You ought to have seen to it. You ought to make up your mind, Monsieur. Either admit to being a courtier or do your duty as an officer." ' As this scene took place only two years before the death of Louvois it bears witness to his lack of success in disciplining the gilded youth of France.

The tough measures employed by Louvois to push through his reforms provided material for the lampooners who were trying to blacken the reputation of France in the eyes of Europe. It provoked Louvois to an act of self-justification – *La Réponse au livre intitulé La Conduite de la France* which appeared in 1683. 'It is reported of our wartime officers', he wrote, 'that they are continually under threat of imprisonment, obliged to consume their private fortunes and to end up in the hospital [presumably Les Invalides] without hope of recompense.' Louvois replied: 'This happens only to bad officers and not to those who do their duty.' To the charge that officers were ruining themselves in the service of the King, he replied that this was applicable only to those guilty of 'an insane expenditure which does not contribute to the service of the King . . . Does it, in fact, contribute to a man's service that a Captain in the Chevaux-Légers should possess thirty horses, as thousands do in our army; that he should wear a doublet costing 500 écus, that he gambles away 100 pistoles in a quarter of an hour and, in fact, commits a thousand suchlike follies?'

He then turns to the more positive side of the picture. 'There is no position in which one might make one's fortune more quickly . . . The fortune of an officer of merit has no limits with us. From an ensign he becomes a lieutenant, from a lieutenant a captain [and rises finally] from lieutenant-general to maréchal de France.' He cites the example of a Monsieur Le Bret, 'of obscure origins, without fortune, without support, without useful contacts', who had died a lieutenant-general and Governor of Douai.

There were certain rewards to be especially coveted by deserving officers. There existed an institution, the Order of Saint-Lazare, of which Louvois was Chancellor, for the support of 150 officers 'disabled in the service of the King'. There was the possibility, even, of becoming a Knight of the Order of the Saint-Esprit, which began to open its ranks to military distinction. Needless to say, Saint-Simon was hostile to the change. The promotion of 2 October 1688 he described as 'the first promotion at which men of purely military merit had a place as such. M. de Louvois, who was all-powerful at that time . . . persuaded the King to bestow, as a reward for military service, that which had always been according to birth.' It was not until after the death of Louvois that the purely military Order of Saint-Louis was founded, but he had paved the way for it. There is a painting at Versailles by Jean Marot of a group of officers kneeling before Louis to receive the accolade of this Order. The scene, it must be admitted, is an anachronism. The occasion recorded took place in 1693, but the bedroom depicted was not created until 1701.

As regards recruitment of ordinary soldiers, France had, like most other countries, to resort to *racolage* – the press gang – but there is evidence to show that in hard times recruitment was easier: 'Misery is the best recruiting agent.' Louvois wanted quality as well as quantity – he wanted his soldiers well built, well dressed and well armed. He noticed, however, that recruiting officers showed a preference for tall men. On 25 February 1685, Louvois sent an instruction to the inspectors that 'His Majesty does not wish that soldiers should be measured. An old soldier should not be dismissed because he is short, nor a young and hopeful man turned away.'

The feeding of the 387,000 soldiers was both a high priority and a major administrative problem. Above all it needed to be regularised. In April 1689 the daily ration was fixed at 700 grammes of bread, 'between white and wholemeal'; the cavalry received a kilo of meat, the dragoons three quarters and the infantry half a kilo. To this was added half a litre of the *boisson du pays*. In the north this was normally beer.

Another problem was that of accommodation. Louvois and Vauban together pioneered the building of barracks, much to the relief of local populations, many of whom were victims of the system of billeting.

An important element in the morale of soldiers is the self-respect which is bred of a distinctive uniform. By the end of the Dutch war all the troops were provided with uniform – blue for the royal regiments and Gardes Françaises, red for the Suisses and grey for the rest. 'It is the intention of the King', wrote Louvois to Inspector Montbron in June 1683, 'that you should notify the cavalry which are under your orders that His Majesty desires that . . . the officers of each regiment are to be dressed uniformly and that their outfit should be regulated in such a way as to incur a minimum expenditure.'

It was with an eye to economy that Louvois insisted that 'there must be a piece of leather on the left shoulder of each soldier so that he can more easily carry his musket without wearing out his jerkin'. The piece of leather seems to have been the forerunner of the epaulette.

Perhaps the most delicate of problems confronting Louvois was that of the religion of the troops. It is always possible to treat religious belief as a means to an end and to enrol it in the service of good behaviour and obedience to the law. Louvois encouraged the practice of religion in the army and this could have been done merely with an eye to its beneficial effect on discipline. But there is evidence that he pursued it for its own ends as well. In 1690, when raising two regiments in Alsace, he insisted on the appointment of extra chaplains who spoke German. 'It would be better to incur this expense', he wrote, 'than to allow soldiers in the said regiments, who do not understand French, to die without making their confessions.'

The spiritual welfare of the French army seems to have been catered for reasonably well. The marquis de Feuquières records that 'for some time the hospitals of the army have been followed by a number of Récollets for ministering to the religious needs of the sick and wounded; their vehicles and their horses are paid for by the King, as well as the carts for transporting the baggage and furnishings of the chapel'.

Before a battle it was customary for the chaplains to give a blessing to the troops accompanied by a homily which was only too often too long. The marquis de Valfons records an occasion when a commander interrupted with the words: 'Soldiers! What *Monsieur l'abbé* is saying is that there is no salvation for cowards. *Vive le Roi!*'

One of the points at which poverty can hurt most is the inability to pay for a decent funeral. This need was recognised and provided for in Louis' army. The funeral of a soldier, Albert Babeau records in his study of military life, was a dignified and reverent occasion. The whole Company paraded for the event. The arms of the deceased soldier were carried ceremonially behind the coffin, which was escorted by flambeaux.

This was, of course, for the Catholics. Huguenots were fairly numerous among the officers and other ranks in the army. Corvisier puts the overall proportion as high as one tenth, but in Swiss and German regiments it was more like one third. Louvois was naturally anxious not to bring such pressure to bear on them that might cause them to defect to the enemies of France. He allowed Huguenots in the forces freedom to worship in their own way. Where his own domain of Barbezieux was concerned, however, he was more anxious to rid himself of the Protestants and gave orders that the persecution should be carried out on his own lands 'more harshly than elsewhere'.

On 7 November 1685, less than a month after the Revocation of the Edict of Nantes, Louvois wrote to the maréchal de Boufflers on the subject of the newly converted. 'You must be on your guard against letting them believe that we wish to establish the Inquisition in France, and it would be better to make use of the way of kindness.'

He hoped to achieve conversion by bribery. The tariff was straightforward: 2 pistoles for a private soldier, 4 for a sergeant; an annual sum of 200 livres for a lieutenant and 300 rising to 600 for captains. It was a system, however, open to abuse. Corvisier records Catholic soldiers becoming Protestant in order to claim their pistoles for converting back to Catholicism.

It is generally true that those who excel in any particular area of competence tend to overrate its relative importance. Louvois excelled in administration; but he does not seem always to have understood that administration exists for the army, not the army for administration.

Had Louvois confined himself to matters of administration, all might have been well. Unfortunately he did not. He tried to take over the direction of the campaign. This was noticed by Spanheim. 'Although the command of the armies', he observed, 'during the whole course of this war was given to generals of such high reputation as the prince de Condé and M. de Turenne ... nevertheless they were not ordinarily entrusted with more than the responsibility for the execution, and thus to conduct no operations or proceedings that were not stipulated in the orders of M. de Louvois, who was authorised by the King.' Not unnaturally this set Louvois at loggerheads with first Condé and later Turenne, 'who both endured with impatience', writes General d'Ambert, 'this subordination in a profession of which they believed they had a sufficient understanding not to need to be ruled by the opinions of M. de Louvois and to depend on his orders'. There can be little doubt, however, that most of the orders came from the King. On one occasion Louvois wrote to Turenne: 'I feel obliged to tell you that it would be very advisable, when you do not think that you can carry out something which His Majesty commands you, for you to explain to him at full length the reasons which prevented you, he having taken great exception to the fact that you have not yet done so.'

In September 1673, Turenne, one of Louis' greatest generals, received a communication from Louvois giving him a comprehensive plan of campaign and ending: 'Here is what His Majesty thinks about the action of his army which you command, and in respect of which, to anyone other than yourself, he would send a positive order to execute it. But in view of the confidence which he has in you, and since what might seem, from a long way off, difficult or ruinous to the army, could appear the exact opposite to those who are present on the site, His Majesty leaves you entire liberty to do what you judge appropriate.'

In spite of that concluding vote of confidence, Turenne was not pleased with the tenor of the letter. He wrote in reply: 'I can see clearly the King's intentions and I will do all that I can to conform with them.' He ends with a sarcastic twist: 'you will permit me to say that I do not think it was in His Majesty's interests to give precise orders from so far away to the most incapable man in France'.

Louvois used to say that administration was not, like a victory, a matter of improvisation. That is perhaps true. A single victory may well be won by improvisation, but, as General d'Ambert insists, this is not the case with a skilfully conducted campaign. 'In order to plan the whole and to conduct it day by day, a man must meditate. That was the merit of Turenne, who never carried off a spectacular victory like Austerlitz or Wagram, but conducted his warfare step by step and was a master of it beyond compare.'

This was clearly recognised by Louis. Turenne shared with him the passion for detailed information. 'M. de Turenne', wrote the Duke of York (later James II), 'wanted to see everything for himself; he went and reconnoitred, and at close range, the town which he was going to besiege; he always marked out the place at which it was necessary to open the trenches and was present there himself.'

Louvois was more ready to operate through the King's Intendants than through the King's generals. In 1673 the prince de Condé was commanding the troops in Holland. The Intendant Robert was putting extreme pressure on the local inhabitants to extract all the money that he could from them. On 6 March he wrote to Louvois: 'I can assure you that I am following so well your intention not to spare the country that I am very sure you would never, if you were present, allow all the cruelties which I commit in order to gain the small amount of money which I obtain from them.' A month later Louvois wrote back to him: 'I have received the statement of the contributions. The total sum exceeded my hopes. I beg you not to tire of your aggression but to push these matters with all the rigour imaginable.'

In April Condé arrived at Utrecht and was indignant to see such pillage committed by the French government. Generals are often capable of magnanimity towards the conquered, and Condé was no exception. On 25 April he wrote to Louvois: 'I cannot forbear from saying to you that I find the attitude of these people here quite other from what it was a year ago. They are all in despair on account of the insupportable taxes which are imposed upon them every day. It seems to me that the profit derived from this, taking into account what could have been obtained by lenience, is very mediocre and not worth the cruel hatred which it has attracted. I do not know that it is in the King's interest to continue thus.'

Louvois' answer was true to form. 'The King knows perfectly well that the taxes which he has ordered M. Robert to levy on the people of Holland cannot have put them in a good humour, nor made them wish to live under his dominion; but His Majesty decided that the money was worth more than their good graces . . . That is why He desired that Your Highness should show himself as aggressive and pitiless as you would be the opposite if you followed your natural inclination.'

At the same time Louvois wrote to M. Robert, asking him to omit no severities in order to get all the money out of the country that he possibly could and assuring him of Condé's support. Louvois even went so far as to use Robert to intervene in what could be legitimately regarded as a matter of military discipline. On 3 July he wrote: 'You must prevent the troops from committing disorders, of which His Majesty has often received complaints, and make your authority felt.'

Turenne was killed at the battle of Salzbach on 27 July 1675 and it was noticed that he was replaced by generals such as the maréchal d'Humières or the duc de Luxembourg, who were submissive to Louvois. 'That is to say', concludes Spanheim, 'that M. de Louvois was able to establish and to maintain himself as absolute master in his department of the War Office, in which the King relied on him completely.'

A constant problem in the high command was that of rank. The upper aristocracy would often consent to serve under a prince of the blood royal and their endless jealousies and jostling for position could cause serious problems of discipline. The maréchal de Bellefonds felt it beneath him to serve under Turenne. Louis' reaction was as swift as it was severe. Through Louvois he ordered Bellefonds 'to leave this very day for Tours [he had a property near Bourgueil] and to remain there until further notice, and with the prohibition to exercise the functions of a maréchal de France'. Louvois adds on his own account: 'You must recognise His Majesty's disposition against those who will not obey. The point at issue here, Monsieur, is not just one of not serving during this campaign, or of incurring His Majesty's displeasure, or of going off to spend the rest of your life in a province, but also of losing all your positions ... You will permit me to say that there is no other course of action open but to obey a master who says that such is his wish.'

One of Louvois' limitations was his inability to appreciate other men. He might, grudgingly, have admitted that Turenne or Condé understood the art of war and that Vauban understood the art of fortification, but he did not admit that their opinions on other topics might be worth listening to.

On 15 August 1683, Vauban wrote to Louvois suggesting possible terms of a treaty on typically humanitarian lines. 'In so doing,' he concludes, 'His Majesty would destroy the opinion of him which the Germans hold, and which his enemies are striving to establish on all sides, that he has designs on the Empire and even on universal monarchy.' Louvois reacted immediately against this intrusion, as he saw it, by an engineer into the affairs of the Conseil du Roi: 'As for the memoir,' he wrote, 'which I return to you in order that you may destroy it, as well as the draft which you made of it, I would say to you that if you were not more capable in the matter of fortification than the contents of your memoir give reason to believe that you are in the matters dealt with therein, you would not be worthy of serving the "King of Narsingue", who had an engineer who could neither read nor write nor draw.' Vauban had the good sense not to answer.

Anyone so close to the King and so powerful as Louvois was certain to incur the hostility of the envious; anyone who used such power in such a bullying and aggressive way was certain to have many enemies. Louvois has attracted, both from his contemporaries and from later historians, much hostile criticism. He was, for all his faults, a big enough man to admit a mistake and to take the blame for it on himself. In early 1690, when negotiations between Louis and Victor-Amadeus of Savoy were critically tense, Louvois was detained at Chaville with a high fever. In dictating instructions to the maréchal de Catinat he said 'or' when he meant to say 'and'. His two requirements therefore appeared as alternatives. A few days later he discovered his mistake. He immediately confessed this to Louis and wrote to Catinat assuring him: 'I did not fail to give an account of this to His Majesty so that he may know that you are not at fault.'

On 16 July Louvois died suddenly. The duc de Saint-Simon, who had no love for him, wrote describing Louis' apparent emotions on hearing the news. 'Although I was hardly fifteen years old, I wished to see the countenance of the King on an occasion of this quality.' Louis was about to begin his *promenade des jardins*. 'I went and waited for him and followed the whole promenade. He appeared with his customary majesty, but with a little indefinable *je ne sais quoi* of freedom and deliverance which I found sufficiently surprising . . . I noticed that, instead of going to see his fountains, he walked up and down the length of the balustrade overlooking the Orangerie, from which he could see, on turning back towards the Château, the Maison de la Surintendance in which Louvois had just died.'

Louvois' son, the marquis de Barbezieux, was only twenty-three at the time and not really a person capable of filling the post, to which he had, however, a hereditary right. Louis would have preferred the marquis de Chamlay, but Chamlay would not interfere with the right of succession. The result of this was that Louis had to take a far greater hand in the management of the army. His letters are written in a very different style from that of his former Minister of War.

12

Louis in Court and Camp

The marriage alliance between Louis and the Infanta of Spain had been agreed on the condition that she renounced all claims to the Spanish succession in return for which a dowry of 500,000 écus d'or was to be paid. As the dowry was never paid, the 'rights', which were nowhere defined, of Marie-Thérèse could be claimed as being still valid. The claim, however, was only strong enough to provide a pretext for resuming the war.

The marquis de Saint-Maurice, the newly appointed ambassador from Savoy, describes the situation. Alone among the ambassadors at that time he was privileged to accompany Louis into Flanders. He was thus particularly well placed to report on the activities of the army and the intrigues of the Court, on the policies of Louis' ministers, on the decline of Louise de La Vallière and on the rise of Mme de Montespan.

He was an acute observer of events and a skilful painter of portraits. He offers a picture of Louis which was drawn from life. 'In contrast with the mask of impassability with which Saint-Simon depicts him,' writes Saint-Maurice's editor Jean Lemoine, 'we find ourselves in the presence of a character that is both human and alive ... rejoicing openly at good news, vexed by bad news, sometimes giving his ministers a good dressing-down and treating them *de haut en bas*, but also indefatigable when on campaign, sleeping on straw, unshakeable in danger ... kind and generous to his servants; "on ne vit jamais roi si honnête homme".'

But Saint-Maurice's admiration for the character of the King and for the power of France did not blind him to the signs of approaching decadence. 'He was appalled at the enormous sums which the King spent on his household, on his pleasures, on his buildings ... He points to the dangers of excessive protectionism ... He gets a glimpse of the day when France will succumb before the combined efforts of a European coalition.'

On 6 May 1667, Saint-Maurice wrote to the Duke of Savoy that war was imminent. 'It is certain that at the end of the month the King will enter Flanders.' A few days later the matter was beyond doubt. 'The King wishes to be at the head of his army ... Everyone wants to follow the King ... Everyone is getting into debt, pledging their silver plate and jewellery, obliging their tenants to provide them with more money; there are no more horses [in Paris], everything is horribly expensive and it is no longer possible even to find heavy canvas for making tents.' The *Gazette* caught the same note of excitement. 'Everyone is on fire with a noble ardour to seize the opportunity of distinguishing himself, inspired by the presence of this great King, whose continual activity one cannot cease to admire – His Majesty himself giving those orders, by day and by night, which he judges necessary and taking less repose than any officer in the army.'

On 16 May the King set out from Saint-Germain for Amiens with an army of 35,000. The Queen also went to Amiens. 'The King has left her Regent,' continues Saint-Maurice; 'that is the right of a Queen who has produced a Dauphin.' The Queen travelled in a large coach, capable of holding eight persons, and always escorted by M. de Bissy with 700 horsemen. The King joined her and rode beside the carriage, bringing a further escort of 200 light cavalry, sword in hand; Saint-Maurice observed: 'I have never seen anything so fine.'

With the Queen went her ladies, and among the ladies were Louise de La Vallière and Mme de Montespan. The Governor of the Low Countries, the marquis de Castel Rodrigo, in an attempt to retain the loyalty of the Flemish, turned this to his advantage and put it about that Louis was a tyrant and also 'a soft and effeminate man who always takes his mistress with him in the very coach of the Queen'.

It was to be an eventful journey. As they approached Landrécies the river overflowed and the occupants of the royal coach were obliged to spend the night in a very small house with only one bed. The Queen, protesting that the idea was horrible, claimed the bed. Mattresses were found for Louis, for Monsieur and Madame, for Mademoiselle and finally for Louise de La Vallière and Mme de Montespan. It would have made a good scene for a Mozart opera – the Queen outraged by la Montespan; La Vallière bewailing her lost position; Mademoiselle jealous of La Vallière because of a rumour that Lauzun was her lover; Monsieur and Madame deeply distrusting each other; and Louis, unembarrassed by so much embarrassment.

There was much speculation as to whether Louise would retain the King's favour. Louis had just, on 13 May, created her a duchess, conferring upon her 'the highest and most honourable of titles which a singular affection, aroused in our heart by an infinity of rare perfections, has inspired us for several years in her favour'. When the Premier Président had come to Saint-Germain to receive the King's orders for the creation of the dukedom, Louis, holding the parchment in his hand, said: 'Monsieur le Premier Président, when you were young did you never indulge in the follies of youth?' It was a time for tact. The Premier Président made 'un joli discours' in which he demonstrated to his sovereign that at that age there were very few who were not guilty of 'quelque légerté'.

With the dukedom of Vaujours and the barony of Saint-Christophe went the opulent estates attached to them. This endowment of La Vallière must be seen in connection with Louis' desire to make provision for their daughter Marie-Anne, who was on the same occasion declared legitimate. The timing of this act – shortly before Louis departed for the campaign in Flanders – was perhaps significant. In his memoirs he stated that 'having no intention of going to the army in order to remain at a safe distance from all danger, I felt it was justice to secure for this child the honour of her birth and to give her mother an establishment appropriate to the affection which I have had for her for the last six years'.

Louise's only reaction to her elevation and endowment was to feel ashamed. Mme de Sévigné described her as 'the violet which hid in the grass and blushed alike to be a mistress, a mother and a duchess.' All that she wanted was Louis' love and this was precisely what she was losing. She had been paid off. Saint-Maurice noted that 'the King has been in an ill humour these last days, either on account of La Vallière or because of the war'.

From 14 to 24 May the new duchess continued to follow the Court, but when Louis left to rejoin his army she was ordered to retire to Versailles. On 20 June, however, when the Queen and her ladies were awaiting the King at La Fère, it was suddenly announced that Louise had come back. Mme de Montespan declared: 'I marvel at her effrontery in daring to present herself before the Queen . . . It is certain that the King did not send for her.' Later she added: 'Heaven forbid that I should ever become the King's mistress! But if I were I should be shamefaced in the presence of the Queen.'

This sort of situation afforded exactly the material which was hoped for so eagerly by the gossips of the Court, but their speculations as to the movements of the King's heart were somewhat out of place. Louis was much more interested in the course of the war. Saint-Maurice was no doubt right when he reported back that La Vallière 'was unable to recognise that it was time for her to retire . . . It is thought that la Montespan will succeed her; however, all this is mere conjecture, the King applies himself entirely to the war and to glory and gives evidence of not bothering about the women.'

On 16 June Saint-Maurice wrote from the camp at Charleroi. It had been a long march and Louis had gone on foot with his troops. Turenne told him that he was fatiguing himself too much and that he risked falling ill. Louis replied: 'Monsieur le maréchal, you are no lover of my glory if you speak to me like that.' There were times, however, when Louis was able to live in greater comfort. His camp was truly royal. 'The King's tents', observed Saint-Maurice, 'are the most spacious and superb that it would be possible to see, all of them lined with damask or satin and in each of them there are hung three or four chandeliers of gilded wood.'

Two things particularly impressed the ambassador: that 'the King paid for any damage done by his soldiers' and that he had never seen 'so good a discipline among troops'. Louis was out to win the attachment of the people, not to conquer them. In June the *Gazette* reported, in its usual glowing terms: 'One thing which will be of no small advantage in gaining the affections of the people is that His Majesty's army observes a discipline so strict that the cattle graze in front of the camp and the labourers plough their fields without being in any way incommoded.' Louis claimed in his journal (18 July): 'I have observed such order at the outset of the march that no harm was done to the inhabitants of the places whom I hoped to win round by this good treatment – even to the extent of paying for all the corn which I was obliged to commandeer for forage.'

Louis commanded his own army himself, wrote Choisy, 'with a clearness of vision, an understanding of the art of war and a good fortune, the like of which has never been seen. Everyone knows how this great prince exposed himself to danger and himself went into the smallest details of the commandment of an army.' The correspondence between Louvois and Chazerat, Director of Fortifications at Ypres, gives a typical example of the latter. 'At Elverdinghe they were making use of lime of inferior quality; the King desires that in future they use the lime of Warneton.'

Louis, in fact, seems to have possessed all the qualities of a great general. The chevalier de Quincy, author of *Maximes et Instructions sur l'Art Militaire*, gives his own list of what those qualities should be. The general must have a complete familiarity with all the functions of those under his command and an accurate knowledge of the lie of the land. 'It is even of importance that he should be born of a noble family, because the more illustrious it is, the more it inspires respect in subordinates. He must make every effort to gain the confidence of his troops, which he may acquire by his affability towards the officers and other ranks, by the soundness of his planning, by the well-directed execution of his intentions. He should be both magnificent and magnanimous; he should expend a great deal on spies in order to be perfectly informed of the movements of the enemy and to avoid causing unnecessary fatigue to his men.'

De Quincy commends an almost puritanical morality and earnestness. 'He must exercise a considerable severity in all that pertains to military discipline, must have religion not only in his heart but in his outward conduct . . . He must punish without exception any impiety or irreligion in order to prevent, as far as possible, those disorders which sometimes accompany warfare.'

Even before the Flanders campaign, in 1665, a medal had been struck showing Louis, on a rather baroque-looking parade ground, drilling the Gardes Françaises in person. It bears the inscription: 'Prelude to Victory. Discipline restored to the militia.'

Another aid to discipline was the regular holding of military reviews. In the spring of 1666 Louis reviewed his troops near Mouchy. It lasted three days. 'There were fifteen hundred soldiers,' wrote Lefèvre d'Ormesson; 'it is generally agreed that it would be impossible to see finer or more magnificent men, the officers having gone to great expense.'

Louis was obviously delighted with his army and was in his element when on campaign with them. This was not necessarily true of those who followed him. They were for the most part left to look after themselves and often suffered considerable hardships. In May they had very bad weather, cold and extremely wet. 'I learnt that the King', wrote Saint-Maurice, 'had called a halt at Charleroi to do some repairs to the place and to give some rest to his soldiers, who were in a state of unwonted fatigue; the baggage wagons not having followed, no one, not even the greatest of seigneurs, has either changed his linen or slept on a bed these last eleven days, and the King was obliged to sleep in his coach.' Between Charleroi and Tournay, Saint-Maurice never saw his bed, but was obliged to sleep under a tree wrapped in his cloak. Only on one occasion did his coach catch up with him and the packhorse carrying his food often failed to arrive.

In June the weather turned hot and dry. What Saint-Maurice now suffered from most was the dust. On one occasion he described it as being 'so thick that we cannot see one another at three paces'. But, whatever the difficulties, the discipline and morale of the troops were maintained; 'they always marched and camped in good order, the King always with them at the head of the army and at the camp between the two lines. He is indefatigable and Monsieur also; they never leave each other's side.'

Monsieur's first reaction to the declaration of war was to provide himself with tents that were elegant, suited to his rank and well provided with mirrors and crystal chandeliers. His senior chaplain, Daniel Cosnac, Bishop of Valence, saw this as evidence that the young prince's first concern was still only with vanities and bagatelles. Seeing in the Flanders campaign Monsieur's last chance of rescuing his reputation, Cosnac did not mince his words. 'I spoke to him as a member of his household who believes that he has the right to treat his master roughly because he loves him.' Monsieur accepted the rebuke. 'You shall be satisfied,' he promised; 'follow me to Flanders.' Cosnac then proceeded to brief him on how he should behave at the front. 'I suggested that he should consider building up his reputation by being liberal with his money, his praise and his affection, because all those things, if well managed and conducted, were more capable of winning him esteem than even courage. Above all I exhorted him to show no signs of becoming weary of the life which he will be leading but, on the contrary, to make it clear to everyone that this is the sort of life which he finds most agreeable and that he must never abandon the army even when the King had returned.'

Monsieur put the document containing this advice safely away, promising to turn it to good account. It appears that he did so. The abbé de Choisy tells how he inspected the guards and visited the trenches before the King got word of it, and encouraged the troops by a lavish distribution of money. On the next day 'he showed himself valiantly at the most advanced posts'.

The Queen also proved herself equal to the rigours of a campaign. On 23 July Saint-Maurice wrote: 'We have been on the march from nine o'clock until six ... The Queen and the ladies arrived at Arras all horribly fatigued by the long marches and by the heat and the dust ... but this does not dishearten them in any way, but only goes to show that their beauty becomes greater in sufferings and in labours. They have a pride which demonstrates that they are resolved to surmount any danger and only seek for enemies to fight.'

At Tournay on 21 June, writes the chevalier de Quincy, Louis made a reconnaissance with Turenne in the course of which he exposed himself 'with such audacity that Turenne threatened to resign his command if the King would not put himself in safety'. It is exactly this scene which is depicted in one of the series of Gobelin tapestries, *Histoire du Roy*. The King, instead of being represented, as in all the others, in the forefront of the scene, is shown in the middle distance. He is the most highly placed figure in the composition and easily identified by his red plumes: he is thus among those closest to the enemy and offering an easy target. Ormesson records in his journal for 9 July 1667: 'This morning the Parlement considered remonstrating with the King on his exposing himself in the trenches like an ordinary soldier, and begging him to take care of himself.'

On 24 August Saint-Maurice wrote from the camp before Lille: 'The King is all night and part of the day on horseback and completely unprotected; he never misses a bivouac and visits the batteries but not the trenches, because the officers of the army do not want him to.' The other ranks did not want him to either. 'We were to see him in the trenches before Lille,' wrote Choisy, 'attracting by his courage the fine words of a common soldier who, seeing him exposed to musket fire, and one of the pages of the Grande Ecurie killed just behind him, took him roughly by the arm and said: "Get out of it! This is no place for you." '

Louis had arrived on the scene on 10 August and on the night of the 17th the Governor capitulated. 'My orders had been executed with such zeal', the King wrote in his memoirs, 'that the town was reduced to the last extremities before the Spanish had even heard that it was in danger.'

Choisy relates an anecdote about the siege of Lille which illustrates a sort of *esprit de gentilhomme* between adversaries. 'The comte de Brouai, who was Governor on behalf of the King of Spain, sent every morning some ice to the King, having learnt that he had none in the camp. One day the King said to the gentleman who came on his behalf: "Tell M. de Brouai that I am most obliged to him for the ice, but could he please send me a little more?" "Sire," replied the Spaniard without hesitation, "he thinks that the siege will last a long time and is afraid that he may run out of it." He made his bow and went off. But the old Charost, who was standing behind the King, shouted after him: "Tell M. de Brouai not to behave like the Governor of Douai who capitulated like a knave!" The King turned round and said: "Charost, are you mad?" "I beg your pardon, Sire," he replied, "but the comte de Brouai is my cousin." ' Not all Louis' enemies respected his desire for iced drinks. Lefèvre d'Ormesson noted, in July 1667, that 'Castel Rodrigo is guilty of further brutishness disgraceful in a gentleman; he has had all the ice houses broken down in order to deprive the King of the satisfaction of having his drinks chilled'.

The capture of Lille provides the subject-matter for another of the tapestries. Louis, in his red plumed hat, and seated on his light bay horse, is receiving the news from the marquis d'Humières. Behind him are two other men on horseback. One can easily be recognised as Turenne; the other was to play an increasingly important role in the vital areas of siegecraft and fortifications: Sebastien Le Prestre de Vauban.

'You are right to esteem Monsieur de Vauban as highly as you do,' wrote Boileau on 21 May 1684 to his friend Brosselle; 'in my opinion he is one of the men of our century of the most outstanding merit and to say in a word what I think of him, I think there is more than one Marshal of France who, on encountering him, would not blush to be a Marshal of France.' It was not until January 1703 that the dignity of Marshal was finally conferred upon Vauban, and he took his elevation with a becoming humility. He was the first engineer to be thus honoured.

Saint-Simon has left one of his brilliant little pen portraits of the man. 'Vauban, whose name was Le Prestre, was, at best, a *petit gentilhomme* of Burgundy, but perhaps the most honourable and the most virtuous man of his century, and, while he had the highest reputation as the man most skilled in the art of siegecraft and fortification, remained the most simple, the most genuine and the most modest of men. He was of medium height, thick-set and with the bearing of a soldier, but with an outward appearance that was boorish and coarse, not to say brutal and ferocious. He was nothing of the sort; no man was ever more meek, more obliging, more civil, more respectful, but without any artificiality; protective to the point of miserliness of the lives of his men, and possessing a valour that took everything upon himself and gave the credit for everything to others.'

His contribution to the military successes of the reign was prodigious. In the first place his undertakings were on a colossal scale. At Longwy the operation involved the shifting of 640,000 cubic metres of earth and the erection of 120,000 cubic metres of masonry. It was this capacity to 'think big' which contributed so much to the *Grand Siècle*. 'We do not live in a reign', wrote Colbert, 'which is content with little things. With due regard to proportion, it is impossible to imagine anything which can be too great.' Without the financial backing of Colbert, Vauban might never have been able to realise his genius.

But it was Louvois who was really responsible for recognising the genius of Vauban. It is difficult, sometimes, to separate out the opinions of Louis and of Louvois. The latter seems often to be a sort of interface. But Louis was very clearly in possession of all the facts. There is no reason to doubt that Louvois' letter to Vauban of 23 November 1668 means what it says: 'it is His Majesty's desire that Vauban's plan [for Lille] should be put into execution point for point'. The fortification of Lille was the first great work of Vauban and perhaps the most important – 'sa fille ainée dans la fortification', as he called it himself. It was in September 1667 that Louis determined on the newly captured citadel of Lille as the key fortress to the north-east defences of his realm. The chevalier de Clerville was still Chief Engineer and produced a plan which did not meet with the royal approval. Vauban was given his chance and he set himself to the task with energy – 'Il travaille', wrote the marquis d'Humières, 'avec la dernière application.'

In plan, Vauban's design for the citadel had the geometrical precision of a snowflake – one five-pointed star superimposed upon another and circumscribed by a ten-pointed star. In section the three 'stars' are seen as three levels, each overtopping the one in front. The points of each star were elongated, forming a projection the shape of a bishop's mitre, and the cross-fire made possible by the superimposition of these projections was devastating. The long, sloping parapets enabled the infantry to use their muskets in almost complete safety and to move with ease and under cover from one position to another. The effect upon morale which such a system must have produced was not the least of its virtues.

The demands of a campaign in Flanders did not, however, put a stop to the ceremonial functions of the Court. Even before the signing of the peace of Aix-la-Chapelle, on 25 March 1668, the Dauphin was baptised at Saint-Germain. It was an occasion for regal heraldry and papal pomp. The courtyards of the Vieux Château had been made to resemble something between an opera house and a cathedral. A large royal box had been constructed on the north side and a gallery to the south, where Lully conducted his musicians. A massive silver cuvette, 1.5 metres long, 1.5 metres high and 1.25 metres across, served as the font. The Pope, Clement IX, was godfather and represented on this occasion by the Cardinal de Vendôme, assisted by the Cardinal Antoine Barberini, *legatus a latere*, and Henrietta-Maria, represented by the princesse de Conti, was godmother.

Those involved in the performance – for it can be called little else – processed from the Château Neuf to the main entrance and took up their places. Not much thought had been given to anyone else. The marquis de Saint-Maurice arrived to find such a press at the barrier that he waited for the Introducteur des Ambassadeurs, M. de Bonneuil, to procure for him a more dignified entry. He was amused to observe that Turenne, who was conducting Prince Maximilian of Bavaria, was unable to make any headway; he lost his temper and was hitting out on all sides. Turenne noticed Saint-Maurice and came over, saying, very civilly, 'that the French had no consideration for anybody'. At last M. de Bonneuil managed to clear the way for them.

The peace signed at Aix-la-Chapelle on 2 May 1668 was little more than a truce and a period of consolidation. Louis did not push his demands as far as he might have. Franche-Comté, his latest acquisition, was returned to Spain, but Louis retained his newly won rights in the south of Flanders.

Louis himself was perfectly confident about the treaty and wrote in his memoirs: 'I would not lack opportunities for a breach with Spain whenever I want one . . . Franche-Comté, which I handed back, could be reduced to such a condition that I could become the master at any time.' Great soldiers such as Condé and Turenne disapproved: a military opportunity had been thrown away. Louvois, as Minister for War, felt his position a little undermined. Even Vauban, who was no warmonger, was in favour of continuing the campaign long enough to take the town of Condé. 'A fortnight spent on it would conclude the matter and then you will not come to the conference table with empty hands. There are no judges more just than cannons; they go straight to the point and they cannot be corrupted.' The cannons in Louis' army were embossed with the words 'ratio ultima regum' – 'the final argument of kings'.

The Peace of Aix-la-Chapelle was celebrated at Versailles on 18 July with the Grand Divertissement Royal. This was the supreme moment of the existence of the old Versailles, the colourful *maison de plaisance* of Patel's painting, for in the same year the plans for enlargement were finally agreed and soon after the entertainment the work was put in hand.

The fête began in the cool of a summer evening.

> L'importune et grande chaleur
> Cédant la place à la fraîcheur,
> Ainsi que Phébus aux étoiles,
> La nuit tendit ses sombres voiles.

First came the *promenade des jardins* where Louis showed off the latest additions and embellishments. The ladies were mounted *en calèche*, a vehicle combining the ease of a bath-chair with the elegance of a Roman chariot, with colourful parasols held, like miniature canopies, over their towering coiffures. The men were on foot, swarming round Louis as he stopped here and there, now explaining the latest scheme for the extension of the gardens, now pausing to discuss the mythology relating to one of the newly erected statues.

The gardens had been expanding in all directions for the last four years. The space available made possible the construction of a theatre capable of holding 3,000 spectators and a Salle de Bal in the form of a vast octagon, its walls panelled with marble and porphyry and decorated with swags and festoons of fresh flowers. 'There is not a palace in the world', exclaimed Mlle de Scudéry, 'which has a salon so beautiful, so vast, so tall or so superb.'

When the guests arrived at the Cabinet de Verdure they found the sideboard loaded with delicacies and all the trees around hung with fruits, fat oranges from Portugal, currants from Holland, and every sort of pear, peach and plum there for the plucking. One of the tables supported a palace of marzipan and sugar which, as soon as Louis and his party left, was broken up and consumed by the crowds.

Passing by the Fontaine des Cygnes, soon to be the Bassin d'Apollon, for which the group of the chariot of the Sun was already ordered, the guests arrived at the theatre, erected by Vigarani in the Allée de Saturne. It was constructed entirely of foliage and hung with tapestry on the inside and lit by thirty-two crystal chandeliers. Here was performed 'une agréable comédie de Molière', *Georges Dandin*.

Already at this date Louis was beginning to dream of a new Versailles – a palace without rival in Europe, which could be set in a landscape reshaped by Le Nôtre, extending as far as the eye could see. But for the present the gardens were too small and the crowds were too big. 'There was never so great a concourse of people', noted Saint-Maurice, 'and never such great disorder, and together with that the lack of care and precaution taken by the Sieur de Bonneuil and the lack of experience of the officers and the Gardes du Corps, who only knew how to make war.' The envoys of the Emperor, of the Kings of Sweden and Portugal, withdrew with their suites after having been repulsed and even maltreated at the entrance to the Comédie.

In the small hours of the morning the guests began to make their way through the dark alleys of the Petit Parc towards the Château. But even now a further surprise awaited them. The Château itself and the gardens, right down to the Bassin des Cygnes, were aglow with a phosphorescence which seemed their own; on the last occasion on which it was to serve as the background for Louis' magnificence, Versailles had become 'véritablement le palais du Soleil'. But as the courtiers stood enraptured by the sight, the crash of gunpowder rent the air, and on every side the woods and alleys leapt into a blaze of fireworks; fountains added showers of golden rain to their waters, the monsters round Latona spewed fire and the whole surface of the Bassin des Cygnes appeared to be a sea of flames; so closely were the two elements of fire and water allied that they could hardly be distinguished. No sooner had the fires on the earth died down than a thousand rockets streaked into the air, breaking into great petals of light, and tracing the royal cypher, the inverted Ls, in figures of fire across the sky, where already the day, as if jealous of the splendours of such a night, was beginning to show its morning lustre.

For the professionals, the four years which separated the Peace of Aix-la-Chapelle from the beginning of the Dutch war were to be a period of consolidation. For Vauban they were probably the busiest years in his busy life. But for the Court, life in Paris, Saint-Germain or Fontainebleau resumed the customary round of entertainments and Louis was able to indulge in his favourite sport – *la Chasse*.

'The practice of hunting ought to follow the exercise of warfare,' wrote Buffon. 'To know how to control horses and how to wield weapons are talents common to huntsmen and to warriors.' The stag, being the most noble of the beasts in the forest, is reserved for the pleasure of the most noble among men. 'From time immemorial hunting has been the pastime of heroes.'

Louis XIV was as pleased to see his nobility skilled in the chase as he was pleased to excel in it himself. It was the love of hunting that had led the Kings of France into many of their building ventures. Two of the most important were the creations of François I – Fontainebleau and Chambord.

Louis had visited Chambord on his way back to Paris after his wedding. It was in the autumn of 1668, a few months after the Peace of Aix-la-Chapelle, that Louis first decided to bring his Court here, when October had brought the trees to their most resplendent glory and laid its golden carpet along the rides and alleys of the park. The impact was immediate. 'There is no royal house of a more noble and magnificent design,' wrote Pellisson; 'the park and forest which surround it are full of ancient trees, tall and spreading, which in times past would have been consulted as oracles.' They were more than commonly fortunate with the weather, and the blue skies and autumn sunshine set off to the greatest advantage the blue and gold uniforms of the Court – for Louis, with his meticulous eye for detail, ordained the colours that were to be worn by his followers on their visits to his various palaces.

This sort of magnificence was new to the Blésois – new, almost, to Pellisson; 'Nothing', he wrote, 'could equal the magnificence of the equipages.' Everywhere they went they brought their own atmosphere with them; it seemed as if 'Le Brun, Mansart and Le Nôtre had employed all their talent and all their knowledge on the places passed by the King'. Even the modest château of M. d'Herbault became 'as it were the Louvre or the Tuileries as he did the honours to his King. No one has ever seen a fête prepared in so short a time.'

There exists in the Cabinet des Estampes a collection of drawings from the papers of Robert de Cotte. Among them is a plan of Chambord, with flaps for each successive floor. Such plans would have been of the greatest use to anyone allocating rooms to members of the Court on the occasion of a visit. It shows that there were, in the château proper, 218 apartments, mostly consisting of two rooms, one large, one small, though the more important apartments had the addition of a second small room.

A further 120 beds, arranged with barrack-like uniformity, occupied the mansardes over the stables. Chambord could offer sleeping room in proper beds for some 350 persons. The servants would have had pallets which were unrolled when required and would not have figured on the plan.

The plan provides two other details of domestic interest. Behind the alcove in the King's bedroom was installed a *poêle* – a porcelain stove in the Alsatian style. It was approached by a narrow passage cut in the thickness of the wall, so that servants could maintain the temperature of the bedroom without intruding on its privacy.

The plan also marks ten kitchens on the ground floor, the two largest being in the wing adjoining the apartments of François I in the north-east tower. Under the Valois, Chambord had been the permanent setting for an occasional, rather gorgeous camp. Now its naked walls were clothed in panelling and the house was adapted to more luxurious inhabitation.

In 1670 the visit was particularly memorable. The magnificent opportunities afforded by the great forest for the sport of kings were the *raison d'être* of Chambord. The Grand Veneur commanded a personnel of some thirty experts. It was he who conveyed the news to courtiers of the most coveted of privileges: 'Le Roi vous permet de prendre l'habit d'équipage.'

When there was a hunt the *quêteurs* were out at break of day to identify the quarry. If possible they discovered the *gîte* where the animal had slept. They had to be able to tell by the imprints in the ground, by the *fumées* (the excrements) and any other evidence vouchsafed them, the age, sex and number of points of the stags. This information was brought to the King at his *lever* and when he had decided which beast was to be attacked, the party moved off to the place where the huntsman had made his *brisée*, marking with a broken sapling the spot from which the quarry could be traced. Detachments of hounds were stationed at likely places to be released at critical moments and join with the rest of the pack.

Once the quarry was sighted the musical accompaniment to the hunt began, and announced to the field the quality and movements of the stag. The number of points could be identified by the length of the opening call, the *gresle*. A hart royal was greeted with an appropriately imposing fanfare, and by means of the succeeding calls – *au bois, volcelet, passage de l'eau* – the course of the hunt could be traced through forest and farmland, through village and vineyard, until the horns sounded the *hallali* and the beast was forced to his last stand.

The architecture of Chambord, with its balustraded walk round the donjon at third-floor level, enabled those who were not mounted to follow the hunt. Much of the day was devoted to the chase; in the evenings there was often a comedy. Here on 14 October 1670 was performed the première of the *Bourgeois Gentilhomme* in which Molière and Lully so happily collaborated. It was a difficult moment for Molière, for Louis gave not the least sign of approval or amusement. But he made up for it the next day by explaining that 'he had been carried away by the manner in which it was produced' and ending with the fine compliment: 'Vous n'avez rien fait qui m'ait plus diverti.'

Meanwhile, in October 1668, Vauban had begun his great work on the fortification of Dunkirk, which Louis had bought, seven years previously, from Charles II. Vauban's correspondence with Louvois was almost daily. A lot may be learnt about these two great servants of the King, and, indeed, about the King himself, from these letters.

Louvois, impatient as ever, rebuked Vauban for taking so long. On 8 October, unperturbed, Vauban replied that 'it was necessary to do things

one at a time and still have space to reflect. This is not a children's game.'
Six weeks later (23 November), he wrote again: 'I humbly beseech you
to have a little trust in a man, who is wholly yours, and not to get angry
if, in these letters which I have the honour to write to you, I prefer the
truth, however unpolished, to a cowardly complacency which could serve
only to deceive you and to dishonour me.'

The difference between the two men becomes increasingly obvious as
the correspondence continues. Louvois regarded the army as a machine
which must be made to function with maximum efficiency. Only such
expenditure as was strictly necessary to this end could be justified. Vauban
regarded soldiers as human beings whose welfare needed to be considered.
In November 1670 Louvois allocated a task force of 22,000 men to
accelerate the prodigious earthworks at Dunkirk, Tournai and Ath. The
transport of earth from the excavations to the parapets was achieved by
each soldier carrying a hod-load. This was hard and heavy work and
progress was slow. Vauban applied for a large number of barrows which
would have relieved the workmen and accelerated the work. Louvois
immediately rejected the idea as 'une dépense épouvantable' and foresaw
endless breakages. Hods cost only 6 or 7 sols and were not subject to
accidents. But Vauban's quiet persistence won the day and 2,000 barrows
were provided.

It was not until the spring of 1678 that Vauban had finished his great
work. On 10 May Colbert wrote to him: 'I have no doubt that you would
consider this job as one of the finest things which you have done so far,
for to all appearances it seems that you have given to Dunkirk a port
which will be capable of receiving vessels of up to 700 or 800 tons, so
that the King could keep here a squadron as large as he pleases and,
consequently, greatly increase his maritime strength.' This was a prospect
close to Colbert's heart.

This was a period of consolidation: consolidation of the string of fortified towns which were to mark the eastern frontier of France;
consolidation of the lands attaching to Louis' recent conquests – known
as *les Réunions*.

Nothing could bring to light more clearly the survival well into the
seventeenth century of feudal concepts and systems than the idea of
the suzerain and the fief – the land held from him on the condition
of homage. When a town was captured during a war it was possible for
the victor to claim suzerainty over the fiefs dependent on it. As it was not
always clear what these fiefs were – and they were seldom if ever defined
in peace treaties – there was plenty of room for legal chicanery. France
was beginning to appear to Europe as an aggressive and imperialist regime,
ready to resort to dubious procedures in order to extend her dominions.

In November 1678, Vauban drew up a memoir 'des places frontières de Flandres qu'il faudrait fortifier pour la sûreté du pays et l'obéissance du Roi'. The frontier which he had to rationalise was open and in disarray. It had been compared to a piece of Brussels lace. Vauban insists on a dual role – one defensive: 'fermer les entrées de notre pays à l'ennemi' – and the other offensive: 'nous faciliter les entrées dans le sien'. He recommends a double line in imitation of the order of battle.

His front line, of thirteen *places fortes*, was very nearly the present frontier of France – Dunkirk, Ypres, Menin, Lille, Tournai, Valenciennes, Maubeuge; his second chain of fortresses, anything between 20 and 50 kilometres behind this, followed the line Gravelines, Arras, Douai, Cambrai, Rocroi, Charleville-Mézières. Having built or improved the fortifications of these places, Vauban suggested the dismantling of those which lay outside his scheme of defence. The mathematics of this were simple: 'ten places less would be worth 30,000 men more'.

Next he turned his attention to the frontier between France and Germany, but before he even began to write his reports he stated that the possession of Strasbourg was essential to the security of France. Strasbourg guarded one of the rare bridges over the Rhine, protected by the fortress of Kehl. It had the status of a 'free town' under the Empire but the Emperor did not have direct control over it. Voltaire describes it as a republic. In many ways it was Germanic, as the architecture of the old town suggests. In August 1679 the Chambre de Réunion, sitting at Breisach, declared the whole of Alsace to be under French suzerainty, but a free town could not be caught on this particular hook. It was decided to annex Strasbourg.

Louvois master-minded the takeover. On the night of 27 September some 30,000 French troops encircled the walls of the city. Two days later the magistrates submitted. The city was confirmed in its privileges, its Senate, its university and its civil and criminal jurisdiction; it was not subjected to any taxation and continued to mint its own money. More importantly, the free exercise of the Calvinist religion, which was very strong here, was guaranteed. The cathedral, however, was returned to the Catholic Church, which had built it, and on 24 October the Bishop, François Egon de Fürstenberg, irreverently known as 'Bishop Bacchus', received Louis and his Queen here for the Te Deum. Somewhat typically a medal was struck to commemorate this occasion, engraved with the legend 'Clausa Germanis Gallia' – France closed to Germany.

In January the following year Vauban was sent to survey Franche-Comté and from thence to Provence and Roussillon. He decided to complete the last part of this journey by ship from Toulon. But it was a pirate-infested sea and Louvois would not hear of it. 'As I regard you as quite unsuitable to serve as an espalier stake in a galley, I have received the order from the King to forbid you to use this vessel . . . His intention is that you should make this journey by land.' It was, of course, safer, but it was unbearably slow. It took him five days to cover the 64 kilometres which separate Toulon from Marseille.

As ever there was a certain amount of friction between Vauban and Louvois. In May 1679, Vauban applied for higher pay for his workers in Roussillon. He was met with a refusal. 'They are able, faithful and diligent,' he persisted; 'if you do not increase their salaries they will be obliged to quit or resort to theft.' He felt it necessary to add: 'It gives me no pleasure when I am neglected and counted for less than I am.'

It is pleasing to note, however, that Louvois could, on occasion, rise to expressions of real warmth. When Vauban's daughter became engaged the King's assent was sought. It was Louvois who answered for the King, but he added a postscript of his own: 'As I do not know the son-in-law whom you propose to take, I can only say that I would do him a favour for love of you, with all my heart, on any occasion that I could be of use to him.'

The year 1680 was the most demanding yet. From the north-east frontier Vauban travelled to the south-west – the Pays Basque; he followed the Pyrenees from the Atlantic to the Mediterranean; he returned north and then south again into Alsace and ended up in Flanders. 'Please forgive my bad handwriting,' he wrote; 'I am so tired and so wet that I hardly have the strength to write.'

His business involved, however, the writing of an immense number of letters and memoirs, not to mention drawings. As so much of his time was spent on the roads he devised a sort of mobile study – a sort of *chaise-à-porteurs* for which the *porteurs* were mules and the *chaise* large enough to provide him with a desk-top and even a small library. As the inventory of his books at Bazoches indicates, Vauban had a catholic taste in literature.

In February 1680, his little procession happened to cross the path of the cortège of the Elector of Bavaria, who was escorting his daughter Marie-Christine into France to marry the Dauphin. Vauban gives a typical seventeenth-century pen portrait of her. 'She has large eyes, bright and wonderfully beautiful; she is brunette with a lovely complexion; her nose a little large and just a trifle low over the mouth, which is also on the large side but well-shaped and the lips of a good vermilion colour . . . all these made up a whole which gave her an agreeable and very spirited appearance. I did not see her on her feet, but I am told that she has a good figure; she has a great look of youth and gaiety.' She had the advantage of speaking really fluent French. Voltaire was to record that, to start with, 'she added a note of brilliance and vivacity to the Court'.

But her success at Court did not last. She had brought with her a young Piedmontese girl, Mlle Bessola, who had been one of her ladies and her closest companion in her father's Court. The more the courtiers in France showed their indifference to Marie-Christine, the more she took refuge in this solid friendship: the more she did so, the more the courtiers rejected her. Mlle Bessola had no ambition and no taste for intrigue. She was therefore of no use to courtiers who might have found in the Dauphine's favourite a means of furthering their own interests.

In December 1681, it was announced that the Dauphine was with child, and the proclamation was celebrated by public rejoicings everywhere. Louis took charge of the situation and made an appointment which broke with tradition. All Queens, including his own wife, had hitherto been tended by midwives. The children of Mme de Montespan, however, had been brought into the world by a surgeon named Lefèvre. He had by now been succeeded by his pupil and son-in-law, Clément. Louis decided that the Dauphine should be attended by Clément.

It was on 4 August 1682 that Marie-Christine felt the first pangs. Louis, who had gone to bed early, was woken at five the following morning. He immediately ordered a Mass to be said and that prayers should be offered in all the churches of Versailles, together with a generous distribution of alms to the poor. He spent the next three hours with the Dauphine and then went to the Council as usual.

After the Council was over, Louis returned to the Dauphine's room. She was in constant pain and becoming very weak. Louis himself helped her to take a little nourishment. Later that evening her pains became acuter and he stayed up the whole night with her.

Needless to say, the sufferings which she endured were increased by the fear that the child might be a girl. She felt certain that she was dying. According to the *Mercure* she told Louis 'how much it grieved her to have known so good a father and so good a husband and to have to take leave of them so soon'. She added that she would die happily if she could know that she had given France a prince. Louis replied that he would be quite content to have a girl if only she could suffer less and be delivered sooner.

The second day of her labour, Thursday 5 August, the child was born. It had been agreed with Clément that when Louis enquired what sex the baby was, the answer 'I don't know' would mean it was a girl, 'I don't know yet' would mean a boy.

A little after a quarter past ten the Dauphine was safely delivered of a child. Clément gave the signal: 'I don't know yet', and Louis proclaimed in a loud, triumphant voice: 'We have a Duke of Burgundy!'

13
Mademoiselle, Madame and Lauzun

The period immediately following the Peace of Aix-la-Chapelle began with one of the most astonishing events in the life of the Court.

Antoine Nompar de Caumont, marquis de Puyguilhem (pronounced and usually spelt Péguilin), was the third son of an impoverished member of the provincial aristocracy of Gascony, the comte de Lauzun. He was distinctly ugly. His cousin, the maréchal de Gramont, described his face as resembling 'that of a skinned cat'. Bussy-Rabutin claimed that he was 'one of the smallest men that God ever made'. Of his character the marquis de La Fare summed him up as: 'the most insolent little man that has been seen for a hundred years'. Saint-Simon, who was his brother-in-law, complained that he was 'always pursuing some intrigue, envious, spiteful, bold and audacious in every way, loving very few, impertinent in the last degree with women'.

Spanheim makes the observation that Lauzun 'had nothing in his appearance which could attract the affection of a prince with a well-balanced disposition'. There was nothing attractive in his character either, which Spanheim says was the opposite of the King's. Lauzun was confident enough to oppose Louvois to his face, and opposed him with impunity. He was brazen enough to tell Louis that Mme de Montespan was a whore. His effrontery knew no bounds.

But what Lauzun lacked in physical or personal attraction he made up for by his assiduity. To the astonishment of the Court he managed to insinuate himself into the confidence and affection of the King. 'M. de Lauzun', wrote Saint-Maurice in January 1671, 'has been declared a favourite, the King having given him all the *entrées* into his cabinet and into his bedroom as if to a *premier gentilhomme de quartier*, a privilege which no one else has.' It was thus that he attracted the attention of la Grande Mademoiselle.

She began to notice his gift for conversation; he possessed, she claimed, 'quite extraordinary powers of expressing himself'. She began to notice that she was beginning to frequent the Court more often. 'My long periods of residence were cause for astonishment.' She began to notice that there was something at Saint-Germain 'which diverted me more than usual'. Finally she realised the truth: 'After having agonised over it for several days, I perceived that I was in love with M. de Lauzun.' She said that he 's'était glissé dans mon coeur. Je le regardais comme le plus honnête homme du monde.' She came to the conclusion that, once in a lifetime, 'one needed to taste the sweetness of knowing that one was loved by someone who was worthy of one's love'. Whether she was indeed loved by Lauzun is another matter. His inner feelings are not recorded, but Mademoiselle managed to convince herself that 'the care which he took to come everywhere that we could see one another, made it sufficiently clear to me'.

She sent urgently to Paris for a copy of Corneille's *Suite du Menteur* in which Mélisse confides to Lise: 'Quand les ordres du ciel nous ont fait l'un pour l'autre, c'est un accord bientôt fait que le nôtre.' These words seemed to proclaim a divine predestination to marital life. 'At last, having turned over the arguments for and against again and again, my heart decided the matter, and it was in the Church of the Récollets that I made my final resolution . . . Never have I been to church with such devotion . . . I believe it was the inspiration of God, showing me what he wanted me to do. The next day, which was 7 March, my gaiety was extreme.' It was in this state of mind that she prepared to follow the King on a triumphal tour of his newly conquered possessions in Flanders.

La Grande Mademoiselle might have married a king – in fact, but for her behaviour during the Fronde, she might have married the King of France. A daughter of the House of Orléans, who was reputedly the richest woman in France, was clearly a matrimonial prize of the first importance. It was in the natural order of things that such a marriage should be arranged for purely political reasons. There could have been no place for love or personal feelings in the choice of her husband. Perhaps because, deep down, she knew that this was the inevitable lot of royalty, she had kept Cupid at bay. 'I do not know what sweet sayings are,' she admitted, 'for no one has ever dared address any to me, not on account of my birth, since some Queens we know have heard them, but on account of my humour, which is known to be far removed from coquetry.'

But, as Bussy-Rabutin wrote to Mlle de Scudéry, 'Love is an illness, like smallpox; the later you catch it, the worse you take it.' These words were only too tragically true of Mademoiselle. At the age of forty-three she had fallen hopelessly in love with the most unworthy object for anyone's affections. The prospect of such a misalliance put Louis in a difficult and delicate position.

Louis was at the time secretly negotiating a treaty with Charles II of England. The special envoy to be employed for this task was Louis' sister-in-law, Madame, born Henriette-Anne of England, sister of Charles II and wife of Monsieur, duc d'Orléans.

It was on 20 April 1670 that Louis and his whole Court set out for Flanders. His personal bodyguard was commanded by Lauzun. The purpose of this royal progress was plainly political. Louis wanted to impress his new subjects with the glory that was now theirs as Frenchmen.

An important source of information about this occasion is Pellisson-Fontanier, official historiographer, together with Racine, to the King. Most of his letters were to Mlle de Scudéry. 'It is not possible to tell you', he wrote to her, 'how huge the Court is. It is not like this at Saint-Germain or in Paris. Everyone has come with him.'

Louis not only brought his Court with him, he brought Lully, together with all his singers and musicians, and put on a performance of his *Psyche*. Molière and Corneille were joint authors of the libretto. Louis had already demonstrated to Europe the superiority of the French military machine. He was now displaying the supremacy of France in the arts of music and literature.

'All that you have read of the magnificence of Salome and the grandeur of the King of Persia', wrote Mme de Coligny to Bussy-Rabutin, 'is not to be compared with the pomp which accompanies the King on his tour.' The streets were one long procession of white plumes, gold-embroidered tunics, richly caparisoned mules, caracoling horses and sumptuous equipages. Bussy puts the number of horses required for the courtiers at 30,000. All the great noblemen brought with them a host of chaplains, confessors, treasurers, secretaries, major-domos, cooks, scullions and other domestics. They also brought their furniture.

Louis had two 'bedrooms' with him. On 17 May Pellisson wrote from Tournay: 'The King, who for the whole of this progress, had only his bedroom of crimson damask, had another very magnificent one brought to Tournay and to Lille with the whole suite of furniture needed for him to be lodged at his ease, and the same for the Queen. This includes some very beautiful Gobelin tapestries, a bed embroidered in gold and a great quantity of sconces, branches and chandeliers of silver. In fact the King and the Queen are housed at the Abbey of Saint Martin as if in the Palace of the Tuileries – or very nearly. But although the King's bedroom is very large it is true that they could not find room for a ruelle, because his bed, which is of green velvet with gold embroidery, is of immense size.' Mademoiselle had a bed with a high canopy which presented problems. In one peasant's house the ground level had to be dug several feet deeper in order to accommodate it.

From very early on it was obvious that the progress was achieving its purpose. On 24 May Pellisson wrote: 'Without intending to flatter the King, it is a fact that all the near-by towns in Spanish hands envy the good fortune of those that are in his, largely on account of the lack of discipline in their garrisons and because their citizens cannot pass beyond their walls without being robbed if they have no escort, whereas on entering the French territory one can walk in full security.'

Wherever they passed, the streets were lined with tapestries; they were greeted with firework displays and dinners served with abundant courses; festoons of flowers hung from window to window across the streets together with hundreds of little paper lanterns – 'qui faisaient un berceau de lumière sur la tête des passants'.

The wide horizons of the fields of Flanders, so clearly shown in the paintings of Van der Meulen, revealed a landscape of flat pastures and scattered villages. 'A feature of this country', noted Pellisson, 'was the number of church towers which sounded the hour, the half hour, the quarter and the half quarter with their carillons.' As they were by no means synchronised, there was always something striking and it was never possible to discover what the time was.

There were, of course, problems. Pellisson states that 'His Majesty agreed that it was difficult for so large an army to pass by without causing some disorder, but that he had taken, and still took, all the precautions that he could think of to prevent it.' Though the soldiers were allowed to let their horses browse on the roofs of the thatched houses, 'Louis always summoned the curé or the pasteur and asked him to inform himself of what damage had been done to crops and to forage and gave him money to distribute to those who had suffered, so that many gained more than they had lost'.

A part of Louis' intentions was to bring the Court to one of the sea-ports so that his sister-in-law could set sail for England. On 23 May Pellisson noted: 'On dit hier adieu à Madame.'

All was not well between the King's brother Philippe d'Orléans and his wife Henriette-Anne of England. There is much interesting information on the subject in the letters and despatches of Ralph Montagu, Charles II's ambassador to France. In December 1669 he wrote to the Foreign Secretary, Lord Arlington: 'I will say nothing to you of Monsieur's usage of Madame, but if she had married a country gentleman of England of £5,000 a year, she would have lived a better life than she does here, for Monsieur . . . doth take a pleasure to cross his wife in everything.'

The cause of the trouble was, of course, Monsieur's relationship with the chevalier de Lorraine. In a letter to Lord Arlington, dated 1 February 1670, Montagu gives a typical example of Monsieur's infatuation: 'The Bishop of Langres, that was favourite to the last Duke of Orléans, was possessed of some 4,000 pistoles a year in two abbeys, which upon his death were in Monsieur's disposal . . . This Bishop fell sick about six days ago, and upon Thursday the news came to Saint-Germain that he was dead. I happened to be in Madame's Chamber when Monsieur heard it, who, before a great deal of company, told the chevalier de Lorraine that he should give him the two benefices, though it seems the King had already told Monsieur he would never consent that the chevalier de Lorraine should have them, not thinking him a man of a life fit for Church benefices.'

The marquis de Saint-Maurice, whose account of this episode accords with Montagu's, adds: 'The King also accuses the chevalier de Lorraine of the infamous crime of sodomy with the comte de Guiche and even with those who were burnt for this offence on the Place de Grève.'

The affair of the abbeys provoked a row between Monsieur and the King which ended in the chevalier de Lorraine being arrested and sent to the prison of Pierre Encise at Lyon. 'Monsieur, I believe,' continues Montagu, 'in his heart thinks this is Madame's doing, though she has, in the opinion of all the world, behaved herself the best to Monsieur that can be in this matter, and is gone along with him to Villecotrait [Villers-Cotterets] where he is gone this morning, and pretends never to come back, as he says: "qu'on ne me rend le chevalier". I believe that the King will not send for him in haste.'

To Charles II Montagu wrote of his sister: 'The King has declared more publicly how much he thinks himself obliged to her for her behaviour; but Monsieur cannot help suspecting that all this affair was conducted by Madame and that the King did it to gratify your Majesty.'

The interrelationships between Louis, Charles and Henriette-Anne, and therefore indirectly with Philippe d'Orléans, were to become of first importance for diplomatic reasons. Although England had entered, in 1668, into an alliance with Holland, Charles was already beginning to formulate in his mind a different arrangement of the powers in Europe which he called the Grand Design. At first only Lord Arlington had any knowledge of the project. Henriette-Anne became Charles' closest confidante. 'I must again conjure you', he wrote in January 1669, 'that the whole matter be an absolute secret.' In March Lord Arundell of Wardour, a prominent Catholic, was sent on a special mission to discuss the matter with Louis.

In brief it was a plan for Louis to subsidise Charles – whose Parliament would not vote him sufficient funds – to support his claims against Spain and to join him in a war against Holland. Charles, for a further subsidy, was to declare his conversion to the Church of Rome – a move which would clearly be very unpopular in certain circles. It was this condition that created the delicacy and the danger underlying the negotiations.

What Charles really felt about the Catholic Church was only revealed on his death-bed. Bishop Burnet, who knew him well, wrote: 'He seemed to have no sense of religion; both at prayers and sacrament he, as it were, took care to satisfy people that he was in no sort concerned . . . He once said to me that he was no atheist, but that he could not think God would make a man miserable only for taking a little pleasure out of the way.'

He may have been thinking of his adulteries, but they were as much an offence in the eyes of the Anglican Church as of the Roman. Burnet makes an interesting suggestion. 'When he talked freely, he could not help letting himself out against the liberty that under the Reformation all men took to enquiring into matters of religion, for from their enquiring into matters of religion they carried the humour further to enquire into matters of state. He said often that he thought government were a much safer and easier thing where authority was believed infallible and the faith and submission of the people implicit.' Catholic doctrine was more akin to Charles' belief in the authority of Kings. 'He made such observations on the French government that he thought a King who might be checked, or have his ministers called to account by a parliament, was but a King in name.'

The part played by Henriette-Anne in the conduct of these negotiations was all-important. On 21 September 1669 she wrote from Saint-Cloud a long letter to her brother. It is a remarkable document. It shows a clear understanding of all the issues involved and a far-reaching perception of the probable consequences. It also reveals that her first concern was to serve her brother's interests rather than her brother-in-law's. Ralph Montagu was right when he assured Lord Arlington (September 1669) that 'some of the most understanding people of France apply themselves to Madame, having a great opinion of her discretion and judgement . . . In England you ought not to slight any advices that come from her, because she is so truly and passionately concerned for the King her brother.'

Her letter affords important insights into the affairs of France: 'I write to tell you that the order into which the King has put his finances has greatly increased his power and has put him more than ever in a position to make attacks on his neighbours.' She was also perspicacious about her brother's hope of turning Roman Catholic (abbreviated to 'R' in her letters). 'The matter takes on a different aspect, firstly because you have need of France to ensure the success of the design about R, and there is very little likelihood of your obtaining what you desire from the King except on condition that you enter into a league with him against Holland.' She concludes: 'What is there more glorious and more profitable than to extend the confines of your kingdom beyond the sea and to become supreme in commerce, which is what your people most passionately desire and what will probably never occur so long as the republic of Holland exists.'

It became a necessity that Henriette-Anne should pay a visit to her brother, but Monsieur, in his hatred and his jealousy, refused to allow her to go. On 11 January 1670 Ralph Montagu reported: 'The King has resolved here that on Easter Monday he will set forwards to Flanders to visit all the new conquered places and fortifications. He will go first to Callice [Calais] and so to all the towns he has on the sea coast ... The Queen and all the Court go with him.' Montagu was not at the time aware of the secret treaty.

Louis, of course, had in mind the possibility of overruling his brother, if necessary, when they had arrived at a convenient port. 'The voyage culminated in a visit to the seaboard towns', wrote Choisy, 'and Madame was to embark from the most convenient port. Never was a secret so seemingly well-kept as that which was to conduct Madame to England.'

A few weeks before her departure, however, Monsieur horrified Louis by talking of the secret treaty as one already in the know. Apart from Madame there were only two people in France who could have leaked the information – Louvois and Turenne. Louis managed to extract from his brother the admission that he had his information from the chevalier de Lorraine. But who could have told him? Louis confronted Turenne and asked him point-blank whether he had revealed the information to anyone. 'Speak to me as you would speak to your confessor,' he demanded. To his great credit, Turenne made an honest avowal that he had told a certain Mme de Coatquen that Madame was to go to England to see her brother. The King, relates Choisy, burst into laughter. 'Monsieur,' he said, 'then you are in love with Mme de Coatquen?' 'No, Sire,' answered Turenne, 'not exactly – but she is a very good friend.' 'Ah well,' concluded Louis, 'what has been done has been done, but don't tell her any more: for, if you do love her, I am sorry to have to tell you that she loves the chevalier de Lorraine to whom she passed on everything and the chevalier de Lorraine passed it on to my brother.' Madame, however, was permitted to cross the Channel; Charles sent an English fleet under Lord Sandwich to fetch her from Dunkirk, and, in the early hours of Sunday 26 May, Henriette-Anne arrived before Dover. She was met by the royal yacht with her two brothers, the King and the Duke of York, accompanied by the King's illegitimate son, the Duke of Monmouth, and their cousin Prince Rupert. On 1 June, the secret Treaty of Dover was signed by Lord Arlington, Lord Arundell, Sir Thomas Clifford and Sir Richard Bellings on behalf of England and by Colbert de Croissy on behalf of France.

Colbert de Croissy, a brother of the famous minister, had been appointed French ambassador in order to negotiate this treaty. He formed a very high opinion of Madame. 'It has appeared during her stay', he wrote to Louis, 'that she had much more power over the King her brother than any other person in the world, not only by the eagerness which the other Ministers have shown to implore her favour and support with the King, and by the favours which he has granted simply at her request ... but also the King's own confession and the tears he shed on bidding her farewell.'

'Madame now returned from England', writes la Grande Mademoiselle, 'where it seemed that she had at least found health, for she was looking very pretty and happy.' She had reason to; she had returned, according to the marquise de La Fayette, 'with all the glory and the pleasure which could be given by a visit begun by friendship and followed by a successful business transaction. Her brother the King, whom she loved dearly, had shown her an extraordinary tenderness and consideration ... She saw herself, at the age of twenty-six, the link between the two greatest kings of the century; she had in her hands a treaty upon which depended the fate of a part of Europe; the satisfaction and the esteem which comes from public affairs, united in her with the pleasantness of youth and beauty, produced a grace and sweetness diffused throughout her person. This attracted a sort of homage which must have been all the more acceptable to her since it was accorded to her person rather than to her rank.

'This condition of happiness was troubled by her estrangement from Monsieur ever since the affair of the chevalier de Lorraine ... but, to all appearances, the good offices of the King furnished her with the means of escaping from this embarrassment. At last she had arrived at the most agreeable situation in which she had ever found herself, when, suddenly as a thunderclap, death put an end to so beautiful a life and deprived France of the most loveable princess that ever lived.'

On Tuesday 24 June, shortly after her return from Dover, Madame and her husband were back at Saint-Cloud. She went, of course, to Versailles. La Grande Mademoiselle describes her appearance. 'She came into the Queen's apartment looking like a corpse dressed up and to which some rouge had been applied. When she left everyone said, and the Queen and I remember having said, "Madame has death painted on her face." She told the Queen, however, that she was not feeling too bad that day. It was noticed that when she left she had tears in her eyes.' Next day she complained of a pain in her side and in her stomach – pains to which she was subject.

On the Saturday, at about ten in the evening, the marquise de La Fayette arrived at Saint-Cloud; she found Madame in the gardens. 'She told me that I would find her looking ill and that she was not in good health: she had her supper and walked by moonlight until midnight.' The next day, Sunday 29 June, she had dinner as usual and lay down afterwards on some cushions. She went to sleep with her head on Mme de La Fayette's lap. 'During her sleep such a change came over her that after looking at her for some time I was astonished, and I came to the conclusion that her spirit must contribute much to the embellishment of her face, since it made her so charming when she was awake and so little so when she was asleep.'

A little later Madame came down to the salon, where she asked for a cup of *eau de chicorée*. As she was replacing the cup in the saucer she suddenly clasped her hand to her side and said, in a voice which betokened real agony: 'Ah! what a stitch! Ah! what pain! I cannot bear any more!'

'We got her to bed', continues Mme de La Fayette, 'and as soon as she was there she cried out even more and tossed from side to side like a person in infinite pain. At the same time her Premier Médecin, M. Esprit, was sent for, who said it was a colic and prescribed the remedies usual in such a case . . . Madame continued crying out that she had terrible pains in the pit of her stomach. All of a sudden she said that we should inspect the water which she had drunk; that it was poison; that perhaps they had mistaken one bottle for another; that she had been poisoned, that she felt sure of it; that they should give her some antidote for poison.'

Monsieur suggested that some of the chicory water should be given to a dog, but Mme Desbordes, first lady of the bedchamber, who was completely devoted to her mistress, said that she had mixed the potion and had drunk some of it herself. Mme de La Fayette had also drunk some of it. Antidotes were administered but without success.

Meanwhile at Versailles the Queen was preparing to make an excursion on the Canal; Mademoiselle was to accompany her. The duc de Longueville came to escort her to the Queen's coach. 'As I came out of my room', she writes, 'I found the comte d'Ayen, who said to me: "Madame is dying! I am looking for M. Vallot; the King has ordered me to take him there." I ran to find the Queen, who was waiting for me . . . As I got into the coach she said: "Madame is dying, and do you know what she has said? That she believes herself poisoned!" Oh! how horrible! I cried. It threw me into despair.'

On their way to Saint-Cloud the party from Versailles met Vallot returning. 'He told us that it was just a colic, that the pain would not last and that there was no danger at all. That was what we read on the faces of all whom we met on arriving; hardly anyone was looking mournful.'

They were therefore quite unprepared for what they were to see. 'Madame was on a little bed which had been made up in the ruelle beside her bed; she was all dishevelled, her chemise undone at the neck and sleeves so that, thin as she was and with her face pale and taut, she had every appearance of a person already dead . . . I have never seen anything so pitiful as the state she was in. She talked to the King for some time in a low voice. She kept asking for an emetic. I told the doctors several times; they said it would be useless. The King tried to reason with them. They did not know how to answer him. I said: "No woman has ever been left to die without being given some remedy." They looked at each other and said not a word.'

It was decided that the time was come for Madame to receive the last rites of the Church. Louis took his leave of her. 'He kissed her,' continues Mademoiselle; 'she spoke many tender words to him, which the King told us of; but I believe she said things to him of which he did not tell us.' Perhaps, now that the moment of parting was come, Louis' mind went back to that lovely summer at Fontainebleau when he and Henriette had come so dangerously near to falling in love.

Madame herself had little doubt that her end was near and she called for her confessor, a Capuchin monk, but the curé of Saint-Cloud, Nicolas Feuillet, came instead. D'Ormesson describes Feuillet as 'a man of very strict devotion and rather out of the ordinary in his doctrines, so that he had been inhibited from preaching'.

Feuillet has left his own account of the interview. 'At eleven o'clock that night she sent in great urgency to summon me. When I had arrived at her bedside she made all the others retire and said: "You see, M. Feuillet, to what condition I am reduced." "In a very good condition, Madame," I replied: "you now confess that there is a God whom you have known very little during your life." "It is true, my God, that I have not known you at all," she admitted with the deepest signs of emotion. That gave me good grounds for hope. "Very well, Madame," I said; "you have made your confession?" "Yes," she replied. "I do not doubt then", I continued, "that you must have confessed that you have broken so often the vows of your baptism by the love you have had of grandeur, having spent your life surrounded by pleasures and delights, by games and entertainments, in all the luxury, the pomps and vanities of this world . . ." "No," she said, "I have never confessed such things, I was never told that they would offend God." Feuillet speedily put her right on that count. "O my God, what must I do then? I see clearly that my confessions and my

Communions have been in vain." "It is true, Madame, that your life has been nothing but sin; you must employ such little time as remains for you in doing penance." '

Having made a further confession, Henriette-Anne now asked for the Viaticum and received it, but immediately her physical pains returned. 'My God, will these terrible pains not finish soon?' she asked. 'What, Madame,' pursued her confessor; 'do you forget yourself? You have been offending God for so many years, and you have only been repenting for six hours!'

As Henriette-Anne was receiving the Viaticum, Bishop Bossuet arrived at Saint-Cloud. He had made the acquaintance of Madame during the winter months before her visit to Dover and she had asked him to instruct her in her religion, 'of which I am very ignorant, and I want to think seriously about my salvation'.

Bossuet was a more merciful pastor than Feuillet and spoke to her 'with that eloquence and spirit of religion which were evident in all his speaking', with an infinite gentleness that opened up to her the way to heaven'. He held a crucifix before her eyes, saying: 'Behold our Lord Jesus Christ opening his arms to you.' Presently he spoke again: 'Madame, you believe in God, you hope in him, you love him?' She managed to answer: 'With all my heart.' Those were her last words.

Back at Versailles, Mademoiselle began to think about herself. She was of royal blood and immensely rich. What if Monsieur should decide that he wanted to marry her? But the King and Queen, not to be distracted, spoke only of Madame. At last Bossuet arrived, having been with Henriette until the end. His words were words of comfort. 'He told us that God had been very gracious and that she had died a very good Christian.' In a letter to his brother, Bossuet describes the occasion. 'I found her fully conscious, speaking and doing everything with great ease and no ostentation . . . so appropriately and with such courage and piety that I can still hardly believe it . . . I was with her for a whole hour and I saw her breathe her last, kissing a crucifix which she held in her hand.' The King, writes d'Ormesson, 'was deeply afflicted by this death and made a very remarkable comment on Madame's steadfastness. 'I am not a great preacher', he had said to her, 'but it seems to me that, in the condition in which you now find yourself, a great steadfastness is not what is needed, and that it is better to keep one's thoughts on dying in a Christian manner rather than strongly.' Perhaps the right word for it would be 'submissively'.

On 21 August, Bossuet preached her *oraison funèbre* at Saint-Denis. 'Bossuet's genius had been conspicuous in his funeral oration over the Queen of England,' wrote Cardinal Bausset, his biographer; 'he put forth the whole tenderness of his soul in that spoken over her daughter.' It remains one of the great classics of the French language. 'Woeful night, when, like a thunderclap, the startling news was spread abroad – *Madame se meurt! Madame est morte!*' He dwelt with earnestness on the vanity, the emptiness of all things mortal, returning again and again to the particular subject of his discourse. 'Madame met death gently and sweetly as she had ever met all else.' He did not fail to point his moral to his princely congregation. 'As you gaze upon these courtly places where she no longer moves, remember that the glories you admire were her greatest dangers in this life.'

Among those present at her death was Ralph Montagu. In a letter to Lord Arlington, dated from Paris, 30 June, at four a.m., he begins: 'I am sorry to be obliged, by my Employment, to give you an account of the saddest Story in the World, and which I have hardly the courage to write.' He repeats the details of how it all started: 'She continued in the greatest Tortures imaginable till Three a Clock in the Morning, when she dyed: The King, the Queen, and all the Court being there till about an hour before. God send the King our Master Patience and Constancy to bear so great an Affliction. Madame declared she had no reluctance to die but out of the Grief, she thought, it would be to the King her Brother.'

Louis XIV at once despatched the maréchal de Bellefonds as Ambassador Extraordinary to Charles II; 'who, besides his Condolence,' wrote Montagu, 'will endeavour, I believe, to disabuse our Court of what the Court and People here will never be disabused of, which is Madame's being Poisoned . . . but to me in particular, when I asked her several times, whether she thought her self Poisoned, she would answer nothing: I believe being willing to spare the addition of so great a trouble to the King our Master, which was the reason why, in my first Letter, I made no mention of it; neither am I Physician good enough to say she was Poisoned or she was not'.

In a letter to Charles II, dated 15 July, Montagu tells his King: 'As soon as I came in, she told me: "You see the sad condition I am in; I am going to die; how I pity the King my brother! For I am sure, he loses the Person in the World that loves him best." ' They were speaking in English. Montagu continues: 'I ask'd her then, if she believ'd her self Poison'd: Her Confessor that was by, understood that Word and told her: "Madame, you must accuse no Body, but offer up your Death to God as a Sacrifice"; so she would never answer me to that Question tho I asked her several times, but would only shrink up her shoulders.'

In a further letter, partly written in code, Montagu refers to the reappearance at Court of the chevalier de Lorraine. 'If Madame were

Poisoned, as few People doubt, he is look'd upon by all France, to have done it.'

Ralph Montagu had carefully avoided expressing his own opinion on the question. He was, however, in his official capacity, present at the post-mortem. The event is described by a secretary at the embassy named William Perwich. 'My Lord Ambassador went to Saint-Cloud to see her opened, and what might be the cause of her so sudden departure.' With him went the duc de Bouillon, described as 'Chamberlain', and Mr Beaucher, who was Henrietta-Maria's surgeon. It is probable that Perwich obtained his information from the latter. He records that 'the doctors and ladies deferred the opening till eight at night notwithstanding that the Ambassador pressed to have it done sooner because of better light. No sooner was the upper skin entered but all the house was filled with the most horrible stench that anybody ever smelt. She was all over rotten within, her liver wasted, and this the general opinion of the Doctors, that they wondered not why she died then, but that she lived so long. She was stuffed up with bile. Beaucher spied a little hole in her stomach, which the other chirurgiens excused to be the hast [sic] of the incisor, though it was blackish within.'

Vallot was also there and describes the gruesome event himself, speaking of his surprise that 'this princess should have resisted so long against the corruption of those organs which support life and conserve it, particularly the lungs and liver'.

At the same time Lionne wrote to Colbert: 'Given the considerable corruption in the body, she has only lived these last three or four years by a miracle. He [Vallot] assured us that in all his life he has not seen two corpses in which there was so much corruption . . . The King told us that for more than three years she had been complaining of a stitch which obliged her to lie on the floor for three or four hours without finding rest in any position. I must not omit . . . that M. Vallot observed to the company that the inside of the stomach is always livid when there is any poison because it is principally there where it operates, whereas that of Madame was found to be the best in the world.'

Unfortunately some of the doctors, having accepted the findings of the post-mortem, went back on their opinion afterwards, so a small question mark remains.

Recently, it has been suggested by Ida Macalpine and Richard Hunter, mother and son and both doctors of medicine by profession and historians by inclination, that Henriette-Anne may have died of porphyria, the so-called 'madness' of George III, the symptoms of which include 'sudden onset, agonising abdominal pains and prostration followed by rapid improvement or precipitate death'. Her grandfather James I had suffered from the same symptoms and his eldest son, Henry Frederick, Prince of Wales, died at the age of eighteen in circumstances similar to those attendant upon the death of Madame.

The majority verdict is that Henriette-Anne died from natural causes. Less clinical in her concern, Mme de Sévigné wrote: 'With her were lost all the joy, all the charm and all the pleasures of the Court.'

No sooner had the news of Madame's death reached Versailles than Louis took Mademoiselle into the Queen's bedroom and said: ' "My cousin, there is a position vacant: do you wish to fill it?" I went as pale as death and said to him: "You are the master, I shall never have any will but yours." He pressed me further; I said, "I have nothing to say about that." "But do you feel any aversion to it?" I said nothing. He said to me: "I will study the matter and I will let you know." '

Mademoiselle's feelings are better imagined than described. 'I went out and joined those who were walking with the Queen; there was no talk but of the death of Madame, of her suspicions regarding the suddenness of her death; of the way she and Monsieur had lived together; that he would soon be consoled; that he would marry again, but to whom? Everyone looked at me. I said nothing.' In the end Philippe d'Orléans married Charlotte-Elizabeth, Princesse Palatine, known in Germany as Liselotte von der Pfalz.

At the beginning of December 1670, the Court moved to Paris for the season of Advent, which was marked by a series of sermons. Mademoiselle and Lauzun were planning the magnificence with which his brigade would be mounted and equipped thanks to her money; the caparisons of the Spanish horses were to be covered with fleurs de lys.

It was about this time that Mademoiselle wrote to the King asking him to permit their marriage. 'It is upon Monsieur de Lauzun', she told him, 'that I have cast my eyes: his merit and his attachment to Your Majesty are what have pleased me most about him.' Louis sent his answer at once. 'It was very honest,' she wrote; 'he indicated the astonishment which he felt; he begged me not to do anything without due reflection; to consider the matter well; that he would never compel me; that he loved me.'

A little later, 'le jour de Notre-Dame', Mademoiselle was forced to take decisive action. Lauzun approached her after the sermon and said in her ear: 'Guilloire [her secretary] has discovered the affair and has gone to Louvois to inform him.' She sought an interview with the King.

She had to wait until two in the morning. ' "You are up very late, my cousin," he said. "It is that I have something to say to Your Majesty." ' Louis took her into the space between the inner and the outer door. She suggested that they might sit somewhere, but he answered: 'No; I am all right like this.' 'Sire, it is to say to Your Majesty (my heart was beating) what I have already written; I have not changed my resolution; the more I think, the more I examine the matter, the more I feel that I shall be happy. Sire, I esteem Monsieur de Lauzun; I love him.'

Louis repeated the advice given in his letter, but he went on: 'You are old enough to know what is good for you. I should be sorry to constrain you in any way ... I do not advise you to do it; I do not forbid you ... make your arrangements.' 'Sire,' she replied, 'if your Majesty is for us, no one can harm us.' 'I wanted to kiss his hands; he embraced me and thus we parted.'

On 15 December Mme de Sévigné wrote to the marquis de Coulanges, who was at Lyon, one of her most famous letters.

'I am about to tell you the most astonishing thing, the most surprising, the most marvellous, the most miraculous, the most triumphant, the most bewildering, the most unheard of, the most singular, the most extra-ordinary, the most unbelievable, the most unexpected, the greatest, the smallest, the most unusual, the most common, the most dazzling, the most secret until today, the most brilliant, the most enviable; in short a thing whose parallel is only to be found in bygone centuries, and even this comparison is not exact; a thing which we cannot credit in Paris, so how can it be credited in Lyon? A thing which makes everybody cry Mercy on us! a thing which fills Mme de Rohan and Mme de Hauterive with delight; a thing, finally, which will take place on Sunday when those who witness it will think their eyes have tricked them; a thing which will take place on Sunday and will perhaps not have taken place by Monday. I cannot bring myself to give it away; guess; I give you three guesses. Do you give it up? Well then, I must tell you: M. de Lauzun is going to marry, on Sunday, at the Louvre, guess who? I give you four guesses, I give you ten, I give you a hundred. Mme de Coulanges says, "That's easy; it is Mme de La Vallière" – not a bit of it, Madame – "Then it is Mlle de Retz?" Not a bit of it; how provincial you are. Ah! you say, "How silly we are, it is Mlle Colbert" – even less likely – "Then it must assuredly be Mlle de Créqui?" No, you have not got it. So in the last resort I must tell you: M. de Lauzun is marrying on Sunday, at the Louvre, with the King's consent, Mademoiselle, Mademoiselle de ... Mademoiselle ... guess the name; he is marrying Mademoiselle, my faith! by my faith! my sworn faith! Mademoiselle, la Grande Mademoiselle, daughter of the late Mon-sieur, granddaughter of Henri IV, Mademoiselle d'Eu, Mademoiselle des Dombes, Mademoiselle de Montpensier, Mademoiselle d'Orléans, Made-moiselle, first cousin to the King, Mademoiselle destined to a throne, Mademoiselle, the only match in France worthy of Monsieur.'

The King's consent to such a match was too good to be true, and there were those who advised Mademoiselle to lose no time in making the step irrevocable. She delayed three days and those three days were fatal. The Queen was outraged and told her that she had far better not marry but to leave her fortune to the King's second son, the duc d'Anjou. The duc d'Orléans flew into a rage; Louvois protested; the prince de Condé and the maréchal de Villars begged Louis to reconsider his decision. Louis yielded.

The marquis de La Fare put the final responsibility on Mme de Maintenon, still only Mme Scarron – 'a woman with much wit whom Mme de Montespan had placed with the children which she had borne to the King, and was at that time her principal confidante. Mme Scarron, I say, made Mme de Montespan recognise the storm which she would attract by supporting Lauzun in this matter. She did this so well that the person who had begun this affair was the one who put an end to it, and after three or four days, Lauzun and Mademoiselle were ordered to proceed no further.

'As this event caused a great stir throughout the whole of Europe, the King felt obliged to send a circular letter to all his ambassadors.'

The story is thus told by Louis himself: 'About ten or twelve days ago my cousin, not as yet having the courage to speak to me in person on a matter which she well knew must surprise me very much, wrote me a long letter to announce the resolve which she said she had taken to make this marriage, begging me, by all the justifications of which she could bethink herself, to agree to give my consent . . . My reply, in a note which I sent her, was that I would ask her to think again about it and above all to be careful to do nothing with precipitation in an affair of this nature, which could lead to long repentance with no remedy. I was content to say no more, hoping to be able, by word of mouth . . . to recall her by gentle means to change her opinion. She continued, however, to send me more notes and, by any other means which came to her mind, to press me to give my consent to what she was asking, as being the only thing which could, she said, be the source of her happiness and contentment in life, just as my refusal would make her the most unhappy woman that ever lived.'

Mademoiselle, Louis continued, had summoned the duc de Créqui, the duc de Montausier, the maréchal d'Albret and the marquis de Guitry to support her cause. These pointed out to Louis that he had willingly allowed Mademoiselle's sister to marry the duc de Guise and that if he would not consent to Mademoiselle's marrying Lauzun, Louis would, in effect, be saying that he made a great distinction between the younger sons of sovereign princes (Guise was a younger son of the duc de Lorraine) and the Officers of the Crown; that this could not happen in Spain where *les Grands* had precedence over *les princes étrangers*, and that for him to make such a distinction would mortify all the nobility in the land. Louis accepted their argument. 'In the end I yielded and gave at least my tacit consent to the marriage. I shrugged my shoulders with astonishment that my cousin should be so carried away, merely saying that she was forty-five and could do as she pleased. From that moment the matter was regarded as settled; they began to make preparations; all the Court went to pay their respects to my cousin and their compliments to the comte de Lauzun.'

The next day it came to Louis' ears that Mademoiselle was putting it about that she was making this marriage because the King had wanted it. He had summoned her and asked her, before witnesses, if this was true. She firmly denied it. But Louis was hearing on all sides that the majority opinion was something very insulting to him, which was that 'all the opposition which I had put up in this case was pretence and play-acting, and that in fact I was only too pleased to procure so great a good for the comte de Lauzun, whom everybody believed that I loved and esteemed highly – which was true; I resolved immediately, since I saw that my glory was so deeply concerned, to break off this engagement and to give no further consideration to the satisfying of either the princess or the count'. He had therefore sent for Mademoiselle and told her that she could marry any nobleman in the land with the exception of Lauzun, and had even offered to give her away in Church. He described her anguish – 'as if I had stabbed her a hundred times . . . I then made it known to the comte de Lauzun . . . and I can say that he received the news with all the constancy and all the submission that could be desired.'

Segrais, in his *Mémoires-anecdotes*, states that 'when M. de Lauzun learnt that it was Mme de Montespan who had prevented his marriage with Mademoiselle from being accomplished, he conceived an implacable hatred for her'. It is not clear what date Segrais had in mind. The final rupture occurred a year after the engagement was broken off. On 28 October 1671, the *Gazette* announced that the maréchal de Gramont had resigned from his post as colonel of the Regiment des Gardes Françaises and had been replaced by the duc de Roannes. Gramont was Lauzun's cousin. Racine, in his capacity as Historiographer Royal, mentions the same appointment at the same date. 'It is asserted that M. de Lauzun passionately desired to have this regiment of the Gardes . . . It is said that he spoke to Mme de Montespan about it and that he then hid himself to see how Mme de Montespan would put it to the King.' Saint-Simon, however, puts it some two years earlier.

Lauzun's hiding-place was under Mme de Montespan's bed; here he could overhear her conversation with Louis in which she advised the King not to grant him the post. That evening he escorted the royal mistress to the ballet and repeated verbatim the conversation which he had overheard. Summoned next day by the King to give an account of himself, he lost his temper and snapped his sword in two, swearing that he would not use it again in the service of a master who broke his word at the bidding of a whore. It was then that Louis performed what Saint-Simon called 'perhaps the finest action of his life' – he opened the window and threw his cane out of it, 'saying that he would have regretted having struck a gentleman'.

That was the end. On 25 November Lauzun was arrested at Saint-Germain and taken to the fortress of Pignerol where he was to pass the next ten years of his life.

14

The Grand Dauphin and Bossuet

Louis' commitment to the planning of his campaign and to the care of his army did not prevent him from keeping an attentive eye on affairs at home. Whether it was information about the ever-increasing elaboration of Versailles or on the day-to-day health of his children, he insisted upon full and frequent accounts – 'le détail de tout'. Where buildings were concerned his correspondent was Colbert, but on the subject of his children his letters were addressed to the maréchale de La Mothe-Houdancourt.

On 3 September 1664, he wrote to her: 'My cousin, having need to appoint a governess for my son, I believe it would not be possible to make a better choice than yourself. For that reason, if there is no obstacle to your occupying that position, I offer it to you with joy because of the particular esteem that I have for you personally.'

Mme de La Mothe succeeded the duchesse de Montausier, who, brilliant, witty and worldly, was more suited to take her place in a Salon than to be appointing wet-nurses or to speak the language of the nursery. Mme de La Mothe was of a more maternal and practical nature, capable, as la Grande Mademoiselle puts it, 'of choosing a broth or deciding on the merits of a gruel'.

Some forty letters from Louis to the Gouvernante have survived and have been studied by Charles Dreyss. Most of them date from the year 1667 when the King was on campaign in Flanders. They shed an interesting light on the domestic side of Louis' character.

The first of these letters, written from Amiens on 21 May of that year, sets the tone. 'I am very pleased that my children have arrived safely at Compiègne in good health and with the good behaviour of my son [aged five and a half]. Make use of the time when you are alone with him to make him fear you. I can think of nothing more necessary at this moment. I beg you not to stand on ceremony when writing to me.'

In the following month the health of the Dauphin took a turn for the worse. On Sunday 12 June, Louis wrote to the Chancellor Séguier, who was at Compiègne: 'I was not a little relieved to see from your letter of yesterday that there is nothing untoward to be feared from the indisposition of my son. It does cause me some anxiety . . . I hope that the illness will come to an end soon.'

It had, in fact, only just begun. On 13 June a rather virulent form of measles declared itself. The story is taken up from Compiègne by the valet Du Bois. 'Monseigneur was in a condition of torpor and sweated a lot. On 16 June M. Elliant [the surgeon] identified an inflammation of the left cheek and concluded that it was caused by "a malignant humour" – probably an abscess. He insisted on lancing it and there was a considerable evacuation of pus. "Monseigneur," said Elliant to the young prince, "I have the strongest desire to be of service to you, but this is perhaps the greatest service which I shall ever render you." On Sunday 19 June, the Dauphin slept until nine o'clock and woke up *beau comme le jour*.'

On the previous Thursday Louis had written to Mme de La Mothe from Charleroi at five in the evening. 'I was in a fever of anxiety when your letters arrived. They have put my mind somewhat at rest.' He was just about to enter enemy territory for the sieges of Tournai and Douai. There are no letters known between 16 and 28 July.

Concern for the health of the heir to the throne might not be evidence of paternal affection on the part of a King, but Louis shows an equal interest in the health of his daughter. Marie-Thérèse bore Louis three daughters; the first two only lived for a few weeks, but the third, *la petite Madame*, named after her mother, was born on 5 January 1667, and survived until 1 March 1672. It was of her that he wrote from Chambord on 25 September 1669: 'The last phase of my daughter's fever caused me a little disquiet . . . I have so much confidence in your care, and it has been so happy so far that I only await comforting news from you.' But on 9 October, still at Chambord, he was still uneasy about the indisposition of his daughter. 'I trust that you will not fail to send me the details of everything and nothing but the pure truth.'

On Saturday 26 February 1672, the marquis de Saint-Maurice noted in his despatch: 'It was thought yesterday that *la petite Madame* was dying. The King was distraught during all her illness. I have never seen him so upset; he has hardly slept at all . . . and sent every half hour to enquire of her condition.' She died on the Tuesday at ten in the morning. 'Their Majesties', continues Saint-Maurice, 'are in a state of affliction which it is difficult to imagine. The King could be seen almost the whole time in Madame's room; tears filled his eyes. They returned yesterday to Versailles and finished the carnival in the most profound melancholy.'

Louis' letters to Mme de La Mothe say something about his character in general. The letters also give evidence of a discreet but affectionate relationship with his children's governess. 'I have known for a long time the feelings which you have for me and for all that concerns me. You are too good a Frenchwoman not to rejoice at all the honours which come my way.' Her quality of *bonne française* was probably her truest title to oversee the upbringing of the heir to the throne of France. But she only held that position until 1 November 1667; for when the Dauphin reached his sixth birthday he was transferred from female to male tutelage. He was described at about that time by d'Ormesson as 'the most beautiful and the brightest child that it would be possible to see'.

Louis appointed the duc de Montausier, husband of the boy's first governess, to be Governor to the Dauphin with Jacques-Bénigne Bossuet, Bishop of Condom, and soon to be Bishop of Meaux, as Preceptor. Bossuet had been born on 27 September 1627 in Dijon – the name Bénigne reflects that of the city's oldest church building. One of his biographers, Victor Giraud, calls the Burgundians 'a race of poets and orators, of Parliamentarians and Councillors of State, in whom good, solid sense is set off by a sonorous and colourful speech in which logic avoids all dryness and willingly adorns itself with a poetry, an eloquence, an idealism, where the sense of public speaking takes on some of the generosity and warmth of the local wine'. Montausier had a fine military record, and his wife was now *dame d'honneur* to the Queen and closely linked with Mme de Montespan. But his own qualities, Spanheim assures us, 'the probity and personal merit of the Duke, his character upright, rigid and in strong contrast to the weakness and complaisance so common among courtiers', qualified him for the post: he could be accounted the most learned among the noble and the most noble among the learned. It was all this, continues Spanheim, 'which easily determined the King to entrust the education of the Dauphin to him'.

Another reason for Louis' making this particular appointment is suggested by Spanheim. 'He judged, from certain traits of a stubborn and intractable nature in the young prince, that he needed to be ridden with a tight rein and, rather than given his head, to be treated with more than usual severity.' The duc de Montausier has often been supposed to have been the original for Molière's *Misanthrope*. The play had come out some two years before Montausier's appointment as Governor, but at least in one respect he is true to the principles of Alceste – 'On devrait châtier sans pitié' ('One must chastise without pity').

Mme de Caylus wrote that the Dauphin 'was believed to have understanding and ability because he ought to have had them[.] One can imagine the details which have made known to us the temper of M. de

Montausier and which reveal him as more likely to discourage a child like Monseigneur – born soft, lazy and stubborn – than to inspire such sentiments as he ought to have. The harsh way in which he was forced to study gave him so great an aversion to books that he determined never to open one when he became his own master, and he has kept his word.'

The details do not need to be imagined, as Mme de Caylus suggests; they are provided in abundance by the same valet de chambre, Marie Du Bois, who had recorded anecdotes of the young Louis XIV. During the summer of 1670, when Du Bois was in service, he kept an almost day-to-day log of the number of canings (the word used is *férules*) administered to the boy, who was then aged eight and a half. 'Tuesday 4 July, in the morning Monsieur de Montausier gave him four or five strokes with the cane so hard that it made the poor child limp. After dinner it was worse: no supper, no walk and in the evening . . . at prayers, at which everyone was present as usual, this precious child was saying the Lord's Prayer in French; he left out a word; M. de Montausier threw himself upon him and hit him with his fist as hard as he could. I thought he would knock him unconscious. M. de Joyeuse merely said: "Hey! Monsieur Montausier!" He made him start again and the dear child made the same mistake – which was really nothing. M. de Montausier stood up, took hold of him by his two hands and dragged him into the Grand Cabinet, where he did his lessons, and there gave him five strokes of the cane on each of his beautiful little hands.' On another occasion Du Bois noticed that the Dauphin's hands were all swollen and trembling so that he could not continue his work.

One might have hoped for evidence of more gentle treatment from Bossuet, but Du Bois insists that 'M. de Condom had very little tenderness for my little master, who often received a caning which he could have spared him'. On another occasion 'there was a difference of opinion between Monseigneur and M. de Condom, who ordered me to go and find M. de Montausier to come and beat him, which was something I never wanted to do'.

After the episode of the Lord's Prayer Montausier was afraid that he might have gone too far and 'for five or six days the Dauphin was treated far more kindly than usual, and this for two reasons; the first in order to take care of his health; the other to prevent Their Majesties from discovering the details of his cruel anger'. How much the King and Queen really knew about what went on is difficult to ascertain. The Dauphin had his establishment in the Louvre, whereas his parents lived in the Tuileries. They did not meet very often.

'A few days later', continues Du Bois, 'the Queen came and took her son for a walk. The next day all went well, but the following day the cane came out again.' On another occasion the Queen came to watch her son at work. 'So long as she was there all went as well as one could wish. When she left all was far from well; a great trumped-up quarrel, so much so that M. de Condom broke off the lesson and was going to find the King, who was at the Council ... Monseigneur was crying bitterly and said to me: "Du Bois, I beg you not to let him go." '

Du Bois went to the door and said to Bossuet: 'Monsieur, you will not leave. Please will you make it up with Monseigneur. I am asking you for mercy.' Bossuet did not go to the King. He resumed his place and went on with the lesson. Du Bois went for his dinner. When he came back the Dauphin was alone with Monsieur Millet, the Assistant Governor, who greeted him with the words: 'Monsieur Du Bois, you are looking at a prisoner.' 'I looked at my little master and replied: "That is the best-looking prisoner I have ever seen." I went to him and kissed his hand; then, turning to M. Millet, I said: "Allow me to go and fetch his little dog." Permission was given and Monseigneur played happily with it. A little later I said that the Queen was with Madame [the Princess Marie-Thérèse, aged four] and that Monseigneur usually went to see her at about this time. M. Millet went and arranged this meeting with the Queen, with the result that Monseigneur went to Madame's door and stood behind a small tapestry screen, without entering the room, and could hear all that was said.

'Madame threw herself on her knees before the Queen and said: "*Belle maman*, I ask you to pardon my *petit papa*, who will not be naughty again. I beg you to see him." The Queen said to her. "I am afraid I cannot see that naughty boy who will not learn his lessons. Do not speak to me about it." Madame did not give up and once again she went down on her knees before the Queen and said: "*Belle maman*, once again I ask you to forgive my *petit papa*, who will not be naughty again, and if he should be, I offer myself to be beaten in his place." The Queen said: "My daughter, be careful of making that offer, for you will suffer on his account. All right! I will see him on those terms." Monseigneur le Dauphin appeared and, kissing the Queen's hands, he burst into tears.'

Later that evening he went to say good-night to his father, who said to him: 'I want you so much to be an *honnête homme* and you don't want to be one! We shall see which of us wins. All right! If you do well this evening at your catechism' – which was the lesson he had every evening – 'and tomorrow morning at your studies, I shall decide whether you come in my coach, with the Queen, or if you go alone in yours to Saint-Germain.' After Monseigneur's *coucher* Du Bois went up to the Queen's room, where she was playing cards. 'The King came in and said to the

Queen: "Well, is our little man not repentant? I have put tomorrow's journey in the balance." The Queen said: "Yes. I found him very chastened." The next day,' concludes Du Bois, 'which was the last of my quarter, the morning's work had been good enough and Monseigneur went to Saint-Germain in Their Majesties' coach.'

Bossuet was assisted by Octave Périgny, soon to be succeeded by Pierre-Daniel Huet – later to be Bishop of Soissons. Together they formed ambitious plans for the publication of a whole library of new and specially annotated editions of the greatest writers of Greece and Rome. As well as the classical authors the curriculum was extended to include mathematics, geometry, geography, architecture and lessons in drawing for which, says Spanheim, the Dauphin had a real taste. François Blondel taught him geometry and Israel Sylvestre, whose beautiful engravings enable us to visualise so much of Louis XIV's world, both drawing and engraving.

So far as the academic subjects were concerned, the combined efforts of Montausier, Bossuet, Périgny and Huet cannot be said to have been productive. 'If they had treated the Dauphin with more consideration,' asserts Spanheim, 'if they had paid more attention to making his studies agreeable, to bringing him to taste them more from inclination than from sense of duty, they might have been more successful.'

No doubt Bossuet's broad intellect and profound learning enabled him to create a syllabus which matched the high destiny of a future King of France. Since the Grand Dauphin died before his father, that destiny was never achieved and Bossuet's formation of the young prince was never put to the ultimate test; but to all appearances it failed. A teacher needs more than a syllabus: he requires an understanding of the juvenile mind and the ability to relate to the young. Men of broad intellect and profound learning do not necessarily possess these qualities. It is quite possible that Bossuet did not.

It is also possible that the Dauphin was an unreceptive vessel, as Saint-Simon claimed: 'radically incapable of receiving instruction'. Certainly he does not appear on the pages of history as a shining example of a well-educated man. If we make allowance for Saint-Simon's capacity for exaggeration and personal dislikes, we still find someone whom the duchesse d'Orléans could describe as being content to spend a whole day lying on a sofa tapping his shoes with a cane.

In 1674, when the Dauphin was thirteen, Montausier addressed a memoir to the King complaining of the young prince's 'lack of attention'. He insists, however, that he has plenty of intelligence. 'When he wants to he listens, he understands and remembers with a wonderful ease'; but, he added, 'unfortunately, too often, he does not want to'.

Bossuet was not unaware of the apparent failure of his efforts. In July

1677, he wrote to the maréchal de Bellefonds: 'Everything is so little established that the least influence of the world can overthrow all. I would dearly love to see something more solidly founded, but perhaps God will do it without me.' All sorts of people, however, can be quoted as offering praise for the prince, but it is difficult to penetrate the ingratiating and obsequious language used by those speaking of royalty to royalty. A parliamentarian of Dijon, Le Gouz de Sainte-Seine, sums it up in his journal thus: 'Monseigneur has plenty of intelligence, but his intelligence is hidden.'

Not only was the Dauphin in constant fear of his Governor's severities, he lived in an ever-increasing awe of Louis, who was, says Saint-Simon, 'always King with him and only too seldom father'. One of those closest to the Dauphin was the chevalier de Grignan who held the position of *menin* from the Spanish *meninos*, meaning a young nobleman closely attached to a prince. Whenever he heard any disparagement of his master, Grignan would say: 'Just you wait!'

It was not until 1688, when he first went on campaign, that the Dauphin really showed his metal. The sudden blossoming was compared to a 'fig-tree laden with the finest fruits, of which no one had seen the flowers'. He showed much the same qualities as his father, 'having a real taste', said Vauban, 'for the trenches'. His success at the front earned him praise from his former Governor, Montausier, who, noted Mme de Sévigné, applied to him the adjectives 'liberal, generous, humane, and intent upon making full use of the services of his companions in arms'; and on his return from Philippsburg he passed through Meaux where he was fêted at the episcopal palace by his boyhood Preceptor, Bossuet.

Bossuet had become famous as a preacher and urged other preachers, in his *Panégyrique de Saint-Paul*, to reject 'the artifice of rhetoric'. All that is needed is a thorough understanding of the subject. He does not disapprove of a certain measure of light relief, but he insists: 'At least let us distinguish between the solid nourishment and the sauce.' In 1671 Bossuet had published his first important work, *L'Exposition de la doctrine catholique sur les matières de controverse*. This was written, in the first instance, for the conversion of Turenne, in which it succeeded.

In our own century Lord McLeod of Fuinary has advocated the same rules of Christian controversy – 'earnestly to draw out the best in your opponent's case, rather than to wrest a victory by exploiting its weakness, is the only principle for advancing thought'. It is a principle which churchmen and politicians ignore at their peril. With Bossuet the principle was absolute: 'ne pas prendre sur ses adversaires de faux avantages'. As a controversialist, Bossuet urges the double duty of total intellectual honesty and fully Christian charity. 'He would rather be indulgent than unjust,' claims his biographer, Alfred Rébelliau. 'He would consider it equally dishonest to conceal his own beliefs as to misrepresent those of his adversary, because if, by means of the first, he betrays both his religion and his conscience, by the second he reveals himself the sworn enemy of fraternal charity.'

Perhaps it was precisely because of this happy blend of honesty and charity that Bossuet was responsible for so many conversions. He did not treat the Huguenots in his diocese as vermin to be exterminated but as *frères séparés* to be encouraged to rejoin the family. His *Histoire des Variations des Eglises Protestantes* is described by Owen Chadwick as 'one of the sharpest weapons in the armoury of Catholic apologetic'. It is the work, however, of a theologian rather than an historian. 'Bossuet', continues Chadwick, 'had declared the axiom that variation in religion was always a sign of error; that the Christian religion came from its Lord complete and perfect; that the true Church had maintained immutably – *must* have maintained immutably – the deposit of truth which had been given to it.' Jansen had expressed this by asserting that theology was an affair of the memory, not of the reasoning faculty.

Firmly convinced that the true Church had never varied, Bossuet never varied either. 'Touch the bell anywhere', wrote Chadwick, 'and it sends forth the same note, deep and serene, across the fields.'

The most respectable alternative to invariability is the doctrine of legitimate development. Where matters of church order, rather than matters of theology are concerned, this is particularly important. The full Catholic definition of a bishop or a priest may or may not be a legitimate development of the apparently interchangeable terms of *Episcopos* (bishop) and *Presbuteros* (priest) in the vocabulary of Saint Paul. It has certainly not come down to us 'unchanged from the teaching of Jesus Christ'. So far as we know he never mentioned the subject. The full doctrine of papal authority may or may not be a legitimate development of the authority conferred upon Peter. His apparent position at the Council of Jerusalem, described in the fifteenth chapter of the Acts of the Apostles, is hardly a blue-print for the papacy as Bossuet knew it. Bossuet was, however, by no means blind to some of the mistakes of his Church. 'He is severe in his judgement of Mary Stuart', writes Rébelliau, 'and condemns the Massacre of Saint Bartholomew. Never did Coligny [its most distinguished victim] – "Français jusqu'au fond du coeur" – receive more magnificent praise than from Bossuet.'

Bossuet was quick to detect the real weakness of Protestantism, which is its capacity for fragmentation. It seems that the further Protestantism moves from its Catholic roots the greater is the proliferation of sects. Bossuet was right to underline the *unité dans la continuité* which is the ideal, but he takes little account of the Great Schism of 1054 when the 'Catholic' Church in the west broke away from the 'Orthodox' Church in the east. The 'unity in continuity' was lost five centuries before the Protestant Reformation provoked the further disintegration of the One, Holy, Catholic and Apostolic Church.

Further evidence of Bossuet's honesty is in the lengths to which he went to gain a true understanding of his opponents' position. 'There can still be seen', continues Rébelliau, 'in the Séminaire at Meaux the enormous notebooks, in his handwriting, which prove that he had gone through many *in folio* editions of Luther, many works by Calvin, Melancthon, Erasmus and a score of others.'

It was this combination of integrity and reasonableness which gave Bossuet the courage to confront Louis with the sin of his matrimonial infidelity and with his responsibility for the misery of his people. Of Louis' passion for Mme de Montespan he wrote: 'I do not require, Sire, that you should extinguish in a single moment a flame so violent; that would be to ask of you the impossible; but, Sire, try, little by little, to diminish it; beware of entertaining it.' Louis was ready to listen to those who spoke to him in that spirit and from that altitude.

Even bolder, but just as reasonable and realistic, was Bossuet's appeal to Louis to take note of the sufferings of his people. In a letter dated 10 July 1675, when the Dutch war seemed to be dragging on interminably, Bossuet confronted the King with his true responsibility to the poor – 'the very strict obligation which it imposes on you to keep a watchful eye on their misery'.

Bossuet also played an important part in the management and affairs of the Gallican Church, which was trying to remain within the bounds of Catholicity while claiming a certain measure of independence from the Vatican. Relations between Louis and the Pope had never been good, but matters came to a head when, in 1681, Pope Innocent XI excommunicated the vicars-general nominated by Louis for two vacant dioceses. The cause at issue was the *droit de régale* – the right to enjoy the revenues of the see during an interregnum. Both Louis and the Pope laid claim to this right.

A General Assembly *extraordinaire* was summoned to consider the crisis. Colbert, assisted by one of his sons, the Archbishop of Rouen, and Le Tellier, assisted by one of his, the Archbishop of Reims, wanted a formal declaration of 'the doctrine of France'. It is probable that Louis would have welcomed this, but he made an opening move which showed that he was prepared to listen to reason and which, he must have known, was likely to lead to moderation: he appointed Bossuet to preach the opening address. Bossuet chose as his title 'the Unity of the Church'. It was the theme nearest to his heart and an important part of it was his desire to facilitate the return of the Protestants to the bosom of the Church.

This made it difficult for Bossuet to accept, without modification, the position of the ultramontanists – the zealots for papal authority, who seemed to reduce the voice of the Church to the pronouncements of the Pope. This was belittling to the voice of the bishops and to the ancient custom of appealing to the common mind of a general council. But it was equally difficult to countenance any substitution of royal for papal power, as in the Church of England. He could not go so far 'as to find good the right of the King'. And yet he believed that there was an aura of divinity – *un je ne sais quoi de divin* – attaching to the French monarchy. An English ambassador had been heard to say that soon there would be no difference between the Church of England and the Church of France. But the Gallicanism of Bossuet was more concerned with the Church *in* France than with the Church *of* France.

Bossuet produced what was not only a masterpiece of French literature and an important statement of theology but also a triumph of pacification. His address contained, writes Aimé-Georges Martimort, 'a moving presentation of the mystery of the Church, a magnificent hymn to unity and a paean of praise for the Chair of Saint Peter'. To this he added a delicate allusion to the reserves felt by the Gallican Church about ecclesiastical authority. He asserted that a broadening of the base of its authority did not imply 'the slightest diminution of the true greatness of the Holy See', but he required that such authority shall be exercised 'in the manner understood by bishops and not in the manner understood by magistrates'.

There are times when his arguments could be said to contradict each other, but it is done with such finesse and with so delicate an avoidance of clear-cut definitions that one hesitates to reproach him. He was certainly prepared to admit a principle but to regard the time as not ripe for putting it into practice. It could be, in his own words, 'hors de saison', and to enforce it at that moment might only increase the divisions which they were trying to heal. He claimed that 'he would have preached it in Rome with the confidence with which he had preached it in Paris'.

15

The Louvre, Versailles, the Navy, Trianon and Clagny

Thanks to Colbert's financial reforms Louis was rich enough to indulge a very real taste for military exercises and the art of war. He was beginning also to cultivate the equally expensive arts of peace. The construction of sumptuous buildings and the laying out of appropriately elaborate gardens was to become his ruling passion until the end of his days. The way of life which this required for the Court extended the field of interest to music, drama and literature. To Louis these were undoubtedly seen as means of ministering to his pursuit of glory.

On 23 February 1663, Colbert created the Petite Académie, consisting of four men of letters, of whom the best known was Charles Perrault. They were to meet regularly on Tuesdays and Fridays. 'You may judge, *Messieurs*,' wrote Louis, 'the esteem which I have for you, because I am entrusting to you the thing which is the most precious in the world – my *gloire*. I am sure that you will do marvels; I will try for my part to furnish you with material to be put in hand by men as capable as yourselves.' Their work led to the creation of the Académie des Inscriptions et Médailles. Louis' glory needed to be eternalised in art and literature.

It is in this light that the setting up and maintenance of the great Academies should be seen. Two were already in existence, the Académie Française, founded by Richelieu in 1635, which was still flourishing, and the Académie de Peinture et de Sculpture, founded by Mazarin in 1648, which was not. To these Colbert added the Académie de France à Rome (1666), the Académie des Sciences (1666), the Académie d'Architecture (1671) and the Académie de Musique (1672).

The Académie Française had been at work for some thirty years on its great Dictionary, a colossal undertaking which was expected with impatience, but which did not finally appear until 1694, twelve years after the death of Colbert. The foundation of the academies bears witness to the breadth of Colbert's vision, but Louis demanded from Colbert 'the detail

of everything', and it is in the innumerable little details of his administration that the enormous scale of his undertaking and achievement can
best be appreciated.

Mazarin's Académie de Peinture et de Sculpture had run into heavy
opposition from its medieval predecessor, the Guild, and strenuous efforts
had been made by the Parlement de Paris to counter what they saw as an
attack on their ancient privileges. New regulations were drawn up by
Colbert, who nominated Charles Le Brun as Master. A more despotic
ruler would be difficult to imagine. For twenty years Le Brun was in
charge of the artistic ensemble of the royal palaces.

It had been the practice for some time to award bursaries to promising
students of art to study in Rome, but it was soon recognised that 'the
greater number of those who had been to Rome came back with no more
knowledge than they started with, which was the result of debauchery or
of wasting time with small private commissions'. To remedy this state of
affairs Colbert created the Académie de France à Rome.

The Academy was placed under a rector appointed by the King. The
first to be appointed was Charles Errard. Under his supervision there were
to be twelve pupils who had to be both French and Catholic. Six of them
were to be painters, four sculptors and two architects. Their regime was
strict. The day began with prayers at five in summer and six in winter.
They had to be in bed by ten. They studied arithmetic, geometry, perspective and anatomy and made copies of the works of the great masters.

In July 1667, Colbert wrote to the French ambassador, the duc de
Chaulnes, asking him to visit the Academy from time to time to assure
them of the King's interest. 'His Majesty, loving the fine arts as he does,
will cultivate them with all the more care since they could serve to
eternalise his great and glorious actions.' In 1671 it reached Colbert's ears
that Charles Errard was not satisfied with the standard of discipline.
Colbert immediately demanded details, adding: 'It is my desire that you
have full and absolute authority to expel any who fail to observe this.'
He took an active interest in the individual pupils and followed their
progress throughout their time at the Academy.

The Académie d'Architecture consisted of only seven men and the
secretary, André Félibien, the historiographer of the royal palaces. They
studied the works of Vitruvius, Vignola, Philibert de l'Orme and Androuet
du Cerceau. Their object was to discover whether it was possible to assert
the existence of an objective standard of beauty. The analogy of musical
and architectural proportions was a subject upon which Vitruvius,
Vignola and Philibert de l'Orme had much to say. De l'Orme claims that
it is possible to reduce '*symmetry to symphony* and the *Harmony of sound*
to a kind of *Harmony of Sight*'. 'There is', they decided, 'in architecture a

certain arrangement, rhythm, disposition, grandeur and proportion in the parts which produces this union of harmony which we call beauty and is perhaps no less inherent in nature than the rhythm, the disposition and arrangement of sounds which produces that harmonic unity in music which pleases us.' The idea that architecture can be regarded as 'frozen music' dates back at least to Boethius. Harmony in music is a matter of objective truth. The human ear is so constituted as to register the octave. Saint Augustine had been impressed by the fact that harmonic intervals can be represented as intervals of length along the string of a musical instrument. From here it is an easy step to the theory that these intervals of length constitute harmonic proportions which are as satisfying to the eye as their equivalents in sounds are pleasing to the ear.

The basic position of the academicians was that painting and sculpture should make their appeal to the reason rather than to the eye – hence the primacy, in their view, of composition, perspective and proportion. Colour, which appeals chiefly to the eye, was of secondary importance. Everything must be done according to the rules. Le Brun even produced a treatise on the *Méthode pour apprendre à dessiner les passions*. As Anthony Blunt comments: 'the reader will not be surprised to learn that this restrictive teaching did not produce remarkable or individual artists. The painters trained at the Academy by Le Brun are uniformly competent.' They were trying to do for the visual arts what Boileau did for literature in his search for objectivity in the art of poetry.

But Colbert was not content with theories. The works of art still had to be created. By the setting up in Paris of such manufactures as the Savonnerie and the Gobelins, created by Fouquet near Vaux-le-Vicomte and transferred to Paris in 1664, he ensured their production and, according to Félibien, 'obtained from His Majesty new favours for these illustrious workmen in order to stimulate them the more by the desire for rewards and honours', 'for nothing contributes more to the glory of the prince than these immortal works which the painters and sculptors leave to posterity'.

Some of this encouragement was achieved by a straightforward system of pensions and gratifications. In January 1664, assisted by Charles Perrault and Jean Chapelain, 'the regent of Parnassus', Colbert drew up a list of 58 men, eleven of whom were foreigners, among whom 77,500 livres were distributed. In 1665 the sum of 82,000 livres was shared between 75 men; in 1666 the sum rose to 95,000 and the number of recipients sank to 72. The highest sums seem to have gone to the foreigners; Christian Huygens, a physicist from Holland, received 6,000 livres while Jean-Dominique Cassini, astronomer, received 9,000. At the other end of the scale the sieurs Lacrois and Dippi shared 600 livres for six months' work translating the Arabic manuscripts in the King's library and the sieur Dupuy obtained a pension 'in consideration of his application to the study of mathematics'. Mathematics was, in fact, the most highly subsidised of subjects. The best-known names were not the most highly paid. Molière received 1,000 livres for his 'ouvrages de théâtre' and Racine 1,500 for his 'belles pièces de théâtre'. Indispensable to such varied activities was the need to discover where true talent was to be found. In June 1683, a circular went out to all Intendants asking for information: 'since the King makes gratifications to men of letters, and since His Majesty is Protector of the Académie Française and has established various academies of science and of the arts, it is much to be hoped that, in all the provinces of the realm, there could be found literary men who devote themselves to some particular branch of science, or even to the history of a particular province'.

Colbert was very conscious of the importance of history, especially history that would eternalise the memory of Louis le Grand, and he saw that local histories were needed to provide the details necessary for this. He knew that Louis was prepared to encourage local men of promise and he knew that there is nothing so discouraging as the fear that one's gifts and abilities may pass unrecognised. 'If there should be any of this kind, His Majesty could perhaps offer them some gratification, in proportion to their merit. I beg you to examine whether, in the extent of your area, there is anyone of this quality, and, if so, to let me know.' Colbert was keen on encouraging the young: 'if you were to find some young man of twenty-five or thirty, who has talent and a natural aptitude for applying himself to research into all that might make up the history of a province, you may stimulate him to undertake this work ... in which case, according to his industry and his merit, I could obtain for him some gratification from His Majesty'. One cannot help noticing that, when Louis was looking for men of special skills, he nearly always found them.

In appointing Colbert, at the end of 1664, to the post of Surintendant des Bâtiments, Louis set his architectural ambitions upon a firm foundation.

During the first years of Louis' effective reign the Court had divided its time mainly between Paris and the Châteaux of Saint-Germain and Fontainebleau. In Paris the two palaces of the Louvre and the Tuileries were both being enlarged and embellished. But Versailles was already coming into an ever greater prominence in Louis' mind. The history of its creation has, perhaps, more to teach us about Louis as a King than anything else. It involved him in serious disagreements with Colbert.

Colbert had a vision of Paris as the centre of France: 'Paris', he wrote to his eldest son, the marquis de Seignelay, 'being the capital of the kingdom and the seat of the King, it is certain that it sets the pace for all the rest of the country and that all internal affairs begin with it.' But Paris, in terms of seating the King, could only mean the Louvre. Colbert's great ambition was to see the King housed in splendour at the heart of his great metropolis.

For reasons which remain obscure, he did not like Le Vau, whose plans for the Louvre were regarded as accepted. 'Colbert', wrote Charles Perrault, 'was not satisfied with this design; it became a matter of honour with him to provide this palace with a façade worthy of the Prince who was having it built. He began by causing the design to be examined by all the architects in Paris . . . Nearly all the architects found fault with Le Vau's project.' They were, of course, all hoping to get their own designs accepted. None of them, with the exception of François Mansart, succeeded in solving the basic problem. There is a limit beyond which a classical or baroque façade can be extended without monotony. By varying the height of the various roofs and by the insertion of a large central pavilion, which looks more like a church than the gateway to a palace, Mansart at least avoided monotony. Unfortunately he was always ready to pull down what he had just built if he did not quite like it, and was, from the point of view of the client, an expensive and exasperating architect.

Colbert now turned to Italy. 'It is a question', he wrote to Poussin at Rome, 'of bringing to perfection the most beautiful building in the world.' Only in the imagination of a visionary could the Louvre ever have been so considered. The only project from Rome to be taken seriously was that of Bernini – a great architect but an extremely difficult personality. Arrogant as an artist, temperamental as a prima donna, and radically incapable of appreciating anything French, he flew into a temper at the least criticism of his designs and personally insulted most of the people whom he met. He was invited to submit a design and the design which he produced met with certain criticisms which he bitterly resented.

The duc de Créqui, Louis' ambassador in Rome, had the difficult task of trying to smooth him down. 'I went last Thursday', he wrote on 2 December 1664, 'to see the cavalier Bernin, and, the discourse turning on the new design which you told me that the King wishes him to do for the Louvre, he appeared to be utterly scandalised by the manner in which the one which had already been sent was treated. His very words were: "a greater number of observations were made and faults found than there would be stones needed for the whole building; that if he did another the same thing would happen, because the architects of France would never fail to blame anything he did as it was in their own interest not to put into execution the design of an Italian".'

When Bernini arrived in Paris, towards the end of April 1665, he found that he was not up against 'the architects of France'. He was up against Colbert.

The duel between Bernini and Colbert which ensued makes good reading. 'It would be difficult to find two spirits more opposite,' declared Perrault. Bernini was simply and solely concerned with creating theatrical effects and architectural perspectives. Colbert, with his usual eye for detail and for the practical, insisted on asking: 'Where and how was the King to be lodged, how the service could be effected most commodiously.' He wanted to know everything about the distribution of the rooms, 'even to the smallest which are no less necessary than the most important'. Bernini, however, 'did not understand and did not wish to understand any of these details, fancying that it was beneath the dignity of a great architect like himself to condescend to such minutiae'.

Colbert drew attention to the need for a certain measure of security 'without it being necessary to construct a fortress, but just to ensure that the entrances cannot be too easily approached and that the whole building should impose respect'. He required that Bernini should visit the Louvre several times between ten o'clock and midday to observe the number of coaches and the concourse of people so that the *place* before the palace would be sufficient to contain them. He insisted that the architect should always bear in mind 'our climate and the way of life of our Kings'. Since France had only four or five months of summer, during which the King was practically never in Paris, it was necessary to regard the Appartement d'Hiver as the one which he would most normally make use of. Bernini's design would have been more suited to an Italian summer.

Colbert goes on to underline the need for all the water conduits to be 'extraordinairement faciles', as also the drains 'for the easy disposal of excrement and the cesspools of the privies so that evil smells should never incommode the apartments ... It is necessary to regard this point as one of the most important and on which depends the health of the royal family.'

Louis had originally expressed the desire to preserve the work of his predecessors, but he finally agreed, or pretended to agree, with Bernini's advice 'de tout jeter par terre'. Bernini would have created an immense palace in an uncompromisingly Italian style. He made no concession to the difference of climate, let alone to the difference of architectural tradition. It would have looked out of place in the middle of Paris. Somewhat surprisingly, however, Louis accepted his modified design and the foundations were even begun. But the moment Bernini left the country, his project was abandoned.

In April 1667, the Petit Conseil des Bâtiments was appointed. From this group originated the design, which is often attributed to Perrault alone, of the colonnade. This formed the east front – much as we see it today. It is difficult to say exactly to whom the credit is due, but, in a batch of designs, marked in Perrault's handwriting: 'divers plans and elevations of the Louvre – useless', is an exquisite drawing by François d'Orbay, showing the right-hand pavilion and part of the façade adjoining it. It contains most of the features of the actual building but avoids two which might be regarded as grounds for adverse criticism – the disproportionately large central window to the end pavilions and the monotony of the skyline. D'Orbay has filled the semicircle above the window with a bas-relief, thus reducing its height, and he has crowned his balustrade with an impressive array of trophies.

Henri Sauval, a contemporary historian of Paris, makes the interesting statement that 'these great works were begun in 1667 and continued to the state at which they are seen at present in 1670, under the oversight and from the designs of Le Vau ... François d'Orbay, his pupil, made no mean contribution to the perfection of this beautiful work and it is to these two excellent artists that should be given the glory for the design and execution of this superb edifice.'

Ever since 1665 Colbert had been fearing the worst. 'Your Majesty is returning to Versailles,' he wrote on 28 September; 'I beseech you to permit me to say to you two words on the subject.' He admits how much this matter has been on his mind and asks forgiveness for his zeal.

'This house concerns far more the pleasure and diversion of Your Majesty than His glory. However, if Your Majesty would like to search at Versailles where is the sum of over 500,000 écus which has been spent over the last three years, he will have great difficulty in discovering where it has gone. During this time that He was spending such great sums on this house He has neglected the Louvre, which is assuredly the most superb palace in all the world and the most worthy of the greatness of Your Majesty ... Oh! what a pity that the greatest and most virtuous of Kings, of that true virtue which makes the greatest of princes, should be measured by the yardstick of Versailles.'

Sometime towards the end of 1668 Colbert was still marshalling his arguments to dissuade the King from what seemed to him a very extravagant folly. 'It is impossible to make a great house in this space. The site is hemmed in, not only by the parterres, but also by the village, the church and the lake. The steep slope of the parterres and avenues do not permit of expansion nor of any advantageous use of the terrain without turning everything upside down and incurring a prodigious expense ... which would be more appropriate and more glorious to spend on the Louvre.' But Louis had already made up his mind. Versailles was to be considerably enlarged. The new additions were known as the 'Enveloppe', for they surrounded the old building on three sides, leaving the courtyard of the Petit Château open as an inner court, now known as the Cour de Marbre.

Early in 1672, just before the beginning of the Dutch war, Charles Perrault describes another rather violent disagreement when 'M. Colbert, and nearly all the Court' tried to induce the King to have the Petit Château pulled down 'in order to be able to complete the whole palace in the same order and the same architecture as that which had just been built'. 'But the King still wanted to preserve the Petit Château. In vain did they say that it was in danger of falling down and was caving in in several places; he was suspicious of their intentions and said in a strong and angry voice: "Do what you will; but if you pull it down I will have it rebuilt just as it was without changing anything." '

Seen from the gardens, the Enveloppe presented an entirely new aspect. It was all of stone, three storeys high, with the first floor proportioned by an Ionic Order. Two long buildings, containing the Grand Appartement to the north and the Appartement de la Reine to the south, flanked the Petit Château on either side, each presenting towards the west a stately façade of seven windows with a portico at first-floor level marking the centre. These two blocks were connected at ground-floor level by a long arcade supporting a terrace behind which the central portion of the whole façade was deeply recessed. The terrace was overlooked by three windows on each side. There is an architect's drawing in the collection of the Ecole des Beaux Arts which gives the details of Le Vau's façade and the manner in which it was attached to the Petit Château. The three windows of the first floor come right down to floor level and each is surmounted by a bas-relief. The attic storey is what we see today.

Despite many changes in plan, the new building progressed with little interruption. The accounts for 1669 show an expenditure of 335,000 livres for masonry, which rises to 586,000 and 428,500 in the following years. In 1672 it dropped to 54,500 as the new structure rose above the gilded rooftops and chimney-stacks of the old Versailles.

Louis frequently visited the scene of operations himself with a sharp and critical eye, and the prospect of his next visit was kept as a perpetual incentive to the workmen. When he was absent, especially on his campaigns, he maintained a correspondence with Colbert so voluminous that the Superintendant, fearing that his labours might be *de trop*, asked whether he desired long or short despatches. 'De longs,' came the answer; 'le détail de tout.' It was by his close interest in detail, during the many years of its construction, that Louis imprinted his personality upon Versailles, which made it, not a prosaic essay in classical architecture, but something individual and made to measure.

It is not clear why Louis abandoned Paris for Versailles. Some have linked this with a supposed dislike of the capital caused by the humiliations of the Fronde. But Louis' long periods of residence both at the Louvre and at the Tuileries and his evident concern for the modernisation of Paris do not support this theory. In an edict issued in March 1667 for the setting up of a Conseil de Police, Paris is described by Louis as 'le lieu de notre résidence ordinaire'. Two other considerations suggest themselves. One is that the isolation of Versailles had a symbolic value in representing the unique position of the monarch. However magnificent the Louvre might become, there was perhaps implicit just the slightest suggestion that the King might be sharing there his own supremacy with that of his capital. The other is simpler still. Versailles was not only a palace; it was a palace with a garden. The latter was, if anything, the more important; Louis was a great lover of the open air.

This was appreciated by the English philosopher John Locke, who visited Versailles in June 1677: 'A beautiful house', he wrote, 'but even more a beautiful garden.' Unfortunately Locke did not have the gift of lucid description and his account of Versailles is disappointing. The château was still the 'Enveloppe' of Le Vau, but the gardens were already, in broad outline, assuming their familiar form. Above all the great cruciform Canal had been created, which set the scale for the whole gigantic lay-out.

Seldom can 100 hectares (some 250 acres) of land have undergone such a metamorphosis. The duc de Saint-Simon described the original site as 'the most sad and barren of places, with no view, no water and no woods'. But Louis was undeterred. The more difficult the undertaking, the greater was the glory of the King who succeeded in overcoming those difficulties. Since Nature had not provided the Val de Galie with any features of distinction, Le Nôtre set out to create a landscape worthy of its destiny, and he went about the task with that broadness of vision which was his title-deed to greatness.

It was he who ordained the lay-out of the Grand Design, giving the land itself a new symmetry and a new shape – now making use of the natural declivity of the site (there is a drop of some 32 metres from the Palace to the Canal) to form a series of terraces; now hollowing out a vast amphitheatre for the Parterre de Latone; now clothing the slopes with woods and hedges within which were contrived bosquets of an astonishing variety.

It is impossible to appreciate the work of Le Nôtre without seeking to answer the question: 'What was the purpose of this elaborate creation?' We might begin by taking note of the nomenclature of Le Nôtre's garden. The words which are used to describe the various features are largely drawn from the vocabulary of the interior of a house – names like the *Galerie* des Antiques, the *Salle* du Conseil, the *Salle* des Festins, the *Cabinet*, or even the *Appartement* de Verdure; words like the *Tapis* Vert, the *Buffet* d'Eau or the Parterre de *Broderie* are all suggestive of indoor architecture and furnishing. It is as if the gardens were conceived as a vast open-air extension of the palace, and in fact the uses to which these Cabinets de Verdure were put reflect, as often as not, those of the State Rooms. We find them serving for supper parties, for theatricals, for dances: was not one of the most elaborate of the bosquets known as the *Salle* de Bal?

The principle of the bosquet is clearly illustrated by the painter Jean-Baptiste Martin. His view of Versailles from the north, showing the huge Bassin de Neptune in the foreground, accurately portrays two thickly wooded enclosures which lay to either side of the central Allée d'Eau: to the left the Bosquet de l'Arc de Triomphe and to the right the Bosquet des Trois Fontaines. A water-colour of the latter, now in the Bibliothèque de l'Institut, bears the caption: 'De la pensée du Roi, executé par M. Le Nôtre'. In the mid-eighteenth century the architectural critic Jacques-François Blondel praised the manner in which the Trois Fontaines had been designed, adding that 'this bosquet alone would have sufficed to establish the reputation of Le Nôtre'. In the centre of each of these bosquets is an open space, closely embowered by the surrounding trees, exposed to the sun but sheltered from the wind, set off by an elaborate architectural feature and decorated with an alternation of statues and fountains.

As if to heighten the impression of being outdoor rooms, the statues were set against a wall of foliage in the form of a *charmille* or hornbeam hedge. In 1685 the transfer of 2,870,000 hornbeam plants from the Forêt de Lyon to Versailles took place. The bosquets provided a *raison d'être* for many of the features of the garden, but there was more to it than this. The whole lay-out was an attempt to impose upon the landscape a form conceived by the human intellect – a form in which every part was related to the whole in a manner which was easily grasped and readily understood. The principles underlying such a composition are laid down by the critic Roland Fréart de Chambray as built on 'proportion, symmetry and agreement of the whole with its parts, taught above all by geometry, the source and guide of all the arts'.

In the eighteenth century, the gardens of Versailles became unfashionable. Already such expressions as 'beau désordre', 'heureuse négligence' and 'piquante bizarrerie' were beginning to appear in the vocabulary of gardening. 'Le Nôtre massacred nature,' claimed the vicomte d'Hermenonville; 'he invented the art of surrounding himself, at great expense, with a belt of boredom.' In 1752, however, Jacques-François Blondel showed himself by no means unappreciative of the work of Le Nôtre. He saw the need for formality in the immediate surroundings of the house. The gardens were to provide a delicate and graduated transition from the refinements of architecture to the beauties of Nature. 'After having ornamented the parts nearest the building', he continued, 'one should find in Nature enough to satisfy the view.' He was more ready to praise the work of Le Nôtre at Meudon or Saint-Cloud. Here the natural contours of the ground and the delightful prospects afforded by the site provided a continual contrast between 'the regularity of the forms and the beautiful disorder of the valleys, hillsides and mountains, the one setting off the other to its best advantage'.

Another feature of the gardens is provided by the numerous groups of statues. Charles Mauricheau-Beaupré, Conservateur of Versailles in the 1950s, described the gardens as 'a great mythological poem'. Mythology was a language still understood in the seventeenth century by the educated man, and even its more subtle allusions were probably picked up by most of the courtiers. André Félibien, writing in 1674 his *Description Sommaire du Château de Versailles*, makes the point that 'just as the Sun is the device of the King, and as the poets make no distinction between the Sun and Apollo, so there is nothing in this superb residence which does not relate to this divinity; consequently, since all the images and ornaments that one sees are not placed at random, they all have reference either to the Sun or to the particular locations in which they have been put'.

The two most prominent groups of statuary in the main perspective towards the Canal are the Bassin d'Apollon and the Bassin de Latone. Latona was the mistress of Jupiter by whom she had two children, Apollo and Diana. One day, while fleeing from the wrath of Juno, Jupiter's espoused wife, she was prevented from quenching her thirst by the peasants of Lycia, who troubled the water with stones and clods of earth. She appealed to her lover to avenge the insult. He did so by turning the offending peasants into frogs. The group shows Latona and her children in the act of appealing, while around her a number of frogs continue to spit water where once they had thrown stones. Some still retain their human form, save for the hideous grin and emaciated fingers which betray their metamorphosis. Nathan Whitman, an American historian, has drawn attention to a difference in style between the figures of Latona with her children and those of her attackers. The former, 'a standard example of baroque classicism' executed in 1668 by Gaspard Marsy, contrasts with the grotesque treatment of the other figures in which Gaspard collaborated with his brother Balthasar. This 'stylistic discrepancy' is most effective and expresses the social distance between royalty and peasantry.

As the mother of Apollo, Latona could claim a place of honour in the 'mythological poem' of Versailles, but in the choice of this particular event it is possible to see in Latona an allusion to Anne of Austria, the mother of the Sun King, and in the hideous figures throwing mud and stones at her, a grim reminder of the Fronde.

Much the same symbolism can be detected in the Fontaine du Dragon, today the Bassin de Neptune, at the bottom of the Parterre du Nord. The dragon was Python – the 'monster bred of mud and slime' – who dominates the group of statues, transfixed by an arrow. Python appeared also in the mural paintings of the Escalier des Ambassadeurs. This was described in the *Mercure Galant* of September 1680. Louis, it claimed, 'put an end to the civil wars. These revolts are represented . . . by the serpent Python, because it derived its origin solely from the coarse impurities of the earth and because it was pierced, almost at birth, by the arrows of Apollo, who, in this subject, represents the King.' The King, in fact, writes Nathan Whitman, 'restores order by destroying the monster of civil rebellion'.

One of Louis' greatest pleasures was to take visitors of distinction and show them round his gardens. On 12 September 1671, the Venetian ambassador, Francesco Michiel, spent the day at Versailles. The maréchal de Bellefonds received him and offered to take him round. It was an opportunity not to be missed, first for its own sake, but secondly as an acceptable way of paying one's court to the King – 'the works of Versailles being occupations which delight the mind of the King'. The visit to the gardens was kept for the afternoon and Louis was informed of this at his dinner.

The tour began with the Grotte de Thétis, where the ambassador duly admired the figures by Girardon and Regnaudin, which he found to be 'equalling, both in the proportions of their design and the delicacy of their draperies, the marvels left by the sculptors of antiquity'. While they were there the King arrived in a small coach which he drove himself. 'He drew rein before the grotto, descended with a joyful countenance and with the most open graciousness, invited me to accompany him on a tour of the gardens.' During their inspection, Louis asked Michiel's opinion on the statues and on the appropriateness of their positioning. 'For two hours on end it was his good pleasure that I should accompany him into the remotest parts and the most delicious retreats where he can repose from the fatigue occasioned by his demanding occupations.'

Not only did Louis show the ambassador the full extent of the gardens as they were, he gave him a preview of what they were to be. 'His Majesty was good enough to put the finishing touch to his kindness by showing me, with the assistance of his architects, the drawings of all his projects and by helping me to comprehend the vast designs which are intended to make perfect this domain, which is destined to surpass all that is magnificent in Italy, or in any other country, as much in the abundance of the statuary and the quality of the fountains as in the varied and delightful circuit of the gardens'.

Perhaps the thing which most interested Michiel was the central feature of the whole lay-out. 'One of the most remarkable of the creations within the vast enclosure of this domain', he continues, 'is a great canal of no ordinary breadth.' The Canal was being lengthened between 1671 and 1672 and Michiel often uses the future tense – 'it will have the length of one league'. Its finished length was in fact 1,800 metres. It was also being deepened in order to accommodate a whole flotilla of ships and boats which Louis was beginning to collect. 'The King told me that he had, for the navigation of the canal, various sorts of craft such as the little *feluccas* of Naples.' Michiel, seeking to discern the mind of the King, replied that 'to part the waters of a canal there could be nothing more appropriate than the gondolas of our City, which the King acknowledged with a gracious and courteous smile'. The hint was taken and on 28 November the Senate of Venice passed a resolution that 'two large gondolas, of the most beautiful design, should be offered to the King of France'.

An engraving by Perelle of about this time shows the Canal with a fleet of small boats and ships and a large, three-masted man of war. Pierre de Nolhac, in his book *La Création de Versailles*, quotes a text from 1681 showing how the construction of model warships for the Grand Canal by the carpenters at Versailles was used for the improvement of their design for the navy. 'If by the execution of this design the promise is crowned with success, all future frigates will be built according to this model.' There were also on the Canal two yachts built in England. Charles Perrault reported on them to Colbert: 'I think these two vessels are really beautiful. The carvings are half by English and half by French artists. The difference in style is very great and the English are a long way behind the French.'

This was doubtless welcome news, for Colbert set almost as great an importance on the beauty of a sailing ship as on its efficiency as a man-of-war. 'I agree that the works of sculpture on the three great vessels just recently constructed at Toulon has taken up a lot of time,' he wrote to the Intendant de la Marine, 'but you will yourself acknowledge that there is nothing more striking to the eye or more evocative of the magnificence of the King than the quality of the ornament, as with the finest of those which have already gone to sea, it appertains to his glory to surpass in this respect all other nations.'

This was acknowledged by two young Scottish noblemen, Lord Drumlanrig and Lord William Douglas, sons of the Marquis of Queensberry, who were doing the Grand Tour with their tutor, James Fall. In the summer of 1682 they were at Toulon, 'the most secure harbour the King of France hath for his warships... That which is most admired is the *Grand Louis*, a ship of prodigious bigness, rich in gildings and in all other tackling, which makes her esteemed the stateliest ship in the world, whereof at least the French must be persuaded since these two lines are engraven in gold letters on her:

> Je suis l'unique sur l'onde
> Comme mon maître l'est dans le monde.'

James Fall concludes his account with the observation: 'The ships and magazines are extremely fine and well kept.'

Typically, Louis' chief interest in his fleet was the opportunity which it offered to assert his primacy over other nations. No French ship was ever to strike its flag to a foreign vessel. Special buttons were made with the device of an eagle soaring above the waves with the motto 'Tout me cède ou me fuit' (All yield to me or run away).

Colbert, in his efforts to raise the country to the status of a maritime power, was not able to enlist the whole-hearted enthusiasm of the King, but his campaign received considerable support in terms of royal money and royal time. Louis' lack of personal interest had something to do with individual bravery. He did not deny the potential advantage of a strong navy, but wrote in his memoirs: 'Warfare on land is an opportunity for valour which has more advantages than naval warfare, in which even the most valorous almost never have occasions to distinguish themselves from the most weak.'

'Whoever has the mastery of the sea', wrote Richelieu, 'has great power over the land.' It was a principle, however, which he was never able to put into practice. Colbert was an avowed admirer of Richelieu and in many ways tried to follow the Cardinal's principles and to carry them further than he had been able to himself.

For Colbert the development of a strong navy and mercantile fleet was a matter of logical necessity. The idea of bringing in more bullion was fundamental to his policies. 'The tangible fruits of the success of all these', he wrote to the King, 'would be by attracting a very large amount of money into the Kingdom through trade; not only would he soon succeed in re-establishing the balance which there must be between money in trade and the taxes paid by the people, but he would also increase both the one and the other.' On the one hand, the more the people were earning the more they could afford to pay in taxes; on the other hand, increase of bullion meant trade, trade meant ships and ships meant trained and experienced mariners and a full back-up service.

But France was not a maritime power. During the fifteenth and sixteenth centuries, Genoa, Venice, Portugal, Spain, England and Holland had all engaged in the great upsurge of maritime exploration and colonial expansion. France had been conspicuously absent from the scene; and yet, geographically, with a seaboard on the Channel, a seaboard on the Atlantic and a seaboard on the Mediterranean, she seemed ideally placed for such activities. But for much of the sixteenth century the energies of France were largely absorbed by her internecine religious wars. It seems also that there was something in the national psychology which created a reluctance to take to the seas.

In 1663 Colbert himself outlines, in a memorandum to Louis, the position which he found when he took over the navy. 'For more than ten years no more than two or three French warships have put out to sea; all the naval magazines are completely empty; the total number of vessels is reduced to twenty or twenty-two, several of which are no longer fit for service, having rotted in port from lack of maintenance; the captains are inexperienced because of the long cessation of operations; the best sailors, and many others, have taken service abroad, finding no work in France.'

Clearly a colossal undertaking of closely interconnecting reforms needed to be set in motion, but the first necessity was that Colbert should have undisputed control over the whole field. Needless to say there were men occupying places of authority which they were not qualified to exercise but who clung tenaciously to their prerogatives. At the top of this list was the duc de Beaufort, an illegitimate son of Henri IV and Gabrielle d'Estrées. The position of Amiral de France had been abolished by Richelieu, but Beaufort held the title of Grand Maître. On 25 June 1669, Beaufort was killed in action in Candia. It was somewhat providential, for it enabled Colbert, by an edict of the same year, to suppress the position and to revive that of Amiral de France, which was immediately bestowed upon the comte de Vermandois, an illegitimate son of Louis XIV and Louise de La Vallière. As he was only four years old, Colbert could exercise his function in his name.

A little before Beaufort's death, Louis had written to him almost in despair. 'The difficulties which one encounters on all sides in the raising of ships' crews for my vessels are such that it is impossible that I should be able to think of making any large commissions unless I can find means to change the ill will and the almost insurmountable aversion which mariners have to engage in the service of my fleet.' Colbert's most effective measures for recruitment were the establishment, in September 1673, of a mutual insurance system for 'Les Invalides de la Marine', and a general improvement in the standard of living of those on board. From 1669 a central Munitionnaire Général took responsibility for all the catering. The standard of food became higher and the cost to the King lower. But Colbert never had enough men to meet his needs.

Another important consideration was the prospect of promotion. 'Naval administration was never based on venal office holding', writes Geoffrey Symcox, 'so that it was largely free from the built-in inertia characteristic of venality, and though advancement might not have been purely dependent upon merit, it was still probably more accessible to unsupported talent.' This is illustrated in some of the letters of Mme de Maintenon to her sailor cousin, the comte de Villette-Mursay. 'I must compliment you', she wrote to his wife in February 1676, 'on the marvels which M. de Villette has achieved; I had my first news of it from the King, who did me the honour to tell me that my cousin had distinguished himself.' In another letter, written a few days later to Philippe himself, she states frankly: 'I could not have asked for more from you in order to support my good offices; I will certainly do the best I can, but do continue to help yourself, for my credit is mediocre and what you have done will do you more good with the King than the good offices of all the ladies in France.' Her letters shed light on the interdependence between personal merit and credit at Court. One needed both.

Philippe de Villette had with him on board his twelve-year-old son, the comte de Mursay. He was wounded at Agosta in April 1676. Mme de Maintenon was delighted to hear of this and lost no time in recounting the fact to Mme de Montespan. It all helped to build up the young man's reputation – his *nom* at Court – and from *nom* one could hope to graduate to *renommée* (fame).

Another indispensable factor was the creation of naval bases. Colbert was reluctant to make use of the large city ports, partly because, once again, he was up against vested interests and divided responsibilities. At Toulon, for instance, the gigantic chain which could be drawn across the entry to the harbour could be raised or lowered only by order of the Council. Unfortunately neither Dunkirk nor Le Havre was deep enough to harbour really large vessels. Colbert had to look as far afield as Brest. Brouage had silted up and Colbert proceeded to a new creation – Rochefort. Built, like Brest, on a simple grid system by the architect Le Vau, with the assistance of Blondel and Clerville for the dockyards and fortifications, it had all the necessary buildings to house the manufactures needed – a rope-walk and drying room (which still exist) for the construction of cables, a forge for making the anchors, a foundry, the hangars and timber pond for the making of masts, and the powder magazines, besides the quays and dry-docks. By 1670 Rochefort was fully equipped for the building of ships of the very latest design. These took into account the latest development of naval tactics. The old system of trying to board the enemy ship was less and less employed; the new system of line-of-battle tactics, writes Symcox, 'was developed as the best way of co-ordinating a fleet's broadsides, so that naval tactics became an artillery duel between lines of warships sailing parallel courses'.

But the Canal at Versailles was not merely a stretch of water which was useful for trying out miniature naval ships. It was the centrepiece of the whole garden lay-out, joining the bosquets with the Ménagerie.

One of Louis' favourite pastimes in summer was to embark on the Canal 'to enjoy the freshness of evening'. Mme de Montespan was naturally his companion. It was as a destination for these expeditions that Trianon was planned. It was first conceived as a garden. This was not an area greatly endowed by Nature and there are frequent mentions in the accounts of the transporting of 'good earth' to provide the gardens with topsoil; an immense quantity of manure was imported also. Thus cared for, Trianon flourished. André Félibien was among the earliest to record its charms: 'One could with reason name it the "Abode of Spring", for in whatever season one goes there, it is enriched with flowers of every kind and the air which one breathes is perfumed by the jasmines and orange trees beneath which one walks.'

The orange trees lined the parterres; they did not stand in cumbersome tubs waiting to be trundled back into some vast orangery for the winter, but were planted in the soil. At the coming of the first frosts the gardener, Le Bouteux, erected a greenhouse over them which was removed in the following spring. It was the only concession made to the elements, for the gardens were kept supplied with flowers throughout the year by the expedient of planting them out fresh every day from the hothouses. Thus even in midwinter Louis was able to take his guests for a walk in a spring garden.

The accounts for the period are full of references to the purchase of flowers on a gigantic scale. Colbert's letters and instructions illustrate the same concern. On 5 May 1670, he wrote to Louis: 'The garden is pro-gressing well; Le Bouteux is being provided with all that he needs.' Louis noted in the margin: 'It will be well to urge Le Bouteux on and not let him lose a minute.' It seems that he was a man who needed supervision. 'Visit Trianon often,' wrote Colbert to Petit. 'See that Le Bouteux has flowers for the King for the whole winter and that he has enough workers . . . You must render an account to me every week of the flowers that will be available.'

To the Intendant des Galères at Marseille, the Sieur Arnould, Colbert wrote: 'I beg you to buy me all the jonquils and tuberoses that you can possibly find.' In answer to his request came 3,000 jonquils, 1,300 hyacinths and a promise of further supplies. In order to maintain this continual transformation scene, Le Bouteux kept, according to the duc de Luynes, the almost unbelievable number of 1,900,000 flower-pots. Louis' victory over the seasons was asserted in verse by the duc de Saint-Aignan:

> Pour le plaisir des yeux changé l'ordre du temps,
> Fait des plus grands hivers un éternel printemps.

The gardens required an architectural focus: Louis required a private retreat for himself and Mme de Montespan. In 1669 Le Vau was commissioned to design a little pavilion which would serve both purposes. Some five years earlier, the west of Europe had become acquainted with the fabulous Tour de Porcelaine at the imperial palace of Nankin, 'built with such propriety, proportion and symmetry that the foremost architects of the universe could find nothing to say against it'. The taste for chinoiserie (the word is comparatively modern; *lachinage* would have been the word familiar to Louis) had already come to France under Mazarin, and in Delft the factories were producing beautiful tiles of blue and white porcelain for decoration. It was in this style that Louis decided to decorate his Palais de Flore. The architecture remained, however, strictly classical. Having planned his pavilion with a disposition reminiscent of the Villa Pia at the Vatican, fixed its proportions with a Doric order and loaded it with a high and highly decorated mansart roof, Le Vau relied upon a profusion of ornaments for an effect which he hoped might pass as a tolerable imitation of the architecture of the Far East.

The roof was entirely covered with porcelain tiles, blue and white with a little yellow or green. The roof ridge at both levels carried a great quantity of china urns; between the urns were grouped a number of gilded *amorini*, while on the tier above them a line of birds, painted in natural colours, presented to those standing in the forecourt a jagged skyline suggestive, perhaps, of the temples of Nankin.

The furnishing of the apartments betrayed the purpose of the building. The central salon, the largest of the rooms, merits the shortest entry in the inventory. Two armchairs and eighteen tabourets suggest a merely formal use. According to Félibien, the walls were of stucco 'very white and highly polished with ornaments of azure'. A curious fact revealed in the accounts is that this work was done by Carmelite monks 'who sent two of their brothers to paint white the apartments of Trianon'. The fact that all the rooms in the four attendant pavilions were consecrated to the preparation of food 'pour la table des Princes et Seigneurs' suggests that Louis was prepared to entertain here at a high gastronomic level.

To the right of the central salon was a bedroom known as the Chambre des Amours. It was furnished with 'un lit extraordinaire' in the form of a couch with a large mirror for the bedhead and overhung by a canopy of great complexity, with curtains flounced up into festoons, 'the whole of white taffeta with blue embroidery . . . the said bed trimmed with gold and silver lace and with tasselled fringes and braid also of gold and silver'. The Chambre des Amours, of course, reveals the principal purpose of the building. Louis' passion for Mme de Montespan is clearly expressed.

It must be said, in fairness to Mme de Montespan, that she had not yielded too easily to Louis' embraces. But having once succumbed, she remained the *maîtresse déclarée* for some twelve years and bore him six children. 'The pregnancies and the childbirths were common knowledge,' wrote Saint-Simon; 'the salon of Mme de Montespan became the centre of court life – the centre of pleasures, of fortunes, of hopes, the terror of ministers and generals and the humiliation of all France.'

Everyone seems to have been in agreement as to her looks. Mme de Sévigné, writing in July 1676, said: 'She was dressed entirely in French lace, her hair done in a thousand curls . . . with black ribbons on her head and the pearls of the maréchale de l'Hôpital enriched with bows and pendants of the most lovely diamonds possible . . . In a word, a triumphant beauty to present to the admiration of ambassadors.' Mme de l'Hôpital's pearls were, according to Mademoiselle, even larger than those of the Queen. They had been offered to Mazarin as a bribe for the post of *dame d'honneur* to Marie-Thérèse.

Athenaïs de Montespan was one of the most expensive of mistresses, but the largest expenses which she incurred were in connection with the Château de Clagny. This was built almost at the gates of Versailles, somewhere near the present Lycée Hoche. The official pretext was that the building was needed to house Louis' natural children. Through the influence of Le Nôtre the commission was given to a new architect, Jules Hardouin-Mansart. At the age of twenty-eight he had been commissioned by Louis to design the Château du Val, a small hunting-lodge at the extremity of the long terrace at Saint-Germain. The ground plan shows some ingenuity in the arrangement of four little cabinets around a central *poêle* or stove. Now in 1674, he was given the important commission of designing Clagny.

Such an opening must have been the fondest dream of all young artists of his age, the tide in his affairs which 'taken at the flood leads on to fortune'. Within ten years he was to enjoy a position of confidence with the King which gave almost unlimited scope for his creative powers. He put all the care and skill which he could command into the building of Clagny, which earned the description of 'perhaps the most regularly beautiful house in France'. It was built between four pavilions round three sides of a quadrangle; a fifth pavilion marked the centre of the entrance front. It presented a façade of nineteen windows westwards towards its gardens.

The work started with the gardens, which soon formed a favourite promenade for courtiers. On 12 June 1674, Louis wrote to Colbert: 'Mme de Montespan greatly desires that the garden should be ready for planting this autumn; do everything that is necessary in order that she should have this satisfaction and keep me informed of the measures which you have taken.' A year later, on 5 June, Louis wrote from his camp at Latines: 'Continue to do whatever Mme de Montespan wishes, and let me know what sort of orange trees have been brought to Clagny.'

Louis followed each stage in the construction with his usual attention to detail, while his mistress presided in person. Some of Mme de Sévigné's friends had been to the building site. 'They found the Beautiful One so occupied with the works and the enchantments which are being created for her, that, for myself, I think of Dido on the walls of Carthage . . . You cannot imagine how triumphant she is, in the midst of all her workmen, who number twelve hundred.' On 7 August, Mme de Sévigné visited Clagny herself. 'What shall I say? It is the palace of Armida. The building rises while you watch it. The gardens are finished. You know the style of Le Nôtre. He has left a little dark, shady coppice, which is very good. There is a plantation of orange trees in large tubs; one can walk about between them; they form alleys where one is in the shade. There are palisades on either side, elbow high, all ablaze with polyanthi, roses, jasmines and carnations. It is certainly the most beautiful, the most surprising, the most enchanting novelty that it would be possible to imagine.'

In one of his letters to Colbert, of 8 June 1675, Louis had admitted that the expense was excessive, but he added: 'I can see from this that, in order to please me, there is nothing that you cannot do.' The total cost of Clagny had been reckoned at some 2,862,000 livres – nearly a quarter of the vast sums spent by Colbert in that year on building up Louis' navy.

16

The Dutch War

'I have often gone to war too lightly and pursued it for vanity's sake. Do not imitate me.' This admission, made by Louis on his death-bed, formed part of his last words of advice to his great-grandson and successor, then aged five. We cannot, of course, know exactly which occasions he was thinking of, but of all the wars which punctuated the reign of Louis XIV, the war with Holland (1672–3) seems to be the one to which these words apply most obviously. It is commonly condemned as one of his gravest errors. It is not easy to say exactly what his objective was, but it is clear that he regarded the whole campaign as ministering to his glory and that he thoroughly enjoyed it.

In trying to understand Louis' motivation for the conduct of the Dutch war we must place it in its historical context. The spirit of feudalism, as the events of the Fronde had shown, was by no means dead. In the eighteenth century Montesquieu could still write: 'The essence of monarchy is war and the enlargement of dominion.' The King was a military leader. Louis had been brought up to play soldiers. Before the age of five he was taking a personal interest in the battle of Rocroi. He was encouraged to take Henri IV as his role model. He was also the undoubted leader of a warrior class. As Joseph Schrumpeter puts it: 'These did not fight for material acquisitions or specific goals but rather because it was only in battle that they could fulfil themselves and achieve their identities as dictated by the traditions of their social class.'

Saint-Maurice quotes an anecdote about the old maréchal de Biron who, as a young man, boasted that he would exterminate the troops of Spain and of the League. His father, also a maréchal de France, made the observation that, having done so, 'he would have to go and plant cabbages at Biron', adding that it was necessary to prolong the war 'in order to have some occupation and to gain a living'. Warfare was the *raison d'être* of the French nobility: it was therefore to some extent the *raison d'être* of the King. In 1664, Jan de Witt had noted with foresight that France 'has a twenty-six-year-old King, vigorous in mind and body . . . who possesses a kingdom inhabited by an extremely bellicose people'. Such a King, he continues, would have to possess 'an extraordinary, almost miraculous moderation if he thrust aside the ambition which is so natural to princes and did not extend his frontiers where they are most restricting'. He saw that a clash was inevitable between France and Holland.

There was not much love lost between the two countries. Since the reforms of Colbert they had become rivals in the world of commerce and colonialism. France was a Catholic monarchy: Holland was a Calvinist republic. It was also, to a certain extent, the centre of anti-French propaganda. Libellous material, which could not be published in France, was often printed in Amsterdam or The Hague. One medallion was struck showing Joshua causing the Sun to stand still. It had about the status of a political cartoon in a modern newspaper. Perhaps the worst offence of the Dutch Republic was, having signed a treaty with France in 1662, to have joined with England and Sweden in the Triple Alliance of 1668. But Louis also hoped that Spain would join in, which would give him a respectable pretext for attacking the Spanish Netherlands.

Sir William Temple, who had lived for two years in Holland and later became the English ambassador there, makes a contemporary comparison between the Dutch and the French. 'The States of Holland, in point of both riches and strength, is the most prodigious growth that has been seen in the world . . . the conduct of their ministers, the art, the industry and the parsimony of their people all conspiring to drive almost the trade of the whole world into their circle [while their neighbours were taken up either in civil or in foreign wars] they have grown so considerable in the world that they have treated upon an equal foot with all the great Princes in Europe . . . Their only danger they apprehend is from France, and not immediately to themselves but to Flanders, where any flame would soon scorch them.'

A little later Temple began to discern in this very strength the causes of their failure. 'I take their vast trade, which was the occasion of their greatness, to have been one likewise of their fall, by having wholly directed the genius of their native subjects and inhabitants from arms to traffic and the arts of peace, leaving their whole fortune to be managed by foreign and mercenary troops, which much abased the courage of their nation and made the burghers of so little moment towards the defence of their towns.' This lack of military training and experience and the consequent lack of confidence made them an easy prey to France. Temple contrasts the military might and efficient organisation of the French with the 'abased courage' of the Dutch.

'The Crown of France, considered in the extent of the country, in the number of people, in the revenues of the King, the greatness of the land forces now on foot and the growth of those at sea (within these two years past), the number and bravery of their officers, the conduct of their ministers and chiefly the genius of their present King, a Prince of great and aspiring thoughts, unwearied activity in all that is in pursuit, severe in the institution and preservation of order and discipline . . . I say that considered in all these circumstances, France may be designed for greater achievements and empires than have been in Christendom since Charlemagne.'

There was, however, a wider political perspective to the diplomacy and warfare of Louis' reign than lust for conquest. 'France' was not so much an area defined by the dictates of geography, as by the legacy of history. To the south, of course, there were the Pyrenees, but between France and Germany there was no 'natural' frontier but the Rhine – and that was a long way east of the political frontiers of Louis' reign. Northern France was a country wide open to invasion – as the history of Europe has often demonstrated. Only an artificially created frontier, such as Vauban's idea of a *ceinture de fer*, a pattern of fortresses controlling the high roads to Paris, could protect the sanctuary of the nation. Louis' policy was ultimately defensive in its aims, but it is sometimes true that attack is the best method of defence.

In April 1671 Saint-Maurice was reporting on the climate of opinion at Court. 'War does not seem likely. They want to damage the Dutch, but they do not know how to go about it.' April 17 still found Louis at Versailles 'where he is occupied in making the most beautiful fountains that have ever been seen. He has made up his mind to incur a horrific expense and has set aside eight millions for that.'

It was, however, officially known by then that the prince de Condé had been offered the command of the company of *gendarmes*. Condé was in fact re-establishing his reputation both as a loyal subject and as a great commander. His capture of Franche-Comté in 1668 had been as swift as it had been successful. He was to play an important part in the attack on Holland, but first he gave a display of opulent entertainment by inviting Louis and most of the Court to three days at Chantilly. The fête recalled the lavishness of that given, ten years previously, by Fouquet at Vaux-le-Vicomte. Mme de Sévigné has left the most readable account of it.

The King arrived on Thursday 23 April, towards evening. The entertainment began with light refreshments in an area 'carpeted with daffodils'. This was followed after dark with a stag hunt in a part of the forest illuminated with a thousand lanterns. It was clear moonlight and the firework display with which it ended was, according to Mme de Sévigné, 'a little effaced by the brightness of our friend; but after that the evening, the supper, the cards – all went beautifully'. There were twenty-five tables each served with five courses. At two of the lower tables there was a shortage of roasts. No one thought anything of it, but in the small hours of the following morning a tragedy occurred.

The arrangements for this sumptuous occasion were the responsibility of Condé's *maître d'hôtel*, François Vatel (who had master-minded the fête at Vaux-le-Vicomte). He was ably seconded by Herbaud de Gourville, Condé's right-hand man. A *maître d'hôtel* was a very important person with his own apartments and his own domestic servants. He filled approximately the place occupied by the steward of a great house in England under the Tudors or Stuarts.

Vatel had, by his own confession, not slept for twelve nights and his head was reeling. The lack of roast meat at two of the tables had upset him disproportionately. 'I have lost my honour,' he told Gourville; 'this is a disgrace which is more than I can bear.' Gourville reported the matter to Condé who went at once to Vatel's apartment and tried to comfort him. 'Vatel, *tout va bien*,' he insisted; 'nothing could have been finer than the King's supper.' 'Monseigneur,' replied Vatel, 'your kindness is the last straw. At two tables there was a shortage of roasts.' Nothing the prince could say would console him. The next day being Friday, and for Catholics, therefore, a day of fasting, Vatel had ordered cartloads of the finest fish from the nearest sea-ports. At four in the morning a small cartload arrived. It contained only two draughts of fish. 'Is that all?' asked Vatel, aghast. 'Yes, sir,' came the answer. Imagining, while of unsound mind, that this represented the whole order, he went up to his room, fixed his sword against the door and leant on it.

When the rest of the household got up the next morning great quantities of fish began to arrive from all sides. They ran to find Vatel. They found him dead. Mme de Sévigné could hardly hold her pen to convey the news to her daughter.

By this time there were already rumours of war. The Dutch were proposing that Louis should retain Franche-Comté but that he should restore Lille to the Spanish. 'That was something', wrote Saint-Maurice on 24 April, 'about which they did not want to hear.' In his next letter he continues: 'The King certainly desires to make war; his ministers, to please him, are urging him on.'

The Treaty of Aix-la-Chapelle was more of an armistice than a lasting peace. During the four years that it continued, the French diplomats Hugges de Lionne and, following his death in 1671, Simon Arnauld, marquis de Pomponne, were busy trying to detach the allies of Holland and at least to secure their neutrality. The appointment of Pomponne, noted by Mme de Sévigné as 'un changement si extraordinaire', raised many eyebrows. He was a nephew of Antoine Arnauld, the leader of the Jansenists, and his wife was a relative of Fouquet. These relationships could have constituted an insuperable barrier to his preferment, and it is a tribute to Louis' single-mindedness that he made the appointment. 'As for M. de Pomponne,' wrote Saint-Maurice, 'never has a choice been so generally agreed as his ... He is extremely wise, good-humoured and is an inspired speaker and writer. I have no doubt that he will follow faithfully the inclination of the King.'

The diplomacy of Lionne and Pomponne had a large measure of success. England, or rather Charles II, had already been bought out of the Triple Alliance by the secret Treaty of Dover. Sweden was to realign itself with France. The Elector of Cologne and the Bishop of Münster openly sided with Louis. The Elector of Brandenburg signed a treaty of neutrality.

Meanwhile Vauban had been busy upgrading the fortifications of Ath, Oudenarde, Charleroi and Dunkirk. In May 1671, Louis arrived at Dunkirk and on 14 May Saint-Maurice reported back to Savoy: 'They are making at Dunkirk the finest fortifications I have ever seen ... Nine thousand men are at work every day with the greatest order and diligence that has ever been put into practice ... They are divided into three brigades; one begins the work at five in the morning; it is relieved at nine by the second which remains until two and the third until nightfall. Thus they work fifteen hours without interruption, which would not be possible if they all worked the whole day.'

The marquis de Saint-Maurice, involved as an ambassador in the complexities of diplomacy, was also the eyes and ears of the Duke of Savoy in France. As such his job was to be both observant and perceptive. The balance of power between Colbert and Louvois was of some importance to the likelihood of war. Colbert, chiefly for economic reasons, favoured peace: Louvois, chiefly from personal ambition, favoured war. At the end of September 1671, Saint-Maurice reported: 'It is said that what has mortified Colbert most is that the King, asking him for the latest news about commerce, made it known that he knew that it was decaying and, taking him by the hand, said to him that what had been done had been done with the best of intentions, that he was grateful for it and that he did not grudge the expenditure that he had made and that, if the affair could not succeed, it was no use persisting in it, but better to pull out of it and to apply oneself to something more advantageous to the welfare of his crown and of his subjects.

'Everyone at Court believes that this was a stroke by M. de Louvois whose vanity is flattered that everything appertaining to his own ministry is going as well as he could wish, either in the fortifications, in the maintenance of the troops and the arsenals, where every possible economy is observed, which is not the same with things needed for navigation, where at the present moment considerable expenditure has been made.'

By the middle of December the Dutch were beginning to become alarmed. The Dutch ambassador, Peter de Groot, received a letter from the States General to pass on to Louis. The substance of it was, according to Saint-Maurice, that 'they had been assured that the great armament which His Majesty was making is in order to wage war upon them, and that they found this difficult to believe because they had never been lacking in respect nor done anything against his interests; that they had not wished to listen to the suggestions made that they should attack him; that they had carried out punctiliously all the latest treaties made with his Crown and thus, feeling their consciences to be clear, they could not imagine that he had anything against them; that if they had done him any disservice, or if, without knowing it, they had failed him in any respect, if His Majesty would have the goodness to let them know, they were ready to give him any appropriate satisfaction.'

Louis' reaction was to make an appointment with de Groot and then, saying that he had other business that day, to put him off. Louis was not prepared to show his hand. In the end the Dutch ambassador was granted an audience; he reported to the States General that Louis had appeared more lofty than ever and had said: 'We tell you that we will increase our armament by land and by sea, and when we are in the position which we plan to be in, we will make such use of it as we consider appropriate to our dignity, of which we render account to no man.'

Later in January Louvois made a personal visit to the Electorate of Cologne arranging for the provisioning of the French army, and treating with the Elector and the Bishop of Münster for their support, which he obtained. 'I must say a little about his tour,' wrote Saint-Maurice, 'about his diligence and his overworking, the treaties which he negotiated and all the splendid arrangements which he made for the subsistence of the troops and the preparations for the war. He wanted to let me know about the incompetence and irresolution of the Dutch.' Louvois instanced his own method of dealing with the problem of transporting gunpowder to Neuss – a town on the Rhine downstream of Cologne: he persuaded German merchants to purchase large quantities of gunpowder from the Dutch themselves. He said that the Dutch could easily have become the masters of Neuss with a mere 4,000 men. At the end of April 1672 Louis was ready to attack.

He himself wrote: 'Future generations will find it hard to believe that I was able to provide troops, artillery and ammunition in sufficient abundance . . . I had made such adequate provision for all things and my orders were carried out with such regularity and precision, thanks to the marquis de Louvois, that nothing was lacking at any of the sieges.'

The King's presence with his army was essential because only he or a close relative could impose order on the line of command. It was a necessity, too, for a successful siege. On Wednesday 27 April Louis left, somewhat abruptly, from Saint-Germain and on Thursday 5 May he was at the camp at Charleroi, where he was joined by Saint-Maurice. Here he reviewed his troops as they arrived, the cavalry first. The Royal Piémont Regiment, under M. de Lucinge, impressed him most. 'The King said twenty times to M. de Lucinge that he had no more beautiful cavalry.' Then he reviewed the infantry. 'There has never been any so fine in France', claimed Saint-Maurice, 'and I do not know if the Roman legions were their equals.'

Saint-Maurice was full of enthusiasm for all that he saw and relayed it in great detail to his sovereign. 'The army marches in very good order and is well paid. The King does everything himself and without fuss; without saying an angry word to anyone; he gives the orders for the marches, sets up all the camps, marks out the guard posts and visits them and works harder than any other officer.' It is interesting to find a foreign ambassador confirming the account by Pellisson, who says: 'There is no general who could apply himself more thoroughly to such a matter, nor enter more fully into all the details of a march, nor give his orders better, nor be so quick to notice the slightest irregular movement in the country, nor apply a prompter remedy than we have seen the King do in these days.'

'The King is almost continually on horseback,' continues Saint-Maurice; 'he takes great care that his army lives and marches in good order. He acts like a great captain and this campaign will certainly teach him much of the profession of arms; he always has a map of the country in his hand, he talks to all the officers, listens to everyone and gives his orders without consulting anyone.' Good leadership is the first requirement for good morale, and Saint-Maurice claims that 'the King's armies are in a position to undertake anything; their numbers are great and never have troops been more keen to do well'.

On 31 May Louis marched eastwards from Juliers and reached the Rhine near Neuss. In a letter to Colbert he wrote: 'I have estimated that it is of greater advantage to my plans, and no mean advantage to my glory, to attack, all at the same time, four places on the Rhine and to command in person all four sieges. I have chosen for this purpose Rheinberg, Wesel, Burik [Büderich] and Orsoy.' Condé was to attack Wesel, Turenne, Büderich, and Monsieur, Orsoy. Louis himself was to start at

Rheinberg, where he was near enough to hear the cannons of the three other sieges.

On 9 June Condé laid siege to Wesel. That night the King attacked Rheinberg and, as usual, exposed himself to danger. Pellisson recorded that 'the chevalier d'Arquien was wounded there by a cannon ball, of which he died today, and this was at six paces from the King, without exaggeration'. Louis used the direst threats to the Governor of Rheinberg, saying that if he did not surrender there would be no quarter given, that he would be hanged and his soldiers put to the sword. The Governor capitulated and Louis, wrote Saint-Maurice, 'with his usual generosity, permitted the said Governor to retire to Maastricht with arms and baggage for his whole garrison'. The great coup was over. 'In three days, there he is master of four well-fortified places.'

One of the consequences of the defeat of a Protestant stronghold was the reinstatement of the Catholic religion. The Cardinal de Bouillon blessed the churches and had the Mass said in them. Some of them had not heard it for a hundred years.

On 12 June Condé led his troops across the Rhine. According to Voltaire, who obtained his information from Pellisson – an eye-witness – and from his own later researches on the site, Condé had received information that, in dry weather, there was a ford over the river at Tollhuys ('toll-house'), where there was an old tower which acted as the customs office. The comte de Guiche was sent to do a reconnaissance. The ford was passable on foot except for about 18 metres in the middle, which would have to be swum. Across the river there were 'two feeble infantry regiments with no cannons'. This was clearly the place to cross. The French artillery directed a devastating fire against the Dutch troops.

The river would probably have been crossed with no casualties, but when the Dutch laid down their arms the young duc de Longueville, Condé's nephew, 'his head filled with the fumes of wine, fired his pistol at the enemy, who were on their knees asking for grace, shouting "No quarter for this *canaille*!" and shot one of the officers'. The Dutch infantry, in their despair, took up their arms again and fired a volley which killed the duc de Longueville. At about the same time a Dutch cavalry captain named Ossenbroek fired his pistol at Condé, whose raised hand, thus deflecting the bullet from his head, was seriously wounded.

Opinion has been divided as to the merit or demerit of the operation. Napoleon dismissed it as 'a fourth-rate military operation'. Louis deemed it worthy of being one of the scenes illustrated on the ceiling of the Grande Galerie at Versailles. For Louis took good care that his conquests should be recorded for posterity. He did, however, have the good taste to modify the inscriptions proposed by Charpentier – '*l'incroyable* passage du Rhin' or 'la *merveilleuse* prise de Valenciennes' – by omitting the adjectives.

Adam Frans van der Meulen kept a record of his work as official painter of battles. 'I accompanied the King on the campaign in Flanders, where I drew the town of Douai from both sides with all the particularities.' He adds Tournai, Lille and Courtrai and, during the campaign in Franche-Comté, both sides of the city of Dôle. These preliminary sketches formed the basis of later paintings and tapestries.

With the crossing of the Rhine the way was clear for a full-scale invasion of Holland. Condé urged the King to strike swiftly at Amsterdam. Louis preferred to continue adding names to his list of spectacular, if minor conquests. On 20 June the Dutch played their last, but highest, trump card. They opened the sluices from the Zuyderzee at a point not far from Muyden and flooded the polders – the vast area of flat lands below sea level. Amsterdam became an island. The opportunity of taking the most important city in Holland was lost.

The situation in Holland triggered off a revolution. Jan de Witt, who had the title of Grand Pensionary, and his brother Cornelius, representing the oligarchy of rich merchants and magistrates, would have been content with an honourable peace. But the populace, inflamed by the preaching of fanatical Calvinists, were determined on a war to the bitter end. The de Witts were murdered and the Dutch found their leader in the young Prince William of Orange, who now had the title of Stadthouder. He was twenty-two at the time and was acclaimed as the new Samson, divinely destined to destroy the Philistines.

'He was a Prince', wrote William Temple, 'frugal in the common management of his fortune, and yet magnificent upon occasion; of great spirit and heart, aspiring to the glory of military actions, with strong ambition to grow great, but rather by the service than by the servitude of his country. In short, a Prince of many virtues without any appearing admixture of vice.'

Voltaire, commenting on the renewed spirit of resistance among the Dutch, drew attention to one particular aspect. 'It is a matter worthy of the notice of posterity that Holland, thus overburdened on land . . . continued redoubtable at sea. This was the true element of these people.'

It was just about this time that France was first able to take part in a major naval encounter. On 18 March 1672, Saint-Maurice reported that the marquis de Seignelay was busy with a zeal which greatly pleased his father. 'He leaves tomorrow to launch the vessels which the comte d'Estrées is to command.' They were to join forces with an English fleet commanded by the Duke of York with Edward Montagu, Earl of Sandwich, second-in-command. These set sail on 22 April to meet the French at Portsmouth.

The Dutch admiral van Ruyter, with a fleet of some seventy ships, appeared in the mouth of the Thames too late to prevent the English and French from joining forces. On 3 May Charles II reviewed the combined fleets at Spithead. There were three squadrons: the English mustered fifty-two ships (these figures do not include smaller vessels and fire-boats) in two squadrons: the Red, commanded by the Duke of York on the flagship *Prince*, and the Blue, commanded by Lord Sandwich, on the flag-ship *Royal James*; in the White were thirty French ships-of-the-line, under Amiral d'Estrées on the flagship *Saint-Philippe*. There were three divisions, the other two being commanded by the Amiral Duquesne and the Chef d'Escadre Des Rabesnières. Between them they carried 1,664 guns. It was agreed, perhaps prudently, that if anything happened to the Duke of York, Lord Sandwich was to command the combined fleet.

On 16 May John Evelyn was at Dover and saw the whole fleet sail past. 'Such a galant and formidable navy never, I think, spread sail upon the seas. It was a goodly yet terrible sight to behold them, as I did, passing eastward by the straits betwixt Dover and Calais in a glorious day. The wind was so high that I could not well go aboard and they were soon got out of sight.'

On Tuesday 21 May, the allied fleet put into Sole Bay, on the Suffolk coast near Southwold, for victualling and careening. On the 28th de Ruyter appeared on the horizon. When the alarm was given the *Prince* was still partially heeled over for careening. It was rather a scramble to get her upright and launched: a somewhat inauspicious start.

'The English were to form their line of battle', writes Richard Ollard, 'in conjunction with the French whose quality was unknown and whose experience of fleet action against a first-class power, let alone the Dutch under de Ruyter, was nil. Even in an all-English fleet the primitive state of signalling made communications tricky to say the least. With a foreign ally it would be open to disaster.'

The only first-hand French account stresses the swiftness of the Dutch approach with an east wind and an incoming tide behind them. 'We only had time to learn that the order from His Highness the Duke of York was "to hold to the wind for as long as possible".' It was an ambiguous order. 'The Dutch were sighted to the north-east of the allied fleet', continues Richard Ollard, 'coming in line abreast. Allied reaction was confused by the fact that the Van or White Squadron, commanded by d'Estrées, was the southernmost and Sandwich's squadron, the Blue, the northern. Thus for practical purposes the Rear became the Van, since to engage the Dutch a northerly, or north-eastern course had to be steered.

The French, misunderstanding the Duke's signal, set off on a southerly course, doubtless thinking that they were to get to windward of the enemy and then tack once they were clear of an all too close and probably too little-known lee shore.' The Dutch sent a detachment to engage them which, not without a brisk exchange of fire, managed to hold the French off from the main battle.

Bishop Burnet gave de Ruyter 'the glory of surprising the English fleet, when they were thinking less of engaging the enemy than of an extravagant preparation for the usual disorders of the 29 May' – that is to say the celebration of the King's birthday – 'which he prevented, engaging them on the 28th in one of the most obstinate sea-fights that has happened in our age; in which the French took more care of themselves than became gallant men, unless they had orders to look on and leave the English and Dutch to fight it out while they preserved the force of France entire'.

Burnet was being unfair. The French loss has been estimated at 450 killed and wounded. Des Rabesnières was mortally wounded and his ship, *Superbe*, badly damaged. The French lacked one vital quality – experience. Colbert had advised d'Estrées 'to observe everything that the English do'.

The battle of Sole Bay, according to Roger Anderson, was indecisive, 'but the Dutch had more reason than the allies to be pleased with the result . . . they had, with an inferior force, inflicted enough damage to prevent the enemy from attempting any action on the Dutch coast for some time'. The allies had suffered the loss of their flagship *Royal James* and well over 700 men killed, including Lord Sandwich.

After the flooding of the polders, and an ill-judged attempt to march across the ice, the duc de Luxembourg attacked a small Dutch force at Swammerdam, which was then savagely pillaged. The same lot befell the little town of Bodegrave. This became the deliberate policy of Louis and Louvois. The country already in French hands was subjected to an enemy occupation of the utmost severity. It may have succeeded in striking terror into Dutch hearts, but it created something more lasting: it created a bitter hatred of the French which was to find its incarnation in the Prince of Orange.

The Dutch took the occasion to sue for peace. On 30 June 1672, Saint-Maurice wrote from Utrecht: 'De Groot and his colleagues arrived the same evening and were received by Louvois and Pomponne. Their conference lasted long; it was noticed that the deputies from the States went in cheerfully enough but that they came out in the deepest melancholy.' De Groot said that they had been treated 'avec la dernière rigueur'.

Their first offer was rejected. Their second, more generous, offer was rejected. Louis now proposed his own terms, more costly and more humiliating. They included an indemnity of 24 million livres and the opening of all public offices to Roman Catholics together with the free exercise of their cult. These terms the Dutch rejected. As Voltaire puts it: 'the pride of the conqueror inspired the courage of despair in the conquered'.

Bishop Burnet, who was usually well informed about the affairs of France, has left an interesting account of this phase of the negotiations: 'The King had none about him to advise with but Pomponne and Louvois, when the Dutch sent to him to know what he demanded. Pomponne's advice was wise and moderate, and would in conclusion have brought about all that he intended. He proposed that the King should restore all that belonged to the Seven Provinces, and require of them only the places that they had outside them; chiefly Maastricht, Bois le Duc, Breda and Bergen-op-Zoom: thus the King would maintain an appearance of preserving the Seven Provinces entire, which the Crown of France had always protected. To this certainly the Dutch would have yielded without any difficulty. By this he [would have] had the Spanish Netherlands entirely in his power, separated from Holland and the Empire, and might have taken them whensoever he pleased. This would have an appearance of moderation, and would stop the motion that all Germany was now in . . .

'Louvois on the other hand proposed that the King should make use of the consternation that the Dutch were then in and put them out of a condition of opposing him for the future. He therefore advised that the King should demand of them, besides all that Pomponne moved, the paying of a vast sum for the charge of that campaign; the giving of the chief church in every town for the exercise of the popish religion; and that they should put themselves under the protection of France; and should send an ambassador every year with a medal acknowledging it; and should enter into no treaties and alliances but by the directions of France.

'The Dutch ambassadors were amazed when they saw that the demands rose to so extravagant a pitch. One of them swooned away when he heard them read; he could neither think of yielding to them, nor see how they could resist them.'

In June 1673, Louis renewed his offensive. Of all military manoeuvres, the siege of a town was the one which appealed most strongly to him. There was an element of the spectacular about it. He has given his own account of his decision to attack Maastricht. 'I had carried my conquests so far in 1672 that I feared not being able to do something in 1673 that would compare with what I had already done.' His conquests, however, were remote from France and he needed a safe approach to be able to protect them. 'Only Maastricht would do.' Maastricht, says Ekberg, 'was strategically important as covering the middle reaches of the Meuse which provided the best route from France to the French-occupied territories of the Dutch Netherlands'. Louis had chosen well. On 1 May 1673, Louis, accompanied by the Queen and both his mistresses, set out from Saint-Germain. 'Never', wrote Pomponne to the duc de Chaulnes, 'was there a more splendid army.'

On 6 June Louis attacked Maastricht with a force of 25,000. The town was strongly garrisoned under Jacques de Fariaux; he was 'a brave man with a good record' and his hopes were high, but he reckoned without Vauban.

Vauban's intimate understanding of the principles of defence made him the master also of the possible methods of attack. With a task force of 20,000 peasants he proceeded to dig his way towards the fortress. The process is described by Christopher Duffy: 'Parallel gave way to zig-zag saps, zig-zag saps to a further parallel and so on until the French were close enough to take the hornwork and ravelin of the Tongres Gate by battering and assault.

'The siege parallels had the simplicity of genius . . . The first of the parallels was dug just out of effective cannon range . . . As further parallels were dug closer to the fortress, so they offered to the besiegers secure sites for their batteries, a defence against sorties and start lines and supports for assaults. Thus Vauban assailed the fortress with a marching fortress of his own and stole for the siege attack the tactical advantage which had hitherto been the preserve of the defence.'

The success was immediate. Fariaux reported that 'from the first day' his side had lost hope, and he admitted that 'he who conducted the trench work must have been the craftiest man in the world'. From the other side Louis recorded in his memoirs that 'the way in which we conducted the trenches prevented the defenders from doing anything against us, for we advanced towards the fortress in great parallel lines, broad and spacious, almost as if we were drawn up in battle formation. Neither the Governor nor his officers had ever seen anything like it.' It needs to be remembered that, according to the marquis de Quincy, who wrote his *Histoire Militaire du Règne de Louis le Grand* in 1726, the French casualties were fairly high. The list included the celebrated name of d'Artagnan.

On 1 July Fariaux capitulated. Mme de Sévigné wrote at once to Bussy-Rabutin: 'What do you think of the conquest of Maastricht? All the glory goes to the King.' That was the comment of a courtier. The true merit of Louis was to have appreciated the ability of Vauban and to have provided him with all the facilities which he needed in order to make full use of it. Louis, in his own account of the siege, makes no reference to Vauban, but he paid him a 'gratification' for his success at Maastricht which enabled him to purchase the Château de Bazoches, near Vézelay in Burgundy.

On 10 August, some six weeks after the capitulation of Maastricht, Louis invited the prince de Condé to inspect the place and to comment on the situation. Vauban was there to receive him and show him round. 'The place', wrote the prince, 'seemed to me to be the finest in the world and the most considerable; the more I examined it the more I felt that it was of the utmost importance to fortify it. M. de Vauban has done two designs; the big one is the most beautiful thing in the world.'

To refortify Maastricht was a costly business. In August 1673, Colbert wrote to Louis to say that, in order to carry on, it would be necessary to raise 20 million livres 'by extraordinary means' – that is to say by going back to the sale of offices, the alienation of the royal domain and new excise taxes. William Perwich, secretary to the English Embassy in France, wrote in October to Lord Arlington that Colbert had sought an advance of 14 million livres, but had been told that this was unthinkable 'because of the deadness of trade'. In December he added that 'M. Colbert has been a long while in a small disgrace'. It was Colbert, however, who wrote to Louis after the taking of Maastricht to tell him that 'Paris has never been so jubilant. On Sunday evening the bourgeois, on their own initiative and without being ordered, lit bonfires of joy.'

In the autumn of 1673 Louis suffered his first set-back. The Austrian army under Raimondo Montecuccoli was advancing up the Rhine towards Bonn while the Prince of Orange was trying to come down and join forces with him. On 23 October Louvois wrote to the duc de Luxembourg, who was commanding the French army at Utrecht: 'What the King hopes to achieve with the army which he is ordering you to assemble is to prevent Montecuccoli from crossing the Rhine. Everything depends on the arrival of an army near Bonn as soon as is humanly possible.'

It was not humanly possible. On 4 November the Austrian army crossed the Rhine, joined Prince William and invested Bonn, which surrendered a week later. The Elector of Cologne, one of Louis' few remaining allies, had lost his capital. This defeat for France was an encouragement to other German states to form an alliance against Louis.

The marquis de La Fare gives a rather different account of the same occasion, suggesting that 'either from lack of foresight or out of malice, Louvois, the declared enemy of Turenne, put no troops into Bonn, allowed the place to be taken and then put the blame on the Marshal ... The courtiers, in order to please the Minister, strongly blamed M. de Turenne.'

Meanwhile attempts were being made by the Congress of Cologne to find acceptable terms for peace, but England made a separate peace treaty with Holland in February 1674. In April the Bishop of Münster withdrew his support from France, followed a few weeks later by the Elector of Cologne. On 28 May, at the Diet of Ratisbon, the Emperor declared war on France. The Dutch war had become a European war.

The success of the first phase of the war says much about the military competence of Louis and his generals, of Louvois and Vauban, but above all of the soldiers and task forces. Louis was prepared to admit this. In May 1674 he wrote to the maréchale de La Mothe-Houdancourt: 'You know me well enough not to give me the credit for the taking of Besançon; my soldiers have a large share in it and, besides, I must recognise that it was chiefly due to God.'

Louis now took Franche-Comté after a rather long siege at Besançon and a rather short one at Dôle. On 8 June, la Grande Mademoiselle accompanied the King and Queen to Dôle – 'that is to say, the camp; one did not enter the town' because of the bad air. Most of the cavalry had been sent into Germany, but all the infantry regiments were still there. 'One could easily see how much they had suffered; there were lots of officers and soldiers with their arms in slings, their heads bandaged and plasters everywhere.' Some of the mines were still smoking and there was blood on the walls. The King took them to the site of the battle 'and explained everything to us so well that you could have believed that you had witnessed the siege'.

They were lodged in the houses of peasants, which did not always have glazed windows or even proper ceilings. 'Mine', continues Mademoiselle, 'was very pretty; they had put tapestries all round and a carpet on the floor. I slept as well as if I had been at the Luxembourg.' They took their meals in one of Louis' tents which they made as like Versailles as possible. 'There were always violins and oboes at the King's dinner and supper. We had the idea of playing cards after dinner when the King was with his Council and the Queen at her prayers.' Nevertheless, when Louis announced that on 19 July they were going to Fontainebleau, there was great rejoicing.

In August Condé repulsed William of Orange at the battle of Seneffe, but with heavy losses. With 45,000 men he attacked the rear-guard of William's army of 60,000. In a succession of fierce encounters, in the course of which Condé recovered some of the fire of the victor of Rocroi, there were some 20,000 killed, of whom nearly 8,000 were French. According to Voltaire, one of his officers remarked that 'the Prince de Condé was the only one left who had any desire to fight'. Mme de Sévigné's comment was that, 'apart from the Te Deum and one or two flags, we would have imagined that we had lost the battle'. There were, in fact, 107 flags captured. This was to be Condé's last great feat of arms. When, at the end of the campaign, he put his sword back in its scabbard it was never to be drawn again.

It was also to be Turenne's last campaign. Once again, Mme de Sévigné tells the story. 'We are just off to Fontainebleau – but no, we *were* just off to Fontainebleau; all was ready when we received a staggering blow which put an end to our joy. M. de Turenne has been killed. There is general consternation. There goes M. le Prince off to Alsace, and here is France devastated. No one knows where they are – we look for someone with whom to talk about Turenne – we flock together. Everyone in the streets is in tears.'

She then goes on to describe the event according to the information received. 'It was after three months of conducting his campaign with a miraculous success, which the professionals are never tired of admiring, that he reached the last day of his glory and of his life. He had the satisfaction of seeing the enemy decamping before his eyes, and on the 27th, which was a Saturday, he went up a little hill to observe their departure . . . A distant cannon fired a shot at a venture, which struck him in the middle of his body.'

She then proceeds to philosophise. 'What more could he have asked for? . . . his reputation could hardly have risen higher; he was reaping the benefits of all that he had achieved. He did not feel his death.' She then turned to the spiritual aspect of the event. 'Everyone speaks of the innocence of his way of life, the purity of his intentions, of his humility – far removed from any affectation . . . of his generous and Christian charity. Such a soul is worthy of Heaven; it comes too directly from God not to return to Him.'

Meanwhile at Salzbach, the scene of the disaster, a French surgeon, accompanied by a single groom, rode off at the gallop to convey the news to Turenne's opposite number, Raimondo Montecuccoli. After a respectful silence the great General said: 'There has died today a man who did honour to the human race.' Montecuccoli was a soldier worthy of Turenne's metal. There is usually solidarity among such experts. Voltaire comments that 'together they had reduced war to a fine art'.

It could have been a good moment for talking of peace. Honoré Courtin, a French diplomat who was both honest and perceptive, explains the position in a letter to Louvois dated 16 September 1673: 'The King is doubtless the world's greatest prince . . . He can remain so with a peace settlement that all Europe would consider honourable for him and very advantageous for his state. Thus I have trouble understanding why His Majesty wants to jeopardise this happiness and risk exposing himself to future troubles, which might indeed serve to show off his courage and his valour, but will doubtless be the ruin of his subjects . . . If it is not recognised that funds are depleted, that most of the money that has left the kingdom will not return while the war continues to ruin commerce. Can it not be understood that the taxes on the people, who will become impoverished [and in fact already are] cannot be raised without a violence that is very dangerous?'

Courtin had been an Intendant before he became a diplomat and he knew what he was talking about. Ekberg sums up thus: 'To Courtin, Louis' search for military *gloire* was incredibly short-sighted because, in trying to achieve it, the King was precisely destroying his instrumentality for further *gloire*, that is, the richness and well-being of his realm.'

Courtin's views were largely shared by Bossuet. On 10 July 1675, when the Dutch war seemed to be dragging on interminably, he had written to Louis: 'I am not unaware, Sire, how difficult it is for you to give [your people] this relief in the middle of a great war, in which you are obliged to make an extraordinary expenditure, both to resist your enemies and to support your allies.

'But the war which obliges Your Majesty to make such a great expenditure obliges him at the same time not to allow his people [through whom alone he can sustain it] to be overburdened. Therefore their relief is just as necessary for your service as for their ease. Your Majesty knows that; and to go on from there I must tell him what I believe to be his clear and indispensable duty: that he should above all apply himself to understanding thoroughly the misery of the provinces, and especially those things which they have to suffer that are of no profit to you, partly from the licentiousness of the soldiery, partly from the cost of raising the *taille*, which attains to unbelievable excesses. Although Your Majesty doubtless knows well to how great an extent injustices and extortions are committed, what sustains your people, Sire, is that they cannot believe that Your Majesty is aware of all that is going on. It cannot be that such great evils, which are capable of destroying the State, are without possible remedy; otherwise all would be lost and without resource. But these remedies could not be found without much care and patience, for it is not easy to examine praticable expedients, and it is not for me to hold forth on such matters.' This last sentence is typical of Bossuet's humility. In his view it is the function of the Church to draw attention to the moral necessity, but it is not the function of the Church, as such, to propose the remedies.

Despite Courtin, despite Bossuet's admonition of the King, the campaign was reopened in 1676 with a new attempt to establish a practicable eastern frontier to France – what Vauban called the *pré carré* (this could mean a square piece of land, but it was also the technical term for a duelling field). The immediate targets were Condé (the place) and Bou-

Versailles, Louis' *Maison de Plaisance* in 1668, by P. Patel.
Colbert wrote: 'The King has a particular affection for this house.'

The Louvre from the Pont Neuf, showing the long gallery joining it with the Tuileries.

The Collège des Quatre Nations, as seen from the windows of the King's apartment in the Louvre, by I. Silvestre.

The Louvre.
The Colonnade, showing the machinery used to hoist the stones, by C. Perrault.

(*Bottom left*) Colbert, by C. Lefèbvre. 'The whole figure of the minister,'
writes Inès Murat, 'evokes the image of saturnine severity, terrifying to those who
approached him, but reassuring to the King.' (*Bottom right*) Père de La Chaise,
by P. Simon. Louis' slightly accommodating confessor, derided by Mme de Montespan
as 'une chaise de commodité.'

Saint-Germain on the occasion of the baptism of the Grand Dauphin, showing the *Château Neuf* at the top of the picture. Engraving by P. Brissart.

The Tuileries as completed by Louis, by J. Rigaud.
Described by the Grande Mademoiselle as 'the most agreeable habitation in the world and one which I greatly loved.'

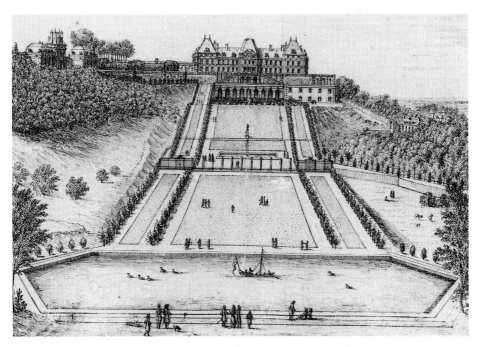

Meudon in the days of Louvois, engraving by I. Silvestre.
It later became the seat of the Grand Dauphin.

(*Above left*) Michel Le Tellier, engraving by R. Nanteuil. He was described by Louis as 'both prudent and wise, and of a modesty which I greatly valued.' (*Above right*) Le Tellier's son, marquis de Louvois, by an unknown artist. According to Spanheim, he was 'by nature uncouth, his haughty manners…seemingly brusque and hot-headed.'

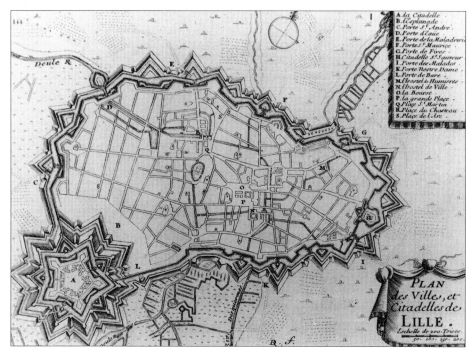

Plan of Vauban's fortifications of Lille, showing the citadel, bottom left,
'with the geometric precision of a snow flake.'

(*Above left*) Vauban: 'His principal care,' said Lazare Carnot, 'was the preservation
of his men…His kindness of heart, so characteristic of him, impregnates all his
maxims and ideas.' (*Above right*) Turenne, by C. Le Brun. He was, according to his
adversary, Montecuccoli, 'a man who did honour to the human race.'

Bossuet, engraving by P. Drevet after Rigaud. His *Histoire des Variations* is described by Owen Chadwick as 'the sharpest weapon in the armoury of Catholic apologetic.'

A Huguenot cartoon on forcible conversion. Vauban wrote of Languedoc, 'a country whose streets are paved with the newly converted who are as Catholic as I am Mohametan.'

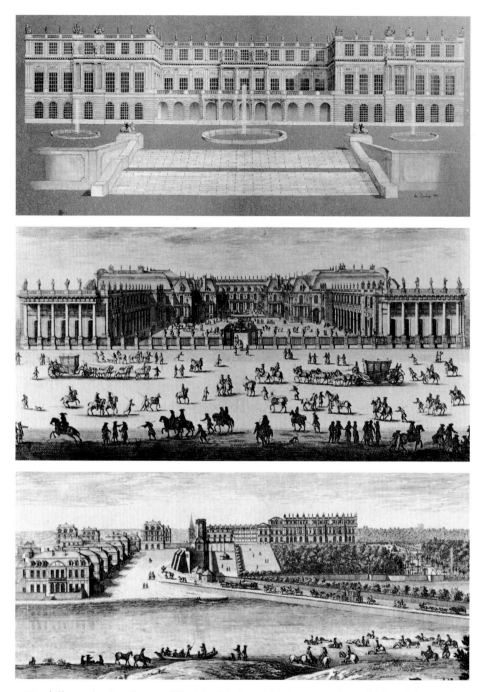

Versailles – the Enveloppe. (*Top*) Le Vau's palatial garden front, before Mansart's remodelling and enlargements. Reconstruction by Ian Dunlop. (*Middle*) Engraving by I. Silvestre. An unsatisfactory jumble of styles because Louis insisted on retaining his beloved *maison de plaisance* at its centre. (*Bottom*) Seen from the north, engraving by I. Silvestre showing the Etang de Clagny and watertower.

chain, which would open the way to taking Valenciennes and Cambrai. On 23 April the bombardment of Condé began. The siege of Bouchain Louis, 'jealous for his brother's glory', left to Philippe d'Orléans. Louis placed his own army between his brother's and Valenciennes. It was here that an incident occurred which involved him in adverse criticism ranging from cowardice and a fear of personal injury, which had no place in his character, to vanity and a fear of failure, which were most improbable under the circumstances. The event is described by the marquis de La Fare.

'At the beginning of the campaign of 1676 the King lost the most wonderful opportunity . . . All those who knew the country had no doubt that they [the Dutch] were lost and that this day would put a glorious end to the war.' Louis had already arrived on the site, named from a near-by village Heurtebise, a cannon shot from Valenciennes, and was in full battle order when William of Orange began to ascend the heights of Valenciennes. The maréchal de Lorges declared that he could rout them with a single brigade, but Louis, as was his wont, sought the counsel of his military advisers. The advice was not to attack. La Fare, who detested Louvois – 'as timorous as he was insolent' – puts the blame on him. He preferred no action, 'either because he did not want to see the war end so soon, or that he feared for the King's person or his own'.

Dangeau was later to write that Louis always spoke of this occasion with regret: 'He never thinks of it without sorrow and recalls it in the night and wakes up angry.' Dangeau supports La Fare in putting the blame on Louvois.

But Louis' advisers may have been right. The days when a King could, like Henri IV, lead a charge into the thick of the battle, were beginning to look out of date. If Louis had been killed at Heurtebise he would have been succeeded by the Grand Dauphin. That might well have proved a disaster. The place of the King should be at the head of the country rather than at the head of the army.

In May 1677, Philippe d'Orléans had his moment of glory when he caused William of Orange to leave Cassell with such precipitation that he left behind him not only his gold plate but 'the most magnificent plans of all the strongholds of Europe'.

It was not until then that Louis became serious about the peace talks which had begun at Nijmegen. 'I do not know', wrote William Temple, Charles II's ambassador at The Hague, 'what need France had of peace, but I know well that there was a very strong desire and that France tried every imaginable means except those which would have laid her necessity bare.'

The necessity was fundamentally financial. By 1676 there was a deficit of some 24 million livres and Colbert was reverting to the very expedients which he had condemned in Fouquet. But the greater part of the burden, as ever, fell upon those least able to support it. There were revolts and uprisings in the provinces which became insurrections in some of the towns. Bordeaux, which had a bad record during the Fronde, was among the first, while in Brittany the resort to violence spread rapidly until the number of rioters reached some 15,000. They were certain in the end to lose and reprisals were severe. According to the Governor of Brittany, the duc de Chaulnes (always *notre bon duc* to Mme de Sévigné), 'the trees began to bend under the weight imposed on them'. Mme de Sévigné showed herself devoid of compassion. 'The mutineers from Rennes escaped long ago; the innocent will suffer for the guilty, but I find everything very good provided that the four thousand soldiers who are in Rennes do not prevent me walking in my woods, which are of a wonderful height and beauty.'

The most serious plot was that of the chevalier de Rohan, a penniless and embittered scion of that noble house. He went so far as to make treasonable approaches to the comte de Monterey, the Governor of the Spanish Netherlands, with a project of an armed invasion of Brittany by William of Orange. The conspiracy was betrayed and Rohan and a few of his companions in treachery were executed.

In May 1677, the peace talks were begun in earnest at Nijmegen. 'One can say', claimed the marquis de La Fare, 'that it was there that the King appeared as the master of Europe. He could virtually choose between subjugating it and granting it peace ... He preferred peace to war and his action was masterly.' La Fare even went so far as to give credit to his enemy Louvois for the brilliant capture of Ghent and Ypres in 1678, which enabled Louis to offer to Charles II the restoration of Ghent as the price of peace.

France ended up with a part of its frontier on the Rhine, the final acquisition of Franche-Comté and the chain broken that had linked the possessions of the Habsburgs from Milan to Luxembourg.

Voltaire rather pleads the case for Louis: 'These conditions were fixed with the loftiness of the conqueror; they were not, however, so extreme that they must reduce his enemies to despair and oblige them to unite once more against him in a last effort. He spoke to Europe as a dictator, but at the same time he acted as a moderate. He succeeded, at the conference at Nijmegen, in sowing the seeds of jealousy among the allies.'

But it is sometimes true that 'nothing fails like success'. La Fare sums up: 'It is impossible to pass over this period of our history, which was the cause of all that has happened since, without making the reflection that a State should never act against certain interests which are fundamental unless it is resolved to push matters to extremes and to envisage the possibility of the total overthrow of the party attacked. It was never our intention to take Holland, but merely to punish her: a bad idea because we implanted fear and hatred in the hearts of a people who, in their own interest, were our natural allies . . . we caused them to abandon themselves to a leader who had made them warlike, and a republic which, in the state it was in, could never have been a danger to us, has become the strongest of our enemies, and one without which the others were not capable of resisting us.'

17

The Affaire des Poisons

So far as Louis' amours were concerned, history seems to have repeated itself. His mistresses overlapped each other. In March 1679 it was becoming evident that the King's affections were no longer exclusively engaged with Mme de Montespan. It was Mme de Maintenon who seems first to have mentioned it. She wrote to the abbé Gobelin: 'I ask you to pray, and to have prayers said, for the King, who is on the brink of a great precipice.' On 15 March Mme de Montespan had left Saint-Germain rather suddenly 'as the result of the jealousy which she had conceived against Mlle de Fontanges'.

Mlle de Fontanges was a lady-in-waiting to the duchesse d'Orléans, who wrote of her: 'she was as beautiful as an angel from head to foot . . . She loved the King very much, like the heroine of some novel. She was passionately romantic but devoid of wit.' The marquis de La Fare observed that Louis' confessor, the Père de La Chaise, 'was less particular about the love of Mlle de Fontanges than about the double adultery, which inspired Mme de Montespan to make one of her witticisms, saying that the Père de La Chaise was "une chaise de commodité" '.

Mme de Montespan, perceiving perhaps that she was at least in partial eclipse, profited from the circumstances by renewing the only request which Louis ever denied her – the post of Surintendante de la Maison de la Reine. In 1671 this had been regarded by Louis as being out of the question. Now that she had declined in his favour he was prepared to grant it. At the end of March she wrote to the duc de Noailles: 'Everything is very peaceful here; the King only comes to my room after Mass and after supper. It is far better to see each other seldom but with pleasantness than often but with trouble.' Bussy-Rabutin commented: 'Mme de Montespan is thus Surintendante de la Maison de la Reine, and she is no longer mistress.'

In the same odd way in which Louise de La Vallière had put the finishing touches to Athenaïs de Montespan's attire, so now Athenaïs was prepared to adorn her new rival for a masked ball. On 6 March 1680 Mme de Sévigné wrote: 'I have it on good authority that there was a ball at Villers-Cotterets [*chez* Monsieur]; they were wearing masks. Mademoiselle de Fontanges made a brilliant appearance, dressed by Mme de Montespan.'

Mlle de Fontanges did not last long in Louis' favour but was, like La Vallière before her, pensioned off with a duchess's tabouret. Mme de Maintenon tells of her decline. 'I remember one day the King sent me to go and talk with Mlle de Fontanges. She was in a rage because of the complaints which she had received. The King was afraid of an outburst and had sent me to calm her down. I was there for two hours and spent the time trying to persuade her to cast off the King and to convince her that it would be a fine and praiseworthy action. I recall that she replied with some vivacity: "But, Madame, you talk to me of my getting rid of a passion as one might cast off a shirt!" '

Liselotte, the new duchesse d'Orléans, who was not too careful about what she said, compared the two rivals. 'La Montespan was a devil incarnate, but la Fontanges was good and ingenuous; they were both beautiful. The latter is dead because, it is said, the former poisoned her with some milk. I do not know whether this is true, but what I do know for certain is that two of la Fontanges' servants died and it was said openly that they were poisoned.' She herself died in the abbey of Port-Royal in the quartier Saint-Jacques on Saturday 28 June 1681, attended by the great preacher Bourdaloue. The duc de Noailles was also present and informed Louis of the death. Louis included in his answer: 'As to the desire that there should be a post-mortem, if it is possible to avoid it, I think that would be best.'

Louis' reluctance to order an autopsy might imply that he had suspicions. Such suspicions were amply justified by evidence taken before the new Procurator-Général, Nicolas de La Reynie, in a court specially set up in April 1679 by Louis. Its official title was the 'Commission de l'Arsenal', but it was widely known as the 'Chambre Ardente'. Its transactions were to be in secret and its decisions without appeal. La Reynie was at the time occupied with one of the scandals which had shaken Paris and the Court – the *Affaire des Poisons*. In the next two years 441 suspects were to come before the Chambre Ardente; 377 were arrested, 36 condemned to death, 5 sent to the galleys and 23 banished.

One of the real weak spots in the *Grand Siècle* was in its attitude to the treatment of disease. It is probably true to say that more people died of the remedy than of the complaint. The art of the physician had not advanced very far into the realm of science and there were certain 'grey areas'. There was no clear dividing line between the practice of medicine and the belief in love potions and spells or the administration of poison. When Mme de Sévigné relates that Mme de La Fayette made use of a 'broth made from vipers' one is entitled to wonder whether that was prescribed by a doctor or purchased from some back-street alchemist.

It was a short step from medicine to magic and from magic to the Black Mass, or at least to a most improper misuse of the Mass. A crudely literal interpretation of the words 'This is my blood' gave a quasi-magical power to wine consecrated by a priest, and an extract of toad – usually referred to simply as a 'powder' – if passed beneath a chalice after consecration, was widely held to gain efficacy as a love philtre.

The central figure in the *Affaire des Poisons* was a Mme Monvoisin, usually referred to as 'La Voisin'. She was prepared to claim that her supernatural powers were gifts 'which God had given her'. In October 1679 La Voisin gave evidence that a number of ladies of high rank had sought her aid in order to attract the affections of the King, or to rid themselves of a husband, or to do both. The most distinguished of these was none other than Hortense de Mancini, comtesse de Soissons. Other names were Mme d'Alluye, the Scottish-born comtesse de Gramont, Mme de Polignac and her sister-in-law the comtesse de Roure. In January the following year the order was given for their arrest. Mme de Soissons – probably warned by Louis – and Mme d'Alluye fled to the Netherlands; Mme de Polignac retreated into Auvergne.

Louis' first reaction was to insist on a full enquiry into the situation. On 27 December 1679, La Reynie noted: 'His Majesty has commended to us the cause of justice and our own duty in the strongest possible and most precise terms, and impressing upon us that it is his desire, for the public good, that we should penetrate as deeply as possible into these unfortunate dealings with poison, in order to cut them off at the roots, if that is possible. He has commanded us to observe the strictest justice without any distinction of persons or of rank or sex.'

On 12 March 1679 Mme Monvoisin was arrested and interrogated. In February the following year she was burnt at the stake for sorcery.

Besides her daughter she had at least three confederates. One was the abbé Etienne Gibourg, a priest from the parish of Saint-Eustache, currently chaplain to the comte de Montgoméry at the Château de Villebousin, near Monthléry. The second was another priest, François Mariette, whose mistress was a professional dealer in poison. The third was known as the abbé Lesage, but he was not a priest and his name was not Lesage but Coeuret. Mariette passed the magic potions of La Voisin beneath the chalice while he was celebrating Mass; Lesage pronounced the magic formulas.

On 26 June 1680, Gibourg was being interrogated by La Reynie's commission. He admitted to having celebrated a Mass on the naked stomach of a woman. A baby was then sacrificed. Astaroth and Asmodeus were invoked. The woman who had served as the altar then said: 'I demand the friendship of the King . . . and that he should abandon and not look again at La Vallière.' The authenticity of this evidence is affirmed in the archives of the Bastille. The truth of the assertions is another question. But the fact is that during that summer of 1680 the name of Mme de Montespan was mentioned by more than one witness.

In July Mme Monvoisin's daughter and a woman named Filastre made statements to the effect that Mme Monvoisin had had dealings with Mme de Montespan; that the occasions of these dealings were the times when Mme de Montespan 'feared some diminution of the King's good graces'; that La Voisin had caused sacrilegious Masses to be said and had provided powders that were love philtres to be given to the King; that one of the Masses had been said by the abbé Gibourg.

On 21 July Louvois informed La Reynie that Louis had read Mlle Voisin's deposition and stated 'that the King much hoped that he [La Reynie] would discover the truth'. It seems that at this period La Reynie was inclined to the opinion that Mme de Montespan had indeed asked for powders which could well have killed the King. On 6 October, however, La Reynie advised Louvois not to name Mme de Montespan in the matter. Louis' reaction to the implication of his mistress was immediate. The clerks who took down the prisoners' depositions were forbidden to use ledgers, but told to write on loose sheets of paper. He was then able to withdraw those on which Mme de Montespan's name was mentioned. He kept them until July 1709, two years after Mme de Montespan's death, when he burnt them.

At an early stage in the process Colbert had decided to take cognisance of the affair. He sent La Reynie's memoranda and the depositions of those examined to a lawyer named Claude Duplessis. Duplessis made the observation that Mme Monvoisin, if she had been having dealings with Mme de Montespan, could have had no motive for concealing the fact and that Mme de Montespan could have no motive for taking an action which might have killed the King. On Colbert's advice the whole matter was hushed up.

To Louis he wrote at some length, pointing out the various discrepancies in the evidence, but his real appeal was to the King's own judgement. 'Could there be a witness more reliable or a better judge of the falsity of all this calumny than the King himself? His Majesty knows in what sort of way Mme de Montespan has lived with him himself; he has witnessed all her behaviour, all her wit, all her proceedings at all times and on all occasions, and a mind as clear-sighted and penetrating as Your Majesty's has never noticed anything which could attach to Mme de Montespan even the least of these suspicions.'

According to the interrogations, Mme de Montespan had been seeing La Voisin since 1673. 'Now, His Majesty knows that the little anxious moments of jealousy, which her affection could have produced on the mind of Mme de Montespan, only began in 1678, and His Majesty knows in what tranquillity of mind Mme de Montespan lived as much in 1673 as before then.' But in any case the whole idea was illogical. 'What! to conceive the idea of poisoning one's master, one's benefactor, one's King, a person whom one loves more than life itself; to know that in losing him one would lose everything, and to proceed with the execution of this mad venture and yet to preserve all the peace of mind that the most pure innocence could produce! Such things are inconceivable: and His Majesty, who knows Mme de Montespan to the very depths of her soul, could never persuade himself that she could have been capable of such abominations.'

Colbert may have touched the right notes in Louis' heart, but he must have known that during the year 1680 all was not well between Louis and Athenaïs. It was just then, on 6 April, that Mme de Sévigné had written to her daughter that the new duchesse de Fontanges was holding court openly and receiving courtiers while in bed. 'Mme de Montespan is enraged; she cried a lot yesterday. You can imagine the martyrdom which her pride has suffered.'

The figure of Nicolas de La Reynie links the *Affaire des Poisons* with a very much larger and more important venture – the modernisation of Paris. Colbert had dreamed of establishing the greatest King in the world in an appropriately sumptuous palace at the heart of the greatest capital in Europe. In 1664 both the Louvre and the City of Paris fell sadly short of Colbert's vision. The Louvre was soon to be eclipsed in Louis' priorities by the creation of Versailles. Louis was, however, willing to give his full support to a campaign intended to transform Paris into a city worthy of its King and country.

When, on 1 January 1664, Colbert was given the charge of Surintendant des Bâtiments, a colossal enterprise was put in hand for the modernisation of Paris. In spite of certain very beautiful additions, such as the Place des Vosges, Paris was still much as it had been in the Middle Ages, with its narrow, tortuous streets and close-packed houses whose upper storeys, built out on corbels, almost shut out the light; with its open drains and muddy, unpaved streets; with few quays and fewer bridges: it was unhealthy, unsightly and unsafe.

As so often occurred in the course of the *Grand Siècle*, the right man had appeared at the right time for the task. Once again Louis' assertion that in a great state there were always men suited to every sort of activity was shown to be true; once again it appeared that all that was needed was to know them and put them in place. For the direction of the many-sided task of modernising Paris, Colbert found the man suited to the activity, *l'homme de la situation*, Nicolas de La Reynie. Saint-Simon said of him: 'He was a man of virtue and of valour and of a very great ability, who, in a position which he had himself created, was to incur the hatred of the populace, but was nevertheless to win for himself universal esteem.'

To pull France out of a medieval morass, Louis and Colbert looked to the days of ancient Rome. This was in no spirit of archaism or sentimental revival. With the mathematical proportions of its architecture, the orderly planning of its urbanism and the clear logic of its legal system, Latin civilisation provided the only precedent for progress. To Louis and Colbert nothing could have looked more modern than ancient Rome.

On 15 March 1667, the Parlement registered an edict creating the new post of Lieutenant de Police in favour of La Reynie. For the first time the complementary but often incompatible functions of police and justice were separated. Within the competence of the new Lieutenant de Police were included a variety of responsibilities.

The word 'police' in those days still covered the whole area of civic administration. This included the security of the city, the prevention of crime, the detection and arrest of criminals. But it extended also to the disposal of sewage, the cleaning and lighting of the streets, the construction of more quays, the provision of an adequate water supply and the safeguarding of health.

One of the first functions of a police force is the detection and punishment of crime. When Louis took over the reins of government, theft and murder were daily events in Paris, as were the public executions in the Place de Grève. Guy Patin had complained, just before the Fronde, that 'day and night they rob and kill here . . . We have reached the dregs of the centuries.' Louis Bernard, in his well-documented study of the emerging city of Paris, states that there were 372 murders in one year and a record 14 in one night. But daylight robbery was also common. One victim cried out to the thieves: 'Messieurs! You open shop very early today!'

The only official agent against the cut-throat and the cut-purse was the system of nightly patrols known as the Guet. Needless to say it had not been working well. La Reynie's first move was to double the men's pay, treble their numbers and increase their self-respect by providing them with a distinctive new uniform. The 400 thus equipped were divided into groups of four or five who were constantly on patrol. The King insisted that they should keep altering their routes, 'sometimes in one place, sometimes in another', so that their arrival was always unpredictable.

These measures were sufficiently successful for the historian Colletet to write in 1674: 'As for robbers, they are now so little feared that – astonishing to relate – where, in the past, there was no security on the Pont Neuf after nightfall, one could now walk with as little fear as in broad daylight as the result of the increase that has been made of the Guet, which is on the march at all times and who even conduct drunkards back to their homes.' Criminals arrested by these patrols were handed over to a now independent justiciary and, if convicted, either condemned to death or sent to prison.

One of the most important tasks imposed upon La Reynie was the inspection of prisons, described by Bourdaloue as 'the living image of hell'. We must remember that this was over a hundred years before the work of Elizabeth Fry in England. Conditions in the prisons of Europe were appalling and they were rendered the more odious by the financial exactions of the warders. Life was just tolerable for those who could pay their way. Perhaps the most shocking of these exactions was that a prisoner who was officially released still often had to bribe his way out. Inability to do so could render ineffective the order for release. There is no doubt that some of those detained were in fact innocent and had been incarcerated on the deposition of a single individual.

Louis sometimes made personal interventions. In September 1676 – to take a single instance – three prisoners who had been at the Châtelet for three months, having been denounced by a man named Gelet, managed, through a friend, to convey their *placets* to the King protesting their innocence. Louis ordered 'that this affair be settled promptly' and that La Reynie 'should inform himself of the reasons for this delay'.

Too long a period of confinement could lead to the disappearance of a prisoner's name from the records. In 1685 a certain Lamotte managed to complain to Colbert's son, the marquis de Seignelay, that he had been in the Petit Châtelet for twenty-five years. Louis instructed La Reynie to draw up regular lists with the names, the causes for detention, the length of the sentence imposed and the amount of it that had been already served.

Complaints were taken seriously and their validity scrutinised. On 6 February 1684, La Reynie received a letter saying: 'His Majesty desires that you do all that is possible to discover if that which the so-named Valerio has said of the treatment of prisoners in the Bastille is truthful.' Louis always wanted to know the details.

The Bastille was by far the least horrific of the prisons of Paris. Most of its inmates were from the upper classes and were sent by a *lettre de cachet* from the King. It was even possible to take one's own servant and to have one's own meals cooked.

Louis appears, in all these reforms, in a not unfavourable light, but Louis was not one to hide his light under a bushel. He understood the art of publicity and propaganda. As early as 1661, Colbert had encouraged the striking of medallions 'to consecrate for posterity the great deeds which the King has already accomplished' which would henceforth be 'eternalised in metal'. It is significant that among the 286 medallions actually struck, alongside the countless victories on the battlefield, as many as 8 were consecrated to the transformation of Paris into a safer, cleaner, healthier and more agreeable place to live in. The first of these was issued in 1666 and commemorated 'the regulations concerning the filth and the lanterns of Paris'.

The problem of the disposal of sewage and the cleansing of the streets was typical of those confronting La Reynie. The principle that each householder should be responsible for the cleanliness of that portion of the street which was fronted by his property had been vaguely established since the Middle Ages. A tax was supposed to be paid by householders in order to pay for entrepreneurs who were to collect the refuse in tumbrils and dispose of it. But the system never worked; taxes were not always paid; there were far too many entrepreneurs and far too few tumbrils.

The new Lieutenant of Police set about the task with imagination and determination. He was admirably supported by the King. Louis was so keen on the cleaning up of his capital that, on 10 November 1666, he told the Parlement through the mouth of the Chancellor Séguier 'that he would walk through the streets on foot in order to know more accurately their condition'.

First La Reynie turned his attention to the proper financing of the project. A new tax was imposed on all householders and owners of land. It fell alike on royal and ecclesiastical properties and the private houses of noblemen. The only exceptions allowed were the Mendicant Friars and the Hôtel Dieu.

This tax enabled the regular payment of entrepreneurs at 2,000 livres a year for each tumbril used. Each quartier was obliged to employ an inspector who checked each day the number of tumbrils in use.

Householders were under a strict obligation to sweep the street in front of their houses every morning. Anyone who threw ordure out of the window – and there is plentiful evidence that this was the practice – was liable to a fine.

The daily scene was described by Colletet. 'At seven in the morning in winter, workmen paid by the city go into all the quartiers sounding a little bell, which serves as a warning to the citizens to have the street before their houses swept by their servants and to put out all the refuse from their offices, chambers and kitchens ready for the dustmen to collect them in half an hour's time. The result is that Paris, in spite of the prodigious number of people with which it is filled, is in a state of cleanliness which has not hitherto been usual.'

Street cleansing and street lighting appear to have been inseparable in the minds of the authorities. The tax which financed the two operations was called the *taxe des boues et lanternes*. Not much had been done about the lanterns before the advent of Louis XIV. Optimistic attempts had been made to encourage householders to keep candles burning in their ground-floor windows and the Parlement had even considered providing lanterns for them, but, as so often, the system just did not work. La Reynie put the responsibility for financing the street lighting onto committees formed in each of the seventeen quartiers. These were also responsible for appointing each year a number of *commis-allumeurs* to act as lamp-lighters.

La Reynie's lanterns were simple frames of metal and glass each containing a candle of 'good and trusty tallow of Paris', weighing more than a pound. Some 200,000 were used each year. These maintained about 6,500 lanterns. According to Martin Lister the lanterns were hung at a height of about 20 feet and set at intervals of 60 feet. That could have provided for nearly 65 miles of street to be illuminated for most of the night. There were strict precautions to deter hooligans from smashing the lanterns. Lister tells of 'three young gentlemen of good Families who were in prison for having done it in a Frolick'.

The dangers from insanitary conditions, the dangers from criminals and the dangers from darkness had thus been at least greatly diminished by the vigorous administration of La Reynie. There remained a fourth peril, which was in a somewhat different category and rather more difficult to deal with: the danger from fire. La Reynie's appointment as Lieutenant de Police came only a few months after the devastating fire which had destroyed so much of London. It had been an awesome spectacle, 'a most horrid, malicious, bloody flame', as Pepys recorded, 'not like the fine flame of an ordinary fire . . . It made me weep to see it; and a horrid noise the flames made and the cracking of houses at their ruin'.

What had happened in London could just as easily happen in Paris. The means of fighting even an ordinary house fire were limited. A combination of human chains passing buckets from the nearest source of water and the demolition of houses which stood in the path of the flames was about all that La Reynie had at his disposal. The most that he could do was to try to ensure the efficient functioning of the system.

The first warning of a conflagration was likely to come from the nightly patrols of the Guet. The alarm was sounded by the ringing of the tocsin, but the patrol was required to remain on the spot to prevent pillage.

If the fire began to spread, the only remedy was the destruction of buildings which stood in its path. This required the professional assistance of masons, carpenters and slaters. These were now obliged to register their names and addresses with the local *commissaires* and to be on call. Householders who tried to obstruct this process were made liable to heavy fines.

It was not until 1699 that La Reynie, 'having learnt of the use of pumps in Holland, made a most careful study of this invention and grasped its potential'. These pumps were the invention of a certain Jan van der Heyden and were capable of playing a jet of water 'as thick as a man's arm up to the roof crests of the highest houses'. Thirteen such pumps were immediately purchased for Paris.

In 1670 a medallion had been struck to celebrate the 'embellishing and enlarging of Paris'. The accompanying text claimed that 'while the King had in mind the greatest of projects, he did not neglect to devote his attention to everything which could make the capital of his kingdom more beautiful. Streets were widened, new quays built, the number of fountains [that is to say, public water supply] increased for the commodity of the citizens. But what is greatest and most magnificent is the continuation of the rampart begun by Henri II.'

This rampart was transformed from a defensive wall, extending from the Bastille to a point on the Seine downstream of the Tuileries, to a boulevard 'of prodigious width and planted with elms which formed long alleys providing a very pleasant shade. The old gateways to the town which were situated at points along this rampart have been replaced with as many triumphal arches.' Louis' intention was not to facilitate traffic but 'to provide promenades for the bourgeois and inhabitants'.

These new boulevards are clearly marked on the map which Louis ordered in 1676 to be drawn by François Blondel and Pierre Bullet. The map, as Louis himself stated, was to include projects which were not completed until later. Blondel's writings show that Louis played an important creative role in the embellishment of his capital. A medallion struck in 1669 to commemorate the new paving stones of Paris claims that the capital 'has felt the effects of the solicitude and the magnificence of the King even in the smallest matters. The paving stones of this great city had been neglected for a long time . . . which caused a dirtiness which was not only disagreeable but most unhealthy. The King gave orders for the re-paving of the whole city and the work was carried out with such carefulness that, for cleanliness and convenience, Paris is now superior to all the cities of Europe.'

In 1698 this improvement was noted by Martin Lister, who had previously visited Paris in 1665. 'The pavements of the streets are all of square stone, of about eight to ten inches thick, that is, as deep in the ground as they are broad at the top; the gutters shallow and laid round without edges, which makes the coaches glide easily over them. However it needs to be said that the streets are very narrow and the passengers a-foot no ways secured from the hurry and dangers of coaches, which are always passing down the streets with an air of haste, and a full trot upon broad, flat stones betwixt high and large resounding houses, makes a sort of music which would seem very agreeable to the Parisians.'

The streets of Paris afforded a colourful and animated, if sometimes distressing spectacle. 'No sort of people', wrote Lister, 'make a better figure in the town than Bishops, who have very splendid equipages and variety of fine liveries, being most of them of great families who had obtained preferment as such, learning not being so necessary a qualification for those dignities as with us ... 'Tis to be wished that they exceeded others in merit as they do in birth.' Among pedestrians, 'the Counsellors and chief officers of the Courts of Justice make a great figure; they and their wives have their trains carried up, so there are abundance to be seen walking about the streets in this manner'.

But at the other extremity of the social spectrum Lister remarked upon 'the great multitude of poor wretches in all parts of the city, such that a man in a coach, a-foot or in the shop is not able to do any business for the numbers and importunities of beggars, and to hear their miseries is very lamentable, and if you give to one you immediately bring a whole swarm upon you'.

An attempt had been made in 1656 to remedy this evil with the foundation of the Hôpital Général. A medallion was struck to commemorate this and the text refers to 'three separate houses for people of every age and sex' and claims that the poor were treated with every care. This is something of a euphemism. In November 1677 Louis was urging La Reynie to resort to stricter measures. 'His Majesty understands that you will have all vagabonds and Bohemians whom you can find arrested ... He orders me to say that if you need new commands to send them to the galleys you are to let me know immediately.' A life sentence to the galleys was the punishment prescribed for those who 'escaped' from the Hôpital Général.

It was in many ways more like a prison than a hostel. The inmates had to work, and to work hard. Apart from compulsory attendance at the chapel, they had no respite. The very architecture of the chapel followed the arrangement most often used for penitentiaries – its eight naves radiating out from a central sanctuary, which thus enabled a much larger congregation to be assembled within earshot of the celebrant than was possible with a single nave. The vagabond, the vagrant and the beggar were treated more or less as criminals. Their way of life – *le fainéantisme* – is described in the text of the medallion as an industry. It was to a large extent organised, almost like a guild, and its headquarters in the north of Paris, behind the Couvent des Filles-Dieu, was known as the 'Cour des Miracles'. The name derives from the simulation of various wounds, diseases and deformities calculated to touch the hearts and open the purses of the passers-by. On returning to their headquarters at the end of the day the beggars put off their faked deformities and – as if by a miracle – resumed their proper appearance.

Henri Sauval, a contemporary historian of the antiquities of Paris, describes how he once penetrated this sanctuary. It was like going 'into another world . . . one must often lose oneself in the narrow, wretched, stinking, unfrequented streets; to enter it one must descend a long, tortuous and uneven slope. I saw there a half-buried mud hut, a square not eight yards long, tottering from age and rottenness, in which, however, more than fifty households are lodged.'

In 1667 La Reynie used armed force to enter the Cour des Miracles and disperse its inhabitants, some to prison and some to the Hôpital Général. It was a courageous move and for a time it may have been successful. Colbert, in a letter to the Intendant of Poitou, boasted that robbers had been eliminated from Paris. But of course it did not last. In October 1691, Louis, 'deeply wounded by the number of crimes committed every day in Paris', insisted on the night patrols continuing to circulate until seven in the morning and instructed La Reynie to arrest some ten or twelve notorious pick-pockets 'in order to intimidate the others'.

The projects of Colbert for the ennoblement of the capital were not confined to those entrusted to La Reynie. The personal rule of Louis XIV saw also the construction of some magnificent and important public buildings, in particular the Collège des Quatre Nations, the Observatoire and Les Invalides.

The first, often known also as the Collège Mazarin, had been under discussion between Colbert and the Cardinal, but it was only after the death of the latter that any action was taken. Mazarin bequeathed 2 million livres for a college that would provide free education for the sons of noblemen from the four 'nations' that had been annexed to France by the treaties of Münster and of the Pyrenees. Louis Le Vau was to be the architect and it was he who chose the site of the old Tour de Nesle, across the Seine and directly opposite the windows of the Louvre. His design, which was meant to have included a bridge, was one of the most dramatically effective in France. No city palace could have a more distinguished outlook. It is perhaps the most satisfactory of Le Vau's creations.

The Collège des Quatre Nations owed more to Colbert than to Louis; the Observatoire was of equal interest to both. It was part of the Académie des Sciences. On 17 March 1667, the land was bought at the entrance to the Faubourg Saint-Jacques. The building was designed by Claude Perrault and was destined to house, in his own words, 'tous les principaux instruments d'astronomie dont on se sert pour les observations'. The main block was exactly orientated. There were octagonal pavilions at either end. One of the windows in these faced the point of sunrise at the winter solstice and another the point of sunset. The text of the commemorative medallion claims that 'the disposition and orientation provide the Astronomers with every convenience necessary for the exact observation of the stars in their courses'.

It has to be said that the astronomer Jean-Dominique Cassini was somewhat critical of the plan. This led to a modification of it proposed by Colbert. It was here, in 1686, at the new Observatoire, that one of the finest astronomical discoveries was made: that of the satellites of Saturn. The discovery, of course, was celebrated by another medallion.

Martin Lister was particularly impressed with the quality of the construction, especially the stereotomy of the vaulted ceilings. 'I was, by the invitation of Monsieur Cassini, at the Observatoire Royale ... The building is very fine and great art is used in the vaulted cut roofs and winding staircases. The stones are laid, inside and outside, with the most regularity I ever saw in any modern building.' But neither the architecture of these two buildings nor the purpose for which they were built entitles them to the first place in the order of merit: that must be awarded to the Hôtel des Invalides.

Perhaps the greatest act of recognition of the worth of a soldier was the provision of a comfortable and dignified retirement. In April 1674, Louis signed the foundation deed for the Hôtel des Invalides. 'We have deemed it no less worthy of our piety than of our magnificence', he states, 'to rescue from misery and beggary the poor officers and soldiers from our armies who, having grown old in our service or, in the past wars, having been disabled, were not only in no condition to continue to serve us, but also to do anything to enable them to survive.' It was also stipulated in the deed that the Director and Administrator should be the Secretary for War – at that time Louvois.

The idea that the King had some responsibility for his disabled soldiers was nothing new, but it had originally been entrusted to the religious orders. A brutal and licentious soldiery, however, did not make welcome guests in a monastery and the penitential regime of a monastery was not likely to appeal to those who had lived by violence, pillage and rape. As

André Corvisier puts it, it was difficult for them to drop the habits contracted in camp.

In December 1668, during his first campaign in Flanders, Louis asked for information about the existing provision for disabled soldiers. On 24 February 1670, he issued a decree for a new provision, which was to be met from monastic revenues, for wounded and crippled soldiers, who were to be lodged 'in a hostel which His Majesty is resolved to build for this purpose'. The architect Libéral Bruant was given the commission to produce the design and the builder Pierre Pipault to realise it. But Bruant was only made responsible for the residential part of the complex. In 1676 Louvois called in Jules Hardouin-Mansart for the more prestigious ecclesiastical buildings. There were to be two churches sharing a common sanctuary. One was for the pensioners, and the other, beneath one of the finest domes in France, was for the King. The cupola was painted by Charles La Fosse.

In 1802 the Hôtel des Invalides received its accolade of praise from a source innocent of any motive of flattery – Chateaubriand. In his *Génie du Christianisme* he exclaims: 'What good taste in this simplicity! What beauty in this quadrangle which is, however, nothing but a military Cloister in which Art has brought together notions of warfare and notions of religion and married the image of a camp of old soldiers with the moving memory of a hospice! It is at the same time a monument to the God of Battles and to the God of the Gospels. The rust of centuries which begins to cover it gives it a noble consonance with these veterans, these living ruins, who stroll beneath these ancient arches.'

It is possible that the nobility of the architecture ministered to the self-respect of the old soldiers, but there can be little doubt that the creation of so vast and sumptuous a building in Paris was intended also to proclaim the glory and the liberality of the creator. The finished building contained twelve courtyards and covered an area of 10 hectares (approximately 25 acres). In its dimensions it measured up to Versailles.

The accommodation offered was spacious. The men slept in small dormitories with four or six beds. There were eight heated rooms known as *poêles* or *chauffoirs*, two of which were reserved for smokers. A high standard of personal hygiene was required and water was provided in abundance with conduits in the corners of the courtyards. The latrines had the rare refinement of seats. The infirmary contained 300 beds. It seems a large number, but, contrary to the usual custom, each patient had a bed to himself. In 1676 Louvois appointed a doctor, a surgeon and an apothecary, each with a number of colleagues or assistants.

Soldiers were to receive two thirds of a kilo of bread a day, half a kilo of meat and a quarter of a litre of wine. One of the minor punishments was to be put on water and to sit at a special delinquents' table in the centre of one of the long refectories. Discipline was strict. The punishment for begging was expulsion, but blasphemy was regarded as the most serious offence of all. It could be punished by a transfer to the prison of Bicêtre.

The inmates were not condemned to idleness. They were offered the possibility of earning some money and of what would be called today 'occupational therapy'. In 1682 an English merchant named Povey, the author of a *Description of the hostel of the Invalides*, recorded that some 400 of the pensioners were employed in the manufacture of military uniforms and stockings, and another 300 at the looms. That would have accounted for about one third of the inmates.

The spiritual needs of the community came within the oversight of the Archbishop of Paris. The standard set was somewhat demanding. All pensioners were required to make their confession and to attend Mass regularly. Twelve resident chaplains provided the pastoral care and shared responsibility for the services which were accompanied by 'exhortation, preaching and catechism'.

Shortly before Louis' death, Montesquieu devoted number 75 of his *Lettres Persanes* to the military hostel. 'Yesterday I went to Les Invalides; I would much rather have created this establishment, were I a prince, than to have won three battles. One sees on all sides the hand of a great monarch. Of all the buildings in the world, this is the one most worthy of our respect.'

The Hôtel des Invalides was certainly Louis' greatest building in Paris and, as all creations say something important about their creators, so Les Invalides tells us much about Louis – almost as much as does Versailles. But what it says is something different. At Versailles we are dazzled by the apotheosis of the monarch: at Les Invalides we see a different side of his character, which he claimed in his memoirs – that of *le Père du Peuple*. Here we see a more caring side of his nature.

Louis made a number of visits to Les Invalides, two of which are recorded in some detail. On 19 May 1701, he came incognito, accompanied only by Mansart. It is only thus that a genuine inspection of the normal conditions of a large institution can be carried out. Two months later he made an official visitation. According to the marquis de Sourches, 'he inspected it down to the last detail and saw the officers and soldiers having their supper'.

On 28 August 1706, Louis made his last visit, 'with no other motive than to give pleasure to M. Mansart'. The great architect was at the entrance to meet him. 'Sire,' he said, 'I have the honour to lay at the feet of Your Majesty the key of this sacred Temple which was raised by your piety to the glory of God, happy if this task, which you entrusted to my care thirty years ago, could answer the high ideal which Your Majesty set before me, and to his wise guidance. This superb monument to your religion will proclaim to the remotest posterity the greatness of your reign.' Louis replied by returning the key to his architect 'in such a manner as to make it clear to him and to all the Court . . . how contented he was with him and his achievements'. Noticing Mansart's wife among the spectators, Louis advanced towards her. 'Madame,' he said, 'seeing you here I cannot forbear to compliment you on the share which you must have in the glory which your husband receives today.'

Voltaire, whose attitude to Louis was usually favourable without being obsequious, adds his own appreciation. 'The foundation of Les Invalides and its chapel, the most beautiful in Paris, and the establishment of Saint-Cyr, the last of so many constructions undertaken by this monarch, would alone suffice to cause his memory to be blessed.'

The establishment of Saint-Cyr was the achievement of one of the most important figures in the latter part of Louis' reign – the Widow Scarron, Governess to Louis' children by Mme de Montespan. The King rewarded her so generously that she was able to purchase the Château and Seigneurie of Maintenon on the River Eure. Louis now addressed her as Madame de Maintenon, but Mme de Sévigné, foreseeing the phasing out of Mme de Montespan, spelt it 'Madame de Maintenant'.

18
Madame de Maintenon

It reads like a fairy story. Françoise d'Aubigné, granddaughter of the famous Huguenot soldier and poet Agrippa d'Aubigné; born in 1635 in the prison at Niort, where her father was serving a sentence at the time; taken with him, on his release, to Martinique; brought back to France on his death by a mother who embraced her only twice in her life; looked after at the Château de Mursay by her aunt, Mme de Villette, a strict Calvinist; converted by the nuns at an Ursuline convent; married at the age of sixteen to Paul Scarron, a crippled poet, who specialised in the burlesque, and widowed at twenty-five, she did not seem marked by Fortune for any particular celebrity in life.

She was, however, a woman of great personal charm and with a natural wit which made her *persona grata* in the demanding atmosphere of a salon and within a society which was precious without necessarily being ridiculous. It was in the salon of the maréchale d'Albret that the Widow Scarron found her spiritual home, in the secular meaning of that term. Here she met and became attached to the marquise d'Heudicourt; through Mme d'Heudicourt she met the marquise de Montespan; Mme de Montespan was just at the crest of the wave which was to lift her to the position of *maîtresse déclarée du Roi*; as a mistress she almost inevitably became a mother. It was important to find a discreet and devoted person to look after the steadily increasing number of illegitimate children. The Widow Scarron seemed to possess all the qualities required. In March 1669, she took up her position officially. From governess she advanced to companion and from companion to confidante. It was not long before she became acquainted with the King.

Looking back in later years, after she had started a school for the daughters of impecunious noblemen, she told her charges: 'You must believe that the foundation of my astonishing fortune, without my having given it a thought in the world, was all the kindness which I showed to Madame d'Heudicourt, who was our mutual friend [with Mme de Montespan] at whose house we met often.' Her 'astonishing' fortune was to lead to a deeper relationship with Louis than that of acquaintance. She was to become his wife.

It was her relationship with Mme de Montespan that first paved the way to her preferment. She could state, some thirty years after the events: 'Mme de Montespan and I were the greatest friends in the world; she very much appreciated me, and I, simple as I was, contributed to our friendship. She used to speak to me very confidentially and said all that she thought. But later we got up against one another.'

It was, above all else, the Widow Scarron's discretion which qualified her for the job of looking after the King's natural children. The most complete secrecy had to be maintained. This required her to make no noticeable change in her social life. 'I sometimes spent the whole night with one of the children, if one was ill, in a little house outside Paris.' Sometimes she even had to wear disguise. 'I came back home in the morning, entering by a little back door, and when I was dressed I got into my coach at the front door and went to the Hôtel d'Albret or the Hôtel de Richelieu, so that those whom I normally met did not notice anything and did not even suspect that I had a secret to keep.' The winter of 1671–2 was spent thus.

In January 1672, Mme de Sévigné began to form a friendship with her and gives us her own account of her. 'We have supper every evening with Mme Scarron; she is of a lovable nature and very straightforward. It is a real pleasure to listen to her describing the horrible agitation of *a certain place which she knows well* [the Court], of the desperation of that Mme d'Heudicourt, of the tantrums of the little Lauzun and the sad premonitions of the ladies of Saint-Germain. These conversations led us on a long way, from moralities to moralities, now Christian, now political.' To have received such acclaim for her powers of conversation from one of the greatest conversationalists of her time was praise indeed.

On 20 December 1673, Louis declared all his children legitimate and there was no more need for secrecy. Mme de Sévigné made haste to inform her daughter of Mme Scarron's new fortune: 'a large and beautiful house, which one does not enter, a large garden, large and beautiful apartments. She has a coach, servants and horses; she dresses in a manner both modest and magnificent, like someone who spends her life among persons of quality.' She sums up with her usual precision: 'Elle est aimable, belle, bonne et négligée.'

The Widow Scarron was now officially a member of Mme de Montespan's household and, as such, attached to the Court. She did not let this go to her head. Writing in March 1674 to her confessor, the abbé Gobelin, she stated: 'I am resolved to try and acquire a profound indifference to the places and the way of life to which I am destined.' She saw it as a threat to her integrity and promised the abbé that she would quit the Court if ever he told her to do so. Bussy-Rabutin was confident of her sincerity: 'I know the generosity of Mme Scarron and her virtue and I am persuaded the corruption of the Court will never spoil her.'

She ran true to type. Looking back in November 1702, she could write to Mme de Glapion: 'Do you not see that I am dying of tedium in the midst of a fortune which it would be difficult to imagine? I have been young and pretty; I have tasted pleasure; I have been loved on all sides. At a later stage I spent many years in the society of the wise and witty and I protest, dear daughter, that all these conditions leave a fearful emptiness.' It was not given to Mme Scarron to see the features of this world 'apparelled in celestial light'.

Soon she began to recognise a need to have a place of her own somewhere where she could be by herself and could be herself. In 1674 she admitted to Gobelin that she had a strong desire to purchase an estate. It was just at this time that the duchesse de Richelieu and Mme de Montespan made an attempt to marry her to the elderly duc de Villars, a man 'very far from being an *honnête homme* and very short of money'. She merely saw such a position as a source of further vexations and embarrassments. 'I have enough of those in my unusual situation as well as being the envy of everyone.'

The one thing which tethered her to the Court was her almost maternal devotion to the little duc du Maine. 'Born beautiful and beautifully made,' wrote Languet de Gergy, 'he had at the age of three some trouble with his teeth which threw him into such convulsions that it caused one of his legs to shrink and made him lame. Mme Scarron, who had a good and tender heart, together with a natural penchant for the education of the young, conceived an affection for those who had been entrusted to her, and if they called her *Maman* for love of her, she felt for them the yearnings of a real mother. Their sufferings were her sufferings, and she gave up more of her sleep to ease them than most mothers.' But she had to convince herself – 'nothing could be more foolish than such an inordinate affection for a child that is not my own'. She could not just enjoy the relationship.

It was this very attachment to her children which caused the breach with Mme de Montespan, who seemed to be at once pleased to be relieved of her responsibility and annoyed by the preference which her children felt for their governess. 'The tenderness which I feel for them', wrote Mme Scarron in September 1674, 'makes me insupportable in the eyes of those to whom they belong.' In February 1675, she wrote: 'The most dreadful things happen between Mme de Montespan and myself. The King was witness to one yesterday, and this behaviour, together with the continual harm which it does to the children, puts me in a state which I shall not be able to endure for long.'

Her relationship with Mme de Montespan was steadily deteriorating. In August she had confronted her mistress, 'saying that the matter was serious; that I could see, without any room for doubt, that she did not like me and had set the King against me. She gave very bad answers to these accusations and we had a most animated conversation, and yet very reasonable.'

On 13 September she had another conversation 'fort vive' with Mme de Montespan, which she described to her confessor: 'and, as I am the one who suffered most, I cried a lot. She gave an account of it to the King as usual. I admit to you that it grieves me a lot to remain in a position where I have scenes like that every day. A thousand times I have longed to take the veil.'

She was still at this time hoping to purchase an estate in the country, but if she was dreaming of a little château not too far from Versailles, she was also able to spend long hours 'building imaginary castles in Spain'. Louis had given her 100,000 francs, but that would not have bought what she was looking for. But in October he repeated the gift. She eagerly told the abbé Gobelin about it, but begged him to keep it a secret. In November she could write to her brother: 'I am buying an estate: it is Maintenon.' She bought it without seeing it, but when, one morning next February, she visited it she was immediately captivated. 'I have been to Maintenon,' she wrote to her brother, 'with which I am very pleased; it is a big château at the extremity of a large market town, a situation very much to my liking and in some ways comparable with Mursay; all set about with meadows and a river flowing through the moat.' She summed up her appreciation with the words: 'This is where I shall end my days.' On 15 January 1675, she added: 'It is true that the King has given me the name of Maintenon.'

A year later, on 20 December 1676, she wrote to the abbé Gobelin from Versailles. 'I came here yesterday from Maintenon, where I spent eight days in a *douceur* and a peace of mind which makes one find *this place* worse than ever. If I followed my inclination, as I have always done, there is not a minute of the day that I would not be demanding to retire.'

The first signs of favour on the part of the King were followed in a few weeks' time by a change in his attitude to Mme de Montespan. Louis was never comfortable about his departures from the strict requirements of his religion. 'The major festivals', wrote Mme de Caylus, 'caused him remorse; he was equally troubled at being unable to make his devotions and by making them inadequately. Mme de Montespan had the same sentiments, and it was not simply in order to conform with those of the King . . . She used to fast so austerely during Lent that she had her bread weighed. One day the duchesse d'Usèz, astonished at her scruples, could not forbear from speaking to her about it. "What, then, Madame," she answered; "just because I do one wrong, is it necessary that I do the others?" '

In Holy Week 1675, 'the two lovers, oppressed by their consciences, separated in good faith. Mme de Montespan moved to Paris, went to several churches, fasted, prayed and wept over her sins; the King, for his part, did all that a good Christian should.' On Easter Day Bourdaloue preached before Louis a somewhat outspoken sermon which many courtiers felt was 'lacking in discretion'. Louis, however, complimented Bourdaloue and added: 'You will be very content with me; I have sent Mme de Montespan to Clagny.' Bourdaloue answered him bluntly: 'Sire, God would be more content if Clagny were forty leagues from Versailles.'

When the sacred season was over, the question arose: should Mme de Montespan return to Court? 'Her friends and relations, even the most virtuous among them, were saying "Why not?" She was entitled by her birth and by her charges to be there. She could live there in as Christian a manner as elsewhere. The Bishop of Meaux was of the same opinion.'

Mlle de Scudéry, however, remained cynical. She wrote to Bussy-Rabutin: 'The King and Mme de Montespan have separated, although it is said that they are still madly in love with one another. The rumour is that when she returns to Court she will no longer be living in the château and will only be seeing the King at the Queen's. I very much doubt this to be the case, for it seems to me that there is more than a chance that their love will prevail.' It turned out that she was right. It was decided that they should meet again, at first in public, before a well-chosen company of pious and respectable ladies. But Louis drew Athenaïs into a window recess; they talked in low voices for a long time; there were tears. 'Then they made a profound reverence to these venerable matrons and passed into another room. Mlle de Blois, the future duchesse d'Orléans, and the comte de Toulouse were the result.'

On 28 April 1675, Mme de Maintenon took the duc du Maine down to Barèges in the Pyrenees. The waters were highly reputed for their healing qualities. This expedition kept her away from the Court until 20 November. She arrived back on the day before she was expected. The little Duke was by no means cured, but he was walking better. 'Nothing could have been more agreeable', wrote Mme de Sévigné, 'than the surprise which it gave the King. He saw him come into his room, held only by Mme de Maintenon's hand. He was in transports of joy.' On 16

October she had written to her brother from Belfort to share her pleasure. 'M. le duc du Maine is walking, and, although not very vigorously, there is ground for hope that he will walk like you and me. You do not know the depth of my affection for him, but you understand enough not to doubt that the happy success of my journey brings me great pleasure.'

On 8 June 1677, Mme de Maintenon took the duc du Maine again to Barèges. This time the cure was not successful. In September she took him to Bagnières, where she nearly despaired of his life. 'If he is in the state which they think he is it will be impossible to save him, and he is the sweetest creature on earth whose intelligence surprises twenty times a day. But these agitations are not the only ones I am suffering; I am tormented by continual information from the Court.' This probably refers to the renewed relationship between Louis and Mme de Montespan. On 2 July Mme de Sévigné had written: '*Quanto* [Montespan] and her friend are together longer and more intimately than ever; the eagerness of their early years has returned and all restraint is lifted . . . One has never seen anyone more solidly in power.'

One of Mme de Maintenon's earliest biographers was a much younger first cousin, who always called her 'aunt', Mlle de Villette de Mursay, later marquise de Caylus. During a long absence at sea of her father, a staunch Huguenot, her mother, a converted Catholic, removed her, almost by force, to Paris and put her under the care of her cousin with the undisguised intention of converting her to Catholicism. She was taken to Saint-Germain in floods of tears, but on the next day she went to Mass in the Chapel Royal and was so impressed by the beauty of the service that she agreed at once to become a Catholic – but on condition that she would henceforth be spared the rod.

It did not result in her being spoilt. She claimed in her memoirs that she was given an upbringing 'with a care for which it would be impossible to give Mme de Maintenon too much praise'. The details reveal a curriculum which was both demanding and rewarding. 'I have entered into this detail', she continues, 'to mark by these achievements, which are beyond all praise, the conduct and character of Mme de Maintenon; it seems to me that it would be impossible to reflect on the position which she occupied without admiring the attention which she gave to a child, of whom she was only in charge because she was good enough to take it on.'

What Mme de Maintenon herself needed was, in her own words, 'the friendship and the esteem of all. I had no desire for the love of anyone in particular, whoever it might be. I wished to be loved by everyone, to be spoken well of by all; to cut a fine figure and to win the approval of honest people was my idol.' One may perhaps see behind these words the insecurity bred of some of the privations of her past. But she was beginning to find a place in the heart of the King. He was becoming tired of Mme de Montespan. 'Louis', writes Mme de Caylus, 'saw a great difference in the humour of Mme de Maintenon. He found a woman always modest, always in control of herself, always reasonable, but who combined with such rare qualities the charms of vivacious conversation.' The more she rose in the estimation of the King, the more difficult became her relations with Mme de Montespan. Her correspondence with the abbé Gobelin often tells of their encounters. 'How pleasant it would be for me to regain my liberty,' she writes on one occasion; 'I cannot understand why it should be God's will that I should endure Mme de Montespan. She is incapable of friendship and I cannot do without it.'

But friendship was something for which Louis was beginning to feel the need. On 17 July 1680, Mme de Sévigné wrote: 'Mme de Coulanges is always surprised at the sort of favour enjoyed by Mme de Maintenon. No other friend shows such care and attention to her ... She has introduced him to a new world that was unknown to him, which is the relationship of friendship and of conversation, without constraint and without wrangling.'

An obvious failing of Mme de Montespan was her hardness of heart. This showed itself when her coach ran over a poor man on the bridge at Saint-Germain and she rebuked her companions for their pity and compassion. 'To this hardness was joined a continual caustic humour ... It often happened that the Queen was the butt for her raillery.' Louis once had to rebuke her, saying: 'Remember, Madam, that she is your mistress.'

The marriage of the Dauphin in 1680 and the placing of Mme de Maintenon as lady-in-waiting to the Dauphine brought about a separation between the two women. It also began to bring about an improvement in the relationship between the King and the Queen, but it was not to be for long. 'This princess departed this life just at the time when the increasing age and piety of the King was making her happy. He showed an attentiveness towards her to which she was not accustomed. He saw her often and sought to amuse her, and since she attributed this happy change to Mme de Maintenon, she loved her and gave her all the marks of consideration that could be imagined. But the poor princess had such a fear of the King and so great a timidity that she no longer dared to speak to him or to expose herself to a tête-à-tête with him.' Mme de Maintenon, writing to the abbé Gobelin, was highly critical of the Queen's confessor. 'If only the Queen had a director like you, there is no end to the good one might hope for in the royal family, but the Queen's director, as I see it, led her in a way more appropriate for a Carmelite than a

Queen.' Languet de Gergy, chaplain to the duchesse de Bourgogne and later Archbishop of Sens, who knew Mme de Maintenon well and was one of her first biographers, records that 'she used to tell her friends that if this good princess had had more wit and kindness in her humour, the King might perhaps never have thrown himself into the extraneous passions which corrupted his youth'.

Since Mme de Maintenon could not have known that the Queen was going to die so young and so soon, it could hardly have been her ambition to succeed her. Her intention seems to have been simply to separate Louis from his mistresses and to reunite him with his wife. This is what she did and with immediate success. The Queen, of course, was extremely grateful, saying that 'God has raised up Mme de Maintenon to give me back the heart of the King', and she told those who were closest to her that she had never before been treated so well by her husband.

On Friday 30 July 1683, Marie-Thérèse died. The death of the Queen offered the Court only a moving spectacle. Mme de Caylus summed it up. 'The King was more touched than afflicted . . . The Court was sad that he was suffering.' Louis went first to Saint-Cloud and then to Fontainebleau. 'With him in the coach', wrote Choisy, 'were Monsieur, the duchesse de Bourbon, the princesse de Conti and Mme de Maintenon. The favour of the latter increased more and more at Fontainebleau. She had a very beautiful apartment on the same floor as that of the King, who began to spend his evenings with her, as he had been accustomed to do with Mme de Montespan.'

It was at this point that Mme de Caylus began to have her first intimations that something important was happening in the King's heart. 'During the Voyage de Fontainebleau . . . I saw such an agitation in Mme de Maintenon's mind that I have since come to the conclusion that it was caused by a deep uncertainty about her position, her fears and her hopes.' She pretended to be suffering from the vapours and made frequent expeditions into the forest accompanied only by Mme de Montchevreuil. By the time the Court returned to Versailles, on Sunday 10 October, all was calm. Mme de Caylus, reading through her cousin's correspondence with the abbé Gobelin, noticed that those letters written before the Queen's death were full of disenchantment with the Court and of her desire to leave it as soon as she decently could, but that those written after the Voyage de Fontainebleau were full of her duty to remain at Court. The moment after the Queen had died she had wanted to retire to her Château, but the duc de La Rochefoucauld, who was not a friend of hers, took her by the arm and said: 'This is no time to leave the King: he has need of you.'

It seems probable that the secret marriage which united them for the rest of Louis' life took place soon after the return to Versailles and before the beginning of Advent. This may be inferred from the colour of the stole worn for the marriage service. Languet de Gergy records that 'the Archbishop of Narbonne told me often enough that the marriage had been celebrated by the Père de la Chaise in the presence of Monseigneur Harlay de Champvallon, Archbishop of Paris, and of Monsieur Bontemps, Premier Valet de Chambre du Roi, *avec cette circonstance que le Père de la Chaise avait une étole verte*'. La Baumelle, writing in 1756, quotes the Archbishop of Narbonne saying that 'one day in the winter Harlay got up very early in the morning and said to his senior chaplain: "Get me my green vestments and a Missal marked for *De Matrimoniis*" ... The Archbishop put them into a coach and drove off to Versailles.'

The green of vestments and stole was the colour in ordinary use from Pentecost to the beginning of Advent. But for a wedding which offered 'the full treatment' the celebrant would have worn a white vestment and stole. It may be inferred from the use of green that this was regarded as a *mariage de conscience* – in other words a quiet wedding.

There was no public announcement of the marriage and there were some at Court who remained uncertain. Liselotte d'Orléans, the second Madame, writing to her aunt, the Duchess Sophia of Brunswick-Lüneburg (whose son was to become George I of England), on 13 May 1687, said: 'Your Grace desires to know whether it is true that the King is married to Mme de Maintenon, but honestly I am not able to tell you. Not many people doubt it, but as long as this marriage is not made public I find it difficult to believe. And because of what I know of marriage in this country', she added cynically, 'I do not believe that if they were married they would be as much in love as they are.' A year later she still did not know, but added: 'What is certain, however, is that the King has never had the same passion for any of his mistresses as he has for this one; when she is present he cannot wait fifteen minutes without whispering something in her ear and talking to her in secret.'

Alone among the royal family, the duchesse d'Orléans hated Mme de Maintenon. 'I do not believe that a more wicked devil can be found in the whole world than she is, for all her piety and her hypocrisy, and I find that she is a fine example of the old German proverb: "Where the devil cannot go he sends an old woman." ' In June 1701, however, on the occasion of her husband's death, she completely changed her mind. Mme de Maintenon came to see her. 'I immediately told her that I desired her friendship. I also confessed that I had not liked her in the past, thinking that she had deprived me of the King's favour and hated me; that I had heard this from Mme la Dauphine also, but that I would be happy to forget all this now if she would be my friend. To this she replied with many beautiful and eloquent words, promised me her friendship and we embraced.'

Mme de Maintenon's relationships with the royal family might have presented her with a difficult and delicate problem, but she seems to have won the respect of all. Shortly after her death, King James II wrote to the superior at Saint-Cyr, Mme de Boufflers: 'I could not fail to have been a witness, during many years, of the respect which the royal family bore for her and of the dignity and modesty with which she upheld the position in which Providence had placed her – a manifest proof of the solidity of her mind and virtue and of the discernment of the late King.'

Solidity was the key-note. The abbé de Choisy relates how Louis conferred upon her the title, saying: 'One accords to Kings the title of Your Majesty, to the Pope that of Your Holiness, to ambassadors that of Your Excellency; we must address you as *Votre Solidité*.' Languet de Gergy sums up her position thus: 'I have lived for fifteen years in the middle of this Court, and it seemed to me to be united. It was Mme de Maintenon herself who, by her prudence and her modesty, was as it were the common centre in which they were all united and who maintained a good relationship between them and the King.'

Certain historians have looked for evidence that Mme de Maintenon was responsible for the 'conversion' of Louis. That he showed a steady increase in piety after his break with Mme de Montespan seems to be beyond doubt. But his 'conversion' was neither dramatic nor sudden. One of the most interesting sources of information comes from the letters written by disaffected Jansenists living in Rome who were trying to damage Louis' reputation in the eyes of the Pope. The central figure in this group was the Bishop of Vaison, a diocese in the Comtat d'Avignon which was still a papal possession. This bishop entertained hopes of having Louis excommunicated and France placed under an interdict.

Among the correspondents of the Bishop of Vaison were the abbé Dorat and the abbé Bizot. Their letters were full of animosity against Louis, but they had to admit the deepening of his faith. Bizot, writing on 3 October 1687, included the news: 'We are receiving letters from many places which tell us that the King has changed his way of life, that the Père de La Chaise has brought him back to himself in an unimaginable manner.' Shortly afterwards the Père Dorat says much the same thing: 'It is true that the King has changed his life in a surprising way. The Père de La Chaise has brought him back by slow degrees, to where he wants him to be.' Dorat concludes: 'It is the abbé de Vauborel who has written all that I have told you; you know that he is not a man to be untruthful or to give false advice.' These letters, written four years after the marriage between Louis and Mme de Maintenon, bear witness to the slow and steady progress of the King towards a deeper devotion. Both the writers give all the credit to Louis' confessor rather than to his wife.

That does not mean that she played no part in furthering Louis' devotion, but it is not really possible, nor is it necessary, to assess the contribution made by Mme de Maintenon to Louis' spiritual recovery. That his closest companion was a deeply religious woman is proved by her correspondence with her confessor. But she, like Louis, was progressing in spirituality as she advanced in age. She possessed the somewhat rare combination of piety and charm. It was still the same person who had once so delighted Mme de Sévigné who was now to help coax the King into a deeper devotion. In one of her letters to Gobelin she wrote: 'I would very much like you to make a little extract or collection – I do not know what to call it – but some maxims on the duties of a prince, which will give him the opinion which he ought to have of religion, and a form of devotion, short and solid, for daily use. I beg you to work on this project however involved it may be.' It was entirely natural that she should do whatever she could to encourage Louis in his new way of life.

19
The Revocation of the Edict of Nantes

On Thursday 18 October 1685, the King signed the Edict of Fontaine-bleau, usually known as the Revocation of the Edict of Nantes. It forbade any exercise in public of *la Religion Prétendue Réformée*. To be a practising Huguenot was henceforth to be outside the law.

Most of the Catholics in France went into ecstasies over the news. Bossuet, preaching the *oraison funèbre* of Michel Le Tellier, one of the chief architects of the Revocation, spoke for the majority. 'Let us publish abroad this miracle of our times; let us indulge in an outpouring of the heart over the piety of Louis; let us raise our applause to the very heavens themselves; let us say to this new Constantine, to this new Theodosius, to this new Marcion: "This is the worthy achievement of your reign; this is its true character; through you heresy is no more; God alone has made this marvel!" '

On the other side Saint-Simon, who saw the affair with the perspective of history, condemned the action as morally inexcusable and politically inept: 'the Revocation of the Edict of Nantes, without the slightest pretext and without the least necessity . . . which depopulated one quarter of the realm, which ruined its commerce and weakened it in all its parts, which gave it over for so long to pillage, both public and admitted, by the Dragoons, which authorised the tortures and executions in which thousands of people of both sexes died, which ruined so many . . . which lost our manufacture to other countries and caused them to flourish and abound at our expense'.

There is hyperbole on both sides. Bossuet seems undecided as to whether to give the credit to Louis or to God. Saint-Simon exaggerates somewhat in claiming that the Revocation 'depopulated one quarter of the realm': Scoville has estimated that the Huguenots accounted for only 10 per cent of the population and that only 10 per cent of those emigrated.

The Edict of Nantes had granted a measure of tolerance to Huguenots.

Tolerance enjoys a high moral status in Western civilisation today, but it exists in inverse proportion to a general decline in commitment to any creed or moral code. Total tolerance denies, in effect, the possibility of any objective truth in either religion or ethics. Intolerance, a logical outcome of total commitment or total conviction, is therefore more typical of the seventeenth century because of the often fanatical firmness with which the differing faiths were held. In England, in the late seventeenth century, the Marquis of Halifax was ahead of his time in writing: 'There should not always be storms and thunder: a clear sky would sometimes make the Church look more like Heaven.' To Louis XIV, however, and to all good Catholics, a clear sky could only be one from which the clouds of heresy had been dispersed.

Louis had certain rather particular ideas about the nature of God. They interconnected with his ideas about the nature of kingship. 'To tell you the truth, my son,' he wrote, 'we are not only lacking in gratitude and in justice but in prudence and common sense when we are lacking in veneration for Him whose lieutenants we are. Our submission to Him is the guide and example of that which is due to ourselves. The armies, the councils and all the ingenuity of man would be but a feeble means of maintaining us on the throne if everyone believed he had the same right as us and did not reverence a superior power of which our own power is part.' He regarded himself as exercising 'a truly divine function'. Moreover, he was on his guard against hypocrisy. 'My rebel subjects, when they have had the audacity to take up arms against me, have perhaps provoked me to less indignation than those who, while remaining close to my person, paid me more respect and with greater assiduity than all the rest, when I was well aware that they were betraying me and had no true respect for me or true affection of the heart.' Thus Louis could argue from the danger of hypocrisy in the adulation of a courtier to the danger of hypocrisy in the sanctimoniousness of the worshipper.

Louis had acquired, by virtue of his anointing and coronation, an aura of divinity and the sacramental power to cure scrofula – 'the King's Evil' – by the laying on of the royal hand with the formula 'The King touches you; may God heal you.' But this, together with the titles of *le Roi très chrétien* and *Fils aîné de l'Eglise*, left his actual authority over the Church in France undefined. This could easily lead to friction with Rome.

Although the Gallican Church, more or less independent of the papacy since the Pragmatic Sanction of Bourges in 1438, had been brought back under papal jurisdiction by a Concordat signed at Bologna in 1516, the signing had been fiercely opposed in France and a certain spirit of independence had survived. In exchange, François I had obtained for the Kings of France the right of nomination to all the most lucrative posts in the Church – a right which was to be frequently abused. Less clearly defined was the right of *régale* which entitled the King to receive the revenues of a vacant bishopric. It was this which brought Louis into controversy with the new Pope Innocent XI, elected in 1676. Pious, virtuous, authoritarian and very conscious of the prerogatives of his position, Innocent was soon in conflict with Louis and even threatened ecclesiastical sanctions.

In 1680 the Assemblée Générale du Clergé reaffirmed their 'strong attachment' to the King and added: 'it is extraordinarily difficult for us to accept that the Eldest Son and Protector of the Church should be subject to threats . . . We are so closely attached to Your Majesty that nothing could possibly separate us.' The death of the Bishop of Pamiers, who had supported the Pope against Louis, led to the excommunication of the new Vicar-General appointed by the Archbishop of Toulouse. It was a potentially explosive situation.

Louis needed the full support of the General Assembly and in March 1682 they passed the 'Four Articles'. The first of these stated that the political power of Kings was not subject to the control of the Church, which can neither depose princes nor release their subjects from their oath of fidelity (precisely what Pope Pius V had done in 1570 when his bull *Regnans in excelsis* claimed to depose Queen Elizabeth I and to release her subjects from their allegiance to her). The second postulated the superiority of an Ecumenical Council over the Pope and could cite the councils of Constance and Basle in the fifteenth century which dealt with the anomaly of there being three claimants to the papacy. The third article laid down that although the Pope is Head of the Church, he is obliged to govern according to its laws and to respect the privileges of the particular – that is, the national – Churches. The fourth maintained that whereas the Pope exercised the chief role in questions of doctrine, he had no personal infallibility; his judgement was not irreformable until it had received the consent of the Church. How such consent was to be obtained is not clear.

The prime mover of this declaration was Charles-Maurice Le Tellier, Louvois' brother and Archbishop of Reims. Predictably, the Vatican rejected the decisions of the Assembly, which provoked their response: 'The Gallican Church governs itself by its own laws.' In 1683 those bishops who had subscribed to the 'Four Articles' were ordered to send written apologies to the Pope, admitting themselves to be 'sorry and angry, more than words can say, about what happened in the Assembly in 1682'.

On 13 November 1685, the duc d'Estrées conveyed the news of the Edict of Fontainebleau to Pope Innocent XI. 'His Holiness could not refrain from embracing him tenderly.' Louis had hoped that his meritorious action would earn him the Pope's gratitude in some tangible form, and d'Estrées tried to take advantage of the situation by asking for certain concessions – some arrangement over the *régale*, or the immediate despatch of papal bulls confirming the appointment of those bishops whom Louis had nominated. But Innocent, a doctrinaire quite capable of refusing the most advantageous of deals rather than sacrifice a principle, resumed his customary coldness and gravity, which prevented the Duke from proceeding any further.

The dates of these manoeuvrings between Rome and Louis, backed by his clergy and his Parlement, coincide with the years immediately preceding the Revocation of the Edict of Nantes. Both the General Assembly of the Clergy and the Parlement de Paris were strongly anti-Protestant. On 1 July 1682, the clergy addressed an *Avertissement Solennel* to the Huguenots, threatening 'misfortunes far more fearsome and fatal than those which you have already incurred by your rebellion and schism'.

This reference to rebellion added a political dimension to their ecclesiastical abhorrence of schism. Not only was the theology of Calvinism in important respects irreconcilable with the dogmas of Rome, but also its political structures, with their parochial independence, their elected elders and their provincial and national synods, did not accord with the pyramidal hierarchy of French society in which all authority flowed from the top. Not only were the Huguenots heretical: they were democratic. Even Sully, the Huguenot Minister of Henri IV, castigated in his memoirs 'those who wished to make of Calvinist France a sort of republican state'.

In 1661, long before the Revocation of the Edict of Nantes, Louis had recorded in his memoirs his attitude to the Protestants in his country. He makes it quite clear that their beliefs and their right to live by their beliefs were not acceptable. 'As for the great number of my subjects of the *religion prétendue réformée*, which is an evil which I have always regarded, and still do regard, with much pain, I formed at that time the policy of my whole attitude towards them.'

His policy was quite simply their conversion to Catholicism, but in his approach he shows a more generous readiness to understand than his ministers or his parlements. In 1661 he wrote in his memoirs: 'It seemed to me, my son, that those who wished to employ extreme or violent remedies did not understand the nature of this evil, partly caused by the fierceness of men's spirits which one must allow to pass off and die out imperceptibly, rather than to make it flare up again by a strong opposition ... Insofar as I have been able to understand it, the ignorance of the clergy in the last century, their luxurious living, their debauchery, the bad example which they have set and those which they were obliged to tolerate in others, in fact the abuses which they allowed to be authorised in the behaviour of individuals, which were contrary to the rules and the public opinion of the Church, gave rise more than anything else to the wounds which the Church has received through heresy and schism. The new reformers were manifestly speaking the truth over many matters of this sort which they reproved with some acrimony; but, on the other hand, they were guilty of imposture in all matters which concerned not facts but faith.'

Louis realised also that the political interest of certain princes and even such factors as the love of novelty played a large part in establishing the heresy.

His gentleness and reasonableness at this early stage in his personal rule say much about him, but it seems that he had little understanding of the Protestant zeal which had faced the tortures of the Inquisition in Spain and the fires of Smithfield in England and was soon to face the dragonnades – the billeting upon them of brutal soldiery – and the hell on earth, *l'enfer anticipé*, of his own galley slaves. Not that all Calvinists in France were cast as martyrs. Thousands of them abjured, sometimes more than once when there was a financial reward attached. The dragoons who plundered the Protestants were joined by the citizens and among these were some of the newly converted, anxious no doubt to prove the sincerity of their conversions.

The persecution of the Huguenots had begun long before the Revocation. Looking back on the year 1678, Mme de Caylus wrote: 'The Peace [of Nijmegen] having been concluded, the King, tranquil and glorious, believed that all that was lacking to his glory was the extirpation of a heresy which had made such ravages in his country. This project was great and beautiful and even prudent if it is considered independently of the means by which it was achieved. The Ministers and several Bishops . . . were largely responsible for some of these means and for determining the King to adopt some which were not to his taste but also in deceiving him about the manner in which those agreed to were executed.' Furthermore, it was claimed in a pamphlet, printed at The Hague, entitled 'Considerations on the Circular Letters of the Assembly of the Clergy of France in 1682', that the rigours against the Protestants did not originate with Louis: 'The greater part of the decrees against the Protestants were formally demanded by the Clergy.'

Mme de Caylus, however, saw Louvois as the real culprit. He was Minister for War and as long as the war lasted his supremacy in the Council was secure. But he was afraid that the coming of peace would give the advantage to the others, especially Colbert and his son Seignelay. 'He wanted, at no matter what cost, to bring the military into a project which should have been based on charity and gentleness . . . M. de Louvois asked the King's permission to send into the town which had the most Huguenots a regiment of dragoons, assuring him that the mere sight of his troops would determine their minds to listen more willingly to the voice of those who were sent to them. The King yielded, against his better judgement and natural inclination, which always inclined him to gentleness. His orders were passed on and, unknown to him, they committed cruelties for which they would have been punished if he had known about them.'

There is evidence that Louvois himself tried to restrain the cruelties. On 16 October 1685, Louvois wrote to the Intendant Foucault: 'His Majesty has learnt with regret that a company and a half of dragoons was billeted on a woman in Poitiers ... I have told you so often that these violences were not to the King's liking that I can only be astonished that you should not comply with his orders ... It would be greatly in your interest not to fail again.' On 5 November, less than a month after the signing of the Revocation, Louvois decided that, in the absence of any official declaration, he could authorise 'quelques logements un peu forts', sufficient to correct the simple-minded, and he informed the marquis de Vérac that 'those who would have the stupid glory of wanting to be the last (to abjure) should be pushed to the last extremities'.

But if Louvois knew of the violences and cruelties, the question must be asked how much he passed on to the King. Benoist insists that Louis was made 'inaccessible through the care taken by those in high office to prevent anyone from speaking to him about matters on which they had not yet had time to forewarn him'.

The idea of the dragonnades seems to have come in the first place from the Intendant of Poitou, Marillac. Louvois first rebuked Marillac, insisting that the Protestants must be given 'no legitimate pretext that they have been subjected to violence or threats when they refused to change their religion', and in February 1682 Louvois obtained from the King the recall of Marillac and his replacement by the less violent Nicolas de Lamoignon, Seigneur de Basville. The instructions given to him were clear. 'It is not fitting to the service of His Majesty that they [the dragoons] should make any disorders among those upon whom they are billeted, nor that there should be any violence like that which was complained of in the days of Marillac.'

It is possible that the soldiers were more violent than the officers required them to be and that the officers were more violent than the Intendants required them to be and so on up. Mme de Caylus did her best to exonerate Louis by blaming Louvois, but it was unlike Louis not to demand full information on any matter; he had always required 'le détail de tout'.

It is precisely the details which are horrific. One of the first accounts of the dragonnades comes from the pen of one of the victims – Jean Migault, a schoolmaster with the title of *lecteur* at Moulle in the commune of Aigonnay, not far from Niort in Poitou. The events which he described took place in 1681 when Marillac was still Intendant. Migault detailed his experiences in a journal written for his children, who had been evacuated to safety. Early in 1681 a declaration by the King was published 'which excluded Protestants from all public offices, abolished all the charges which were connected with our religion and which deprived most of the brethren of any means of earning their livelihood'.

On 13 February Migault and his family moved to the near-by village of Mougon. All was quiet for four or five months, which was lucky, for during that time Mme Migault gave birth to her eleventh child. She had a very difficult confinement and was still in great pain and badly needing rest when the dragoons arrived. They were distributed among the villages and billeted on the Protestants. The results were soon apparent. 'Every day we saw people, who had hitherto confessed the true faith, flocking to the Mass – behaviour which was all the more reprehensible and astonishing because they renounced their religion at the very moment when the soldiers crossed the threshold and before they had suffered the least inconvenience.' This was just what Louvois had predicted.

The readiness of the majority to become Catholic greatly increased the sufferings of those who remained staunch. Since Catholics were exempt from the billeting, the ever-decreasing number of the faithful Protestants had to find accommodation for an ever-increasing number of dragoons. It was not long before Migault's house was invaded.

'It would be difficult to forget the heartbreaking scene which I was to witness.' It was Tuesday 22 August. In the course of the morning, 'as we were coming out of the church, where we had just made our customary prayers, we saw a troop of cavalry, commanded by M. de La Brique, advancing towards us at the gallop; they took up their positions round the churchyard and by their behaviour struck terror into the hearts of the most courageous. I had scarcely returned home when the quartermaster presented himself, holding in his hand a *billet de logement* and, without dismounting, asked us in the most uncompromising voice if it were our intention to become Catholics. On being assured that we had no such intention he rode off.'

'We were alone in the house, for a few days earlier we had taken the precaution of sending you [their children] away ... Within a minute of the quartermaster's departure we had a visit from M. de La Brique himself.' He had come quite simply to barter; the more they offered to pay the fewer the soldiers who would be billeted on them. They had no money with which to barter. After a thorough inspection of the house the commanding officer left.

'A few minutes later we saw two soldiers arrive who produced their *billets de logement*, who, having put their horses in my stable, demanded a dinner, the menu of which would have been, with no exaggeration, enough for twenty. While we were preparing this frugal repast two of their comrades entered, billets in hand, who likewise took their horses to the stable; they had scarcely gone to do so when another soldier presented himself.

'The presence and the insults of these five soldiers, the most insolent of men, as insatiable in their demands as they were ferocious in their manners, was not regarded as sufficiently vexatious . . . The fifth was almost immediately followed by four more.' To obtain sufficient provisions to meet this ever-increasing demand Migault was obliged to go to Niort, but on leaving the house he slipped next door to the home of some Catholic ladies. They were interrupted by the appearance of six horsemen who were asking for his address. He now had fifteen guests.

Their Catholic neighbours begged him not to return to his house, assuring him that the troopers were intent on his destruction. They promised to procure a means of escape for Mme Migault, who was still suffering from the effects of her confinement. They were nearly too late. One of the soldiers had discovered the unfortunate woman and forced her to come downstairs. 'There, this man, mixing the most barbarous irony with the most revolting ferocity, suggested that, in her condition, it was necessary to keep her as warm as possible.' They flung her into the corner of the chimney and proceeded to light a blazing hot fire. 'The soldiers made a sport of increasing the furnace with pieces of our furniture, and, in the vain hope of overcoming the constance of their victim, began to outrage the holy name of God in terms which I dare not repeat, threatening to burn her if she did not at once abjure her Protestantism.' The heat of the fire was so insupportable that these men themselves had not the strength to remain near the fireplace, but replaced each other every three minutes.

By this time the Catholic ladies from next door had entered and, falling on their knees, begged the officer to have mercy on the woman. They pleaded in vain. Then, by what seemed like the grace of God, the curé of the parish, who had come to stand in for the absent prior – an excellent man and an old friend of the Migaults – arrived and was told what was going on. 'He came immediately to our house, and using the influence which his position and his reputation gave him, succeeded in rescuing your mother from the hands of her executioners . . . It would be superfluous to recount in detail the abominable behaviour of the soldiers when they saw that their victims were out of reach of their tyranny. Their rage knew no bounds.'

'The next day all the Protestants in our parish made a formal abjuration of their religion, except for twenty families who, abandoning their homes at the approach of the cavalry, had taken refuge in the woods. Our beds, our linen, our clothes, everything that we possessed was either sold or destroyed; the entire contents of the abandoned houses suffered in the same way and, when M. de La Brique was well assured that there was no more damage to be done at Mougon, he took his troop off to Souche.'

The good neighbours of the Migaults, in the meantime, had made the best arrangements which they could. As soon as darkness fell, and while the troopers were preoccupied with drinking their wine, husband and wife were reunited in the middle of the forest. A cabriolet was awaiting them. 'I experienced an inexpressible feeling of joy', concludes Migault, 'to see these good Catholics uniting their thanksgivings with ours to the Father of us all who had granted us such a happy deliverance.'

Daniel de Cosnac, Bishop of Valence, has left his own account of the impact of the Revocation upon his diocese. Already before 1685 Cosnac was boasting that he had destroyed all the Protestant temples within his jurisdiction. He claimed to have done all that he could to bring about conversions, 'either by instruction, or by granting favours or money. My efforts were not without success.' But he added: 'I admit that fear of the dragoons and of billeting in the homes of heretics could have contributed more than I did.'

This went on for a whole year, when a large number of conversions were brought about by the reprisals after an armed rising, at which nearly 4,000 men turned out 'in order to defend and maintain their heresy'. M. de Saint-Ruth, who commanded the local militia, attacked and routed them, and burned some 200 who had taken refuge in a barn. 'A large number', continues Cosnac, 'were taken prisoner and all were condemned to die by the hand of the executioner. All the prisons in my diocese were filled with these unfortunates . . . It was a terrible spectacle.' Cosnac wrote to the King, detailing the continual executions, and beseeching him to pardon all who repented. Louis accorded this on condition that they were converted. 'I therefore accompanied the Intendant wherever there were prisoners, and while he was instituting proceedings against them and condemning them to death, I was receiving their abjurations. More than two thousand were saved in this way, which gave me considerable credit among those whom I had snatched from the gallows; I can say that out of this large number . . . there was only one who chose the rope rather than his life.'

On another occasion at Tournon – also in his diocese – Cosnac learnt that two ministers had been arrested with arms in their hands and condemned, one to be broken on the wheel and the other to be hanged. 'I felt it my duty to go to Tournon in order to try and rescue them from their unhappy condition and to save, if possible, both their souls and their lives. I left at once and with incredible speed.' When he arrived at the place of execution the second minister was already at the foot of the gallows with the rope round his neck. 'I shouted as loud as I could, "*Arrêtez!*" ' He conducted the prisoner to a near-by house and in less than an hour had persuaded him to recant.

The first prisoner, however, Isaac Homel, was quite prepared for martyrdom. The Intendant informed Cosnac that Homel was expressly excluded by the King from pardon even if he did convert. This was, of course, a case not just of heresy but of rebellion. Cosnac spent nearly four hours with him. 'I told him that I had the power to open Heaven to him, but not to enable him to live in this world.' It was in vain. Homel died the next day upon the wheel. Cosnac's account provides first-hand evidence of the situation which suggests that Louis was fairly closely in touch with what was going on.

Another source of information is from an eye-witness who was a Catholic priest named Jean-François Bion. He served as a chaplain on the galley *La Superbe*. He was so afflicted by the savagery with which the *galériens* were treated and so impressed by their courage and resignation that he became a convert to Calvinism. He records that the Turks who served on the galleys avowed that they would rather be 'turned into dogs than embrace a religion where they witnessed the exercise of so much cruelty'.

Bion's *Relation des tourments que l'on fait souffrir aux protestants qui sont sur les galères de France* is quoted by Van Malssen. Bion draws attention to the non-observance by subordinates of any regulations which were humanitarian. Having described the appalling conditions of those chained to the oars, he goes on to affirm that 'the lot of those who were ill was even more hideous than that of the others. When a galley is commissioned the medicaments taken on board are good. But the surgeon sells them in the town . . . The King's orders are that all the sick are to be given half a kilo of fresh bread, half a kilo of fresh meat and 50 grammes of rice a day' (that was not far short of the daily rations at Les Invalides), 'but the steward, who ought to provide it all, wants to make his fortune in five or six campaigns: instead of broth he serves only boiling water.'

In 1704 Bion went to Versailles and gave information to Chamillart, Ministre pour la Marine, on the disgraceful practices of the stewards. Louis approved his report and granted him a gratuity.

Another group of galley slaves were the *faux-sauniers*, dealers in contra-band salt who were dodging the *gabelle* – the tax on salt. These were not sentenced for life and ought to have been released upon the expiry of their sentences, but this did not always happen, 'especially if the man had the misfortune to have a strong body'. This was, of course, the act of a subordinate, 'but the King is not the less guilty,' continues Bion, 'for a prince is never absolved from the obligation of vigilance with regard to his Ministers'.

Much interesting information, also, about the persecutions can be obtained from the letters on the subject sent to the Grand Condé by his agents. Even before the Edict of Fontainebleau had been published, reports were coming in of mass conversions and temples razed to the ground. The marquise de Portes, a cousin of Condé and daughter of a notable campaigner against the Huguenots, was invited by Louis to spend the next two years back in Languedoc where 'he was persuaded that she would make a great stir on her lands'. She reported her successes to Condé – 'which shows, if one could ever have doubted it, that their religion is not that which has filled Heaven with so many martyrs'. This statement, as it turned out, was not entirely true.

Du Rosel, a Jesuit who had been preceptor to Condé's son, and was with the Court at Fontainebleau and therefore close to the events, reports on the eve of the Revocation how the Père de La Chaise, the King's confessor, had been commenting after dinner on the increased numbers of conversions in Languedoc and had suggested as a devise or symbolic picture a parterre full of sunflowers (in French *tournesols*) and above them the sun with the motto 'ab eo conversio' (our conversion is his work).

Immediately after the publication of the Edict of Fontainebleau the marquis de Givry, one of Condé's former officers, reported from Metz that orders had been given to pull down the Protestant temple. 'The edict will be read tomorrow, registered and published. The ministers have received orders to quit the kingdom unless they abjure their Calvinism within a fortnight. Councillors who are of the *Prétendue Religion* have been ordered to lay down their offices . . . and all children born henceforth are to be baptised into the Church of Rome.'

On 21 October Du Rosel provided further details. 'The King offers members of that religion who have left France a free entry into the kingdom and into their property (on proof of their conversion) and to ministers a third as much again as they were paid by the Huguenots, freedom to take up offices and to be called to the bar without examin-ations. So there you have any exercise of the Protestant religion forbidden in all the kingdom and complete liberty to become converted.'

Du Rosel then goes on to describe a particular incident at the Château de Fontainebleau. 'The King has had performed a ceremony of solemn abjuration during the Mass.' The candidate was the Duke of Richmond, the illegitimate son of Charles II and Louise de Queroualle, Duchess of Portsmouth. 'The Bishop of Meaux gave a very fine and very fair dissertation by applying to it the gospel for the day. It was the parable of a King who invites to a solemn banquet people of every sort and who, when these decline to come, desires that both the good and the bad should be obliged to come in – *compelle intrare*'. Saint Augustine was responsible in the first place for the misuse of this text to justify the savagery of religious persecution.

On the same day, Sunday 21 October, the comte de Briord, also at Fontainebleau, wrote to say that the papal nuncio had had an audience with the King who had complained 'that the Huguenots were retreating as into an asylum into the city and county of Avignon'. Avignon had been, since the days of the papal schism, annexed to Rome.

On Monday the 22nd, the Père Alleaume, another Jesuit also at Fontainebleau, announced that the King was sending the famous preacher Bourdaloue to Montpellier for Lent. 'It is a pleasure that he wants to give this town which has become converted with such a good grace.' Mme de Sévigné mentions the same occasion, adding that 'so many people [in or near Montpellier] had been converted without knowing why. The Père Bourdaloue will teach them and make them into good Catholics. The dragoons have been good missionaries up till now.'

From all quarters Condé was receiving assurances of the great numbers of abjurations. On 2 December, Delarue, his Capitaine des Chasses, who was one of the more active of missionaries, assured him that 'he knew of no more of the religious remaining in all the dependences of Chantilly'. At the same time Jacques de Thésut, one of Condé's former officers, writes from Dijon: 'In the Charolais all are converted by the ministry of le Père de Langeron, rector of the Jesuits in Paray-le-Monial.' The same was true of Arnay-le-duc and at Avallon only one Huguenot remained obdurate.

On 12 December de Thésut drew up a table of figures showing the number of former Catholics in Dijon (2,002), the number of converts (5,207), the number of those who refused to convert – *restés dans leur opiniâtreté* (240) – and the number of those who had left France (2,426). But statistics do not always reveal the whole truth. What the letters to Condé convey again and again is that very many of those classified as *nouveaux convertis* were not behaving as converts should.

On 4 December, Dom Tixier, a Benedictine monk, writes from Rouen that 'the greater part of the newly converted do not go to Mass or Vespers – that their excuse was that they could not understand anything of the prayers [which were, of course, in Latin], that as for the sermons they found very little instruction, and in any case no one ever asked other Catholics if they went to Mass. But the greatest difficulty was in going to confession, and only a very few could resolve to do so.' And those who did not go to confession were unable to receive Communion.

Matters were much the same in the south. The comte de Lusson, writing from his château near Nîmes, complained that 'our new converts fulfil their obligations very badly. I find them more opinionated and mutinous than they were before; it seems that they repent of what they have done and they act in concert to put the matter right. They only go to Mass if forced. They refuse to be instructed or to have their children instructed. The missionaries have very little success in the towns and less in the country. I have just been told that they [the Huguenots] chant the psalms in public.' Presumably it was not the psalms themselves which were offensive to the Catholics but the fact that they were sung in French and not in Latin. Vauban sums up, in a typically outspoken manner, the situation in Languedoc – 'a country whose streets are paved with the newly converted who are about as Catholic as I am Mahometan'.

Saint-Simon had claimed that the Revocation 'lost our manufacture to other countries and caused them to flourish and abound at our expense'. The history of Burgundy provides many examples. Colbert had gone to great lengths to establish manufactures of linen and serge *à la façon de Londres*, and the cultivation of flax and hemp. He saw in this the only means 'by which the people can be raised from their misery'.

Conservatives in Burgundy had opposed such innovation in a land traditionally divided between agriculture and viticulture, but Colbert's persistence prevailed. But those who took to the new manufactures were almost invariably Calvinists. There were about 2,200 of them in Burgundy, of whom some 1,400 emigrated. The persecution of these serious-minded and hard-working men put an end to many of Colbert's ventures. Two towns in particular felt the painful effects of their departure. At Beaune the manufacture of broadcloth, employing some 2,000 people, came abruptly to an end. At Paray-le-Monial the linen mills closed and the business was taken out of France.

But the loss was not merely financial; the horrors of the persecution, as Saint-Simon perceived, had yielded the moral high ground to the enemies of France, who, even in an age well acquainted with cruelty, viewed with indignation the spectacle of 'a prodigious number of people proscribed, naked, fugitive, wandering, innocent of any crime, seeking asylum far from their native land; which sent men who were noble, rich, elderly, men often highly esteemed for their piety, their learning, their virtue; men of ease, frail and delicate, to the galleys under the lash, only too effective, of the officer in charge of convicts – and all because of their religion and nothing else'.

In 1758 there appeared in London a book entitled *The Memoirs of a Protestant Condemned to the Galleys in France for his Religion. Translated from the original by James Willington.* James Willington was in fact Oliver Goldsmith. The author of the book, who was 'still alive and known to numbers, not only in Holland but in London', was Jean Marteilhe, born in 1684, son of a trader in Bergerac, who seems to have been fairly prosperous – for when the dragonnades reached Bergerac in 1700, their house was large enough to have twenty-two troopers billeted on them.

The persecution, conducted by the duc de La Force and four Jesuit 'bloodhounds', was particularly fearsome. 'There were no conceivable cruelties which these booted and spurred missionaries did not exercise to oblige the poor citizens to go to Mass, make their public abjuration and swear, with horrible oaths, never to abandon the practice of the Roman religion. The Duke had a form of this oath filled with imprecations against the reformed faith, which he made them sign and swear to.'

Jean Marteilhe determined to make his escape. He was only sixteen, but he was of the stuff of which martyrs are made. Together with his friend Daniel Le Gras he left Bergerac by night and reached the little town of Mussidan the next morning. 'There we resolved, whatever the perils might be, to continue our journey as far as Holland, resigning ourselves wholly to the will of God . . . and as we implored the Divine protection we made a firm resolution not to imitate Lot's wife in looking back, and that whatever might be the result of this perilous enterprise, we would remain firm and constant in confessing the true reformed religion even at the risk of the punishment of the galleys, or of death.'

The crossing of the frontier without a passport was as difficult as it was dangerous. They were arrested at Marienbourg. They were put in charge of a Major de La Salle who actually came from Bergerac and knew the Marteilhe parents. He tried to help them, but unfortunately a Minister of State, the marquis de La Vrillière, was in Marienbourg at the time. He ordered the Governor to condemn both the young men to the galleys for life. They were told that the abjuration of their faith would procure their immediate pardon and release. They both refused.

It was not until January 1702 that they exchanged prison, where they had sometimes been fairly comfortable, for the convict ships. They were fortunate enough to be taken to the galleys at Dunkirk and were thus spared, for the time being, the horrors of the long walk to Marseille. The galley to which they were assigned was named *L'Heureuse.*

Marteilhe's first experience was to have to watch the infliction of the bastonnade upon another convict. 'I was terrified at witnessing this punishment, which takes place without any form of trial and immediately . . . The manner in which this barbarous punishment is inflicted is as follows. The unfortunate victim is stripped naked from the waist upwards; they then make him lie upon his face, his legs hanging over his bench and his arms over the bench opposite. Two convicts hold his legs and two more his arms, his back is bare and exposed.' The flogging was administered by 'a muscular Turk', also stripped, so that the officer could whip him if he slackened in his efforts, 'to urge him on to belabour the back of the poor victim with all his strength, which he does with a thick rope . . . He applies his blows with all his force, so that each cut raises a bruise about an inch in height . . . I have seen fifty, eighty, even a hundred strokes given; in such cases the victim scarcely ever recovers.'

The next day the under-officer came, without warning, to Marteilhe's bench and, to his horror, ordered him to strip at once to receive the bastonnade. He had been accused by a fellow convict of 'horrible blasphemies against the Catholic Church and the Virgin Mary'. Fortunately, being chained to his bench, he could not have uttered such blasphemies without all those nearest to him hearing. These all testified to his innocence and the punishment was not inflicted.

During his time at Dunkirk, Marteilhe was severely wounded in an engagement with an English frigate. This would have earned an ordinary convict his freedom, but not one condemned on account of his religion. He was, however, soon to leave the English Channel for the Mediterranean.

'Everyone knows that in the year 1712, the Queen of England made peace with France, and among other articles it was stipulated that the English should occupy the town, fortifications and port of Dunkirk.' The sight of the convicts moved the English soldiers to great pity and indignation and the French authorities deemed it prudent that they should all be transferred to Marseille. This condemned them to the horrors of the 'long walk'.

At Calais they were landed and were linked together to form a procession. An under-officer 'fettered us two and two, each by a leg and then passed a long chain through the rings of the chains which coupled us all, so that eleven couples were all chained together . . . Amongst us there were old people who, by the feebleness of their age or by their infirmities, could not walk a quarter of a league even if they had not been laden . . . None of us had walked at all for a very long time.' Carts could be provided for those who were really unable to walk, but the regulations required that these should be subjected to a severe whipping to make certain that they were not malingering.

From Calais the chain-gang made its painful, cumbersome way to Le Havre and from Le Havre to Paris. At Le Havre they enjoyed relative comfort and were allowed to receive visits from the Calvinists who had abjured, many of whom were now made ashamed of their conversion. 'The conduct of these new converts showed very plainly that the Roman Church, instead of converting, only makes hypocrites.' But with the help of the 'hypocrites' they were able to worship according to their own religion. 'We had prayers morning and evening, and, after hearing the good sermons which we had with us, we sang psalms, so that our prison was something like a little church.'

The prison of La Tournelle in Paris, once a royal palace, far from being like a little church, was more like a vast torture chamber. 'I confess that, accustomed as I was to dungeons, fetters and chains . . . I had not the strength to resist a fit of trembling with which I was struck on beholding this fearful place. It was furnished with huge beams of oak, placed at a distance of about three feet apart . . . To these beams thick iron chains are attached, one and a half feet long and two feet apart, and at the end of each chain is an iron collar. When the wretched galley slaves arrive at this dungeon, they are made to lie half down so that their heads rest upon the beam; then the collar is put round their necks, closed and riveted on an anvil with heavy blows of a hammer. As these chains with collars are about two feet apart, and as the beams are generally forty feet long, twenty men are chained to them in file.' As many as 500 could be thus accommodated. 'There is nothing so dreadful as to behold the attitudes and postures of these wretches thus chained. For a man so bound cannot lie down full length – the beam upon which his head is fixed being too high; neither can he sit nor stand upright – the beam being too low . . . Thoroughly inured as we were to pains, fatigues and sorrows, the three days and three nights which we were obliged to pass in this cruel situation so racked our bodies and all our limbs that we could no longer have survived it, especially our poor old men who cried out at every moment that they were dying and that they had no more strength to endure this terrible torture.' The only mitigation to this horror was that the food was tolerably good. This was thanks to the nuns of a Catholic order known as the Grey Sisters, who brought soup, meat and good bread in abundance, and even medicines.

The prison of La Tournelle was under the spiritual direction of the Jesuits. Marteilhe was shocked by the 'absurdities' of their preaching and deeply shocked to see them administer the Holy Sacrament, 'which they made them take in this frightful attitude with their heads nailed down upon the beams, a proceeding which appeared most irreverent to us . . . and which filled us with horror. I noticed that after they had given them the host they made them drink some wine out of a chalice. I asked one of them if they received Communion in both kinds. He replied that they did not and that the wine was not consecrated – that it was only a precaution which they took at La Tournelle to make them swallow the Host.' This was apparently to prevent any convict from preserving a consecrated wafer in his mouth in order to make a pact with the devil.

The Bishop of Saint-Pons, Percin de Montgaillard, in his pastoral letter of 1686, referred to 'the reproach, which he had heard made by some, that we do not ourselves have a strong belief in the real presence of Jesus Christ in the Eucharist since we give it so freely to people who do not scruple to reveal that they hold very different beliefs'. Vauban was to make much the same point: 'This practice, wrongly applied, caused many to think that, since they made so light to expose them [the sacraments], they did not themselves have much faith.'

On 17 December 1712, the chain-gang set out from Paris. It arrived at Charenton by moonlight that evening. It was freezing hard, but thanks to the 150-pound weight of the chains that each of them carried, they arrived streaming with sweat. 'At nine o'clock when it was bright moonlight with a very hard frost and a north wind, they unfastened all our chains and turned us out into a spacious courtyard; then they ordered us, holding huge whips in their hands, blows from which fell like hail upon the slothful ones, to strip off all our clothes and to put them down at our feet ... After we had stripped completely naked ... we were exposed to the north wind for two long hours during which the archers [their armed escort] searched and examined all our clothes.' At the end of this ordeal they were so stiff with cold that they were most of them unable to move when ordered. The lash was the only means used to warm them up. By the following morning eighteen of them were dead.

From Charenton they proceeded to walk, still chained, through Burgundy to Lyon – a distance of some 500 kilometres. They covered only three or four leagues a day. At Lyon they were loaded onto barges where their chief suffering was from the cold. On 17 January 1713, they arrived at Marseille. 'Thus ended a journey during which I suffered more, especially after leaving Paris, than I did during the twelve years of my imprisonment and servitude in the galleys.'

One of the most vivid descriptions of conditions on the galleys comes from John Evelyn, who had visited Marseille in October 1644. The Captain of the Galley Royal invited him and his companions on board. 'This galley was richly carved and gilded,' he wrote, 'and most of the others were very beautiful.' They offered a striking contrast with the appearance of the galley slaves. 'The spectacle was to me new and strange, to see so many hundreds of miserably naked persons, their heads being shaven close and having only high red bonnets and a pair of canvas drawers ... doubly chained about their middle and legs, in couples and made fast to their seats and all commanded in a trice by an imperious and cruel seaman.' The captain took the party out to sea. 'The rising-forward and falling-back at their oar is a miserable spectacle, and the noise of their chains, with the roaring of the beaten waters, has something of the strange and fearful in it to one unaccustomed to it. They are ruled and chastised by strokes on their backs and the soles of their feet, for the least disorder and without the least humanity, yet they are cheerful and full of knavery.'

Another Englishman to record his impressions of the circumstances of the Revocation was Gilbert Burnet, author of the *History of his own Time* and later to be Bishop of Salisbury. He spent some time in France during the summer of 1685. In Paris he called on Ralph Montagu, now Earl of Montagu, 'with whom I conversed much and got from him most of the secrets of the Court'. Burnet describes the scene a few months before the actual Revocation. He noted the low morale of the Huguenots – 'a dismal consternation and feebleness ran through most of them, so that great numbers yielded'. Some were won by bribery – 'the hopes of pensions and preferments wrought on many'; some were converted by 'the plausible colours that the Bishop of Meaux, then Bishop of Condom, put on the errors of the Church of Rome'. But many were victims of cruelties, especially at Valence. Those in the streets 'could have known the new converts as they were passing by them by a cloudy dejection that appeared in their looks and deportment'. He was horrified that 'the Intendants and other officers that had been mild and gentle in the former parts of their lives, seemed now to have laid aside the compassion of Christians, the breeding of gentlemen, and the common impressions of humanity'.

In April 1713, the Treaty of Utrecht brought the long war between France and England to an end. It led to the emancipation of some of the convicts. The marquis de Rochegude, a Calvinist refugee in Switzerland, obtained letters from the Kings of Sweden, Denmark and Prussia and other Protestant rulers, asking Queen Anne to intercede strongly with Louis for the release of the Huguenot convicts. A fortnight later the Queen, meeting him in Saint James's Park, said to him: 'M. de Rochegude, I beg you to tell all those poor fellows on board the galleys of France that they will be released immediately.'

Louis must have ordered this, but he reckoned without the Jesuits. At the end of May the order came to the governor at Marseille to release 136 of the Protestant convicts. This caused dismay and perplexity, says Marteilhe, since there were more than 300 such men; 'imagine the affliction of our poor brethren whose names were not on the list. The Queen of England had asked for and obtained the release of us all. But what does one not suffer between fear and hope?'

The Jesuit 'missionaries' at Marseille were outraged by the order for release and did everything that they could, first to have the order revoked and then, when that failed, to postpone for as long as possible the actual release of the prisoners. In the end they had, reluctantly, to let them go.

Marteilhe is not lavish with his dates, but sometime in October, having arrived safely in Geneva and having passed from there to Amsterdam, he was invited to join a deputation which was being sent to England to beg Queen Anne to renew her intercessions for the release of the remaining convicts. After thirteen years of the living hell of the French galleys, Jean Marteilhe found himself a free man in a free country and being presented to its Queen. But a number of Protestant galley slaves had still not been released. Queen Anne died on 1 August 1714. Her successor George I took the matter up again.

'The Earl of Stair', writes Scoville, 'while serving as the English ambassador in Paris wrote home to Secretary Stanhope on March 2, 1715, that he had recently spoken to the French Statesman M. de Torcy about the *galériens* as a thing of little consequence to France and for which the King, my master, interested himself out of pity to these poor people that suffered so much for their religion.' De Torcy replied that he could do little to alleviate their suffering, for 'that was the one point in all the world that the French King was the most delicate upon and the hardest to be managed'.

Louis' stubbornness may have been a refusal to admit failure. Heresy had not, as Bossuet had so proudly proclaimed, ceased to exist in France. Vauban had the courage and integrity to remind the King that 'the blood of the martyrs has been an infallible method of strengthening a persecuted religion'. Scoville brings evidence to suggest that the true conversions had been more numerous where persecution had been the least severe. He draws attention also to the growth, during the latter years of Louis' reign, of a new and more insidious heresy – dangerous to Catholic and Protestant alike: atheism.

Leibniz was quick to draw attention to this development. 'It is now necessary to apply ourselves more to combating Atheism and Deism than our own heresies.' If Christians could only be reconciled with one another, 'they would save the Church of God'. No such reconciliation took place. Leibniz continues: 'Insofar as it is possible to insist upon a date to determine the movements of thought, it is true to say that 1685 marks the culmination of the victorious efforts of the Counter-Reformation: after that comes the turn of the tide.' The age of the Enlightenment had arrived.

20

Marly and the Completion of Versailles

The year 1678, with the annexation of Franche-Comté and the Peace of Nijmegen, 'perhaps the most glorious', wrote the marquis de La Fare, 'that France has ever made', marked the flood-tide of Louis' glory. He had had some spectacular successes; he was acting as arbitrator of Europe. He had also thoroughly enjoyed it. He was in his element when on campaign with his troops. The art of war was probably his first and greatest passion. But in time of peace he had more opportunity for indulging his other great love: building. It was no longer endurable that his magnificence should be inadequately housed. The years following the Peace of Nijmegen saw a period of very considerable activity on the architecture front. The final enlargements of Versailles were put in hand.

It is difficult to say when the idea of making Le Vau's 'Enveloppe' into the gigantic palace which we see today began to take shape in Louis' mind. In 1670 the allocation of building sites to the east of the Château reveals the intention to provide a satellite town. In 1678 all expenditure on the Louvre ceased and a budget for buildings of 2.5 million livres – more than twice the expenditure of the previous year – was agreed by Colbert.

An interesting light is shed on Louis' intentions for Versailles by his simultaneous desire to add another vast architectural ensemble, far more important than Trianon or Clagny, to the existing constellation. Early in November 1677, Louis was out hunting in the forest near Saint-Germain, Jean-Antoine du Bois relates, and 'finding himself in a kind of marsh where the situation seemed to lend itself to his plan . . . he found there a fine vista opening towards the river and the place surrounded by several magnificent woods, its whole aspect determined the King then and there to choose and to take this plot'. What Louis' plan was can only be deduced from what he created here – the Château de Marly.

'I must needs say', wrote the English traveller Martin Lister, 'it is one of the pleasantest places I ever saw, or, I believe is, in Europe. It is seated in the bosom or upper end of a valley, in the midst of and surrounded by woody hills. The valley is crossed at its upper end, and gently descends forward by degrees, and opens wider and wider, and gives you the prospect of a vast plain country and the river Seine running through it.' What Lister called a valley was in fact a deep re-entrant of which the principal contour takes the form of a capital U. The open end of the U, which commanded the prospect referred to, was to the north.

This, then, was the natural conformation which Louis identified as the one which 'lent itself to his plan'. The first known plans and drawings for Marly were made by Jacques Hulot in 1679, but the inscription describes the work as being already begun after 'designs and models had been approved by His Majesty'. Louis did not waste any time; he knew exactly what he wanted to do. Hulot's drawings reveal the broad outlines of the design and set the scale. At the focal point of the rounded end of the U was to be a large house, smaller than the main block of Chatsworth, but in some ways resembling it. The west front of Chatsworth is 170 feet; the façades of Marly were 132. This great house, the Pavillon du Roi, was for lodging the whole royal family.

On the same contour line which forms the two arms of the U were twelve separate pavilions for the guests, each of two storeys, set some distance apart and linked by a trellis pergola. Within the area thus circum-scribed the land continued to slope downwards and was cast into terraces between which were contrived a succession of ornamental lakes.

Louis' intention seems clear. Versailles was no longer the charming *maison de plaisance* of Patel's painting. He still felt the need for somewhere to which he could invite the privileged few and offer them exclusive entertainments to which invitation would be greatly coveted. In due course the highest hopes of ambitious courtiers were to be summed up in the formula of application for an invitation: 'Sire, Marly?'

There was something about the site, something which may still just be recaptured today, which had first attracted Louis. The high, wooded hills give a pleasing sense of privacy, and with it intimacy and exclusiveness. To the north the prospect opened across the wide meanders of the Seine towards Saint-Germain, Le Vésinet and Argenteuil. But although the gardens were thus left open to the north, their insulation was secured by the skilful use of ground levels. In order to make sufficient space for the last of the lakes, the Pièce des Nappes, the lower gardens were consider-ably banked up and ended abruptly in a high terrace overlooking the Abreuvoir. The privacy, the intimacy and the exclusiveness were main-tained. 'He who planted this garden', wrote Diderot in the mid-eighteenth century, 'realised that it was necessary to keep it out of sight until the moment when one could see it in its entirety.' It was only to those privileged to enter the precincts that the whole glorious lay-out of Marly was revealed.

The first impact – what in French is called *l'annonce du Château* – was carefully planned. Turning in at the gates, the carriages crossed a wide circular court flanked by quadrant arcades, and began cautiously the steep descent of the Allée Royale. From this moment the gardens were beginning to become visible and with them the Pavillon du Roi, framed between two neat outbuildings, nestling comfortably amid the luxuriant foliage of a short avenue.

The impression created was one of extreme richness. The balustrade, with its statues and vases, was brilliantly gilded; the bas-reliefs which ornamented the panels above the windows were picked out in gold against a royal blue; the tall pilasters were of marble, *rouge de Languedoc*, set upon a podium of *vert antique* – or so it seemed at a distance. A closer inspection revealed that the entire decoration of the façades was painted in *trompe l'oeil* upon a flat wall.

This external painting made Marly extremely colourful. The *Mercure Galant* gave the credit to Le Brun for the whole décor, which was done 'from his designs and under his directions'. The Comptes des Bâtiments record the payment of 74,476 livres to the painter, Jacques Rousseau, compared with the total of 49,495 divided among twelve others, which leaves no doubt as to who played the major part in the execution.

But Rousseau was a Huguenot and was driven out of France by the Revocation of the Edict of Nantes. He came to England and received an important commission from Ralph Montagu, who was rebuilding his house in Bloomsbury after a disastrous fire. Together with Charles La Fosse and Jean-Baptiste Monnoyer, Rousseau executed the superb decorations of which Horace Walpole wrote: 'It would be impossible to take the art of painting to greater lengths.'

In 1679 Louis was forty-one; he had reached the prime of life and the high point of his glory; he had behind him eighteen years of experience in building; he knew his artists and their measure. It is not surprising that here at Marly, starting with an unencumbered site of his own choosing, he should have produced his masterpiece, acclaimed by Louis Bertrand as 'the complete and perfect realisation of the thought of Louis XIV, and assuredly his *chef-d'oeuvre*'. It is all the more tragic therefore that the buildings of Marly should have so completely disappeared. They would have told us a lot about Louis. Fortunately a magnificent set of coloured drawings from 1714, now in the Archives Nationales, showing every detail of the finished design, enables us to picture Marly as it was in its pristine perfection. It may be visited in the imagination.

The main buildings were completed by 1683, but the first recorded house party took place three years later. Racine was one of the earliest to have recorded his impressions: 'You could not believe how agreeable this house of Marly is,' he wrote; 'it seems to me that the Court is quite different here from what it is at Versailles.'

There was nothing more flattering to the courtier than to be allowed to lay aside for a few days the etiquette of the Court. Those who had been to Marly formed an inner ring which placed them in a position of quiet superiority over those who had not. It was one of the privileges of Marly for men to remain covered in the presence of the King, but it still required the royal command. As Louis left the Pavillon du Roi to conduct his guests round the gardens, he would say: 'Chapeaux, Messieurs.'

The whole design of Marly was conceived to sustain this flattering sense of privacy and exclusiveness which lent their savour to an invitation. In the area immediately adjacent to the Pavillon du Roi everything was closely packed and heavily overhung by high banks and steep woodlands. To east and west were four *cabinets de verdure* whose very names – *Cabinet Sombre* – *Cabinet de la Rêverie* – *Cabinet Secret* – *Cabinet de l'Ombre* – suggest that atmosphere of intimacy which was one of the delights of Marly. 'What strikes me most', wrote Diderot, 'is the contrast between refined art in the plantations and pergolas, and rude nature in the solid mass of luxuriant foliage of the great trees which dominate and form the background. This continual interplay between nature and art and between art and nature is truly enchanting.'

During all this time the final extensions of Versailles, under the direction of Mansart, were progressing steadily. By 1689 the two new wings, the Aile des Princes and the Aile du Nord, had been completed. On the other side, facing the twin blocks of the magnificent stables, the integration of the whole vast compendium of buildings had been achieved. Apart from the Grande Chapelle, this was already the palace so skilfully depicted by Pierre Denis Martin. Not everyone applauded its architecture.

'When you arrive at Versailles', wrote Voltaire, 'from the courtyard side you see a wretched, top-heavy building, with a façade seven windows long, surrounded with everything that the imagination could conceive in the way of bad taste. When you see it from the garden side, you see an immense palace whose defects are more than compensated by its beauties.' Voltaire writes with all the confidence of eighteenth-century 'good taste', but he underlines the duality of Versailles. Le Vau had already created this duality with the building of the Enveloppe, but the junction between this and the brick and stone façades of the Petit Château was architecturally awkward.

It was decided that Versailles would become the permanent seat of the Court and the Government. In order to accommodate both these Louis had to make the palace so extensive that the architecture of the entrance courts can never be seen at the same time as the garden fronts.

The man chosen to design the enlargements was a nephew of the great architect François Mansart – Jules Hardouin-Mansart, who had distinguished himself in the building of Clagny.

On the garden front of Versailles Mansart continued the architecture of Le Vau, but with certain important alterations. He raised the height of the first-floor windows by half their width in the form of a semicircular arch. He also raised the apparent base of each window by inserting a balustrade. This gave a sort of 'face lift' to the façades. But the greatest change came from the construction of the Grande Galerie, which, with its two attendant salons, occupies the entire length of Le Vau's west front. The dramatic relief, achieved by his deep-recessing of the central portion, was perforce sacrificed. The Grande Galerie was more important to the glory of the King and to the life of the Court. The Aile du Nord and the Aile des Princes continued the architecture of the main block.

One of the earliest appreciations of the new Versailles comes from a slightly unexpected source – Mme de Maintenon. She was usually severely critical of the Court as an institution, but it did not cloud her aesthetic judgement. On 2 May 1681, she wrote to the marquis de Montchevreuil: 'Versailles is of an astonishing beauty and I am delighted to be there; we will taste pleasures of all sorts; there is often a ball in the King's rooms, comedy in Monsieur's, walks everywhere and *médianoche* with us.' *Médianoche* was a meal just after midnight which sometimes marked the termination of a fast. 'The King wishes everyone to enjoy themselves.'

When Mansart had finished with it, the buildings of the Château covered some 30 hectares of ground; there were 2,143 windows and 1,252 fireplaces. Towards the gardens it presented the vast length of 670 metres, the square block of the state apartments projecting proudly against the elongated architecture of the two wings. Towards the town it deployed its ever widening procession of forecourts – the Cour de Marbre, the Cour Royale and the Cour des Ministres. But when all had been built, the original hunting lodge – the façade seven windows long which Voltaire derided – remained embedded in the fabric and formed the inner sanctuary. A flight of three steps secured it from the intrusion of coaches.

Beyond the Cour des Ministres and across the spacious Place d'Armes, in the angles formed by the convergence of three avenues, the Grande Ecurie and the Petite Ecurie offered a panorama of architecture to the windows of the palace. The names are misleading: they were both the same size. The Grande Ecurie was for saddle horses and the Petite Ecurie for coach horses. They were capable of holding 600 horses each. The Petite Ecurie also contained accommodation for 200 coaches. The Grande Ecurie, being largely stocked with hunters, was the obvious place for the kennels and beyond these was the Manège or Riding School. This made it the proper location also for the Ecole des Pages, where some 200 young noblemen received a good, if spartan, education. To become a royal page one had to be able to show proofs of nobility dating back for at least 200 years. South of the Cour des Ministres was a large block known as the Grand Commun. It contained 600 rooms and offered sixty apartments to high functionaries of the Court, including, for instance, Le Nôtre. It had its own social life and its own chapel.

The Great Kitchen was also in the Grand Commun and here was prepared the food for those who had *bouche à la Cour* – the right to eat and drink at the King's expense. The Bouche du Roi, where food for the King's table was prepared, was required by etiquette to be within the palace. The King's Kitchen was in the main building between the Grand Commun and the Aile des Princes. The food, the *viande du Roi*, was taken in solemn procession through the Château to the room in which the King ate. What was left after he had eaten went to the table of the Gentlemen Servants, known as the 'Serdeau'. What *they* left was sold to the townspeople at a special market called the 'baraques du Serdeau'.

The remarkable painting by Van der Meulen in Buckingham Palace, showing the forecourts of Versailles during the final enlargements, portrays the conditions in which the Court often had to live. A procession of royal coaches is seen arriving in the middle of crowds of workmen and all the clutter of their materials and machinery. The courtiers were often obliged to occupy a palace much of which was under scaffolding, and to endure the proximity of thousands of workmen who laboured both by day and by night. In May 1682, when the Dauphine was about to give birth to the duc de Bourgogne, she had to move from her room, the hammering of the carpenters being so loud that she could not sleep.

The years 1684 and 1685 were those of the greatest activity. In the first, 4,598,190 livres were expended, and on 14 August Dangeau noted that 'during the last week there was an expenditure of 250,000 at Versailles. Each day there are 22,000 men and 6,000 horses at work.' In 1685 the financial total rose to just over 6 million, which was the highest total ever recorded.

In 1684, Louis spent the autumn hunting, first at Chambord and then at Fontainebleau. The date of 15 November had been fixed for the return of the Court to Versailles and Louvois went on ahead to hasten the works. Every evening a courier arrived from Fontainebleau to collect Louvois' report which Louis received at his *lever* the next morning. His comments, written in the ample margins, reached Louvois the same day. Bad weather was delaying the work and Louis had to decide on his priorities. He had no doubts about their order. 'Pay more attention to my bedroom than to the rest,' he ordered; 'the smell of gilding is most unpleasant.' Louvois replied: 'Bontemps, Premier Valet de Chambre, has been instructed to keep a large fire going and to open the windows from time to time.' Louis, although by nature impatient, was reasonable about unavoidable delays.

But the good news was that the Grande Galerie would be completed. On 15 November 1684, the very day fixed from the beginning for its completion, the Court returned from Fontainebleau to find the Grande Galerie in all its glory and lit by a thousand candles. It met with immediate acclaim. 'Nothing could equal the beauty of this gallery at Versailles,' exclaimed Mme de Sévigné; 'this sort of royal beauty is unique in the world.'

It was the apotheosis of Louis. Measuring 238 feet long by 35, the gallery was lit by seventeen windows, each reflected on the opposite wall by a corresponding mirror. To do honour to the supremacy of France, even the classical Orders had been set aside; in place of the Doric, the Ionic and the Corinthian, Le Brun had been charged to design an *Ordre Français* which incorporated the Sun, the fleurs de lys and two cocks.

The supreme glory of the gallery was its ceiling. Here Charles Le Brun produced what must be regarded as his finest work. One of the problems confronting Mansart had been the necessity of providing sufficient daylight for the painted ceiling to show to advantage. Light from the attic windows was too far overhead to be much use. The earlier drawings show a barrel-vault of a full semicircle. The final form has a flattened arch which reduces the distance from the source of light. The raising of the height of the windows, already noticed, brought the light nearer to the ceiling and the reflections from the mirrors would have doubled the amount of light in the gallery. Jacques-François Blondel, writing two generations later, was not uncritical of the *style Louis Quatorze*, but he could describe the gallery as 'the most beautiful place in the world' and write of Le Brun's ceiling that the painting there 'ensures the immortal glory of the French school'.

'School' is the right word. Anthony Blunt, while claiming that 'Le Brun produced no single work which one is tempted to linger over', admits that 'in creating such an ensemble as the decoration of Versailles he was a master'.

Le Brun himself was a man of his age – respectable, reasonable, 'noble in all his tastes and in all his ways; at home in the company of men of letters; at ease in the presence of princes; apart from his devotion to the King, everything about him seemed to be subject to proportion – even his virtues'.

And yet . . . he seems in his paintings to dwell on the subject of human aggression. Of course the crucifixions and the martyrdoms required by the Church and the scenes of battle required by the historiographer demanded an artist capable of conveying the pain, the horror, the anger and the terror appropriate to such occasions; but it may be asked if it was necessary to go so far; it is possible to suspect that there was something of an obsession – an outlet for an aggression within himself which had to be either repressed or sublimated.

'Le Brun', writes Jacques Thuillier, 'had made a profound study of the human passions and the facial expressions which portray them . . . he sought to discern beneath the mask of humanity the face of the beast and those deep-seated instincts which it betrays.' This is particularly clear in his studies of human eyes in their various expressions. His sketches show a tireless interest in the human form in every imaginable position and seen from every possible angle; an interest also in the relationship between bodily position and the folds and drapes of human clothing. This is the secret of the seemingly endless permutations of position which enabled Le Brun to produce any number of crowd scenes which are wholly convincing.

Seldom can such an opportunity have been offered to any artist: a young King in the full flood of his fortune – a Minister devoted to the role of the Arts in the interest of national supremacy and political propaganda – the greatest palace in Europe, with gardens to match, in course of construction and the challenging task of co-ordinating the work of hundreds of artists, so that everything, from the statues in the gardens to the paintings and furnishings of the interior, should form an overall harmony of style. That was the prospect which opened before Charles Le Brun.

The first theme accepted for the subject-matter of the ceiling of the Grande Galerie was the Labours of Hercules. The theme could easily be adapted to depict the labours of Louis, but the King and his secret council decided to change this and to demand a direct representation of the actual achievements of the reign.

Le Brun had to start all over again. His nimble imagination, however, and the versatility of his style were equal to the occasion. One of his pupils, Claude Nivelon, writes: 'M. Le Brun shut himself up for two days in the old Hôtel de Grammont, and produced the first drawing of this great work, which is the central painting and the point of departure for all the others; on the strength of this he was given the command to

continue the series on the same lines and with the same beautiful ideas –
but with the prudent proviso, added by Colbert, that "nothing must be
brought in which was not consistent with the truth, nor too oppressive
for the foreign powers which might be involved".' The glory of Louis'
victories was not to be enhanced by dwelling on the humiliation of those
whom he defeated.

Next to the magnificence of the painted ceiling, it was in the furnishings
that the greatest richness of the gallery was to be seen. Against the
background of the marble pilasters and the tall windows, each reflected
in its answering mirror, we must set two enormous Savonnerie carpets;
curtains of 'thick white damask brocaded in gold with His Majesty's
monogram' framed the windows; between the windows stood sixteen
solid silver tables of the most exquisite workmanship, and in each
window-recess stood a massive silver tub containing an orange tree; seventeen great silver chandeliers, twenty-six smaller ones and countless
candelabra on gilded guéridons lent an indescribable lustre to the scene.

It must always be remembered, when looking at Versailles, that much
of the life of the Court took place at night and the rooms are seen at
their best by candlelight. The marble and the gilding, which can look
oppressive by day, spring magically to life when highlighted at a thousand
points by the flattering flames of the candles. 'Figurez-vous', exclaimed
the abbé Bourdelot, 'l'éclat de cent mille bougies dans cette grande suite
d'appartements.' 'Add to that', writes the author of the Mercure Galant,
'the brilliance of the Court in full dress and the sparkle of the precious
stones with which most of the ladies' costumes are adorned.'

The abbé Bourdelot was attached to the household of the duc d'Enghien
in the capacity of physician and was invited to Versailles during the
carnival of 1683. He gives a vivid account of a Jour d'Appartement, a
reception given every Monday, Wednesday and Friday when the Court
was in residence.

Bourdelot waited in the crowded vestibule to be summoned into the
royal presence. Presently M. de Joyeux, who happened to be a friend of
his, entered and called him by name: 'the door closed, and I found myself
in the middle of the Royal Household. The Queen was there with Madame
la Dauphine, Madame and Madame la duchesse [d'Enghien] who had
with her Mlle de Bourbon and the princesse de Conti.'

From the Cabinet des Raretés, where he had thus been introduced, the
abbé returned to the reception rooms. 'At one's first entrance', he wrote,
'one's eyes are dazzled. I was enchanted . . . In the Grand Appartement
the flower of the Court was gathered, all the princes and princesses, lords
and ladies, officers of the Crown, generals of the Army, besides an infinite
number of persons of quality, superbly dressed, left hardly a space vacant.

I found myself in the middle of all this pomp, the only man from the University and accustomed to a life of retirement.'

The first two rooms, the appropriately named Salle d'Abondance and the Salle de Vénus, were set aside for the refreshments, the tables being constantly replenished during the course of the evening. There were suppers for those who wished to make a serious meal; there were sweet-meats and chocolate for those of less hearty appetite; there were liqueurs for those who were not really thirsty and the finest wines for those who wished. Madame, always nostalgic for her native Germany, puts the finishing touch: 'It looks just like the children's table on Christmas Eve.'

The next room Bourdelot found 'full of tables covered with cards and dice'. This room, the Salon de Mars, was situated at the centre of the suite; six portraits by Titian adorned the walls, which were hung with crimson velvet braided with gold. Among the gaming-tables Louis moved informally and with ease, the players being allowed to remain seated if he came and joined their table. 'The throng was dense', continues Bourd-elot, 'but without any noise or tumult. There is something august about the place which imposes respect, and especially the presence of the King, who was near by, where there was a billiard table of extraordinary size.' Louis was a most accomplished player. 'The accuracy with which the King executes that which he has judiciously thought out passes belief.'

The billiard table was in the Salon de Diane. From here the abbé went through into the Salon d'Apollon, 'a room which pleases by every object which meets the eye. The throne of the King is raised here; the hangings of crimson velvet with pilasters of gold thread, stitched and double-stitched, impose respect. These pilasters are raised in relief; the bases and capitals seem to be the work rather of the goldsmith. Nothing could be more august and majestic. I inspected them attentively and could not tear myself away, although I had before me five of the most beautiful Italian paintings done by the greatest masters. Ought one not to go down on one's knees before that by Paul Veronese of Our Lord at the Last Supper?' Bourdelot mistook the subject-matter; the painting, acquired by Louis in 1665, represented Christ eating with Simon the Pharisee.

The Salon d'Apollon was being used as a ballroom. 'There were many ladies there, both young and beautiful, and scintillating with diamonds. The princesse de Conti, *la belle*, carried off the prize for dancing; all eyes were fixed upon the young princess ... but the greatest figure, in which was the centre of all the charm, was that of the King. He did not sit on his throne; there were four stools on the edge of the dais; I was surprised to see him sitting there, turning to this side and to that to give an order for the music or for the dance ... I admired the tunes which His Majesty ordered to be sung; they were well selected, moving and of a neat composition. His Majesty took much pleasure in them and it was evident that he was himself satisfied that all the troop were contented, talking familiarly with those who were placed near to him. I thought what a difference it was to see him at the head of his formidable and victorious armies, where he is the terror of terrors, whilst here among his own he is accessible to everyone.'

It is easy to imagine the feelings of this quiet, academic man, accustomed, it is true, to the more rough-hewn grandeur of Chantilly, as he drove away from the brilliant Court of which he had been the privileged spectator; the vividness of the impression which it made is clear from the liveliness of the account which he wrote. In strong relief against all the marble and crimson velvet, the silver filigree and gold embroidery, and in contrast with the more than ordinary splendour of the guests, stands out his picture of the King, 'faisant les honneurs de chez-lui en galant homme', magnificently informal against the formal setting which he had created for his own person. 'Ce qui plait souverainement', concluded Mme de Sévigné, 'c'est de vivre quatres heures entières avec le souverain, être dans ses plaisirs et lui dans les nôtres.'

Spanheim makes the same point. 'He had the happy gift of being able, in his private conversation, to strike the balance between grandeur and familiarity and to conduct himself equally without loftiness or baseness.' The theme is developed further by the Duke of Berwick. 'There was no trace of pride in him except in his appearance. He was born with an air of majesty which impressed everyone so deeply that one could not approach him without being struck with fear and respect; but when you wished to speak to him, his face became more relaxed and he had the art of putting you at once completely at ease with him ... in his replies he said so many obliging things that, if he was granting you a favour, you felt that he had given it twice; and if he refused it, it was impossible to complain. Since the beginnings of Monarchy you will never find a King who was more human.' It was Louis' particular merit to have been able to combine the humanity of Louis de Bourbon with the majesty of the Sun King.

The sun was his emblem, and, since the sun is never seen at a greater advantage than at its rising and at its setting, it was appropriate that the beginning and the ending of the royal day should be marked with due decorum. 'Who is there that does not admire this beautiful Heavenly Body?' asked Bossuet in one of his higher flights of hyperbole. 'Who is not ravished by the brilliance of his midday and by the superb parade of his rising and his setting?'

The two ceremonies of the rising and setting, the *lever* and the *coucher*, were of an almost religious significance. Voltaire states that the Frenchman regarded his King as 'a sort of Divinity' and the theology of the Coronation had brought this home to Louis. He exacted and was accorded a deference not far removed from worship. The courtiers became as it were the priests and acolytes in the royal liturgy. The height of honour was to hold the candle to him at the *coucher*. Courtiers made their low obeisance before the royal bed, even when Louis was absent. So greatly was this Holy of Holies revered that the customary precedence in leaving the room was reversed, it being the greater honour to remain a moment longer in the royal presence. It is with this in mind that the extreme richness of the decoration of Versailles should be considered.

It was in the winter that Bourdelot had made his visit and his account affords an interesting comparison with that of Nicodemus Tessin, a Swedish architect who visited Versailles in the summer of 1687. His description of the throne room is very different, for in every important apartment there were two sets of hangings – one for winter, usually a rich velvet or damask – and one for summer of a lighter, more colourful invention. In the Salon de Mars the *meuble d'été* was of a gold and silver brocade; there were seventeen pieces of silver furniture 'of a prodigious size and weight'. Bourdelot also marvelled at the furniture 'of solid silver and of an inestimable price'.

The windows of the Grande Galerie looked out on to the gardens and park. The areas of the garden nearest to the palace were treated on the principle that 'the eye is best satisfied by seeing the whole at once'. Louis' own advice – the *Manière de voir les Jardins* – was to walk out of the ground-floor vestibule and proceed straight to the edge of the Parterre de Latone, and there, having first admired the prospect before you, to turn and look at the façades of the palace. If this were really one's first view of Versailles the impact would be overwhelming. In order to give full power to this impact, Le Nôtre designed the Parterre d'Eau, where everything is kept flat in order not to intrude upon the great panorama of architecture. In pursuance of this end the figures representing the mighty rivers of France – the Seine, the Loire, the Rhône and the Garonne – are all recumbent.

Thus Le Nôtre not only provided an area surrounding the Château which set off the buildings to the best advantage, but he also made necessary one of the greatest of Louis' triumphs, the creation of a water supply at Versailles. 'Though a place naturally without water,' wrote John Locke, 'yet it hath more jet d'eaus and waterworks than are to be seen anywhere, and looking out from the windows of the King's apartment [there was as yet no Grande Galerie] one sees almost no thing but water for a whole league forwards, this being made up of several basins . . . and a very large and long canal.'

The waters were conducted by a network of underground pipes to the basins and there translated into an infinite number of *jets d'eau* of an astonishing variety of forms. In April 1672, the author of the *Mercure Galant* recorded: 'I would never come to an end if I were to tell you all the marvels which the waters produce in this delectable spot. Le Sieur Denis conducts them by means of the most admirable pumps and aqueducts and Monsieur de Francine makes them do things which are beyond our imagining.' But today when the Grandes Eaux are turned on, they chiefly consist of jets spouting in different directions; the art of François Francini, the second generation of his family to work as *fontaniers* to the Kings of France, is seldom if ever practised today and not many of the original achievements have survived. One of the best is at Schloss Hellbrunn, near Salzburg, where nozzles and other fittings so direct the water as to form spheres, hemispheres, urns, bells and other improbable shapes. One of the most elaborate creations was made at the suggestion of Mme de Montespan. In the centre of the Bosquet du Marais was an artificial tree, cast in bronze with leaves of tin, which were, according to Félibien, 'so cleverly made that they seemed natural. From the extremities of all its branches come an infinite number of little jets.' The bosquet was framed by three tiers of marble steps 'from which water played, by means of special fittings, which took the shapes of ewers, of goblets, of carafes, and of other sorts of vases, which looked as if they were made of rock crystal garnished with silver gilt'. This particular skill earned Francini the handsome salary of 10,000 livres a year, and to procure this sort of decoration and animation to the gardens Louis was determined to achieve an adequate water supply.

Locke was fortunate in being able to see Louis and Mme de Montespan surveying the gardens. 'The King seemed to be mightily pleased with his waterworks, and several changes were made then and there to which he himself gave sign with his cane, and he may well be made merry with his water since it cost him dearer than so much wine, for they say it costs him three shillings for every pint that runs here.'

When Locke saw the gardens the water was still being circulated by a system of windmills and horse pumps which returned it from the Canal to the Etang de Clagny. The ten windmills – 'the best sort of windmills I have seen anywhere' – worked a chain of copper buckets. Working in relays of forty, 120 horses laboured night and day.

In spite of its admirers, the system left much to be desired. Certain fountains – Latona, the Dragon and the Pyramid – played only when Louis was in that part of the gardens. It must have required a certain nimbleness on the part of the staff to ensure that the right fountain was playing at the right time. Claude Denis, the overseer, was liable to a fine in case of failure. A letter from Louis to Colbert, dated from Alsace in 1673, suggests that failures of a purely mechanical nature were common. 'You must arrange that the pumps at Versailles work properly, so that when I come back I will find them in a condition that will not exasperate me by their breaking down at all times.'

Moreover the water, whether from stagnation or from the ordures thrown into the Etang de Clagny, made the place unhealthy. Primi Visconti, commenting in 1681 on the foulness of the air caused by all the excavations, added: 'and the waters, which are putrid, infest the atmosphere, so that during the month of August everyone was taken ill, except the King and myself only'. Mme de Sévigné was inclined to be defeatist. 'Kings, by reason of their wealth, can give to the ground a form different from that which it received from Nature, but the quality of the water, and that of the air, is not within their jurisdiction.' It was even thought by Perrault that Louis might abandon Versailles 'and go and live in a more happy situation'.

Louis, however, had no intention of doing any such thing. The greater the obstacles, the greater the honour to the King who overcame them. Just as the creation of Versailles had revealed artists of the first quality in every branch, so the search for water was to bring forth engineers equal to the seemingly impossible task. But it was a costly and a wasteful undertaking. It became a point of pride with Louis, and the matter was pushed to ugly excess. There was not only an enormous expenditure, but a considerable loss of human life. This was chiefly caused by the gases released by the excavations. Mme de Sévigné refers to the 'prodigious mortality' among the workmen, whose bodies could be seen at nightfall being carried off to surreptitious burial.

Of the three deficiencies listed by Saint-Simon – 'no view, no water, no woods' – the lack of water was by far the most difficult to overcome. Le Nôtre's design ultimately comprehended 1,400 fountains, which required a continual and very copious supply.

Two great names were associated with the first attempt to obtain water from a wider area: the abbé Jean Picard, an astronomer who was the first to apply telescopic lenses to instruments of surveying, and a Dane, Olaüs Romer, the first scientist to calculate the speed of light. To these two men Colbert turned for help, and their scheme for collecting water from the plateau beyond Saint-Cyr was the first to be successful. Louis reacted with enthusiasm and impatience. 'What I urge you most', he wrote to Colbert in March 1678, from the camp at Gand, 'is with regard to the reservoirs and channels which are to provide water. This is what you must make them work on without respite.' Later in the year the water arrived at the reservoir situated on the roof of the Grotte de Thétis; Louis was present when the taps were opened and expressed himself vastly satisfied with the force with which it flowed.

Louis and his Minister, however, still continued to entertain hopes of a more spectacular water supply. Their first success in this quest was the Machine de Marly. A certain baron Arnold de Ville, alderman of Liège, brought before Louis a project for raising the waters of the Seine to the summit of the high ground at Louveciennes by means of a gigantic pump. He brought with him to Saint-Germain Rennequin Sualem, also of Liège, who was the constructor, and possibly the deviser, of the machine.

A working model was made towards the end of 1680 and tried out in the presence of the King; it succeeded in raising the waters of the Seine to the level of the terrace at Saint-Germain. A site was selected near Bougival and in 1681 the construction was put in hand. Fourteen water-wheels, each 11.6 metres in diameter, communicated their movement to 221 pumps, which worked in relays up the hillside. These raised the water to the height of 165 metres above the river.

The machine produced an average of 3,200 cubic metres of water every twenty-four hours. This figure needs to be compared with Nicolas Blondel's estimate for the consumption of water at Versailles. For the fountains to play à l'ordinaire, from eight in the morning until eight in the evening, 12,960 cubic metres were required. But many of the jets were only at half pressure. For the full glory of Les Grandes Eaux – a spectacle only laid on for an ambassador or other very important person – the fountains consumed 9,458 cubic metres in two and a half hours. Although the Machine de Marly greatly helped, it by no means solved the problem of water. On 13 June 1684, the Machine de Marly was inaugurated by Louis. Contemporary writers noted with astonishment the complexity of the mechanism and the perpetual grinding of the levers and crankshafts, but it was claimed that, apart from the constructors, Vauban was the only man in France who fully understood it.

It was Vauban who was to be in charge of the most ambitious project of all. In August 1684, the Truce of Ratisbon seemed to promise at least four years of tranquillity and Louis announced at his *lever* at Fontainebleau that there was to be a new undertaking: the diversion of water from the River Eure at Pontgouin, some 40 kilometres upstream of Chartres, to the reservoirs of Versailles, a total distance of some 80 kilometres.

The most spectacular portion of the works necessitated by this scheme started at Berchères. Vauban proposed a *tranchée ouverte*, like a long, deep railway cutting, leading towards the point where the river was to recross its own valley, a little upstream of the Château de Maintenon. This he proposed to negotiate by means of an underground siphon – *un aquéduc rampant*. The Romans had already made successful use of such a system, but Louvois, backed by the opinion of the Académie des Sciences, did not believe that it could work. In February 1685, he wrote to Vauban: 'In reply to the memoir you sent me which has the heading "problem of the weight of water in subterranean aqueducts", I can tell you that you are grossly wrong.' It was unwise, but typical, of Louvois to state such an opinion to the greatest expert on the subject in France, but Louvois knew that he had Louis behind him. 'It is useless to think of an *aquéduc rampant* of which the King does not wish to hear any more. If the memoir enclosed does not suffice to make you understand the reason, the Master's wish must prevent you from ever mentioning it again.' Louis may have had his own reasons for preferring an aqueduct above ground to a siphon: it would provide a more conspicuous monument to his glory.

In December 1684, Mme de Sévigné heard of the project from her daughter. 'Nothing has ever been so pleasing as what you tell me of this great beauty that is to appear at Versailles, so totally fresh, so totally pure, so totally natural and must eclipse all the other beauties. I assure you that I was anxious to know her name and that I was expecting some new *belle* to arrive at Court; suddenly I discover that she is a river which is diverted from her course, precious though that is, by an army of forty thousand men.'

The number of soldiers employed was more like 30,000. Their first task was one of preparation. The Eure had to be made navigable upstream of Maintenon for the transport of the materials needed; quarries had to be opened to provide the stone; brick kilns and lime kilns had to be set up; the necessary instruments, carts, shovels and pick-axes had to be made and white wood ordered for scaffolding; specialist workmen had to be taken on and camps set up for the soldiers who provided the unskilled labour. All this Vauban accomplished in three months, and in May 1685 the work began. Nearly 9 million livres were poured into it. In July 1686, Dangeau noted that the works were well advanced and that the success of the enterprise seemed assured.

But in August an outbreak of fever put 1,600 soldiers in the hospitals of Chartres and Coulombs; then the war of the League of Augsburg required the withdrawal of the troops. They did not return. The granting of a pension to M. Pigoreau, 'çi-devant directeur des travaux de l'aquéduc de la rivière de l'Eure', seemed to admit that the project was abandoned.

Saint-Simon hurled not unmerited abuse at Louis for his 'cruel folly . . . Who could count the cost, in money and in men, of this obstinate endeavour?' Napoleon adopted an attitude of quiet superiority. Referring specifically to this project he wrote: 'It would not have been abandoned if I had undertaken it, because, before I started, I would have seen everything, examined everything and I would have assured myself that it could all have been finished.'

The Aquéduc de Maintenon, much of which survives today, was over 500 metres long and would have attained a height of just over 33 metres. It was to have had three tiers of arcading. We must imagine another row of arches surmounting the present arcade and a further storey, half the height of the lower ones, on top of that. Here, more than in any of the works of architecture or statuary, would have been a monument worthy to recall the achievements of ancient Rome, had it been accomplished. Instead the gaunt, ruined arches remain, a noble but melancholy reminder of an Augustan age which just failed.

The abandoning of this huge project, however, did not in any way imply a lessening of Louis' mania for building. The somewhat fragile decorations of the Trianon de Porcelaine necessitated continual repairs. It may also, owing to its close association with Louis' double adultery with Mme de Montespan, have become an embarrassment to him. For whatever reason, it was decided to pull it down. In July 1687 the marquis de Sourches noted that Louis' intention was to replace it with a larger building, 'in order', he said, 'to be able to give a few *fêtes* and *divertissements*. That was the pretext, but they thought he was having the building put up in order to withdraw himself more, and it was of this that they were mortally afraid.'

Perhaps nothing at Versailles illustrates more clearly Louis' method of building. It was the way of the amateur – a succession of trials and errors, of building and pulling down and rebuilding, which may have produced the desired result but was certainly the most expensive procedure possible.

From the outset Louis exercised the closest supervision over the construction. 'He even often went', continues Sourches, 'to pass the *après-dîners* in a tent where he worked with M. de Louvois and cast an eye over the works from time to time to see that they were advancing.'

As at Versailles, so at Trianon, Louis began with the intention of retaining the central pavilion and surrounding it with new buildings. He was soon dissatisfied. On 18 September Louvois wrote to Mansart, who was taking the waters at Vichy: 'The King, not being content with the effect produced by the building on the garden side, ordered that it should be demolished. His Majesty did not wish the continuation of work on the roofs either, which he found too heavy and to give to Trianon the appearance of a big house.' These mansard roofs, it was decided, were to be replaced by flat roofs concealed behind a balustrade. The chimneys were to project no more than 30 cm above the roof, 'His Majesty preferring the risk that they might smoke to their being visible from the outside'. At the same time Louis decided to fill the gap left by the demolition of the old pavilion with an open peristyle. This may well have been inspired by the 'Perspective', painted by Rousseau in *trompe l'oeil* on one of the buildings at Marly. 'His Majesty desires that it should be something very light, upheld by columns in the form of a peristyle, and it is for this that he would like you to make a design at your earliest convenience – understanding as he does that, while you are taking the waters, it is difficult for you to apply yourself.' Two days later he gave the commission to Robert de Cotte.

On 2 October the Court left for Fontainebleau. Letters from Louvois continued to pass on the King's instructions on the minutest of details, always accompanied by the insistence that the work must be carried out 'the earliest that it is possible to do'. On 13 November Louis returned to Versailles between two and three in the afternoon 'where he took coach immediately to go to Trianon'. Fortunately for all concerned the work had progressed equal to his expectation. Dangeau records that he found it 'very well advanced and very beautiful'. He made six more visits before the end of the month, during which 'he walked a great deal about the buildings which he is having put up and with which he is very pleased at present'.

There can be little doubt that Louis' was the controlling mind throughout the creation of Trianon and that his architects were little more than the interpreters. The result was a building which no architect was ever likely to have built. Its extraordinary plan can only be explained in relationship to the gardens as they had been laid out for the Trianon de Porcelaine.

The controlling factor was a garden room known as the Cabinet des Parfums. It was situated at the north-west corner of the parterre. The whole length of the north side of this parterre was occupied by a trellis pergola. In the finished design of the new Trianon, this pergola was replaced by the Gallery and the Cabinet des Parfums by the Salon des Jardins. Finally, since there was nowhere else to put it, a further block of lodgings was appended at right angles to the Gallery which was known from its sylvan setting as the Trianon-sous-Bois. It was an architecture dictated by the lay-out of a garden.

By the end of 1688 the Trianon de Marbre – as it was now called – was finished and furnished. Some sixty years later, when it was no longer fashionable to admire the architecture of the *Grand Siècle*, the duc de Cröy asserted that 'it is the most charming piece of architecture in the world', but he added: 'the view from the entrance court is admirable, but the rest does not answer to it'. The entrance courtyard is of a size proportionable to the single-storey Ionic Order, but seen from the parterre the château deploys its somewhat monotonous length, interrupted only by the peristyle, turns at right angles to present the fourteen windows of the Gallery and its attendant salon, and finally regains its original orientation in the wing known as Trianon-sous-Bois.

One could easily believe that the Trianon-sous-Bois, with its two storeys, its smaller windows and its rather conspicuous absence of marble, was a later addition. This is not, however, the case. Trianon was conceived and built as a whole. The King's guests were lodged in the Trianon-sous-Bois and here Madame, the duchesse d'Orléans, found a lodging to her heart's delight. She looked out over a little garden known as Les Sources. It must have been a very attractive corner – 'a little bosquet so closely planted that at high noon the sun did not penetrate'. Beneath the trees some fifty little springs gave birth to as many rivulets and the rivulets created a diversity of islets, some of them large enough to set a table and chairs for a game of *tric-trac*.

Within doors Trianon contained a suite of rooms which still afford, in their carved friezes, panelling and overdoors an important souvenir of the *Grand Siècle*, although most of the décor was modified either by Napoleon or Louis-Philippe, both of whom made use of Trianon. In order to imagine the rooms as they were under Louis XIV we need the evidence of the inventory. We must see the walls hung with crimson damask or tapestries, in much of which the Chinese taste was still in evidence. Fourteen rooms are marked as having furniture 'upholstered with Chinese stuffs' and beds hung with satin 'sprinkled with flowers and animals from China'. Only the Gallery seems to have reflected the style of the parent palace. The furniture was carved and gilded and upholstered in crimson damask.

But the real décor of the Gallery comes from the set of paintings which lined the walls – twenty-four of them, mostly by Cotelle, representing the chief beauties of the gardens and park of Versailles. The paintings in the Galerie des Glaces told of the civil and military accomplishments of the *Grand Monarque*; those at Trianon commemorated another achievement of which Louis could feel equally proud. As he walked down his Gallery he could compare with advantage the successive views of parterres, bosquets and fountains with the state of Versailles as he first remembered it – 'the most sad and barren of places', as Saint-Simon had said, 'with no view, no water and no woods'. Cotelle's paintings recorded the incredible transformation which had been accomplished in the last quarter of a century. But the last and loveliest of the views came, not from a painting, but from the windows of the Salon des Jardins at the end of the Gallery – over the parterre and across to the Ménagerie. No longer could it be said that Versailles was lacking in views nor in woods nor in water.

On 11 July 1691, Dangeau describes an idyllic evening at Trianon. 'A great supper party was given under the peristyle for seventy-five ladies, who were joined by the King and Queen of England. They came by the Canal, where all the orchestra remained. Arriving in gondolas and chaloupes, they landed at Trianon, which was brilliantly illuminated; they walked in the gardens; then supper was served at five tables.'

The French word *féerie* is needed to describe these nocturnal occasions, these spectacles of *son et lumière*, in which the sound was that of Lully's music, enhanced by the strange echoes of a woodland setting, and the light was the warm, smokeless glow of dry faggots, which lit the façades from below, inverting the normal shadow projection so that they appeared as figures before the footlights.

Understandably, an invitation to Trianon was one of the most coveted privileges which could be conferred upon a member of the Court. Saint-Simon reveals how the niceties of etiquette could be used to his discomfiture. When a lady was invited to Marly, her husband accompanied her without need for a personal application, but this was not the case with an invitation to Trianon. By consistently inviting the duchesse de Saint-Simon to Trianon and equally consistently refusing her applications for Marly, Louis was able to convey, in no uncertain manner, his displeasure with the Duke.

21

The War of the League of Augsburg

The Peace of Nijmegen had left Louis at the zenith of his glory. He had acted as arbiter of Europe and his campaigns had been marked by spectacular successes. He had thoroughly enjoyed it.

It was a dangerous position to be in. It carried with it the risk of over-confidence in his own position; the risk of underestimating the strength, singly and in combination, of his opponents. It required an almost prophetic ability to read the signs of the times and, if not actually to foresee the future, at least to identify what was inherent in the situation. As King Louis-Philippe was to put it: 'Gouverner c'est prévoir.'

The events which the diplomat would particularly like to be able to predict are, not infrequently, the deaths of certain individuals whose positions are pivotal. Obviously there is an inevitable unpredictability here which the diplomat must not be reproached for failure to foresee.

There is also another force which is almost incalculable, and that is the risk of counter-productivity; it lies behind such expressions as: 'nothing fails like success'. It concerns one's regard to public opinion which it is often unwise to neglect. As Europe in the 1680s began to move in the direction of war there were a number of uncertainties which hung in the balance.

In England the uncertainty was largely concerned with religion, particularly in the royal family. In November 1677 Princess Mary, the elder daughter of James, Duke of York, by his first marriage, was married to William of Orange. Sir Henry Coventry, Secretary of State, observed: 'You will think we have been quicker than ordinary that a Prince should come and woo, marry, bed, and carry away the Princess Mary all in a month's time.' James himself was a declared papist. He had married, some three years earlier, the Catholic princess Mary of Modena and the prospect of a Catholic heir to the throne of England provoked an angry response from the Commons.

The King, Charles II, was still pursuing his somewhat equivocal policy of hoping for subsidies from Louis without giving back very much in exchange. He had spent the summer of 1684 more or less as usual, making his annual visit to Windsor Castle and to his still unfinished palace at Winchester. There he had asked Sir Christopher Wren how soon it might be completed and was told that about a year should suffice. He had answered that a year was a great period at his time of life. He was fifty-four.

The summer had been hot and the drought excessively prolonged. It was followed by a winter which was so sharp that the Thames froze over on several occasions. On 27 January 1685 John Evelyn was at Whitehall. 'I saw this evening such a scene of profuse gaming, and the King in the midst of his three concubines, as I have never before seen – luxurious dallying and profaneness.' There was nothing in that to alarm the Chancelleries of Europe.

On Wednesday 4 February, however, Charles was 'surprised in his bedchamber with an apoplectic fit'. It was soon evident that the end was near, but Charles seemed ill at ease with the Anglican divines who were in attendance upon him. His brother noticed and understood. He whispered something in his ear. The reply was faintly audible: 'With all my heart.' By a happy circumstance a Catholic priest, Father Huddleston, who had risked all and achieved much to help Charles to escape after the battle of Worcester, was present in the palace. Charles died reconciled with the Church of Rome and fortified by its sacraments.

James duly came to the throne. He was known to be a practising member of the Church of Rome. His second marriage was, however, childless and according to the laws of succession the Crown would naturally pass to his elder daughter Mary, already married to William of Orange, and from her, in default of issue, to the younger daughter, Princess Anne. Mary and Anne were both staunch supporters of the Church of England.

The new Queen, Mary of Modena, was, in Bishop Burnet's words, 'in an ill habit of body and had an illness that was thought would end in a consumption, and it was believed that her illness was of such a nature, that it gave a very melancholy presage that, if she should live, she could have no children'. The prospect of the Protestant succession seemed secure.

James's solitary concern for his new kingdom was that it should be reconciled with the Church of Rome. He pursued his end with an almost uniform ineptitude and he failed completely. Voltaire claims that it was being said in Rome that James ought to be excommunicated on the grounds 'that he would lose what little Catholicism remained in England'.

But at least James had the perception to appreciate that the last thing which would serve his purpose was to be seen in close alliance with Louis XIV. The anger and horror with which Protestant Europe saw the persecutions associated with the Revocation of the Edict of Nantes were not likely to facilitate the conversion of a strongly Protestant country. The best that French diplomats could hope for was a prolonged period of internal strife and civil war which would keep England out of European affairs. They were to be disappointed.

The treatment of the Huguenots did nothing to endear Louis in the eyes of Pope Innocent XII, who commented that 'Christ did not use armed forces to further the Gospel'. He was angry with Louis for not sending armed forces to succour the Christian Emperor against the Infidel. Louis would much rather have given active support to the Turks and kept the Emperor's troops, which might otherwise become available for use on the Rhine, fully occupied on their eastern frontier. Just how long the army of the Grand Vizier would be able to hold out was one of the most important diplomatic uncertainties which Louis was up against.

His relationship with the Pope was steadily deteriorating, and this was to have serious repercussions on his relationship with the Emperor. Innocent XII, a strong believer in the temporal authority of his office, had rejected the 'Four Articles' proposed by the Gallican Church and ably, if unsuccessfully, put across by Bossuet. They were to remain a cause of contention. Innocent first retaliated by refusing to ratify any episcopal appointment made in France. As diocese after diocese became vacant, the situation became increasingly untenable. By the end of 1687 some fifty sees were without pastors.

At the same time the Pope withdrew diplomatic immunity from foreign embassies in Rome. There may have been good reasons for doing so, but it could be construed as an act of aggression towards France. Louis first reacted by trying to barter certain concessions in return for accepting this restriction. When Innocent declined any such concessions, Louis sent his new ambassador, the marquis de Lavardin, to the Palazzo Farnese with a small armed force.

It was, of course, a purely political issue, but Innocent countered it with a purely spiritual weapon: Lavardin was excommunicated. But the Pope did not stop there. At the beginning of January the following year he made it secretly known to Louis that he and his ministers were included in the excommunication. Colbert de Croissy declared that 'if anyone had the audacity to speak to the King of excommunication, whoever it might be, would have paid for it with his life'. Louis asked the Archbishop of Reims, Louvois' brother, what he should do in the event of his being excommunicated. The Archbishop assured him that the decree would be null. He received the news calmly but imposed an absolute silence on the subject. It was, however, not possible to keep the secret. On 7 June 1689, John Evelyn learnt of it from the Archbishop of Canterbury.

Such was the situation between France and the Holy See when, early in 1688, the question of the succession to the Electoral Principality of Cologne was becoming urgent.

Cologne was a site of capital importance to Louis' hopes of establishing a frontier between France and Germany on the Rhine. At the beginning of 1688 the Prince-Bishop of Cologne was the Elector Maximilian-Henry, a member of the ruling house of Bavaria, the Wittelsbachs. Bishop also of Hildersheim, Münster and Liège, he was now an old man and not likely to live long. He had been a good ally to Louis XIV. It was a matter of vital importance that he should be replaced by someone equally friendly towards France.

The obvious candidate from Louis' point of view was Prince Egon von Fürstenberg, Bishop of Strasbourg. Louis was successful in obtaining for him the post of coadjutor to Maximilian-Henry. This position could normally be regarded as a stepping-stone to the episcopal throne.

The alternative candidate was Joseph-Clement von Wittelsbach, the younger brother of the Elector of Bavaria. He was not yet seventeen, and as such under age to be a Bishop, in spite of which he was – with papal dispensation of course – the incumbent of the two wealthy dioceses of Freisingen and Ratisbon. He was a person quite unsuited to be a Bishop at all, but the idea of a Bishop being the spiritual leader of a Christian community had been lost sight of completely. The great dioceses of Europe were simply regarded as sources of income and political power.

On 3 July 1688, Maximilian-Henry died. The contest began. Fürstenberg, since he already held four bishoprics, needed papal dispensation to become eligible for any more. He held the important card of being already on the spot, and, until a new appointment was made, acting Archbishop. Both candidates therefore needed a papal dispensation in order to proceed with the candidature. Although the game was of an entirely secular nature, the Pope held all the trump cards.

During all this time William of Orange was now seeking to strengthen his alliances against France. But an event, as important as it was unexpected, focused the attention of diplomats once more on England. On 15 January 1688, John Evelyn had recorded 'a solemn and particular office used at our church, and all the churches of London and ten miles round, for a thanksgiving to God for Her Majesty's being with child'. On 10 June Evelyn made one of his shortest entries in his diary: 'A young prince born which will cause disputes.' The first dispute was as to whether the rather healthy boy, when finally produced and exhibited to the Court, was in any sense the offspring of James and Mary. Bishop Burnet strongly suggests that he was not. There were a number of suspicions surrounding the birth, which, according to one account, was the classic 'warming-pan baby'. But these suspicions did not greatly affect the political situation. For all practical purposes England was regarded as having a Catholic heir to the throne. This profoundly altered the situation in England and the relationships between England and Europe.

By the beginning of June 1688, overtures were already being made to William of Orange to come and establish his own and his wife's claim to the throne. But William wanted to be able, if Louis were to send troops into Cologne, to oppose him with armed force. William therefore established himself at Nijmegen. According to which claim came first, he could march south down the Rhine or sail north for England.

In July Louis made a last effort to negotiate with the Pope, sending the marquis de Chamlay on a secret mission. The Pope refused to see him. It was at this juncture that Louis determined to resort to military force.

The failure of Chamlay's mission to the Vatican was followed closely by the news arriving from Vienna that the Turkish Empire was opening negotiations for peace. Anything that Louis could do to prevent, or at least to delay, the signing of such a treaty was clearly of vital importance to him. Military activity on the Rhine and a strengthening of his still incomplete line of frontier fortresses appeared to be the best option open.

On 22 August 1688, he wrote to his ambassador at Vienna, the marquis de Girardin: 'You may easily judge what effects this will produce, and that the Emperor will be forced to withdraw his troops from Hungary in order to send them to the Rhine . . . This, of course, could encourage the Turks to renew their offensive.'

On 6 September 1688, Louis sent a letter to the Cardinal d'Estrées in Rome. It was in fact a manifesto to the Pope. He stated 'that he could no longer prevent himself from making a separation between the quality of the Head of the Church and that of a temporal Prince who openly espoused the interests of the enemies of his crown; that he, for his part, no longer looked for justice on the differences which concerned him'. As a result he no longer recognised the Pope as 'mediator' over the succession to the Palatinate.

Louis then threatened to send troops into Italy to remain there until the States of Castro and Roncignione were returned to his ally, the Duke of Parma, and at the same time to 'take possession of Avignon, either in order to return it to His Holiness upon the entire execution of the Treaty of Pisa, or to give it to the said Duke of Parma'. The Pope listened in silence and two days later confirmed his appointment of the young Joseph-

Clement as Archbishop of Cologne. On 16 September, Louis ordered Tessé to seize Avignon.

Louis' main diplomatic policy at this juncture was to try to unite Catholic Europe against the Protestant William and to make permanent the clauses of the Truce of Ratisbon. The Emperor had consistently refused to agree to this. Louis sent him a letter declaring his desire for peace and an assurance of the purely defensive nature of his territorial demands.

The most important gap still in Louis' defences was the town of Philippsburg, which Louis now proceeded to attack. The French forces were put under the nominal command of the Grand Dauphin, now aged twenty-six. 'In sending you to command my army', Louis instructed him, 'I am giving you an opportunity to make known your merit; go and show it to all Europe, so that when I come to die it will not be noticed that the King is dead.' The maréchal de Duras was the real director of operations and he had Vauban to advise him.

The strength of Philippsburg was in its situation, surrounded as it was by marshes. The siege was opened at a time of torrential rain and Vauban records that the men in the trenches were 'up to their bellies in mud'. The Dauphin insisted on visiting the trenches, which were under heavy fire. Vauban was understandably reluctant to expose the heir to the throne to real danger. He contrived a look-out place for the Dauphin. In order to see out of it, 'he raised himself up with me holding the edge of his jacket to pull him back when it was necessary'. On 29 October Philippsburg surrendered. The Dauphin was so delighted by the experience that he presented Vauban with four of the captured cannons, which were duly mounted at Bazoches.

The duc de Montausier wrote to his former pupil in an old-school-masterly way: 'I shall not compliment you on the taking of Philippsburg; you had a good army, bombs, cannons and Vauban. I shall not compliment you because you are brave. That virtue is hereditary. But I rejoice with you that you have been liberal, generous, humane, and have recognised the services of those who did well.'

In November, after the taking of Philippsburg, Louis wrote to Vauban: 'You have known for a long time what I think of you and the confidence which I feel in your knowledge and in your affection; be sure that I will not forget the services which you render and that what you have done at Philippsburg is most agreeable to me.' He then refers to the Dauphin's experience. 'If you are as content with my son as he is with you, you must get on well together, for it seems to me that he knows you as well and esteems you as highly as I do. I cannot finish without giving you my express command to preserve yourself for the good of my service.'

In November Louis ordered Boufflers to bombard Coblenz in order to 'punish' the Elector of Trier for refusing to surrender the city. The word 'punish' says a lot about Louis' attitude to his smaller neighbours.

On 15 November William of Orange landed without opposition at Torbay, claiming the throne of England in the name of his wife and of himself. There was probably little that Louis could have done to prevent this, and in any case he was more concerned with defending his frontiers against the Empire. In view of the reduction of the Turkish threat to Austria and the correspondingly increased ability of the Emperor to send troops to the Rhine, that may have seemed the most important thing for Louis to do; but in the long run the accession of William to the throne of England was a disaster for Louis.

The enthusiasm with which the accession of William and Mary, described by Burnet as a 'double-bottomed' occupation of the throne, was greeted by the English showed that Louis had been wrong in hoping that a long period of civil strife might keep England out of the coalition. On the contrary, it put a greatly increased power and prestige in Europe into the hands of the man who hated Louis most and was intent on his destruction.

The flight of James II covered him with ignominy in the eyes of Gilbert Burnet. 'It seemed very unaccountable, since he was resolved to go, that he did not choose to go in one of his yachts or frigates, than to expose himself in so dangerous and ignominious a manner. It was not possible to put a good construction on any part of the dishonourable scene which he then acted.'

He was held in some contempt in France also. Voltaire records that the Archbishop of Reims, Louvois' brother, said openly in James's ante-chamber: 'Look at this fellow who has sacrificed three kingdoms for the Mass.' Voltaire also states that when William was setting sail for Torbay, a Catholic priest at The Hague said a Mass for the success of the enterprise.

Louis, however, received James with open arms, accorded him a generous pension and made over the Château de Saint-Germain to him. This act of generosity moved Mme de Sévigné to one of her highest flights. On 24 December 1688, she wrote to her daughter: 'The King's magnanimous soul enjoys playing this grand role. What could be more in keeping with the image of the Almighty than to stand by a King who has been expelled, betrayed and abandoned like this one?'

Louis respected James's position if not his character. He was by birth the undoubted King of England, Scotland and Ireland (but not, as was still somewhat archaically claimed, of France). It was the birthright which counted. It was the divine right. William was not only a usurper: he owed his crown not to God but to an Act of Parliament.

Louis would no doubt have liked to have seen James, a militant Catholic and a believer in the divine right of Kings, back on his throne, but the prospect of a second civil war in England would not have been displeasing either. It could have kept England out of any effective alliance with Louis' enemies. Louis was therefore ready to give active assistance to James in his attempt to re-enter England by way of Ireland. On 12 May 1690, James left France to recover his kingdom. Louis' last words to him were: 'The best that I could wish for you is that we should never meet again.'

It was here that the French navy, patiently prepared by Colbert, and now at last staffed and led by competent seamen, came into its own. It was the French fleet, under Amiral Tourville, that landed James safely in Ireland. It was a forlorn hope. The eye-witness account of John Stevens, himself a devoted supporter of James, reveals the fundamental weakness of the Jacobite position – lack of leadership and lack of morale. Stevens himself, when he volunteered, was snubbed and humiliated.

The reinforcements sent by Louis brought 'great satisfaction to all good men and no less vexation to the rebellious party'. Stevens describes the occasion. 'In the spring arrived at Cork the French fleet, bringing, besides wheat and ammunition, eight battalions of foot, well clothed, armed and disciplined.' Louis had put his former favourite Lauzun in command, who won the respect of the native population by issuing an order to his men 'by which he forbade their taking anything but what they paid for and also prohibiting their molesting Protestant assemblies'.

The French troops offered a striking contrast with the Irish volunteers, whom Stevens portrays as an ignorant and cowardly rabble. 'When they perceived how dear they were to buy their bread and liberty ... they deserted in vast numbers.' They were wholly unacquainted with the lot of the soldier – a people, continues Stevens, 'used only to follow and converse with cows ... It was difficult to make many of them understand the common words of command, much less obey them. Many regiments were armed and sent on service who had never fired a shot ... and it is hard to guess, when these men were upon action, whether their own or the enemy's fire was most terrible to them.'

The officers were scarcely better. 'The commanders have not only wanted valour to lead on ... but through ignorance have run themselves into dangers and then, cowardly and basely, been the first that betook themselves to shameful flight.' In this they resembled their leader and King, for whose sacred cause they were fighting. On 1 July, at the battle of the Boyne, writes Bishop Burnet, 'King James staid all the time with his guards and never came to the places of danger or action; and when he saw his army everywhere giving ground, was the first that ran for it, and reached Dublin before the action was quite over'. It was the French fleet which carried him back.

The French navy, however, was to achieve greater things than these. The British fleet, newly returned from an unsuccessful attempt to provide a convoy for the Queen of Spain and to blockade Toulon, was commanded by Admiral Arthur Herbert, now Lord Torrington. He was, according to Burnet, 'a man of pleasure and did not make the haste that was necessary, nor did the Dutch fleet come over so soon as was promised, so that our main fleet lay long at Spithead. The French understood that our fleets lay thus divided and saw the advantage of getting between them; so they came into the Channel with so fair a wind that they were near the Isle of Wight before our fleet had any advice of their being in the Channel'. The news had had to come overland, 'yet the fleet sailed as fast as the post could ride'.

On 10 July 1690, Tourville, with 78 vessels, was able to confront the English and Dutch fleets, numbering only 58, off Beachy Head – the Cap de Béveziers in French. Seventeen English or Dutch vessels were lost with all their cannons. Louis was delighted: 'I now find myself master of the Channel, after having defeated the English who prided themselves for several centuries on being its masters, even though they were supported by the Dutch.' A single victory, however, does not secure permanent mastery, as Louis was soon to discover.

On 3 November of the same year Jean-Baptiste Colbert, marquis de Seignelay, died and Louis' navy was bereft of its presiding genius.

In Europe Louis now determined on a policy of 'scorched earth' to prevent his German enemies from occupying the land on their side of the boundary. It was common practice for the protection of a fortress to make the ground in front of it uninhabitable, but to treat France itself as a fortress was to magnify the scale of the operation beyond all measure. Louvois drew up a list of the cities to be destroyed, which included Mannheim, Tübingen, Heidelberg, Worms and Bingen: 'not one stone left upon another'. John Wolf, in his biography of Louis, has made a valuable study of the letters of Louvois in the archives of the Ministère de la Guerre, which show that the orders to destroy these cities were not carried out fully. The duc de Montclair seems to have been constantly in default. 'I am surprised not to have letters from M. de Montclair, telling me that he has abandoned Heilbronn, Tübingen, Eslingen and other places after having put them in the condition that I ordered ... His Majesty is not accustomed to see that one argues with orders that he gives, when these are so precise.' 'It is amazing that you left Pfortzen in a condition that the enemies can establish a base there. The failure to execute the orders that His Majesty gave you on this point has not been agreeable to him.' None the less, many of the glories of medieval Europe were destroyed.

Liselotte d'Orléans was, of course, horrified and heart-broken by this action – 'this terrible and deplorable distress which has assailed the poor Palatinate; and what pains me most of all is that my name is being made use of to plunge these poor people into the extremity of misery'. She here refers to Louis' attempt to lay claim to her inheritance in the Palatinate. 'Indeed', she continues, 'I have such a horror of all that has been done that every night, as soon as I have had a little sleep, I imagine myself to be in Mannheim or Heidelberg and looking at all the devastation, and then I start up in bed and cannot get to sleep again for at least two hours. Then it comes back to my mind what it was all like in my own day and in what condition it is in now, and what a state I am in myself, and I cannot restrain my tears.'

Louis was presumably behind all Louvois' instructions in this policy of frightfulness It is perhaps not altogether surprising to learn that the Germans, according to Hubert Gillot, described the French as 'Huns' long before they earned that title for themselves.

In September 1689, the Emperor formed an alliance with the United Netherlands in order to force France back behind her former frontiers as defined by the Treaty of Nijmegen. Spain and Savoy duly followed suit and William was able to bring in his new Kingdom of England. The League of Augsburg had been formed. Louis was now facing the most formidable opposition which he had yet encountered. He needed a strong army with which to confront the threat, which meant, of course, that he needed money.

On 3 December 1689, Louis gave the order for nearly 1,200 pieces of solid silver furniture, mostly from the Grande Galerie, to be melted down. Each article was marked on the register: 'Déchargé, ayant été porté à la Monnoie' (the Mint). A sum of just over 2.5 million livres was realised by this expedient.

In June 1689, Louis had chosen the maréchal de Luxembourg to command the army in Flanders. Louvois hated Luxembourg as he had hated Turenne. Louis wrote to reassure his new commander-in-chief. 'I promise you that I will see to it that Louvois goes straight. I will oblige him to sacrifice the hatred which he has for you for the good of my service; you will write to me direct; your letters will not pass through his hands.' In July 1690, the maréchal de Luxembourg won an impressive victory over the Prince von Waldeck at Fleurus. Louis was so pleased that he informed the Sultan of Turkey of it, hoping, no doubt, to encourage him to keep up his struggle with the Emperor.

In May 1692, Louis decided to lay siege to Namur, a nearly impregnable fortress which, in French hands, would constitute a threat to both Brussels and Liège. Ably seconded by Boufflers, Louis himself commanded the army, 40,000 strong and with powerful artillery. He also had with him

Vauban. At the same time another army, 20,000 strong, under the maré-chal de Luxembourg, was keeping watch over William to prevent his attacking the besiegers. Racine, in his capacity as Historiographer Royal, wrote to his colleague Boileau on 3 June: 'In three days Vauban had pushed his main trench as far as the little stream which flows at the foot of the counter-escarpment, and from there, in less than sixteen hours, he had taken the whole of the covered way . . . with the result that so tremendous a place . . . saw all its outworks carried away . . . and without it costing the King more than thirty men.'

Vauban was most intrigued to see the whole of the great Spanish fortress. He was even more intrigued to meet the engineer who had designed and built it, a Dutchman named Coehorn, whom he praised and who praised him.

Vauban then wrote to the King, outlining the measures which he pro-posed to take to restore the fortifications of Namur. 'I will carry that out to the best of my ability and I hope that His Majesty will be contented with me, alive or dead.' Louis returned the letter with his annotations in the margin, but adding: 'It is quite certain that I shall be contented with you. I hope that it will be alive and for a long time.'

Louis was maintaining a war on all fronts against almost the whole of Europe. Nevertheless he planned an invasion of England. 'This winter', writes the Duke of Berwick, James II's illegitimate son, '*Le Roi Très Chrétien*, being convinced that the quickest means of ending the war would be to re-establish the King in England . . . gave the order to equip a great fleet, of which forty-four vessels would be at Brest and thirty-five at Toulon. All the Irish troops, together with a few French battalions and squadrons, were in readiness to reach La Hougue and Le Havre-de-Grâce, where the embarkation was to take place.' According to Burnet, in April 1692 when William was in Holland, James II was preparing to set sail again from France, with some 14,000 Englishmen and Irishmen, plus the maréchal Bellefonds and 3,000 Frenchmen. 'The heavens fought against them more effectively than we could have done. There was, for a whole month together, such a storm that lay on their coast that it was not possible for them to come out of their ports, nor could Marshal d'Estrées come out with the squadron from Toulon.' The 'Protestant wind' gave the English time to prepare and by 24 April the news of the invasion plans was out.

Meanwhile the French were fuming at their lack of luck. Berwick wrote that contrary winds prevented the comte d'Estrées for six weeks from leaving the Mediterranean with the Toulon fleet, so Louis ordered the 'chevalier de Tourville, Admiral of the Fleet, to come into the Channel with the Brest fleet without waiting for the squadron of the comte d'Estrées, and to engage the enemy, strong or weak, if he found them'.

Pontchartrain, Minister of War, showed himself to be Louvois' successor in the style of his letters. 'His Majesty', he wrote to Tourville, 'desires that he shall leave Brest on 25 April, even if he has warning that the enemy are outside in superior numbers. If he should encounter them on his way to La Hougue, His Majesty desires that he should engage them in combat, whatever their numbers are.' Louis appended in his own hand: 'These orders are my will and I want them to be observed exactly.' It is remarkable that when Louis was writing to his generals, whose *métier* he understood, he usually deferred to their professional opinions and local knowledge; when dealing with admirals, of whose professionalism he was largely ignorant, he was peremptory in conveying his decisions. According to La Roncière, Tourville commented: 'Those men there have no knowledge of the navy.' He obeyed, however, and therefore did not receive a further despatch from Pontchartrain warning him 'it is not for you to dispute the decisions of the King'. Pontchartrain threatened to replace him with someone 'more obedient to His Majesty and less circumspect than yourself'.

It was a simple failure to appreciate the merits of Tourville. 'This admiral,' states Berwick, 'the most capable seaman there was in France, or perhaps in the whole world, was piqued because, during the previous campaign, someone had done him a bad turn at Court and even accused him of not liking battles. So he did not hesitate to carry out the order which he had received. He came round into the Channel with his 44 ships of line, and, having ascertained that the combined fleets of England and Holland, numbering 85 ships, were off Spithead, he set sail for them ... Tourville attacked the English with vigour; the combat continued until nightfall, and never was action so brilliant, so daring, so glorious for the French navy. Tourville, although surrounded by the enemy, fought like a lion, without the enemy being able to take a single vessel or daring to penetrate the line.' But Tourville could not continue against such heavy odds and when the light faded he retreated towards the coast of France, pursued by the allied forces.

The tide was now against Tourville and most of his ships had to drop anchor, but the strong currents dragged the anchors and they had to cut their cables. Twenty-seven vessels managed to reach Brest, some by sailing right round the British Isles. Tourville himself sought refuge with the remainder in the bay of La Hougue, where King James and his expeditionary force were still waiting to be ferried across to Sussex. But the allied fleet put in their fire-boats and destroyed all the French ships.

The total losses amounted to only fifteen vessels, but the intended invasion of England had to be called off.

In the eyes of Villette-Mursay the operation was a source of pride. 'Everything that the comte de Tourville did on that day is so great and so beautiful that there is nothing to excuse or to defend. He did, during ten to thirteen hours, everything that is heroic.' But the last word was left to Louis. His reception of Amiral de Tourville was magnanimous. 'I have more joy', he said, 'on learning that forty-four of my vessels have fought against ninety of my enemies for a whole day than I have chagrin at the loss which I have suffered.' What would have been the result if Louis had had the patience to wait for the arrival of d'Estrées is matter for conjecture, but in the following year Tourville was made a Marshal of France.

Louis also paid public tribute to the ordinary seamen who had contributed by their valour to the glory of his fleet. In 1693 he had a medal struck. But this was no mere addition to some connoisseur's collection. It was meant to be worn. It was accompanied by the usual explanatory text. 'The particular attention which the King pays to everything which concerns the navy, has maintained it in the flourishing condition to which he has brought it. As he has always recompensed bravery even in the humblest soldiers, so he has desired that all good sailors and skilful pilots should feel the effects of his liberalities; with this in view, and in order to arouse a noble emulation, he has caused medals to be struck which are being distributed among those who are the most conspicuous. They will wear it as a public and honourable sign of the satisfaction with which His Majesty regards their services.'

22
Louis' Fistula and the Death of Condé

The year 1686 saw two important events – the death of the prince de Condé and the successful operation on Louis for a fistula.

Bossuet was invited to preach the *oraison funèbre* for Condé. In a memorable passage he compared Condé the master of the art of war with Condé the lover of the arts of peace. 'Always great, both in action and in repose, he appeared at Chantilly as he appeared at the head of his troops. Whether he was embellishing this magnificent and delectable mansion, or whether he was provisioning a camp in the middle of enemy territory and fortifying a position, whether he was marching with an army through places of peril, or whether he was conducting his friends through these superb alleys to the sound of so many fountains which were never silent by day or by night, he was always the same man, and his glory followed him everywhere.'

Saint-Simon describes how the great general would review his gardens, followed by a troop of secretaries armed with pen and paper, ready to take down on the spot the ideas which came to him for the elaboration of the lay-out. These would be turned into realities by Le Nôtre.

The two sides of Condé's character were reflected in the fabric of his main seat, the Château de Chantilly. He had inherited through his mother the great sixteenth-century castle of the Montmorency family. Rising from the waters of a wide moat and set about with seven massive towers, Chantilly was still outwardly a fortress; but the Connétable Anne de Montmorency had added the Petit Château to the south, a building in Renaissance style and of a purely domestic nature. War and Peace were already juxtaposed in the architecture. Chantilly never looked more magnificent than with the Petit Château in the foreground, backed and overtopped by the tall, gabled roofs, the *poivrières* and pinnacles of the older building. Condé himself made no significant alterations to the outward appearance of the château, but he filled the rooms with pictures and tapestries, created a library stocked with over 10,000 books and gave the gardens their gargantuan flights of steps and their glittering expanses of water.

In many ways Chantilly under the Grand Condé resembled Rabelais' 'Abbey of Thelema' – a temple for free-thinkers. Rabelais had placed over the doors of his abbey the motto 'faict que voudras' (Do what you wish!). The abbey was a club and the condition for membership was a lust for living. All lived for pleasure, but their pleasures were those of men who thirsted for knowledge as keenly as they thirsted after wine; 'so nobly were they instructed that there was not a man or woman amongst them who could not read and write, sing, play musical instruments, speak five or six languages and compose in them both verse and prose'.

All the great names of the *Grand Siècle* occur in the annals of Chantilly, for Condé understood men of letters. Bishop Burnet declared that 'there was not in France a better judge of wit or knowledge'. La Fontaine, a frequent guest, wrote of him: 'he has an extreme love of disputation and never has so much wit as when he is in the wrong.' As a general he had been at his best when faced by superior numbers and apparently insurmountable difficulties. It was the same with the intellectual battles of his retirement. 'He is never more contented', continues La Fontaine, 'than when he is confronted by a mass of authorities, reasonings and examples – it is in these circumstances that he triumphs.' His pugnacious attitude towards the pursuit of Truth earned him the respect that he enjoyed among men of letters. Praise from him was praise indeed.

Although for many years Condé was not a practising Christian he always enjoyed religious controversy. The son of a devout Catholic and grandson of a fighter for the Protestant cause, he was equally accessible to men of both persuasions. As the duc d'Aumâle wrote: 'It was his pleasure that his house should be neutral ground.' He was a great friend of Bossuet, who introduced Fénelon to the delights of Chantilly, where the two could be seen arguing beneath the shade of the Allée des Philosophes.

In 1683 the abbé Malebranche was invited to pass a few days as the guest of Condé, who was reading with interest his *Recherche de la Vérité*. 'Monsieur le Prince has a lively mind,' he recorded; 'penetrating and clear-sighted, and he is, I think, steadfast in the truth once he has accepted it, but he wants to see clearly.'

Early in 1686 the prince de Condé went to Versailles to plead for the royal pardon for his nephew, François-Louis, prince de Conti, who had gone with a number of young noblemen to fight the Turks in Hungary – that is to say, to fight under the duc de Lorraine, the general commanding the troops of the Emperor. They received from Versailles, records the marquis de Sourches, a lot of correspondence filled with abuse about the King, which was intercepted at the frontier. Louis made his pardon conditional on Conti's revealing the names of some of these correspondents, which Conti, as a matter of honour, felt unable to do.

Louis, at the time of Condé's visit to Versailles, was far from well. During the previous summer, his physician d'Aquin writes, 'the King was enjoying such perfect health that he had no grounds for taking any purgatives . . . This good health, however, was not of long duration and served as a prelude to the most troublesome and pernicious of all indispositions.'

On 5 January 1686, Louis complained of a tumour, which was situated 'two fingers' breadth from the anus'. By the end of the month his doctors were pressing him to consider various remedies. On Monday 11 February, Dangeau noted that the King did not go to the opera 'because he would have been incommoded by being seated for three hours'. A week later the pain had increased to a point at which he was unable to walk and took to his bed. Among the various treatments tried was the application of a plaster named *manus Dei* – 'the hand of God'. It did not work. The complaint was by now diagnosed as a fistula of the anus. Dangeau politely calls it 'une tumeur à la cuisse'. Louis' morale, however, was high. 'The King's illness', wrote Choisy, 'did not make him down-hearted; he wanted everyone to enjoy themselves in his absence.'

During the summer Louis appears to have had some remission, for on 22 May it was recorded that he was able to mount his horse 'without any incommodity'. On 6 August, however, he woke with a fever, 'his teeth chattering and his head aching'. Later in the month he was given quinine, which was apparently successful. Dangeau was consistently optimistic. But towards the end of August the reception of a rather spectacular embassy from the King of Siam had to be postponed because of a bad attack of the fever.

The Siamese emissaries were lodged in the Hôtel des Ambassadeurs in Paris. They had brought with them a Letter – the *Mercure Galant* always spells it with a capital L – from their King. It was written, as all royal letters were written in Siam, on a sheet of gold thin enough to be rolled up. It was placed in an ornate casket which was housed within an elaborate baldachino somewhat resembling a monstrance and always treated with the same reverence, for it represented the King. 'Every time they pass in front of the Letter', continues the *Mercure Galant*, 'they make the most profound obeisance.' It was carried like a sedan chair by twelve acolytes.

The ambassadors declined to see anyone, let alone to eat with anyone, because they felt obliged to deny themselves any pleasure before they were presented to Louis. On Sunday 1 September, it was decided that the reception could take place. Louis was clearly out to impress. The maréchal de La Feuillade and M. de Bonneuil, Introducteur des Ambassadeurs, went with the King's coaches to announce that 'the happy day, for which they had crossed so many seas, had at last arrived', and to convey them, together with their sacred Letter, to Versailles. They each wore a special *bonnet d'honneur*, a sort of toque rising from a golden coronet.

The route had been carefully chosen to offer an impressive view of Saint-Cloud and Meudon on their way. A guard of honour of a thousand soldiers awaited them in the forecourts of the palace. They were received by M. de Blainville, Maître des Cérémonies, who conducted them up the great Escalier des Ambassadeurs, through the successive salons of the Grand Appartement and into the Salon de La Guerre. Louis, surrounded by various members of the royal family, awaited them on a silver throne, raised on a dais at the far extremity of the Grande Galerie.

It was one of the accomplishments required of a Siamese ambassador to be able to make a reverence so profound that his head touched the ground without losing his balance or his *bonnet d'honneur*. Every time that the King spoke they all performed this feat, and when they rose they kept their faces turned towards the ground. Louis graciously said that 'they had come from too far away for them not to be permitted to see him'. When they presented the Letter he rose to his feet and uncovered. He was paid the compliment of being told that 'the knowledge of his great qualities and of his victories had reached the extremities of the Universe'.

At the end of the reception the ambassadors were served with a magnificent collation. Not only were they very appreciative of the French cuisine; they wanted to know every ingredient to each of the ragouts, 'in order not to return to their country without taking everything which had regard to the art and customs of France'. But they were more concerned to take back maps of the country, plans of the fortifications, paintings and engravings of the royal houses and of the King, both at the head of his troops and engaged in the various forms of hunting.

By the beginning of October Dangeau was still optimistic. 'The King had become so well from the effects of the quinine that he is stronger and more vigorous now than he was before his fever.' A week later the Court set off for the annual Voyage de Fontainebleau. It was the usual round of hunting, gambling and theatrical performances. During the comedy on Saturday 9 November, the duchesse de Bourbon was taken ill. Two days later the smallpox had declared itself.

Louise-Françoise, daughter of Louis and Mme de Montespan, known before her marriage as Mlle de Nantes, was only thirteen. She was the hope of the Condé dynasty. On 11 November her grandfather-in-law, the prince de Condé, left Chantilly and arrived at Fontainebleau at midnight. He was himself far from well. On Wednesday the 13th the young Duchess was so ill that she made her confession and received Communion. At about this time Louis decided to pay her his last visit. He found, according to the Père Bergier, the way barred by the figure of the prince de Condé, who said: 'I have no longer the strength to prevent you passing; but if you wish to enter you will at least have to tread on my stomach.' The next day the smallpox had worked its way out and the duchesse de Bourbon was no longer in danger.

Louis was still at Fontainebleau when he resolved to have the operation for the fistula. On 15 November he was back at Versailles and Monday 18 November was fixed for the event. It was to take place in his bedroom first thing in the morning.

The utmost secrecy was observed. Only the surgeon, Félix, Mme de Maintenon, Père de La Chaise, Louvois and those directly concerned with the operation were in the know.

The evening before, Louis went on horseback round the gardens and reservoirs; Dangeau noted that 'he appeared very tranquil and gay throughout the promenade'. Louis' calmness and peace of mind were not put on for show. On the following morning, the marquis de Sourches records: 'eight o'clock having sounded, they entered the King's bedroom and found him in a deep sleep, a great sign of his inward composure in a situation where others would have had so much anxiety. When he had been awoken, he asked if everything had been prepared and whether M. de Louvois was in the antichamber. When told that M. de Louvois was there and that everything had been prepared, he knelt by his bed and prayed. After which, having risen to his feet, he said aloud: "My God, I place myself in your hands." Then, getting back onto his bed, he ordered Félix to begin the operation, which he did right away, in the presence of Bessière, the most skilled surgeon in Paris, and of M. de Louvois, who held the King's hand throughout the operation, for Mme de Maintenon stood near the fireplace.'

The instrument in use for such an operation was that invented by Galenus in the second century AD, but Félix had made his own improvement on it for use on the King. The new lancet acquired the name of *bistouri à la royale*. Vallot, who was of course one of the doctors present, describes how the lancet was introduced inside a sheath to the top end of the fistula and then drawn back, 'opening it easily enough'. Félix then inserted his scissors and severed all the connections with the intestine, 'which the King supported with all the steadfastness possible'.

An hour later the astonished courtiers who had presented themselves for the *lever* were told of the whole affair by the King himself. It was reported at length in the *Mercure Galant*, the official journal of the Court.

The story was a splendid opportunity for propaganda. 'His Majesty, who saw that he ran the risk of suffering for the rest of his life from this sort of incommodity ... took a resolution worthy of his fortitude, and this prince desired to suffer in order the better to be able to work without ceasing for the welfare and repose of his subjects.

'Those whose business it was, or whose presence was necessary, entered by different ways to prevent anyone from having any suspicions. Although I will not give you here the detail of what happened, I can tell you that a thousand things happened worthy of the unshakeable courage of the King. As soon as the operation was over, the door was opened to what is known as *la première entrée*, that is to say those who have the first right of entry to the *lever* ... The news of this operation went quickly round Versailles and anguish was portrayed on every face so that one would have said, on seeing the King, that this monarch was the only one who was well.'

A courier was immediately despatched to Fontainebleau where the prince de Condé and the duc de Bourbon were still looking after the convalescent duchesse de Bourbon. Louis expressly forbade them to come to Versailles. The Dauphin, however, who was out hunting, galloped back to the palace in floods of tears. Mme de Montespan, Dangeau adds, 'left in haste to come to the King, but having learnt at Essonne that he had made a good recovery, went back to Mme de Bourbon'.

Choisy records the impact of the news upon the capital. 'Everyone felt at that moment how precious was the life of such a King; everyone felt themselves to be in the same danger that he was; fear, horror and pity were painted on every face ... I heard with my own ears a *porteur de chaises* say through his tears: "They gave him twenty cuts with the lancet and the poor man did not breathe a word! What pain it must have caused him!"

'Nothing else was spoken of in any of the streets and all Paris knew of it within a quarter of an hour. The churches filled up in a matter of minutes.' Félix was praised for having over the last two months 'exercised himself in these sorts of operation and carried them out in the hospitals of Paris. His example, so unusual in men of high position, produced an admirable effect; young surgeons redoubled their diligence on seeing their leader work with his own hands like the others and not disdain from healing the poor as well as the greatest of seigneurs.

'After the operation', continues Choisy, 'Félix recommended that the King should remain quiet ... but he would have none of that; the duties of kingship were pressing. He sent for his Ministers and wanted to hold a council; he did not do so, however, in the morning; he was in too much pain; he had to yield that much to nature. The next day he gave audiences to Ambassadors, Ministers and foreign Princes and talked with them with a presence of mind and a gaiety which made them write to their masters on what they had seen and admired. One could see, however, his suffering painted on his face; his forehead was nearly always covered in sweat.'

It was already becoming evident that the prince de Condé was dying. He wished to die at Chantilly and had made plans for a journey in three stages on 11 December, but he did not live to do so. Herauld de Gourville, who was acting as confidential secretary to Condé, took down his last will and testament. His family, his household, the poor were all remembered. He also wished to distribute, writes Gourville, 'fifty thousand écus in the places where he had caused the greatest disorders during the civil war'. Chief among them was Rethel.

On 3 December the prince de Condé wrote to Louis what he knew would be his last letter. 'I humbly beseech Your Majesty to be pleased that I should write to Him for the last time in my life. I am in a condition in which it does not seem I shall remain long before I go to render account to God for all my actions. I could wish with all my heart that those which concern Him were as innocent as those which concern Your Majesty.' His mind went back to his behaviour during the period of the Fronde.

'It is true that in the middle of my life I behaved in a way which I am the first to condemn and which Your Majesty has had the goodness to forgive me. I have since then endeavoured to make repairs for this misconduct by an unbreakable attachment to Your Majesty and it has been the cause of considerable distress to me that I have not been able to achieve anything sufficiently great to have merited the goodness which you have had towards me.'

There followed a last plea for the pardon of the young prince de Conti, but in the early hours of 4 December, before the letter was sealed, Condé's son, the duc d'Enghien, arrived from Versailles. He brought with him the tremendous news: 'The King pardons the prince de Conti!' Condé added a postscript to his letter: 'My son has just arrived and told me of the mercy which Your Majesty has had the goodness to grant me in forgiving M. le prince de Conti . . . I die happy.'

Between the hours of seven and eight that evening, having received the last rites of the Church from Father Etienne-Agard de Champs, an old schoolfriend from the Collège Sainte-Marie at Bourges and the priest who had brought him back into the Catholic faith, the Grand Condé breathed his last. When Louis, still in a state of convalescence after his operation, heard the news, he said: 'I have just lost the greatest man in my kingdom.'

23
Saint-Cyr and Fénelon

One or two historians, notably César Pascal, have tried to make out that Mme de Maintenon was almost personally responsible for the persecution of the Huguenots connected with the Revocation of the Edict of Nantes. That she began, as Louis had begun, in a spirit of understanding and *douceur*, is clear from a letter to her brother Charles in 1672. 'I beg you not to be inhumane towards the Huguenots; people must be won by kindness. Jesus Christ himself has given us the example.' By the end of 1680 her attitude had hardened somewhat. She was determined to convert the younger members of her near relations. On 19 December 1680, she wrote to her brother d'Aubigné about a cousin named Minette de Sainte-Hermine: 'I love Minette and if you could send her to me it would give me very great pleasure; no other method than force is possible since the family will be very upset on hearing of the conversion of the Mursay children. It will therefore be necessary for you to get her to write to me that she wishes to become a Catholic. You will send me her letter and I will send you a *lettre de cachet* with which you will take Minette to live with you until you find an occasion to send her to me.' It appears to be a case of legalised abduction. It has no connection with the methods used to obtain conversions by the dragonnades.

But as Mme de Maintenon grew older her Catholicism became more rigid. Her attitude towards the persecution seems to have been very much in line with that of almost all devout Catholics. She hated heresy and schism and rejoiced at the thought that both would be extirpated in France. That was Louis' attitude also. But there is no evidence that she was responsible for his attitude. Louis was not easily swayed, especially by women. There was strong anti-Protestant influence from the General Assembly of the Gallican Church and on the secular side from Louvois and the Parlement de Paris.

Among the various gifts with which Françoise d'Aubigné was endowed by nature, the gift of teaching was perhaps the most fundamental – but the word 'teaching' must be allowed to include all the varied forms of care and attention of which the young have so much need. She had given evidence of this as the governess of the royal bastards, but by far her most important contribution in the field of education was the foundation of the Maison Royale de Saint-Cyr.

It began with her meeting Mme de Brinon, a nun whose convent had been closed and who was running a little school for the children of the poor at Montmorency. Mme de Maintenon was sufficiently impressed to want to take it over and had it moved to Rueil, nearer to Versailles. There she undertook to teach the girls their catechism. The social teaching, as was usual in those days, attributed the distinction between rich and poor to divine providence, but Mme de Maintenon put in some ideas of her own.

'God wills that the rich are saved by giving their money and the poor by not having any.' 'The rich will have more difficulty in achieving salvation than the poor.' 'Never murmur against the rich; God has willed that they should be so, just as He has willed that you should be poor. Your heart is content while your body labours; most of those in high positions are disquieted at heart, whereas you seem to be happy.'

From Rueil the school was moved to better accommodation at Noisy. Louis began to take an interest in the project, even on one occasion making an unexpected visit on his way back from hunting. He soon realised that this could be an important contribution to the benefit of the realm and the glory of the King. In due course they were regally housed at Saint-Cyr near Versailles.

In September 1686, the *Mercure Galant* printed one of its most laudatory articles. 'How happy we are, as well as those Frenchmen who will follow us, that God has given us a monarch who, as well as the infinite number of great things which he has done for the glory and the benefit of his people, has now done three so worthy of his greatness!' The three deeds referred to were the foundation of Les Invalides, the setting up of companies of young gentlemen for military training and the founding of the community of Saint-Cyr. The first and second were concerned with the rewarding of old soldiers and the training of new officers – 'which will show that Louis le Grand will always be invincible'. The third would ensure that 'there will always be pure souls who will pray continually for the prosperity of his army'.

The foundation of Saint-Cyr, however, had wider aims than providing a spiritual power-house for the armed forces. Louis himself, in the letters patent of 7 June 1686, decreed that there should be two Masses said each day 'with the special intention that it might please God to give to us and to our successors the enlightenment necessary to govern our state according to the rules of justice, and the grace to increase our devotion to Him'. He saw Saint-Cyr as a spiritual power-house for the King.

The Foundation Deed was drawn up by Louis himself. He refers at some length to his arrangements for the training of young soldiers and goes on to say that he had considered it no less just and no less useful to provide an education 'for young ladies of noble extraction, especially for those whose fathers had been killed while serving or who were impoverished by the expenses which they had incurred and found themselves without the necessary means to give them a good education'. It is clearly stated that they would be brought up 'on the principles of a real and solid piety', so that when they left – at the age of twenty – 'they will be able to take into all the provinces of our Kingdom the example of modesty and virtue and contribute either to the happiness of their families or to the education of convents where they can devote themselves wholly to God'.

The choice of Saint-Cyr as a site for the new school was made by Louvois and Mansart. The contract was signed in April 1685; Mansart drew up the designs and building began in May. Louis gave permission for soldiers to be employed and with a task force of some 2,400 the work was completed in fifteen months. Louis took his usual interest in the building operation and drew up the agenda, which included the item: 'Provisions, in advance, so that nothing is lacking for 1 July, the day the young ladies will enter Saint-Cyr.'

The institution was to be not so much a religious community as a community of religious people. It was to have the virtues of the cloister but not its detachment from the world. The draft constitution had been submitted not only to the Bishop of Chartres and Père de La Chaise but also to Boileau, Dépréaux and Racine, who shared the position of Historiographer Royal. It provided for the reception of 250 daughters of impoverished noblemen – who had to show proofs of their nobility and a letter from their Bishop confirming their poverty – thirty-six teachers and twenty-four *soeurs converses* who ran the household. It was assured a regular income paid for out of the revenues of the abbey of Saint-Denis, the Generality of Paris and the estate of Saint-Cyr.

Mme du Perrou, the author of the *Mémorial de Saint-Cyr*, and since July 1686 one of the original staff and *Maîtresses des Novices*, who was to succeed Mme de Maintenon as the Superior and was 'close enough to her to speak with certainty', has left her own appreciation of the character of the school. 'We were taught to be simple and straightforward in our way of thinking, in our manner of speaking and in our conduct. Nothing was so pleasing to Mme de Maintenon as this simplicity, and she used to say that those who had real intelligence were more capable of it than the others.'

They were taught also the importance of relationships between teachers and pupils – and here she is very much in line with the principles of Fénelon: 'You speak to your children', she wrote to the mistress in charge of the youngest group, 'with a dryness, a peevishness and an abruptness which will turn all hearts against you. They must sense that you love them and that you are only vexed at their faults for their own sakes, and that you are full of hope that they will put matters right themselves.'

Mme de Maintenon recognised the need to develop the poise and elocution of her pupils. One of the means of achieving this was to engage them in theatrical performances, but here she was up against a not inconsiderable difficulty. Almost anything to do with the stage was regarded with disapproval if not with horror by the authorities of the Church. 'A man who writes novels and plays', claims the author of a popular pamphlet, 'is a public poisoner – not of the bodies but of the souls.'

The Churches of the seventeenth century, both in Catholic France and in puritan England, seemed to have forgotten – possibly because they wanted to forget – that 'the natural instincts and affections implanted by God' could actually be 'hallowed and directed aright' and that the boundaries of sex and sin were not co-terminous. A sometimes pathological fear of sex was matched by a resultant over-emphasis on virginity and celibacy and the states of mind which went with them. Some such outlook underlay the invincible mistrust of the devout for the activities of the stage and of those authors who promoted them.

This attitude was expressed at an individual level by one of the nuns at Port-Royal, Soeur Agnès de Sainte-Thècles, who wrote, towards the end of 1663, to her nephew: 'I heard a few days ago a piece of news which hurt me deeply. I write this to you in the bitterness of my heart and with my eyes full of tears . . . But I have learnt with sorrow that you frequent more than ever the people whose name is abominable to every person who has even a tinge of piety – and with good reason, since they are cast off from the Church and from the Communion of the faithful even in death, unless they recognise the error of their ways.' In her nephew's manifestly unredeemed condition she declined so much as to meet him. The people thus condemned to perdition were those shameless hussies who disported themselves upon the stage. The nephew was Jean Racine.

Jean Racine is one of the greatest dramatic poets that France has produced and a name which adds its particular lustre to the *Grand Siècle*. After an education at Port-Royal des Champs, which would have been a better preparation for life in a cloister than for the mixture of Court and theatre to which his natural talent orientated him, Racine quickly established himself as a poet and a writer of tragedy.

Born in December 1639, he was twenty-five when he wrote his first tragedy, *La Thébaide*, which was produced by Molière's company. He had already been awarded a pension of 600 livres a year and was sometimes to be seen at Court. In November 1663, he wrote to his friend the abbé Le Vasseur: 'at the King's *lever* today I found Molière, whom the King praised very highly. I was glad for his sake. He was glad, too, that I was there.' A little later he wrote again: 'You see that I am half a courtier. In my opinion it is a very boring business.' But, as so often in France, success depended upon a certain balance between real ability and powerful patronage.

The relationship between Mme de Maintenon and Racine came about through Mme de Brinon. This lady, though very devout, had a passion for the theatre and longed to indulge in theatrical productions at Saint-Cyr. Not feeling equal to producing the great works of Corneille and Racine, she wrote her own. They were, wrote Mme de Caylus, 'détest-ables'. Mme de Maintenon expressed a desire to see one – 'and found it as it was, that is to say so bad that she had to ask her not to produce others like it'. She suggested that the young ladies might present those works of the two great authors 'in which there were the fewest references to love'. Racine's *Andromaque* was chosen. It is arguably the most erotic of his tragedies. 'The piece was performed only too well,' continues Mme de Caylus. Presumably the young ladies put too much enthusiasm into the more passionate scenes. Mme de Maintenon reacted predictably. She wrote to Racine: 'Our young ladies have just played *Andromaque* and played it so well that they shall never play it again, or any other of your pieces.' But she still needed to develop the poise and elocution of her pupils. In the same letter she asks Racine if he could not compose 'a moral poem . . . from which love is entirely banished'. His response to this was *Esther*.

'Mme de Maintenon was charmed by it', wrote Mme de Caylus, 'and her modesty did not prevent her from finding in the character of Esther . . . certain allusions flattering to herself.'

This new form of theatrical production, created to meet the special requirements of Saint-Cyr, gave Racine the opportunity to introduce a new element into the cast – the chorus. This was, of course, as Mme de Caylus states, 'in the imitation of the Greeks'. Racine had always wanted to bring this back to the stage, and it found its place quite naturally in *Esther*.

Both *Esther* and its successor *Athalie* were taken straight from the Old Testament – or nearly straight. 'It seemed to me', wrote Racine in his preface to *Esther*, 'that without altering any of the smallest circumstances of the Holy Scripture (which in my opinion would be a kind of sacrilege) I could construct the whole of my action from the scenes which God himself – in a manner of speaking – had prepared.' He did, however, omit all references to the King's concubines and trod delicately when referring to the position of Esther in the royal household. He also has Haman lynched, 'by the fury of the people', instead of hanged as the sacred text asserts.

Mme de Maintenon was by now, of course, the legal but morganatic wife of Louis. In the summer of 1686, at the time of the final trans-migration of her academy for young ladies to Saint-Cyr, she wrote to the abbé Gobelin a letter which reveals much of what she thought of her new status. 'I am not in any way more of a *grande dame* than I was in the rue des Tournelles ... and if the favour in which I stand puts all the world at my feet, it should not have this effect on a man in charge of my conscience, and whom I require earnestly to conduct me without any consideration along the route which he believes the best for my salvation.'

At the end of December 1688, Mme de Brinon fell from favour and was dismissed. At about the same time Mme de Maintenon's confessor Gobelin retired. A new *dramatis personae* began to appear on the scene. Mme de Brinon was replaced by Mme de Maisonfort. She had a cousin named Mme Guyon, who was a well-known exponent of an approach to religion known as 'Quietism'. She had an admirer in the abbé de Fénelon. 'God wants of you', she wrote to him, 'something simple and childlike which reduces the soul to guilelessness and spiritual infancy, which only experience can enable you to understand.'

Perhaps no controversy of the seventeenth century is so remote from the secular thought of today as that which surrounded quietism. If it is true that only experience of it can enable a person to understand it, these must be few indeed.

Mme Guyon has left some forty volumes of her writings. During the winter of 1681–2 she produced her first spiritual treatise, *Les Torrents*. It sounds the key-note to her spirituality. She wrote it, without re-reading it, driven by some inner force; 'it welled up from the depths and did not pass through my head'.

The same bypassing of the human faculties was the essential condition for her prayer. It was 'empty of all forms, all particular ideas or images. None of my prayer took place in my brain, but it was a prayer of joyful possession of the will, where the flavour of God was so strong that it attracted and absorbed the other potentialities of the soul in a profound recollectedness, without actions or language.'

The elimination of human mentality was one important step in the approach to God; the elimination of human experience was another. It took the form of a passionate desire for infancy. 'It would be impossible', she wrote to Fénelon in June 1689, 'for you to be too small or too child-like.' In pursuance of this ideal she had contracted 'a mystic marriage with the Child Jesus'. It is not very clear what such a marriage entailed. An exclusive concentration on the infant Jesus seems, at the very least, to ignore his ministry, his teaching, his crucifixion and resurrection. Everything in Heaven and on earth was eliminated: 'everything vanishes away and only God is left, as he was before the Creation'.

As he was before the Creation: the whole history of Judaism and Christianity, with its emphasis on God's self-revelation to his people, becomes irrelevant. God before the Creation is a God about whom we lack information.

To Bossuet this looked like the elimination or marginalisation of all that was specifically Christian. It seemed to dispense with the Gospel, the gift of the Holy Spirit, the sacraments and, perhaps worst of all in his eyes, the Church. His was a far more down-to-earth religion, with its respect for history, its acceptance of the Scriptures and its insistence on Christian morality: a religion for the ordinary human being. Quietism had something rarefied and elitist about it. It may be significant that four of Mme Guyon's closest supporters were duchesses.

Mme Guyon's impact on the young ladies of Saint-Cyr was immediate and disastrous. They neglected their academic and religious duties in order to indulge in prostrations on the floor of the chapel. Godet des Marais, the Bishop of Chartres, was horrified. Mme de Maintenon was in a position which was difficult if not dangerous.

Fénelon was intrepid enough to write in support of Mme Guyon. An inquest into her beliefs and behaviour was chaired by Bossuet. It resulted in her doctrines being declared heretical and her incarceration in the Bastille, but it left Fénelon for the moment untouched. In the spring of 1694 he was appointed to the Archbishopric of Cambrai. But he went further in his injudicious behaviour. In the following year he wrote an anonymous letter to the King. Whether Louis ever saw it is open to doubt.

The letter is a head-on attack on Louis' regime, and almost unbelievably outspoken. 'You thought you were governing because you regulated the limits of those who were governing [his ministers]. They were hard, haughty, unjust, violent and dishonest. They knew no other rule, both for internal and foreign affairs, than to threaten, to crush and to annihilate all who resisted.' In particular he condemned the Dutch war. 'It had no other foundation than the motives of glory and vengeance, which can never make a war just.' Through such actions 'your name has become odious and the whole French nation insupportable to all its neighbours' and 'you have spent your whole life outside the paths of truth and justice and, as a result, outside the Gospel'. It calls into question the balance of mind in a man who has just been made an archbishop by the King to write such a letter which might well have reached him.

Four years later, in 1699, another work of his was published, probably without his knowledge, which spelt out the same criticisms, albeit in milder language. Written for the edification of the duc de Bourgogne, this would become Fénelon's most famous book – *Télémaque*. In March that year he was deprived of his position as Précepteur des Enfants de France and exiled to his diocese. It made Mme de Maintenon tremble for her own position. Languet de Gergy records that she confided in him that 'she had never felt a more lively fear. It made her ill.' In the end Louis said to her: 'Come, madame, are we to see you die of this matter?'

Her position was more secure than she imagined. It had even been recognised by Pope Alexander VIII, who wrote to her in 1690: 'Dear daughter in Jesus Christ, noble lady, your distinguished virtues and commendable privileges are so well known to us that they invite me to show you the most particular marks of our fatherly affection.' He was trying to enlist her support for his 'very dear son Toussaint, Cardinal de Forbin'. 'We beg you to be so good as to give all the assistance and protection possible in a Court in which your merit has justly earned you a favour approved by everyone.' It is a letter that might have been written to a Queen.

Her epitaph in the chapel at the Château de Maintenon reads splendidly with its typically eighteenth-century crescendo of virtues, but within the harmless hyperbole of its style it contains truth. 'Tranquil amid the agitations of the Court, Simple in the midst of grandeur, Poor at the fountainhead of wealth, Humble at the height of her honours, Revered by Louis le Grand.' Neither her epitaph nor her *acte de décès* makes the slightest allusion to her position as Louis' wife. But it was as such that she played her most important role.

When La Bruyère wrote the chapter on the Sovereign in his best-known book, *Les Caractères*, he must have been thinking of Mme de Maintenon. 'A King may lack nothing except the sweet joys of a private life; he can only be consoled for so great a loss by the charms of friendship and by the fidelity of his friends.' Louise de La Vallière and Athenaïs de Montespan represent the springtime and the summer of Louis' life. Françoise d'Aubigné represents the autumn. With her he knew for the first time the joys of a simple, homely relationship. With her he was to grow old. But the domestic scene was to be completed by the young wife of the duc de

Bourgogne – Marie-Adélaïde de Savoie. In 1697 she had come from Turin as a girl of eleven, to all the stale solemnity and settled routine of Versailles. As Saint-Simon so aptly puts it: 'elle l'animait toute entière'.

24
The Duke and Duchess of Burgundy

The peace treaty with Savoy had been signed on 10 September 1696. It was to be cemented by the marriage between Louis' eldest grandson and heir, Louis, duc de Bourgogne, and Marie-Adélaïde, daughter of Victor-Amadeus II of Savoy and his wife Anne-Marie. Anne-Marie was the daughter of Henriette-Anne d'Angleterre, Louis' former sister-in-law. Marie-Adélaïde was only eleven at the time.

France was at this time badly in need of peace. The people were at their last extremity. As Voltaire puts it: 'they died of hunger to the sound of Te Deums'. For the poor it meant the all too familiar condition of *la misère*; for those at the top it took the form of a general feeling of *ennui*.

One cannot help being conscious, when reading the accounts of life at Versailles written by Saint-Simon, La Bruyère, Mme de Maintenon or the duchesse d'Orléans, of a great change that had come over the Court as the seventeenth century neared its close. Gone were the gallant crowds who had swarmed after Louis on his *promenades des jardins*, applauded the fêtes, complained of the lack of accommodation and rolled wearily back in their great coaches at the break of day to Paris or Saint-Germain. They may not have come from purely disinterested motives – 'jeunesse du Prince, source des belles fortunes' – but there was a spirit of enthusiasm and an unfeigned appreciation for the delights which were offered. Now the courtiers had settled down to the regular routine of interest and backbiting. At the beginning of the century Saint François de Sales had written: 'It is a great loss of time being at Court, and for many it will mean losing Eternity also.' Now, at the end of the century, La Bruyère could write in the same vein: 'Life at Court is a serious, melancholy game which needs application.' Even Mlle de La Fayette, once so enthusiastic about Versailles, commented on the sameness of everything: 'always the same pleasures, always at the same hours and always with the same people'. A cold wind of austerity had chilled the summer landscape and

333

ominous clouds were gathering on the horizon. It was to this world of disenchantment that Marie-Adélaïde was to bring a new breath of life. She started by causing a great rejuvenation in the heart of the King which was soon imparted to Mme de Maintenon.

On 7 October Marie-Adélaïde left Turin for France. Her arrival was eagerly awaited. Dangeau, who had been appointed her Premier Ecuyer, kept Mme de Maintenon fully informed. 'You are giving us some pleasing impressions of the princess,' she wrote; 'we are most impatient to greet her . . . We are fortunate in having a child with a sweet nature to bring up, and I am glad to hear that she is still childish, because I do not think precocious children ever make much progress.' Her maternal instincts had been thoroughly aroused and the schoolmistress in her was finding full expression. Together with the comte de Govon, the ambassador from Savoy, she started to plan the details of the young princess's education.

Louis was equally expectant. The Court had moved to Fontainebleau, but he could not resist the temptation to go ahead and meet Marie-Adélaïde at Montargis. He granted her in advance the precedence which would become hers as duchesse de Bourgogne, after her marriage, which greatly upset his brother, her grandfather.

The princess's cortège arrived at Montargis at about five o'clock. 'The moment the coach that was carrying her came into the street the King, who was on the balcony, came down . . . As soon as the door was opened, without giving the princess time to alight, while she was still on the step, he caught her in his arms and embraced her, saying: "Madame, I have been awaiting you with much impatience." ' She replied that this was the happiest day in her life.

She was then allowed a little repose during which Louis wrote to Mme de Maintenon: 'She is the most graceful person and has the most beautiful figure that I have ever seen. Her dress and her coiffure were a perfect picture; her eyes bright and very beautiful . . . her complexion very simple and as pink and white as one could wish . . . the most beautiful dark hair that one could possibly see . . . her lips a bright red but thick, her teeth white but uneven; she speaks little, but so far as I can see she is not in the least embarrassed when one looks at her . . . I am wholly satisfied.'

One member of the royal family who was not present on this occasion was the one whom it affected most closely – the princess's future husband, the duc de Bourgogne. He seems to have been kept deliberately in the background. He saw her first on the following day as she passed through Nemours.

When the coach appeared he broke away from his tutors and ran to meet it. He jumped in and just managed to kiss her hand before being relegated to a back seat. The royal party then proceeded to Fontainebleau.

The ceremonial entrance to the palace was, in those days, still by way of the town and through the central pavilion of the Aile des Ministres. The cavalcade thus entered the great forecourt, the Cour du Cheval Blanc, and swung left in order to draw up before Du Cerceau's impressive double-horseshoe staircase. As the carriage entered the courtyard, Marie-Adélaïde was confronted not only by the magnificent panorama of architecture, but by the Court of France arrayed in all its glory.

'A truly magnificent spectacle,' wrote Saint-Simon; 'the King led the princess, so small that she seemed to be sticking out of his pocket, and, after walking slowly the length of the terrace [at the top of the horseshoe staircase], they entered the Chapel for a short period of prayer and went on to the late Queen Mother's suite [in the Cour de la Fontaine], which had been specially prepared to receive her.' After dinner they all drove round the Canal and watched the cormorants catching fish. This form of aquatic falconry, which had been learnt from the Chinese, was one of the specialities of Fontainebleau.

Marie-Adélaïde expressed her appreciation of everything. 'The stay at Fontainebleau is very pleasing for me,' she wrote to her grandmother, Jeanne de Savoie-Nemours, 'above all because it is the place in which I had the honour of seeing the King for the second time and I hope one thing, my dear Grandmama, that I shall be happy not only at Fontainebleau but everywhere, being resolved to do whatever depends upon myself in order to be so.' But her real love was not for Fontainebleau: it was for Louis.

It is noticeable that she wrote far more often to her grandmother than to either of her parents. Granddaughter to grandparent was a generation gap which she crossed with ease. The same was true of her relations with Louis. 'The King had for her', wrote the marquis de Sourches, 'all the friendliness and all the kindness that it would be possible to imagine.' Louis lost no occasion for seeking her company and she had the unique privilege of being allowed to scratch (one never knocked) on the door when Louis was in his Council.

But the affection was deeper than that suggested by Sourches. As the result of a fall while hunting, Louis no longer rode to hounds. He followed the chase in a little vehicle drawn by four small horses, which he conducted himself with much skill. Marie-Adélaïde could sit beside him and thus, in the long, straight alleys of the forests of Marly, Compiègne and Fontainebleau, they could be alone together. It seems that there existed between Louis and Marie-Adélaïde one of those loving relationships in which an old life touches a young life, where flame touches flame and both are fed. On one occasion, relates Dangeau, she pretended not to have toothache in order not to deprive the King of his hunting.

She had a special habit made for these excursions – a skirt and justau-corps of red velvet with broad gold braiding and a coiffure *de chasseuse*. 'Everyone', wrote Sourches, 'found that this outfit suited her to perfection.' The evenings were usually spent with Mme de Maintenon where they were sometimes joined by the duc de Bourgogne. Etiquette was banished and with it the dignified figure of the Maître d'Hôtel, presiding over the ceremonial like a maréchal de France with his baton. Marie-Adélaïde's relationship with Mme de Maintenon was slightly remoter than with Louis. 'It is true that I have a good friend in Mme de Maintenon', is how she put it, 'and it would not be her fault if I were not perfectly happy.' She always addressed her respectfully as *ma tante*.

This happiness was marred only by the departure of a loved one. In October 1698 her aunt by marriage, Elizabeth-Charlotte d'Orléans, left Versailles to marry the duc de Lorraine. Madame – the bride's mother – even found it possible, on this occasion, to praise Marie-Adélaïde. 'The duchesse de Bourgogne has at last proved that she has a virtuous disposition, for she was so sad that she could not eat. She shed the most bitter tears while saying farewell to her aunt.'

More usually Madame wrote of the duchesse de Bourgogne in terms of utter disapproval and disgust. According to her, neither Louis nor Mme de Maintenon was capable of saying 'No' to her. The result was that the little princess was thoroughly spoilt. It was the subject of a long outburst to Sophia, Electress of Hanover on 22 October 1698. 'On a journey she does not remain for an instant in the same place; she sits on the knees of those in the coach and jumps about like a little monkey. They find all that charming. She is absolute mistress in her own room ... sometimes she has the whim to run out of doors at five in the morning. They allow it; they admire it. Anyone else would chastise a child who behaved in that sort of way. They will come, I believe, in due course to repent of having allowed the girl to do anything she wanted.'

Madame goes on to give a list of excesses, chiefly at mealtimes. 'In the middle of dinner she will start singing; she will dance on her chair, pretend to salute all the company, pull the most frightful faces, tear a chicken or a partridge apart in her hands, dip her fingers in the sauces ... She treats her father-in-law without any respect and addresses him as "tu". It is said that she treats the King with even greater familiarity.'

There is evidence, however, of a certain measure of discipline. Neither the Duke nor the Duchess of Burgundy was permitted at first to attend a theatrical performance. In November 1698, however, this rule was relaxed. Both of them, as well as the two young princes, Bourgogne's brothers, were allowed to go to a comedy. It was the *Bourgeois Gentil-homme*. The choice was a good one and the performance seems to have been brilliant. 'The duc de Bourgogne', wrote Madame, 'completely lost his gravity. He laughed until he cried. The duc d'Anjou was so entranced that he sat with his mouth open, as if in ecstasy ... The duc de Berry laughed so much that he nearly fell off his chair. The duchesse de Bourg- ogne, who knows better how to hide her feelings, held herself back to begin with. She did not laugh much but was content to smile. But from time to time she forgot herself and got up out of her chair in order to see better.'

In the early days of her marriage Marie-Adélaïde took little notice of her husband: she was much more concerned with his grandfather. The young Louis de Bourgogne had been in many ways a problem child. 'This prince', wrote Saint-Simon, 'was born a little terror and in his early infancy one trembled for him; of a difficult and angry temper, even to the extremest of transports and even against inanimate objects; furiously impulsive; unable to endure the least opposition, even if caused by the passage of time or by the weather, without getting into a passion which made one fear that he would do violence to his own body; opinionated in the extreme.'

To handle such a situation it required someone of the calibre of his Governor, the duc de Beauvilliers. Described by Louis as 'one of the wisest men in the Court and in the Kingdom', he was the only *grand seigneur* to hold a high position in the State. Saint-Simon, who suspected him on account of his excessive devoutness, admitted that 'he surpassed himself by his application, his patience and the variety of his remedies'. One of these was to allow the young Duke to develop an apparently natural interest in military matters. He even went on parade. It was pouring with rain, but that did not deter him. He handled the situation, says the marquis de Sourches, 'with an application, a precision and a dexterity far superior to anything of which children of his age could normally be capable, it being unheard of that a child who was not yet seven should give evidence of such adroitness and self-control as a man of twenty-five'.

Beauvilliers was supported by his brother-in-law the duc de Chevreuse and above all by the Preceptor Fénelon and the Valet de Chambre Moreau – 'fort au-dessus de son état'. Together they achieved what might have seemed impossible. 'From this abyss there arose a prince who was affable, mild, humane, moderate, patient, modest, penitent and, as far as and even further than his position admitted of, humble and austere in himself.' Mme de Maintenon added her own interpretation: 'We have seen the faults that caused so much concern for the future disappearing one by one. Religion has so transformed him that, though passionate by nature, he is now even-tempered, gentle and obliging. One feels that this is his true character.'

Of the gifted team who brought about this metamorphosis the most important was Fénelon. His impressive appearance is described by Saint-Simon. 'This prelate was a man tall and thin, pale, with a large nose, with eyes from which his spirit sparkled like a stream and a physiognomy the like of which I have never seen . . . There was gallantry, seriousness and gaiety; it savoured equally of the Professor, the Bishop and the Grand Seigneur. But, as in his whole personality, that which predominated was the delicacy, the wit, the charm, the decorum and above all the nobility. It needed an effort to take one's eyes off him.'

And yet there was something discordant about Fénelon. Both Louis and Bossuet began by admiring him and ended by rejecting him.

He first appears on the stage of history as the director of *nouvelles Catholiques*, the instructor of converts from Calvinism. In 1689 the duchesse de Beauvilliers, who had eight daughters, encouraged him to produce his first work: *Le Traité de l'Education des Filles*. In it he outlines a new approach to teaching, much of which was applicable to boys also, which was well in advance of his times. In place of strict intellectual discipline stimulated by corporal punishment, his aim was to make study enjoyable and interesting and therefore to be pursued for its own sake. So far as personal demeanour and deportment were concerned he set before the girls 'the noble simplicity which is apparent in the statues and other representations which remain of the women of Greece and Rome'.

Not only was study to be made agreeable: the relationship with the teacher was of prime importance. 'There is another sort of feeling', he wrote, 'which is more difficult but more important to communicate: that of friendship. As soon as the child is capable of it, it is just a question of turning his heart towards the people who are useful to him. Friendship will guide him towards all that one might wish for him. One has a bond guaranteed to draw him towards the good – provided that one knows how to make use of it.'

Fénelon most certainly did know how to make use of it. His one undoubted success was to have secured the deep and lasting affection of the young duc de Bourgogne. The pupil paid the highest tribute to this himself with the words: 'I leave the duc de Bourgogne behind the door and with you I am just *le petit Louis*.'

Like many tutors of princes Fénelon preferred to write his own texts. He had the idea – not unknown to the Greeks – of composing a series of conversations, *Les Dialogues des Morts*, in which two characters from history, some of them Kings of France, confront each other and invite the judgement of the reader. But his most important work was *Télémaque*, in which he creates a sequel to the *Odyssey*. There is much political teaching, sometimes satirical, contained in *Télémaque* and it is full of implied criticisms of the regime of Louis XIV.

The allusions are fairly easy to 'read'. When he says that the Phoenicians 'are to be feared by all their neighbouring states on account of their innumerable ships and the trade they carry on, right to the Pillars of Hercules, brings them a wealth which surpasses that of the most flourishing nations' – is this not a clear allusion to Louis' arch-enemy the Dutch Republic and an endorsement of Colbert's policy? With it goes advice on how to become a maritime force. 'Give to all foreigners an open and easy welcome; see that they find in your ports security, comfort and total liberty. Never let yourself be led by avarice or pride. The true means of gaining a lot is by not wishing to gain too much.' This is merely sound advice, but when he starts describing the oarsmen in the galleys – 'well paid for their services, well fed, well looked after when they are ill, and when they are absent, their wives and children are cared for' – it is impossible not to make the contrast with the shameful treatment of the *galériens* of Louis XIV. The portrait of Idomeneus seems to fit uncomfortably closely the figure of the *Grand Monarque*.

Fénelon vehemently denied that there was any such intention. He wanted to warn his pupil of the evils of warfare and luxury. He wanted to warn him not to trust too much in aggressive, war-loving ministers, but of course the figure of Protésilas was not aimed at Louvois! But most of all Fénelon seemed to be determined to warn the young prince of the dangers of sex and the importance of the Christian moral teaching – but of course he was not thinking of the marital infidelities of the old King! In this last matter Fénelon was successful: the duc de Bourgogne was an unusually chaste young man.

'He has not been subject', wrote his confessor, the Père Martineau, 'to the vices to which youth is so often prone, particularly in the most agreeable milieu in the world.' He exhibited an extreme bashfulness: always modest in the way he looked at people, always reserved in what he said, he conducted himself in perfect conformity with the maxim of Tertullian: 'it is not enough to be chaste: one must be seen to be so'.

Fénelon personifies three levels of love in three nymphs on the island of Cyprus: Calypso, representing the carnal affections – passionate, sensual, culpable; Eucharis, representing a tender, eager attachment which could exist, however, within the bounds of Christian morality; and Antiope, typifying the *mariage de convenance*, something dutiful and chaste and to be entered into only with parental consent. This was, of course, the normal arrangement for members of the royal family.

Telemachus, who had fallen deeply in love with Eucharis, responds to the call of duty and sees her no more. 'But for Antiope', he admits, 'I have no such feelings. This love is not passionate; it is a taste for someone; it is esteem; it is a feeling that I would be happy to pass my life with her.' But he needed the consent of Ulysses. In the event, Louis de Bourgogne married 'Antiope', but his relationship with her contained a strong element of Eucharis and perhaps even a touch of 'Calypso'.

Towards the end of the year 1698, when the duc de Bourgogne had reached the age of sixteen, Louis decided that the time had come to initiate him into the various aspects of the art of war. To this end he laid on a series of military manoeuvres, on a very large scale, based on a camp in the vicinity of Compiègne.

The young Louis was to be the titular commander, or *Chef de l'Armée* – in sartorial terms 'il portait l'écharpe blanche'. But in fact the maréchal de Boufflers had oversight of the whole operation. He rose magnificently to the situation, according to the chevalier de Quincy; 'he kept open table from morning till evening', employing 72 cooks and 340 domestic servants.

The young Louis set himself to the task with ardour. First he went into training. 'The duc de Bourgogne', noted Dangeau, 'went to Maisons and back on foot in order to accustom himself to marching at the head of the troops which he was to command at the camp.' The King himself designated the troops which were to participate. Fifty battalions, each made up of 700 men; fifty-two squadrons of cavalry, each made up of 50 men; forty pieces of artillery, six mortars and eight pontoons – some 60,000 men in all.

The particular tasks which the young Louis was to learn were listed by the King: 'the way in which orders are issued; the distribution of bread, meat and fodder; the setting up of a hospital; the business of foraging; the dividing of an army into two halves, a skirmish, a cannonade, the fording of a river, a general combat, the setting up of a siege, the assault and capitulation of a stronghold and, lastly, the retreat of an army in three columns without any confusion or disorder'. Although this was not the first of Louis' camps it was on a far larger scale than any of the previous ones. It had a secondary purpose which was political. The death of Carlos II of Spain was thought to be imminent, and with it the possible partitioning of his empire, and Louis, according to de Quincy, 'wanting to show the Spanish that he alone, the King of France, was in a position to prevent this dismemberment, deemed it necessary to make this demonstration before the whole world of his magnificence and power'. The camp at Compiègne took place a month before the terms of the partition treaty were drawn up.

So far as the Court was concerned, anyone who wanted to come could do so. The problem of lodging them was the main difficulty. Compared with the other palaces to which the courtiers were accustomed, Compiègne had little to offer in the way of accommodation or comfort. Louis had been heard to say that at Versailles he was lodged like a King; at Fontaine-bleau like a Prince; and at Compiègne like a peasant. It must not be forgotten, however, that the courtiers who had followed the King on previous campaigns – such as the Grande Mademoiselle – had shown themselves prepared to occupy the houses of genuine peasants. Even Saint-Simon did not complain of having to share a room with another duke.

Mme de Maintenon, however, appears to have been a reluctant guest. 'It seems to me', she wrote to the Archbishop of Paris, 'that some charitable assembly would be more fitting for me – but *One* [the King, of course] wishes to have everything as it suits him.'

Everything went according to plan – except the weather. 'Never has the month of September been so atrocious,' wrote de Quincy; 'it did not stop raining for one single day during the twenty-one that we were there.' Dangeau observed of the duc de Bourgogne that 'all the works and all the attacks gave him great pleasure and were most instructive for him'. When it came to siegecraft, the young Louis made his engineers explain all the details of mounting a siege and showed his concern for the workers by ordering a distribution of beer.

The siege was to be that of Compiègne itself. The long rampart, which is now the terrace of the Château, offered front-row, dress-circle seats for the spectators. One of the most assiduous of these was the duchesse de Bourgogne. It was a new experience for her and she was a lover of novelty. 'I would never have believed, my dear Grandmama, that I would find myself in a besieged town and woken in the morning by the sound of cannons, as I was this morning . . . I am getting a truly great pleasure out of it all.'

The culmination of the whole operation was the *bataille rangée* – a mock full-scale encounter. The opposing force was commanded by Conrad, marquis de Rosen, a Swede formerly in the service of Queen Christina. Although not yet a maréchal de France, he was regarded as the most experienced of Louis' lieutenant-generals. He was determined to make the whole occasion as realistic as possible and refused to beat the retreat until positively ordered by the King. Louis commented: 'Rosen does not relish playing the part of the defeated.' As for the duc de Bourgogne, the whole operation was a triumphant success. He had given proof of his manhood.

He had not, however, as yet consummated his marriage. Neither one of the young couple seemed to be in a hurry, but the decision as to when this was to be permitted lay with Louis alone. The event had to be preceded by a reconstruction and a rearrangement of the Duke's apartment

at Versailles. These rooms have since been replaced by the Petits Appartements de Marie-Antoinette. They connected directly with the Queen's
bedroom, which, since there was no Queen, was his wife's.

Work started in July 1699. It was not completed until the end of
October. The 'first night' was treated rather as some official occasion
of the Court. The Grand Maître des Cérémonies, the baron de Breteuil,
was closest to the event and it is from his memoirs that many of the
details are known. He first records that Louis mentioned at the *petit
coucher* that when the news had been conveyed to Marie-Adélaïde, some
five days earlier, 'her threatened modesty brought tears to her eyes'.

The event was timed for the return of the Court from Fontainebleau to
Versailles on 22 October. Marie-Adélaïde spent the evening as usual with
Mme de Maintenon, but went to her own room at about ten o'clock,
which was so unexpectedly early that some of her ladies were not yet
present. Soon afterwards Breteuil, in his capacity as Master of Ceremonies,
went to conduct the young Duke to his wife's bedroom. 'His hair was
well curled and the magnificence of his *déshabillé* and generally well-
groomed appearance were suggestive of the wedding night. He left his
room in a manner brave and bright, and, since I had the honour of
carrying his candle, I conducted him to the door of the battlefield.' All
this happened so quickly that Louis, who had expressed his intention of
coming privately to see them into their bed, arrived too late and did not
go in.

It seems probable that the real relationship between Marie-Adélaïde
and the young Louis dates from about this time. In the early days she
had shown little interest in her husband. In her not very copious correspondence with Turin the duc de Bourgogne himself merits only a single
mention – and that of no importance.

It is in the nature of things that the relationship between a young royal
couple should be of consuming interest to the gossips of the Court: it is
in the nature of gossips that their interest in a marriage decreases in direct
proportion to its happiness. Had the duc de Bourgogne and his wife
outlived Louis XIV, France would have had the somewhat rare spectacle
of a King and a Queen who were in love with each other. It seems that it
was more passionate on his side than on hers, and on her side there was
a fondness of the sort which is increased by absence.

Two of the most convincing accounts of the marriage come from
Dangeau, who had been close to Marie-Adélaïde since her betrothal. At
the very beginning of 1701 the young Duke was returning from the
Spanish frontier after he had accompanied his brother, the duc d'Anjou,
thither to claim the Spanish throne. 'Madame la duchesse de Bourgogne',
records Dangeau, 'had her dinner taken through to Mme de Maintenon's

apartment, although Mme de Maintenon was not there, because from her rooms one can see right down the avenue [de Paris] and she wanted to have the pleasure of seeing the arrival of M. le duc de Bourgogne from afar off. As soon as she saw him in the avenue she went to await him in the King's apartment. It would be impossible to witness a greater joy than that which they both exhibited on seeing each other ... That evening the King sent them to bed the moment after they came into his cabinet.' In the following year the young Duke returned from his first campaign. He arrived at Versailles the day before he was expected, a little before midnight just as the courtiers were leaving the *coucher*. He and the King embraced each other tenderly and then Louis said: 'Go quickly to the duchesse de Bourgogne who is waiting for you with the greatest impatience.'

The same mutual affection is at once apparent in their letters to each other. Their correspondence during the summer of 1703, when the young Louis was at the siege of Breisach, began with a disappointment. On 12 June he wrote to express his astonishment at how seldom he received a letter from his wife. 'I was really angry yesterday evening to have no letters in the ordinary delivery from Franche-Comté.' On 3 July his tone was very different. She had written to him using her own blood as ink. 'I cannot wait for a single moment before replying to you, and far from having heart-ache at the adorable blood which I received, I kissed it a thousand times ... I have just drawn some of mine to send to you.'

Their love was, however, the attraction of opposites. The abbé de Proyart, in his biography of the Duke, states the case thus: 'they never agree on any subject, but their hearts are always united. I do not know if there have ever been seen two characters so unlike who love each other so tenderly.'

By the turn of the century Marie-Adélaïde was, by the standards of her own age, a young woman. She had been accorded the title of duchesse de Bourgogne on her arrival in France, but it was now that she really entered into her position at Court. Saint-Simon gives us one of his brilliant little pen portraits.

She combined in her person qualities which are not often found together. There was an elegance, a dignity and a nobility in the way she carried herself and the way in which she held her head – 'un port de tête galant, gracieux, majestueux'. When she walked she moved like a goddess walking upon the clouds – 'une marche de déesse sur les nuées'. But in this grace and grandeur there was no hint of pride or pompousness. It was combined with a simplicity and an almost naive charm – 'un air simple et naturel ... elle plaisait au dernier point'.

It was the result of a complete lack of self-consciousness. She had that great gift, which all royal personages should pray for, the ability to appear to be exclusively interested in the person to whom they are speaking – 'on était tenté de la croire toute uniquement à celle avec qui elle se trouvait'. If there had ever before been such a presence in the Court of France it was her grandmother, Henriette-Anne d'Angleterre, whom she resembled chiefly in her desire to give pleasure to all – 'elle voulait plaire aux personnes les plus inutiles et les plus médiocres'.

The impact of such a presence upon a crowded ante-room was like that of a gust of wind over a cornfield – 'comme un tourbillon qui remplit plusieurs lieux à la fois et qui y donne le mouvement et la vie'.

Seen at closer quarters, Marie-Adélaïde was almost ugly. The bust of her by Coysevox bears out the frank admission of Saint-Simon – baggy cheeks, the forehead too prominent, an insignificant nose, thick lips and a rotten set of teeth. She did not conform to the rules of beauty – 'régulièrement laide', asserted Saint-Simon. The sculptor was obliged to reproduce these features faithfully. The painter would have had wider scope. Her skin and complexion were really beautiful; her eyebrows and her hair were of a lovely chestnut brown. But for the artist of the pen portrait there are even further lengths to which he can go. For it was in the movement of her expression that beauty shone forth. It was the smile, both on her lips and in her eyes, which made one forget the lack of regular beauty. It was the expression of her personality – 'les yeux les plus parlants et les plus beaux du monde . . . la sourire la plus expressive'. It was this combination of charm and vivacity which qualified Marie-Adélaïde to become the animating spirit of the Court.

Without interesting herself particularly in architecture, she was the source of a great rejuvenation in the heart of the King which found its expression in the redecoration of much of Versailles in the year 1701. First the Ménagerie was enlarged to form a little private residence for Marie-Adélaïde. Mansart was instructed to draw up the plans and, as usual, Louis noted his comments in the margins; they are most significant. 'It seems to me that there is something to be changed,' he observed of the decorations, 'that the subjects are too serious and that there must be youth mingled with what is done.' In another directive he struck the same note: 'Il faut de l'enfance répandue partout.' That was to be the key-note of the new style at Versailles.

These youthful figures also invaded the ante-room adjoining the King's Bedroom. The whole suite overlooking the Cour de Marbre was rearranged and redecorated at the beginning of the century. The old bedroom and its ante-room were joined into one large salon which takes its name from the oval window above the cornice – the Salon de l'Oeil de Boeuf. The two rooms were of different heights and to resolve this problem the coving of the ceiling was of two tiers. The lower tier provided the opportunity for a decorative frieze of considerable depth of which the happiest use was made. Louis himself determined what the subjects were to be: *Jeux d'Enfants*. Six sculptors, of which the best known was Van Clève, worked, in a special studio fitted up for the purpose in the Orangerie, on the realisation of this command. Together they produced a masterpiece. The playing boys form a sort of garland to the ceiling and the flowing lines of their scant garments endow the room with an almost Grecian elegance. The figures are not just the fat-buttocked babies so dear to the eighteenth-century artist, but are of varying ages and height, the tallest of them already partaking of the slender elegance of youth.

At Fontainebleau changes were made at the same time of a very different nature. Louis undertook a certain amount of bowdlerisation of the paintings. In 1701 he gave orders 'during the visit to Fontainebleau to abolish two of the pictures in the Galerie [François I] in which the postures were somewhat irregular and have placed there two others by Boulogne le Jeune of decent subjects taken from the *Metamorphoses*'. There was another painting – *Les Amours de Jupiter et Semélé* – in the little projecting cabinet which marked the centre of the gallery on the north side. This painting, 'jugée impudique', was also removed by Louis and replaced by a more proper allegory of Minerva and the Arts by Boulogne. This puritanism may have been due to the influence of Mme de Maintenon. There is no evidence, however, that she interested herself in the new style at Versailles.

It was at Marly that this new influence was chiefly felt. The Comptes des Bâtiments reveal the years 1699, 1701 and 1703 as those of greatest activity, the total often surpassing that for the year at Versailles. 'Another block of lodgings is being made here,' sighed Mme de Maintenon; 'Marly will soon be a second Versailles.' Whatever influence she had upon her husband, she never succeeded in curbing his passion for architecture.

In the gardens, hitherto devoted to impressive scenic effects, a lighter note was struck in the creation of the Bois de la Princesse – named in honour of Marie-Adélaïde – and the multiplication of outdoor amusements. The new bosquet heralded a new style of garden design, for in and out of the straight alleys, which were still held to be *de rigueur,* little tortuous paths wandered with the completest inconsequence, opening unpredictably into little *cabinets de verdure*. In one of these a charming miniature temple was placed to give shelter in case of rain. It was made up of two semicircular benches beneath a blue dome supported on marble columns, and the whole painted inside like trellis-work, powdered with birds and flowers. It was the work of Bellin de Fontenoy and Louis was so delighted with his achievement that he granted him a special bonus.

Besides the Bois de la Princesse, a number of new amusements were installed. There were two courses laid out for *mail*, one round the Bosquets de Marly and the other up at the south end of the Rivière. *Mail* is a relative of golf. The course was in the shape of a long horseshoe and lined with boards. One tried to drive the ball round in the minimum number of strokes. More exciting was the *Roulette*. A steep incline, starting near the Reservoir du Trou d'Enfer at the southern extremity of the gardens, had been equipped with a sort of switchback railway on which ran a toboggan, richly carved and gilded, in which the Duchess could descend at exhilarating speed into the valley below. The spirit of informality was everywhere apparent. Marie-Adélaïde collected carp of the most beautiful colours for the fish-ponds. She gave them each a name and claimed that they answered to it; she and her ladies went for a swing on the *Escarpolette*; they walked up into the forest or went down to the river to bathe.

As often as not the comparative intimacy of the surroundings and the relative freedom from etiquette brought out the worst in them. The princesses smoked pipes, composed obscene verses and not infrequently indulged in horse-play, none of it in the best taste. Their behaviour did not pass unrebuked. Amid these scenes of a sometimes juvenile but rejuvenated Court moved the dignified figure of Madame, carrying beneath her capacious bustle 'the imposing rotundity of a part which shall be nameless'. She observed with rising indignation the duchesse de Bourgogne walking arm in arm with her ladies, men remaining seated in the presence of the Dauphin and covered before the King. She could not forbear from remarking: 'It no longer bears the slightest resemblance to a Court.' Those invited were becoming more numerous.

The spirit of informality soon spread to Versailles. It really began with the carnival of the year 1700. It was a period of uninhibited abandonment to pleasure; as the marquis de Coulanges wrote to Mme de Grignan: 'It is the King's wish that the duchesse de Bourgogne shall do whatever she wants from morning until night ... It is all visits to Marly, visits to Meudon, comings and goings to and from Paris for operas, balls and masquerades.' Everyone was striving to gain the good graces of the young princess. It was all enormously expensive. Dress materials were anything from 100 to 150 francs a yard, and to have worn a dress more than once would have been to invite ridicule. The *Mercure de France* for that period reads rather like a modern fashion magazine.

Naturally all eyes were upon the latest creation for the duchesse de Bourgogne. She was often in fancy dress – now appearing as Flora with a train of attendant nymphs, now in the simplicity of a milkmaid, now in the gorgeous finery of a Sultana, now dancing the *entrée* for a village wedding procession – everywhere she was acclaimed with rapture.

Not only was it ruinously expensive – it was utterly exhausting. Saint-Simon claims that for three weeks they never saw the daylight. 'I was delighted by the arrival of Ash Wednesday.' Marie-Adélaïde, on the contrary, found the carnival far too short and declared that the next year it would start in October. She cannot have meant it seriously, but it brought a rebuke to Mme de Maintenon from the Cardinal de Noailles.

All this hectic hedonism must have posed problems to the duc de Bourgogne. The austerities of Lent were more to his taste. What the courtiers cannot have failed to notice was his careful avoidance of the young ladies. 'He pictured himself in the Court', wrote the abbé Proyart, 'as if he were in the middle of that island of voluptuousness [described in *Télémaque*] of which his beloved Mentor [Fénelon] had underlined the dangers. He was forever on his guard against the insidious invitations of those treacherous nymphs who rivalled each other to obtain the glory of having triumphed over the virtue of the son of Ulysses.' As Madame puts it: 'Never has such prudery been seen.'

Four of the formative years, from 1697 to 1701, when the young Louis was between the ages of fifteen and nineteen, were just those during which Fénelon was exiled from him. It was the duc de Beauvilliers who exerted the strongest religious influence – and Beauvilliers was a puritan. Fénelon maintained a slightly anxious correspondence with him about their former charge. 'If he were to commit some serious fault, may he feel that he has in you an open heart, like a port in a storm.' On another occasion he wrote: 'Piety is something agreeable, accommodating, simple, exact; firm without being harsh.'

It seems as if the duc de Bourgogne's religion had not so much transformed his nature as diverted his impetuosity into new and very different channels. He was not one to do things by halves. His long retreats into the sanctuary of his study may well have included an element of escapism. Temptation might not have been the only experience which he avoided encountering.

In 1701 Fénelon and his pupil were able to take up their correspondence again. The Preceptor, however, had clearly been kept well informed. 'Do not make long prayers', he advised, 'but pray a little in the name of God, every morning and secretly.' The young Duke's reply was full of self-abasement and self-reproach. 'Redouble your prayers for me,' he insisted; 'I have more need of them than ever, being always as weak as I am and miserable. I become more and more aware of this every day.'

Fénelon's answer was to dwell on the love of God. 'This love does not demand of all Christians the austerities, such as those practised by the hermits of old, nor their profound solitude nor their contemplations.' Christianity does not require the separation of one's self from God's creation. This world provides the stepping-stones to Heaven.

This obvious concern to temper the spirit of self-abnegation in the young prince does not appear to have entirely achieved its object. Madame, who was one of those people in whose eyes religion is desirable provided that it is not taken to extremes, spoke her mind on the subject. 'I am convinced', she wrote in December 1704, 'that when the duc de Bourgogne comes into power, bigotry will rule. It is unheard of that a man of the Duke's age should be devout to such a degree. He receives Communion every Sunday and every Saint's Day; he fasts – and it is pitiful to see; he is as thin as a rake.' Even Mme de Maintenon was prepared to qualify her approval of the young man's devoutness. In July 1706, she wrote: 'Monsieur le duc de Bourgogne is filled with piety, love and scrupulosity, but he becomes more reasonable every day.'

This scrupulosity was beginning to disturb his confessor, Père Martineau. In his eyes it made the heir to the throne 'unable to act on his own, so that there are times when he does not know which course to take'. Lack of self-confidence, which can sometimes be mistaken for humility, caused him always to seek advice but often prevented him from acting upon it. 'This ignorance, the fear and the lack of judgement', observed Saint-Simon, 'which always accompanies devoutness in its early days, made him over-zealous in reacting against his faults and inspired in him an austerity which was overdone.' The long hours spent by the young Duke with his confessor caused Saint-Simon to fear that one day the role of confessor would become the most important in the Council of the King, and 'to think with anguish that the business of the Council would no longer be separable from theology'.

25
Spain

As the seventeenth century drew towards its close the eyes of all Europe were focused on Spain. It was a dying country with a dying King. There was no heir to the throne whose claim could not be disputed.

Henry Kamen, who has written a recent and well-documented account of the situation, gives a number of quotations from French and Venetian ambassadors which all tell the same tale. In May 1689, François de Rébenac reported: 'if one examines the government of this monarchy at close quarters, one will find it in an excessive state of disorder . . . Enlightened people agree that the government of the House of Austria is leading them inevitably into total ruin.' Ten years earlier Girolamo Zeno assured the Venetian Senate that 'the ancient valour of Spaniards has perished. Consumed by idleness, they live as they please.' His successors at the embassy added their own disparagements. 'The whole of the present reign has been an uninterrupted series of calamities' – 'It is incomprehensible how this monarchy survives.'

Such was the Kingdom to which Carlos II had succeeded in 1665. He was four years old at the time and was the product of a marriage that was a mixture of inbreeding and incest. Philip IV had married Princess Maria-Anna of Austria, his sister's daughter, whose father was also a Habsburg. He was forty-four at the time and his bride fourteen. It was twelve years before they produced Carlos. He was weak in body and feeble in mind. When he came to the throne he was still being breast-fed and was unable to walk. At the age of nine he could neither read nor write. For some time the only words that he could pronounce were *Cubrios vos* – *couvrez-vous*. They were at least among the most important words of Spanish etiquette. The Grandee had the right to keep his hat on in the presence of the King.

When he was twenty-five the papal nuncio gave a pen portrait of him. 'The King', he wrote, 'is frail, not badly formed; his face is on the whole ugly; he has a long neck, a broad face and chin, with the typical Habsburg lower lip . . . He has a melancholic and faintly surprised look . . . He is as weak in body as in mind. Now and then he gives signs of intelligence, but not at present; usually he shows himself slow and indifferent, torpid and indolent and seems to be stupefied. One can do with him what one wishes because he lacks his own will.' Kamen completes the picture. 'For most of his reign he did not attend Council meetings, did not confer with ministers and did not countersign Council deliberations, which were usually approved by a minister . . . It is possible that he did not make a single important decision throughout his reign. The government lacked an effective head.'

The monopoly of power was therefore in the hands of the higher aristocracy – the Grandees. Cardinal Porto-Carrero, Archbishop of Toledo, writing to Torcy in 1703, stated: 'In the last few years of the reign of the late King our Lord Carlos II, the nobility were brought up without any application, in pure idleness, accustomed to the fact that, with the aid of the Palace . . . they could obtain the principal employments in military and political government, without knowledge or experience or merit of their own, exercising these appointments thereafter with ambition, pride and self-interest, so that the natural results of this unhappy procedure were repeated ill successes, squandering of the Treasury and the ruin of the State.'

Besides the Grandees a large proportion of the population was classified as 'noble'. The lowest rank – the 'hidalgos' – had no other apparent title to nobility than the right to carry arms. The French traveller Muret noted with amusement that 'the cobbler wears a sword when he is mending shoes, the barber when he is shaving, the apothecary when he is dispensing'. But even the Grandees were far from being rich. In 1681 the Venetian ambassador Frederico Cornaro reported: 'There is hardly a Grandee who does not live off the King's treasury or who, in the absence of royal pensions, could keep himself on his own income.'

The Spanish were becoming insulated from the rest of Europe. In the past there had been a sort of international brotherhood of scholars. Ideas passed quickly and easily from one country to another. Of seventeenth-century Spain Kamen comments: 'The foreign observers were correct to note that Spain had lost touch with world scholarship. This happened because of the rarity of creative contact with foreigners and because of the policy of censorship . . . The siege mentality which typified the "closed society" of Habsburg Spain induced the authorities to treat all non-Spanish influences as suspect.'

Rather like the Nazi regime in 1930s Germany, the Spanish Inquisition was as much concerned for purity of blood as for purity of doctrine. This fits with the treatment as suspect of all that was not Spanish. By the late seventeenth century it was a relatively moderate organisation. In the *autos da fé* of 1691, nevertheless, thirty-seven *conversos* were burnt at the stake. The Inquisition seldom took the initiative in prosecution. It worked largely on denunciations made by neighbours and relations. It existed for the protection of orthodoxy rather than for its enforcement. Kamen refers to the 'deep-rooted and officially encouraged distrust of all things foreign. The phrase *tierra de herejes* [a heretical country] keeps recurring in the papers of the Inquisition.' A notary in Barcelona was accused, in 1689, of visiting such a country. The country was France.

It was in Spain that the belief in the Immaculate Conception first took hold. Philip IV tried to persuade Rome to adopt this doctrine, but it was not until 1696 that the Immaculate Conception was even allowed the status of a second-class rite. Perhaps with an eye to the growing likelihood that the next King of Spain would be French, a diplomatic attempt was made to obtain Louis' support for the doctrine. Dangeau notes, on 27 October 1699: 'In the morning the King gave a private audience to the ambassador from Spain. He strongly urged His Majesty to establish in his kingdom the Immaculate Conception of the Virgin.' Carlos II included in his will a plea to his successor to pursue this cause.

The last will and testament of King Carlos was to be the most significant diplomatic document of the turn of the century, for it was in his power to decide the future of the vast possessions of the Spanish Crown.

In June 1690 Spain joined the Grand Alliance against France. The Duke of Villahermosa had just been appointed Viceroy and took the trouble to make a tour of places of military significance. Gerona, the most important fortress in Catalonia, he described as being 'in the most miserable state conceivable since, like the other fortresses in the principality, it lacks everything'. Here, as elsewhere, he found the defences in ruins, the artillery out of action and soldiers reduced to begging in the streets. The Intendant of Rousillon, Raymond de Trobat, writing to Louvois after the capture of Camprodon, assured him that 'it is almost unbelievable to see the state in which the Spaniards kept this fortress . . . The barracks are like a pigsty.'

The French, using their new *galiotes à bombes*, attacked Barcelona and then Alicante, causing very considerable destruction. The high-trajectory mortar not only made possible the mass destruction of built-up areas, but it could inflict unprecedented casualties on civilians.

These savage attacks did much to unite Spain. Louis XIV was regarded as the country's most dangerous enemy – and yet there existed what Kamen calls 'a reluctant admiration for France' in Madrid. Sir William Godolphin, when he was ambassador to Spain, had made the observation:

'there is nothing which the people of this country ... abhors more than war with France. I have heard people say that a war between them and France would be very unnatural, the French King being next in succession to this crown, and by all the notices I have of the present temper of this people I am persuaded that, if the young king dies as things now stand, they would tamely go into the obedience of France.'

It was not to prove quite so simple. The question of the Spanish Succession was to dominate the diplomacy of most of Europe. England, Holland and Austria were all deeply concerned – and of course Spain. In the late summer of 1693 Carlos became seriously ill and on 14 September he signed a will leaving the whole of his inheritance to the infant Prince Elector Joseph-Ferdinand of Bavaria. It was arguably the best choice at the time.

Louis stood firm by the doctrine of divine right which included the principle of heredity. He applied it to the question of the Spanish Succession and he applied it in his continued support of James II and his son and his consequent reluctance to recognise William III and Mary II, Anne or George of Hanover as sovereigns of Britain. But with the claims to the Spanish throne there were a number of complications.

Unlike the crown of France, that of Spain could pass through the female line. Had this not been so there would have been no heirs to the throne of Spain on the death of Carlos II. The genealogy of the situation is fairly straightforward. Philip IV's sister, Anne of Austria, had married Louis XIII and was Louis XIV's mother. Philip IV had three children: Carlos II, Marie-Thérèse, the elder daughter, who married Louis XIV, and Marguerite-Thérèse, who married the Emperor Leopold I. They had a daughter, Maria-Antonia, who married Max-Emmanuel, Elector of Bavaria. *They* had a son, the Prince Electoral Joseph-Ferdinand, to whom Carlos left the Spanish crown in 1693. By merely genealogical rules, however, Louis XIV had the best claim.

This genealogy, however, was complicated by renunciations. Anne of Austria had renounced her claim on marrying Louis XIII. Marie-Thérèse had renounced her claim on marrying Louis XIV. Louis claimed that Marie-Thérèse's renunciation was conditional upon the payment of a large dowry. As the dowry was never paid, he argued, the condition remained unfulfilled and the renunciation was null and void. The acceptance of this argument would have made Marie-Thérèse's son, the Grand Dauphin, the undoubted heir. He had three sons and could pass on his claim to either of the younger two. There were less grounds for rejecting the renunciation by Anne of Austria except by stating that no princess had the right to deprive her prospective sons of their inheritance.

From the Spanish point of view there was an understandable desire to keep the inheritance undivided. This meant that the whole would go to the French or the Bavarian or the Austrian candidate.

The alternative to this was a partitioning of the somewhat scattered elements of the Spanish possessions. France had much to gain from a partition treaty which might give her, for instance, the Spanish Netherlands and Luxembourg, which would make a lot more sense of France's eastern frontier. The acquisition of Milan, Naples and Sicily would cut into the encirclement of France by a Habsburg hegemony.

Owing to the intransigence of William III, however, Louis had to be content with much less than that. On 15 July 1698, Louis wrote to Tallard, who was in charge of his negotiations in London. He favoured continuing the negotiations. 'In breaking with the Prince we would indirectly force him to enter into relations with Bavaria and the other princes of the Empire. With a league formed before the death of the King of Spain it would be impossible for me to assert the legitimate rights of my son to this succession ... without causing a new war as great as the last one.' Although he was optimistic about his chances of winning, he did not relish the prospect of war. 'Nothing is more assured than the calamities which it would bring in its wake, and than the sufferings of the peoples, and after having sacrificed such great gains in order to give my subjects peace, no interest seems to me to be more urgent than that of preserving the tranquillity which they now enjoy.' As Mark Thomson comments: 'That is not the language of pride or reckless ambition, but of humanity and realistic statesmanship.'

The terms of the partition treaty, as drawn up in October 1698, named Joseph-Ferdinand as principal heir to the Spanish throne. But it would have separated the Spanish from their Italian possessions, which were to be divided between Austria and France. The Spanish were predictably indignant at this breaking up of their empire.

On 6 February 1699, however, the little Joseph-Ferdinand died. The succession now became a straight issue in the first instance between France and Austria, with Savoy in third place. Maria-Antonia of Bavaria renounced her claim in favour of her half-brothers, Joseph and Charles, the Emperor Leopold's sons by his third wife, Leonora von Neuberg – this was never accepted by Spain.

The partition treaty was signed by the Dutch at the end of May 1700. William said that he had 'made a treaty to avoid war and did not intend to go to war to implement the treaty'. Austria still refused to sign. Louis wrote: 'The share that I give to the Archduke is so great that [considering] the power that I have to sustain the just rights of my son, one would have difficulty understanding that I should leave such important states to the House of Austria if I had not already made it known that the conservation of the general peace is the first aim that I put before myself.' One never knows the degree of sincerity in a diplomatic statement. That was Louis' official position.

Carlos had lost his wife, Marie-Louise d'Orléans, in March 1689, and had married Maria-Anna von Neuburg, sister of the Empress of Austria. Their father became the Elector Palatine. The family was strongly anti-French. In view of the devastations of the Palatinate by Louis, this was to be expected. Had Carlos and Maria-Anna produced a son or a daughter, the whole problem of the Spanish Succession would have disappeared. But they did not – which, under the circumstances, was hardly surprising. 'It would be a piece of luck for the whole of Europe', wrote Liselotte on 1 October 1699, 'if the Queen of Spain could have a child; a boy or a girl would be equally good if only there were a child and it remained alive. One does not have to be a prophet to see that war is inevitable if the King of Spain should die without heirs.'

The party supporting the French candidature was led by Louis' ambassador at Madrid, the marquis d'Harcourt, but the Spanish, who were not without their pride, were deliberating about their own answer to the problem. Voltaire brings this out in his *Siècle de Louis XIV*. 'The Cardinal Porto-Carrero, Archbishop of Toledo, the Count of Monterey and other Spanish Grandees wanted to save their country. They got together to forestall the dismembering of the monarchy. Their hatred of the German government strengthened in their minds the needs of the State and rendered a service to the Court of France without their knowing it. They persuaded King Carlos to give preference to a grandson of Louis XIV rather than to a prince remote from them who was in no position to defend them.' The proximity of France and the reputation of its army, and above all its navy, gave it the character of protector.

The interpretation of the renunciation by Maria-Antonia implicit in this stance was regarded by the Spanish as a vindication of the rights of the blood, and it guaranteed the preservation of the Spanish empire undivided. The King, sick as he was, wrote to Pope Innocent XII to consult his opinion. 'Being obliged to appoint an heir to the Spanish crown from a foreign country, we find such great obscurity in the law of succession . . . that we are unable to form a settled determination. We are anxious to act rightly, and we have recourse to Your Holiness, as to an infallible guide, entreating you to consult with the cardinals and divines whom you judge to be most able and sincere, to decide by the rules of equity.'

On 16 July, the Pope replied, supporting his claim to integrity with the imminent prospect of his own death, 'being in a situation similar to that of His Catholic Majesty, on the point of appearing at the judgement seat of Christ'. Carlos, he said, 'ought not to put the interests of the House of Austria in competition with those of Eternity . . . neither should you be ignorant that the children of the Dauphin are the rightful heirs of the crown and that in opposition to them, neither the Archduke, nor any member of the Austrian family, has the smallest legitimate pretension'.

The Pope, comments Voltaire, 'who thought he saw in the weakening of the House of Austria the freedom of Italy, wrote to the King that "the laws of Spain, and, indeed, of Christianity, required that he should give preference to the House of France" '.

Towards the end of July Saint-Simon records an event which had no connection with the Spanish Succession. Louis was obliged, after all, to continue conducting the affairs of State and this particular incident is of interest because of the light which it throws on the way Louis exercised his royal power.

'At about the same time' (27 July 1700) 'the King did something which he did only five or six times in his life. The Chapter of Chartres was totally independent of its Bishop. It had full authority in the Cathedral where the Bishop could not officiate without its permission except on rare, specified occasions . . . It owned a large territory in which there was a great number of parishes, which formed a little diocese of its own, where the Bishop could do nothing, and a number of very strange rights directly incompatible with the hierarchy. One of these strange rights obliged the Seigneur de Maintenon to present to the Chapter on the Feast of the Assumption one sparrow hawk.

'Godet des Marais, Bishop of Chartres, and one who carried out very assiduously and very religiously all his duties, found his path blocked in a thousand ways. In the close relationship which he had with the King and Mme de Maintenon he tried to make the Chapter see reason about these rights, so contrary to usage, but without inducing them to listen to any moderation. He had hopes in his patience and returned to the charge from time to time, but always without any success . . . In the end he resorted to legal prosecution. He knew perfectly well that he could not succeed, but the moment the proceedings started he appealed to the judgement of the King. A commission was set up under the chairmanship of a Maître des Requêtes. But the usurpation was so ancient, so often confirmed by a Pope or a King, that the commission maintained the cause of the Chapter.

'The King', continues Saint-Simon, 'let them say all that they wanted without exhibiting any impatience or partiality. When everyone had finished he said: "Messieurs, I have fully understood the matter and your opinions on all of it; but your opinion is not mine, and I find religion, reason, good order and the hierarchy so damaged by the usurpations of the Chapter, that I will on this occasion, contrary to my usual custom, make use of my right of decision. I pronounce, at all times and in all places, in favour of the Bishop of Chartres."

'The astonishment was general; they all looked at each other. The Chancellor, who disliked the Bishop of Chartres . . . made certain representations. The King listened to him and then said that he would persist.'

Louis exhibited, in this case, not only an authoritarianism, which Saint-Simon states was rare, but also a readiness to use it in the service of common sense, which he stated in his memoirs was the primary requirement of government. Godet des Marais, according to Saint-Simon 'a great and saintly Bishop', sought only to restore good relationships with his Chapter, which he succeeded in doing by his moderation and 'by the esteem which it was impossible to refuse him'.

Meanwhile events in Europe were moving towards a climax. On 20 October Louis wrote to Villars stating once more that his chief objective was to maintain peace, but adding that 'if the Emperor should resort to armed force before the death of Carlos he ought not to think that my forces will remain unused. I have reason to believe that, joined by my allies, it will be enough to maintain the complete execution of the treaty . . . It is up to the Emperor to prevent this choice by accepting the treaty.'

On 1 November, Louis wrote to his ambassador in Constantinople: 'For some time the health of the King of Spain has been reduced to such an extremity that the news of his death is already spread about, but even though he lives the peril seems the same and the events foreseen by the treaty are on the point of happening.' He then repeats his intention of resorting to force. 'Everything is prepared in such a manner that . . . I can confront those who wish to oppose the execution of the treaty. My troops are on the frontiers of Spain and I have sent the marquis d'Harcourt as commander. I have others on the Rhine front and I have others in Dauphiné and Provence. My ships are armed at Toulon and ready to sail at my order.'

It was the time of the annual Voyage de Fontainebleau. The Court went, in the first place, to enjoy the magnificent facilities for hunting afforded by the surrounding forest, but there was something more relaxed about the atmosphere which made a pleasant change after Versailles. For the King, of course, business had to be as usual, but Dangeau's journal makes it clear that he managed to hunt most days. But this particular visit was overshadowed by the imminent prospect of the death of King Carlos and the agonising uncertainty about whom he would designate as his successor to the vast possessions of the crown of Spain.

On Saturday 25 September, according to Dangeau, 'a courier arrived from Blécourt [the French chargé d'affaires], despatched from Madrid on the 15th. Blécourt had declared to the King of Spain that if he allowed the troops of the Emperor to enter any of his States ... for any reason whatever, the King would regard that as an infringement of the peace. The Spanish Council replied, in the name of the Catholic King, that he had enough troops and in sufficiently good condition not to have need of any foreign help, but that they would in no circumstances accept any from the Emperor.' There may have been more of Spanish pride than of accuracy in that statement. Most of the evidence suggests that Spanish forces were few and in poor condition. But the agreement was reassuring.

A week later there came more letters. 'The news received by private individuals from Madrid about the health of the King of Spain is very bad; they say that he is declining every day. We have large numbers of troops and magazines', adds Dangeau, 'and there are neither troops nor magazines in any of the Spanish territory.' On Saturday 9 October, it looked as if the anxious period would soon be at an end. 'At the King's *lever* we learnt of the extremity in which the King of Spain was. When the last despatch from Blécourt left Madrid he had received all the sacraments. The doctors have abandoned him and even the Queen had quitted his chamber.'

Unfortunately the information was not always accurate. On 12 October 'M. de Torcy came to tell the King that he had passed a courier from the Elector Palatine on his way from Madrid; his envoy from that country informs him that the King of Spain had died on the second of this month.' Hopes must have been high at Fontainebleau until another despatch sent on the same day assured Louis that Carlos was feeling better.

Meanwhile the life of the Court pursued its even course. Louis went shooting in the morning, or followed the hounds in his little *calèche* accompanied by the duchesse de Bourgogne; the Dauphin rode off with his wolf-hounds; the regular Councils were held in Mme de Maintenon's apartment. In the evening there was a comedy, or gambling or the reception for all known as an *Appartement*.

On Saturday 6 November, the King took out his stag-hounds; the duchesse de Bourgogne went with him. They returned only at nightfall. 'On his return the King told us he had never had so good a hunt.' The following day, while the King was with the Council, a courier arrived from Blécourt that the King of Spain was in his final agony; that he had received Extreme Unction and had lost the power of speech. In the same entry Dangeau wrote: 'The King of Spain, a month ago, made a will which he signed with his hand and five or six Grandees witnessed the signature; it is believed that the will is made in favour of Monseigneur le duc d'Anjou or Monseigneur le duc de Berry.' On Tuesday the 9th, 'in

the morning the King was at the Council of Finance when M. de Barbezieux came with the news of the death of the King of Spain'.

Another observer to record his impression of events was the baron de
Breteuil, the Grand-Maître des Cérémonies. 'Since the ambassadors who
were following the Court had received letters from their correspondents
in Madrid, it became public knowledge, but leaving minds in the uncertainty as to whether His Majesty would take the side of the partition
treaty or that of the will; everyone awaited with impatience what would
be the outcome of the conference.

'But since it was not possible for His Majesty to make a definite decision
which could be made public until such a time as the will was made known
to him in a more authentic manner, the Council only made conditional
resolutions, which remained a close secret.

'The next day the King received a copy of the testament signed by all
those who were members of the Junta, and in the Council which His
Majesty then held, with the same persons already named, the Dauphin,
the duc de Beauvilliers, the marquis de Torcy and the Chancellor, Louis
Phélypeaux, they made a formal resolution to execute the will and to
declare Monseigneur le duc d'Anjou King of Spain; but he postponed the
making public of it until his return to Versailles, which was to be
the following Monday.

'The duc de Beauvilliers, governor of Monseigneur le duc d'Anjou, was
the one who, on leaving the Council, was the first to inform him of his
destiny. The same day the King shared this confidence with Monseigneur
le duc de Bourgogne, and either then or the next day did the same to
Monsieur and told them not to mention it at all.'

According to the marquis de Sourches, 'the King wished to stand by
his word in the succession treaty. Monseigneur stubbornly insisted that
he ought to accept the crown of Spain for the duc d'Anjou, and maintained
it so strongly that the King finally gave in.'

All this, of course, was kept a close secret. The eager and expectant
courtiers had to content themselves with the deductions they could make
from the crumbs of information which fell from the rich King's table. After
the King had dined, Dangeau noted, the Chancellor left Fontainebleau. His
departure was correctly interpreted as a sign that the final decision must
have been made.

On Thursday, Friday and Sunday, the Spanish ambassador received
couriers from the Regency Council with despatches for His Majesty full
of prayers, even more pressing, to grant them the duc d'Anjou. 'On the
Friday the King despatched a courier to the Regency Council with a letter
from His Majesty which informed them that he accepted for the duc
d'Anjou, his grandson, the will and testament of the late Catholic King

and that he would make him leave forthwith to go and take possession of his kingdom.

'On Friday the 12th it became known that the King had had a long conversation in his cabinet with Monseigneur le duc d'Anjou, the Dauphin, and Monseigneur le duc de Bourgogne. It was the general opinion here that during this conversation the King informed him [Anjou] that he was King of Spain. Monseigneur le duc d'Anjou did nothing and said nothing which could have revealed to the courtiers that he had been informed of his destiny.' Louis decided to withhold the announcement until the Court had returned to Versailles, which was scheduled for the following Monday.

'Tuesday 16 November. At Versailles no one yet knew that the moment was approaching when this important decision was going to be proclaimed. At the end of the *lever* the ambassador was conducted into His Majesty's cabinet by M. Sainctot, Introducteur des Ambassadeurs for the half year, at the time and in the manner of private audiences, that is to say with no one there but M. de Torcy, Ministre d'Etat des Affaires Etrangères. As soon as the ambassador had entered, the King called the duc d'Anjou, who was in the *arrière-cabinet* with his brothers, and having taken him by the arm, offering him his right hand, His Majesty said to the Ambassador: "Monsieur, here is the King of Spain." At these words the Ambassador made his obeisance kneeling at the feet of his master, kissed his hand and made him a compliment in Spanish. His Majesty answered, saying: "It is for me to speak; he does not understand Spanish", and in his response he gave praise to the Spanish nation and to the Ambassador in particular.

'The audience over, Sainctot returned in order to take the ambassador back, but in the moment when the door was open to let him leave His Majesty said: "Let everyone come in." In an instant every courtier who was present crowded into the cabinet and the King said: "Messieurs, Monsieur le duc d'Anjou is King of Spain. God places him on the throne to which his birthright calls him; the testament of the late King proclaims him the inheritor; all the Grandees and the people are asking me for him; all that is lacking is my consent and I give that with joy." Then, turning towards the King of Spain, he said to him: "This is clearly an act of God, for which you should be eternally grateful. Be a good Spaniard; that is your first duty; but never forget that you were born French. Remember that on the union of the two crowns depends the repose of Europe and the happiness of your people." ' According to Dangeau, Louis now turned to the ambassador and said: 'If he follows my advice, you will soon be a *grand seigneur*. At present he could not do better than to follow your advice.'

It was at this moment, according to Breteuil, that Castel dos Rios, the Spanish ambassador, said that 'the Pyrenees had just melted away and that the two nations would henceforth no longer be separated'. There are other sources which mention this saying. They are sufficiently numerous to leave little doubt that some such remark was made, but sufficiently different in their wording for it to be impossible to decide exactly what was said. The new King's two brothers then embraced him and all three burst into tears. They were tears of joy at Anjou's good fortune and tears of sorrow at the prospect of his departure.

That night Philippe slept in the ceremonial bedroom, the Salon de Mercure in the Grand Appartement. From the moment that Louis had announced that he had accepted the throne of Spain for his grandson he treated him with full royal honours.

Saturday 4 December was the day finally fixed for the departure. Philippe spent much time alone with his grandfather and then with his father. They all attended Mass together in the tribune of the old Chapel. 'The crowd of courtiers there', wrote Saint-Simon 'was unbelievable.' The royal family, surrounded by an escort far larger than usual, then proceeded – or rather processed – to the Château de Sceaux, now the seat of the duc du Maine, where they arrived at about midday.

'At last the moment of separation had come,' continues Saint-Simon; everyone was in floods of tears; 'the King conducted the King of Spain to the last room of the suite of apartments, embracing him again and again and holding him for a long time in his arms; and Monseigneur likewise. The spectacle was profoundly moving.' It was not in the nature of things likely that they would ever see each other again. His brothers Bourgogne and Berry were to accompany him as far as the frontier.

One of the best résumés of the early reign of Philip V is to be found in the instructions given to the marquis de Bonnac on his appointment, at the beginning of the year 1711, as ambassador to Spain. The words are Torcy's but they certainly express the mind of Louis and have his *imprimatur*. The preamble to the instructions is in the form of a review of the past eleven years. It can be regarded as the view which Louis took, or at least wished to be accepted, as the true account of the events.

'The difference in the general state of affairs since the beginning of the war gave rise to the difference in the approach of the King to the affairs of Spain since the King his grandson became master of this monarchy. The first object of His Majesty in accepting the will of the late King Carlos II of Spain was to maintain the peace of Europe, and, far from thinking of his own aggrandisement by the acquisition of so many powerful States which God had added to the royal House of France, the King had no other intention than to leave the Spanish to take care of their own government in accordance with their own principles and their ancient customs, and only consenting to offer advice when the King of Spain asked for it.

'But this moderation did not accord with the desires of the Spanish nation. They attributed their misfortunes to the bad administration of their public affairs, and the imminent danger of dismemberment to which the monarchy had been exposed had so impressed the minds of a country conscious of its glory, that they desired to conduct themselves entirely by the order of the King, being persuaded that this submission was the only means of conserving the States, the dividing up of which they had only avoided by throwing themselves into the arms of His Majesty. He therefore saw himself as obliged by the unanimous representations of the whole nation to enter in detail into the government of this kingdom, and of those States which are dependencies of it, once the King had arrived at Madrid. And since the whole weight of the war, which had to be undertaken immediately afterwards, fell upon France alone, the King felt the necessity of allowing his ambassador to be present at all the Councils of the King his grandson and that he should become as it were his Prime Minister.'

When Philip arrived in Spain the country had been for so long without an effective king that he had a role to create. He had not, however, received any training in the art of kingship. It is astonishing how the spectre of Gaston d'Orléans, the rebellious younger brother of Louis XIII, haunted the minds of those most closely concerned with the government of France. Louis XIV's brother had been kept at a distance from the throne and encouraged to lead a life of dissipation. The younger brothers of the duc de Bourgogne were likewise kept firmly in second place. Considering the risks of early mortality, mainly caused by medical ignorance, it is difficult to account for the lack of that foresight which might have provided for the possibility of a younger brother succeeding to a throne.

Madame was outspoken on the subject of Philip's education. 'Monsieur de Beauvilliers', she asserted, 'is a brave and honest man, but he is far too devout to bring up the young princes properly. He has not taught them enough about life nor let them see enough of the world, with the result that they are shy and have no conversation. They have not even been taught who the people are who concern them most closely.' She also made observations about Philip's appearance which are significant. 'The duc d'Anjou certainly has the look of a Spanish King. It is extraordinary how grave and serious he is ... Physically he has a distinctly Austrian appearance: the mouth always open. I have drawn his attention to it a hundred times; when he is told he shuts it, for he is very docile.'

Philip had to make up for his lack of training as best he could. But

Louis had to tread delicately in advising him. He desired his ambassador, the duc d'Harcourt, to speak to Porto-Carrero in such a way 'as to remove all suspicion, if he could have any, that you have it in mind to interfere with the government of Spain. He must be persuaded, and the whole country with him, that I wish to have no part in the government of this monarchy, that I will never enter into the affairs of Spain except insofar as the Spanish may desire it themselves for the good and for the maintenance of a perpetual understanding between my crown and that of Spain.' Louis needed, however, to give belated advice to his young grandson on how to govern without appearing to interfere with the government of Spain.

'Do not have any dealings with the Queen Dowager', he advised, 'except those which are indispensable; see to it that she leaves Madrid and, wherever she may be, prevent her from leaving Spain . . . regard as suspect any who have too much to do with her.' Maria-Anna had, of course, been a fierce opponent of the French candidature. Louis goes into small but not insignificant details. 'Treat your servants well, but do not show them too much familiarity; never make them your confidants and never take their side against the Spanish.' As for the Spanish, Louis was apprehensive that his grandson might see a lot that was ridiculous about them. 'Do not appear shocked at the extraordinary figures which you will find. Do not laugh at them . . . You will soon become accustomed to what at first you may find surprising.' He urges the young man to love his wife and to ask God for a suitable one, but with the provision: 'I do not think you ought to take an Austrian.'

Certain items on the list were touched on rather lightly. 'Try to restore your finances . . . think about commerce.' He commends a reasonable measure of *divertissements*; 'there are few so innocent as the chase and a liking for some country house provided that you do not incur, with regard to this, too much expense'. Anyone at all familiar with the accounts published by Guiffrey for the expenditure on Louis' buildings must be astonished at this statement. It was just at this time, when Louis wrote these words, that he undertook an extensive programme of redecoration, and the construction of the new Chapel at Versailles, and that the expenditure at Marly surpassed that of the parent palace. Louis was preaching what he had never practised.

More relevant to his style of kingship was some advice which he had given previously to the Dauphin. 'Do not prefer those who flatter you; value most highly those who, in your own interest, risk your displeasure. These are your true friends.' But the essential message is the last: 'I end with one of the most important counsels that I could give you. Do not let anyone govern you; be the master. Never have a favourite or a First

Marly, the entrance court: it was only to those privileged to enter the precincts that the whole glorious lay-out of Marly was revealed.

The Machine de Marly, which produced 3,200 cubic metres of water every 24 hours. Vauban was said to be the only man in France who understood it.

Versailles, the north gardens by J-B. Martin, showing in the centre the
Allée d'Eau with the Bosquet de l'Arc de Triomphe left and the Bosquet des
Trois Fontaines right and the Bassin de Neptune in the foreground.

Versailles, the Grand Canal with its flotilla, engraving by A. Perelle.
Models of naval vessels were tried out there.

The poop of the *Soleil Royal*,
by J. Bérain. Colbert claimed
that there was 'nothing more
evocative of the magnificence
of the King than the quality
of the ornament.'

(*Clockwise*) Marie-Adélaïde, duchesse de Bourgogne by T. Gobert. When she arrived at Versailles, says Saint-Simon, 'elle l'animait toute entière.' Liselotte von der Pfalz, duchesse d'Orléans, by H. Rigaud. She complained of Marie-Adélaïde's behaviour at Marly, saying 'it no longer bears the slightest resemblance to a Court.' Fénelon, by Vivien. Saint-Simon described his eyes 'which sparkled like a stream.' Madame de Maintenon, after Mignard. Her epitaph claims a crescendo of virtues: 'Tranquil amid the agitations of the Court, Simple in the midst of grandeur, Poor at the fountain head of wealth, Humble at the height of her honours, Revered by Louis le Grand.'

The creation of the Order of Saint-Louis, by J. Marot. The scene represented took place in 1695 but Louis' bedroom took the form shown only in 1701.

Louis with his son, the Grand Dauphin, grandson, the duc de Bourgogne, and great-grandson, the duc d'Anjou, later Louis XV, attributed to F. de Troy or N. Largillière. The descent of the throne is marked by the straight line from the bust of Louis XIII, the head of Louis XIV and the figure of the future Louis XV.

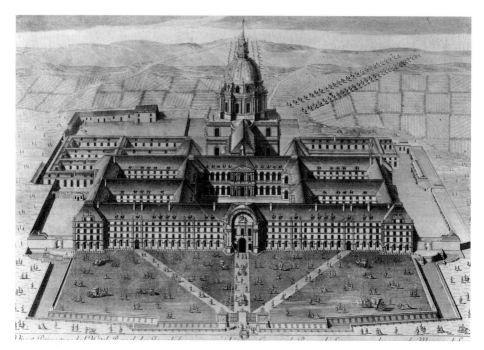

Les Invalides from the north. Built by Libéral Bruant, it covers ten hectares – approximately twenty-five acres – and in its dimensions measures up to Versailles.

Les Invalides from the south with Mansart's beautiful chapel, P-D. Martin. 'One sees on all sides', wrote Montesquieu, 'the hand of a great monarch.'

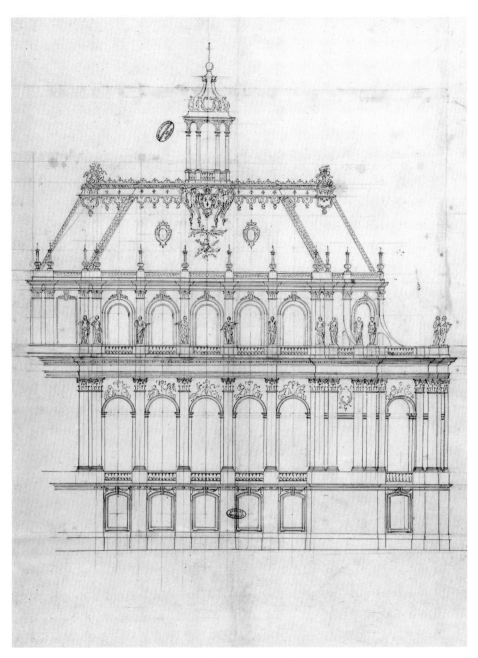

Versailles, the Grand Chapelle. Consecrated in 1710, it was derided
by Saint-Simon as presenting 'the mournful appearance of an immense catafalque.'

(*Following page*) The Grande Chapelle, by C. Cochin.
Louis' last addition to Versailles. According to Mlle d'Aumâle,
'Mme de Maintenon has done everything she can to oppose this magnificent
new Chapel... because the misery of the people was very great at that time.'

Ceremonie du Mariage DE LOUIS DAUPHIN DE FRANCE AVEC MARIE THERESE INFANTE D'ESPAGNE.
Dans la Chapelle du Château de Versailles le xxiii Fevrier MDCCXLV.

Minister. Listen, consult your council, but make the decisions yourself. God, who has made you a King, will give you all the understanding necessary so long as your intentions are good.'

The King's instructions to Philip were supplemented by the duc de Beauvilliers. They start, somewhat predictably, with questions of religion. Philip should place his country, as Louis XIII had placed France, 'under the protection of the Holy Virgin'; he should oppose Jansenism, establish seminaries and reduce the severity of the Inquisition without attacking it openly. He was also advised 'to prevent the increase of papal authority in Spain'. Beauvilliers ends on a personal note. He told Philip that he was too cold and too taciturn, both of them defects which would alienate his peoples and rob him of their affection, 'something which is so necessary for a King if he is to prosper'. He may well have had a share of responsibility for that.

The wave of enthusiasm which greeted Philip on his arrival in Spain was of short duration. As early as July 1701, Blécourt, who was chargé d'affaires during the illness of the ambassador Harcourt, was writing to Torcy: 'I observe with distress that the great love which the people had for the King has almost entirely disappeared in the provinces as well as in Madrid.' The duc de Noailles, formerly comte d'Ayen and married to Mme de Maintenon's niece, describes in his memoirs the irregularity of Philip's habits. He often rose much later in the morning than he had arranged to; he kept the Council, which was summoned for nine o'clock, waiting until eleven; he was sometimes as much as three hours late for his supper. He left his letters unopened for days and hardly spoke to anyone.

A caricature was published depicting Philip as a child; Porto-Carrero is leading him on a rein while Harcourt is holding his hand and saying: 'Walk, walk, my child; the Cardinal wants you to.' The marquis de Louville, who had been one of Philip's preceptors and had followed him to Spain as a sort of mentor, declared that 'he is a King who does not reign and never will'. But he went further: 'if anyone gets possession of his mind he could make him do anything'. This is exactly what happened.

On 5 September 1701, Philip married Princess Marie-Louise of Savoy, the younger sister of the duchesse de Bourgogne. Torcy was informed that 'she has the wit and the penetration of a woman of thirty'. Marie-Louise was twelve. At about the same time Tessé wrote a pen portrait of her to her sister, with whom he compares her, with a delicate tact, as not quite so good-looking as herself – 'the eyes the same colour as yours, but smaller and less sparkling'. Phélypeaux adds a character-sketch. 'She is full of pride, haughtiness and ambition . . . In conversations within the family she made it clear that she would consider herself offended if she were offered [in marriage] anyone less than a King.' Her ambition, however, seems to have been not so much to marry a king as to become one. The comte de Marcin, the new ambassador to Spain, was told that 'the Queen will probably assume complete domination over the King'. Her letters to her mother and grandmother were intercepted and passed by the King's barber to Marcin. 'We read them all', he admitted, 'and we found nothing that was not very good ... She appears to be very much in love with her husband and is extremely happy.'

Since it was certain that she was going to govern the King, the important thing was to ensure that she governed him well.

The duc de Gramont described the characters of Philip and Marie-Louise. 'The King of Spain has both wit and intelligence. He always thinks straight and speaks accordingly; he is of a soft and virtuous disposition and incapable, of himself, of doing any wrong, but timid, feeble and lazy in the extreme. His weakness and his fear of the Queen are such that, although born virtuous, he would go back on his word if ever he could see in it a means of pleasing her. I have experienced this on more than one occasion. You can believe me and count upon it once and for all that so long as the King of Spain has the Queen he will just be a six-year-old child and never a man.' Those observations do not reflect any credit on the young prince's upbringing.

'The Queen', continues Gramont, 'has an intelligence well in advance of her years. She is proud, secretive, vainglorious, undecipherable, haughty and wholly unforgiving. At the age of sixteen she has no love of music or the comedy or conversation or walking or hunting – in a word, of any of the amusements of someone her age. Her only wish is to be the sovereign master, to keep the King her husband on a leading rein and to depend as little as possible on the King her grandfather.'

But if Marie-Louise dominated the King, she was herself dominated by another woman, Anne-Marie de La Trémoïlle, widow of the comte de Chalais, widow of the Duke of Bracciano and best known as the princesse des Ursins. She was to become the confidante of Mme de Maintenon and the recipient of a great number of letters from her which vividly depict the emotions of the Court of Versailles during the difficult years of the War of the Spanish Succession. Her intimate knowledge of France, Spain and Italy made her the ideal unofficial ambassador to the Court of Philip V. Torcy went so far as to say: 'If one had been wanting to create someone specially to occupy this place, one would have had to take her for the model.' She was exactly the person that France needed; she was exactly the person that Spain needed. She lost no time in taking possession of the young Queen, heart and soul. In March 1702, she wrote to Torcy: 'Her confidence in me could hardly be taken to greater lengths, and I think I shall always have sufficient mastery over her to make her do what I want.'

With Torcy's approval she was given the all-important post of Camerera-Mayor – First Lady of the Bedchamber. She shared the same carriage as the King and Queen, was present at audiences given by the Queen to ministers and ambassadors, and sat beside her at the Council, more or less in the capacity of a *duenna*, claiming that it was not proper for her to be alone among so many men. Saint-Simon, who knew her well, gives her the highest praise. 'She was a person so exceptional throughout the whole of her long life and who played a part everywhere so nobly and so conspicuously ... whose intelligence, courage, industry and resourcefulness were so rare; in fact her rule in Spain, so absolute and so open, and her character so stately and so unique, that her biography ought to be written; it would take its place among the most curious passages in the history of her times.'

After a short period of leaving the government of Spain to its new King, Louis decided that it was necessary to take over. His ambassador, the duc d'Harcourt, and Jean Orry, who was to try to improve the finances of the country, were Louis' chief agents. Harcourt, however, fell ill and was replaced in July 1701 by the comte de Marcin. His instructions, signed by Louis and Torcy, constituted 'un véritable plan de renovation de l'Espagne'.

The Spanish were beginning to want the firm hand of Louis at the helm. In May 1701, a Monsieur Ozon wrote to Torcy that 'it was absolutely the desire of the people that the King should govern until his grandson was ready to do so himself'. Louville warned Torcy that Spanish hopes of a French government were impatient and exaggerated. 'The one thing that frightens me is that they have formed such high hopes that, unless God sends them angels to govern them, they will be difficult to live up to. A kingdom which is rotten from top to bottom cannot be reinstated in a short time.'

A little later in the year the marquis de Montviel pointed out that the imminent prospect of war 'ought to have awakened the Spanish from the lethargy in which they have lived so long, but they seem to rely completely on the strength and protection of the King of France'.

During that summer Louis' communications with Spain became more imperative and imperious than ever. On 3 June he ordered Blécourt to go at once to see Porto-Carrero about an alliance with Portugal. 'If he continues to hesitate, say to the King my grandson, in my name, that I am the master and it is for me to decide on a matter of such importance, that it is in his interest to conclude the treaty with the King of Portugal and that if his Council advises to the contrary I will take no account of them.' His orders were obeyed without question. In March 1702, Marcin wrote to Torcy: 'We await in all things the decision of the King, which is regarded here as an absolute command, just as in France.' To Louis Marcin wrote in a spirit of humble obedience: 'The King of Spain will conform in all matters which the King ordains . . . I await the orders of Your Majesty on the manner in which the King of Spain ought to conduct himself.' If Louis was not the ruler of Spain *de jure* it is clear that he was *de facto*.

All important appointments were made by Louis directly. 'It is in the interest of the King my grandson', wrote Louis to Marcin on 24 July 1701, 'to strengthen them in the opinion which they have that my recommendation to him is the most certain way of obtaining favours.'

Those who begged Louis to come and put their country to rights soon began to resent the implied insult to themselves. The Spanish were neither capable enough to manage their own affairs nor sensible enough to want Louis to. Their pride, which was their dominant characteristic, was offended. Louis' assistance was not making any apparent improvement in Spain: it was threatening to ruin France.

In July 1702 Torcy wrote a long and unusually frank letter to the Duke of Medina-Celi, one of the most francophile of the Grands d'Espagne. He complained that when something went wrong the Spanish were quick to blame the French, but that if anything went well 'they will never believe that France had any hand in it'. Such judgements, continues Torcy, 'would be of little importance if their affairs were in the condition in which they ought to be; but the trouble has always been that the principal persons of the realm have been far more concerned with their own pretensions, their own interests and their particular passions (Your Excellency will pardon me if I speak with such confidence) than they are with the welfare of the State.'

Torcy goes on to defend the position of Louis. 'When this monarch refused to concern himself with their government, they murmured and said that he was content to put his grandson on the throne of Spain, but he would not inconvenience himself enough to remedy the disorders of Spain: when he did give his opinion they protested that no decisions were ever made except at Versailles.'

This letter does not appear to have had the effect intended. A month later Louis obliged his grandson to address an open letter to him, which of course he dictated himself.

'I have a duty', he was to say, 'for the greater satisfaction of Your Majesty, as well as for my own, to blaze abroad the infinite obligations that I owe to Your Majesty, and in particular my gratitude for the succour which I receive from him and his Kingdoms, the numerous armies which he employs in my defence, and in short for the fortune which he has spent on the maintenance of the troops which he has sent . . . Now is the time of crisis, Sire, for the misfortunes of my Kingdom. Your Majesty alone can save it.'

Faced with the particular mixture of incompetence and wounded pride of the Spanish, there may not have been any right course open to Louis and Torcy, but the course which they pursued seems to have been counter-productive. At the end of November 1702, Mme des Ursins wrote to Torcy that 'many of the Spanish already regarded it as possible that the Archduke should become their King'.

The matter, however, was not going to be settled by peaceful means. On 7 September 1701, the Grand Alliance between England, Holland and Austria had been signed. On 15 May in the following year England, the Dutch Republic and the Emperor declared war on France. The War of the Spanish Succession had begun.

26

The Camisard Revolt

There seems to be a curious geographical infrastructure to the Reformation. Generally speaking it was the northern countries of Europe which followed the reformers and the southern countries which retained allegiance to Rome. But within these broad divisions there were further distinctions to be observed. Lutheranism and Calvinism differ from each other in many important respects. Anglicanism fits neither of these categories.

The 'geography' of Calvinism is interesting also. Scotland reacted quickly to the reforming zeal of John Knox. There was something about 'Caledonia, stern and wild' which responded to that somewhat dour and moralistic creed. It appears that, in the same way, the district of the Cevennes in Languedoc had some affinity with the Lowlands. 'There was something in this landscape', wrote Robert Louis Stevenson, 'that explained to me the spirit of the Southern Covenanters, those who took to the hills for conscience's sake in Scotland.' For above the little valleys of the southern coastlands, with their ubiquitous forests of sweet chestnut, rose the barren rocky uplands of the north, described by the duc de Noailles as 'that rampart of heresy'. It had been so in the late twelfth century, when the Protestants in Albi provoked the launching of the Albigensian crusade by Pope Innocent III in 1209. The Roman Catholic Ronald Knox describes the Languedoc as 'a country which seems designed . . . to foster the growth of heresy'. In seventeenth-century France it was still one of the great strongholds of the Huguenots.

The Revocation of the Edict of Nantes had many repercussions in Europe of a largely political nature. Within France it led to a movement, partly spiritual, partly political, but more often a mixture of both – the rise and fall of the Camisards, probably so-called because of the *chemise* which they wore outside their clothing. In the eyes of the government it was a revolt; in the eyes of the Catholic Church it was an outbreak of heresy; but in the eyes of the Camisards themselves it was a spiritual revival. It began with a girl of fifteen talking in her sleep.

On 3 February 1688, Isabeau Vincent, a young, unlettered shepherdess of Dauphiné, was heard calling for repentance and announcing the imminent judgement of God. She was apparently sound asleep. On the night of the 23rd she again spoke in her sleep and her words were recorded. What was astonishing was that, instead of speaking in the local dialect, the *langue d'oc*, which was the only language known to her, she proclaimed her message 'en fort bon français'. A group began to form around her, consisting mostly of young people. Her condition was infectious; the infection soon reached the proportions of an epidemic. The symptoms were fairly uniform – periods of physical rigidity, frothing at the mouth and ecstatic utterances were normal. Sometimes those possessed spoke, like Isabeau Vincent, in a French which was not their language; sometimes they spoke 'with tongues'.

The phenomenon known as 'speaking with tongues' is a sort of inspired utterance which requires, but does not always receive, an equally inspired interpretation. It has a long history in the annals of the Church, dating back to the writings of Saint Paul. It is not uncommon today. It must be distinguished from 'prophesying', which Paul defines as speaking intelligible words which have the power to edify, to exhort and to comfort. As he wrote to the Christians in Corinth: 'I would rather speak five words with my understanding than ten thousand in an unknown tongue.' He did, however, commend the practice of speaking with tongues.

But it was neither the language used nor the message proclaimed which was the mark of one possessed. It was a sort of physical seizure. Jean Cavalier, who emerged as a leader of the Camisards, describes his own experience. 'I felt something like a blow with a mallet which struck my chest hard; it seemed as if this blow stimulated a fire which seized hold of me and which flowed through all my veins. This led to a feeling of faintness which made me fall down.' These 'convulsionaries' heard voices and received instructions which they never doubted were the dictation of the Holy Ghost.

The eighteenth-century word which covered most of these manifestations was 'enthusiasm'. The enthusiast expects more evident results from the grace of God than most men. The 'ordinary' Christian, perhaps more content to qualify than to excel, is regarded with suspicion if not hostility. Orthodoxy, especially Roman Catholic orthodoxy, is the enemy. 'Our traditional doctrine', writes Ronald Knox, 'is that grace perfects nature, elevates it to a higher pitch, so that it can bear its part in the music of eternity.' Not so the enthusiast. For him or her, grace must destroy nature and replace it. 'The saved man has come out into a new order of being with a new set of faculties proper to his state.'

The enthusiast, therefore, has an instinctive distrust of anything intellectual, Man's intellect being fatally flawed, if not totally depraved, by Man's fall. There was, however, behind the Camisard enthusiasts, an element of theology. Pierre Jurieu, a pastor at Rotterdam, was a prolific writer whose books, judging by the numerous translations, had a wide readership in England and Scotland. Their titles are significant. *The Accomplishment of the Scripture Prophecies and approaching Deliverance of the Church, Faithfully Englished*, appeared in 1687 and was followed the next year by *A New System of the Apocalypse, or Plain, Methodical Instructions of all the visions of the Revelation of Saint John.*

The 'scripture prophecies' gave ample space to the Book of Daniel. Daniel and Revelation are, to the ordinary mortal, the most obscure and difficult pieces of writing in the whole Bible, which can be a mystification if not a stumbling block. It is significant that the more extreme and emotional religious positions always seem to concentrate on these passages – the interpretation of which can be more than somewhat arbitrary. Notorious examples of this are the identification of the 'Scarlet Woman' with the Pope and of Babylon with the Church of Rome. It requires the resort to cryptograms which are at best unconvincing and at worst dishonest.

Much the same may be said of the predictions of the end of the world or at least of the liberation of the Church from its oppressors. Jurieu, writing in 1686, boldly predicted that the 'Beast' would be overcome in three years' time. Confidence in the inevitability of the event did not, however, deter the enthusiasts from taking active steps to hasten its consummation. The successful ousting of James II from the throne of England and his replacement by William of Orange, 'the Joshua and the Judas Maccabaeus of Protestantism', were encouraging signs and the epidemic which had started in the Dauphiné now spread to the Vivarais and the Cevennes.

It was largely a one-class movement. Very few of the nobility or richer bourgeois supported it. The typical Camisard was a rural artisan – one of the carders, combers and weavers of the wool trade, smallholders and gatherers of chestnuts and, rather curiously, castrators of pigs. The Intendant Basville dismissed them as 'miserable wool carders and peasants'.

There was little or no sign of political motivation which, in other areas, was aroused by the excessive taxation. None of those who reported to Versailles on the situation, Broglie, Montrevel or Villars, makes mention of such a thing.

The movement is perhaps best seen as an attempt to reverse the Revocation of the Edict of Nantes – to win back to Calvinism those whose conversion to Catholicism was often so manifestly insincere, rebuild the temples and restore the worship of the Protestant religion. This was, in the early days, frequently accompanied by protestations of loyalty to the King. In Louis' eyes, however, loyalty implied obedience and the Camisards were guilty of disobedience.

Basville was quick to recognise the original nature of the uprising. 'One must consider this as a kind of revolt without precedent and which takes a form which is all the more dangerous because it is very difficult to suppress.' The marquis de Montrevel, appointed to master-mind the operation, admitted, shortly after his arrival: 'these wretches are so well supported and so diligently alerted that I regard it as a sort of miracle to manage to make contact'.

Under the leadership of Claude Brousson, an avocat of the Parlement de Toulouse, a policy of non-violence was pursued. His preaching and organising ability did much to rally the Huguenots and to structure their resistance movement.

Louis and Pontchartrain countered the rising mood of revolt with a typical demand for detailed information. It was addressed to the Intendants of the district. Forty-five of their replies have survived. Their message is unanimous: the *nouveaux convertis* had not been converted. 'The greater part neither go to Mass nor listen to sermons; they content themselves with reading the sermons of their own ministers. They prevent their children from going to Church or receiving the sacraments or attending catechism and their mothers handle them roughly if they do.' The Bishop of Montauban sums up – the greater part of the *nouveaux convertis* in his diocese were 'either in a state of half-heartedness or one of total indifference'. The policy of forcible conversion had been a failure.

The Bishops of Languedoc took a rigorist line, openly approving of the methods of the Inquisition in the days of the Albigensian heresy. Esprit Fléchier, Bishop of Nîmes, can speak for them. 'I conclude, together with Saint Augustine, that to be concerned for the salvation of our brothers is to love them; the question is not *whether* to push them, but where we are pushing them to.'

On 3 October 1698, Basville received with joy the news that Brousson had been detected and arrested. 'He has done a lot of harm and would have done a lot more. No fanatic has ever been more dangerous.' On 1 November he wrote to Fléchier about the trial. 'He gives me a lot of trouble, not by his skill, but by the appalling prolixity of his replies.' To be in the dock was, for a man like Brousson, a God-given opportunity for preaching. On 4 November Brousson was condemned to be broken on the wheel. He walked to his ordeal, according to one witness, 'as one would go to a festival'. He did not then know that Basville had commuted the sentence and decreed that he should be strangled – 'in order to end the spectacle promptly'. The spectacle of a martyrdom often does more good to the cause of the martyr than to that of his executioners.

Later in November, Basville wrote to the duc de Beauvilliers. 'It is easy to see', he claimed, 'that the trouble one has taken to beat them down has merely united them and drawn them close together . . . Thirteen years of proscribed worship, far from detaching them from their religion, has attached them more strongly than ever.' It had been hoped that by taking children away from their parents and educating them as Catholics, the Church would ultimately put an end to Protestantism, but the younger generation were becoming more Huguenot than ever. Pierre Carrière stated that 'as a schoolboy I never presented myself for confession or went to Mass. I preferred to suffer all the ill treatment to which the schoolmaster subjected us when we refused to obey.' Young girls imprisoned in convents became missionaries for the Protestant faith.

The government had to decide between a policy of brutality or one of comparative moderation. On 23 December 1698, Louis opted for the second alternative. He ordered that no *nouveau converti* should be forced to approach the sacraments. He sent directives to all Bishops and Archbishops, calling upon them 'to abstain from saying anything untrue or doubtful or puerile; to try and make piety attractive to them and not to insist on practices which are not demanded by the Church and which might distance them from it'. One of these practices he specifies – that of dragging on a hurdle the corpse of any *nouveau converti* who had refused the Last Sacraments. As for the true doctrines of the Church Louis stood firm. 'Nothing could ever be more dangerous than to yield the slightest ground.'

In May 1702, the Camisards finally abandoned Brousson's policy of non-violence. The preacher and prophet Mandagout issued the first call to arms. 'Tear down the Churches; kill all the Catholics.' A Camisard named Abraham Mazel dreamed that some fat, black steers were eating the cabbages in his garden. The garden was interpreted as the true Church of Christ and the black steers as Roman Catholic priests. He, Mazel, was the chosen of God to drive out the intruders by force. It was his sacred duty to commit murder: in July he killed the abbé du Chaila, a notable persecutor of the fanatics, and, under his orders, a Catholic schoolmaster named Parent was castrated – perhaps by one of the professional castrators of pigs – and died shortly afterwards. 'Such was the incident', writes Le Roy Ladurie, 'that touched off the war: a dream; a compulsive delirium; murder; castration.' Mazel himself died at the stake.

On 25 May 1703, Basville wrote at some length to his friend Jean Hérauld de Gourville. 'The first article in the instructions given to M. de Montrevel, and which the King has recommended most strongly, is to take good care never to make any concessions to the rebels . . . and that if it was proposed to give fifteen or twenty livres to those who are foreigners to the Province to make them retire that would be a contravention of what His Majesty seems to have most at heart; besides, there are very few foreigners among these rebels, who are nearly all locals. The suggestion that one might give them an exemption to any sort of tax for a period of two years would most certainly not be to the mind of His Majesty.' The deportation of leaders of the revolt to work in the mines in Spain had appealed to Basville, but he felt sure that 'fundamentally the King would have difficulty in making up his mind to send them, because he has never wished to send the women fanatics to the American islands, as I have often proposed'.

Louis seems to have been on the side of moderation. He was also practical and positive. 'The King has sent missionaries, who have preached, and urged those people to come and listen. They came. They have received instruction. But that was never brought about by violence.' That is to say that the conversion of heretics was not to be brought about by violence. The war against the rebels, however, continued.

The Cevennes, more than any other area, offered a refuge for the persecuted and a perfect landscape, with its rocky ravines and crumbling ruins, for guerrilla warfare. The wilderness had a biblical significance and it was both creative and expressive of the character of the insurgents. The duc de Noailles was not far from the truth when he wrote: 'the harshness of the climate and the temperature of the air breathe into them a wild and savage nature.' Basville tried, by the construction of a system of roads and forts, to penetrate this natural fastness and to make it accessible to more regular military manoeuvres. It cannot be said that he was often successful.

The time when the fugitives were most at risk was when they were engaged in corporate worship. These assemblies took place often after dark in some cave or ruin with sentinels posted. Occasionally the royal troops burst in on them and there were massacres, arrests, trials and executions – mostly by hanging, but sometimes by breaking on the wheel.

Liliane Crété states that nearly a thousand Camisards were condemned to the galleys and some seventy, five of whom were women, were hanged or broken on the wheel. It was becoming clear that the policy of frightfulness did not work – it was even counter-productive.

The Camisards were many of them prepared to give their lives for their faith. Fulcran Rey, tortured and condemned to the gallows, wrote to his father just before his execution: 'Oh what happiness it would be to me if I could be one of those whom the Lord has set aside to pronounce his praise and to die for his cause!' He, and many others like him, walked with light-hearted step to enrol their names in the noble army of martyrs. Whatever one might think of their cause, it is difficult not to admire the courage which went with their convictions.

In March 1704, Montrevel was recalled and replaced as Governor of Languedoc by the marquis de Villars, maréchal de France. In making this appointment Louis must have known that he was sending them a man who was by nature a moderate and by experience a skilled negotiator. He had already made his name in the course of a distinguished embassy to the Court of Vienna.

Basville had by this time moved away from the barbarous methods of Montrevel and was more inclined to the paths of gentleness and peace (probably more from considerations of prudent policy than from truly humanitarian sentiments); he and Villars understood each other and could work together. Villars' first move was to have all the scaffolds dismantled and the gibbets taken down. It was a conspicuous means of announcing his new policy. Soon he could write to Chamillart: 'I have gained the confidence of the *nouveaux convertis*. It is certain, Monsieur, that the people, and especially these people, like to be talked to.'

Villars quickly observed that there was a great difference between the townsmen and the countrymen. He also publicly repudiated the excesses of some of the Catholic clergy.

On 6 May 1704, a meeting eventually took place between Villars and the Camisard leader Jean Cavalier. The ground had been carefully prepared beforehand. They met in the garden of the Récollets at Nîmes. They talked for a good two hours. Claude Du Bosc quotes Cavalier's own account of the interview. 'At last the Marshal stepped forward and passed a very civil compliment on me, which I answered in the best manner I was able; but I looked at M. Basville as if I had not known him, which made him, when I began to make my demands to the Marshal, to break out and say in a rage that the King was very merciful to condescend to treat with such a rebel as I was. I answered that that was not the business I had come about; if they had nothing else to say to me, I might as well have stayed away, and that I should retire; adding that he alone had forced us to take up arms by his tyranny and his cruelty. The Marshal, observing his passion, interrupted us that the King's intentions were to spare his subjects and use easy methods to reduce them to their duty. Then the Intendant fell into a great passion as put me in some apprehension. The Marshal, who, to do him justice, is a polite and fine gentleman, interposed saying: "Take no notice of what M. Basville is saying. I told you that it is with me that you are to treat." Accordingly I delivered my demands by word of mouth and when I had done, "you insist", says he, "upon liberty of conscience. The King is willing to grant it you. You shall live as you see fit. He will also permit you to meet and have service in your own way, but not to build churches. You ought to be satisfied with this." '

The principal leaders of the Camisards agreed to submit totally and unconditionally to the mercy of the King, offering either to leave the country or 'expiate their fault' by enrolling in the service of the King. Villars was able to report to Louis that, on the matter of religion, no words had been spoken and no demands made. On 6 November, Bishop Fléchier wrote to Villars: 'You are right, Monsieur, to congratulate yourself on the tranquillity which we enjoy at the present. There is no more killing and burning and the roads are almost completely safe. Most of the fanatics are surrendering with their arms.'

The pacification of the Camisards, however, was viewed with amazement and horror by many Catholics. Séguier's own secretary, the abbé Bégault, exploded. 'Everyone thinks he is dreaming that in one moment the situation should have altered in so extraordinary a manner, and that a beggar, a little urchin – for Cavalier was not more than twenty and looked more like sixteen with the air of a child – should treat, as if between two crowned heads, with the King by the mediation of a maréchal de France, and that the greatest criminals ever vomited from Hell, blackened by crimes and by the most appalling outrages, should come brazenly into Nîmes under the protection of the authorities and with hostages and other safeguards.'

At the end of the year Fléchier could say: 'The maréchal de Villars has conducted this affair very prudently and has calmed it without bloodshed, which has pleased us very much.' Villars regarded his work as having been accomplished. Chamillart had said to him, before he left for Languedoc, that if he succeeded in pacifying this country he would be rendering a service to the King greater than winning three battles on the frontiers. Villars now reminded him of this and asked to be made a duke. He did not receive that title until after the battle of Malplaquet.

In March 1705, Villars was given command of Louis' army on the Moselle and was replaced in Languedoc by the Duke of Berwick. Born in 1670, he was the illegitimate son of James II and Arabella Churchill. He was thus a nephew of the Duke of Marlborough. His contemporary, the Président de Montesquieu, who knew him well, gave him high praise. 'Never has a man followed more closely the laws of the Gospel which cost most to men of the world. Never has a man practised religion so much and talked about it so little.' Lord Bolingbroke, in a short obituary, likened him to Turenne, 'of whom it could well be said that he did honour to humanity'.

Berwick lost no time in taking up his new duties. 'In March', he wrote in his memoirs, 'I went to Montpellier where I found matters to all appearances very calm; nevertheless at heart the Huguenots were merely hankering for opportunities to renew the revolt. The maréchal de Montrevel, by means of a veritable army, had defeated them in 1703; the maréchal de Villars, who had succeeded him, found means of dividing the leaders and dispersing the members; but the evil remained embedded in their hearts, so that only by taking great care and by a strict severity was it possible to prevent the fire from reigniting. Assisted by the insights and counsels of M. de Basville, the most judicious man there is in France, I applied myself to forestalling anything that could cause trouble and I declared that I had not come as a persecutor, nor as a missionary, but firmly resolved to render justice to all alike, to protect those who behaved as loyal subjects of the King and to punish with the extremest severity those who persisted in contravening.'

It was not long before his fears were realised. While staying with Basville at Montpellier he learned of a plot against them. He ordered that the gates be closed and all the houses searched. The conspirators were betrayed by one of their number and all were arrested. Among them were the leaders Ravanelle and Catinat (so named after one of Louis' generals under whom he had once served). Both were guilty of 'the most horrible sacrileges'. Both were condemned to be burnt at the stake, and two others, Du Villar and Jonquet, to be broken on the wheel. When Basville passed sentence on Du Villar he expressed surprise that a man of his parts should associate with such villains. He received the reply: 'Ah! Monsieur, please to God that I should have a soul as beautiful as theirs!' Whatever Villars and Berwick had achieved, they had by no means put an end to the fanaticism of the Camisards.

Berwick, however, was not content to be 'idle in a province when there was a brisk war being waged. I would have wished to find myself once more back in my natural element.' He turned his attention towards the situation in Spain. In April Louis had appointed Michel-Jean Amelot ambassador to Spain. Saint-Simon called him 'a man of honour, of great good sense, a great worker . . . He had been a success everywhere.' He was instructed to work in concert with the princesse des Ursins.

The policy which Amelot was to pursue was the humbling of the Grandees, the subordination of the religious orders and the destruction of all national institutions except for those of Castille. The most divisive force in Spain was in the spirit of provincialism enshrined in the local rights or *fueros*.

In June there was a plot against Philip's life and the marquis de Légarès was implicated and arrested. Public opinion was clearly on his side and Philip wrote to Louis begging him to restore order at all costs. Louis' answer was to give his support to the right of freedom of judgement. 'I wish that we could put a stop to the rumours of which Your Majesty complains: but it is not possible to deprive the public of their freedom of speech. It has been claimed by them at all times and in all countries, and in France more than anywhere. One must try only to provide them with occasions for approval and praise. I hope there will be found frequent occasions for this in the course of your reign.'

'During the summer of 1705', he writes, 'the enemy took possession of Catalonia.' Voltaire, in his *Siècle de Louis XIV*, gives us a eulogy of this region on the east coast of Spain nearest the French frontier – 'one of the most fertile lands on the Earth and the most happily situated; as well watered by beautiful rivers, streams and springs as both Old and New Castile are devoid of them; it produces all that is necessary for the needs of Man and all that could gratify his desires in the way of trees, of corn, of fruits and vegetables of every species ... Its capital, Barcelona, is one of the finest ports in Europe and the country provides all that is needed for the building of ships ... Catalonia, in fact, can do without the whole Universe, but her neighbours cannot do without her.'

This victory of the Grand Alliance was attributed by Berwick 'less to their strength than to the defection of the inhabitants and to the negligence of the Courts of Versailles and Madrid ... The King of Spain [Philip V] even thought he might have lost his throne as the result. The principal cause of this misfortune was that the Minister who was most in favour' (he clearly means Chamillart), 'on whom such matters depended, possessed neither the talent to have foreseen the evil nor the intelligence to remedy it: consequently, through his incapacity, he brought France to the edge of a precipice from which it was only saved by a miracle.'

The loss of Catalonia would almost inevitably have entailed the loss of the other east-coast regions, Aragon and Valencia. These regions were usually referred to as 'kingdoms' and the provincial governors known as 'viceroys'.

On 22 August an English fleet with sixty warships, and thirteen 'bomb-boats' equipped with high-trajectory mortars, arrived at Barcelona and laid siege to it. With them was the Archduke Charles, now referred to by their side as Charles III of Spain or just 'the King'. The English troops were led by Charles Mordaunt, Earl of Peterborough, a colourful and highly controversial figure. Barcelona was duly taken and Catalonia came out in support of the Archduke.

Charles's influence spread south into Aragon, chiefly by means of the *miquelets*. These were 'freedom fighters' to those on Charles's side and rebels in the eyes of Philip's supporters. Most of their leaders were monks who were surprisingly ready to commit acts of violence. One, belonging to the Order of Minimes, was arrested on a charge of nine murders and conspiracy. But the Council of Castille insisted that no secular judge could try a member of a religious order without papal consent. Papal consent was not given and the criminal was not brought to justice. 'This flagrant act', wrote the princesse des Ursins, 'gives to other monks the courage to be leaders of all the revolts.'

The situation was becoming critical. Louis, writing to Amelot, the new ambassador, on 15 November 1705, saw that the last hope for Philip was to put himself at the head of his armies and fight for his throne. 'I have enough confidence in his courage', he wrote, 'to believe that he will not regard his cause as lost and that, working to preserve his crown, he would rather expose himself to every extremity than to despair too easily of being able to keep himself on the throne.'

The year 1706 began with military activity in Spain, where the combined French and Spanish forces were preparing to lay siege to Barcelona. Louis wrote to his grandson: 'The defence of Barcelona will be stubborn, but its conquest will bring closer the end of the war.' He ends on a typically religious note: 'The outcome is in the hands of God; we must await with submission whatever he wishes to do for the good of Europe.'

In February 1706, Berwick was made maréchal de France and put in charge of the French and Spanish troops in Spain. It was not an easy assignment. 'The Ministers, although they were wholly ignorant of our profession, wanted always to act as our leaders; this is what made my position difficult, having to fight Madrid as well as the enemy . . . The two armies made, so to speak, the tour of Spain: they began near Badajos and after having marched across Castille, ended up in the kingdoms of Valencia and Murcia . . . This year [1706] saw many events which were unhappy for France and Spain: Flanders lost by the battle of Ramillies; Italy by that of Turin and Spain by the raising of the siege of Barcelona and by our retreat from Madrid; but we were the only ones who had the good fortune to recover from our losses.'

The final victory was that of Almanza. It was typical of the crossing causes in this war that the French troops were commanded by an Englishman – the Duke of Berwick – while the English troops were commanded by a Frenchman – Henri de Massué, marquis de Ruvigny, a Huguenot who had been raised to the English peerage as Earl of Galway.

On 28 April Lord Galway wrote to Stanhope an account of the battle. He ended with a review of the prospect before them. 'All the generals that are here have assembled yesterday to consult what is now to be done.

All agreed that we were not in a position to think of defending this kingdom [Valencia] and resolved to retire to Tortosa [on the borders of Catalonia] . . . These are too bad news for me to write to the King [Charles III] which I broke to you, and acquaint him with it that he may send us his orders, if he has any to give us.'

On the same day he wrote to Admiral Byng: 'I suppose you have already heard of the battle having been lost . . . You are sensible that with that we shall not be in a position to form an army able to protect the kingdom of Valencia.'

On 3 May, the Archduke Charles wrote to Marlborough deploring the event. 'Our cavalry, and particularly the Portuguese, gave way without waiting for any charge, abandoning all alone on the plain our infantry without a commander, my Lord Galway having been wounded by a sabre over the eye, and the marquis das Minas and the greater part of the generals having retired with the cavalry in such disorder and precipitation, without looking behind them, and without drawing rein until they reached Xativa, a good eight leagues from the field of battle.' Marlborough himself wrote: 'This ill success in Spain has flung everything backwards, so that the best resolution we can take is to let the French see we are resolved to keep on the war so that we can have a good peace.'

27
Blenheim, Ramillies, Turin, the Death of Vauban

In 1703 Louis had the idea of making a bold attempt to put an end to the war by attacking Vienna. In May the maréchal de Villars – probably Louis' greatest general at the time – led an army into Bavaria, France's ally, and joined forces with those of the Elector, Max-Emmanuel. The duc de Vendôme was to join them by bringing up his army from Italy by way of the Brenner Pass. Vendôme was distracted by the activities of the Duke of Savoy, Victor-Amadeus, who was at that time in the somewhat odd position of being at war with his two sons-in-law. Of his two daughters Marie-Louise was already Queen of Spain and the other, Marie-Adélaïde, married to the duc de Bourgogne in direct succession for the throne of France.

The joint attack on Vienna never took place. The Duke of Marlborough, who commanded the British forces, determined to confront the French army. He found the perfect partner in the commander of the Imperial troops, Prince Eugène of Savoy, whom Napoleon was to describe as one of Europe's greatest generals. The blood of the Habsburgs flowed in his veins through the Infanta Catherine and that of the Bourbons through his grandmother, Marie de Bourbon-Soissons, princesse de Carignan. His mother, Olympe, comtesse de Soissons, a niece of Mazarin, had been involved in the *Affaire des Poisons*. Louis had allowed her to escape from France, but she was thereby an exile. The young Eugène – according to Jonathan Swift 'an ugly-faced fellow' – was destined by his family for Holy Orders and had, much against his will, received the tonsure. In spite of this he presented himself at Versailles and asked for a company in the French army. But there was something insolent and insubordinate about his bearing which told against him. Louis was later to say: 'No one has ever dared to look at me with such impertinence, like a hawk taking the measure of his prey.' Louis' rejection of him confirmed him in his attitude of raptor. Two years later, in 1685, he left France to fight in the Emperor's army against the Turks and earned the rank of Field Marshal. In 1697 he won the decisive victory of Zenta.

At the end of May (1704) Marlborough set out from near Bonn for his epic 250-mile march to the banks of the Danube. An interesting description of this march comes from Colonel Blackader of the Cameronians. He was a zealous Calvinist of the Cromwellian type. Mentally he was marching against the Amalekites – 'Thus saith the Lord of Hosts . . . Go and smite Amalek and all that they have.' His account of his military and religious experience is largely introspective and egocentric. 'June 4. Marching all day. Kept as much alone and retired my thoughts for prayer and meditation as much as I could among such a crew, and was serene and spiritual . . . June 8. Marching all day. Great fatigue, bad weather, bad roads, whereby my mind was not so easy and serene.'

Captain Robert Parker has left another account of the experience. 'We frequently marched three, sometimes four days successively. We generally began our march about three in the morning, proceeded for about four to four and a half leagues [about twelve miles] and reached our ground about nine o'clock.' Their efforts were supported by excellent administration. 'As we marched through the countries of our allies, commissioners were appointed to furnish us with all manner of necessities for man and horse; these were brought to the ground before we arrived and the soldiers had nothing to do but pitch their tents, boil their kettles and lie down to rest. Surely never was such a march carried on with more order and regularity and with less fatigue both to man and horse.'

It is evidence of Marlborough's genius that he managed to overcome one of the greatest problems facing an army commander in those days – the problem of logistics. David Chandler has recently made a study of the statistics which tell their own tale. As the seventeenth century drew to its close there was a noticeable increase in the size of armies. 'What had changed dramatically', he notes, 'was the improvement in the means and methods of state administration which made it possible to mobilize, equip and marshal more and more men in pursuit of national objectives. It did not, however, make it commensurately easier to feed them.'

The usual method was to collect large quantities of supplies in magazines in the expected area of a coming campaign. Although these could be moved with convoys to follow the army, the system clearly imposed restrictions upon the line of country that could be followed. 'The sheer bulk of provisions', continues Chandler, 'was staggering. Most armies tried to issue each man with a kilogram of bread a day.' But of course officers, 'expert craftsmen' and other privileged persons required more. Puységur was not far wrong in estimating that for 60,000 soldiers, 90,000 bread rations were needed. Thus Chandler could calculate that an army of that size would require, for a six-month campaign, 43 million kilograms of bread. Bread has to be baked. To supply the same number of soldiers, 60 ovens would be necessary, and 240 bakers. The bakers had to be fed. A single oven required 500 bricks; the transport of these necessitated 60 carts. The carriers had to be fed. Ovens need fuel. A single baking consumed 200 loads. Over a period of one month 1,400 wagon-loads of fuel were needed. The wagoners had to be fed. Flour had to be milled. Mills could be destroyed in advance by the enemy. Marlborough was the first to introduce small hand-mills. He was able to boast that 'everything has been so organised, and there has been so little cause for complaint, that all know our army in Flanders has been regularly supplied with bread during the war'.

That, however, was just for the men. There were also horses. An army of 60,000 soldiers required 40,000 horses. They had to be fed and would have consumed one million kilograms of oats and straw a day in winter. The transport of this would have required some 500 carts. Carriers and horses had to be fed. When summer came and the grass began to grow, the situation was different, for grazing was possible. But grazing takes time. It could have exercised an important effect on the planning and progress of a campaign. In 1676 Lord Orrery, in his *Treatise on the Art of War*, observed that the French, 'with great prudence, attack places in the beginning of spring, when there is no army to relieve them, and then in summer, when the whole confederacy is in the field, they are usually on the defensive and cover what they have taken . . . They do at least as much by their always providing well to eat, and by their entrenched camping, as by their good fighting.' After an early victory the commander had the whole campaigning season before him.

This all had a controlling influence on the timing of a campaign. The regular baking of bread and the need for foraging dictated one day's pause every four or five days. The men needed the rest also. Chandler suggests that an average major battle took several months to prepare, often leaving the victorious general only about 100 days before the end of the campaigning season. 'But no less than 70 of these days would be taken up by basically administrative considerations. The 24-hour halt every 4 days for foraging and issuing bread used up some 25 days . . . We find a mere 30 days for true military advances. Few days' marches averaged above 10 or 12 miles.'

It need hardly be added that the overriding necessity in all these factors was the ability to pay for them. Dutch and English money played as large a part in the successes of Marlborough and Eugène as their own brilliant leadership. It was especially noted in the ease with which Marlborough obtained provisions for his march to the Danube.

On Monday 8 June, the Duke of Marlborough and Prince Eugène met for the first time. Eugène and Wratislaw rode out to the Duke's camp at Mundelsheim on the Neckar. It was to be the beginning not only of a fruitful partnership, but of a life-long friendship. When Eugène put down on paper his first impressions of Marlborough, he described him as 'a man of high quality, courageous, extremely well disposed and with a keen desire to achieve something. With all these qualities he understands thoroughly that one cannot become a general in a day and he is diffident about himself.' Schulenberg, one of the generals of the allies, describes the conference between Eugène and Marlborough on the eve of the battle of Blenheim. 'The map was spread out before him on the table like a chess-board and Eugène studied the moves. He was all fire and flame. At last he had found a being who understood him, who appreciated the circumspection of his plans and thought the same way as he did. Marlborough's handsome face glowed! But he listened with the cool ardour of the Englishman and was amazed at all Eugène's precautionary measures.' Later Schulenberg adds: 'It is part of Eugène's character to see difficulties and obstacles before beginning a task. When the moment for action arrives, then he is all strength and activity.'

This spirit of mutual understanding and co-operation, together with the healthy note of diffidence, contributed not a little to the success of their joint campaigns. It contrasts significantly with the lofty independence and arrogant self-confidence of the duc de Vendôme. It was to bear immediate fruit in the battle of Blenheim.

Their bold march down to the Danube reversed the situation of the French armies. As Winston Churchill puts it: 'In May they had been choosing between the prizes: now (in early June) there was only a choice of evils.' At about the same time Tallard wrote to Louis: 'In view of the superiority of the enemy forces between the Rhine and the Danube, assistance to Bavaria is so difficult as to appear almost an impossibility.' On 12 June, Louis wrote to Villeroy: 'Matters of this importance demand long meditation and a perfect knowledge of the land. The maréchal de Tallard has been at war there for several years; he has made a thorough examination of all the different courses which it would be possible to take; he could not make up his mind to any one of them. I send you the one which I consider the best, but I am not giving you any positive orders that would put you under the necessity of carrying out the one which seems to me the most advantageous.' Villeroy replied: 'Your Majesty understands war better than those who have the honour to serve you.' The general who was supposed to be in command of the French army was putting the responsibility back onto the King and asking for instructions. On 23 June Louis sent explicit orders to Villeroy as to how the

French armies were to be divided up and where they were to go. The manoeuvring all led to the decisive battle of Blenheim.

On 12 August Marlborough and Eugène mounted the church tower at Dapfheim and observed the French and Bavarian forces taking up their position near the village of Blenheim. 'The post of which they were possessed', writes Burnet, 'was capable of being, in a very little time, put out of danger' (by raising earthworks) 'of all future attacks; so the Duke of Marlborough and Prince Eugène saw how important it was to lose no time and resolved to attack on the next morning.'

On the same evening, Dangeau records, Louis was offering a magnificent entertainment at Marly to the King and Queen of England. It began with 'a sumptuous repast with new services of porcelain and glass on tables of white marble without cloths'. When darkness came, the sound of music announced the beginning of a firework display. The centre-piece was a triumphal arch brilliantly illuminated. A triumphal arch was the symbol of victory. In the course of the following day Louis' troops suffered their first major defeat.

Claude Du Bosc, in his *Military History of the late Prince Eugene of Savoy*, prints a letter from 'a French General Officer to M. Chamillart'. It is dated 30 August 1704. At a critical moment in the combat, when Tallard was trying to extricate his troops from the village of Blenheim, 'our Horse had faced the enemy; but on a sudden they were ordered to wheel about, which, you will imagine, was done with great disorder. In short this was so precipitate a flight that many cast themselves into the Danube and the enemy let loose three regiments of Dragoons after them. M. de Tallard was environed with the fugitives and taken in that rout. The taking of M. Tallard was a great misfortune to the King, for 'tis certain that with his infantry he might have made an honourable retreat, whereas that infantry is now the laughing stock of the Nations.'

That evening, 13 August 1704, Marlborough, still on horseback, wrote to Duchess Sarah. The letter has survived. 'Of all the thirty-five thousand documents housed in Blenheim Palace,' writes David Green in his history of that great house, 'none is more treasured than a note hurriedly pencilled on the back of a bill of tavern expenses.' On it Marlborough wrote: 'I have not time to say more than but to beg you will give my duty to the Queen and let her know her army has had a glorious victory. Monsieur Tallard and two other generals are in my coach and I am following the rest.'

Colonel Blackader records his comment. 'We fought a bloody battle and by the mercy of God have got one of the greatest and most complete victories the age can boast of.'

When the news of the precipitate French flight from Blenheim reached the French troops in Italy, Vendôme refused to believe it. Sevin de Quincy describes the general reaction: 'Consternation, sorrow and dismay immediately spread throughout the army.' The French were and are easily dejected. Francis Hare quotes Colonel Wynne, who was guarding the French officers taken prisoner at Blenheim: 'Some were blaming the conduct of their own generals, others walking with their arms folded, others were laid down lamenting their hard fortune and complaining for want of refreshment, till at last, abandoning all reflections of this nature, their chief concern was for the King, abundance of muttering and plainly saying: "O! que dira le Roi?" '

What the King said, if he said anything, is not recorded. He first heard the news in an indirect manner. Letters were arriving at Versailles from officers who were prisoners of war to reassure their families of their survival. 'These letters', Louis wrote to Tallard, 'leave me no room to doubt that there has been an action at Höchstedt in which the enemies have had a considerable advantage . . . I still hope that the situation is not as bad as the enemies have asserted.' But such optimism could not last. On 23 August he wrote: 'I have no room to doubt that the infantry of the army of M. de Tallard and our regiments of dragoons have been cut to pieces.' He then crossed out the last three words and inserted 'entirely defeated and taken prisoners of war'.

Dangeau states that Louis 'sustained that misfortune with all the constancy and the courage imaginable; one could not give greater evidence of resignation to the will of God or of greater strength of spirit; but he could not understand how twenty-six French battalions could have given themselves up as prisoners of war'. Louis knew that it was incumbent upon him to restore morale as quickly as possible. To the Elector Max-Emmanuel he wrote a comforting letter ending with the hope that 'M. de Marlborough would give him an opportunity for revenge'.

A week before the battle of Blenheim an event took place which, though not of great immediate consequence, was to be of capital importance to the history of the British navy. At the beginning of August Admiral Sir George Rooke, who had been manoeuvring somewhat aimlessly in the Mediterranean, decided to attack Gibraltar. His bombardment was not effective. Gilbert Burnet describes the occasion. 'He spent much powder bombarding it to very little purpose.' It was not the artillery, however, which achieved the victory; 'some bold men ventured to go ashore', continues Burnet, 'where it was not thought possible to climb up the rocks; yet they succeeded in it; when they got up, they saw all the women of the town were come out, according to their superstition, to a chapel there, to implore the Virgin's protection: they seized upon them, and that contributed not a little to dispose those in the town to surrender'.

All attempts to retake the Rock ended in failure. 'The King', writes Voltaire, 'having sent thirteen vessels to attack Gibraltar, while the maréchal de Tessé besieged it on land; this double temerity caused the loss of both the army and the fleets . . . Since that day we have no longer seen the great French fleets, neither upon the ocean nor on the Mediterranean; the navy reverted to nearly the same condition from which Louis XIV had raised it – like so many spectacular things which had both their sunrise and their sunset under his rule.' 'All the resources that Philip V had at his disposal', writes Baudrillart, 'were to melt away in this extremity of the peninsula.' It looked as if Spain was wide open to a determined attack by the Archduke. Gramont wrote to Louis that Philip had cried like a child on receiving such disheartening news. Indeed, in Gramont's opinion 'he seemed like a child of six, so shy and subjected he was before the Queen'.

During that summer the duchesse de Bourgogne had been expecting a child. She had been filled with fear at the prospect. The duchesse du Lude wrote to the duchesse de Savoie: 'She is in terrible fear of childbirth, which gives her the vapours and leaves her in a sorry state.' Nearly two weeks after the battle of Blenheim she gave birth to a son, the duc de Bretagne. France was once more in a state of general rejoicing and on the night of 27 August Louis attended a magnificent firework display at Meudon. But the little prince died.

The British were still exulting in their victory at Blenheim. 'England', wrote Gilbert Burnet, 'was full of joy, and addresses of congratulation were sent up from all parts of the nation; but it was very visible that, in many places, the Tories went into these very coldly.' On 7 September, John Evelyn recorded 'the thanksgiving for the late great victory' at Saint Paul's. It was Joseph Addison who wrote the paean of praise:

> 'Twas then Great Marlbro's mighty Soul was prov'd,
> That, in the shock of Charging Hosts unmov'd,
> In peaceful Thought the Field of Death survey'd,
> To fainting Squadrons sent the timely aid,
> Inspir'd repuls'd Battalions to engage
> And taught the doubtful Battel where to rage.

The importance of Blenheim was partly psychological. It had the effect on morale that might be caused by a first goal scored by a team habituated to defeat. Louis no longer seemed unbeatable. But the victory did not lead to any immediate follow-up. 'Now our army,' writes Burnet, 'that was got so far into the bowels of the Empire, marched quickly back to the Rhine.' The Emperor offered to reward Marlborough by making him a Prince of the Empire, but 'he very decently said he could not accept of this till he knew the Queen's pleasure; and upon her consenting to it, he was created a Prince of the Empire and about a year after Mindelheim was assigned him for his principality'.

Marlborough decided to make his winter quarters at Trier. He only had to take Traerback to open an unbroken communication by water with Holland, so that, as Burnet noted, 'during the winter everything that was necessary could be brought up hither from Holland, safe and cheap'.

The year 1705 began quietly in the Rhineland. In May the maréchal de Villars scored a minor victory near Trier over Marlborough, causing him to decamp. The occasion affords an example of the mutual respect which often exists between great captains and overrides their mutual enmity. Marlborough sent a note on this occasion to Villars saying: 'Do me the justice to believe that my retreat is the fault of the Prince of Baden' (who had arrived too late) 'and that my esteem for you is greater than my anger against him.'

In May the Emperor Leopold I died. His departure did not make much difference. George Stepney, who had filled a number of posts in various German Courts, wrote that Leopold was 'of an irresolute, wavering temper, on which the last impressions ever make the deepest marks; this occasions that he is frequently torn several ways by the different inclinations of his Ministers, who, in a manner, governed him by turns'.

In the same month Louis wrote to Villeroy: 'the situation in Flanders requires great precautions on your part to avoid having a combat forced upon you. You understand the smallness of the advantage if you should win and the terrible results of losing.'

In the Netherlands the Elector Max-Emmanuel and Villeroy commanded a force of 96 battalions and 150 squadrons. Voltaire claims that Villeroy was over-confident in his own abilities and that this was fatal to France. He was encamped near the village of Ramillies. He could have avoided an encounter; his generals advised him to do so, but he overrode them. On 23 May 1706, he launched his attack. The scene was described by an eye-witness, Colonel La Colonie, author of the *Chronicles of an Old Campaigner.*

'So vast was the plain at Ramillies that we were able to march our armies on as broad a front as we desired, and the result was a magnificent spectacle. The army began its march at six o'clock in the morning, formed into two large columns, the front of each consisting of a battalion. The cavalry squadrons, in battle formation, occupied an equal extent of ground and, there being nothing to impede the view, the whole force was seen in such a fine array that it would be impossible to view a grander sight. The army had but just entered on the campaign; weather and fatigue had hardly yet had time to dim its brilliance and it was inspired with a courage born of confidence. The late marquis de Goudrin, with whom I had the honour to ride during the march, remarked to me that France had surpassed herself in the quality of these troops; he believed that the enemy had no chance whatever of breaking them in the coming conflict' – but he added: 'If defeated now we could never again hope to withstand them.'

On 6 May Louis had written to Villeroy: 'It would be very important to pay particular attention to that part of the line which will endure the first shock of the English troops.' Winston Churchill comments: 'With this the Marshal was in full agreement. He had, therefore, no doubt what to do. He saw with satisfaction that this dreaded attack . . . was about to fall upon that part of the French army which was most strongly protected by the accidents of the ground.' This high optimism made the ensuing crash all the more resounding.

The first and fundamental question to be asked is whether the French should ever have undertaken the encounter here at all. Voltaire states that Villeroy, 'carried away by the blind desire for glory', was claimed to have made 'a formation such that not a single man of experience would have failed to foresee that it could not succeed; newly levied troops, incomplete and without discipline, occupied the centre; he left the baggage between the lines of his army; he positioned his left behind a marsh, as if he wished to prevent it going for the enemy.

'Marlborough,' continues Voltaire, 'who noted all these mistakes, drew up his army in such a way as to profit by them. He noted that the left of the French army was unable to attack his right; he withdrew his right in order to be able to swoop down on Ramillies with superior forces. M. de Gassion, Lieutenant-General, who observed this movement of the enemy, shouted to the maréchal: "You are lost if you do not change your order of battle. Withdraw the troops from your left so that you can face the enemy with equal numbers. Draw your lines together; if you delay for a single moment, there is no further resource." Several officers supported this salutary advice; the Marshal would not listen. Marlborough attacked; he had to deal with enemies in a battle array such as he would have positioned them himself in order to beat them. This is what everyone in France was saying, and history is, to some extent, the account of the opinions of men.

'It was a total overthrow. The French lost twenty thousand men, the glory of their country, and their hope of being able to carry on any more. Bavaria and Cologne had been lost at the battle of Höchstedt [Blenheim]: the whole of the Spanish Netherlands was lost by that of Ramillies. Marlborough entered victorious into Antwerp, into Brussels; he took Ostend; Menin surrendered to him.'

As soon as the battle was over, Marlborough wrote to Sarah, giving himself 'the satisfaction of letting her know that on Sunday last we fought, and that God Almighty has given us a victory'. He was in the extremity of fatigue, 'having been on horseback all Sunday and after the battle marching all night, my head aches to that degree that it is very uneasy for me to write'. Next day he sent fuller details to Godolphin. 'I shall only add that we beat them into so great consternation that they abandoned all their cannon . . . The General Officers which were taken tell us that they thought themselves sure of a victory by having all the King of France's Household and with them, the best troops in France.' On 27 May he wrote again: 'the consequence of this battle is likely to be of greater advantage than that of Blenheim; for we have now the whole summer before us, and with the blessing of God I will make the best use of it'.

On the same day he wrote again to Sarah, still complaining of fatigue and headache. Godolphin, he tells her, is going to show her his letter, 'by which you will see that we have done in four days what we should have thought ourselves happy if we could have been sure of in four years'. These words found their way to France rather quickly. On 20 June, Mme de Maintenon wrote to the princesse des Ursins: 'M. de Marlborough dit qu'il a fait en quatre jours ce qu'il eût été bien content de faire en quatre ans.'

Mme de Maintenon's copious correspondence with the princess had only begun on 31 May, a week after Ramillies. In her first letter she wrote: 'the King bears it all like a great man, but he suffers. First of all he was deeply hurt to hear it said that his Household had done nothing of any value; he is very sensitive to the honour of the nation. It is certain that there were some units which did not do well and there was great disorder.' This is usually the sign of lack of leadership at the top. Mme de Maintenon's piety required her to attribute the defeat to God – 'One must worship God above all' – but it left her puzzled. 'Our two Kings [France and Spain] are the supporters of religion and justice – and they are unlucky; our enemies attack both of these – and they triumph. God rules.' In her next letter she takes up the same theme. 'The intentions of God are incomprehensible.'

The disaster of Ramillies ended with the reception of Villeroy at Versailles. 'Monsieur le Maréchal, at our age we are not lucky,' was all that Louis said.

But in the eyes of most of France the person held responsible for the decisive defeat of Ramillies was Villeroy. Louis, who had a great affection for him, was in a difficult and painful position. 'Our friend the maréchal de Villeroy', wrote Mme de Maintenon on 27 June, 'is in despair, and with all too good reason; but his pain is arid and sour and he cannot enter into the mitigations that the King would like to offer. I have never seen him more deeply moved than he was by what he was obliged to do on this occasion, but he could not avoid doing it.' Villeroy had to be relieved of his command. 'There has never been such a general outcry, and all the stronger for its moderation; they are not saying that M. de Villeroy was negligent, that he was lacking in affection or in zeal for the interests of the King, but that he lacked the esteem of the army.' That is another way of accusing him of professional incompetence. 'The maréchal de Villeroy is only accused of incompetence and misfortune,' continues Mme de Maintenon. 'The King has seen so certainly and so closely the little confidence that the army has in him and the outcry in Paris has been so great, that he was forced to make this change and he would always have repented if he had not done so. I have seen close-to how much it cost the King to do it; his friendship for this Marshal is even greater than I thought it.' At the end of June Louis wrote to Villeroy: 'Your letter of the 28th confirms the good opinion that I have always had that you would forget yourself if it were for the good of my service. Your presence is necessary in Flanders until the arrival of the duc de Vendôme.'

This last appointment was received by Mme de Maintenon with certain misgivings. 'Paris and the army are reassured by the nomination of M. de Vendôme. May God grant that he comes up to expectation.'

Perhaps in the hope of compensating for this defeat, Louis now put his main efforts into the siege of Turin. It was a difficult, though not untypical, family occasion. Victor-Amadeus had turned against both France and Spain – that is to say, against both his sons-in-law. The situation drew upon the Duke of Savoy the wrath of Louis.

Marie-Adélaïde felt it acutely. On 31 December 1707, not daring to address her father directly, she wrote to her mother: 'It would give me the greatest pleasure that I could have in this life if I could bring my father to see reason. I do not understand at all how he does not come to some arrangement, especially in the unfortunate situation in which he is placed without any hope of relief . . . I am in despair about the condition to which my father is reducing himself by his own fault . . . I assure you that all the King wishes for is to see his country, and that of his grandson, at peace. It seems to me that my father ought to desire the same for his.' It would be difficult to express feeling so natural in a manner more straightforward. The appeal met with no success. The siege of Turin went ahead.

Louis put the duc de La Feuillade, who had married Chamillart's daughter, in charge of the operation. Chamillart did all that was in his power to ensure the success of his son-in-law. Voltaire quotes the long list of munitions provided and dismisses it all as 'this immense and useless apparatus'. Having accepted all this, La Feuillade rejected the one offer which might have saved him from failure. Vauban, who knew more about the fortifications of Turin than anyone, volunteered his help.

He had, on 2 February, been admitted to the highest order of the land – he became a Knight of the Saint-Esprit. It required proof of nobility. Saint-Simon dismissed his claim as 'if he was a gentleman, that was the very most'. But Louis went ahead with the nomination.

La Feuillade rejected Vauban's advice on how to lay siege to Turin. At the beginning of September he wrote to Chamillart: 'Have confidence in me and you will find yourself, and the King, the better for it.' Then he added with a sneer: 'There are those who are born to command and there are others [the engineers] born to carry out the commands which they are given.'

Vauban, who had no pride to swallow, offered to serve as a volunteer – as Saint-Simon puts it: 'to leave his Marshal's baton behind the door'. Vauban wrote to Chamillart: 'since the King stands next to God in all things, I will always carry out with joy anything that he might be pleased to order me, even if I knew it would cost me my life'.

La Feuillade's manoeuvres were to a certain extent dictated from Versailles. 'I very much wish that I had the power to besiege the city of Turin before the citadel,' he wrote to Chamillart, 'but such a change could only come about from the Court. I would not dare to oppose the opinion of Vendôme. I beg you to reflect a little. It is a very difficult undertaking to attack the citadel before the city. The honour of your son-in-law is involved.' The opinion of Vendôme, expressed in a letter to Chamillart dated 10 July, was that 'as to the siege of Turin, you can count on it definitely that Prince Eugène cannot upset it; there are plenty of places where we could stop him if he is thinking of coming to the rescue'. During July and August Eugène was advancing steadily along the valley of the Po. Thanks to English subsidies, he could pay his troops and was free to leave his magazines in the Tyrol behind him. The weather was very hot and his men had to march by moonlight. When he finally arrived before Turin he immediately detected a vulnerable point. 'They seem to me half beaten already,' he observed.

When Louis withdrew Vendôme to replace Villeroy he decided to put his young nephew, Philippe, duc d'Orléans, in command of the French armies in Italy with the maréchal de Marcin as his mentor. Philippe showed real signs of military intelligence – more, perhaps, than Marcin and La Feuillade. These both ignored the suggestions of the young Duke and were defeated on 7 September by Prince Eugène at the gates of Turin in an encounter in which Marcin was killed. After only a short resistance the French capitulated: 5,000 men and 3,000 horses were captured. Marlborough was delighted. In a letter to Sarah he wrote: 'It is impossible for me to express the joy it had given me; for I do not only esteem, but I really love the Prince.'

It is possible that had Marcin and La Feuillade listened to Philippe they might have been more successful. It is almost certain that they would have succeeded had La Feuillade listened in the first place to Vauban.

In December 1706, it was already six years since Vauban had submitted to the King his *projet d'une dîme royale*. Louis had shown polite interest but had not taken any action. Vauban was getting on for seventy-four and he was not well. His twelve volumes of memoirs and observations which he called his *Oisivetés or Various thoughts of a man who has not much to do*, were still unfinished. That was a task for the coming winter.

In line with his great contemporaries, the duc de La Rochefoucauld and La Bruyère, he had noted down a number of *maximes*. But the most important subject of his thinking was about the true welfare of his country. On several occasions he had drawn Louis' attention to the pitiful state of his people and to his own crippling lack of means, but the *projet d'une dîme royale* had been overlooked.

He decided to print the text. He did not seek the King's authorisation, which was required for all publications. This suggests that he only intended it for a limited circulation – less than 300 copies were printed – to be distributed among his friends. In the preface he affirms his loyalty. 'I am a Frenchman and I love my country dearly; I am very grateful for the favours and the kindnesses with which it has pleased the King to honour me for so long.'

His thinking has a curiously modern ring about it. It is clearly out of tune with the presuppositions of the *Grand Siècle*. 'It is not so much by the extent of a State', he affirms, 'or by the revenues of the King that his greatness is to be judged, but by the number of his subjects who are well united and well contented.'

He outlines the conditions for a new, properly recruited and well-trained army which almost anticipated Napoleon's principle *la carrière ouverte aux talents*: the rank of officer should be open to all who were worthy of it. 'God laughs at the distinctions which we make and distributes good sense wherever he chooses.'

But Vauban was not just preaching social theories: he was advocating compassion. 'I feel myself bound in honour and in conscience to make representation to Your Majesty that it appears to me that not enough consideration has ever been given in France to the humbler classes; that too low a value has been set on them; they are the most ruined and miserable section of the population. It is, however, the section most worthy of consideration by its size and by the real and effective service which it pays.'

Vauban, who easily saw things in terms of mathematics, broke down the population into ten categories. One tenth, he claimed, was reduced to begging; of the other nine tenths, five were not in a position to provide alms; three of the four tenths remaining were encumbered by debts and litigation. There remained the top 10 per cent – the *noblesse d'épée*, the *noblesse de robe*, the high ecclesiastics, those holding important charges, rich merchants and bourgeois, which he put at no more than 100,000 families, only a tenth of which could be considered really well off.

Vauban attributed this state of affairs to 'the abuses and malpractices in the imposition and collection of taxes such as the *taille* and the *aides* and the customs duties in the provinces'. The tax which he proposed, the tenth, had its origins in Scripture and the ancient world; the Church had accepted the principle of the tithe. It would be applied in proportion to the taxpayer's revenues; it would be easy to collect and would eliminate the notorious intermediaries, the *traitants*. It was to be applied *tout entier* or not at all.

France was, in fact, on the verge of bankruptcy. On 16 October 1706, Chamillart, Contrôleur Général des Finances, wrote to the King in despair. His statement of the accounts showed 32 million livres *mangés d'avance*, and some 73 million still owing from the years 1704–6, the years when Marlborough had won his victories; there were only 51 million livres in the royal coffers and his budget required the spending of 214 million. The poverty of the poor was daily increasing; they were 'only skin and bone, reduced to hunger and thirst, to beggary and death'. The duc de Vendôme declared that such an emergency required the summoning of the States General. They were not summoned until 1788.

None of this escaped Vauban. 'The kingdom is exhausted,' he concluded; 'it has reached a degree of weakness which puts it in danger of succumbing.'

Some of Vauban's friends offered their comments on the scheme. Puysieulx wrote: 'Your project is too beautiful to succeed; in being realised it would encounter terrible obstacles, as much on account of its novelty as for other reasons which you have foreseen better than I.'

Vauban had indeed foreseen them. He devotes a whole section to the various bodies whose interests were threatened. 'It is for this reason', he concludes, 'that the King should be even more on his guard against those who will make objection to this system, since the poor people in whose favour it is proposed, having no access to His Majesty to represent to Him their miseries, are always exposed to the avarice and cupidity of others . . . to the extent of being deprived, as often as not, of the sustenance necessary for life, always exposed to hunger, to thirst, to nakedness, and, to conclude, reduced to a miserable poverty from which they never recover.'

Perhaps the most important person to speak in his favour was the duc de Bourgogne. 'I love to listen to Vauban reasoning about agriculture,' he wrote; 'his views on the taxation of the public also seem to offer a number of real advantages. It is certain that the unification of taxes has a pleasing look.' But the opposition was more serious than the support. In December 1706, the Chancellor Pontchartrain had summoned bookshops not to sell anything that did not carry the *privilège du Roi*. On 14 February a council held in secret ordered that all copies of Vauban's work be seized and pulped.

A few days later, Vauban was walking with Le Peletier in the Tuileries gardens and caught a severe cold. He wrote the following week to say that he could not come to Versailles before the next Voyage de Marly. It is significant that he had been invited. All invitations to Marly were at Louis' discretion and were signs of the greatest favour.

It was not until March that Vauban learnt of the condemnation of his book. By now he was seriously ill. He sent one copy to his confessor and another to a priest at the Couvent des Jacobins asking if he should regard anything in it as 'contrary to his conscience'. He did not live to receive their replies.

On 29 March Dangeau records: 'Yesterday, while the King was at dinner, M. Fagon came to tell him that the maréchal de Vauban was *in extremis* and begged that M. Boudin, Premier Médecin to the Dauphin, could be sent to him. The King ordered that he should be sent at once and spoke of M. Vauban in terms of great esteem and friendship; he praised him on many counts and said: "I am losing a man who had a great affection for me and for the State." '

When Fontenelle pronounced his *éloge* a few weeks later, he made no mention of the *dîme royale*. It was not until 1784 that Vauban received the *éloge* that was his due. It was pronounced before the Academy at Dijon by Lazare Carnot, at that time a young officer in the Engineers. 'Vauban's principal care', he asserted, 'was always the preservation of his men. This kindness of heart, so characteristic of him, impregnated all his maxims and ideas.' Carnot may have been thinking of the *dîme royale* when he said: 'He was in advance of his century and perhaps his language will only be understood by posterity.'

Of the many people who have left contemporary accounts of these troubled times, one was uniquely placed to be well informed – Mme de Maintenon. Most of the important meetings of the King's Council took place in her room and she knew better than anyone what the King was feeling. Her correspondence with the princesse des Ursins provides a vivid picture of the atmosphere at Versailles, of her own emotions and those of the principal courtiers. On 21 May 1707, she wrote from Marly: 'Marlborough est arrivé!' The name already carried an ominous ring. 'The armies should be assembled in three days' time and you, Madame, expect me to be tranquil. Every day I hear it said at Court that if we lose a battle in Flanders all will be lost, but that if we win one we will hardly be the better for it . . . I have only too many grounds for feeling anxious.'

Marlborough had indeed arrived and he was ready with a plan of campaign which he believed would be 'irresistible and final'. His descendant and biographer, Winston Churchill, describes the general plan. 'His conception was now a double invasion from north and south . . . Marlborough and the Dutch would hold and press hard upon the principal army of France in the fortress zone of the Netherlands. Simultaneously Eugène, with the forces of the Empire sustained by the allied mercenaries and the whole strength of the English and Dutch fleets in the Mediterranean, and based on seaborne supplies and munitions, would invade France from the south. For this purpose they must first of all seize a safe, fortified harbour through which the amphibious power of England could exert itself to the full and also animate the Imperial armies. The mighty French monarchy would be taken between the hammer and the anvil.' That 'safe, fortified harbour' could only be Toulon.

Marlborough faced the opposition of Austria. The chief, if not the only, interest of the Habsburgs was the conquest of Naples. They saw the attack on Toulon as a distraction from this objective. But to capture Naples the Emperor needed the support of British and Dutch naval power. In the end he was forced to agree to the taking of Toulon. Reluctantly it was agreed that Prince Eugène should command the attacking force. The Earl of Manchester, the new ambassador in Vienna, observed that 'they have no great mind to take Toulon . . . Their whole mind is on Italy.' Churchill also notes that Eugène was not in his real element in such a campaign. He describes him as 'a land animal . . . He did not understand the sea; what he knew of it he disliked and distrusted. He had no comprehension of amphibious strategy.' Nevertheless Eugène and Victor-Amadeus, supported by the British fleet under Admiral Sir Cloudesley Shovell, set out to take Toulon.

In the eyes of Mme de Maintenon the outlook was becoming blacker. 'Well, Madame!' she wrote on 23 July, 'now we have the Duke of Savoy burning everything and marching on Toulon: you will believe me if I say that I already see the city on fire, all the King's vessels burnt and our enemies established in Provence.' Her correspondence reveals a strongly pessimistic streak in her. She may have been aware of it. 'I hope to God', she ends, 'that I am mistaken.' In the same letter she observes that 'M. de Vendôme has no fears. He is confident in the extreme.' Later she was to add: 'this confidence cannot fail sometimes to be dangerous'.

The real difficulty lay in the fact that the French forces were too extended. Later in July she wrote: 'We received yesterday the news that twenty-nine battalions had entered Toulon, that they lack for nothing, that there is goodwill everywhere and their resistance will be vigorous . . . But look, Madame: the Kingdom of Naples is lost and with it Sicily: it is not possible to be strong everywhere.' On 7 August she made the same point. 'You chide me that M. le duc d'Orléans does not get his provisions at the right moment; we are just as annoyed as you are, Madame; it is the misfortune of having too many undertakings to support and for too long.'

A fortnight later she was becoming really alarmed. 'How could we possibly be fortunate on all fronts?' Later she adds: 'a happy outcome at Toulon would change the complexion of things; but an adverse one would push us down a very long way. It is this uncertainty which causes me to pass the nights so sadly that it is not possible for the days to be happy.'

On 28 August, however, there was great news. 'Well, Madame! What shall we say of our judgements? M. le maréchal de Tessé has just rendered to France the greatest service which she could receive: the siege of Toulon has been raised; the navy has not been annihilated; the fortress has not been taken; M. de Savoie will have to leave Provence; it has cost us two mediocre vessels and ten or twelve houses burnt. He has failed in his enterprise; he has lost ten thousand men through desertion, through illness and through the actions which have taken place.' A sudden euphoria replaced the months of anxious pessimism.

In September the Court went to Fontainebleau as usual. Mme de Main-tenon states that one of their reasons for going was that it would spell ruin for the local inhabitants if they did not. The widowed Mary of Modena and her son James, the 'Old Pretender', and her daughter Louisa Maria Theresa were among those invited. 'The English Court is here,' wrote Mme de Maintenon. 'The Queen appeared very dejected, although she insists that she is well; the King is large and well made; he is dying to go to war and has been agitating all the summer to serve *incognito*; there are considerable difficulties about this . . . The Princess is large and well made, far more vivacious than her brother and in transports of joy to be at Fontainebleau.'

On 17 October Mme de Maintenon renewed her praise. 'The Princess of England seemed beside herself with joy at all that goes on here; she has been a great success; she has delighted everybody and Madame la duchesse de Bourgogne has conceived such an affection for her that they can hardly leave each other without tears.'

It seemed that Louis was underlining his recognition of the claim of the 'Old Pretender' to the throne of his fathers by the regal manner in which he entertained him and his family. 'Never has the Court been so magnificent as when the Princess was here,' continues Mme de Maintenon. 'Every morning at her *toilette* there are forty or fifty ladies of quality in sumptuous apparel . . . We counted eighty-two coaches in the promenade round the canal, where all the young men were riding beside the windows of the King's coach.' The duc de Bourgogne had restored the beautiful Appartement des Reines Mères on the west side of the Cour de la Fontaine, 'which makes a very beautiful courtyard. We shall be very sorry to go back to Versailles.'

28

Scotland, Oudenarde, Lille

Meanwhile across the Channel certain events were taking place which were to lead Louis into one of his least successful ventures. On 6 September 1701, James II had died. His death raised the question of the status of his son, usually known as the chevalier de Saint-George in France. James had always been referred to by Louis and in the language of Versailles as 'the King of England'. Simple logic suggested that his son should succeed to the same title. Burnet recounts that the French Council debated the matter and the ministers advised that the King should not declare himself, 'but the Dauphin interposed with some heat, for the present owning him King. He thought the King in honour bound to do it; he was of his blood and was driven away on account of religion; so orders were given to proclaim him at Saint-Germain . . . This gave a universal distaste to the whole English nation; all people seemed possessed with a high indignation upon it to see a foreign power, that was at peace with us, pretend to declare who ought to be our King.'

In March 1702, William III died and the throne passed to his sister-in-law Princess Anne. A convinced Calvinist had been replaced by a High Church Anglican. It was in Scotland that the change was most significant. On 1 May 1707, the Act of Union between England and Scotland was passed. It was the signal for the malcontents to unite. Under the leadership of the Duke of Atholl it was decided to ask for French help to restore James – the 'Old Pretender' – to his rightful inheritance. A memorial was drawn up which was to be delivered to Louis by Nathaniel Hooke. It was concerned only with a restoration to Holyrood House and not to St James's Palace.

The first requirement was the presence of the young Prince in Scotland. On his arrival, it was claimed, the nation would rise in support of him and an army of 25,000 foot soldiers and 5,000 cavalry was promised. But a general was needed capable of taking command. The most highly favoured candidate was James's illegitimate half-brother, the Duke of Berwick. Weapons and ammunition were essential, but above all they needed money – 600,000 livres immediately and a regular monthly subsidy. The date proposed for the invasion was September of the same year.

Hooke took upon himself the arduous and sometimes delicate task of obtaining signatures and spent the next month travelling all over Scotland. The response was encouraging: many of the great names of Scotland were on his list. By the middle of June he was in a position to sail for France, where he made contact with the duc de Chevreuse. Chevreuse was close to the centre of events and well informed, but his position was unofficial. This made the relationship easier. His advice to Hooke was clear. 'Have translated the letters to the King which you have brought from the Scottish nobility; give Torcy the original copy but do not show it to Pontchartrain.' He also recommended that the Court of Saint-Germain should know as little as possible. It was not renowned for keeping secrets.

On 1 August 1707, the duc de Chevreuse, together with the marquis de Callières, met Hooke in Paris and drew up a plan of action, which was to be passed to Pontchartrain. The first objective, after having rallied the clans and established control in Scotland, was to capture Newcastle. The supplies of 'sea-coal' from Newcastle were 'so necessary for firing in London that the inhabitants of that place could not be deprived of them for six weeks without being reduced to the greatest extremity'.

The document is also interesting for the light which it sheds on Louis' motives. His determination to support the House of Stuart both in exile and its claims on the British throne was no doubt constant, but in this particular project the words were used: 'This single diversion . . . will force the English instantly to recall the troops and ships which they employ in different countries against His Majesty.' At an important financial level also 'it will entirely destroy the credit of the Exchequer bills and of the commerce of the city of London upon which all the sums employed against His Majesty are advanced'. This in turn 'would soon force the Dutch, upon whom alone the weight of the war would fall, to ask a peace from His Majesty'.

It was emphasised that the thirteen chiefs who had signed the memorandum 'are the richest and most powerful chiefs of that Kingdom, who must be well assured of the enterprise which they undertake since they thereby hazard their lives and families'. They had, however, declared that they could not trust the Court of Saint-Germain and would negotiate only with the French government.

Conspicuous by its absence was the name of the Duke of Hamilton, 'but this Duke', it was claimed, 'does not act sincerely'. He was thought to have been hoping for the crown of Scotland for himself. Hamilton himself wrote direct to Saint-Germain: 'As to the proposal made by Colonel Hooke to give 5,000 men, I cannot approve it . . . If Scotland alone was aimed at I should not make this difficulty about it; but it is not worth while to come to Scotland alone. England is the object, and although the Union has disposed the west of Scotland favourable to the King, yet that does not remedy the other inconveniences or difficulties with regard to England.'

One of the observers of the situation was Daniel Defoe, who was Harley's chief informant. In July he reported on 'the intolerable boldness of the Jacobite party . . . Unless some speedy care is taken to prevent their disorders, the consequences cannot but be fatal.' On 9 August he returned to the subject. 'I must confess I never saw a nation so universally wild . . . They are ripe for every sort of mischief . . . The very Whigs declare openly that they will join with France or King James or anybody rather than be insulted, as they call it, by the English.' The French invasion seemed to be an assured success.

By mid-September the project was ripe for discussion at Versailles, but Louis could not be persuaded. It was Mme de Maintenon, who had formed a friendly relationship with Mary of Modena, who finally won the adherence of the King. The wealthy banker Samuel Bernard offered to put up a million livres for the undertaking. It was not, however, until the early months of 1708 that the expedition was finally organised. At the end of February 6,000 troops were embarked at Dunkirk under the command of the elderly comte de Gacé. The fleet was put under the command of the comte de Forbin – a somewhat hot-headed character who had once been condemned to death for duelling. Having obtained the royal reprieve he devoted himself to a naval career which was marked by a large number of minor successes. He was by no means inexperienced.

On Saturday 28 February, the chevalier de Saint-George arrived at Dunkirk and went on board. He had with him all the paraphernalia of a royal Court. He immediately succumbed to an attack of the measles. He wrote to his mother: 'Here I am at last on board. My body is weak but my spirits are high. I hope my next letter will be from the Palace in Edinburgh. I should be there by Saturday.' He presumably meant Saturday 6 March. Had all gone according to plan that was the earliest possible.

But all did not go according to plan. All naval activities were perforce dependent on weather conditions. A 'Protestant wind' had contributed largely to James II's failure in 1688, a 'Catholic wind' was needed to assure Forbin's success. Admiral Byng was already in the Channel with twenty-six line-of-battle ships. Forbin's much feebler force – five battle-ships, two large frigates and twenty-one smaller ones – was hardly a match for these. Nevertheless he set sail from Dunkirk, 'upon the top of the high water', in the afternoon of Saturday 6 March. The wind at first appeared to be 'Protestant'. High seas held them off the coast of Flanders and three of the frigates, commanded by Lieutenant Rambures, lost their anchors. Byng, however, was forced to retreat to the Downs. The wind was neutral. The afflicted frigates were refitted hastily and Rambures set off for the Firth of Forth, believing that Forbin was ahead of him. He arrived before Leith on Friday 12 March. A large number of Scottish fishing vessels were waiting to transport the troops and munitions ashore. Rambures was assured that the principal noblemen of Scotland were acting in concert and could count on raising an army 20,000 strong. They were only waiting for James to proclaim him King.

But Forbin and the greater part of his fleet had not yet arrived. They had somehow managed to miss the entrance to the Firth. Early on that Friday morning Hooke, on board *Le Mars*, recognised to his horror that they were sailing up the Aberdeenshire coast.

On Saturday morning Rambures ventured out to look for Forbin's fleet. He saw them at the entrance to the Firth, but bearing down on them was an English fleet four times their strength. Forbin wanted to call off the whole enterprise, but Louis had ordered him to obey instructions from James. James refused to give up.

But the delay had been sufficient to enable Byng to confront them off the Island of May. Forbin had no choice but to make for the north. Here, they had the coast of Angus on their port bow. Angus was one of the strongholds of Jacobitism. James demanded to be put ashore. He was confident that his presence, even if alone, was enough to spark off the uprising. Forbin, who was still hard pressed by Byng, refused. The little fleet returned to Dunkirk. The operation had failed.

The Duke of Berwick, who might well have turned the scales the other way had he been in command, insisted on the nature of the real mistake made by Forbin and Gacé. 'The material point', he asserted, 'was that the troops should land with the young King: all Scotland expected him with impatience and was ready to take up arms in his favour; what is more, England was at that time entirely unprovided with troops, so that he might have advanced, without resistance, into the North, where numbers of considerable persons had promised to join them ... The consternation was so great in London that the bank was like to break, every man hastening to withdraw his money: but the news of the ill success of the enterprise soon restored the credit of the government.'

During the summer of 1708 the French Foreign Minister Torcy was already in touch on possible peace terms with Anthony Heinsius, the Pensionary of Holland, who was often represented by Herman von

Petkum. At the end of May Petkum was insisting that France must yield Spain, the Indies and all recent conquests in the Netherlands and Alsace, and that Louis should acknowledge Queen Anne as the legitimate ruler of Great Britain.

England was also entering into negotiations with France. At the end of October, Marlborough wrote to Berwick: 'In my view it is in our power to take such a step as will produce peace before the next campaign . . . I have no other object than to end this wearisome war.'

England's priority requirement was expressed by the House of Lords in early March 1709: 'That the French King may be obliged to own Your Majesty's title and the Protestant Succession as it is established by the laws of Great Britain; and that the Allies may be engaged to become guarantees of the same. And that Your Majesty would take effectual measures that the Pretender shall be removed out of the French Dominions.'

Berwick, on his return from Spain at the beginning of 1708, had been summoned to Versailles and nominated to replace Tessé in command of the army in Dauphiné. He noted that at the same time the duc de Bourgogne had been given the command in Flanders 'with the duc de Vendôme under him'. The campaign which followed was a disaster.

'The year 1708', wrote Saint-Simon, 'began with thanksgivings and fêtes and pleasures.' It seemed as if Blenheim, Ramillies and Turin had been forgotten. 'Only too soon did we perceive that it did not continue thus for long.'

'On 30 April, after dinner,' records the marquis de Sources, 'when the King returned from hunting . . . he went to the apartment of the duchesse de Bourgogne and informed her that her husband would be leaving on 14 May, with the duc de Berry his brother, to take over the command in Flanders, where he would have under him the duc de Vendôme.' That evening the duc de Bourgogne wrote to his brother in Spain: 'You will easily understand how great is my joy . . . It is a great pleasure for me, after a gap of four whole years, to find myself as it were back in service and not remaining useless at Versailles or Marly or Fontainebleau.'

He made no mention of the appointment of the duc de Vendôme. This general was an illegitimate grandson of Henri IV and Gabrielle d'Estrées. That was enough to secure him the favour of the King and his popularity with the private soldier, but it gave him a sense of his own superiority which, in his own eyes, released him from any of the obligations of decency and decorum. 'Filthy in the extreme', according to Saint-Simon, 'and proud of it.' An atheist and a libertine, he was also a practising homosexual – a condition which Louis abominated, 'full of righteous horror for all the men of Sodom' – except, apparently, those of the royal blood.

On the positive side Vendôme had many of the qualities of a great commander – a quick eye for the situation, a promptness to make decisions and a complete indifference to personal danger made him a leader capable of turning a defeat into a last-minute victory. 'I find that M. de Saint-Frémond is right', the princesse des Ursins wrote to Mme de Maintenon, 'to think he has seen Henri IV rallying his troops, speaking to his soldiers as he used to, and setting them the example of valour which they knew so well.' Such a man could easily become the hero of the armies and the idol of the people. Sourches describes an occasion when Vendôme went to the opera in Paris. All places were booked at least a week in advance and when he arrived he received a standing ovation to cries of 'Vive Vendôme!'

Such was the man, a prey to a natural indolence and a temper which made him sulky when things were not going his way, whom Louis appointed to serve *under* the duc de Bourgogne. In some ways they were complementary to each other. Vendôme was audacious, Bourgogne circumspect; Vendôme was slack about discipline, Bourgogne strict. At their disposition Bourgogne and Vendôme had the finest troops in France; Saint-Simon described them as 'smart and of the highest morale . . . and with a prodigious supply of artillery and provisions'. But there was this one fatal weakness which Louis should have foreseen – it was in fact a divided command. Did the duc de Bourgogne's rank outweigh Vendôme's experience? Who did actually command the army?

In early March 1708, everything pointed towards an encounter between the two armies. Marlborough knew that his position at home was deteriorating. His wife was losing her influence over Queen Anne and the Tory Party was losing its power to the Whigs. He feared that the Dutch might sue separately for peace. A brilliant success on the battlefield was needed to put courage into the Dutch and to restore his own credit in England.

On the French side, the duc de Bourgogne was burning to distinguish himself. On 29 May he wrote to his brother in Spain: 'The army here is fine and in great spirits . . . I hope, my dear brother, that, if we find a favourable occasion, we will be able to restore to your obedience a part of the land which you have lost in the last two years . . . the deep affection which I feel for you would cause me great pleasure to have had some part in it.' At this stage no one seemed aware of the dangers of a divided command except Saint-Simon, who, with greater foresight than Louis, predicted that 'the stronger of the two will be the ruin of the weaker, and that the stronger in this case was Vendôme, who was restrained by no bridle and no fears . . . You will see M. de Vendôme emerge with glory and Monseigneur le duc de Bourgogne lost – lost in the eyes of the Court, of France and of the whole of Europe.'

It started well. Bellerive, whose account of the campaign of 1708 is clearly biased in favour of Vendôme (who was thought to be his father), describes a moving scene. 'Nothing could be so charming as to witness the deference of the duc de Bourgogne towards the duc de Vendôme. One day at table the *Généralissime* rose with a glass in his hand and said to Vendôme: "Come, Monsieur; we must drink to the success of our campaign; I wish to take wine with you." Vendôme raised his glass, but said: "I do not desire any ceremony with you, whom we all regard as the father and the guide of the army." ' More authentic, probably, is Vendôme's letter to Chamillart: 'I observe an intelligence and a kindness in Monseigneur le duc de Bourgogne, which I think are proof against anything. I will not forget the orders which you have given me.'

Marlborough was clearly aware of all this. 'I am very pleased with their changing their generals in France', wrote Godolphin to him, 'and I think it is no good sign for them. I am of the opinion that the Duke of Burgundy and the rest of the French princes that accompany him, will be a hindrance and a perplexity to M. de Vendôme, and not any advantage, but I agree with you that the occasion for action will arise soon, not only because of the superiority of the French forces, but in view of the impetuous nature of the young Prince, who is filled with ambition and eager to acquire a reputation for himself in the world.'

By the end of May the two armies were facing each other at a distance of about ten miles across the plateau of Mont Saint-Jean, later to become the 'bleak plain' of Waterloo. Marlborough's army, however, was not yet at full strength. He had summoned Prince Eugène, who commanded 30,000 men on the Moselle, but, as Marlborough wrote to Godolphin on 28 June, he 'cannot join me in less than ten days and . . . their foot must have 14 or 15 days. If they cannot make greater expedition, I fear the horse of the Duke of Berwick will get before them, which I have writ to the prince, by express, this morning.'

Berwick, a professed Catholic, was very conscious of his semi-royal status and as a maréchal de France he could not endure the thought of taking orders from any but a Prince of the Blood. He begged Chamillart to obtain for him a position directly under the command of the duc de Bourgogne, 'in order to avoid a mortification which would be like a dagger in my heart and would make me, in spite of my goodwill and my zeal, incapable of thought or action'. Berwick and Vendôme were no more likely to get on with each other than Vendôme and Bourgogne.

It would have been a good moment for Vendôme to strike, before Eugène had arrived, but Vendôme was in no hurry. He made a few suggestions – such as laying siege to a little place called Huy – of which Bourgogne did not approve. The matter was referred to the King. The despatch and return of a courier between the army and Fontainebleau took the best part of a week. Louis agreed with Bourgogne. Vendôme then suggested an attack on Brussels, where Marlborough had his head-quarters. Bourgogne saw the considerable hazards involved. 'You know', he wrote to Chamillart, 'that the confidence of M. de Vendôme leads him to regard whatever he wants as easy.' Louis was again asked to decide and again came down against the project.

At the end of June Bourgogne wrote to his brother: 'We have been here in all tranquillity since the beginning of the month. We are in a position to move as we like, to right or left, and to anticipate the enemy, who wait on our movements to make their own plans.' What Marlborough was waiting for was the arrival of Prince Eugène and his army.

It was not until early July that any move was made. The French forces attacked Ghent and Bruges simultaneously and successfully. The news was received at Fontainebleau, recounts Saint-Simon, 'with unbridled joy'. On 11 July Louis organised a *repas champêtre* in one of the clearings in the forest near Moret-sur-Loing. 'A light repast was served to all those invited', records Dangeau, 'and the outing was spent with much gaiety.' At the same hour the battle of Oudenarde began.

Marlborough was disconsolate at the loss of Ghent and Bruges, but Prince Eugène himself arrived in Brussels on 6 July. 'The appearance of the illustrious chief', writes Coxe, 'restored joy and alacrity, and Marlborough welcomed him by observing, "I am not without hopes of congratulating Your Highness on a great victory; for my troops will be animated by the presence of so distinguished a commander." '

Everything seemed to favour the chances of the French. But all the moves which they made were started late and executed slowly; irresolution and perplexity were evident in all their movements. It was not until 10 July that they had reached the banks of the Escaut, at the village of Gavre, a little downstream of Oudenarde. Once again Marlborough acted speedily and decisively. Once again Vendôme procrastinated, and when Biron, who commanded the advanced guard, had crossed the river he was astonished to find the enemy already in force on the other side.

One of the most authentic and succinct accounts of the battle was written by the son of the Musketeer d'Artagnan, killed at the siege of Maastricht. 'It was not thought that they could cross the Escaut so quickly,' he wrote; 'our army was in no hurry and only left the camp at Gavre at ten o'clock, and while we were crossing the bridges [which they had had to construct] Monseigneur le duc de Bourgogne received information that the enemy were crossing the Escaut at Oudenarde and that there were already some twenty battalions and forty squadrons passed across. This obliged the army to accelerate their march.' Vendôme was at once informed and commented that 'it must have been devils who carried them there for such diligence was impossible'. He ordered Biron to attack, but on ground that was either marshy or intersected by numerous hedge-rows which made the use of cavalry impossible.

'We were obliged to begin the attack on the left,' continues d'Artagnan, 'our right being not yet in place, so that it all turned into a number of isolated combats which had no connection with each other.' The battle, in fact, degenerated into a series of improvisations. There was no plan of action, no orders issued, with the result that fifty battalions and eighty squadrons remained on the high ground without ever taking part.

'All this continued from three o'clock until half past eight in the evening, the soldiers disheartened and the enemy in possession of the hedges which surrounded us; we were not able to make our soldiers try again because of the terrible fire which the enemy opened whenever we approached them . . . To add to that the night was falling and our infantry in great disorder, having been obliged to grin and bear it for more than an hour without any ammunition against an enemy which was unsparing with it. I made up my mind to consider retreating, for I had received no orders . . . It all passed in one bitter infantry battle, of the loss of which I have the honour to inform you, but since we have lost no artillery, no flags, no standards and no baggage, that cannot be called a great infantry battle. It is true that it was the fiercest that I have ever seen. I think that the enemy losses were about the same as ours, which, I believe, do not exceed on our side 3,000 men.'

This 'defeat' left the French in a situation which was difficult without being desperate. Quick and vigorous resolutions might still have saved the day. They were never made. Hesitations followed hesitations, counter-orders followed counter-orders: and the campaign which had started under such good auspices ended in the most humiliating defeat of Louis' reign – the loss of Lille and the surrender of Flanders.

On 12 July the Duke of Marlborough wrote to the Duchess 'to bring you the good news of a battle we had yesterday, in which it pleased God to give us, at last, the advantage . . . I thank God the English have suffered less than any other of the troops, none of our English horse having been engaged. I thank God for his goodness in protecting and making me the instrument of so much happiness to the Queen and the nation *if she will please to make use of it.*'

While Marlborough was thanking God for the victory, the duc de Bourgogne was thanking God for the defeat, for chastening him for the inadequacy of his personal piety. 'Success would have swollen my pride,' he wrote to his old moral tutor Beauvilliers. God had spared him this danger by humiliating him to remind him of his own helplessness and emptiness and the imperfection of his faith. He was guilty, in an interesting way, of the same egocentricity in faith as the Calvinist Colonel Blackader had been in his conviction that the Almighty deflected the cannon balls from his person. But if Bourgogne gave the credit to God for chastising him by withholding a victory which might have endangered his salvation, he put the blame for the defeat of the French on the inactivity of the duc de Vendôme.

In a letter to Mme de Maintenon written two days after the battle he said: 'You were only too right when I saw you trembling to see our affairs entrusted to the duc de Vendôme. There are not two opinions here on the matter. I knew well that in the running of the service he was no general; without foresight, without making any arrangements, without taking the trouble to obtain news of the enemy, for whom he had nothing but contempt. This is not from the point of view of courage, because he suffered more himself than all the rest of the army, and on that count one cannot praise him too highly.' That was the only praise that he could give. 'He never enjoyed the confidence of the officers; he has now lost that of the troops. He scarcely does anything but eat and sleep . . . Add to that his extreme confidence that the enemy will never do anything that he does not want them to do; that he has never suffered defeat and that he never will.'

On 12 July, having written to his wife, Marlborough also wrote to Godolphin: 'I believe Lord Stair will tell you they were in as strong a post as is possible to be found; but you know that when I left England I was positively resolved to endeavour by all means a battle, thinking nothing else would make the Queen's business go on so well. This reason alone made me venture the battle yesterday . . . I am very sensible that had it miscarried I would have been blamed. I hope I have given such a blow to their foot that they will not be able to fight any more this year. My head aches so terribly that I must say no more.'

On 14 July, a little after midday, the news of the defeat at Oudenarde arrived at Fontainebleau. Speculation was rife about who was to blame. The courtiers at that time were in a difficult position. When Louis died it would be profitable to have been well thought of by the Dauphin and by his closest associates, known as the *Cabale de Meudon*. In the event of the duc de Bourgogne succeeding the same situation would arise. The *Cabale de Meudon*, however, staked all on the hope of the early succession and long reign of the Grand Dauphin. They heartily disliked the duc de Bourgogne. The duc de Vendôme was one of the familiars of Meudon and the members of the cabal did all in their power to put the responsibility for the failure at Oudenarde on the shoulders of the duc de Bourgogne. The courtiers of Meudon, including Vendôme, were mostly libertines. Bourgogne was a puritan and as such incurred their contempt. Mme de Maintenon naturally sided with the puritans, and her strong affection for the duchesse de Bourgogne, who was on the best of terms with her husband, further attached her to Bourgogne's cause.

Mlle d'Aumale was probably expressing the general opinion at Fontainebleau when writing of Oudenarde to a friend at Saint-Cyr: 'There have been few casualties. M. de Vendôme was over-confident and engaged in combat with no order and almost no preparation. M. le duc de Bourgogne agreed with all the good advice, but he had orders to obey M. de Vendôme . . . Our army wants only to retrieve its losses; it is still fine and fit.' In isolation the 'defeat' at Oudenarde might not have mattered. It was the sequel, culminating in the loss of Lille, that nearly ruined France.

Marlborough's own assessment of the situation is given in a letter to Godolphin dated 26 July. 'That which I think is our greatest advantage consists in the fear that is among their troops, so that I shall seek all occasions of attacking them. But their army is far from being inconsiderable, for when the Duke of Burgundy's regiment shall join that of the Duke of Berwick, they will be at least one hundred thousand men.' He ended with a backwards glance at the battle itself. 'If it had pleased God that we had had one hour's daylight more at Oudenarde, we had in all likelihood made an end of this war.'

On 23 July Mme de Maintenon gave her own account to the princesse des Ursins. 'M. de Vendôme, who believes anything he wishes to believe, wanted to give battle and lost it, and we are in a far worse position than we were, as much through the loss of our troops as by the fear of what may come next and the air of superiority which the enemy now has.' But she looked on the brighter side of things. 'Our troops have done their duty; they are in no way discouraged and ask for nothing more than to retrieve their losses . . . M. le duc de Bourgogne had all the right ideas, but was under orders to yield to M. de Vendôme as being the more experienced.' In her opinion Vendôme was clearly in charge.

She then describes the effect which all this had on Marie-Adélaïde. 'She shows in all this sorry business the sentiments of a good Frenchwoman, as I have always known her to be. I admit that I did not think she loved the duc de Bourgogne to the extent that we now see . . . she was vividly aware that the first action in which he took part was unfortunate; she would like him to expose himself like a grenadier – and come back without a scratch; she feels the pain in which he is on account of the misfortune which has occurred; she shares all the anxieties which his present situation must cause him. She would like a battle for him to win – but she fears it.'

Of Louis, Mme de Maintenon claims: 'The King endures this last turn of events with great submission to the will of God.' Then she touches on the real problem. 'It is not possible that this will not cause a coldness between M. le duc de Bourgogne and M. de Vendôme because of the divergence of their opinions; and how much will people contribute to increase it by their wicked words!'

Immediately after the battle of Oudenarde neither the French nor the Anglo-Dutch army had all their forces at hand. Eugène himself had managed to join Marlborough, but only by leaving his troops behind. They were now in Brussels. The Duke of Berwick, who had been shadowing them, was at Tournai. The advantage would pass to whichever commander could rally his forces first and take the offensive. In the circumstances it was not likely to be the French. Vendôme, who had lulled himself into his habitual sense of security, was advocating inactivity. Even d'Artagnan considered the case of the allies 'a great deal worse than ours'. The French made the most classic of all errors: they underrated the opposition.

Eugène's troops had by now arrived and were stationed in Brussels. They were detailed to escort a large convoy of provisions to Marlborough. Berwick learnt of this. 'I alerted Monseigneur le duc de Bourgogne and M. de Vendôme; I represented to them the necessity of attacking this convoy.' He had worked out all the details, but in vain. 'M. de Vendôme would never consent to it, alleging the reason that he was well placed at Ghent; that while he was there the enemies would not dare to undertake anything and that therefore he would in no way dream of moving.'

Berwick knew that Marlborough intended to attack Lille. He knew that he would be unable to do so without bringing from Brussels the artillery and all the other apparatus which was needed for this. 'Another, more important convoy was being prepared. I proposed that we should take measures to attack it, but M. de Vendôme remained firm in his refusal.'

The reason for Vendôme's refusal to leave Ghent is made clear in a letter from Marlborough to his wife, written on 16 July. 'I was in good hopes that the diligence I have made in getting into the French country (for I am now behind their lines) would have obliged them to abandon Ghent... M. de Vendôme declares he will sacrifice a strong garrison rather than abandon that town, which, if he keeps his word, will give me a great deal of trouble, for till we are masters of Ghent we have no cannon.'

On the same day he wrote to Godolphin: 'We are now masters of marching where we please, but can make no siege till we are masters of Ghent from whence only can we have our cannon.' But Marlborough was not content to leave it at that. A week later he wrote to Godolphin to say that he had ordered twenty 'battering pieces' to be brought from Maastricht and sixty more from Holland. 'The calculation of the number of draught horses, to draw this artillery, amounts to sixteen thousand horses.'

Marlborough, left to himself with an all-British army, might well have got to Versailles. But the Dutch were far less adventuresome than he was. 'It is plain', he wrote to Godolphin, 'that they think enough is done for peace, and I am afraid they will not willingly consent for the marching of their army into France, which certainly, if it succeeded, would put a happy end to the war.' It was an opportunity missed. 'Marlborough', writes Sir Winston Churchill, 'might have moved at this time the whole allied army into France behind the fortress line, fed himself comfortably upon the country, and received his munitions and reinforcements through Abbeville.' Chamillart sensed this and wrote to Berwick: 'You must be very attentive to any movements the enemy may make with a considerable corps towards the Somme and the Authie. That would be the sure way of completing the ruin of Picardy and of spreading terror throughout Normandy and to the very gates of Paris.' That, however, was a dream which was never realised.

On 15 July Berwick wrote to Chamillart: 'I admit to you that I am in a terrible state of anxiety, because if no one is in a hurry to take a positive line there could be the most unfortunate consequences.' On 23 July Chamillart wrote to Vendôme: 'There is no remedy for past mistakes, but the greatest of all that could arise, and the most harmful to the interests of the King, would be to see any continuation of the estrangement between M. le duc de Bourgogne and yourself.' He reminded Vendôme that the duc de Bourgogne would have no superior except the King 'if His Majesty had not conferred it upon you'. This seems clearly to suggest that Vendôme was effectively regarded as the commander-in-chief of the army. His actions do not always seem to support that view. He hardly seemed to regard himself as being in charge. On the same day that Berwick wrote to Chamillart, Vendôme wrote to the King: 'I begged Monseigneur le duc de Bourgogne, every time that I saw him of a different opinion from my own – something that happens often, not to say always – to have the goodness to render an account to Your Majesty, in order that He may know the small share which I have in what is going on here.'

A month later, on 26 August, Louis wrote to Bourgogne: 'In the two armies of the enemy there cannot be more than 136 battalions and 130 squadrons: that which you command and that of the maréchal de Berwick have at least an equal number.' There is no suggestion that Vendôme was in command.

It is clear that it was Louis himself who was regarded as the ultimate authority, but he had perforce to exercise it by remote control. Disagreements between Bourgogne and Vendôme were frequently referred to his decision and in this way much time was lost. Progress was not being made. The laziness and sulkiness of Vendôme, the conscientious indecision of Bourgogne and the constant referring of decisions to Louis gave Marlborough and Eugène the time which they needed.

Between these two generals there existed a close understanding. In a letter to Mr Travers, who was superintending the work on Blenheim Palace, dated 30 July, Marlborough wrote: 'No one can be a better judge than yourself of the sincerity of my wishes [for an honourable peace] to enjoy a little retirement at a place you have contributed, in a great measure, to the making so desirable ... I dare say Prince Eugène and I shall never differ about our share of the laurels.' There was more to it than that. 'It is remarkable, very surprising and almost without precedent', wrote the chevalier de Quincy, 'that there had never been any altercation between these two great men while they were serving together, although they were of different nationality and religion and in the service of different princes whose interests were always very different. They acted together in the common cause without any professional jealousy.' It is not altogether true to say that Marlborough and Eugene never disagreed. After Oudenarde Marlborough wanted to push on into France. Eugène was more cautious. He wanted a firm base behind them. The States General of the Dutch were always on the side of prudence. It was decided to capture Lille.

Louis behaved with more wisdom than Vendôme and with more resolution than Bourgogne. On 27 July he wrote to his grandson: 'I have to tell you that, although I approve the course of wisdom and precaution, there are certain cases in which one finds it necessary to take risks, and I have decided to do so if the enemies determine to lay siege to Lille, as there are grounds for belief. There is not a moment to lose, in conjunction with the Duke of Berwick, to make arrangements for your march and to join forces. Nothing less than the city of Lille could possibly oblige me to take the decision to try all possible means to prevent the enemy from taking it.'

The maréchal de Boufflers, Governor of Flanders, went himself to the city to encourage the defenders. It was an unusual move for a governor to make and it earned him much credit. But it did not bring home to the rival commanders the urgency of the situation.

Louis' despatches became more and more pressing. 'I have sent you an instruction', he wrote to Bourgogne on 30 July, 'that I am determined to help Lille or Tournay in case of a siege. The diligence of the enemy is extreme; they are surpassing their own hopes and they are finding nothing to stop or even hinder them.' To Vendôme he wrote on the same day: 'The heavy artillery which they have taken from Maastricht should by now be in Brussels. It would be greatly to our advantage to fall upon the escorting troops with a superior force and it would be impossible to take measures too precisely for that.'

By this time Bourgogne and Vendôme claimed to be acting in harmony. Ignoring the King's instruction, they agreed to lay siege to Ostend. This was the port from which Marlborough's supplies and reinforcements from England would arive. On 1 August Vendôme wrote to Louis: 'I hope that we will get together a body sufficient to make our enemies repent if they are ever so audacious as to attack Lille or Tournay – which I have always found it difficult to believe.'

The duc de Bourgogne was not only in correspondence with Louis and Chamillart. He was also in constant communication with the duc de Beauvilliers. 'It is certain that we should put our trust in God alone, and although our situation appears good enough at present, He could, if He wishes, completely overwhelm us with a final blow, or raise us up again in a manner that comes only from Him . . . Let us humble ourselves more than ever; let us have recourse to God, let us get right with him and all will be well.' Whether this was advanced as an excuse for inactivity is not clear.

Meanwhile Prince Eugène was taking advantage of the leisure afforded him by this inactivity to assemble in Brussels, 87 miles from Lille, 80 heavy-calibre cannons, 20 mortars, 3,000 munition wagons and 16,000 horses: a column some 70,000 yards long that took 14 hours to march past. On 5 August this convoy, a tempting target to Vendôme on one side and to Berwick on the other, left Brussels, taking at first the road to Mons in order to disguise its real destination, but altering course abruptly at Soignies to make for Lille, successfully using a road which Vendôme had described as 'absolutely impassable because of the rain'. On 12 August Marlborough and Eugène arrived before Lille 'without having encount-ered', wrote Eugène to the Emperor, 'the least opposition'. They began to invest it the same day, but it was not until the 23rd that the trenches were opened. Berwick on his own had not sufficient forces with which to confront Marlborough, and Vendôme did not make the slightest effort to join forces with him. Lille, the taking of which had been one of Louis' earliest triumphs; Lille, the most important of frontier fortresses, the first fruit of Vauban's new system of defence – 'sa fille ainée dans la fortifi-cation': Lille was now itself besieged.

Saint-Simon wrote to Chamillart with some asperity, demanding to know the cause of all this inactivity. He received no answer. The marquis de Feuquières expressed his astonishment. 'How can one understand that the enemy, in such an extended line, could provide such cover to this long procession that neither the army of M. le duc de Berwick nor that of M. le duc de Bourgogne undertook any action against this convoy? That is something which no person with any sense will ever understand.'

In vain had Louis sent orders to Bourgogne, with copies to Vendôme, to get his army on the march within four days, and go to the assistance of the besieged town. Vendôme made no move, explaining that the opposing army would be so enfeebled by the losses sustained in the siege of Lille, which could hold out for at least three months, and that 'we should not move off from here until we have heard the enemy's cannon firing for at least eight days'. On 17 August Vendôme ended a despatch to Chamillart with the words: 'It seems that the conclusion from all this is that we should be in no hurry.' Chamillart answered with some asperity: 'Permit me to say, Monseigneur, that whatever confidence I may have in your predictions, I would have a lot more faith when you are in striking distance of being able to succour Lille.'

On 21 August Bourgogne wrote to Louis: 'We will be at Tournay on the 30th and in a position to see what could be done to save Lille, which we will attempt unless it is morally impossible ... We will not lose a moment to put ourselves in a position to know if Lille can be succoured or not ... It is certain that we cannot proceed with too much prudence and precaution ... We must pray to God that everything will turn out all right.'

'One does not risk giving advice', wrote Mme de Maintenon on 19 August, 'when the stakes are so high; however, this is the situation we are in: the enemies are laying siege to Lille; if they take this place they have a foothold in France; if there is a battle and we are beaten, then we are lost. If we beat them we are conducting the finest campaign in the world.

'I do not know how we can survive the two or three weeks that our uncertainty may last. One does not live when one is in the state that we are at present. It is impossible to think or speak of anything else ... I think that all is lost and I do not allow myself the tiniest hope.'

Mme de Maintenon must not be taken as reflecting Louis' own opinions. 'You know the King too well to judge of his sentiments by mine; although I have the honour to see him often, he cannot communicate to me the smallest part of his courage and I cannot inspire him with the smallest part of my fears.'

A week later she reported again on the duchesse de Bourgogne and her anxieties about her husband. 'In a word, Madame, she is fasting for him. In the agitations that she is in, she no longer lives ... She continually studies the countenance of the King and she is in despair if she thinks she sees any sign of gloom ... she tries to amuse herself, but she does not succeed; her heart beats at the arrival of every courier; she fears for the life of her husband; she fears for his reputation ... she would be most upset if he did anything of which the King did not approve; in fact she is at present one of the most unhappy people in the world.'

Louis was apparently reluctant to issue direct commands. It had been his policy in the days of Condé and Turenne to leave them a wide margin of liberty in the details of the execution. On 22 August he wrote to Bourgogne: 'If you are pressed by the maréchal de Boufflers you may, without waiting for my approval or consent, follow whatever way you think advisable for my interests and the best suited for the deliverance of Lille.' Two days later he stressed: 'Your true and only objective is to keep hold of Lille.'

At last, on 29 August, Vendôme and Berwick having joined forces, the former could write to Louis: 'The army is marching to the relief of Lille with a goodwill that is a great pleasure.' Their progress, however, was needlessly slow. Two days were spent in Tournai, partly so that Bourgogne could follow a religious procession led by the Bishop. It was here that animosity between Vendôme and Berwick broke out. The former wanted to make a detour towards Douai to collect some heavy artillery; the latter wanted to make straight for Lille. Bourgogne wavered between the two counsels. But the route proposed by Vendôme turned out to be impracticable and Bourgogne sided with Berwick. After two days of heavy going through difficult country the French armies found themselves face to face with Marlborough and Eugène. Marlborough was conscious of his superior position. On 3 September he wrote to Godolphin: 'The ground is so very much for our advantage that with the help of God we will certainly beat them, so that it were to be wished that they would venture, but I really think they will not.'

He was right. The rival commanders referred the decision to Louis. By the same courier Vendôme wrote privately to Chamillart: 'It is pitiful to see how the goodwill of this army has been rendered useless by the counsels of the Duke of Berwick and a few of the generals, who have destroyed in one minute, in the mind of Monseigneur le duc de Bourgogne, all that I have been able to inspire in them.' He concluded by asking to be relieved of his command.

On 6 September Berwick wrote to Chamillart: 'With an infantry already discouraged and the small number of our battalions, we would run the risk not only of being driven back but of being completely overthrown.

It is sad to see Lille lost, but it would be sadder still to see the loss of the only army left to us which could halt the enemy after the loss of Lille. If there were any likelihood of succeeding one might take the risk, but I have to admit that I cannot foresee anything good if the decision is made to attack the enemy where they are.'

Bourgogne, at the same time, wrote to Louis asking for his decision. 'On the one hand the extreme confidence of M. de Vendôme is to be feared, on the other hand the counsels of timidity are equally so.'

Louis was beginning to show signs of exasperation. On 7 September he wrote to Bourgogne: 'It would not be possible for anything to happen more embarrassing in the end, nor more dishonouring to you, than for you to have approached Lille with an army which you command and to have the mortification of seeing it captured by the enemy.' Louis is putting the responsibility on the duc de Bourgogne with the words *which you command.* To Vendôme he wrote: 'I persist in wishing that you come to the assistance of this place and that you do all that is humanly possible to achieve this.'

In the evening of 9 September, Chamillart took the post-chaise to Flanders. 'Many people', wrote the marquis de Sourches, 'have formed the opinion that it is in order to put an end to the contentions of the generals.' Chamillart was sufficiently successful in his mission of reconciliation to obtain agreement between Vendôme and Berwick. By 10 September their armies had crossed the little stream of the Marck and were confronting the enemy. None of the French generals, however, advocated attacking. On 15 September the French re-crossed the Marck. Eugène was in favour of attacking them, but the Deputies from Holland opposed the idea. 'If Alexander or Caesar', wrote Eugène, 'had had in their camp *Messieurs les Députés de Hollande*, their conquests would have been less rapid.' But Eugène was probably right; Berwick himself admitted that 'if this project had been executed, we would have been utterly routed, in as much as our flanks were exposed and we did not have enough room to manoeuvre'. The French were lucky to get away with it.

On 12 September Bourgogne wrote to Beauvilliers: 'I am more embarrassed than ever, seeing that I bear the weight of a matter of such consequence and which is of great concern to the State. My resource is in God, but this does not mean that I do not suffer a lot in myself... May God enlighten and assist us, for, as for me, I tremble at every step.' It is clear that Bourgogne was steadily losing confidence in himself.

During all this time the life of the Court was more or less suspended. There was no gambling, no theatricals. All Bishops were required to arrange for public prayers; churches were full. 'Truly there was a great need', wrote Sourches, 'to have recourse to the mercy of God at a moment when the State was so near to ruin.' Saint-Simon adds a few touches: 'Fear was painted on every face in a shameful manner. A horse is heard passing a little fast: all start running, they know not where. Chamillart's apartment is besieged by lackeys reaching right down into the street. Everyone wants to know the moment a courier arrives, and this horrid situation lasted nearly a month.'

On 9 September Mme de Maintenon wrote to the princesse des Ursins: 'I have not had a moment's repose since Lille was invested. The King, who had foreseen this, though he found it difficult to believe, first sent word to M. le duc de Bourgogne and M. le duc de Vendôme that if it should happen it would be absolutely necessary to relieve it. M. de Vendôme was determined not to leave, whatever was said, clinging to the belief that it was a ruse of the enemy's to make us abandon Ghent and always maintained that he would not leave until he knew that the trenches were open and he could hear the cannons firing. 'Our anxiety was very great about their joining up with M. de Berwick; it was accomplished very fortunately and we have not received any letters that do not assure us that the soldiers are raring to fight. Since we have known them to be in reach of Lille we have ceased to live. I cannot convey to you the agitation of our dear princess, and all the prayer that she offers and has been offering day and night. Everyone has an interest that is both general and particular. I see nothing but tears and trembling and groaning. Everyone around me is even more apprehensive than I am.'

In the midst of all this anxious agony Louis remained calm and inscrutable. 'The King alone is firm in his desire for a combat for the relief of Lille and for the honour of our country.' He was to be disappointed. On 16 September Mme de Maintenon passed on the news to the princess. 'Finally, Madame, all our generals in Flanders have informed the King unanimously that the enemies are inaccessible on account of the entrenchments which they have had the time to make and perfect.' This use of earthworks was something that Prince Eugène had learnt from the Turks in one of his previous campaigns.

At the army's headquarters, however, there was an atmosphere of optimism. On 20 September Vendôme wrote to Chamillart: 'One might hope, without flattering oneself, that it will end to the contentment of the King. There is ground for thinking that the enemies will suffer much in a day or two from lack of provender and lack of communication with their countries.' The new policy was to cut the communications of the Anglo-Dutch army so that no reinforcements, ammunition or provisions could reach the besiegers. It was exactly what Marlborough was most afraid of.

In mid-September the English fleet landed 4,700 troops and a large quantity of munitions at Ostend. On 23 September Louis wrote to Bourgogne: 'All depends on your attention to giving the comte de La Mothe sufficient means to prevent the enemy from getting anything out of Ostend . . . Do not lose a minute to put him in a position to oppose the march of the convoy which is being prepared.' La Mothe, however, launched his attack before the reinforcements sent by Bourgogne had arrived and was driven off. The English commanders Webb and Cadogan delivered their supplies intact to Lille.

Bourgogne accepted the inevitable but suggested that in the following spring his army might recapture Lille. Chamillart wrote a somewhat quenching reply. 'I could not be of the same opinion as you in thinking of retaking Lille, supposing that it is already lost. I assure you that it is still a lot easier to save it, in the condition in which it is, than it would be to lay siege to it if it were in the hands of the enemy.'

Louis wrote to Bourgogne: 'I cannot persuade myself to make any decision which presupposes the loss of this important place, which it would have been easy to retain if the convoys of the enemy, especially this last one, had been intercepted.' Louis, however, refused to fight their battles for them. 'I will not give you positive orders as to what you will have to do in the different circumstances that may present themselves. It is for you to think them out with the duc de Vendôme and the maréchal de Berwick.' He adds: 'it is a matter of honour that you should not remain inactive on the other side of the Escaut, but do all that is humanly possible to deny the enemy the means of enabling convoys to pass through, either while the siege of Lille continues, or even after the taking of the city, if it has the misfortune to be taken'.

Vendôme's only reaction was to write to Louis on 30 September: 'We are going to take such effective measures that no more convoys will pass.' His 'effective measures' were to open the sluices and flood the land. But he did not know what he was doing. The flood was only partial and Marlborough had no difficulty in obtaining flat-bottomed barges that could carry his provisions as far as the roads which led to Lille. When Vendôme tried to answer with his own ships they turned out to be useless since they drew too much water.

On 22 October Bourgogne wrote to Louis that he hoped he would 'do him the justice to believe that I have always acted for what seemed to me to be the best'; but he added, 'I fear, nevertheless, that we shall see Lille taken whatever we do.' He was, it seems, in no sort of a hurry. He told Louis that he would muster his army on 24 October, cross the Escaut on the 25th and join forces with Vendôme on the 26th. On 23 October the city of Lille capitulated.

In December the duc de Bourgogne and the duc de Vendôme were recalled. On Saturday the 8th Bourgogne wrote to Beauvilliers: 'I hope to be at Versailles on Tuesday. I cannot make much haste because of the ice and snow, but I will try and arrive to meet Mme la duchesse de Bourgogne three or four leagues this side of Versailles.' Etiquette, however, required that he should not see anyone before presenting himself to the King. He may well have awaited this reception with some trepidation; there is a certain air of relief about his account of it. 'I am very content', he wrote to Beauvilliers, 'with the audience I have just had with the King, and I have reason to believe that he is content with me. I followed your advice. I admitted my faults and spoke freely. He gave evidence of much tenderness and I am deeply touched by it.'

Vendôme, according to the marquis de Sourches, was also received 'très agréablement'. His audience, however, only lasted for one hour whereas Bourgogne had been with the King for three. Louis studiously avoided any criticism of either of them. There may have been in this the tacit admission of his own mistake – that of dividing the command of an army between a Prince of the Blood and a veteran campaigner.

At the beginning of the year 1709 Marlborough wrote to Godolphin: 'This has been a very laborious campaign, but I am sensible that the next will be more troublesome; for most certainly the enemy will venture and do their utmost to get the better of us; but I trust in the Almighty that he will protect and give success to our just cause.'

At the end of the year 1708 the curé of Lamothe-Landeron in the Bordelais wrote in his register: 'Nothing extraordinary has happened except in the field of war. May God grant us peace and a good year.'

29

Peace Talks and Malplaquet

The year 1708 had not been a good one for agriculture. The harvest had been late and consequently poor. The vendanges had been disappointing. The first result of this was a rise in prices. In the district of Toulouse the cost of corn had shown an increase of 75 per cent in the course of the year. Wines in the cabarets had doubled their prices.

The winter had arrived early. Louis Morin in Paris, usually an accurate recorder, noted the first frost on 19 October. In December he recorded ten consecutive days of frost. This was succeeded by a mild period and Christmas that year felt more like Easter. On 5 January, the eve of the Festival of the Three Kings, the thermometer reading was 10.7. But on Sunday 6 January the temperature dropped to 3.1. A vivid account of this is given in the *Chronique de Jean Taté* of Château Porcien in the Ardennes. 'There fell so heavy a quantity of rain that night that the ground was saturated and hardly had the rain ceased than we began to feel a terrible cold, so that the whole surface of the land was a sheet of ice; the frost started at the break of day, and by midday the ice was bearing... This great freeze lasted fifteen days. No one had ever seen or heard of such a freeze.' The curé of Saint-Symphorien-de-Laye noted that on 7 January one could cross the Loire 'by a bridge of ice'.

A bridge of ice across the Loire could be a local convenience; the sudden transformation of a river which was a frontier barrier into a bridge could create a military crisis. Even the Rhine could now be crossed. One recorder at Belfort stated that a gang of peasants was armed and provided with axes and set to guard the frontier to prevent the Germans passing into Alsace, 'since it was possible to cross the said Rhine with loaded wagons, and the said peasants were to cut the ice with the said axes and to mount guard'.

At a domestic level the cold was terrible – 'one froze in the corner of a good fire'. Parochial registers often provide the details. According to

419

the curé at Esseintes in the Bordelais, 'one could not even eat bread, because it was frozen'. It had to be cut with an axe rather than with a knife. One had to be careful when drinking that one's lips did not freeze onto the glass and during the Mass the wine froze in the chalice. The only possible place for warmth was in bed. Old people were heating tiles to use as warming pans.

In May the Comité de Charité in Paris published a leaflet entitled 'Nouvel advis important sur les misères du temps', quoting from the reports of country clergy. 'Entering today into Vendôme,' wrote one, 'I was besieged by five or six hundred poor people whose faces were hollow-cheeked and livid, the horrible food with which they try to nourish themselves produces a sort of deposit on their faces which is strangely disfiguring. In the outskirts of the town men were lying on the ground and dying.'

Attempts to relieve the sufferings of the poor were, of course, wide-spread. Bonfires were lit in the public squares and open places of towns – some 200 in Paris. At Toulouse the Conseil des Seizes opened an account of 300 livres for the purchase of faggots. In the city of Reims, where the population was estimated at 30,000, some 12,000 were classified as poor. In an attempt to bring relief to those who were starving, a Bureau de la Miséricorde was set up which organised a daily distribution of bread. This attracted thousands of sufferers from the country round about, seeking bread. On 2 May, the officers recorded an influx of 4,000 'who trampled on each other for fear that it would run out'.

But charity usually only dresses the wounds. It seldom seeks to remedy the cause of the ills. In a powerful sermon preached in Lent 1709, Massillon condemned from the pulpit those who were content to give of their superfluity and those who actually made a profit out of the famine: 'Do you take upon yourselves a share in the calamities of your brothers? Do you not perhaps make the penury of the people a barbarous occasion for profit?' Marcel Lachiver, in his detailed study of the years of misery and famine, puts the case against the profiteers succinctly. 'Once they are sure that there will be no harvest of grain in 1709, they know that they only have to wait to harvest a fortune in gold.' Jean Taté stated that 'many have certainly made their fortunes this year'. In April 1709, the Contrôleur Général wrote to the Intendant of Berry urging severe measures against those who hoarded grain – those guilty of 'usury with corn'. 'Have those proprietors who refuse to open them [granaries] at the first request that you make sent to prison and then distribute half their grain to the people and poor of the district.' At the same time the Government was buying corn abroad, particularly from such places as Dalmatia and northern Africa.

'Our greatest evil', wrote Mme de Maintenon, 'is famine; everything is to be feared from people who are dying from hunger and who are being stirred up deliberately; they say that the King takes away the corn and enriches himself by selling it at a high price.'

It was Fénelon, writing on 14 August 1710 to the duc de Chevreuse, who went to the heart of the matter. 'It is not only a question of putting an end to the war in Europe; it is a question of providing bread to people who are at death's door, of re-establishing agriculture and commerce, of condemning the luxury which is the gangrene at the root of all the morals of the nation, of recalling the proper form of the Kingdom, of tempering the despotism which is the source of all our ills.' At about the same time M. Trudaine, Intendant of Lyon, was in despair. 'I am beside myself with suffering from what I see every day; it is more than humanity – not to say Christianity – can endure.'

The mortality rate was extremely high. The poor, the sick and the old were the chief victims, but the very young also found survival difficult. The curé of Chéroy in the Yonne recorded: 'There died of cold a lot of people and especially little children, of which there were 22 buried in the Parish in the month of January.'

The extreme cold did not only affect the poor. It affected Versailles. 'The strongest elixirs and the most alcoholic liqueurs', noted Saint-Simon, 'broke their bottles in rooms where there was a fire.' Louis, now aged seventy, who was said to be himself immune to cold, cancelled the visits to Marly and Trianon out of consideration for the guards and officers who would have accompanied him. The Dauphin, equally impervious, cancelled visits to Meudon. On 14 January the marquise d'Huxelles managed to write that the ink was freezing on her pen.

Many were driven by the extremity of their suffering to acts of theft. The same curé of Saint-Symphorien-de-Laye records that the families of those who were buried 'listened to the Mass from their houses on account of the thieves'. The difficulty of digging a grave was one of the problems which they had frequently to face – often by burying people under the church floor.

There were numerous records of Christian self-sacrifice, especially on the part of the clergy. The Reverend Father Thomas Madur of Saint-Pierre-de-Lezoux was praised at his funeral 'for his charity towards the poor, who were always so dear to him that in 1709 he was seen to divest himself of everything – even to selling his horse and his books'. On 16 April 1709, Antoine Préveran de la Racquetière died at Montenay-sur-Loire. 'He deserves to be canonised', it was stated, 'for his great works of charity on behalf of the poor, having given them 15,000 francs for corn or bread.' He had truly earned the title *le Père des Pauvres*.

By the beginning of April it was becoming apparent that the winter corn was definitely lost. 'This unfortunate winter', wrote Jean Taté, 'lasted until 8 or 10 March, by which time the ice had melted. The labourers went out to inspect their land, where they could no more see their corn.'

It was the signal for the central authority to take the matter in hand. On 19 April the Parlement de Paris issued an edict requiring all parishes and cities to take responsibility for their own poor. It instituted a compulsory contribution amounting to about one thirtieth of a man's income. The sums were to be paid in monthly to the Bureau de Bienfaisance or Comité de Charité which administered it.

The royal family was not excluded. At Versailles, so Narbonne relates in his journal, five 'directors of the poor', all of them former church-wardens, drew up the tarifs. The King was to pay 4,220 livres, the Dauphin 2,110, the duc de Bourgogne 397. Overall, this system, according to Lachiver, would have provided 1 pound of bread per day for each adult.

Jean Taté records how Louis' action was received in the country. 'Commissioners from the King were sent out into all the provinces forbidding all work on ground sown with wheat before 8 May . . . The King found himself very much embarrassed: a people ready to rise in revolt and enemies on all sides ready to invade France. There was an order from the King that everyone should be obliged to make a declaration of the corn which he possessed before the local Clerk of the Court, on pain of confiscation of the said corn. He sent out commissioners to make visitations of the granaries in order to supply the great cities and put a stop to the seditions and uprisings.' Although the reactions by those in authority appear to have been vigorous they did not solve the problems. In Paris there were uprisings led, as so often, by the women and sometimes ignored by the police. On one occasion the Dauphin was surrounded by a mob when going to the Opera. He bought his way out with promises, but he did not go to Paris again for some time. Louis was the object of abusive lampoons. One was a parody of the Lord's Prayer: 'Our Father who art in Versailles,' it began, 'unhallowed is thy name. Thy Kingdom is no longer great. Thy will is no more done by land or sea. Give us our bread which we lack on all sides. Forgive our enemies who have beaten us, but not your generals who let them do so. Do not succumb to all the temptations of La Maintenon but deliver us from Chamillart.'

Chamillart became in part the victim and in part the scapegoat of the situation. On 12 May 1709, he was openly attacked at a meeting of the Council of War by Villars and Boufflers. On 9 June Mme de Maintenon wrote to the duc de Noailles: 'The outburst against the man you know gets stronger every day, and it reaches the Master; he cannot bring himself to sacrifice him because he pities him.' But Louis did dismiss Chamillart and replaced him with Daniel Voysin de Noiraye. It does not seem to have been a bad appointment, but it was not like Louis to yield to pressure of this sort.

Meanwhile peace talks were starting at The Hague that were to bring Louis to his knees. Prince Eugène represented the Empire, Heinsius the Dutch Republic and Marlborough Great Britain, ably seconded by Lord Townshend, described by Burnet as 'by much the most shining person of all our young nobility . . . a man of great integrity and of good principles in all respects'. The main clauses demanded were the recognition of the Archduke Charles of Austria as King of Spain; the departure of Philip V within two months; the undertaking that no prince of the House of France should ever occupy the Spanish throne; the recognition of Queen Anne as the lawful sovereign of Great Britain and consequently recognition of the Protestant succession; the yielding of nearly all the frontier fortresses – Strasbourg and Kehl, Lille and Tournai, which in fact amounted to the undoing of most of the achievement of Vauban.

Representing France was Jean-Baptiste Colbert, marquis de Torcy, grandson of the great Colbert and one of the ablest negotiators of the time. His particular skill lay in his ability to understand and to express the mind of his Master, who welcomed him, in 1696, as Secretary of State for Foreign Affairs with the words: 'We are very fortunate to have you; what would we have done if you had had a different character?'

'It was at the end of the month of April', wrote Torcy in a review of the year 1709, 'and the imminent opening of the campaign only held out the final misfortunes to be feared. Everyone believed that we would see the enemy advance during the coming summer, right to the gates of Paris. We discussed the options that were open to the King and the places to which he could retreat in order to find any security.

'These melancholy reasonings were based on the general want of every-thing. Money was lacking; the arsenals were empty; no provision was made for supplies and the winter, more harsh than had been seen within the memory of man, had destroyed the hope of harvesting the crops which the freeze, following the thaw, had killed in the earth. Goodwill, ruined by misery, could no longer be found among the troops, and capable generals, if there were any, were extremely rare.

'It was, however,' continues Torcy, 'necessary to go to war without any means of sustaining it. We were no better off for making peace, at least not on terms that could be said in any way to approximate to reasonable-ness. The sufferings of His Majesty seemed to me so acute that I proposed to him to go myself to Holland.' He then describes 'the dismal conferences that I had with men intoxicated with their good fortune'.

During March and April the allies had come to realise that Louis was defeated and that they could make any terms they liked. France was in a difficult and dangerous position. 'Torcy's plan', writes Winston Churchill, 'was to gain the Dutch by extreme concessions on the Barrier [the frontier fortresses] and then to induce them to bring pressure on Marlborough and at the same time to win Marlborough's goodwill by a colossal bribe . . . A precise tariff was set up. If Philip V received Naples and Sicily – two million francs; if the fortifications and harbour of Dunkirk were spared, or Strasbourg was left to France – two millions [more].' Churchill makes the somewhat nice distinction that Marlborough was prepared to accept the sum as a reward but not as an inducement. He did not, in fact, receive anything.

By the middle of May the peace negotiations were progressing. 'Now everyone hastened to put in his claim,' continues Churchill. 'From the Emperor, from the Diet of Ratisbon, from Victor-Amadeus of Savoy and from Portugal there arrived new demands upon the humbled monarchy. All had suffered from Louis XIV in the days of his power. All hastened to reclaim with interest, in this moment of his apparent prostration, what they had lost.' Torcy, writing to the King, makes just this point. 'Every sovereign prince assumes that he has the right to formulate his claims against France and would even consider himself dishonoured if he had extorted nothing to the injury of the French crown.' Churchill adds his comment: 'When we look back on the long years of terror and spoliation to which these princes had been subjected, it would be surprising if they had acted otherwise.'

Van der Dussen, the leader of the Dutch peace party, himself wrote: 'The policy of this province [Holland] . . . depends upon more than five hundred persons, most of whom regard France as having been brought to bay and who are so embittered by their memories of the past that they are resolved without compunction to make an end once and for all of their puissant foe.' Louis was reaping where he had sown, but vindictiveness, however understandable, is seldom a good basis for policy. A person or a nation can be driven too far and the policy can become counter-productive. Churchill identifies the moment at which that point was reached. It was over the question of the Spanish throne. Louis XIV was not really in a position to answer for Philip V. That was a matter for Spain and the Spanish people.

The allies, however, wanted some security or guarantee that their terms would be observed. One idea was to engage Louis to use his own troops to drive his own grandson off the throne. Churchill calls it 'the fatal article'. According to Torcy, Marlborough himself 'suggested schemes to turn the article so as not to commit His Majesty to war against Spain'.

Marlborough, however, had admitted to Godolphin: 'I am far from thinking the King of France so low as he is thought in England.' The clauses, according to Churchill, could have been 'merely a threat of action and that the allies were prepared to accept alternative guarantees'. But the idea was floated. 'The French ministers', wrote Lord Townshend, 'absolutely refused an amendment which might, they said, possibly engage their Master to a condition so unnatural as to make war with his grandson.' Marlborough sympathised with them. Even the duchesse d'Orléans, whose sympathies were still largely with the Germans, condemned the fatal clause: 'to want to set a grandfather against his own grandson . . . is barbarous and un-Christian'.

The allies set a time-limit for Louis' reply: 4 June. The setting of a date, notes Churchill, turned the memorandum into an ultimatum. 'This had not been the original intention. Into this position the allies had been manoeuvred by Torcy's skill.'

On 12 June Louis made a further and even more significant departure from his normal stance. He sent out a manifesto to the people of France in the form of a letter to every provincial Governor, to be disseminated as widely as possible, chiefly by the clergy. It was signed by Louis and countersigned by Torcy. It seemed an impossibility – to convince the people of France, worn out by fighting, weakened by famine, their land impoverished and their commerce in ruins, that peace on the terms offered was unacceptable. But Louis and Torcy had faith in the fundamental love of the French for their country. The cry 'La Patrie en danger!' has often had the power to stir the hearts of the people. It was to this that Louis and his Minister now made their appeal.

'I believe that I owe to the fidelity to which my people have borne witness, during the course of my reign, the consolation of being informed of the reasons which still prevent them from enjoying that peace which I had intended to procure for them.'

'They [members of the League] have made it plain', continues Louis, 'that their intention was merely to increase the neighbouring States at the expense of my Crown and to open up ways of penetrating the interior of my kingdom whenever it suited their interests to begin another war . . . They fixed a time-limit of two months for me to execute my part of the treaty and claimed the right to oblige me to hand over those places which they were demanding in the Low Countries and in Alsace and to raze to the ground those of which they demanded the demolition.'

They were prepared to give Louis until only 1 August to comply, 'reserving the freedom to have recourse to armed force if the King of Spain, my grandson, persisted in his resolution to defend the crown which God has given him, and to perish sooner than to abandon the faithful people who, for the last nine years, have recognised him as their legitimate King'. Then Louis came to the 'fatal clause'. 'I pass in silence over the hints that they have made that I should join my forces with those of the League to oblige and constrain the King, my grandson, to vacate the throne if he did not consent of his own will to live in future with no States and to reduce himself to the simple condition of a private individual. It is contrary to humanity to believe that they even thought of engaging me to form such an alliance with them . . . I am persuaded that they would themselves oppose the acceptance [of peace] in conditions equally contrary to justice and to the honour of the name FRANÇAIS.'

Louis was not demanding obedience: he was appealing to the people for their support. He was not requiring their loyalty to the Crown: he was appealing to their patriotism. His appeal was in general terms and not overstated. 'My intention is, then, that all those who give me such marks of their zeal by contributing, with their suffering, with their money and with their blood, to sustain so heavy a war, should know that the only price that my enemies claimed the right to put on the offers that I had been prepared to make was that of a suspension of hostilities . . . limited to the space of two months. I wish that my people, throughout the extent of your Government, should know from you that they would be enjoying peace if it had depended only on my will to procure their welfare, which they quite reasonably desire, but that it is necessary to obtain it by renewed efforts.' The war continued.

Some interesting light on the situation is shed from Mme de Maintenon's continual correspondence with the princesse des Ursins. On 17 June she wrote: 'The maréchal de Villars is far worse off than the enemy, but he does not lose courage; he complains only about bread and money . . . This beginning of the campaign is difficult; if we can survive until the end of August we will have some resources; if they could work faster at the Mint we could send larger sums to Flanders, because we do not lack for raw materials at the moment because of the quantity of silver plate and old coins that is brought in.' The silver-owning families had been quick in their response.

Mme de Maintenon is consistently pessimistic about the situation. On 14 June she wrote: 'We have undergone a series of misfortunes from which France cannot recover except by a long peace; and the famine, which is the latest and greatest [misfortune] has put us with our backs against the wall. I declare that all my fears had not gone so far as to foresee that we should be reduced to hoping to see the King and Queen of Spain lose their thrones. There are no words, Madame, which express such a pain. The King is pierced by it; Mme la duchesse de Bourgogne is bowed down.'

Marlborough kept himself informed about what was going on in France by means of a spy, who on 10 June reported: 'The King has written that peace is at an end. M. de Villars was delighted at this letter. He read it to the whole army and asked the soldiers and officers if they did not wish to avenge the honour of the King which their enemies were insulting. So saying, he called for cheers from all of them, and when they threw their hats into the air, he threw up his too. It is felt here that this general, although light and vain in his talk, inspires audacity in the soldiers and leads them very well and *as the French like to be led.*' On 14 June the spy wrote: 'There is complete confidence in M. de Villars. It may be said that the fate of the kingdom is in his hands ... Two days ago 500,000 francs were sent to him for the troops. He takes great care of his men, going in detail into everything to do with the provision of the army.' It was a France spiritually renewed and responding bravely to the call of 'la Patrie en danger!' that now faced Marlborough and Eugène.

In July, since no disaster had yet occurred, a note of optimism began to appear in Mme de Maintenon's letters. 'The maréchal de Villars is doing wonders and we are beginning to hope that the enemies will not enter France; but it will not be so if we were to lose a battle.' Marlborough's spy reported: 'I have seen the letters from Flanders which show that M. de Villars is encamped in a very favourable position and that morale in the army is high.' Louis wrote at about this time to Villars: 'I count for much that, by your wise dispositions and the precautions you have taken, all the vast projects [of invading France] are reduced to a single enterprise [the siege of Tournai] and you could not, at the beginning of this campaign, render me more important service.' The siege of Tournai was a preliminary to a major attempt to invade France and even to enter Paris. Both sides, however, wanted a pitched battle.

The encounter took place near the village of Malplaquet. The French, under Villars and Boufflers, took up their position between two woods. 'Marlborough's conception', writes Winston Churchill, 'was the principle of the battle of Blenheim adapted to a new field. The enemy's wings were to be assaulted until Villars was induced by this pressure to weaken his centre. The centre was then to be pierced by the reserve of the infantry ... The enormous cavalry army, nearly thirty thousand strong, was then to pass through the gaps in the defences and fight a sabre battle with the French cavalry on the plain behind. If the French cavalry were routed, all the troops drawn into the two flanks would be cut off.'

The most striking aspect of the battle was the savagery with which it was fought and the unprecedented scale of the casualties. The wounded on both sides were bayoneted and plundered. Such was the blood lust of the Argyle's brigade that, according to a German eye-witness, 'they hewed in pieces all that they found before them ... even the dead when their fury found no more living to devour'. In the course of Villars' big counter-attack, writes Churchill, at least six squadrons of the allied horse were cut to pieces. 'No mercy was shown by the victors and the wounded were slaughtered on the spot.'

Another, more personal, account of the battle comes from Colonel Blackader. 'It was the most deliberate, solemn and well ordered battle that ever I saw – a noble and fine disposition and as nobly executed. Every man was at his post, and I never saw troops engage with more cheerfulness, boldness and resolution. In all the soldiers' faces appeared a brisk and lively gaiety which presaged victory. The Lord of Hosts went forth at our head as Captain of our host ... *I never had a more pleasant day in my life.*'

On 14 September, Mme de Maintenon wrote: 'At last, Madame, this battle in Flanders, so greatly desired in Spain; so greatly feared in France, has taken place on the 11th of this month. M. le maréchal de Boufflers describes this action as "glorious but unfortunate", because we lost it, despite the valour of our troops, from which not a single soldier defected, either in the battle or in the retreat ... It is not yet known how many the enemy lost nor how many we did; but it is thought that both are very considerable, for no one has ever seen such a fierce fight.'

The losses of the British were reported as amounting to 24,000. The figures for the French are less certain, but were much lower – probably somewhere near 15,000. The maréchal de Villars' horse was killed under him and he had his leg shattered by a bullet. Boufflers was there ready to take over.

The French, although technically defeated, managed to retreat in good order. As Churchill puts it: 'The aged, noble Boufflers, unshaken by his prodigious exertions, did not forget his duties as Commander-in-Chief. Both his wings were in retreat. His centre was pierced, his cavalry outnum-bered, but still in order. He devoted himself with his cavalry to the task of covering the general retirement which was now in progress ... So severely and sternly contested had been the battle that the Allies could not pursue.'

Marlborough retired to his tent and sat down to finish a letter to his wife which he had started before the battle. 'I am so tired that I have but strength enough to tell you that we have had this day a very bloody battle; the first part of the day we beat their foot, and afterwards their horse. God Almighty be praised, it is now in our powers to have what peace we please, and I may be pretty well assured of never being in another battle.'

On 13 September, Boufflers, writing to the King about 'the unfortunate outcome of the action', insists also 'how this misfortune was accompanied by glory for the troops and arms of Your Majesty'. He ended on a thoroughly optimistic note: 'The succession of disasters which Your Majesty's armies have suffered for several years had so humiliated the French people that one hardly dared admit to being French. I can assure you, Sire, that the title of French has never been held in higher esteem nor more feared than it is now among all the allied armies.'

The wound which Villars received in the course of the action may have had a serious effect on the outcome. Fénelon wrote to him: 'Permit me, Monseigneur, to express my share in the feelings of all France about the accident which you had in the last battle, without which, everyone agrees, it would have been a total victory.'

Villars himself, writing to Louis, who had raised him to the rank of a *duc et pair*, says that the reception of this honour 'only redoubles my sorrow for a wound which I would have wished to have received two hours later, and which pains me all the more now that Your Majesty's army is altogether more proud and more fearless than it has ever been and demanding with ardour another combat'.

The battle of Malplaquet had boosted French morale, as these letters written in the autumn of 1709 clearly show. By the following spring Villars had come to a more sober estimate. On 29 April 1710, he wrote to the Minister for War, Voysin: 'In a few days we shall be on the eve of a battle which will decide the fate of the country. It would be impossible to take too serious a view of the weakness of the troops.'

The immediate demand of Voysin was that Villars should raise the siege of Douai. Louis wrote to Villars: 'It is not possible for me to give precise orders from this distance. I have explained to you my ideas, and you know well the reasons that make me hope to be able to oblige my enemies to raise the siege of Douai ... However, if you find the enemy too well posted to be able to attack them without too much risk, or if you cannot fight them without believing there are reasonable hopes for success, it would be rash to engage in a disadvantageous battle, and it is not my intention to give you such an order. I put myself entirely in your hands.'

At the beginning of May Marlborough proceeded to invest the fortress; he wrote to Godolphin: 'We would fain be masters of this town in this month of May.' The town was garrisoned by some 8,000 French troops under General Albergotti. As Churchill writes: 'The siege of a fortress so strongly garrisoned as Douai, with the two main armies in close contact around it, created a situation in which on any day one of the decisive battles of the world might explode. The fact that no great battle was fought does not mean that an intense trial of strength and skill was not proceeding between these armies, upon whose interplay all European eyes were fixed.'

On 26 June Douai capitulated and on the 29th Albergotti and his troops marched out.

The penury of the royal finances during these difficult years did not prevent continual and often considerable expenditure on the repair and maintenance of the royal palaces. The four large tomes compiled by Jules Guiffrey of the Comptes des Bâtiments du Roi do not easily yield a picture of the pattern of this expenditure. A large number of entries directly refer to the *Chapelle neuve du Château*, but many others, referring, for instance, to the *cul du four* – a half-dome – presuppose ecclesiastical architecture and need to be added to the total. But the general impression is inescapable: this was by far the most important project to be undertaken during the first decade of the eighteenth century. Not surprisingly, to those who knew her, Mme de Maintenon was against the whole idea. Mlle d'Aumale stated that 'she has done everything that she could to oppose the magnificent new Chapel that the King is having built at Versailles, because the misery of the people was very great at that time and also because she believed that sooner or later Versailles would cease to be the residence of the Court'.

It is not possible to say what Louis' motive was. His piety might well have demanded that God should be housed in as great a splendour as the King of France; he might have found the almost makeshift Chapel which had been in use since 1682 was quite inadequate for the ecclesiastical functions of the Court; but perhaps no motive need be sought other than the passion for building which was one of the key-notes of Louis' personality.

The foundations of the new Chapel were laid in 1689, but the work did not progress because of the war of the League of Augsburg. On 22 December 1698 Dangeau noted: 'The King desires to complete the building of the *Grande Chapelle* . . . Some alterations are being made to the first design.' Louis had changed his mind on two important points. The first was to make a significant increase in the height of the building, so that it stands clear of the surrounding roofscape. It does not present, as Saint-Simon suggested, 'the mournful appearance of an immense cata-falque', but distinguishes the religious from the secular architecture. The Trinity Chapel at Fontainebleau cannot be identified as such from the outside. The Chapel at Versailles declares unmistakably its sacred status.

The other alteration was to the interior. The intended material had been the same multicoloured marble which decorates so much of the palace, but after mature reflection Louis changed his mind. 'In the month of May 1699', wrote La Martinière, author of the *Grand Dictionnaire*, 'the King made the reflection that the marble would cause too great a chilliness and humidity.' He decided to use instead the beautiful white stone known as *banc royal*, which gives the Chapel its particular charm. It creates an entirely different atmosphere – cool and refreshing. If colour is the attribute of royalty, that of divinity is light, and the tall windows, open colonnade and pale stone of the Chapel make the fullest use of this element. The side windows to the ground floor give a restrained illumination to the nave, but those of the apse, where the arcading curves into a graceful ambulatory, provide, by contrast, a dramatic lighting to the altar. Gilding, conspicuously absent from the rest of the Chapel, is used also to focus attention on the Sanctuary and to conduct the eye thence, by way of the organ case, to the brilliant profusion of the painted ceiling – the Promise of Redemption.

It was this ceiling which occasioned one of the largest items of expenditure: 'The enormous work of the vault,' writes Pierre de Nolhac, 'in which Coypel was assisted by Philippe Meusnier for the architectural perspectives, was begun in February 1707 and completed during the first months of 1710. The sum of 103,000 livres had been budgeted for this.' But that was not all; a special gratuity was added. 'To the Sieur Coypel, painter . . . in consideration of the works of painting which he did in the large part of the vault of the Chapel at Versailles during 1709 . . . 25,000 francs.'

One is tempted to compare Louis' chapel with that of Alexander Pope's *Timon's Villa*:

> On painted ceilings you devoutly stare
> Where sprawl the saints of Verrio or Laguerre,
> On gilded clouds in fair expansion lie
> And bring all Paradise before your eye.
> To rest the cushion and soft Dean invite,
> Who never mentions Hell to ears polite.

The bas-reliefs of the arcading on the ground floor, seen from the tribunes, give a delicate, brocade-like texture to the stone. In fact they represent the Passion of Our Lord, but even those seated close enough to observe the details might have been excused for overlooking this fact. A cherub showing the purse of Judas suffices to evoke the Agony in the Garden, and a cock crowing to represent the bitter tears of Saint Peter. These carvings, best studied in Pierre de Nolhac's enormous album of photographs, combine an astonishing variety of invention with a uniform excellence of execution.

Although the Chapel is made up of purely classical elements, the whole

conception is recognisably medieval in form, but with the relative importance of the main arcade and triforium inverted, for the royal tribune was
to be level with the first floor – the *piano nobile* – of the palace. Another
medieval effect is in the clerestory and roof, with flying buttresses replaced
by consoles, pinnacles by statues and the slender belfry doing duty for
the *flèche*. The timbers of the roof differ little in construction from those
of a gothic apse.

The work was carried out with Louis' usual attention to detail. With
the statues, which stand like pinnacles along the balustrade, a wax model
was first submitted to the King's approval; a full-scale plaster copy was
then mounted to try the effect and the final stone figure carved *in situ*.
This system managed to produce a remarkable unity of style from a
considerable variety of artists. There are twenty-eight statues, representing
the major saints. The execution was distributed among eleven sculptors.

By the spring of 1710 the Chapel was completed. On 25 April Louis
had a motet sung in order to try the effect of music in it. A month later
he went again, inspected the whole minutely, and had another motet sung.
The acoustics of the Chapel are magnificent and the music written for it,
by such masters as Lully and Lalande, answered admirably to the stately
dignity of the architecture and the colourful animation of the ceiling.

On 5 June the Chapel was finally consecrated by the Cardinal de
Noailles and two days later Louis attended Mass there for the first time.
On 8 June, the Day of Pentecost, the solemn procession of the Knights of
the Saint-Esprit, their robes of royal blue embroidered with the symbolic
tongues of fire, fittingly inaugurated the Grande Chapelle. Then, and only
then, could Louis' gargantuan creation be regarded as complete.

In order to judge it one must consider the effect which it produced on
the rest of Europe. Along the banks of the Rhine and in the remoter
kingdoms of Würtemberg and Bavaria new and ever larger palaces were
rising from the ruins of the wars of the previous century, and their builders
looked to France for inspiration.

During the early years of the eighteenth century foreign princes were
constantly visiting Versailles. In 1717 Peter the Great came. The fountains
were played for him and he inspected the machines 'with an astonishing
attention'. He took back with him to Russia the French architect Le
Blond, who supplied the designs for Peterhof.

German princes, making that indispensable accomplishment of their
education, the *Kavalierstour*, formed their taste in the galleries of Versailles
and Meudon and in the gardens of Marly, Trianon and Saint-Cloud. 'A
young man', said Frederick II, 'passed for an imbecile if he had not
stayed for some time at Versailles.' On returning to their own lands, the
battleground of Europe for the past hundred years, they tried to recon-

struct their principalities and duchies on the grand lines of the French monarchy. Not only did French become the official language of their Courts, but their clothes, their food, their music, all must be French to be considered in good taste; every Court had its French artists to adorn it and the Prince sought relaxation in the arms of a French mistress. The attempt to ape the magnificence of Louis XIV could lead to absurdities. 'It has always been their misfortune', complained Madame, 'that the Germans not only imitate the French, but always go twice as far as we do here.'

Most particularly was this influence felt upon the Rhine, among the Catholic states near the French frontier, whose families were often connected by marriage with the royal house of France. The historic capitals of the Palatinate, Cologne and Trier, were abandoned and at Mannheim, Bonn and Coblenz electoral palaces arose from foundations sometimes approaching the scale of Versailles. French architects were in demand and, were they not to be had, French models were copied. Even the vocabulary of Versailles was imported, so that each Residenz had its *Trianon*, its *Grotte de Thétis* or its *Bassin d'Apollon* after the manner of its prototype. Robert de Cotte, First Architect to Louis, furnished designs for the palaces of Bonn, Brühl and Poppelsdorf for the Elector of Cologne and a palace for the Prince de Tours et Taxis in Frankfurt. The French influence was also spread through Boffrand, whose magnificent Château de Lunéville, in the progression of its wings towards the town, shows clearly the influence of Versailles.

The result was that in the eighteenth century France became what Italy had been in the Renaissance – the cultural centre of Europe. 'Who could have told', asked Montesquieu, 'that the late King had established the greatness of France by building Versailles and Marly?'

30

The Deaths of the Dauphin and of the Duke and Duchess of Burgundy

The fears of Madame and Saint-Simon about the accession of the duc de Bourgogne and the continuing hostility of the *Cabale de Meudon* were somewhat lacking in urgency since his father the Dauphin would, in the natural order of things, succeed Louis XIV on the throne. In 1711 the Dauphin was fifty and in good health. On 9 April, however, Louis was informed that his son had *une faiblesse*. By the evening the *faiblesse* had become a raging fever and a state of torpor which, on the following morning, declared itself as smallpox.

Louis went immediately to his son at Meudon, forbidding both the duc and duchesse de Bourgogne – neither of whom had had the disease – to follow him. Bourgogne wrote at once to Mme de Maintenon, expressing less concern for his father than for the King, who, in his opinion, 'owed it to the State not to expose himself'.

Marie-Adélaïde wrote also. She saw the difficulties; she appreciated the dangers. But she ended her letter: 'I have got to see the King. Without that Versailles is intolerable to me. You cannot imagine what the atmosphere is like. I have to tell you the whole truth: where the King is absent, everything is lifeless.' For some days, however, Fagon and his assistants continued to assert that Monseigneur's condition was 'beyond what they had dared to hope'.

Fagon's hopes, of course, and those of the *Cabale de Meudon*, were for the Dauphin's recovery. There were many at Versailles, however, in whose eyes his death was more than they had dared to hope for.

The duc de Saint-Simon was one of them. He was spending Eastertide quietly at his Château of La Ferté-Vidame, near Chartres. A pious Christian, he wished to spend Holy Week 'far from Society and the Court'. Nevertheless he could not help brooding. 'Each day the prospect drew nearer of a future when Monseigneur would rule, surrounded by men who were my enemies and who desired my ruin ... For this ill there appeared to be no remedy and it was causing me acute distress, until quite suddenly, at the moment least expected, God chose to deliver me.' On Saturday 11 April, a messenger arrived from Mme de Saint-Simon. He brought the news that the Dauphin had been taken seriously ill.

No news could have been more welcome to Saint-Simon, but he felt that his feelings were sinful and spent the day in a state of conflicting emotions, trying to reconcile the Christian and the courtier within him at this critical juncture 'which gave me a glimpse of a deliverance unhoped-for, sudden and with the most pleasing apparent prospects'.

His hopes were immediately disappointed. 'The courier for whom I waited with impatience arrived on the following day, immediately after dinner. I learnt from him that the smallpox had declared itself and was progressing as well as could be hoped for. I felt that Monseigneur was saved and I wanted to stay at home.' He decided, with much regret, to leave La Ferté and rejoin his wife. On the way he met an old friend who said that the Dauphin was doing very well and could be considered to be out of danger. 'I arrived at Versailles with this opinion filling my mind, which was confirmed by Mme de Saint-Simon.'

It was not, however, the opinion of the Court. 'Versailles presented a very different scene. Monsieur and Madame la duchesse de Bourgogne were openly holding Court, and this Court was like the first moment of the dawn. All the courtiers were assembled there: all Paris was there. Their apartment was not able to contain the crowd.'

Meanwhile at Meudon all was optimism. A deputation from the fish-wives of Paris, with whom the Dauphin was always popular, hired coaches and asked for admission. 'Monseigneur desired to see them, whereupon they threw themselves down at the foot of his bed and kissed it again and again . . . Monseigneur, who was not indifferent to marks of the love of the people, at once gave orders for them to be shown round the house, that they should be treated to dinner and sent back with a sum of money.'

Saint-Simon's apartment at Versailles was on the first floor of the Aile des Princes, almost adjoining that of the duc de Berry, who was enter-taining his father- and mother-in-law, the duc and duchesse d'Orléans. Saint-Simon and Madame were old friends; 'we simply could not wait to see one another and talk to each other in this situation on which we both thought so alike'. The news from Fagon and the doctors continued to be hopeful, which was not, from their point of view, good news. 'To speak frankly and to admit our shame, we lamented together the fact that Monseigneur . . . might still escape from that dangerous disease . . . Sor-rowfully we concluded that we must henceforth reckon on this prince living and reigning for a very long time.'

On 16 April Mme de Maintenon wrote to the princesse des Ursins, who was already aware of the situation: 'We remained in a state of hopefulness and joy until Tuesday, when the King, coming into my room, followed by M. Fagon, said to me: "I have just seen my son, which moved me so deeply that I thought I would weep; his head has swollen prodigiously during the last three or four hours; he is almost unrecognisable; one can hardly see his eyes. But I am assured that this is the normal course with smallpox." ' Both the duchesse de Bourbon and the princesse de Conti, who had had the disease, said the same. But Mme de Maintenon was not to be reassured. 'I thought that I detected a look of anxiety on the face of M. Fagon.'

The King proceeded to take his supper as usual. At about eleven o'clock he received the news that Monseigneur was in a very bad way. 'While the King was calmly having his supper', writes Saint-Simon, 'those who were in Monseigneur's room began to lose their heads. Fagon and the others piled remedies upon remedies without waiting to see if they had any effect . . . The King was just leaving the table and nearly fell over backwards when Fagon, in disarray, appeared before him crying out that all was lost. You may judge the horror that everyone felt at this sudden change from complete security to the extremity of despair.' They went down to his room.

'We found him', continues Mme de Maintenon, 'in convulsions and without consciousness. The curé of Meudon arrived before the Père Le Tellier, and said in a loud voice: "Monseigneur, does it not pain you to have offended God?" Mareschal, who was holding him, assures us that he replied "Yes". The curé continued: "If you were in a condition to make your confession, would you not make it?" The prince replied "Yes". The Père Le Tellier assures us that he [the Dauphin] clasped his hand: on this he gave him absolution.

'What a spectacle, Madame, when I arrived in the Grand Cabinet de Monseigneur! The King, seated on a day-bed, without shedding a tear but trembling from head to foot; Madame la duchesse in despair; Madame la princesse de Conti pierced to the heart, all the courtiers in silence, but a silence broken by sobs.'

The focal point of interest was now in the apartments of the duchesse de Bourgogne. 'I found all Versailles there', wrote Saint-Simon, 'assembled or arriving, all the ladies in *déshabillé*, most of them ready to go to bed, all the doors open, everything in turmoil. I learnt that Monseigneur had received Extreme Unction, that he was unconscious and beyond all hope . . . One only needed to have eyes, without any knowledge of the Court, to distinguish the interests portrayed on the faces, or the lack of interest of those who had none; some unruffled, others pierced with sorrow or gravely concerned with themselves to conceal their emancipation and their joy.' But for those with an intimate understanding of the state of the parties there was a delicious range of nuances to be savoured.

'I must admit', wrote Saint-Simon, 'that for someone who really knows his way about the intricacies of the Court, the immediate spectacle of such rare events as this one, so interesting in so many different respects, is satisfying in the extreme. Every face recalls the cares, the intrigues, the toils involved in advancing one's fortunes, in the formation of cabals and their consolidation; the adroitness at keeping oneself in place and distancing others; every sort of contrivance brought into play for such purposes; the liaisons, more or less advanced, the estrangements, the coldnesses, the hatreds, the ill turns, the little goings-on, the advances, the circumspection, the pettinesses, the basenesses of everyone . . . all this constitutes a pleasure, for those capable of seizing it, which, however insubstantial it may become, is one of the greatest pleasures which it is possible to experience in a Court.'

The death of the Grand Dauphin left the duc de Bourgogne the immediate heir to the throne. Saint-Simon's intimate friendships with the duc de Beauvilliers and the duc de Chevreuse gave him access to the new Dauphin. He began to notice details which he had not observed before – 'a meaningful glance or a concealed smile told me all that I needed to know'. He profited by an occasion in the gardens of Marly, when the Dauphin was nearly alone, to pay his court. The Dauphin said to him, in a low voice, 'that he looked forward with pleasure to their seeing each other more freely'. Saint-Simon rejoiced to find that the views of the heir to the throne were those of Beauvilliers and Chevreuse and also his own. 'It is difficult to express my feelings on leaving the Dauphin,' he concluded; 'a future, magnificent and imminent, opened up before me.'

By the following year, 1712, Louis was beginning to show his age and the prospect of his grandson succeeding him was becoming imminent. Saint-Simon and the duc de Chevreuse began to draw up a list of reforms to be presented to the new Dauphin. Chevreuse spent most of his time in the Château de Dampierre, but he also owned a property in Picardy called Chaulnes, and it was here, during his annual period of residence, that Fénelon, who was forbidden to leave his diocese, managed to pass a few weeks. Dampierre was dangerously near to Versailles. Life at Chaulnes was a mixture of gracious living and political thinking. The political discussions, which were almost plotting, were among its greatest delights. They produced a sort of agenda – *les tables de Chaulnes* – which reveals their evaluation and critique of the reign of Louis XIV. Although it was in many ways a far-reaching reformation, it was still in line with much of Louis XIV's thinking, but it was more concerned with general principles than with actual projects. The three of them, Chevreuse, Fénelon and

Saint-Simon, were preparing to be the future counsellors of the young King.

What little has survived of Bourgogne's writings, for Louis had most of them burnt, does not reveal whether he saw any need for limiting the royal power. It is known that he had received a copy of Bossuet's *Politique tirée de l'Ecriture sainte* and had read it. He would therefore no doubt have been conversant with the Bishop's distinction between absolute power and arbitrary power. He must also have known of Fénelon's reasonings about arbitrary power. 'As long as despotism is wealthy, it acts with more promptitude and effectiveness than any restricted regime; but when it becomes exhausted and without credit it falls into irretrievable ruin.'

The duc de Bourgogne does not seem to have had faith in assemblies. The need for a summoning of the States General was clearly on the agenda, but he said of it that he never thought that this assembly 'could be more than a body whose function was to complain, to remonstrate, and, if the King was pleased to permit it, to make suggestions'. He did not see it as in any way a legislative assembly such as the English Parliament. Bourgogne also stated his disbelief in the value of debating societies. 'I know nothing more ignorant than an assembly of the erudite, nor less clear-sighted than an assembly of the wise.' Such people were by nature unlikely to agree among themselves. He preferred to consult the learning and wisdom of individuals. He may have been content with recognising his need for 'a friend, generous, sincere and well tried, who is authorised and even obliged, on his honour as a friend, to warn him if he ever deviates from his duty, or if wrong is being done in his name'.

He followed Saint-Simon at least some of the way in his respect for the aristocracy. 'He was indignant to see this nobility of France, so celebrated, become almost the same as the common people and only distinguished from them in that these had the right to work, to all sorts of business, even to bear arms, whereas the nobility . . . had only the choice between a deadly and ruinous idleness . . . or to go and get themselves killed in a war.' Bourgogne certainly wanted to see them playing a more important part in the business of government.

He believed that bishoprics should go to members of the upper aristocracy – provided, of course, that they possessed 'the sanctity, the zeal for the salvation of souls and the knowledge needed to direct this zeal'. He claimed that 'religion has something more to be respected in the eyes of the vulgar when it is seen to be proclaimed and practised by a man of high birth'. He did not, however, actually exclude commoners, if sufficiently qualified, from preferment.

Like his grandfather he was opposed to the temporal power of the Pope and the Episcopate. 'Certain Popes have been flattered by an imaginary authority over the temporal powers of sovereigns, but the Saviour of the World was speaking clearly enough when he said "My kingdom is not of this world" and "Render unto Caesar the things that are Caesar's". The ministers of the Priesthood ought to confine themselves within the limits of their ministry, which is purely spiritual.' He was in many ways a Gallican.

He regarded Christian doctrine as a sealed unit, a divine deposit, which was not susceptible of any development, let alone of any improvement, and he regarded as one of the 'seven sacraments of politics' the duty 'to stamp out at its very beginnings any sort of novelty in religious matters'. He had no doubts as to the rightness of Louis XIV's treatment of the Huguenots, though his claim that 'everything happened to the great contentment of His Majesty, without bloodshed and without disorder', is difficult to reconcile with the truth.

He believed, of course, in the divine right of Kings, who owed their position to God and were responsible only to God. It was a responsibility which he took with a deadly earnestness. 'Of all the men who make up a nation, the one most to be pitied, and who is pitied the least, is the Sovereign. He has all the inconveniences of grandeur and yet is scarcely able to enjoy its pleasures. He is, of all his subjects, the one who has the least freedom, the least peace of mind, the fewest moments when he can rest in a pure and peaceful joy.' He might have taken his theme from the words of Agamemnon in Racine's *Iphigénie*:

> Triste destin des rois, esclaves que nous sommes
> Et des rigueurs du sort et des discours des hommes
> Nous nous voyons sans cesse assiégés de témoins,
> Et les plus malheureux osent pleurer le moins.

'I must therefore', he concluded, 'labour much more to live as a Christian than to live as a Prince. I must not make use of the grandeur attached to my station except to raise myself to a more sublime virtue by humiliating myself beneath the almighty hand of God and by doing for others all the good that they might expect from me. A King is made for his subjects and not his subjects for him.'

Saint-Simon describes an evening at Marly on 3 February 1712. The talk began with jokes about the errand boys who slept rough on the steps of Versailles. It was agreed that those should be considered lucky who had not a care in the world. The duc de Bourgogne then proceeded, with growing enthusiasm, to enlarge upon the lot of Kings.

He saw the position of a King entirely in terms of the demands of duty. 'I would not do violence', wrote Saint-Simon, 'to the sentiments and to the natural eloquence of this prince, if I undertook to reproduce them on this occasion; but we all looked at each other in amazement and delight that he could dare to say so much . . . His eyes, more piercing than usual, revealed the sentiments which he expressed with a flamboyant energy; in a word our surprise at hearing him say so much in public was extreme, but each of us was so deeply penetrated that the tears were rising in our eyes.' Their fondest hopes for the future of the Kingdom of France seemed to be in reach of realisation.

The poignancy of the situation was that within a fortnight the duc de Bourgogne was dead. His death was not the only one. During the next four weeks Louis was to suffer, in quick succession, three tragic bereavements: Marie-Adélaïde, her husband, now the Dauphin, but still sometimes referred to as the duc de Bourgogne – and their elder son, aged five, the duc de Bretagne. The first of these was, according to Saint-Simon, 'the deepest affliction, which was the only real one that he had ever suffered in his life'.

On 7 February 1712, a Sunday, Marie-Adélaïde, though not feeling well, had been to Mass as usual. At about six in the evening she was attacked by a sudden and terrible headache. The pain, she said, was worse than childbirth. It lasted all night and all the following day. The customary antidotes of tobacco and opium were applied, but without results. Georges Mareschal, the King's surgeon, then resorted to that most banal of remedies – phlebotomy, the opening of a vein to let blood. It produced a temporary relief for the poor Dauphine. The pain, however, returned and she passed into a state of torpor.

Louis made several visits, but she did not recognise him. Her husband never left her bedside. On Wednesday the 10th, Jean Boudin, her Premier Médecin, diagnosed measles. It was not surprising, for Versailles and Paris were both suffering from an epidemic. She was again given a phlebotomy and again it had no results. Louis forced her husband to take a little air and exercise in the gardens, but he would not stay long. He was not feeling very well himself.

Wednesday and Thursday brought no relief and Marie-Adélaïde's confessor, the Père de La Rue, exhorted her not to delay her confession. This was almost the sentence of death. She looked at him, said she understood and said no more. The Père de La Rue had the perspicacity to see that she might prefer a different confessor. In the end a priest of the Récollets, whose house was next to the Grand Commun, was fetched. His name was the Père Noel.

It was now time for the last rites of the Church, the Viaticum and the Extreme Unction. Louis went to receive the procession at the foot of the staircase. He was in floods of tears. It was nine in the morning. Marie-

Adélaïde received the sacraments with great devotion. She then said to Mme de Maintenon: '*Ma tante*' (her usual form of address), 'I feel quite different. It seems that I am completely changed.' Mme de Maintenon replied: 'That means that you are very near to God.'

But one last attempt was made to keep her in this world. A consultation of doctors was summoned: Fagon, Premier Médecin du Roi, Dodart, Premier Médecin du Dauphin, Boudin, Premier Médecin de la Dauphine, Carlière, Premier Médecin du duc de Berry, Boutard, Médecin Ordinaire du Roi, Dumoulin, Médecin du Roi, and Chirac, Médecin du duc d'Orléans, all the most distinguished men of medicine, conferred together. They prescribed a phlebotomy.

On the morning of Friday 12 February it was clear that the end was near. Mme de Maintenon retired to the Chapel to pray; Louis remained at the bedside. Mlle d'Aumale records that at this moment one of the courtiers brought a powder which he believed to be effective. The dying woman managed to take some and exclaimed: 'Ah! how bitter that is.' Mme de Maintenon returned on being informed that she had recovered consciousness. Marie-Adélaïde was asked if she recognised her. She answered, 'Yes.' Mme de Maintenon said: 'You are going to God.' The Princess replied: 'Yes, *ma tante*.' Those were her last words.

On learning of her death, the Dauphin exclaimed: 'Ah! Lord, preserve the King.' It was as if he already realised that he himself would never reign. The King had already departed for Marly and the Dauphin ordered his coach in order to follow him, but he felt so ill that he returned to his apartment. There was talk of the way in which the doctors had dealt with Marie-Adélaïde. 'Whether the doctors killed her,' he said, 'or whether God called her to himself, we must adore equally what he permits and what he commands.'

The next day, Saturday, the Dauphin went to join the King at Marly. He had to be carried to his coach in a chair, and then into his apartment at Marly, which was on the ground floor, through one of the tall casement windows. When the King was ready for the *lever*, Saint-Simon observed, 'he and his grandson embraced each other again and again, tenderly and for a long time'.

On Sunday Louis wrote to his grandson, the King of Spain. 'I have lost my daughter, the Dauphine, and, although you know to what extent she was dear to me, you cannot possibly imagine the pain which her loss causes me. I know Your Majesty's heart too well to doubt what you will feel when you receive this fatal news.' Philip answered him: 'The great loss which we have sustained by the death of Madame la Dauphine has touched me more deeply than I can express to Your Majesty; but among the many causes which I have to feel it acutely, your suffering, in which I share more than anyone, adds greatly to my own affliction.'

Philip was a dutiful grandson, but he was a really affectionate brother. He wrote at the same time to the Dauphin: 'What can I say, my very dear brother, to make clear to you all the share which I take in the cruel loss to which you have just been subjected, and which has been, for me, keener than I can express? I assure you that it is proportionate to my tender affection for you . . . I am in a terrible state of anxiety about your health, which, I am told, is not too good. In fact I am always thinking of a brother who is infinitely dear to me.' Philip's letter was dated 28 February. The Dauphin can never have seen it. He had been dead for ten days.

When he wrote to the King of Spain, Louis was already beginning to notice the appearance of the Dauphin. Beneath the evident tokens of his sorrow and bereavement, the condition of his health was now alarming. Louis ordered the doctors to feel his pulse. It was poor, but they held their peace, merely recommending that he should go to bed. They persuaded themselves that his illness was merely the effect of his sufferings, which time and rest would cure. He was told that his death, in the present state of affairs, would be the crowning misfortune for France. He asked whether he could, without vanity, believe that he was necessary to the welfare of the State and added: 'God knows what his plans are for me and for the realm. I want what he wants, whether it is life or death. It is for him to order: I am content.'

He was becoming more and more convinced that it would be death. 'Why do you condemn yourself', asked his confessor, 'when the doctors have so much confidence? You must promote the effectiveness of the remedies by more comforting thoughts.' 'Thank God,' replied the Dauphin, 'the thought of death is not one to make me sad. Besides, you know that I desire nothing but the will of God. If he wants me to live, pray that it may be the better to serve him. If he wants me to die, pray that it may be in order to live with him eternally.'

Meanwhile the life of the Court had to continue as best it could. The list of those to be invited to Marly was drawn up; the guests began to arrive; Louis put in three hours' work with Torcy; the routine continued, but underlying its dependable structure was an ever-increasing anxiety.

One of the sources of information on the last days of the Dauphin is the collection of memoirs and letters assembled by the abbé Proyart. On the afternoon of Tuesday 16 February, he records, red patches were beginning to appear on the Dauphin's body and he was in a high fever. They were the same symptoms that had declared themselves in his wife's case, and against which the proposed remedies had proved so useless. No remedy was proposed. The Dauphin began to prepare himself. Gifts to his domestics and money set aside for the poor of the parish were arranged, and a sum of 700 livres to be sent to the Convent of the Récollets in order that prayers should be said for the souls of those who had been killed under his command in the army. He left nothing, Proyart noted, to pay for prayers for himself.

He was asking for the last rites of the Church, but since the doctors persisted in maintaining that he was not in danger, Louis would not give his consent, saying that 'he must be reminded that the rules of the Church, which he would not wish to infringe, do not permit the Viaticum except in the case of real danger, and that it is to the doctors to whom one should refer and not to himself'. It is difficult to see how Louis, in view of recent events, could have had such confidence in the judgement of his physicians. It is possible that he was unable to accept that this second shattering blow was about to fall and was clinging to the slender hope of medical optimism.

The Dauphin asked if he could receive Extreme Unction. He was assured that he was not in need of it. He himself had no doubt that he was dying. He needed the full resources of his faith to accept this final disappointment with humility. 'O my Saviour,' he was heard to say, 'since no one will believe me, I will have to leave this world without the consolation of the help which you have provided for the dying. You can see the desires of my heart; may your will be done.'

Chamillart wrote to the Premier Président of the Parlement on Wednesday 17 February: 'The Prince, whose piety is so well known, wishes to receive Communion tonight and a Mass will be said in his bedroom at which he will receive. Since such news might be capable of causing alarm to the public, the King has ordered me to write this letter to you to inform you and to put you in a position to calm the fears which this might spread.'

It had been agreed that he could receive Communion, fasting, immediately after midnight. 'Those who sought to spare the King so painful a spectacle', wrote Proyart, 'were the first to applaud this expedient, which would satisfy the desires of the invalid and would protect themselves from the reproach of having, from merely human reasons, allowed the Dauphin to die without the sacraments.' As midnight struck, the Mass was celebrated in the Prince's bedroom. 'He followed it with his customary piety and made his Communion with that sweet tranquillity which he brought to it when he was in good health.' After this Mass, continues Proyart, 'he asked to be left alone. Never had he appeared so peaceful as after he had received Communion. The inner joy which he felt manifested itself in outward effects. The fever abated; his agitations were replaced by calm.'

The doctors, of course, tried to take advantage of this spiritual well-being to attempt their own remedies. But their efforts only increased his fatigue.

His fever began to increase and with it his physical pain. 'I feel a fire within me,' he said, 'which consumes me.' The increased pain brought with it a remembrance of his wife's sufferings. 'O my poor Adélaïde!' he exclaimed, 'how much you must have suffered. O God, may it be for the salvation of her soul; unite my sufferings with hers, sanctify them by your own, and grant us peace eternal.'

Since his illness was infectious he was not able to see his son and heir, the five-year-old duc de Bretagne. 'He must be left at Meudon,' he ordered, 'I will see him again soon.' One of the valets, who overheard this remark, ran to tell Mme de Maintenon that the Dauphin was now hoping to be cured. 'Do you not see', she replied, 'that it is in Eternity that he hopes to see his son again? He said "soon" because, in the language of faith, the longest life is but a dream.'

In the early morning of Thursday 18 February, the Dauphin's confessor, the Père Martineau, was saying his Mass. While he was doing so, the Prince entered into his death agony. All he could say when Martineau returned was 'O mon Père . . .'

Martineau began to administer the Extreme Unction and asked him, if he understood, to press his hand. He pressed it. At the end of the prayers for the dying, the Prince opened his eyes once more. He spoke the words 'O mon Jésus' and died. When Louis received the news he managed to say: 'I bless God for the grace which enabled him to die in as saintly a manner as he had always lived.' But this new affliction made him ill and he retired to bed.

On the following Sunday 21 February, Louis wrote to inform his grandson the King of Spain. 'You will understand the increase of my suffering when I inform you of the death of the Dauphin. These are two terrible trials, within a few days of each other, which it was God's will to make of my submission to his will.'

Terrible though these two trials were, there was yet another heavy blow dealt to the King and his family. Both the sons of the duc de Bourgogne, the duc de Bretagne and the duc d'Anjou, went down with the same disease which had killed their parents. The elder, the duc de Bretagne, died on Sunday 7 March. Their governess, the duchesse de Ventadour, absolutely refused to let the physicians have access to the duc d'Anjou and thereby saved his life. He was to succeed to the throne of France as Louis XV.

There hangs in the Wallace Collection a large group showing Louis with the Grand Dauphin, the duc de Bourgogne and the little duc d'Anjou, who is held on a leading rein by Mme de Ventadour. It was in all probability painted after Louis' death. His face is an obvious copy from Rigaud's portrait done in 1701, long before the birth of Anjou. It is therefore not so much a 'conversation piece' as a genealogical tree – 'The Descent of the House of Bourbon'. This is emphasised by the two busts against the wall, one of Henri IV, the first Bourbon King, and the other of Louis XIII. The prominence of the duchesse de Ventadour strongly suggests that the painting was commissioned by her or by her sister, the duchesse de La Ferté. The implication is that, had it not been for her intervention, the senior line of the dynasty would have become extinct. The painting is thus not, as it might seem, an illustration to Louis' claim, made before the disastrous series of deaths, that the succession to his throne had never been more secure.

On 9 March, two days after the death of the duc de Bretagne, the duc du Maine wrote to Mme de Maintenon: 'How many more times will it please God to smite us? . . . If we were to lose the duc d'Anjou also, what great new obstacles to peace! And it all hangs on the life of an infant of two years whose constitution is frail enough. What prospects for the future remain before us? What will not be said by the troublers of public peace in foreign countries? In leaving behind us the fears of a long minority, we fall into those of present evil, of which we can see no end. All these thoughts are simply overwhelming; they increase, from minute to minute, the price of the preservation of the King [of Spain].'

'What great new obstacles to peace!' The sudden disappearance of three of the direct heirs to the throne of France played a highly significant part in the difficult process of agreeing to the terms on which a peace could be signed.

Only one thing seems to have been on Louis' side and that was Time. On 1 September 1710, Torcy noted in his journal: 'In fact this league, up till now so formidable by its union, was showing signs of falling apart, and the slightest division among its parties could change the face of things very much to the advantage of France.'

Affairs in England were leading in the direction of a Tory government, anxious to end an expensive war and even flirting with the idea of the restoration of the Stuarts. Marlborough's own position was far from secure. On 31 July 1710 he wrote to Heinsius: 'You will know, by what I have desired Lord Townshend to tell you, that our affairs in England are in a very desperate condition . . . I could bear my share of it with patience if I did not see immediate ruin to the Common Cause.'

At about the same time Lord Ailesbury wrote to Marlborough: 'I thought you would understand an English Court better than to be surprised by changes. As for our laws, they are excellent, but as for the Court one is as sure of keeping an employment in Constantinople . . . You have a fine family and a noble seat; go down thither, live quietly and retired, and you may laugh at your enemies.'

His enemies had no intention of leaving him in peace. On the last day of the year 1711 the Cabinet made a charge of peculation against him. That evening Queen Anne wrote to Marlborough dismissing him from all his offices. The letter has not survived. He threw it in the fire. Burnet records that 'the Queen wrote him a letter and discharged him of all his employments; this was thought very extraordinary, after such long and eminent service. Such accidents, when they happen, show the instability of all human things.' James Brydges, later to become Duke of Chandos, who had been Paymaster to the Queen's forces since 1705, declared that 'the proceedings were a scandal to the British people'. They were, however, good news to Louis.

With the disgrace of Marlborough and with England clearly losing interest in the war, Eugène decided to act on his own and make an attempt at breaking through and marching on Paris. At Versailles there was talk of the Court retreating to Chambord. But Louis declared that, in the last emergency, he would summon 'all the nobles of his kingdom', put himself at their head and lead them either to victory or to death.

In July 1712, Eugène made his first move. He laid siege to Landrécies, one of the last remaining fortresses between his army and Paris. Louis wrote to Villars to do 'all that is possible to bring aid to Landrécies and to prevent the enemy making themselves masters of that fortification'. His letters show that he was following the course of the campaign with eager interest. 'Your letter does not exactly explain the disadvantages of attacking the enemy between the Sambre and Priche . . . The situation demands the most prompt determination . . . It is up to you to determine both the time and the place for action and to make the best arrangements to ensure success.'

Villars decided that the best way to ensure success was to attack Denain, some twenty miles north-west of Landrécies, which occupied a key position in Eugène's supply system. It was held by the Duke of Albemarle. Villars' plan was to make a feint, marching with his whole army as if he were going to attack the besiegers, and then, under cover of darkness, to strike north for Denain. At seven o'clock in the morning of 24 July he appeared before the citadel. When, in the early morning, Eugène heard of this nocturnal march, it was too late for him to do anything about it.

The French advanced into heavy fire without flinching or breaking order and, according to one witness, with shouts of 'Vive le Roi!', and stormed the parapets. Albemarle's men began to fall back. The only bridge over the Scheldt broke under their weight and they were trapped between the attacking troops and the river. About 1,000 men were killed, some 1,500 were drowned and 2,500 surrendered.

The battle itself was nothing very outstanding except for the successful feint, but its consequences were far-reaching. A hundred years later Napoleon was to state that 'Denain saved France'. The official credit was given to Villars, but there can be very little doubt that the true victor was Pierre d'Artagnan, maréchal de Montesquiou, acting without his orders.

Villars lost no time in consolidating his victory. Marchiennes was taken, Landrécies relieved, Douai, Quesnoy and Bouchain retaken. 'This is a return to prosperity,' wrote Louis; 'it is very agreeable to see.' Villars had already been made *maréchal* and *duc et pair de France*. Now he was given the prestigious post of Governor of Provence. At the end of July the two marshals presented their trophy of captured standards to Louis. 'At Fontainebleau', writes Saint-Simon, 'there was an explosion of joy. The King was so flattered by this that, for the first time in his life, he thanked his courtiers.' Louis was, of course, both relieved and delighted. 'Nothing', he wrote to Villars, 'could more favourably advance and assist the negotiations for peace.'

The time was now propitious to continue negotiations. The allies were no longer united. In March 1712, Eugène made a rather unsuccessful visit to England. He left with the impression that the new Tory government would make its own peace terms with Louis without regard for the other allies.

Eugène was becoming increasingly afraid that the peace would be 'ruined equally by friend and foe'. After the battle of Denain he wrote to Sinzendorff complaining about the Dutch: 'No one would believe what I have had to put up with from these people.' In another letter he stated that 'the poor success of the campaign should not be blamed on the Denain affair but on the mood of fear and irresolution in the Republic'. The Dutch, in fact, represented by Anthony Heinsius, the Grand Pensionary, had all along been implacable in their demands. No doubt the memory of Louis' unprovoked attack on them in 1672 had embittered them. Nothing less than the utter humiliation of Louis would have contented them. For themselves they required their own definition of the 'barrier' of fortresses between Holland and France; they required a commercial treaty that would have excluded French traders. But they required also what amounted to a restoration of the Habsburg Empire as it had been under Charles V.

Austria was not in a co-operative mood and wished to continue the war. Count Wratislaw himself was coming round to agreement about the Spanish possessions, but unfortunately he died on 9 December 1712. This left the English and French to conclude the treaty more or less on their own. It was agreed that Philip V should renounce his claim to the throne of France while retaining that of Spain and control over the Indies. The Archduke Charles would receive the Spanish possessions in the Netherlands and Italy, with the exception of Sicily and Sardinia. The negotiations between France and Austria were left until the following year and were carried on by Eugène and Villars at Schloss Rastadt. Voltaire records that the first words spoken by Villars were: 'Monsieur, you and I are not enemies. Your enemies are in Vienna and mine at Versailles.'

One major issue was the demand of the allies that France and Spain should never share the same King. On 7 December 1711, Torcy had written: 'The King will accept voluntarily and in good faith to take, in concert with the allies, all the measures most proper to prevent the crowns of France and Spain from ever being united on the same head, that is to say that the same prince could never be King of the one and the other together.' Louis had, perhaps unwisely, specified by letters patent of December 1700 that Philip, on becoming King of Spain, had not renounced his rights to the throne of France. The likelihood of his needing such rights looked at the time pleasantly remote, Louis' son and grandsons seemed to provide an assured succession. In 1712, however, with the successive deaths of the princes, the situation took on a sudden urgency.

On 8 March, three days after the death of the little duc de Bretagne, Louis wrote to Philip V to announce the tragic event. 'Bad news follows bad news, and each week I have to inform you of a new misfortune. I have just lost my great-grandson, the elder son of your brother. I have little hope of retaining the duc d'Anjou, who is now the Dauphin, but he has come through the same disease which attacked him at the same time as his brother. Judge, however, how much I can base on an infant of two years. We do not know the secrets of Providence, but Your Majesty is at present regarded by the whole of Europe as the next heir to my throne, and this general opinion will add to the difficulties of the peace. I am persuaded that, in the middle of all these mournful events, you will feel more affection than ever for your family and, if it were possible, a more lively interest in the well-being of a Kingdom which could one day be yours.' The repercussions on Spain had been immediate. 'The affliction and horror', wrote Saint-Simon, 'felt in Spain at these repeated blows was unbelievable.' On the same day Torcy wrote to the princesse des Ursins: 'Up till now matters were progressing as well as one could have wished on the English side. I must admit, Madame, that I begin to fear a change after these sad events and that I can no longer see what safeguards the King, and the King his grandson, can offer.'

On 12 March Don Felix Cornejo, the Spanish chargé d'affaires in Paris, wrote: 'The death of the duc de Bretagne has thrown all France into a general state of uncertainty and confusion. People are beginning to talk of the possibility of Philip V returning to France. The health of the King is the greatest hope of all.' The good health of Louis during these early years of the eighteenth century is constantly referred to in Mme de Maintenon's letters, but it could not last for ever.

Torcy put the full argument in a letter to Henry Saint-John, now Lord Bolingbroke. 'France can never consent to become a province of Spain and Spain can never consent to become a province of France ... It is therefore a question of taking firm measures to prevent the union of the two monarchies, but we should completely lose sight of the end which we have in view ... if we contravene the fundamental laws of the Kingdom. According to these laws the prince nearest to the crown is of necessity the heir ... by the sole right of his birth. He owes this claim to the crown neither to the testament of his predecessor, nor to any edict nor any decree ... but to the law. This law is regarded as the work of Him who has established all the monarchies, and we in France are convinced that only God can abolish it. No renunciation can therefore destroy it, and if the King of Spain made one for the benefit of the peace and in obedience to the King his grandfather, we would be deceiving ourselves in accepting it as an expedient sufficient to avert the evil which we are trying to avoid.'

Bolingbroke's reply was conditioned by the situation in England regarding the claims of the House of Stuart. He accepted that 'you in France are persuaded that God alone can abolish the law upon which your right of succession is founded; but you will allow that we in Great Britain are persuaded that a prince can renounce his right by a voluntary transfer and that he in whose favour this renunciation is made can be rightly upheld by the powers who are guarantors of the treaty'.

In practical terms this meant that if Philip V became King of France, the duc de Berry, the third son of the Grand Dauphin, would become King of Spain. Since the renunciation by Anne of Austria had been annulled, the duc d'Orléans would succeed if Berry had no heirs. All this was in line with the provisions of the testament of Carlos II.

One of the most difficult personalities in the peace process was Philip of Spain. Perhaps because of the sufferings which they had shared with him since the war began, perhaps because he was touched by the loyalty so many of them had shown him, Philip had bonded with his people. He had no desire to exchange his kingdom for some other principality in Europe. But he was confronted with a choice between a principle which he held sacred and the naked necessity of concluding peace. The choice was equally difficult and unpleasant to Louis. Much of the copious correspondence between the two Kings is published by Baudrillart.

Philip persistently refused to agree to renunciation and the argument over this issue continued for two months; but Louis saw that it was a choice between accepting the English demand or losing all hope of peace. He did not, however, bring pressure to bear on his grandson.

On 18 April he wrote telling Philip: 'The demands of the English become more pressing ... The necessity of peace increases from day to day.' He assured his grandson that the terms were equally distasteful to both of them. He urged him to talk to Bonnac, his ambassador in Madrid: 'he will give you my thoughts in a predicament which is so difficult as to rule out any sort of argument'. Louis then appealed to the strength of family ties. 'As I can count on the affection which you have for myself and for your House, I expect you to follow the advice which it is necessary for me to give you and which in no way contradicts the real friendship which I have for you.'

To Bonnac he wrote: 'Make it clearly known to the princesse des Ursins, and through her to the King and Queen of Spain, that all that I have been able to do for either of them was to continue the war until the throne of Spain was secured for them; it is not right that I should complete the ruin of my Kingdom solely with a view to preserving their right either to unite one day the monarchies of France and Spain or to divide them among their children.' He ends with a postscript. 'The ultimate reply from England has arrived. The peace will be broken off completely if the King of Spain does not renounce his claim to succeed me and if the duc de Berry does not at the same time renounce his own claim to the crown of Spain. It only remains for me to decide whether I want peace at this price or the continuation of war. As the second course is not possible to sustain, I will certainly take the first.'

Philip began by making no reply to the demand. Finally, however, he had to agree. On 22 April 1712, he wrote to Louis: 'I am resolved, unless any other expedient can be found, to renounce my claim to succeed to the crown of France in whatever form you judge the most appropriate.'

Charles, duc de Berry, the third son of the Grand Dauphin, was only to make a brief appearance in the limelight of French history. Dangeau provides a portrait of him. 'He was the most handsome and the most affable of the three, and therefore the best loved.' His education, however, had been a waste of time. 'He ridiculed his teachers and their teachings, sometimes also their punishments; he had scarcely learnt to read, and never read anything at all after he had been delivered from his masters.' The result was that he suffered from an appalling shyness and a pitiful lack of self-confidence. 'It caused a diffidence so exaggerated that it gave him an ineptitude for almost everything and even for the proprieties of his rank. He had no conversation and if spoken to he lacked the courage to reply.' Such was the man who was now second in the succession to the throne of France. It looked as if the war might now be brought to a successful conclusion. It ended, as it had begun, with the question of the Spanish Succession. But the principles invoked in the arguments used applied also to the problem which England faced. When Queen Anne was dead, who would succeed her? The War of the Spanish Succession became, to a certain extent, the War of the British Succession. The same arguments which led Louis to believe in the divine right of his grandson to the throne of Spain led him to believe in the divine right of the House of Stuart to the triple crown of England, Scotland and Ireland.

As early as the year 1709 Halifax and Somers had carried through the House of Lords an address to the Queen defining the minimum peace terms to which England could agree. First, foremost and above all came the demand that 'the French King may be obliged to own Your Majesty's title and the Protestant Succession as it is established by the laws of Great Britain, and that the Allies be engaged to become guarantees of the same, and that Your Majesty would take effectual measures that the Pretender shall be removed out of the French dominions'. This was no bargaining about boundaries: it struck hard at Louis' most cherished belief.

In the eyes of someone like Saint-Simon there was no honour but that conferred by Time; ancient nobility and ancient tradition constituted an order which it was not possible to change. But with Louis all things were possible.

Philip was to renounce his claim to the French throne; the duc de Berry was to renounce his claim to the Spanish throne. On 15 November 1712, a courier arrived from Spain with a copy of the renunciation made by Philip, ten days earlier, at a full session of the Cortez and in the presence of the English ambassador. The courier also brought a letter from Philip to his brother, the duc de Berry – 'the most tender, the most strong, the most precise, to express to him his sincerity in this action, which promoted him [Berry] to his place in the succession to the throne of France, and with how great a joy his friendship for him had made him do it'.

The duc de Berry's renunciation, being a matter for the Parlement, took place in the Grande Salle of the Palais de la Cité after a short service in the Sainte-Chapelle. It was an affair of the greatest pomp and protocol. 'All that was needed', comments Saint-Simon, 'to make the occasion more solemn was the presence of the Peers' – those like himself who occupied the highest rank short of royalty, that of the *duc et pair*. Invitation cards were personally delivered to those who were at Versailles by Thomas de Dreux, marquis de Brézé, Grand Maître des Cérémonies: 'The Duke of — is notified by the King that on the 15th of this month he will deal with matters of great importance in the Parlement at which the King desires that he will be present.'

On Wednesday 15 March, Saint-Simon went at six in the morning to the duc de Berry's apartment in Versailles. He was wearing his parliamentary robes. These consisted of a short cloak, a sword and a hat with a plume of white feathers which was the distinctive mark of the peer. He travelled to Paris in the duc de Berry's coach. The duc d'Orléans was with them. He was the soul of gaiety all the way to the Tuileries, recounting tales of his childhood, of his night-time walks round Paris whereby he learnt the names of all the streets, to all of which the duc de Berry paid no attention, but sat in tense and anxious silence all the way. He was deeply perturbed at the prospect of having to make a speech. The Président de Mesmes was to open the proceedings with a little compliment to him and he was to reply.

Saint-Simon had written the speech for him and the Duchess had rehearsed him until he was word-perfect. In the event his memory deserted him. 'The Premier Président made his compliment to Monsieur le duc de Berry. When he had finished it was for him to reply. He took his hat half off, put it on again, looked at the Premier Président and said "Monsieur"; after a moment's pause he repeated "Monsieur"; he looked at the company and said again "Monsieur".' They were the only words he spoke. He turned again and gave a despairing look at the duc d'Orléans. Both were very red in the face and Saint-Simon had broken out into a sweat. 'You may judge what was the embarrassment of all the courtiers present and the surprise of the magistrates.'

Back in his apartment the duc de Berry shed tears of rage and mortification. 'He took it very much to heart', writes Dangeau, 'that he was good for nothing, a figure of contempt and the laughing-stock of the world. He started blaming his education, his ignorance; the care they had taken to humiliate him and to reduce him for fear that one day he might give them trouble.' Once again the spectre of Gaston d'Orléans had haunted the minds of those responsible for his formation. No thought had been given to the possibility that he might one day be called to rule France.

On Good Friday, 14 April 1713, Torcy arrived at Mme de Maintenon's apartment, charged by the maréchal d'Huxelles to bring the eagerly awaited news that the Peace was signed. The deliberations had been concluded on the previous Monday, 'very late at night'. The document was signed by the representatives of England, Holland, Portugal, together with Prussia and Sicily, whose rulers had both been raised to the rank of King. The name of Austria was conspicuously absent. The terms were ratified and the formal announcement made in Paris, on 14 May, 'with great solemnity'. This was followed by a terrific firework display in the Place de la Grève. On the following day the Te Deum was sung in the Cathedral of Notre-Dame. The singing of the Te Deum was usually the response to a victory.

In many ways it was a victory. Thanks largely to the persistence and diplomatic skill of Torcy, terms had been obtained which formed the most happy contrast with the harsh and humiliating conditions proposed at the beginning of the negotiations. Bishop Burnet gives instances when Torcy was arguing from a position of strength. 'The demand of Strasbourg [made by the Emperor] was rejected by the French with so positive an air that our Court did not move in it more.' He adds later: 'we were not at last able to gain any one point on them; they seemed to reckon that they might use us as they pleased . . . All that appeared was that the Pretender was gone out of France.' He had left in February 'with a small suite' and taken up residence in Lorraine where the Château de Bar had been prepared for him. Lorraine was not at that time a part of France, although the Duke owed allegiance to the King of France.

On 26 November Villars and Eugène concluded the Treaty of Rastadt. Louis sent Villars firm instructions. 'I desire peace, but I am under no pressure to conclude it. If the discussions at Rastadt continue you can certainly force Prince Eugène to agree with the principal conditions which I desire. If he breaks off the negotiations, you would do me a greater service, and I would be more grateful to you for the firmness which you have shown in carrying out my orders than if you had concluded a peace which was not in keeping with my *gloire*.' It is the tone of voice of a man arguing from strength.

It was agreed to maintain the frontier between France and Germany as it had been defined by the Treaty of Ryswick. That meant that France retained Alsace and, more importantly, Strasbourg.

Villars left his own summary. 'Thus, after a war of fourteen years, during which the Emperor and the King of France had nearly quitted their capitals, Spain had seen two rival Kings in Madrid and almost all the petty States of Italy had changed their sovereigns; a war, which had desolated the greater part of Europe, was concluded almost on the very terms which might have been procured at the commencement of hostilities.'

Villars did not see further than the dynastic boundaries of Europe. Louis had been obliged to yield on the religious issue behind their dynastic claims. It did not prevent him from giving surreptitious support to the Old Pretender for his ill-starred invasion of Scotland in 1715. It was a French ship that carried him to Scotland and French money which financed the venture. But these were immediate issues. The balance of Europe was never to be the same. The centre of gravity shifted to the trade routes and areas of colonial expansion. The Treaty of Utrecht did not put Britannia immediately on her Imperial throne, but it set her on course.

'The Peace of Utrecht', writes H. A. L. Fisher, 'may conveniently be taken as marking a point after which the religious and dynastic motives, which had previously played so large a part in the moulding of policy, sensibly declined in importance, while their place was taken by the struggle for colonies and markets. The long duel between England and France for colonial power which distinguished the eighteenth century had not in it any particle of either religious or dynastic interest. A new class had come to the front which cared for none of these things.'

At the beginning of May 1714, while hunting at Marly, the duc de Berry had an accident. His horse had slipped and in straining to hold it back he had ruptured a blood vessel in his stomach. On Thursday 3 May, he began to vomit a lot. In the evening his pain increased, but as he had ceased to vomit – which could have prevented him from receiving Communion – his confessor told him that it was time to receive the Viaticum. At four o'clock the following morning he died 'with great steadfastness and religion'.

Another, anonymous, account relates that Louis sent for the duc d'Anjou, now four years old, took him in his arms saying: 'Here is what is left to me of all my family', and burst into tears. Dangeau, however, states that 'the King was not deeply afflicted by the death of his grandson'. He may have become numbed by the succession of blows that had fallen upon him. The duchesse de Berry was pregnant at the time. The child, however, was a girl and died soon after birth.

With the death of the duc de Berry the number of Louis' legitimate descendants was reduced to one – the duc d'Anjou. In the event of his death the throne would pass to the senior member of the cadet branch, the duc d'Orléans, named, like his father, Philippe. Philippe was an atheist and a libertine; he had been widely suspected of poisoning the princes who stood between himself and the succession. Louis appears to have resented the prospect of his becoming the King or even the ruler of France. He took two distinctly high-handed actions to try to prevent either eventuality.

The first was to 'legitimise' his two illegitimate sons, the duc du Maine and the comte de Toulouse, both of them sons of Mme de Montespan. The official view was that it required the co-operation of the Queen to create a legitimate heir. The duc du Maine had always been the favourite of both Louis and Mme de Maintenon. Louis tried to justify his action as necessary because God 'in his anger' might deprive France of the legitimate line, but Louis' daughters had been married to the senior members of the cadet branches – Orléans, Condé and Conti. Their descendants were therefore in the legitimate line. In July 1714, this act of authority was made legal.

In much the same frame of mind Louis made his last will and testament. It recognised the claim of the duc d'Orléans to become Regent, but it created a Regency Council which would have greatly diminished his power. It gave him the title of Chef du Conseil rather than that of Regent. He would have been obliged to respect a majority decision of the Council and would not have possessed his own authority 'to determine, legislate or command'. The maréchal de Villeroy was to be Governor of the Dauphin once the duchesse de Ventadour handed over her charge.

This was very much what Louis' father had done. A Queen who had provided France with a Dauphin had the right to rule in his name, but Louis XIII, perhaps aware of his wife's limitations, had set up a Regency Council. The first act of the new Regent had been to persuade the Parlement to break the will and leave her with full powers. The implication that the Parlement had sufficient authority to set aside the will of a King, and to appoint the ruler of France, had given that Assembly a sense of its own power which had been one of the factors underlying the Fronde. It can hardly have been Louis XIV's desire to re-create that situation, and of course he knew that it would be just as easy to break his own will as it had been to break his mother's.

It is more probable that Mme de Maintenon and the duc du Maine were behind this testament. To the latter Louis said: 'It is what you wished, but know this: that however great I make you and you may be during my lifetime, you will be nothing after I have gone, and it is up to you to make the most of what I have done for you, if you can.'

3 1
The Bull Unigenitus

There is a natural tendency among people of advancing age to look more deeply into the state of their religion and to wonder whether their passports to Eternity are in order and signed by the correct authority. Louis had always been a convinced, if sometimes disobedient, son of the Catholic Church. Encouraged by Mme de Maintenon he had accepted the terrible reverses on the battlefield, the disastrous set-backs to agriculture of the winter of 1709 and the succession of bereavements as Death had cast its shadow pitilessly across his path as resulting from the will of God – not just to be accepted but to be adored. Although he may have been unable to understand how God could favour the armies of Protestant countries against his own, he believed devoutly that all these were to be taken as the chastisement of the Lord.

Towards the end of Louis' reign the conflicts within the Catholic Church took a new turn. Jansenism was by no means dead, but it had changed its form. Its main concern had been originally doctrinal. Now it was becoming more interested in personal devotion. As an aid to this a number of translations of missals and breviaries, and one of the Bible by Le Maître de Sacy, were brought out.

The practice of translation into 'the vulgar tongue' might seem harmless and even commendable, especially when it produced such literary jewels as Cranmer's Prayer Book and Luther's Bible. But in the eyes of the Catholic hierarchy its tendency was to undermine authority – to place at the mercy of individual interpretation the texts of which they were the divinely appointed custodians. It was a choice between the decrees of the hierarchy and the voice of scholarship. It raised the question of the place of the laity. Does 'the Church', as a source of authority, merely mean those in holy orders, or does it mean the congregation of the faithful? In order to understand the situation it is necessary to go back to the publication, in 1671, of a book by Pasquier Quesnel – *L'Abrégé de la morale de l'Evangile* or 'Christian thoughts on the text of the four Evangelists', designed 'to make the reading of them and the meditation thereon more easy for those who are beginning to apply themselves to it'. Quesnel belonged to the congregation of the Oratorians, one of the seed-beds of Jansenism.

Pierre Nicole, a colleague of Antoine Arnaud, had written to Quesnel about this book. 'I am convinced of the excellence of the whole work on the New Testament, and I consider that there is nothing more worthy of a priest, more useful to the Church and more appropriate for everyone, and if I had to choose one book, to the exclusion of all others, to accompany the New Testament, I assure you that it would be this one.'

In November 1700, Cardinal Albani succeeded to Innocent XII as Clement XI. He was known to be favourable to the Jesuits. He was immediately faced with the revival of the old controversy about Jansen's book the *Augustinus*. We have already seen that in 1653 Pope Innocent X had condemned five propositions allegedly to be found in the *Augustinus*. Antoine Arnaud had agreed that the propositions were heretical but denied that they could be found in that book. The next Pope, Alexander VII, issued a further bull stating that the propositions were indeed to be found in it. The community of Port-Royal questioned the competence of the Pope to lay down the law on what was merely a matter of fact. Louis had ordered them to retract.

Now, in 1702, the abbé Fréhel brought the matter up again in what he called 'a Case of Conscience'. He did so by imagining a priest making his confession on his death-bed, who accepted that the propositions were heretical but doubted whether they could be found in the *Augustinus* and maintained a 'respectful silence' on that point. Would it be permissible, asked Fréhel, to grant him absolution?

In May 1703, Quesnel was arrested. He managed to escape, but his papers were seized. Louis appealed to the Pope, Clement XI, to settle the dispute. It was not until July 1705 that Clement issued the bull *Vineam Domini*, condemning the whole Case of Conscience.

The Cardinal de Noailles, not without a little inconsistency, agreed to the condemnation and excommunicated the nuns of Port-Royal who persisted in their rejection of the bull.

Louis went further. He ordered the nuns to disperse. There were only twenty-five, the youngest of whom was over sixty. He then set about the obliteration of the church and conventual buildings. They were to be razed to the ground. All trace of them was to disappear. What Louis did not know was that, some sixty years previously, the floor level of the church had been raised several feet in order to counteract damp. In 1844, when the duc de Luynes, the owner of the near-by Château de Dampierre, had the foundations dug up, he found the original floor and the bases of the pillars intact.

One of the yearnings of the Jansenists was to recover the primitive purity and simplicity of the Church of the New Testament. The New Testament, however, offers no 'blue-print' of the hierarchy and can be used to support the election of 'Bishops' and 'Presbyters' by a democratic process. Nothing could have been less likely to appeal to Louis nor to the Jesuits. The Jansenist threat was pushing Louis into the arms of Rome. But, as often, there was a slightly precarious middle-of-the-road position which still represented the ideas and ideals of Gallicanism. Prominent among those who took their stance here was Louis-Antoine de Noailles, Cardinal-Archbishop of Paris.

In January 1709, Louis' confessor, the Père de La Chaise, died. He was replaced by the Père Michel Le Tellier (no relation of Louvois). He was a rather more militant Jesuit and bent on the destruction of the Jansenists. He made common cause with the group led by the two Dukes, Beauvilliers and Chevreuse. These enjoyed good relationships with Mme de Maintenon.

Fénelon, veering towards the Jesuit position, produced a pastoral letter condemning the heresies in another of Quesnel's books, the *Réflections Morales*, which had, at an earlier stage, been approved of by Noailles. In July 1710 this pastoral letter was placarded all over Paris. Noailles forbade the reading of this letter in his diocese.

Louis now asked the Vatican for a new decree which would condemn in detail the writings of Quesnel. In July 1712, he wrote to his ambassador in Rome, the Cardinal de la Trémoïlle: 'It is certainly necessary that the text should be solid, but if they want to avoid any possible cause for criticism they will never come to an end. However, the evil is urgent and the decree is the unique remedy that can be applied.' It was not until 8 September 1713 that Clement signed the new bull, named as usual after the first word in its preamble: *Unigenitus*. It reached Versailles on 25 September. Mme de Maintenon wrote immediately to Mme des Ursins: 'At last the constitution has arrived and brings the greatest condemnation that one could have desired; it is said that there is nothing in it that can alter our liberties, so we can accept it.' Five days later she wrote again. 'Monsieur le Cardinal de Noailles has already withdrawn the approval which he once gave to this book [by Quesnel]; I hope that we shall see the end of – or at least a diminution of – the row which has been going on for some time in the Church; I would never have thought that we would be better than you [the Spanish?] but it does seem to me that we treat the Pope better.' Clement had extracted from the book 101 propositions which he declared to be anathema.

'We condemn and reject each and all of the Propositions, listed below, as being respectively false, misleading, evil sounding, capable of wounding the ears of the pious, scandalous, pernicious, temerarious, harmful to the Church and to its practice, outrageous . . .'

To the Père Le Tellier this was a triumph. According to d'Agesseau: 'he counted the propositions condemned as Caesar might have counted his victories – "A hundred and one propositions condemned! What a disgrace for those who approved of this book!" ' Louis also was delighted. On 8 October Mme de Maintenon wrote: 'the Bishops who are in Paris are being assembled to receive the bull; God grant that this assembly may proceed smoothly and end quickly'. She was to be disappointed. The opposition was strong and immediate.

It came from such quarters as the doctors of the Sorbonne, the clergy of Paris and many of the monastic orders. The lawyers and magistrates could not consent 'to see forbidden, or even limited, the reading of the sacred texts', as was implicit in article 79 of the bull, which condemned as heretical the claim 'that it is useful and necessary at all times and in all places and to all sorts of persons, to study Scripture, to be familiar with its spirit, its piety and its mysteries'. Article 84 made much the same point. It condemned the proposition which claimed: 'It is shutting the mouth of Christ to Christians to tear from their hands this holy book, or to hold it shut by removing from them the means of understanding it.' This was written in defence of translating the Bible from Latin into French.

As for the quality of the translation, it was claimed in the bull that it departed significantly from the sense of the Vulgate, 'which has been in use in the Church for so many centuries and ought to be regarded as authentic by all who claim to be orthodox. They have carried their ill faith to such a point as to have perverted the natural sense of the text and substituted an extraneous and often dangerous interpretation.' The Vulgate was, of course, itself a translation – into Latin from the earlier texts which were in Greek or Hebrew. Work done during the sixteenth century on the older texts had stimulated a thorough revision of the Vulgate in 1592. It was on the scholarship behind these revisions, rather than on the antiquity of the earlier translations, that its claim to authority should have been based.

The bull and the reaction to the bull in the Parlement de Paris widened the gap between the contending parties. Clement XI seemed to withdraw slightly. Cardinal de la Trémoïlle went so far as to say that 'if the bull were to be rewritten, His Holiness would be more on his guard than he had been'.

Louis was enraged by the opposition from within the Parlement, which was required to enregister the bull. He told the Avocat Général, Joly de

Fleury, and the Procureur-Général, Henri-François d'Aguesseau, that there was no great distance between his study and the Bastille. 'These men', he said, 'will be the death of me.'

D'Aguesseau was emerging as the leader of the Gallican Party, which commanded a good majority in the Parlement. The higher clergy were largely in favour of Louis and the bull, but of the 450 clergy in the diocese of Paris 385 declared their support for Noailles.

It seems that Louis' most ardent desire in all this was the destruction of heresy. There was a threat of schism in the situation. 'It is not a matter of *Gallican liberties*,' he told Joly de Fleury. 'It is a matter of religion; I want only one in my Kingdom and if the liberties are used as a pretext for introducing others, I will begin by destroying the liberties.'

He began to entertain the idea of summoning a national council in order to condemn Noailles and his followers. The Vatican, however, after the stand it had made, could hardly have countenanced the idea of a council exercising authority. In June 1715, Louis' mind was made up. He would call a council on his own authority. The date for its meeting was fixed for 1 September.

The 19 August was the day appointed for the matter to be brought before the Parlement. A collision between the Parlement and the King seemed inevitable, in which case Louis would have been expected to resort to a *lit de justice*. The parliamentary leaders – the Premier Président, the Procureur Général, and the Avocat Général – were solidly behind the Cardinal de Noailles and ready to assert that the declaration was 'contrary to the liberties of the Gallican Church and against the interests of the Crown'.

But the confrontation never took place. A week before, on 12 August, Dangeau had noted that Louis was suffering from 'sciatica' in one leg which gave him considerable pain. On the 13th and again on the 14th Louis was carried in an armchair to the Chapel to hear Mass. On the 15th the Mass was said in his bedroom. On the 17th, in the evening, he ran a high temperature. The visit to Paris and the anticipated *lit de justice* were now out of the question.

It was on 19 August that the Père Timothée wrote from Paris to the Pope. 'I have only the most disturbing news to give to Your Holiness. The declaration should have come out today; it was the day appointed for that; the Parlement was to have assembled for this purpose, but the indisposition of the King not only stops and suspends what was to be done, but it gives grounds for believing that it will never reappear.' He then entered into a diatribe against the Gallican Church. 'It is only too evident that these impudent and ill-intentioned men, together with the Cardinal de Noailles and his followers, are only waiting for the death of this pious prince, so devoted to Your Holiness, so zealous in his upholding of religion, in order to blaze forth what they have been preparing for a long time; and more than that – they want it. This is what makes us tremble and throws us into the greatest consternation.'

Père Timothée then concentrated his anger on the Cardinal, whose charitable and pastoral activities among his flock, which had earned him his great popularity in Paris, he dismissed as mere ingratiation. 'For pity's sake,' he concluded, 'Most Holy Father, save the Church in France; do not let it separate itself from the visible Head of the Faithful!'

32
The Death of Louis XIV

When Timothée referred to the 'indisposition' of the King he was guilty of understatement. Louis was very seriously ill. He had been suffering from considerable pains in one of his legs. By the end of the week the swelling and dark patches were diagnosed as gangrene. This was to be Louis' terminal illness.

The last few days of Louis' life are perhaps the best documented. The main sources have been collected by Boislisle in his great edition of the *Memoirs of Saint-Simon*. These include Mme de Maintenon's own record in a letter to Mme de Villette; the diary written by Mlle d'Aumale, who was in Louis' bedroom whenever Mme de Maintenon was there, which was most of the time; and two accounts by Dangeau – the first, which forms part of his journal and goes as far as 26 August, and a separate document entitled *Mémoire du marquis de Dangeau sur ce qui s'est passé dans la Chambre du Roi pendant sa maladie*. Dangeau was often present in the room and always close to the events. The *Mercure Galant* more or less duplicates his text. Another very interesting and intimate account comes from the brothers Jean and François Anthoine. They both had the title Porte-arquebus du Roi and François was Garçon Ordinaire de la Chambre du Roi. Both were eye-witnesses of much that they recorded. Another source comes from the letters written by the abbé Mascara to the marquis de Grimaldo, Secretary of State to the King of Spain. He was not an eye-witness, but it was his business to be well informed. Equally important is the account of the marquis de Quincy. It has the special interest of having been checked by Louis' confessor, the Père Le Tellier. There is also an anonymous letter from a gentleman of Provence to his father, of which the original is in the municipal library of La Ciota. Finally there is the well-known day-to-day record of the duc de Saint-Simon. As always with him, it is sometimes difficult to disentangle his descriptions of events from his often biased private and political opinions. Many of his descriptions, however, are confirmed by one or more of the above sources.

It would be too much to expect all these accounts to be synoptic. The human mind is seldom an infallible recorder, especially in situations where strong emotions are involved, but there does emerge from their many pages a picture which is convincing in its overall effect even if a little uncertain in some of its details. The events form a day-to-day sequence.

The anonymous Provençal begins by describing to his father the shock which he received on first seeing the King, 'who has fallen, during the last fortnight, into an emaciation so excessive that he can no longer be recognised . . . His complaint has been identified, beyond doubt, as gangrene.' He then passes from Louis' physical condition to his spiritual. 'Nothing could be more heroic and more Christian than the steadfastness with which he faces his last moments.'

On Saturday the 24th, according to the brothers Anthoine, Louis was about to dine as usual in public, when 'he was overcome by so fierce a pain that he ordered that all should leave the room except for the maréchal de Villeroy, with whom he remained alone for two and a half hours, showing him every mark of his friendship and confidence and saying to him that he could see that his time was coming when he must think seriously about dying'. No doubt it was with this in mind that he gave orders, according to Mlle d'Aumale, for a room to be prepared close to his own so that Mme de Maintenon could more easily pass the night near to him when she so desired. Saint-Simon also records that, in the course of this Saturday, Louis 'worked alone with the Chancellor'. It is almost certain that this work resulted in Louis' letter to his little great-grandson, the duc d'Anjou, who was to succeed him as Louis XV.

'In this letter', he wrote, 'you will find the last wishes of your King and father, who, at the time of departing this life, feels a redoubling of his tender affection for you . . . The troubles which he foresees during your minority cause him more anxiety than the fear which is caused by the awe-inspiring prospect of leaving this world which he must soon undergo.' One of Louis' fears for the future was that the enemies of the duc du Maine, who was appointed the Dauphin's guardian, might bring about some adverse changes, which he begs the young Louis to reverse when he comes of age. In the meantime he commends the duc du Maine to him. 'Have confidence in him; follow his advice; he is very competent to be your guide, and if death should deprive you of so good a subject, render to his children, in maintaining the rank which I have bestowed upon them, all the friendship which you owe to their father, who has promised me and sworn only to abandon you at death.

'May the ties of blood and of friendship keep you always united with the King of Spain without any arguments of interest or politics ever coming between you; that is the only way of maintaining peace and the balance of Europe.

'Always keep inviolate your attachment to the common Father of the faithful and never separate yourself, from whatever motive there might be, from the centre and bosom of the Church. Put all your confidence in God; be a Christian before you are a king . . . Set your subjects the same example that a Christian father sets his family; regard them as your children and never incur his wrath upon you for any irregularity in your morals. Make them happy if you wish to be happy yourself. As far as you can, lighten the burden of all the crippling taxation with which the necessity of a long war has overloaded them and which their faithfulness caused them to support submissively. Let them enjoy a long peace, which alone can re-establish the affairs of your kingdom; always prefer peace to the questionable result of war, and remember, my Son, that the most brilliant of victories costs too dear when it is paid for with the blood of one's subjects. If possible, never spill it except for the glory of God; such conduct will bring down His blessing on the course of your reign; receive my own together with my final embrace.'

In this letter Louis was preaching what he had by no means always practised. His desire seems to have been to save his successor from making what he now acknowledged to be his own mistakes. Later in the evening he made his confession to the Père Le Tellier.

Sunday 25 August was the Jour de Saint Louis, a day of special significance for the Kings of France who were his descendants. Louis made a final effort. No change was to be made in the customary forms of celebration. The drums and hautboys played beneath his windows. He insisted on dining as usual in public. 'I have lived among the members of my Court,' he said; 'I wish to die among them. They have followed all the course of my life; it is right that they should see me finish it.' He took some soft refreshment and then talked for about a quarter of an hour to those present. He then dismissed them courteously with the words: '*Messieurs* – it would not be fair that the pleasure, which would be mine by prolonging the last moments which I will pass with you, should prevent you from dining; I bid you *Adieu* and pray you to go and eat.'

Later that evening the ladies came in as usual and at seven the orchestra commanded for them arrived. But Louis fell asleep and the musicians were dismissed. When he awoke the doctors found his pulse so weak that it was suggested that he should receive the last rites of the Church. The Cardinal de Rohan was summoned. The marquis de Quincy gives the most detailed account. 'Since no one had been notified of this ceremony, it was some considerable time before the Cardinal could come with the holy Viaticum.' A numerous cortège, which included the duc d'Orléans and some of the Princes of the Blood, was assembled to process the sacrament in a dignified manner through the palace. Le Tellier heard the King's confession and Rohan administered the Extreme Unction and the Viaticum. Dangeau, returning to his rooms at midnight, sat down and wrote: 'I have just left the greatest, the most touching and the most heroic spectacle that it is possible for a man to witness.'

On Monday 26 August, after a bad night, Louis heard the Mass as usual, after which he remained in conversation with the Cardinals de Rohan and de Bissy. 'He solemnly declared', states Saint-Simon, 'that he died in the faith of and in submission to the Church, and then added that it grieved him to be leaving the affairs of the Church in the condition which they were.' Saint-Simon, corroborated by the brothers Anthoine, quotes Louis as having shifted the responsibility for these affairs on to them – whether this means the two Cardinals or the Church which they represented is not clear. 'If I have perhaps done the wrong thing,' he said, 'it is on your consciences and you will answer for it before God.' Those last words were confirmed by Mme de Maintenon, who entered the room at that moment.

The behaviour of the Cardinal de Noailles must have been in all their minds and the question arose as to whether it would be possible for Louis to see him. The doctors suggested that he should, but Mme de Maintenon, Le Tellier and the two Cardinals were deeply disconcerted. They finally agreed that Noailles should be invited, but on condition that he accepted the constitution of the bull *Unigenitus*. That was a simple way of ensuring that he did not come.

Later that day Louis said his last farewell to the little Dauphin. Madame – the duc d'Orléans' mother – wrote on the following day: 'We had yesterday the saddest and most touching spectacle that it would be possible to imagine. The King, after having prepared himself for death and after having received the Last Sacraments, had the Dauphin brought to his room, gave him his blessing and talked to him.'

The words spoken to the Dauphin were a shortened version of the letter written on the previous Saturday. The words were taken down by the valets and transcribed by a calligrapher named Gilbert. This was then framed and hung at the head of the young prince's bed. The final sentence was 'Do not forget the gratitude which you owe to Mme de Ventadour'. Louis now turned to her. 'Madame, I must embrace him.' He took the boy in his arms and said: 'My dear child, I give you my blessing with all my heart.' This spectacle, admits Saint-Simon, 'was deeply touching'. Mme de Ventadour took the child back to his room.

The King now turned to the princesses who were present. 'He summoned me next,' wrote Madame, 'as well as the duchesse de Berry and all his other daughters and grandchildren . . . He bade me *adieu* in words of such tenderness that I marvel that I did not fall over backwards unconscious . . . I threw myself on my knees and, taking his hand, I kissed it. He embraced me and then spoke to the others.'

On Monday evening incisions were made in Louis' leg which revealed that the gangrene had reached the bone. The Chancellor Voysin, writing to Amelot, mentions 'the cessation of all pain and even of all feeling', which was the sign that the end was near. 'Mme de Maintenon was in his room,' writes Dangeau, 'kneeling alone at the foot of his bed while they were dressing His Majesty's leg; he begged her to leave and not to return, because her presence affected him with too much emotion.' The Père Timothée asserted that 'she behaved herself like a truly Christian lady during the whole of the King's illness'.

The next day, Tuesday the 27th, Louis spent most of the afternoon with the Chancellor and Mme de Maintenon burning letters and papers. In the evening he summoned Pontchartrain and gave instructions that his heart was to be sent to the Jesuits in Paris. Dangeau adds that he ordered it to be placed 'in the same manner as that of the King my father', and notes, 'He gave this order with the most perfect tranquillity.' He was still thinking of everything, arranging everything. Later he sent for a plan of the apartments at the Château de Vincennes, to which the Dauphin was to be taken immediately after his death. Vincennes had not been occupied by the King for some fifty years and needed furnishing. The plan was sent to the Grand Maréchal des Logis.

On the night of the 27th to the 28th, writes Mlle d'Aumale, 'he was very restless, and every minute could be heard reciting all the prayers which he usually said in bed, beating his breast at the *Confiteor* and naming those for whom he prayed'. His list included 'the King my father and the Queen my mother'. It appears from the letters of the abbé Mascara that Louis was expected to die at any moment. The foreign Ministers, who usually came to Versailles on a Tuesday, asked the marquis de Torcy if they were expected on this Tuesday. He replied that they need not come 'because the King could die at one moment or the next'. The uncertainty was almost unbearable, except, apparently, to Louis. 'One needed to have been a witness of the last moments of this great King in order to believe that steadfastness, both Christian and heroic, with which he confronted the approach of a death which he knew to be imminent and inevitable.' Dangeau particularly noticed that Louis conducted himself 'in a manner both simple and natural, as he had always been accustomed to, only speaking to each person about those things of which it was appropriate to speak and with that eloquence, so just and so precise, which had always been his and which seemed to have increased in his last moments'.

On Wednesday 28 August, Louis sent for Le Tellier and, as he was talking with him, he saw in the mirror two Garçons de la Chambre who were seated at the foot of his bed and were in tears. He said to them: 'Why do you cry? Did you think that I was immortal? As for myself, I never thought myself to be so and you ought, at your age, to be prepared to lose me.' The marquis de Quincy tells the same story but adds that the same words were used to two of the doctors. Dangeau relates that Mme de Maintenon came into Louis' room after dinner, fairly late, 'and having found him very drowsy, she left without speaking and went at about seven o'clock to sleep at Saint-Cyr in order to make her devotions there tomorrow morning and to come back *if the King's life lasts*'.

On Thursday there was a sudden change for the better. The abbé Mascara received the news early. 'Everyone is proclaiming a miracle; all who come from Versailles and all the letters which arrive proclaim a miracle and say that an angel has come from Heaven and has saved the King!' It was not an angel from Heaven but a chemist from Marseille. 'He claimed to have a secret, infallible cure for gangrene . . . The doctors questioned him and he told them what the ingredients were . . . They were approved, since His Majesty's health was already despaired of. The King, already prepared for death and imagining that any such attempt would be useless, was unwilling to believe it or to make trial of it; nevertheless he drank it. It is an extraordinary thing', wrote Mascara, 'but it is a fact that the King revived, that he recovered his spirit, his mind and his former vigour and vivacity. He was given some soup, which he held down, and swallowed without difficulty a little biscuit which he had previously not been able to swallow. The King then relapsed into his former condition; he was given more of the *Elixir vitae* and it produced the same excellent result. The King slept peacefully for about four hours.'

Mascara was in Paris. He was not an eye-witness. The story had come from Versailles and had no doubt improved in the telling. Saint-Simon, to whom any recovery in Louis' health was bad news, so anxious was he to see his friend the duc d'Orléans established as Regent, plays it down. 'The morning of Thursday there was an appearance of more strength and a little ray of improvement, which was immediately exaggerated and of which the rumour ran in all directions. The King actually ate two little biscuits in a little Alicante wine with something like an appetite.'

The courtiers, who had recently taken to crowding into the apartment of the duc d'Orléans in order to worship the rising sun, now abandoned it. At two o'clock Saint-Simon went to see his friend. The apartment was empty. 'There is the world for you.' According to Mlle d'Aumale the future Regent had commented: 'If the King eats once again I shall have no one.'

But on Friday Louis was as bad as ever. At four in the morning, Mascara reports, 'he was advancing with great strides towards the final moment'. Only Mme de Maintenon and Mlle d'Aumale were with him now. The latter affirmed that 'during all his illness I was nearly always at his bedside, opposite to Mme de Maintenon. We tried to awaken him a little . . . He had a little dog of which he was very fond and which spent several hours each day at the foot of his bed or in the ruelle, and from time to time he gave it little tit-bits.' On this occasion, when Mlle d'Aumale gave Louis a bonbon for the dog, he said: 'Give it to her yourself.'

At about three in the afternoon, Mascara was told, Mme de Maintenon left the King's room, got into her coach and went off to Saint-Cyr with the intention of never seeing anyone again. 'She gave away and distributed her money, her furniture and all that she had.' The fullest and most authentic account is that of Mlle d'Aumale. Mme de Maintenon saw that the King was unconscious; 'perceiving that he did not ask for her any more and that there was nothing more to wait for than the moment of his death, she left his room and prepared to depart for Saint-Cyr. Before leaving, however, she desired M. Briderey [her confessor] to see the King and to assure her that she could do nothing more by staying with him. She therefore told me to conduct M. Briderey to the King's bedside. And that is what I did; he saw him and came back to tell Mme de Maintenon: "You may leave him; you are no longer necessary to him." On this assurance she left Versailles before the King was dead because she was very much afraid that she would not be mistress of herself at this sad moment.'

On Saturday 31 August, Mascara sent his last account of Louis' agony to Spain. He was dining with the duchesse du Lude when the reports arrived from Versailles. 'The King was still alive, but without consciousness and without feeling . . . Only the Père Le Tellier was now with him. The room was beginning to stink.'

At eleven o'clock that evening the King was sinking fast. The Cardinal de Rohan began the *prières des agonisants*. Louis repeated several times the words *nunc et in hora mortis*. Then he repeated the words of the psalm: *Domine, ad adjuvandum me festina* (O Lord, make haste to help me). Those were his last words. At a quarter past eight on the morning of Sunday 1 September, Louis breathed his last. 'He yielded up his soul', wrote Dangeau, 'without any effort, like a candle going out': 'Il a rendu l'âme sans aucun effort, comme une chandelle qui s'éteint.'

As soon as the death was confirmed the Grand Chambellan went out onto the balcony before the King's Bedroom. He had a black feather in his hat. He said in a loud voice: 'Le Roi est mort.' He went back into the room and then came out again. This time he had a white feather. Three times he cried out: 'Vive le Roi Louis XV!'

Voltaire, the apostle of the eighteenth-century Enlightenment, has written Louis' epitaph. Not all historians would agree with it. But Voltaire was born in 1694. He was alive during the last twenty years of Louis' reign. He knew at first hand what he was writing about. He was fully aware of Louis' faults – 'his zeal against Jansenism, his too great arrogance with foreigners in the days of his success, his weakness regarding certain women'. The King had been justly blamed 'for wars lightly undertaken, for ravaging the Palatinate with fire, for persecuting the Protestants. Nevertheless his great qualities and achievements, when ultimately put in the balance, outweigh his faults. Time, which ripens men's judgements, has put a seal upon his reputation, and despite everything that has been written against him, his name will not be uttered without respect and without associating with it the idea of a century eternally memorable.'

Acknowledgements

First I would like to express my thanks to my wife Deirdre, to whom this book is dedicated, for her sound advice and careful proof-reading; also to Monsieur Jean-Pierre Babelon, Directeur de Versailles and to his staff, especially Monsieur Roland Bossart, Documentalist, for much help with the illustrations; to the Duke of Buccleuch for permission to reproduce the pictures of Louvois and Mme de Maintenon; to Canon Christine Farrington for her hospitality in Cambridge; to Monsieur P. Jan at the Réunion des Musées Nationaux; to the Duke of Richmond and Gordon for permission to reproduce the picture of Princess Henrietta Ann; to Monsieur Roidot at the Bibliothèque Municipale de Versailles; to Madame la baronne Elie de Rothschild and to Monsieur le comte and Madame la comtesse de Talhouet for their hospitality in Paris; to Christopher Sinclair-Stevenson, who first contracted this book and has published most of my books; to Christopher Taylor, Senior Assistant, Foreign books department, and Miss Alison Harvey-Wood, both of the Scottish National Library.

I would also like, retrospectively, to express my thanks to the late Mr J. M. G. Blakiston and Canon J. S. D. Mansel, masters at Winchester College, who nurtured my interest and love of the French language and the history of France; and to the Hon. Mrs Rodd whose introduction to Monsieur Charles Mauricheau-Beaupré, Conservateur en chef, opened all the doors at Versailles to me and made the writing of my first book a possibility.

Bibliography

Amberg, Général, *Louvois d'après sa Correspondance*, 1881

André, L., *Le Tellier et l'Organisation de l'Armée*, 1906

Anon., *Médailles sur les Principales Evènements . . .*, 1702

Arlington, Lord, *Letters to William Temple also containing a Relation of the Death of Madame*, 1701

Armogathe, J.-R., 'Bâville et la Guerre des Camisards'. In *Revue d'Histoire Moderne et Contemporaine*, 1972

Aumâle, Duc d', *Histoire des Princes de Condé*, 1863–1896

Autin, J., *Louis XIV Architecte*, 1981

Avenel, Vicomte, *Lettres du Cardinal Mazarin*, 1893

Avile, H. d', *Cérémonie du Sacre*, 1655

Babeau, A., *La Vie Militaire sous l'Ancien Régime*, 1889

Barbet, A., *Les Grandes Eaux de Versailles*, 1907

Barine, A., *Louis XIV et la Grande Mademoiselle*, 1905

Barthélémy, E., *Mme la Comtesse de Maure*, 1868

Batifol, L., *Le Louvre*, 1930

Baudrillart, T., *Philippe V et la Cour de France*, 1890

Beausant, P., *Lully, Musicien du Soleil*, 1992

Benserade, I., *Oeuvres*, 1981

Bernard, L., *The Emerging City: Paris in the Age of Louis XIV*, 1970

Berwick, Duke of, *Mémoires du Maréchal de Berwick par lui-même*. In Michaud et Poujoulat, Series 3, Vol. 4, 1850

Biver, P., *Histoire du Château de Meudon*, 1923

Blackader, J., *Select Passages from Diary*, 1806

Blondel, J. F., *L'Architecture Française*, 1698

Bluche, F., *Louis XIV*, 1986

Bluche, F., *Villette-Mursay, Campagnes de Mer*, 1991

Bossuet, J.-B., *Lettres de Bossuet*, 1927

Bottineau, Y., 'La Cour de Louis XIV à Fontainebleau'. In *Bulletin de la Société de l'Etude du 17e Siècle*, 1954

Bray, D. de, *Journal de Jean Migault*, 1834

Breteuil, Baron de, *Mémoires de Louis-Nicolas de Breteuil*, 1992

Burnet, Bishop, *History of his own Time*, Vols 3–4, 1818

Campbell, P., *Louis XIV*, 1993

Carré, H., *Enfance et Première Jeunesse de Louis XIV*, 1944

Caylus, Marquise de, *Souvenirs de Mme de Caylus*. In Michaud et Poujoulat, Series 3, Vol. 4, 1850

Cermakian, M., *La Princesse des Ursins*, 1969

Challes, R., *Mémoires de Robert Challes*, 1933

Chandler, D., *The Art of Warfare*, 1990

Chantelou, P., *Journal de Voyage du Cavalier Bernin*, 1889

Chatelain, U., *Le Surintendant Nicolas Fouquet*, 1905

Chérot, H., *Première Jeunesse de Louis XIV*, 1894

Chéruel, A., *Mémoires de Mademoiselle de Montpensier*, 1858

Chéruel, A., *Saint-Simon Considéré comme Historien*, 1865

Chéruel, A., *Histoire de la Minorité de Louis XIV*, 1879

Choisy, abbé de, *Mémoires*, 1979

Christout, M., *Le Ballet de Cour*, 1987

Church, W., *Louis XIV in Historical Thought*, 1976

Churchill, W., *Marlborough*, Vols 3 and 4, 1938

Clément, P., *Madame de Montespan et Louis XIV*, 1868

Colbert 1619–1683. Catalogue de l'Exposition, 1983

Combes, *Mme de Sévigné Historien*, 1885

Corvisier, A., *Louvois*, 1983

Cosnac, D., *Mémoires*, 1852

Coxe, W., *History of the House of Austria*, 1807

Coxe, W., *Memoirs of John, Duke of Marlborough*, 1820

Crété, L., *Les Camisards*, 1992

Dangeau, Marquis de, *Journal*, 1854

Danis, R., *La Première Maison Royale de Trianon*, 1927

Déon, M., *Louis XIV par Lui-Même*, 1983

Dorsanne, A., *Journal* (for Bull *Unigenitus*), 1753

Dreyss, C., *Mémoires de Louis XIV*, 1860

Druon, H., *Education des Princes de la Maison de Bourbon*, 1879

Du Bois, M., *Moi, Marie Du Bois*, 1994

Du Bosc, C., *The Military History of the late Prince Eugene of Savoy*, 1736

Duffy, C., *The Fortress in the Age of Vauban and Frederick the Great*, 1985

Dulong, C., *Le Mariage du Roi Soleil*, 1983

Dunlop, I., *Versailles*, 1956

Dunlop, I., *Royal Palaces of France*, 1985

Ekberg, C., *The Failure of Louis XIV's Dutch War*, 1979

Fabre, J., *Vie et Mort de Madame, Duchesse d'Orléans*, 1912

Feillet, A., *La Misère au temps de la Fronde*, 1862

Ferrier-Carverivière, *L'Image de Louis XIV dans la Littérature*, 1981

Feuillet, N., *Récit de la Mort de SAR la Duchesse d'Orléans*, 1686

Fleury, Comte de, *Le Palais de Saint-Cloud*, 1902

Forster, E., *Letters of Liselotte von der Pfalz*, 1984

Gaxotte, P., *Molière*, 1977

Geoffroy, M., *Mme de Maintenon, Correspondance*, 1887

Gibson, J., *Playing the Scottish Card*, 1988

Gouin, F. and Delteil, F., 'La Révocation vue par les Informateurs de Condé'. In *Bulletin de la Société du Protestantisme*, 1972

Gourville, H. de, *Mémoires*, 1782

Guiffrey, J., *Comptes des Bâtiments*, 1881

Guillaume, J., 'Chambord'. In *Révue de l'Art*, No. 25, 1974

Haggard, A., *Louis XIV in Court and Camp*, 1904

Hamilton, A., *Mémoires du Chevalier de Grammont*, 1883

Hatton, R., *Louis XIV & Europe*, 1976

Haussonville, comte de, 'Les Cahiers de Mlle d'Aumale'. In *Souvenirs sur Mme de Maintenon*, Vol. 2, 1903

Haussonville, comte de, *La Duchesse de Bourgogne*, 1908

Hautecoeur, L., *Le Louvre et les Tuileries sous Louis XIV*, 1927

Hébert, F., *Mémoires du Curé de Versailles*, 1927

Herbet, F., *Le Château de Fontainebleau*, 1926

Hippeau, C., *Lettres de Mmes de Maintenon et des Ursins*, 1862

Hoog, S. and Meyer, D., *Versailles, Musée de l'Histoire*, 1970

Horsley, W., *Chronicles of an Old Campaigner*, 1904

Isherwood, R., *Music in the Service of the King*, 1973

Jestaz, B., *Le Trianon de Marbre ou Louis XIV Architecte*, 1969

Joutard, P., *La Légende des Camisards*, 1977

Kamen, H., *Spain in the Later Seventeenth Century*, 1980

La Colonie, Colonel, *Chronicles of an Old Campaigner*, 1904

La Fare, Marquis de, *Mémoires et Réflexions: Principaux Evènements*. In Michaud et Poujoulat, Series 3, Vol. 8, 1850

La Fayette, Mme de, *Histoire de Mme Henriette d'Angleterre*. In Michaud et Poujoulat, Series 3, Vol. 8, 1850

La Porte, P. de, *Premier Valet de Chambre: Mémoires*. In Michaud et Poujoulat, Series 3, Vol. 8, 1850

La Rochefoucauld, Duc de, *Mémoires . . . de la Minorité de Louis XIV*, 1700

Labrousse, E., *Révocation de l'Edit de Nantes*, 1985

Lacour-Gayet, G., *Education Politique de Louis XIV*, 1898

Lair, J., *Nicolas Fouquet, Procureur Général*, 1890

Lair, J., *Louise de la Vallière et Jeunesse de Louis XIV*, 1907

Lambert, A., *Mme de Maintenon, une Reine sans Couronne*, 1982

Le Brun, C. Catalogue de l'Exposition, 1963

Le Gras, Bishop, *Procès Verbal du Sacre de Louis XIV*, 1694

Le Moine, J., *Trois Familiers du Grand Condé*, 1909

Le Nôtre, G., *Les Tuileries*, 1933

Le Roy, A., *La France et Rome de 1700 à 1715*, 1892

Le Roy-Ladurie, E., *Paysans de Languedoc*, 1966

Lemoine, J., *Mme de Montespan et la Légende des Poisons*, 1908

Lister, M., *A Journey to Paris in the Year 1698*, 1699
Lognon, J., *Louis XIV: Mémoires*, 1860
Lough, J., *Locke's Travels in France*, 1953
Louis XIV, *Oeuvres*, 1806
Macgowan, M., *L'Art du Ballet de Cour*, 1963
Magne, E., *Le Grand Condé, Lettres sur la Cour*, 1920
Maintenon, Mme de, *Lettres Inédites de la Princesse des Ursins*, 1826
Malssen, P., *Louis XIV d'après les Pamphlets en Hollande*, 1936
Marie, A., *Naissance de Versailles*, 1968
Marie, A., *Mansart à Versailles*, 1972
Marie, J. and A., *Marly*, 1947
Marteilhe, J., *Mémoires d'un Protestant*, 1957
Masson, F., *Journal Inédit de J. B. Colbert de Torcy*, 1884
Mazarin, Cardinal, *Lettres du Cardinal Mazarin*, 1872
McKay, D., *Prince Eugène of Savoy*, 1977
Meyer, D., *Gli Arazzi del Ré Solé*. Catalogue of Exposition, 1982
Michaud et Poujoulat, *Nouvelle Séries de Mémoires*, Series 3, Vol. 8, 1850
Michaud, E., *Louis XIV et Innocent XI*, 1882
Montagu, R., *HMC: MSS of Duke of Buccleuch*, 1899
Montpensier, Mlle de, *Mémoires*, 1858
Motteville, Mme de, *Mémoires*, 1806
Moüy, C., *Louis XIV et le Saint-Siège*, 1893
Murat, I., *Colbert*, 1980
Nolhac, P. de, *La Chapelle Royale de Versailles*, 1913
Nolhac, P. de, *La Création de Versailles*, 1925
Nolhac, P. de, *Versailles, Résidence de Louis XIV*, 1925
Ollard, R., *Cromwell's Earl (Lord Sandwich)*, 1994
Orcibal, J., *Louis XIV contre Innocent XI*, 1949
Orcibal, J., *Louis XIV et les Protestants*, 1951
Orléans, Mlle d', *Mémoires sur la Cour*, 1823
Ormesson, Le Fèvre d', *Journal*, 1860
Patin, G., *Lettres du Temps de la Fronde*, 1921
Pelet, Général, *Mémoires Militaires . . . Succession d'Espagne*, 1850
Perrault, C., *Courses de Tête et de Bague*, 1670
Perrault, C., *Hommes Illustres*, 1696
Perwich, William, *Despatches*, Royal Historical Society, 1903
Petitfils, J. C., *Louis XIV*, 1995
Primi Visconti, J.-B., *Mémoires sur la Cour de Louis XIV*, 1908
Pujo, B., *Vauban*, 1991
Pujo, B., *Le Grand Condé*, 1995
Pure, M de, *Idée des Spectacles Anciens et Nouveaux*, 1668
Quincy, Sevin de, *Histoire Militaire du Règne de Louis le Grand*, 1726
Rabutin, Bussy, *Histoire Amoureuse des Gaules*, 1868
Racine, J., *Précis Historique des Campagnes*, 1952

Bibliography

Raymond, J., '*Le Bourgeois Gentilhomme* à Chambord'. In *La Nouvelle Revue*, 1933

Read, C., 'Révocation: Mémoire du Maréchal de Vauban'. In *Bulletin de la Société de l'Histoire du Protestantisme*, 1887

Rébelliau, A., *Bossuet*, 1900

Roncière, C. de La, *Un Grand Ministre de la Marine: Colbert*, 1919

Roncière, C. de La, *Histoire de la Marine*, 1932

Roux, A., *Un Misanthrope à la Cour de France: Montausier*, 1860

Rule, J., *Louis XIV and the Craft of Kingship*, 1969

Sainctot, N., *Sacre de Louis XIV*, 1935

Saint-Germain & Louis. Catalogue of Exhibition, 1988

Saint-Maurice, Marquis, *Lettres sur la Cour de Louis XIV*, 1912

Saint-Simon, Duc de, *Mémoires*. Ed. Boislisle, 1910

Saural, H., *Histoire et Recherches des Antiquités de Paris*, 1969

Scoville, W., *Persecution of Huguenots*, 1960

Sévigné, Marquise de, *Lettres*. Ed. Monmerque, 1866

Sévigné, Marquise de, *Correspondance*. Ed. Duchêne, 1978

Sonnino, P., 'Louis XIV and the Dutch War'. In Hatton, R., *Louis XIV and Europe*, 1976

Spanheim, E., *Relation de la cour de France*, 1882

Stevens, J., *The Journal of John Stevens: War in Ireland*, 1912

Symcox, G., 'Louis XIV & the Outbreak of the 9 Years War'. In Hatton, R., *Louis XIV and Europe*, 1976

Tapié, V., 'Louis XIV's Methods in Foreign Policy'. In Hatton, R., *Louis XIV and Europe*, 1976

Temple, W., *Works*, 1754

Thomson, M., 'Louis XIV and William III', 'Origins of the War of the Spanish Succession' and 'Louis XIV and the Grand Alliance'. In Hatton, R., *William III & Louis XIV*, 1968

Torcy, Marquis de, *Mémoires*. In Michaud et Poujoulat, Series 3, Vol. 8, 1850

Trenard, L., *Mémoires des Intendants*, 1978

Vallier, J., *Maître d'Hôtel du Roi: Journal*, 1918

Vallot, A., *Journal du Santé de Louis XIV*, 1862

Verlet, P., *Le Château de Versailles*, 1985

Vogüé, Marquis de, *Mémoires du Maréchal de Villars*, 1889

Vogüé, Marquis de, *Le Duc de Bourgogne*, 1900

Vogüé, Marquis de, *Le Duc de Bourgogne et le Duc de Beauvilliers*, 1910

Voltaire, *Le Siècle de Louis XIV*, 1910

Walton, G., *Louis XIV's Versailles*, 1986

Wicquefort, A. de, *Chronique Discontinué de la Fronde*, 1978

Wolf, J., *Louis XIV*, 1968

Woodbridge, H., *Sir William Temple*, 1940

Ziegler, G., *At the Court of Versailles*, 1968

Zysberg, A., *Les Galériens*, 1988

Index

477